Understanding China

The series will provide you with in-depth information on China's social, cultural and economic aspects. It covers a broad variety of topics, from economics and history to law, philosophy, cultural geography and regional politics, and offers a wealth of materials for researchers, doctoral students, and experienced practitioners.

Hua Guo

Evidence Jurisprudence in China

北京师范大学出版集团
BEIJING NORMAL UNIVERSITY PUBLISHING GROUP
北京师范大学出版社

Springer

Hua Guo
School of Law
Central University of Finance
and Economics
Beijing, China

ISSN 2196-3134 ISSN 2196-3142 (electronic)
Understanding China
ISBN 978-981-95-3980-2 ISBN 978-981-95-3981-9 (eBook)
https://doi.org/10.1007/978-981-95-3981-9

Jointly published with Beijing Normal University Press (Group) Co., Ltd
The print edition is not for sale in China (Mainland). Customers from China (Mainland) please order the print book from: Beijing Normal University Press (Group) Co., Ltd.
ISBN of the Co-Publisher's edition: 978-730-32-1758-8

Translation from the Chinese Simplified language edition: "证据法学(第二版)" by Hua Guo, © Beijing Normal University Press (Group) Co., Ltd. 2023. Published by Beijing Normal University Press (Group) Co., Ltd. All Rights Reserved.

The original submitted manuscript has been translated into English. The translation was done using artificial intelligence. A subsequent revision was performed by the author(s) to further refine the work and to ensure that the translation is appropriate concerning content and scientific correctness. It may, however, read stylistically different from a conventional translation.

This Springer imprint is published by the registered company Springer Nature Singapore Pte Ltd.
The registered company address is: 152 Beach Road, #21-01/04 Gateway East, Singapore 189721, Singapore

Preface

As a core textbook of law in higher education institutions, this book has been selected and well evaluated by some universities in teaching practice since its publication in 2011; In 2020, it was awarded the title of "Beijing Higher Education High Quality Undergraduate Course" in the selection of the "High Quality Undergraduate Course" project in Beijing universities. In 2023, it was awarded the title of "Beijing Higher Education High Quality Undergraduate Textbook" and included in the "14th Five Year Plan" undergraduate planning textbooks of Central University of Finance and Economics. In order to meet the needs and demands of modern evidence teaching and the application of evidence in judicial practice. This textbook has the following characteristics:

Firstly, in the arrangement of the style, a thinking approach of linking the content before and after guiding case studies and problem thinking is adopted to cultivate a problem awareness in reading.

Secondly, in terms of content arrangement, we not only attach importance to the systematicity of evidence law knowledge, but also pay attention to the interpretability of evidence basic theory, maintaining the integration of evidence law knowledge and evidence theory, selecting extended reading content, highlighting the novelty of the textbook system and the expansion of evidence knowledge.

Thirdly, in the selection of typical evidence cases, controversial cases were chosen to closely integrate the theory of evidence law and the practical application of evidence through evidence cases, strengthen evidence awareness, highlight the enlightenment of evidence rules through controversial cases, and reflect the practicality of evidence law theory guiding practice and the operability of evidence rules.

Fourthly, in the explanation of evidence rules, the key knowledge and systematic knowledge of evidence law should be interconnected, and lively and interesting cases should be communicated with the explanation of citing classics. The "Top Ten" Chinese and foreign meaningful classic cases of evidence law should be attached (obtained by scanning the WeChat QR code on the title page), emphasizing the readability of evidence law knowledge and the modernity of using evidence ability.

This textbook not only emphasizes the content of litigation evidence in traditional evidence law textbooks, but also takes into account the characteristics of evidence rules in administrative law enforcement, arbitration, and disciplinary inspection and supervision cases. It strives to clarify the common problems of evidence from the basic knowledge, principles, and systems of evidence law, and avoid the disadvantage of insufficient content supply in the textbook that leads to a lack of evidence knowledge in learning. Therefore, the revision, supplementation, and improvement of the second edition of the textbook have referred to the latest viewpoints of domestic and foreign experts and scholars, and absorbed the advantages and strengths of other evidence law textbooks. It has made deletions, supplements, and adjustments to address the issues raised by students during their trial reading and learning process. On the basis of following the rules and regulatory requirements of evidence law, it has maintained the practical disciplinary characteristics of evidence law, including its entity, procedure, and applicable norms.

Beijing, China
March 2025

Hua Guo

Contents

Part I
Introduction

Chapter 1
Overview of Evidence Law

1.1 Introductory Case

During the Southern Qi Dynasty, when Fu Yan served as the magistrate of Shanyin County, two individuals appeared in court to resolve a dispute over the ownership of a livc chicken. The first man claimed, "This chicken belongs to my family. I do not know how it ended up in his yard. When I approached him to retrieve it, he insisted it was his and refused to return it. Thus, I seek judgment from the magistrate." The second man responded, "This chicken is clearly mine. I raised it over several months, yet he shamelessly tries to claim it. I cannot simply hand it over." The first man reiterated, "This chicken is obviously mine, but he continues to claim otherwise, which is absurd. This morning, I was feeding the chickens. I intended to lock them up before getting a drink of water, but when I returned, the chicken was gone. I searched around and soon heard clucking in his yard. I went over and saw him seizing my chicken. I said, 'That's my chicken,' but he refused to return it, saying, 'Once it enters my yard, it becomes mine.' I replied, 'I know my chicken—what more proof do I need?' He said, 'I know mine too, why should I give it to you?' Magistrate, do you not agree this is unreasonable?" The second man retorted, "You're twisting the facts. I was feeding the chicken in my yard when he barged in and demanded it. Who's being unreasonable here?" Both parties insisted the chicken was theirs, arguing relentlessly and refusing to yield. As there was no additional evidence beyond the two conflicting statements, Fu Yan initially considered seeking testimony from neighbors. However, he quickly realized that neighbors might provide biased accounts due to personal relationships, which could further complicate the case. Demonstrating his quick thinking, Fu Yan asked, "Since you both claim to have fed the chicken this morning, can you tell me what it ate?" One answered "millet," the other "rice husks." Fu Yan then ordered the chicken to be slaughtered and its crop examined. It contained only millet, with no trace of rice husks. Thus, the man who claimed the chicken ate rice husks inevitably lost the case.

H. Guo, *Evidence Jurisprudence in China*, Understanding China,
https://doi.org/10.1007/978-981-95-3981-9_1

1.2 Chapter Overview

This chapter introduces the foundational concepts of evidence law. It covers the definition, key features, research scope, disciplinary attributes, structural framework, and fundamental functions of the discipline. As essential foundational knowledge, it serves as the basis for the study and research of evidence law and provides conceptual guidance for the content of this textbook.

1.3 The Concept of Evidence Law

Evidence, as the foundation of litigation, is the most reliable means of establishing, proving, and determining case facts, and plays a central role in the legal process. Consequently, the evidence system has become a core component of the litigation framework. The development of the evidence system parallels that of the litigation system. As legal systems increasingly emphasize procedural justice, the robustness of the evidence system has become an important indicator of the completeness and maturity of a country's litigation system. Accordingly, evidence law—focusing on the study of evidence, evidentiary rules, systems, and their review and application—has become a benchmark for assessing the level of legal scholarship in a given country. It is also a core subject in legal education at universities both domestically and internationally, and a required course for future legal practitioners.

1.3.1 The Concept and Characteristics of Evidence Law

The titles of evidence-related textbooks in China have evolved from "Evidence Studies" to "Litigation Evidence Studies," "Litigation Evidence Law," and ultimately "Evidence Law." Although most textbooks refer to the discipline as "Evidence Law," differences remain in its conceptual definition and structural framework. As a course within legal education, its content should remain relatively stable while evolving alongside changes in evidence types and theoretical developments. This not only enriches and improves the discipline but also prevents content deficiencies that may hinder students' knowledge acquisition and skills development. In general, legal activities such as adjudication, arbitration, notarization, law enforcement, supervision, finance, securities, and insurance all involve evidentiary issues.

Due to variations in evidentiary standards, procedures, and regulations across these domains, both broad and narrow interpretations of evidence law have emerged in legal theory. Broadly defined evidence law addresses not only evidentiary issues in litigation but also those arising in non-litigation contexts such as administrative enforcement, arbitration, notarization, supervision, and financial investigations. In contrast, narrowly defined evidence law focuses on litigation-related matters, particularly during the trial phase. These issues involve detailed consideration of evidence theory, systems, norms, rules, and the processes of review and judgment, which are generally more rigorous than those in non-litigation contexts. The evidentiary system's structure and logical framework are more stringent, and its theoretical insights are often applicable beyond litigation. Therefore, focusing evidence law research on litigation-related issues is of particular significance, as it provides a solid foundation for both legal theory and practice.

Issues of evidence law in litigation encompass not only evidence theory, systems, norms, and rules, but also the discovery, collection, preservation, provision, examination, assessment, and application of evidence. Some aspects concern the substantive rights of the parties and fall under the domain of substantive law—for example, the allocation and presumption of the burden of proof, which are addressed in substantive legal provisions. Other aspects fall under procedural law, including evidence collection, fixation, and preservation, as well as procedural mechanisms such as disclosure, cross-examination, and authentication, which are generally governed by procedural norms. The overlap of these issues results in the compatibility of evidentiary norms with both substantive and procedural law, giving evidence law an inherently interdisciplinary character.

Evidence law is a legal discipline that examines evidence theory, evidentiary systems, proof standards, procedural rules, and methods of review, judgment, and identification. It is an essential component of the modern legal system. Its distinct characteristics give evidence law both shared traits with other legal disciplines and unique internal rules that distinguish it within the legal system. As an independent legal field, it holds a distinct position in the structure of modern legal scholarship. Compared to other legal disciplines, it exhibits the following features.

1.3.1.1 Evidence Law Is a Relatively Independent Interdisciplinary Legal Discipline in China

Evidence law originated within litigation law and gradually evolved into one of its essential components. It is closely intertwined with litigation law, and early scholarship largely approached the subject from this perspective, focusing on procedural aspects such as evidence identification, proof, and adjudication. Provisions concerning evidentiary norms, rules, methods of proof, and application procedures were often subsumed under litigation law, leading some scholars to label the field as "litigation evidence" or "litigation proof." However, evidence law differs fundamentally from procedural law. As noted by American scholar Ronald J. Allen, procedural law is localized and context-dependent, whereas evidence law is universal and rooted in human rationality.

When viewed through the lens of evidence discovery, extraction, preservation, and presentation—including rules on cross-examination, authentication, and especially the exclusion of illegal and hearsay evidence—evidence law primarily aligns with procedural law. Given its procedural nature, it is appropriate for national litigation codes to contain extensive evidentiary provisions. However, from the perspective of its fact-finding function—particularly in cases involving factual uncertainty—evidence law also carries substantive legal implications. Since it concerns the substantive rights of the parties, regulation by substantive law is necessary. Substantive laws in China—such as the Criminal Law, Civil Code, Securities Law, and Insurance Law—include provisions on burden-shifting and presumptions that directly affect the parties' substantive rights and interests. Fundamentally, the allocation of the burden of proof lies at the intersection of substantive civil law and procedural civil law in litigation.

The dual nature of evidence law—bridging both procedural and substantive legal domains—makes it unsuitable for complete classification under either category without compromising its scientific coherence and completeness. Given the tensions arising from fragmented regulation across these domains, along with the growing depth of evidentiary theory and the evolving demands of judicial practice, there is an increasing need for evidence law to evolve into an independent discipline. This trend has been reinforced by the emergence of specialized evidence legislation in several jurisdictions. For example, Geoffrey Gilbert's Law of Evidence (1754) is widely considered the starting point of specialized evidence scholarship in the UK and the US. James Stephen's A Digest of the Law of Evidence (1876) further exemplifies the theoretical distinction between procedural and substantive aspects of evidence law. In common law jurisdictions, case-based theoretical developments have driven the codification of evidentiary norms, resulting in independent legal instruments, such as the UK Evidence Act of 1851, the US Federal Rules of Evidence (1975), and the Australian Evidence Act of 1995.

Although China has not yet enacted a unified evidence code, judicial interpretations and normative documents have addressed specific evidentiary issues. For instance, the Supreme People's Court's Several Provisions on Evidence in Civil Litigation (2001, revised 2019), the 2016 joint regulations on the collection and assessment of electronic data in criminal cases, and the 2017 regulations on the exclusion of illegally obtained evidence have all significantly influenced judicial practice. In addition, local judicial authorities have issued departmental rules to meet practical needs. Although these documents lack the formal status of legislation, they provide valuable reference points for legal practice. As a result, evidence law has established an independent research domain within the modern legal system and is poised to emerge as a distinct legal discipline, separate from litigation law.

1.3.1.2 Evidence Law Is a Discipline of Law that Intersects Theoretical and Practical Aspects

Evidence law is characterized not only by the intersection of procedural and substantive law, but also by a close integration of theory and practice. Its scope and depth encompass not only technical and procedural concerns but also foundational theoretical questions, including the core principles and conceptual underpinnings of the discipline. It is essential to articulate the fundamental concepts of evidence law from a theoretical perspective and to examine its basic principles through the lenses of human rights protection and procedural fairness—for instance, in addressing complex or "two possibilities" cases. These theoretical foundations also serve as the basis and justification for developing specific evidentiary norms, rules, and legislative frameworks at the micro level. Such issues underscore the academic character of evidence law, distinguishing it from purely practical evidentiary rules and highlighting its role in providing high-level theoretical guidance.

The primary purpose of evidence law as a legal discipline is to provide a theoretical foundation and normative justification for the use of evidence in fact-finding. Its core function is to support the scientific and accurate determination of case facts. Accordingly, research in evidence law should ensure the conceptual legitimacy and normative coherence of evidentiary rules, while offering theoretical guidance for fair procedures aimed at the timely discovery of evidence, its lawful and systematic collection and preservation, its objective examination and evaluation, and its accurate and effective use. These objectives inherently involve practical evidentiary techniques, underscoring the highly applied nature of evidence law. This practical orientation is particularly evident in Anglo-American jurisdictions, where many evidentiary rules have evolved from case law and reflect a strong pragmatic tradition. Therefore, when drawing on such sources, special attention must be paid to their functional application in practice.

1.3.1.3 Evidence Law Is a Discipline of Law that Combines Rules and Technology

The development of evidence law is closely intertwined with technological advancement. As new technologies emerge, so too do new forms of evidence, accompanied by a gradual shift in proof methods from reliance on "personal evidence" to the growing use of "scientific evidence." Contemporary evidentiary materials include audiovisual recordings, electronic data, emails, online chat histories, digital signatures, and access logs. These forms reflect the ongoing digitization, technologization, and increasing use of intelligent systems in evidentiary processes. For instance, DNA analysis, big data analytics, and algorithmic assessments are now widely applied in the collection and evaluation of evidence. The evolution of the evidentiary legal framework increasingly depends on scientific and technological innovations, with technological progress continuously shaping the underlying logic and trajectory of evidence law.

With the advancement of technology—particularly the widespread application of intelligent systems in everyday life, such as WeChat, Weibo, facial recognition, digital currency, and modern biotechnology—the data generated in these contexts increasingly serve as potential sources of evidence. Emerging high-tech tools, including infrared imaging, brainwave recognition, hand geometry, facial recognition, iris and retinal scans, and even technologies yet unknown, may also become part of future evidentiary systems. These developments require evidence law not only to study and accommodate such technologies, but also to establish standardized legal forms for technology-related evidence, thereby ensuring the protection of human rights in an era defined by digitalization and informatization.

Consequently, the study of evidence law must emphasize the integration of procedural and substantive legal principles while maintaining a balance between theoretical and practical perspectives. Special attention should be given to both general and specific rules of evidence and proof. As this book is part of a textbook series for legal education in finance and economics—rather than a specialized monograph on evidentiary theory—its focus is on foundational concepts, principles, and categories of evidence law. The content emphasizes normative frameworks, such as evidentiary and proof rules, and offers principle-based explanations of practical issues. While theoretical discussion is not the primary focus, this does not diminish the discipline's theoretical depth or the significance of evidence law as an independent and academically rigorous field.

1.3.2 The Relationship Between Evidence Law and Other Disciplines

As an independent legal discipline distinct from both litigation and substantive law, evidence law inevitably intersects with other legal fields due to overlapping research subjects and scope. Clarifying the relationship between evidence law and other branches of law is essential not only for understanding its disciplinary characteristics but also for drawing on insights from related fields. Such interdisciplinary engagement facilitates the development, enrichment, and refinement of evidence law as a distinct academic and practical discipline.

1.3.2.1 The Relationship Between Litigation Law and Evidence Law

Litigation law is grounded in procedural statutes and litigation activities, primarily addressing the initiation, progression, and legal consequences of judicial processes. However, because procedural actions require evidentiary support, evidence-related norms have become an integral component of criminal, civil, and administrative procedure laws. In essence, evidentiary rules play a central role in facilitating the effective advancement of litigation. As litigation law explores general procedural mechanisms, it must also incorporate aspects of evidence law to ensure the coherent integration of evidence with procedural requirements. The combined study of evidentiary theory and practice—particularly the relationship between evidence and procedural law—has laid a strong foundation for the enrichment and development of evidence law as an academic discipline.

Evidence law, as a specialized legal field, focuses on the nature of evidence, evidentiary systems, evidentiary rules, and the application of these norms in legal practice. While it overlaps with some aspects of litigation law, evidence law conducts more comprehensive and systematic research into evidentiary theories, rules, and systems across different litigation contexts, identifying recurring issues and legal patterns. Its research scope is broader and more in-depth than that of litigation law's approach to evidence, and its findings offer valuable guidance for refining procedural rules—particularly in the rational design of litigation mechanisms.

Given the close interrelationship between litigation and evidence law, research in evidence law should remain attentive to developments in procedural law, especially in areas such as judicial reform and litigation procedures. Topics like evidentiary standards, technical investigation results, and the use of big data in the exclusion of illegal evidence illustrate the need for ongoing dialogue between the two disciplines. Likewise, litigation law should continuously incorporate findings from evidence law to meet procedural demands, enhance operational feasibility, and promote the scientific evolution of the legal system.

1.3.2.2 The Relationship Between Evidence Law and Substantive Law

Although the research focus of evidence law differs from that of criminal law, civil and commercial law, administrative law, and economic law (including anti-money laundering, banking, insurance, and antitrust laws), meaningful connections exist between them. In general, substantive law defines the objects of proof, providing a foundation for determining what must be proven within evidence law. Conversely, evidence law offers practical pathways and effective methods for realizing the substantive legal provisions in judicial proceedings.

Criminal law addresses the definition of crimes, criminal responsibility, and punishment. It involves determining the elements of criminal liability, sentencing severity, and various statutory and discretionary circumstances that may mitigate or exempt punishment—all of which require evidentiary support. This reliance on evidence extends to both statutory provisions and authoritative interpretations. For example, the *Guiding Opinions on Sentencing for Common Crimes (Trial)* emphasize the use of evidence to substantiate facts relevant to both conviction and sentencing, including the distinction between conviction evidence and sentencing evidence. Evidence law thus plays a crucial role in guiding how such facts are discovered, collected, examined, and verified. To ensure the proper implementation of criminal law, it must account for what can be proven in practice, making the integration of evidence law research essential to the effective design of criminal legal elements and sentencing frameworks.

Civil law focuses on civil legal relationships, characterized by rights and obligations between private parties. The formation, modification, and termination of these relationships depend on identifiable legal facts, which must be established when disputes arise and enter judicial proceedings. Evidence law provides the tools to ascertain these facts. Furthermore, civil law includes rules concerning burden of proof, presumptions, and exemptions—provisions that must be applied in accordance with the principles and techniques developed by evidence law. In turn, research in evidence law contributes to the rational allocation of the burden of proof and the legitimate use of legal presumptions, offering a sound empirical and theoretical basis for civil law design.

Administrative law governs the legal relationships between administrative agencies and the subjects they regulate. Disputes arising from administrative actions—such as detentions, fines, confiscations, business suspensions, or license revocations—are generally resolved through administrative litigation. Once such disputes reach the courts, administrative actions must be evaluated based on admissible and reliable evidence. Moreover, the administrative agency's own evidentiary basis is critical to judicial review. For instance, in response to evidentiary challenges in administrative penalty cases, the Supreme People's Court issued the *Minutes of the Symposium on Several Issues Concerning Evidence in the Trial of Securities Administrative Penalty Cases* (2011), while the National Copyright Administration issued rules in 2020 to improve the evaluation of evidence in copyright enforcement. These developments underscore the increasing integration between evidence law and administrative law. Evidence law not only informs the evidentiary requirements in administrative adjudication, but also plays a guiding role in administrative enforcement, particularly regarding evidence collection in coercive or punitive actions.

Economic law encompasses a wide array of regulatory frameworks, including anti-money laundering, antitrust, finance, taxation, securities, and insurance law. These laws all incorporate evidentiary norms and require theoretical support from evidence law. For example, under the *Anti-Money Laundering Law*, regulatory agencies may investigate financial and designated non-financial institutions suspected of facilitating money laundering or terrorism financing. Those under investigation are required to provide truthful documentation and information. In such contexts, evidence collection must conform to the general principles of evidence law. Documents at risk of concealment, alteration, or destruction may be sealed in accordance with evidentiary procedures. Both the sealing of materials and the conduct of interviews fall within the purview of evidence law. Accordingly, research in evidence law offers critical guidance for addressing evidentiary issues in the enforcement of economic regulations.

1.3.2.3 The Relationship Between Evidence Law and Evidence Investigation

Evidence investigation is a discipline focused on uncovering the factual circumstances of a case through various methods, including discovery, fixation, extraction, testing, identification, questioning, and inquiry. It primarily examines strategies and techniques for evidence collection. Although there is some overlap between evidence investigation and evidence law, the two fields differ in research perspective and methodology. Their shared areas concern distinct research objects. Evidence law should incorporate the latest advancements in evidence investigation—particularly in techniques for evidence collection, such as DNA typing and electronic evidence acquisition. Conversely, evidence investigation must be grounded in the principles of evidence law to ensure that investigative practices remain within the bounds of legality, are subject to evidentiary rules, and uphold the rule of law.

This interplay is especially important in areas such as standardizing procedures for evidence collection, ensuring proper review and evaluation of evidence, and preventing the misuse of investigative techniques. The pursuit of truth must not justify the use of unlawful or disproportionate means to obtain evidence.

Additionally, the relationship between the *Supervision Law* and evidence law warrants attention. Particular focus should be given to the evidence collection and retrieval provisions outlined in the *Supervision Law* and Chap. 4, Section 2 ("Evidence") of its Implementation Regulations. These provisions must align with the evidentiary standards required in criminal trials, particularly in relation to the collection, fixation, review, and use of evidence by supervisory authorities. Addressing these evidentiary issues requires the normative framework and guidance provided by evidence law.

1.4 The Object of Evidence Law Research

Every academic discipline is defined by its unique research object, which stems from the specific contradictions or tensions it seeks to address. Evidence law focuses on the distinct issues that arise within the evidentiary domain, giving it a research object that differentiates it from other legal fields. In the nineteenth century, the United Kingdom became the first country to establish a specialized system of evidence law, formally recognizing it as a discipline dedicated to studying the application of evidence and the legal norms governing its use.

The research object of evidence law encompasses the core elements of evidentiary inquiry. These include the nature and theory of evidence, the structure of the evidentiary system, rules of proof, methods of proof, evidentiary norms, and the practical application of evidence. Additionally, it covers emerging developments such as the informatization, digitization, and technologization of evidence processes.

1.4.1 The Essence of Evidence

Evidence law, distinct from other legal disciplines, possesses inherent internal norms. These normative foundations are reflected in three primary dimensions: (1) the ontological nature of evidence; (2) issues related to epistemology, value theory, and ethics; and (3) the role of evidence in procedural design.

Early scholarship in evidence law often emphasized ontological analysis, focusing on abstract, macro-level philosophical debates—such as whether evidence possesses "two attributes" or "three natures"—at the expense of practical relevance. This overly metaphysical approach led to conceptual confusion and limited the field's impact on legal practice. In contrast, modern evidence law research has moved beyond purely ontological concerns. It now incorporates evaluative and moral dimensions, particularly those grounded in epistemological inquiry. Contemporary research emphasizes the intrinsic procedural value of evidence and highlights the distinctiveness of evidence law as a discipline. However, excessive emphasis on proceduralism risks devolving into "agnosticism" or "skepticism," thereby weakening the law's capacity to serve its core function.

While the pursuit of truth in litigation remains a fundamental mission of evidence law, it is not its sole normative objective. The discipline must center its inquiry on evidence itself, questioning its normative foundations while critically examining its function in practice. This requires investigating the nature of evidence through a lens that reconciles substantive and procedural compatibility. From the standpoint of practical rationality, evidence should be understood as an objective external entity. By doing so, scholars can contribute to the construction of a disciplinary framework that is scientifically grounded, practically effective, and theoretically robust.

1.4.2 Evidence Theory

Evidence theory represents the refinement and systematization of evidentiary practice. It is the product of summarizing and analyzing practical experience in the application of evidence and reflects the accumulated wisdom of human efforts in fact-finding. Although evidence law is a relatively young discipline compared to procedural law, the sustained efforts and scholarly contributions of legal theorists—both historical and contemporary, domestic and international—have yielded a rich body of research and fostered the emergence of diverse schools of thought. These theoretical debates and divergent viewpoints have laid a solid foundation for the continued maturation of evidence law as an academic field. As such, research in evidence law should be grounded in the development of evidence theory. It should aim to uncover deeper insights into evidentiary issues, while avoiding excessive pragmatism that may lead to the rigid application of rules and hinder their effectiveness in guiding judicial practice. The study of evidence theory not only informs practical evidentiary activities across various legal domains, but also provides a conceptual framework for identifying the underlying principles of the discipline. Furthermore, it offers valuable theoretical resources for constructing a scientifically grounded foundation to improve the evidentiary system in China.

1.4.3 Evidence System

The evidence system refers to the body of legal provisions and rules governing evidence across a country's legal framework. It represents a comprehensive synthesis of evidentiary norms developed at different historical stages or coexisting within the same legal era. As a fundamental component of a nation's legal system, the evidence system evolves alongside changes in societal structure and is shaped by legal traditions, procedural models, political institutions, and cultural values.

Throughout history, different countries have developed distinct types of evidence systems. The historical evolution of these systems has progressed from divine or ordeal-based systems to statutory evidence models, and eventually to systems based on the free evaluation of evidence. In China, the development of the evidence system has been significantly influenced by Soviet and Eastern European socialist legal traditions, particularly through the adoption of the "seeking truth from facts" model. In recent years, growing introspection has led to notable reform efforts aimed at improving the system's practical application.

Within this context, Chinese evidence law must deepen its exploration of the formation, evolution, and transformation of various evidentiary systems, taking into account the structural and cultural framework of China's legal tradition. It is essential to analyze the specific strengths and weaknesses of different evidentiary models under particular historical and institutional conditions. Reform efforts should be guided by the principles of "drawing from the past to serve the present" and "adapting Western ideas for Chinese use."

At present, China's evidence system remains incomplete and requires systematic study of both the successes and shortcomings of foreign models. However, a simple transplant of Western evidentiary theories or rules through legal "borrowing" is neither appropriate nor effective. Instead, reform should also involve a critical reassessment of China's historical legal traditions. Valuable indigenous insights from classical Chinese jurisprudence should be identified and integrated into the development of a modern, context-sensitive evidence system.

1.4.4 Prove the Law

Establishing the facts of a case—identifying or determining facts relevant to a legal matter—is a fundamental objective of evidence law. To achieve this, various types of evidence must be used to uncover the truth, and appropriate rules of proof must be applied to ensure factual accuracy. The primary aim of evidence law research is to identify underlying patterns in evidentiary practices and to develop theoretical frameworks and general principles that govern the use of evidence in fact-finding. These frameworks serve the dual purpose of uncovering the truth and ensuring fairness in legal proceedings.

The act of proof operates on multiple levels. This multi-layered structure includes both general rules for proving facts in legal cases and specialized rules applicable to specific contexts, such as judicial proceedings, law enforcement, arbitration, notarization, administrative supervision, and investigations in the financial, securities, and insurance sectors. It also encompasses procedural rules governing various evidentiary activities—including the collection, preservation, fixation, cross-examination, review, and use of evidence—as well as the treatment of different types of evidence, such as testimonial evidence, physical objects, documents, and electronic data.

Research in evidence law should be grounded in the accumulated practical experience of evidentiary activities across historical and cultural contexts, both domestic and international. It should aim to uncover the inherent regularities in these practices, elevate them into coherent theoretical models, and apply them to legal proceedings to guide evidence collection, evaluation, and adjudication.

1.4.5 Proof Method

Proof requires the application of specific methods, and the choice and implementation of these methods often determine the success or failure of evidentiary efforts. While the methodologies employed in other disciplines may offer valuable insights, the proof methods in evidence law possess distinctive characteristics shaped by legal norms and procedural requirements.

The methodologies in evidence law are diverse and operate at multiple levels. These include: (a) general methods for using evidence to establish facts in various legal contexts, as well as specialized techniques applicable to judicial proceedings, law enforcement, arbitration, and investigations in finance, securities, and insurance; (b) approaches tailored to different legal actors or parties in proving case-related facts; (c) specific techniques for collecting, preserving, analyzing, and applying evidence, with attention to the particularities of different types of evidence, such as documentary, physical, testimonial, and electronic forms; (d) stage-specific methods across the litigation process, including evidence collection, presentation, cross-examination, authentication, and evidentiary adjudication.

Evidence law must also address the methods employed in a wide range of evidentiary activities—spanning judicial, administrative, arbitral, and regulatory domains—including law enforcement, notarization, supervision, and investigative processes in financial and insurance sectors. While interdisciplinary issues merit attention, the core focus of evidentiary research remains litigation, given its representative and paradigmatic role in the legal proof process.

1.4.6 Rules of Evidence

The use of evidence to establish the facts of a case—or other legally relevant facts—must adhere to defined procedures and rules. These evidentiary rules constitute a central component of evidence law. Broadly, evidentiary rules can be categorized into two types: litigation and non-litigation rules. Litigation evidence rules apply to criminal, civil, and administrative proceedings, while non-litigation rules govern evidentiary practices in administrative enforcement, arbitration, notarization, supervision, and investigations in financial, securities, and insurance sectors.

The main categories of evidence rules include those governing the collection of evidence, exclusion of inadmissible evidence, presentation and cross-examination, review and evaluation, and the adoption or acceptance of evidence. Research in evidence law must address not only the content and procedural requirements of these rules but also their function, rationality, and legal validity. It should involve both the interpretation of current evidentiary rules and the development of theoretical foundations and policy recommendations for their reform and improvement.

Given the historical and cultural differences across legal systems, evidentiary rules vary significantly among countries. These differences reflect broader distinctions in legal traditions and procedural models. Accordingly, comparative analysis is essential for identifying the strengths and limitations of different evidentiary frameworks. Such analysis can provide valuable insights for refining China's evidence rules and developing scientifically grounded and contextually appropriate legal norms.

1.4.7 Evidence Application

The application of evidence involves the dynamic use of evidentiary materials in legal proceedings. It includes the principles guiding evidence application; the procedures for collecting, securing, extracting, and preserving evidence; and the processes for presenting, cross-examining, and authenticating evidence during litigation. It also encompasses the procedures for examining and evaluating evidence, as well as applying it to establish the facts of a case.

Evidence can only fulfill its function in fact-finding once it has been introduced into legal proceedings. It must be used in accordance with due process and verified through strict procedural compliance to ensure the accuracy and reliability of the case outcome. The effectiveness of evidence in achieving its purpose depends on whether its use follows proper legal procedures, respects procedural safeguards, and complies with established rules. Additionally, the legal consequences of procedural violations—such as the exclusion of improperly obtained evidence—must be clearly defined and enforced.Therefore, the scientific soundness and procedural legitimacy of evidence application are essential. A well-designed and legally grounded evidentiary procedure not only ensures the validity of the evidence but also prevents its misuse, thereby contributing to the integrity of the judicial process.

1.5 The System of Evidence Law

1.5.1 Overview of the Evidence Law System

The system of evidence law refers to the internal structure and interrelated theoretical framework that organizes the core research components of the discipline. The level of scientific rigor and coherence in this system reflects the maturity of the field and its standing within the broader domain of legal scholarship. Constructing a robust system of evidence law, one that is complete, systematic, and scientifically grounded, is a critical theoretical challenge facing contemporary evidence law research. This endeavor not only determines the internal scientific validity of the discipline but also directly influences the quality and effectiveness of evidence legislation. Moreover, it has a profound impact on the accuracy of factual determinations in legal proceedings.

The system of evidence law differs from both the normative legislative framework governing evidence and the general academic framework used in evidence law research. As a disciplinary system, it comprises the fundamental elements of the field and the structural relationships among them. It must exhibit characteristics of completeness, internal consistency, scientific rigor, and adaptability. Such a system should reflect contemporary scholarly achievements, align with the evolving principles of legal development, and provide a foundation for future theoretical and practical advancements in evidence law.

1.5.2 Evidence Law Textbook System

1.5.2.1 The Debate on the Teaching System of Evidence Law

The system of evidence law is distinct from the normative framework of evidence legislation, but the teaching system of evidence law typically reflects the foundational structure of the evidentiary system. In essence, the textbook system represents a rational selection and organization of the evidence law system's content, tailored to pedagogical needs.

In China, the formalization of evidence law in textbook form developed relatively late. In 1929, Professor Yang Zhaolong offered a course on evidence law at Shanghai Law and Politics University and published the textbook Evidence Law in 1930. In 1948, Soochow University's Law School issued Evidence Law Theory as a general university textbook. This textbook was organized into four major sections: "General Principles of Evidence," "Methods of Evidence," "Preservation of Evidence," and "Debate of Evidence." The first section included chapters on "Burden of Proof," "Exemption Systems," and "Evidence Investigation." The second addressed "Personal Evidence," "Appraisal," "Documentary Evidence," "Investigation," and "Emotional Evidence." The third covered "Civil Evidence Preservation Procedure" and "Criminal Evidence Preservation Procedure," while the fourth section dealt with "Evidence Procedure," "Evidence Debate," "Evaluation Criteria," and "Evidence Illustration."

After the founding of the People's Republic of China, the mainstream structure of evidence law textbooks adopted a binary model centered on "evidence theory" and "proof theory." Currently, the prevailing teaching system follows a tripartite structure: "general theory," "evidence theory," and "proof theory." This structure emphasizes theoretical explanation and interpretation of evidence law norms and is characterized by a formalistic and doctrinal approach.

However, this textbook system is fundamentally constrained by the underlying evidentiary framework. As legal education and disciplinary demands have evolved, this structure has been increasingly questioned by scholars. In many teaching materials, evidence is treated as an external, static, and objective entity, divorced from its functional role in proof activities. This perspective overlooks the subjective, dynamic, and context-dependent nature of evidence in litigation. Similarly, legal proof is often reduced to a purely cognitive activity, stripping it of its procedural and normative dimensions.Therefore, the current textbook system in evidence law requires not only revision but a comprehensive and scientifically grounded reconstruction—one that reflects the complexities of modern evidentiary theory and practice, and better aligns with contemporary legal education and jurisprudential development.

1.5.2.2 The Basic System Structure of this Textbook

The structure of this textbook adopts a pragmatic framework, reflecting the applied orientation of legal education in finance and economics institutions. Unlike traditional evidence law textbooks that primarily focus on criminal evidence, this volume introduces a balanced approach that integrates criminal, civil, and administrative evidence, with particular emphasis on civil and administrative contexts. This adjustment highlights the textbook's practical relevance to the finance and economics domain.Grounded in normative legal provisions, including statutes and judicial interpretations, the textbook prioritizes theoretical explanations for practical problems encountered in evidentiary operations. Its goal is to meet the core educational needs of finance and economics law programs and to support students in their future professional practice.

The textbook is organized into four main parts, comprising a total of nineteen chapters. The first part is called "Introduction". This mainly includes an overview of evidence law, the historical development of evidence system, and the theoretical basis of evidence law. The second part is "Evidence Theory". It mainly includes an overview of evidence, types of evidence, classification of evidence, and rules of evidence. The third part is "Proof Theory". Mainly including proof overview, proof object, proof responsibility, and proof standards. The fourth part is "Program Theory". It mainly includes principles of evidence application, collection and preservation of evidence, procedures for evidence application, examination and judgment of evidence, methods for determining case facts, presumption, and judicial notice.

1.6 The Function of Evidence Law

Evidence forms the foundation of legal proceedings, serving as both the prerequisite for initiating litigation and the core element of litigation activities. Many procedural rules are centered on evidentiary issues, highlighting the pivotal role of evidence in the operation of the legal system. Evidence law comprises the legal norms governing evidentiary matters, while the jurisprudence of evidence focuses on the theoretical and normative study of these laws. This field provides both conceptual guidance and practical support for the development of evidence legislation, the lawful handling of cases by judicial authorities, the protection of parties' legitimate rights and interests, and the realization of judicial fairness.

Broadly speaking, there are two primary methods for resolving disputes: reasoning and evidentiary proof. Reasoning can reveal deception or inconsistency, while evidence provides an objective basis for fact-finding. In litigation, the accurate establishment of facts requires careful evaluation of evidence, guided by common sense, life experience, and ethical principles. One of the primary aims of evidence law is to facilitate the prompt, lawful, and accurate determination of facts, thereby promoting the timely resolution of disputes and ensuring that parties achieve the objectives of both procedural and substantive law in a manner that balances their legal interests.In general, evidence law fulfills several core functions, which will be discussed in the following sections.

1.6.1 The Theoretical Support Function of Evidence Law in Legislation

The depth and breadth of research in evidence law profoundly influence evidence-related legislation, often shaping its scientific rigor. As a foundational theoretical discipline, evidence law not only supports legislative development but also provides critical guidance for judicial practice. Through its theoretical insights, it promotes the continual refinement and evolution of evidentiary rules within the judiciary.Judicial interpretations such as the *Several Provisions of the Supreme People's Court on Civil Procedure Evidence*, the *Provisions on Several Issues Concerning the Exclusion of Illegal Evidence in Handling Criminal Cases*, the *Interpretation of the Criminal Procedure Law*, and the *Interpretation of the Civil Procedure Law* all reflect the accumulated experience of judicial practice. At the same time, scholarly research in evidence law—particularly concerning methods for truth discovery, the rationality and legality of procedural structures, and the evaluation of proof—has informed litigation reform and offered practical solutions to complex evidentiary challenges. These contributions have facilitated timely fact-finding and enhanced the scientific accuracy and reliability of judicial determinations. This influence is especially evident in areas related to the scientific development of evidence provisions in litigation. Ongoing debates surrounding algorithmic governance, personal data, and the exclusion of illegally obtained evidence in the digital economy, as well as judicial deliberations on covert recordings or statistical probability in securities litigation, exemplify how theoretical inquiry directly shapes evidentiary rule-making and addresses difficulties in proof.

To mitigate arbitrariness in judicial evaluation and reduce the influence of misleading information on fact-finding, litigation systems must establish procedural constraints. Evidentiary rules regulate admissibility, the scope of evidence, and permissible methods of investigation. Their design and implementation are fundamentally guided by evidence law scholarship, which continues to inform the development of procedural safeguards and rule-making.

Furthermore, evidence law provides theoretical support to ensure that parties have sufficient access to necessary evidence and that evidentiary mechanisms function effectively to ascertain facts in a timely and fair manner. It also offers a normative framework for assessing the legitimacy of investigative methods and the timing of evidence collection, ensuring that these do not unduly obstruct the pursuit of truth or disrupt procedural order. In addition, it contributes to the development of alternative approaches to fact-finding in exceptional cases, such as burden-shifting rules, presumptions, and judicial notice, thereby reinforcing the balance between procedural efficiency and substantive justice.

1.6.2 The Guiding Function of Evidence Law in Judicial Practice

The development of litigation activities fundamentally depends on evidence for ascertaining the facts of a case, and the design of litigation procedures must likewise center around evidentiary processes. Litigation cannot proceed effectively without evidence, and parties involved must rely on lawful and sufficient evidence to protect their legitimate rights and interests. The influence of evidence law—both conceptually and normatively—shapes the implementation and application of evidentiary rules, thereby playing a pivotal role in guiding the development of litigation systems.

All litigation participants, including investigative authorities and parties, must base their actions on facts, and the determination of these facts relies entirely on evidence. Evidence law provides essential theoretical guidance for determining what constitutes admissible evidence, how evidentiary weight is assessed, and the probative value of different types of evidence. Establishing factual truth through evidence is a prerequisite for proper adjudication, and evidence law serves as a critical framework for ensuring the correct application of evidence.

The process of fact-finding in litigation is inherently a cognitive journey from ignorance to knowledge. It cannot rely on subjective speculation but must instead proceed through legally recognized forms of evidence, such as physical objects, documents, and electronic data. These must be obtained through lawful methods, including witness examination and questioning of parties, in compliance with procedural safeguards. Evidence law informs the evaluative and selective processes by which such evidence is gathered and used, guiding both investigators and litigants toward an objective and scientific understanding of the facts.

For parties to litigation, whose interests are directly at stake, providing persuasive and admissible evidence is crucial to substantiating their claims. Unsupported assertions are unlikely to persuade adjudicators and may result in the denial of legal remedies. Beyond procedural compliance, the evidentiary contributions of parties must align with the standards and methodologies informed by evidence law to ensure their admissibility and probative value. Defense attorneys and legal representatives also play a central role in the evidentiary process. Their responsibility to collect and present evidence is not only foundational to their advocacy but also essential to the realization of procedural fairness. Theoretical insights from evidence law assist these actors in navigating complex evidentiary rules, minimizing the risk of improperly collected or excluded evidence, and ensuring the protection of their clients' legal interests.

Proper case resolution depends on the availability of sufficient and admissible evidence. To avoid wrongful convictions or miscarriages of justice, evidence must be collected in a timely and lawful manner. Evidence law research provides crucial guidance on the timing and methods of evidence collection, ensuring that opportunities are not lost and that fact-finding remains reliable. In particular, where evidence is obtained in violation of legal standards, its admissibility must be evaluated according to the principles and doctrines established in evidence law.

While many evidentiary issues are addressed by statutory law, legislation cannot anticipate every factual scenario. In complex or borderline cases—often involving ambiguous facts or evolving technologies—rigid legal provisions may prove inadequate. In such instances, theoretical frameworks from evidence law are indispensable. They support the flexible and fair application of evidence, inform innovative reasoning within judicial practice, and promote procedural justice. Ultimately, the integration of theoretical guidance ensures the timely resolution of disputes, enhances the efficiency of litigation, and strengthens the pursuit of judicial truth.

1.7 Questions and Reflections

Scholar Chen Pusheng asserts that "determining what kind of information can be used as evidence, how it should be collected and utilized, and whether the established facts and applied law are accurate is of paramount importance. To ensure that the facts established through evidence are true and that the applicable law is correctly applied, a specific legal framework—referred to as the rule of evidence—is essential." Thus, regardless of the size or complexity of a case, factual determination is challenging without supporting evidence. Sole reliance on circumstantial evidence may obscure the truth and increase the risk of wrongful convictions. When key evidence lacks sufficient corroboration, fact-finders may reasonably hesitate in reaching conclusions. To avoid such pitfalls, it is necessary to obtain and evaluate adequate evidence, drawing from life experience to identify the most direct and probative forms of proof. The facts of a case should ultimately be verified through a comprehensive body of credible evidence. Based on the referenced guiding case and the content of this chapter, consider the following questions: (1) What reasoning or observations did Fu Yan rely upon to uncover the truth of the matter? (2) What specific evidence did Fu Yan use to determine the facts of the case? (3) Does the evidence relied upon by Fu Yan align with the definition of evidence in modern evidence law? (4) Which evidentiary theories should be applied or consulted to guide the resolution of such cases?

Extended Reading

Yi, Y. Y. (2005). Zhengjuxue shi yi men faxue ma—yi yanjiu duixiang wei zhongxin de shengcha. Tribune of Political Science and Law, 23(3): 35–51. (in Chinese)

Chen, R. H. (2006). Cong zhengju xue zou xiang zhengju fa xue——jian lun xingshi zhengju fa de tixi he gongneng. Studies in Law and Business, (3): 83–93. (in Chinese)

Long, Z. Z. (2006). Da zhengju xue de jiangou ji qi xueli. Tribune of Political Science and Law, (5): 82–98. (in Chinese)

He, J. H. (2008). Zhengju fa gongneng zhi tantao——jian yu Chen Ruihua jiaoshang shangque. Studies in Law and Business, (2): 27–36. (in Chinese)

Zhang, B. et al. (2019). Zhengju kexue lungang. Beijing: Economic Science Press. (in Chinese).

Chapter 2
The Historical Evolution of Foreign Evidence Systems

2.1 Introductory Case

According to the tenth book of the Old Testament, *1 Kings*, two women once came before King Solomon to resolve a dispute. One woman explained, "Your Majesty, this woman and I live in the same house. She was present when I gave birth to a son. Two days later, she also gave birth. We were alone—no one else was with us. One night, she accidentally overlaid her own child while sleeping. She rose at midnight, took my living son from beside me while I slept, and placed her dead child in my arms. When I awoke to nurse my baby, I discovered he was dead. Upon closer examination, I realized the child was not mine." The second woman contested her account, saying, "No! The living child is mine; the dead one is yours." The first woman replied, "That's not true! The dead child is yours; the living one is mine." The two continued to argue before King Solomon. Recognizing that both women claimed the living child as their own, Solomon devised a test. He commanded, "Bring me a sword." When it was brought, he ordered, "Divide the living child in two, and give half to each woman." Upon hearing this, the true mother, driven by compassion, pleaded with the king: "Please, Your Majesty, do not kill the child. Give him to her instead." The other woman coldly responded, "He shall be neither mine nor hers. Cut him in half." Solomon then declared, "Do not harm the child. Give him to the first woman—she is his true mother."

2.2 Chapter Overview

This chapter examines the historical development of foreign evidence systems, focusing primarily on the evolution of the divine evidence system and the statutory evidence system in both civil law and common law traditions. It also explores the

H. Guo, *Evidence Jurisprudence in China*, Understanding China,
https://doi.org/10.1007/978-981-95-3981-9_2

emergence of the modern systems of free evaluation of evidence and internal conviction. These systems exhibit a degree of historical continuity and have collectively shaped the contemporary evidence frameworks in Western legal systems.

2.3 Divine Evidence System

Throughout the history of human society, various countries have developed distinct types of evidence systems at different stages of their legal evolution. The divine evidence system emerged and was prevalent during the period of Western slavery and early European feudalism. In the legal practices of early societies, it was common to seek assistance from supernatural forces—such as through divination, curses, oaths, and ordeals—to establish the facts of a case.

2.3.1 The Origin of the System of Divine Evidence

The divine evidence system refers to a method of adjudication in which judges rely on divine intervention or revelations to resolve disputes and determine the truth of contested facts in complex cases. Signs interpreted as manifestations of divine will are treated as "evidence" or as evidentiary methods in legal proceedings.[1]

In the early stages of Western slave society and European feudalism, low productivity and limited scientific understanding hindered people's ability to explain natural and social phenomena. Faced with natural disasters, physiological mysteries—especially life and death—and other unexplained events, individuals lacked the tools to investigate or interpret these occurrences rationally. Consequently, they developed a profound reverence for the unknown and attributed incomprehensible phenomena to supernatural forces, leading to the creation of deities or a singular "God" as the omnipotent creator and ruler of all things. In this context, divine intervention became a rationalized means of explaining and resolving problems beyond human understanding. It was believed that God, with infinite power and moral integrity, could perceive and judge all things fairly and justly. People turned to divine revelation to distinguish right from wrong and good from evil, especially in cases where human judgment fell short. This belief laid the foundation for the divine evidence system, in which divine signs or revelations were invoked to resolve legal disputes and determine factual truth in litigation.

The early litigation system was based on an impeachment model, in which proceedings were initiated and driven by the parties themselves. The process advanced through oral statements and mutual debate, while judges played a passive role, making determinations based solely on the arguments presented. At the time,

---

[1] *[E.A. Hobell, "The Law of the First People," translated by Zhou Yong, 229 pages, Beijing: China Social Sciences Press, 1993.*

legal frameworks adhered to the principle of nulla actio sine querela ("no prosecution, no response"), thereby granting litigants the primary responsibility to pursue and argue their cases. This established the foundational structure of the early impeachment-style litigation system. Under this model, when parties presented conflicting claims and the facts remained unclear or indistinguishable, judges often lacked sufficient means to resolve the dispute. In such cases, they would turn to divine intervention, seeking guidance from God to determine truth and justice. When ordinary methods failed to produce conclusive evidence, religious practices became a default mechanism for resolving factual uncertainty. As Hobel noted, when early societies could not obtain sufficient or decisive evidence to settle legal disputes, they routinely sought assistance from religion.[2] The emergence of the divine evidence system can thus be attributed to two main factors. First, the cognitive and evidentiary limitations of human judges, combined with the pervasive influence of religion, created a structural dependence on supernatural guidance. Second, the passive role of judges within the impeachment-style litigation framework made them more inclined to seek external, divine solutions when they could not independently ascertain the facts. Together, these conditions significantly contributed to the development and institutionalization of the divine evidence system.

2.3.2 *The Basic Content of the Divine Evidence System*

In the system of divine evidence, when judges faced doubts or uncertainties regarding the guilt or innocence of a defendant, or the authenticity of disputed facts, they did not rely on empirical investigation or rational methods of inquiry. Instead, they sought guidance from supernatural forces or divine will to determine the truth and resolve legal disputes. Within this framework, three primary methods were used to establish facts: the divine ordeal, the oath, and the trial by combat.

2.3.2.1 Divine Evidence Method

Ordeal, or Gottesurteil, refers to a method of determining the right or wrong in legal disputes by invoking divine intervention or interpreting signs believed to originate from God. This approach typically includes specific rituals such as trial by water, trial by fire, divination, and the casting of lots.

(i) **Water trial**

The "Ordeal of Water" (Kaltwasserprobe) was a form of divine trial that relied on water to assess the truthfulness of a party's statement, particularly in serious cases

---

[2] *[E.A. Hobell, "The Law of the First People," translated by Zhou Yong, 229 pages, Beijing: China Social Sciences Press, 1993.*

such as theft or murder. This ordeal was typically divided into two types: cold water and hot water trials.

The cold water ordeal involved immersing the accused in a river to determine guilt or innocence. The criteria for judgment varied depending on local beliefs and customs. Two main standards were used: one considered sinking as evidence of guilt and floating as a sign of innocence; the other held the opposite—that sinking indicated innocence, while floating indicated guilt. For instance, Article 2 of the Code of Hammurabi from ancient Babylon states that if a person is accused of witchcraft and cannot prove their innocence, they must throw themselves into the river. If the river overcomes them, the accuser inherits the accused's house. However, if the accused emerges safely from the river, the accuser is to be executed, and the accused is awarded the accuser's property. In contrast, under ancient Germanic law, water was believed to be the purest element. If the accused floated, it was taken as a rejection by the pure water of their impurity, thereby indicating guilt. Conversely, sinking was interpreted as the water accepting the person, and thus a sign of innocence.[[3]].

The hot water trial was a form of divine ordeal used to determine guilt by requiring the accused—or both parties—to retrieve an object from boiling water by hand. Guilt was assessed based on whether the individual could remove the object without sustaining burns. If burns occurred, the accused was expected to pray or undergo ritual incantations. The healing of the burns within a specific time frame was interpreted as a sign of innocence; failure to heal was taken as evidence of guilt. In early Japanese practice, a variation known as *Meng Shen Tan Tang* required the accused to retrieve small stones from boiling water. The presence or absence of burns was used to evaluate the truthfulness of their claims.

During the Middle Ages, this method evolved into the "scalding trial," in which the determination of guilt or innocence was based on the severity of burns on the accused's hands—commonly referred to as "judging by the depth of the scald." This practice is documented in both the *Kojiki* and the *Nihon Shoki* in Japan.

The prevalence of water trials stemmed from the belief that water possessed a force beyond human control, a power thought to be derived from divine support. Additionally, water was regarded as sacred and pure—an essential element for human survival and the vitality of all living things. These cultural and spiritual associations elevated water to a revered status, making it an acceptable and authoritative medium for adjudicating right and wrong, and legitimizing judicial actions based on its use.

(ii) **Fire trial**

The "trial by fire" (Feuerprobe) was an ancient evidentiary method used to assess a defendant's guilt or the veracity of disputed facts through exposure to fire or heated metal objects. In this procedure, the accused was required to either walk barefoot over burning embers or carry a red-hot iron in their hand. The burned area would then be wrapped in cloth, and after a set period, the wound would be examined. If

[3] *// [American] Monroe Smith: "A History of the Development of European Law", translated by Yao Meizhen, pages 47–48, Beijing: China University of Political Science and Law Press, 1999.*

it showed signs of healing, it was interpreted as a sign of innocence sanctioned by divine will; otherwise, guilt was presumed.

This practice was codified in the *Lex Salica* (Salic Law) of the ninth-century Frankish Empire, which stipulated that individuals accused of theft must undergo a fire trial. If burned, they were deemed unable to withstand divine judgment and were sentenced to death; if unscathed, they were permitted to pay a fine instead. Similarly, the *Manusmriti* recounts the case of Bardopa, who was falsely accused by his half-brother of being the son of a Shudra woman. To prove his innocence, Bardopa walked through fire and emerged unharmed, which was taken as divine confirmation of his truthfulness. Further, the fourteenth-century Code of Commerce of medieval Serbia (Article 152) required defendants to carry a red-hot iron from a church entrance to the altar as part of the fire trial. The widespread application of such trials, particularly to slaves, stemmed from the cultural reverence for fire as a sacred, purifying force and a medium for divine judgment.

In addition to water and fire trials, other methods were historically used to determine the facts of a case, including divination, drawing lots, and cross trials. Divination involved both parties praying to a deity regarding disputed facts, followed by a ritualistic interpretation of omens or hexagrams. The judge would then decide the case based on the perceived outcome of the divine revelation. When multiple witnesses offered conflicting testimonies on the same issue, the method of drawing lots was sometimes employed to resolve the discrepancy. The cross trial, practiced among Christian communities in medieval Europe, required the plaintiff and defendant to stand face to face with arms extended horizontally, forming a cross shape. The party able to maintain this posture the longest was deemed the victor in the dispute.[4]

2.3.2.2 Eid Law

The Eid law refers to a method of proof whereby a party or witness swears an oath to God to establish the truth of a fact in dispute. Under this method, if a party or witness refuses to swear, exhibits fear or panic while swearing, or appears to suffer divine retribution within a certain period after the oath, these signs may be interpreted as evidence of guilt or as grounds for an adverse judgment.

As a form of divine adjudication, the Eid law is primarily used to verify the authenticity of claims or statements made by litigants or witnesses. Its origins can be traced back to the Babylonian Empire in the seventeenth century BCE, as documented in the Code of Hammurabi. The code stipulates that if a person claims to have lost property and accuses a neighbor of theft, the accused may swear before God to affirm their innocence. If the oath is deemed truthful, the accuser must pay twice the value of the contested goods as compensation. Similar provisions existed in ancient Germanic law, where parties were required to take oaths attesting to the truth of their statements. These oaths could be supported by "auxiliary oaths"—sworn affirmations

---

[4] *[] [Japan] Hero Tingshan: "Freedom of Empiricism", 150 pages, Tokyo: Xueyang Study, 1983.*

by relatives or associates to bolster the credibility of a party's character and claims. Judges could also evaluate the number of oath-supporters as a metric of credibility.

Oaths generally took three forms: (a) voluntary oaths, in which parties swear of their own accord; (b) compulsory oaths, mandated by law; and (c) exculpatory oaths, through which a party asserts innocence. When both parties have taken oaths and the judge remains unable to resolve the dispute based on these declarations, the case may ultimately be decided by interpreting signs believed to reflect divine will.

At that time, religious belief was widespread, and it was customary for people to pray to deities when confronted with uncertainty or disputes. A deep sense of reverence and fear toward the divine prevailed, with the belief that making false statements or deceiving the gods would inevitably provoke divine anger and result in punishment. Within this cultural context, oath-taking served not only as a ritual but also as an effective means of fact-finding, as it exerted psychological pressure on individuals and encouraged truthful testimony.

2.3.2.3 Duel Law

The duel (Zweikampf) was a form of divine adjudication in which both parties used weapons or physical force to resolve legal disputes. When contradictions arose in the parties' statements—particularly when the plaintiff was willing to risk their life to prove their claim and the defendant could not produce exonerating evidence—the judge would order a duel. The victor was deemed innocent, while the loser was considered guilty.

Originally a form of primitive private remedy during the Middle Ages, dueling gradually acquired characteristics of divine judgment after the Germanic peoples adopted Christianity. It was believed that divine intervention would ensure the victory of the righteous party, thereby signaling their innocence. Refusal to engage in combat often led to a presumption of guilt. As a judicial mechanism, dueling was widespread in medieval Europe and remained legally recognized in France until its abolition by Parliament in 1818. Duels typically involved parties of equal social status; in civil cases, it was also permissible to appoint professional duelists to fight on one's behalf.

The weapons used varied according to social class: nobles and gentlemen fought with swords and shields, while commoners used wooden sticks. This practice, particularly the adversarial format of the duel, influenced the development of modern adversarial legal systems.

2.3.3 *Analysis and Evaluation of the Divine Evidence System*

The system of divine evidence refers to a method of resolving legal disputes by appealing to supernatural forces to determine the authenticity or correctness of the facts in a case. As it relies on divine revelation, the system is inherently vague and unscientific, lacking the necessary reliability for accurately ascertaining facts.

Although such methods occasionally led to the discovery of truth in practice, their outcomes were largely arbitrary and unpredictable. Consequently, this system failed to provide consistent protection of parties' legal rights and interests, rendering it one of the most regressive evidentiary systems in legal history.

Nevertheless, the divine evidence system was widely accepted and maintained for a significant period, serving a specific role in resolving complex disputes during its time. In the late stages of primitive society, attributing the resolution of difficult cases to divine will represented a form of historical progress compared to earlier practices centered on personal revenge. Framed as a search for divine truth, the system relied on perceived external authority to assign conclusive evidentiary weight. Within its historical context, this approach held limited yet meaningful value in the evolution of judicial processes.

2.3.3.1 The Emergence of the System of Divine Evidence Has Historical Inevitability

Under the historical conditions of the time, people lacked the scientific means to understand complex natural and social phenomena. When judges were unable to determine the truth of a case, they often found themselves incapable of rendering a judgment based on evidence. Consequently, they turned to widely held religious beliefs, relying on divine intervention and supernatural forces to resolve factual disputes. The concept of an omniscient and omnipotent deity—believed to observe all human actions—provided a framework through which the truth could be revealed. The use of divine evidence reflects an attempt to unify human judgment with presumed divine insight, embodying the convergence of "human adjudication" and "divine judgment."

2.3.3.2 The System of Divine Evidence Had a Certain Degree of Legitimacy at that Time

In the historical context of that time, belief in God was deeply rooted in society, and the law was perceived as divinely ordained—formulated by God and reflecting divine will. As such, the truth revealed through divine intervention was broadly accepted and socially legitimized. Even methods that might now be regarded as primitive or barbaric were considered sacred and justifiable. This acceptance stemmed from the fact that concepts such as rationality and justice were subordinate to religious faith and reverence for divine authority. Consequently, divine will was equated with justice and moral correctness, a notion widely embraced and deemed legitimate by the society of that era.

2.3.3.3 The Method of Determining the Facts of a Case in the System of Divine Evidence Has Historical and Progressive Significance

The system of evidence presentation in early societies employed religious and psychological coercion to ensure the perceived authenticity of case facts. By replacing physical retaliation with formal procedures, it marked a shift from private retribution to public adjudication, representing a relatively "civilized" and progressive development in legal history. As Monroe Smith observed, this system "appeals to the terror of one party, making them feel that if they pretend to be hypocritical, it will inevitably offend the wrath of God, and therefore cannot but be a truthful statement" [5]. Under this system, a party was compelled to swear that their testimony was truthful, relying on the fear of divine retribution to promote honesty. In this sense, the so-called "chosen truth" of God could, in certain instances, reveal the factual circumstances of a case.

One reason this irrational and unscientific system persisted for such a long time was the absence of more reliable methods for determining the truth. In societies that lacked developed evidentiary procedures, divine judgment was seen as the most feasible approach to resolving complex disputes. As Cesare Beccaria noted, "in the barbaric ancient legal system, the tests of fire and boiling water, as well as other unpredictable conflicts, were once referred to as divine judgments, as if the links of the eternal chain in God's hands could be easily broken and disconnected by human reckless means at any time" [6]. Divine judgment effectively transferred the burden of human responsibility onto a higher power, thereby absolving judges of moral accountability for potentially flawed decisions.

2.4 System of Legal Evidence.

The legal evidence system emerged as a successor to the divine evidence system. It refers to a framework in which the types of admissible evidence, the probative value assigned to each type, and the conditions under which judges may rely on such evidence are all predetermined by statutory provisions. Under this system, judges are bound to render decisions strictly in accordance with these legal rules.

---

5 *[] [American] Monroe Smith: "A History of the Development of European Law", translated by Yao Meizhen, 45 pages, Beijing: China University of Political Science and Law Press, 1999.*

6 *[] [Italy]Cesare Beccaria: "On Crime and Punishment", translated by Huang Feng, 38 pages, Beijing: China Legal Publishing House, 2005.*

2.4.1 The Origin of the Legal Evidence System

In the early Roman Empire, a messianic prophecy circulated among the Jewish population. Following Rome's transition from a city-state republic to an imperial system, the empire experienced a spiritual crisis, leading to the adoption of Christianity as the state religion. With the rapid spread of Christianity—particularly after Pope Gregory VII's reform in 1075—canon law emerged as the only universally applicable legal system in medieval Europe. As productivity advanced and human understanding of natural and social phenomena deepened, public faith in the "divine evidence system" declined. With the rise of feudal monarchies, new political realities demanded a more rational and systematic approach to evidence. In 1215, the Lateran Council of the Catholic Church officially prohibited the use of divine evidence. This was followed by its abolition in France (1260), the Holy Roman Empire (1290), and later in England. The legal or statutory evidence system gradually replaced the divine evidence model.

The emergence of feudal monarchies and inquisitorial procedures necessitated a transformation of judicial institutions into instruments of centralized state power. Judges, once serving regional feudal lords, were redefined as enforcers of imperial interests. This shift gave rise to a legal evidence system designed to support centralized authority. Statutory evidence rules were codified in texts such as the *Constitutio Criminalis Carolina* (1532), the Austrian Code of Criminal Procedure (1853), and the 1833 Russian Imperial Code of Laws. Particularly within ecclesiastical courts, highly formalized rules were developed for evidence evaluation. These rules assigned fixed, calculable values to various types of evidence, forming what became known as the principle of statutory evidence.

Beginning in the thirteenth century, canon law began to exert increasing influence over secular legal systems, disseminating the statutory evidence principle throughout major Western European feudal states. This principle became entrenched in their legal traditions, reaching its peak between the 16th and 18th centuries. Elements of the statutory evidence system continue to be reflected in the litigation practices of some European countries today.

2.4.2 The Basic Content of the Legal Evidence System

In the legal evidence system, the law specifies comprehensive evidentiary content and prescribes statutory methods for establishing the facts of a case. These systems generally encompass the following components.

2.4.2.1 Established the Classification of Evidence

In late medieval Europe, certain legal codes categorized evidence into "complete" and "incomplete" types. Incomplete evidence was further classified into three subcategories: wholly incomplete, more than half complete, and less than half complete. For example, the Complete Code of Laws of the Russian Empire defined the following as complete evidence: (a) the confession of the accused; (b) documentary evidence; (c) physical inspection; (d) expert testimony; and (e) testimony from individuals unconnected to the case. In contrast, incomplete evidence included: (a) mutual confessions among co-defendants; (b) information from neighbors regarding personal background and behavior; (c) evidence related to the prerequisites for committing a crime; and (d) confessional oaths. [7] According to this framework, several pieces of incomplete evidence could be aggregated to form one complete item of proof. For instance, if one witness's testimony was considered half evidence, then the consistent statements of two witnesses could amount to one complete item of evidence.

2.4.2.2 Established Rules for Collecting and Assessing Specific Evidence

In countries that adopt a statutory evidence system, legal codes typically provide detailed rules for the collection and evaluation of evidence.

(i) **Rules Regarding the Defendant's Confession**

These rules generally include the following provisions:

(a) Confession as Complete Evidence: A defendant's confession is considered conclusive evidence if it meets certain criteria—namely, it must be voluntarily made by a mentally sound individual, its content must align with established facts, and its authenticity and reliability must be beyond reasonable doubt. A confession made outside of court may also be treated as partial evidence if it is corroborated by a credible third party.
(b) Interrogation Procedures: Legal codes often contain comprehensive provisions governing the procedures, methods, and content of interrogating the defendant. Within the statutory evidence system, the defendant's confession is regarded as the "king of evidence," and historically, coercive methods such as torture were frequently employed to obtain confessions. For example, under the French Edict of 1670, if there was sufficient but inconclusive evidence in a capital case, torture could be used to extract a confession to support a final judgment.

(ii) **Rules for Witness Testimony**

The law prescribes specific rules for the collection and evaluation of witness testimony, which are primarily reflected in the following aspects: (1) The testimony of two

---

[7] [] *[Soviet Union] An Yang Vyshinsky: "Evidence Theory in Soviet Legal Litigation", translated by Wang Zhixiang, pages 92–93, Beijing: Law Press, 1957.*

"typical" witnesses constitutes complete and conclusive evidence. A typical witness is defined as an individual unrelated to the other, possessing full credibility, good character, and providing a statement that is entirely consistent with that of the other. (2) The testimony of a single reliable witness is considered "half evidence" and can only establish a high degree of probability. This is because, despite the witness's reliability, individual observations are susceptible to error or illusion, potentially resulting in testimony that does not align with the facts. (3) When the testimonies of multiple reliable witnesses conflict, the judgment should be based on the view held by the majority. (4) If there is an unequal number of witnesses presenting differing accounts, the following evaluative hierarchy applies: the testimony of men takes precedence over that of women; scholars over non-scholars; individuals of high social status over those of ordinary rank; and monks or priests over secular individuals. These evidentiary rules reflect the influence of the hierarchical structure inherent in feudal autocracy on the legal system.

(iii) **Rules for documentary evidence**

The probative value of documentary evidence is assessed based on several factors: whether the document is official (public) or private; whether it was authored by a party to the case, a third party, or a witness; and whether it is an original or a copy. Greater evidentiary weight is generally accorded to official documents, documents authored by the opposing party or by neutral third parties, and to original documents rather than copies.

2.4.2.3 The Standard Law for Determining Evidence Has Been Established

According to the statutory evidence system, once complete evidence is obtained, the judge is obligated to convict the defendant. If only incomplete evidence is available—evidence that is somewhat credible but insufficient to establish criminal liability—the defendant may be deemed suspicious and subjected to interrogation by torture. If doubts persist even after torture, the court may issue a "judgment under doubt" based on the principle of presumed guilt.

2.4.3 Analysis and Evaluation of the Legal Evidence System

The legal evidence system emerged in response to declining belief in divine creation and was shaped by the constraints of feudal autocracy, ultimately evolving into a tool that served centralized authority. The feudal system not only demanded political unity but also viewed judicial activities as a key mechanism for consolidating central power. Consequently, the development of the statutory evidence system was primarily driven by political factors. As feudal centralized states formed, a unified judicial and procedural system was established nationwide. To preserve the central government's absolute authority, laws were enacted to codify the evidentiary weight and application rules for different types of evidence. This standardization helped eliminate regional disparities in evidentiary practices and transitioned judges from being instruments of local lords to functionaries executing the monarch's legal authority.

The statutory evidence system is closely associated with the inquisitorial model of litigation, which dominated late medieval Europe. Under this model, courts could initiate and prosecute criminal cases without external complaints. Defendants were reduced to mere objects of inquiry, devoid of rights to defense, and trials were typically conducted in secrecy. Judges were not required to assess evidence critically or independently; instead, they applied rigid formulas defined by law to quantify evidentiary value and determine case outcomes. The probative value of evidence was predetermined and static across all cases. Thus, judges merely applied legal calculations to determine facts, a process that, despite its limitations, was more advanced than reliance on divine intervention.

Historically, the statutory evidence system represented a significant advancement over the divine evidence system. One of its primary functions was to curtail judicial arbitrariness. By requiring judges to follow prescribed evidentiary rules, the system introduced a degree of consistency. For instance, it prohibited judgments based solely on the testimony of a single witness and codified distinctions between original and duplicate documentary evidence. Some of these rules reflected practical judicial experience and possessed a degree of scientific validity. However, the system's excessive reliance on legislative authority and its distrust of judicial discretion reduced judges to mere functionaries. As John Henry Merryman observed, judges under this system resembled "mechanical operators" whose sole role was to apply formulas developed by legislators. [8]The result was a rigid legal process with limited adaptability.

The statutory evidence system imposed strict rules on the probative value of evidence, often employing numerical calculations. This formalistic approach emphasized "legal truth" over factual truth. It facilitated presumptions of guilt and frequently led to the use of torture. While divine evidence had emphasized a notion of equality before a higher power, the statutory system institutionalized an unequal power dynamic between the defendant and the state. Moreover, the system universalized localized evidentiary practices and enshrined them in law, leaving little room for judicial interpretation based on the specific facts of each case. Judges were constrained by legal formulas, often unable to assess probative value contextually, thereby limiting their ability to uncover the truth.

Although the statutory evidence system projected an image of objectivity and fairness, in practice, it was far from impartial. Judges ostensibly made rulings based on legal rules rather than personal judgment, but in reality, the law was open to interpretation. Despite its detailed nature, the statutory framework could not address every scenario, allowing judges a degree of discretion. This interpretive flexibility undermined the perceived objectivity of the system and occasionally resulted in inconsistent rulings.

---

[8] *[!] [American] John Henry Merriman, "The Continental Legal System," translated by Gu Peidong* et al., *37 pages, Beijing: Law Press, 2004.*

During the dominance of the statutory evidence system across continental Europe, England remained an outlier. Due to its unique geographical, historical, and cultural conditions, the English legal system—while incorporating some formalistic elements—never fully adopted a rigid statutory evidence framework. Instead, it maintained a more flexible approach, emphasizing judicial discretion and adversarial procedure over codified rules.

2.5 Free Evaluation of Evidence System.

The system of free evaluation of evidence refers to a framework in which judges, guided by their conscience and rational judgment, independently assess the admissibility, credibility, and weight of evidence to form a firm belief regarding the facts of a case. This system originated from the French concept of intime conviction, which was formally codified in the 1806 French Code of Civil Procedure. Japan adopted a similar principle in its 1890 Civil Code, using the term "heart evidence," which was later translated into Chinese as "free heart test." Today, the system of free evaluation of evidence is widely applied in both civil law and common law jurisdictions.

2.5.1 The Origin of the System of Free Evaluation of Evidence

After the victory of the bourgeois revolution, a hybrid form of litigation emerged across continental Europe. The system of free evaluation of evidence was introduced during the French bourgeois revolution and gradually replaced the statutory evidence system by the mid-19th century.

Robespierre, a leader of the Jacobin faction during the French Revolution, was among the first to advocate combining the advantages of legal evidence with the judge's discretionary evaluation. He proposed that judicial trust in legal evidence should be complemented by the judge's inner conviction. The first legislative proposal to abolish the statutory evidence system and establish a framework for the free evaluation of evidence is attributed to the French jurist Dubois. On December 26, 1790, he submitted a reform draft to the Constitutional Council, proposing the elimination of the written trial procedure and the statutory evidence system. Dubois argued that when facts become the object of judicial inquiry, the central task should be the determination of truth. According to him, there are two possible approaches: one, to predetermine which types of evidence can be used to establish truth—thereby requiring judges to reach a verdict based on fixed rules, regardless of personal conviction; and two, to allow judges to consider all available evidence, make their own moral judgments, and render decisions based on their inner belief. He criticized the statutory evidence system as inherently flawed and potentially dangerous to both defendants and society.

Following deliberations, the Constitutional Council adopted Dubois' proposal on January 18, 1791. A decree issued on September 29, 1791, formally required judges to base decisions solely on their own free evaluation of the evidence. Later, the French Code of Criminal Procedure of 1808 codified this principle, stipulating that judges must base their decisions on the facts of the case, the methods of defense, and their own conscience. This was the first explicit legislative endorsement of the free evaluation of evidence system.

Subsequently, several European countries followed France's example. The Italian Code of Criminal Procedure of 1865 and the German Code of Criminal Procedure of 1877 both incorporated similar provisions. This led to the widespread adoption of the free evaluation of evidence system in countries such as Japan, Germany, and Russia.

After the Norman Conquest of England in 1066, led by Duke William of Normandy, the English legal system began to develop independently. Over time, the inquisitorial influences introduced via the English Channel—often associated with the so-called "Frankenstein Inquisition"—gradually diminished, as England adapted to its distinct social structure and political framework. This evolution contributed to the emergence of the jury system and laid the groundwork for the principle of free evaluation of evidence. The newly developed evidence system in England not only granted judges greater discretion in assessing the probative value of evidence but also established specific procedural rules for the examination and evaluation of evidence. [9]For a significant period after the introduction of witness testimony before juries in the judicial process, evidence law remained undeveloped. It was not until the seventeenth century that formal rules of evidence began to emerge in civil courts. [10]

The establishment of the modern jury system in the United Kingdom has significantly influenced the evolution of its evidence system. On one hand, the probative value and admissibility of evidence are assessed freely by the jury, without any legal prescription regarding the weight or effectiveness of specific types of evidence. On the other hand, the long-standing implementation of the jury system rendered the detailed evidentiary rules associated with the doctrine of legal evidence incompatible with jury trials. As a result, the doctrine of legal evidence was gradually abandoned and replaced by the doctrine of free evaluation of evidence, which permits jurors to assess the value of evidence based on their independent judgment.[11] At the same time, to enable professional judges to guide lay judges (jurors) unfamiliar with legal principles in the evaluation of evidence, a series of evidentiary rules gradually emerged through the accumulation of judicial precedents. Following the bourgeois revolution

---

9 [] *Chen Haoran: "Principles of Evidence Science", p. 162, Shanghai: East China University of Science and Technology Press, 2002.*

10 [] *[England]Cecil.Turner: Principles of Kenney's Criminal Law, translated by Wang Guoqing* et al., *p. 504, Beijing: Huaxia Publishing House, 1989.*

11 []*Chen Pusheng: Criminal Evidence Law, p. 547, Taipei: Sanmin Bookstore, 1979.*

in Britain, the evidence system inherited from the feudal era was retained and further developed. These evidentiary rules became increasingly systematic, giving rise to a formalized model of the free evaluation of evidence.

2.5.2 The Basic Content of the Free Evaluation of Evidence System

The core of the system of free evaluation of evidence lies in determining the authenticity, probative value, and factual relevance of various types of evidence. Unlike the statutory evidence system, the law does not prescribe specific rules for this process; instead, judges are granted the discretion to assess evidence based on rational judgment and conscience. Here, "freedom" refers to the judge's ability to evaluate probative value without being bound by rigid formalities. The belief formed in the judge's mind through the evaluation of evidence is often referred to as "inner conviction" or "heart evidence." This conviction must reach a level beyond reasonable doubt. A more complete articulation of this principle is found in Article 342 of the 1808 French Code of Criminal Procedure, widely regarded as a classic formulation of free evaluation of evidence. It states: "*The law does not concern itself with how jurors determine facts... nor does it prescribe any rules as to whether the evidence is complete or sufficient; it only requires jurors to examine the evidence with sincerity and honesty, and to assess what impression it makes upon their minds. The law does not say: 'The fact proved by several witnesses is necessarily true'; it simply asks: 'Have you formed your inner conviction?' That is the sole duty of the juror.*" Similarly, Article 353 of the revised 1863 French Criminal Procedure Code stipulates: "*The law requires the judge to reflect silently and sincerely, to evaluate the evidence and the defense, and to clarify the impressions left by the proceedings. The only question the law asks the judge is: 'Have you formed a belief in your heart?' This is the judge's entire responsibility.*" Importantly, the "freedom" in free evaluation of evidence is not absolute. It is a relative freedom, exercised within the constraints of objectivity. Judges remain bound by the requirement to base their inner conviction on actual evidence and rational deliberation, rather than subjective intuition or arbitrary preference.

Many countries adopt the principle of free evaluation of evidence in their legal systems. Under this principle, a judge's independent assessment of evidence must be based on lawfully obtained materials that possess evidential capacity and must comply with established rules of evidence law. Specifically: (a) Conclusions must be drawn from the overall circumstances of the case; (b) Judgments must be made through comprehensive discretion and consideration of all facts; (c) The evidence should not be assessed in isolation but considered in its totality; (d) Each piece of evidence must be evaluated according to its intrinsic nature and relevance to the case. While the system emphasizes judicial discretion, such discretion must conform to the principles of empirical experience and logical reasoning. The principle of empirical experience refers to conclusions drawn from common human experiences in daily life, not from subjective assumptions. The principle of logical reasoning requires that the evaluation of evidence align with general standards of rationality, and that the judge's conclusions be reasonable and proportionate. Failure to exercise this discretion appropriately may amount to abuse of discretion. In this framework, "evaluation" is the process, and "inner conviction" (or mental evidence) is the result. Inner conviction arises through proper evaluation. The goal of free evaluation is not to remove all constraints, but to ensure a rational and flexible assessment process—unbound by rigid formulas—so as to reach a truthful and just conclusion. Notably, correct inner conviction cannot exist without a proper evaluative process; freedom in judgment does not mean the freedom to disregard logic or experience.[[12]].

2.5.3 *Analysis and Evaluation of the System of Free Evaluation of Evidence*

The system of free evaluation of evidence represents a significant departure from the statutory evidence system. It emphasizes judicial subjectivity by liberating judges from the rigid constraints imposed by formalized evidentiary rules, thereby empowering them to assess evidence and determine facts based on reason, conviction, experience, and conscience. This approach significantly enhances the judge's active role in fact-finding and facilitates the pursuit of substantive truth in judicial proceedings.

As a historical advancement over the statutory evidence system, free evaluation of evidence reflects a partial reconciliation between "personal judgment" and "legal judgment." It marks a return to the authenticity and moral reasoning behind legal provisions. By replacing the authoritarian and rigid evidentiary mandates of earlier systems with a framework grounded in conscience and rationality, this system constitutes a transformative shift in the development of evidence law.

The free evaluation of evidence rejects the formalism inherent in the statutory evidence system. It advocates for a more flexible and discretionary approach, underlining the importance of individual initiative while maintaining a balance between subjectivity and objectivity. This system more accurately aligns with the inherent logic of judicial proceedings, supports the pursuit of substantive truth, and has given rise to a rich and evolving theoretical framework in evidence law.

The system of free evaluation of evidence upholds the principle of evidence-based adjudication, requiring judges to assess evidence through repeated reasoning and comprehensive analysis of all facts and materials related to the case. This approach helps minimize personal bias and arbitrary judgments. Rather than rejecting the normative function of legal rules, the free evaluation model coexists with and complements evidentiary norms, promoting coherence within the broader legal framework.

---

[12] *// Li Xuedeng: "Comparative Study of Evidence Law", p. 712, Taipei: Wunan Book Publishing Company, 1992.*

Its alignment with democratic litigation principles supports the modernization and democratization of judicial processes.

However, the system is not without drawbacks, particularly concerning the principles of evidence assessment. Theoretically, it involves a high degree of subjectivity. In contexts where judges possess strong ethical standards and adhere strictly to procedural safeguards, the system can effectively approximate truth and meet high thresholds of probability. Nevertheless, because it relies heavily on the personal judgment of judges, legal systems that adopt it often impose both internal and external procedural constraints, including the requirement to justify evidentiary conclusions, to ensure objectivity and transparency.

While both common law and civil law jurisdictions embrace elements of free evaluation, their emphases differ. In civil law systems, which typically adhere to the principle of state-led prosecution, the system is geared toward factual truth-finding, particularly through professional judges. The formation of a judge's inner conviction is paramount, though the law often provides limited guidance on how such conviction should be reached, and evidence rules remain underdeveloped in this respect. In contrast, common law systems—particularly those incorporating the jury system and adversarial procedures—emphasize the protection of litigants' procedural rights. Consequently, they have developed a more detailed and complex set of evidentiary rules to regulate the trial process.

2.6 Internal Confirmation Evidence System.

The internal conviction evidence system primarily refers to the evidentiary framework adopted by the former Soviet Union and Eastern European countries. Under this system, judges are required to form a psychological determination of the facts based on a firm belief in the accuracy and reliability of their judgment. In other words, the judge must be subjectively convinced, without reasonable doubt, that their factual determination is correct.

2.6.1 The Origin of the Internal Conviction Evidence System

Following the judicial reform of 1864, Russia abolished the statutory evidence system. On November 7, 1917, the Bolsheviks, led by Lenin, launched an armed uprising, overthrew the bourgeois provisional government, and established the world's first socialist state under the dictatorship of the proletariat. This marked a fundamental transformation of the legal system. The 1918 Regulations on the People's Courts of the Soviet Union stipulated that courts were not bound by formal evidentiary rules and could determine the admissibility and weight of evidence according to the specific circumstances of each case.

The Criminal Procedure Code of the Soviet Union, promulgated in 1922, reinforced this principle by stating that courts were free to evaluate evidence and should base their judgments on inner conviction, formed through comprehensive consideration of all case facts. This approach was further codified in the Basic Principles of Criminal Procedure of the Soviet Union and the Member Republics, enacted in October 1924, which affirmed that judges were not constrained by any fixed evidentiary forms and should evaluate evidence solely on the basis of inner conviction. Influenced by Soviet legislative and judicial practices, several Eastern European countries adopted similar systems of evidence evaluation based on internal conviction.

2.6.2 The Basic Content of the Internal Conviction Evidence System

The Soviet Union, in distinguishing between bourgeois legal consciousness and conscience, placed particular emphasis on establishing an internal conviction evidence system rooted in "socialist legal consciousness." Article 17 of the *Criminal Procedure Outline of the Soviet Union and Its Constituent Republics* states: "Courts, procurators, investigators, and inquiry officers shall evaluate evidence in accordance with the law and socialist legal consciousness, based on their inner conviction formed through a comprehensive, thorough, and objective examination of all case materials. No evidence shall have a predetermined value for courts, procurators, investigators, or inquiry officers." A similar provision appears in Article 19 of the *Civil Procedure Outline of the Soviet Union and Its Constituent Republics*. This evidentiary approach was further affirmed in Article 71 of the 1961 *Criminal Procedure Code of the Soviet Union*, which solidified the principle of internal conviction as a cornerstone of Soviet evidence law.

Professor Cherizov, a prominent Soviet jurist, argued that a judge's inner conviction in the Soviet legal system was grounded in several core principles: (a) Inner conviction reflects the judge's belief in the accuracy and reliability of the criminal facts and their conclusions regarding the perpetrator; (b) It is not an instinctive or uncritical impression, but a conclusion derived from a reasoned evaluation of various facts and forms of evidence, and therefore can be logically explained and defended; (c) It must be based on admissible evidence obtained in accordance with procedural rules; (d) Inner conviction is formed through a comprehensive assessment of all evidence in the case; (e) It is closely intertwined with the judge's socialist worldview, personal life experience, and professional background. In Soviet procedural law—both criminal and civil—the task of evaluating evidence falls exclusively within the court's jurisdiction. The judge's inner conviction, formed through a holistic consideration of the case's circumstances, serves as the sole legitimate foundation for judicial determinations. As Cherizov emphasized, "The conviction of the judge is not merely the recognition of facts, but their determination. It entails not only an understanding of how and why an event occurred, but also the ability to evaluate its legal and social significance. This conviction is inseparable from the judge's ideological beliefs, worldview, and political-legal consciousness."[13]

2.6.3 Analysis and Evaluation of the Evidence System of Inner Certainty

The Soviet system of internal conviction introduced new dimensions to the doctrine of free evaluation of evidence, particularly by emphasizing the decisive role of "socialist legal consciousness" in shaping judicial conviction. Central to this framework is the objective and comprehensive assessment of evidence, which is seen as essential to uncovering the truth. This system asserts that conviction involves not only the recognition of facts but also their establishment. It requires judges to assess the evidentiary significance of events while aligning their understanding with broader societal interests. "The formation of inner conviction itself is free, but the basis and basis for forming conviction are not free." [14]These elements contribute positively to the scientific evaluation of legal facts. However, the system's heavy emphasis on the judge's class background and overarching political-legal consciousness introduces risks of subjectivism. This overreliance on ideological factors may distort the objective application of evidence, potentially undermining the accurate determination of case facts.

The fundamental distinction between the internal conviction evidence system and the free evaluation of evidence system lies in the former's explicit emphasis on "socialist legal consciousness." Nevertheless, both systems share a common opposition to the statutory evidence system, as each affirms that the probative value of evidence should be determined through the judge's independent judgment.

2.7 Questions and Reflections

The decline of divine judgment in legal history gave rise to the use of coerced testimony and forced confessions, as judges, acting as legal agents, assumed the responsibility of examining evidence. In essence, legal truth becomes the product of the cognitive subject's conviction, formed through the interaction between the cognitive subject and object. Although the story of King Solomon's judgment may lack historical accuracy, his exceptional wisdom and fair adjudication have long been admired by the people of Israel—particularly during the barbaric and brutal era of slavery. His legacy reflects an early awareness of justice that transcended

---

[13] *[] [Soviet Union] An Yang Vyshinsky: "Evidence Theory in Soviet Legal Litigation", translated by Wang Zhixiang, pages 196, 215, Beijing: Law Press, 1957.*

[14] *[] [Japan] Hero Tingshan: "Freedom of Empiricism", 4 pages, Tokyo: Xueyang Study, 1983.*

the limitations of divine or supernatural adjudication. Based on the case referenced and the contents of this chapter, consider the following critical questions: (a) What methods did ancient Western societies use to determine the facts of legal cases? (b) Why did those societies adopt such methods for adjudication? (c) How did the fact-finding methods employed by judges reflect the economic, political, religious, and customary traditions of their time? (d) Did these evidence systems contribute to a high incidence of wrongful convictions? (e) How should we understand the notion that the formation of "inner conviction" (or heart syndrome) is free, while the foundation and basis for forming that conviction are not?

Extended Reading

Vyshinsky, A. Y. (1957). Suweiai Falü Shang de Susong Zhengju Lilun [Translation of Теория судебных доказательств в советском праве] (Wang, Z. X., Trans.). Beijing: Law Press China. (Original work published 1950).

Li, X. D. (1992). Zhengju fa bijiao yanjiu [A Comparative Study of Evidence Law]. Taibei: Wu-Nan Book Inc. (in Chinese)

Li, P. F., & Pan, C. (2014). Yingguo zhengju fa shi [British History Evidence Act] [Chinese]. Beijing: Law Press China.

Damaska, M. R. (2003). Evidence Law Adrift (Li, X. J. et al., Trans.). Beijing: China University of Political Science and Law Press. (Original work published 1997).

Damaska, M. R. (2006). Evidence: Comparative Study (Wu, H. Y. et al., Trans.). Beijing: Chinese People's Public Security University Press. (Original work published 1973–2003)

Whitman, J. Q. (2012). The Origin of Reasonable Doubt—The Theological Basis of Criminal Trial (Si, H. Q. & Li, W., Trans.). Beijing: China University of Political Science and Law Press. (Original work published 2008)

Chapter 3
The Historical Development of China's Evidence System

3.1 Introductory Case

During the Northern Song Dynasty, a wandering monk passed through a village late in the day. Seeking shelter, he approached a local household for accommodation. Initially refused, he persisted and requested only to sleep overnight in the carport outside the house. The homeowner eventually agreed. That night, a thief climbed over the wall and entered the house. Shortly after, the monk, who was resting in the carport, witnessed the thief exiting with a woman and a large bundle. Fearing he would be blamed for the theft—especially since he had been denied shelter indoors—the monk decided to flee before dawn. In his haste to escape, he ran across a nearby grassland and accidentally fell into an abandoned well. Surprisingly, he was unharmed. He felt as though he had landed on something soft. Upon investigation, he discovered that he had fallen onto a recently deceased body. In a state of shock and fear, he instinctively rubbed his blood-stained hands against his robe. When daylight came, he realized the corpse was that of a woman who had evidently been murdered and discarded in the well. Meanwhile, the homeowner discovered the theft and his wife's disappearance. He gathered neighbors to search the area. They noticed bloodstains near the well and heard the monk shouting for help from within. They lowered a rope, retrieved the monk, and subsequently recovered the woman's body. Suspecting the monk, they beat him severely and turned him over to the authorities. During interrogation, the monk, fearing torture, confessed to the crime under duress. He claimed he had maintained an affair with the woman and persuaded her to elope. However, concerned about being seen traveling with a woman, he said he decided to kill her and dispose of the body in the well, accidentally falling in himself. He added that the stolen bundle and weapon were left by the well, but he did not know who had taken them. The authorities accepted his confession as fact, closed the case, and sentenced him to death.

When Prime Minister Xiang Minzhong assumed responsibility for the case, he found it difficult to deliver a conclusive verdict. The absence of both the murder

H. Guo, *Evidence Jurisprudence in China*, Understanding China,
https://doi.org/10.1007/978-981-95-3981-9_3

weapon and the stolen property raised doubts. He personally interrogated the monk, who sighed and said, "This is a debt I owed in a past life. In this life, I must repay it—there is nothing more to say." Xiang Minzhong became even more suspicious. After repeated interrogations and careful persuasion, the monk finally recounted the events of that night in detail. In response, Xiang Minzhong ordered the case to be temporarily set aside and initiated a covert investigation into the matter.

3.2 Chapter Overview

This chapter examines the historical evolution of China's evidence system, focusing on four main stages: the brief presence of a divine evidence system in ancient China, the development of an atypical statutory evidence system, the emergence of a modern free evaluation system, and the current pragmatic approach to evidence. Throughout this evolution, the Chinese evidence system has consistently emphasized the role of party statements—particularly those of the defendant—and documentary evidence. It also underscores the importance of investigations conducted by authorities exercising official powers, with the ultimate goal of discovering the truth and accurately establishing the facts of a case.

3.3 Evidence System in Ancient China

In ancient China, the "God Oath Law" was employed as a method for establishing the facts of a case. Historical records indicate that even into the early 20th century, certain ethnic minority regions in China continued to practice forms of "divine judgment." However, foreign methods of divine testing—such as the "fire trial" and "water trial"—were largely absent from mainstream Chinese judicial practice, aside from occasional use in minority communities. For instance, according to Volume 27 of the Yunnan Gazetteer during the Kangxi reign, the Yi ethnic group in Wuding Prefecture resolved disputes by invoking divine authority: "They report to the heavens, boil soup, throw objects, and catch them with their hands. If the hands bend, they decay; if they remain straight, they remain unharmed." China's ancient legal system, shaped primarily during the slave and feudal periods, experienced a brief phase of divine evidence practices followed by the development of an atypical statutory evidence system. Over time, judicial officials accumulated practical experience in the collection, evaluation, and adjudication of evidence. This led to the formation of an evidence system that is distinct from those in both civil law and common law traditions, reflecting a uniquely Chinese approach to evidentiary standards and legal reasoning.

3.3.1 Evidence System in the Slave Society Era

In ancient China's slave society, the ruling class consisted primarily of slave owners. In the early stages of this period, written laws were not yet established, and governmental functions—judicial and administrative—were not institutionally separated. Case adjudication was largely based on traditional customary laws. To safeguard their economic interests and political privileges, the slave-owning class developed rudimentary legal systems characterized by barbaric features, drawing on personal experience and common sense as instruments of class domination. Historical texts indicate that the Xia Dynasty was the first slave-owning dynasty in China, with references to "chaotic governance and punishments under Yu". Subsequent dynasties, such as the Shang, implemented systems like "Tang's punishment", while the Zhou introduced the "rites and measurements" (li and du), and further advanced legal systems such as the "Lü system" and "Lü punishments". These legal frameworks included elements relevant to the administration of evidence. During periods marked by strong theocratic influence, divination was often employed in criminal proceedings to seek divine approval for punishment, reflecting the belief that judicial decisions required endorsement from the gods. In the civil domain, evidentiary practices were mainly derived from precedent and the interpretations of judicial officials. The evidence system of China's slave society exhibited characteristics distinct from those of Western societies. These unique features are outlined in the following sections.

3.3.1.1 Limited Prevalence of Divine Evidence

In the early stages of ancient Chinese society, a limited form of divine judgment was practiced. The traditional Chinese character "灋" (fǎ), meaning "law," reflects this historical connection. It comprises the water radical "氵," signifying balance and fairness, and the component "Zhi" (廌), which refers to a mythical one-horned beast known as Xiezhi (獬豸). According to legend, the Xiezhi could distinguish right from wrong. During the reign of Emperor Yao, the judge Gao Tao would invoke this divine beast when he encountered uncertainty in judicial decisions. The Xiezhi was said to charge the guilty party with its horn, symbolizing divine adjudication in difficult cases. This gave rise to the expression: "Gao Tao governs punishment, and those whose guilt is unclear are judged by the touch of the Xiezhi." During the Shang Dynasty, the Yin people demonstrated strong reverence for deities and frequently engaged in divination for important decisions. Oracle bone inscriptions indicate the widespread practice of divination. However, these inscriptions provide insufficient evidence to support the existence of a formalized system of divine judgment in judicial proceedings. The Book of Rites (Liji) suggests that during this period, oaths and curses were used in lieu of systematic evidentiary procedures. The divine evidence system in ancient China was short-lived and lacked the institutional structure seen in its Western counterparts.

Unlike Western societies where religion often played a central role in governance, religion in China did not dominate public life. Judicial officials primarily relied on tangible evidence when adjudicating cases. Only in especially complex or ambiguous situations did they resort to divine guidance. Even then, such reliance was limited and cautious. As a result, divine judgment never developed into a mainstream evidentiary system in ancient Chinese jurisprudence. By the Zhou Dynasty, only remnants of divine judgment practices remained, and their influence rapidly declined. The brief existence and eventual disappearance of divine evidence in Chinese legal history highlight both the pragmatic orientation of Chinese legal culture and the relatively underdeveloped nature of early evidence systems.

3.3.1.2 Emphasis on Witness Testimony in Determining Case Facts

During the Zhou Dynasty, the system of divine evidence was largely discontinued. In the Shang and Zhou periods, judicial officials were expected to rely on their experience, assess evidence, and make judgments by observing the parties' speech and behavior. According to the Criminal Law of the Lv State, "The two parties appear and speak; five aspects of speech are examined. These five are as effective as the five punishments." This means that during courtroom proceedings, when both parties presented their statements, the judicial officer would evaluate their credibility through an analysis of the "Five Words," using them as a basis for adjudication.

The "Five Words," also referred to as the "Five Listenings," were five methods employed by judicial officers to infer the mental state of the parties during trial. The Zhou Li · Autumn Officials · Xiao Sikou records: "Hear prison cases with the Five Listenings to discern the people's emotions. The five are: listening to speech, observing facial expression, monitoring breath, assessing hearing, and watching the eyes." Zheng Xuan further explained: "Listening to speech involves examining the clarity and consistency of language; observing color refers to watching facial expressions; monitoring breath involves detecting nervousness or shortness of breath; assessing hearing means noticing confusion or distraction; watching the eyes refers to detecting guilt or evasiveness." These methods required judicial officers to closely scrutinize whether a party's statement was logical, whether their demeanor was composed, whether their breathing was steady, whether their attention was focused, and whether their gaze was direct. In essence, the Five Listenings granted judges a degree of discretion in evaluating personal testimony. This practice reflected the significant weight placed on testimonial evidence, particularly in the absence of physical evidence. Ancient judicial texts emphasized this approach: "Carefully understand and investigate the origins of the matter. First apply the Five Listenings, then corroborate through verification. Observe closely to uncover deception, ensuring that the guilty are punished and the innocent protected." Such practices illustrate the emphasis on testimony in ancient Chinese legal tradition—an emphasis that profoundly influenced evidence evaluation throughout the feudal era.

3.3.1.3 Priority of Confessions and the Role of Investigation

In ancient Chinese litigation, a confession was typically considered essential for reaching a verdict. However, defendants were generally unwilling to admit guilt voluntarily. As a result, judges often resorted to the use of torture to extract confessions. Although it is difficult to determine precisely when torture was first introduced, historical records confirm its existence during the Zhou Dynasty. For instance, the Book of Rites: Monthly Ordinances notes: "In the month of mid-spring, officials were ordered to imprison individuals, remove their fetters, refrain from plundering, and suspend imprisonment," indicating that coercive practices were already in use during that period.

The origins of forensic investigation in China can also be traced back to the Zhou Dynasty. In the autumn months, legal procedures involved divination, examining injuries, observing wounds, analyzing causes, evaluating fear, and adjudicating cases. The severity of physical harm was classified hierarchically: surface skin damage was termed "injury," deeper tissue damage as "wounding," broken bones as "fractures," and the complete severance of bone and flesh as "dislocation." These terms represented varying degrees of bodily harm and were assessed visually by judicial officials to determine the seriousness of the offense. This reflects the longstanding Chinese emphasis on physical evidence and practical investigative methods. In civil litigation, judgments primarily relied on contractual documents such as Fu Bie (符别) and Yue Yi (约义), underscoring the importance of written records in dispute resolution.

3.3.1.4 The Leniency Principle for Cases of Doubt in Ancient China

In ancient China, there was a legal practice of treating suspected crimes with leniency, reflecting the principle of "leniency in cases of doubt." A record from the Lv Penal Code during the Zhou Dynasty illustrates this approach. The Code states: "The five punishments are pardoned when there is doubt; fines are pardoned when there is doubt; all should be examined carefully by the court." According to Kong Anguo, this means that when there is uncertainty regarding the imposition of severe punishments—such as tattooing, cutting off limbs, castration, or execution—the penalty could be reduced to a fine. Similarly, in doubtful cases where a fine would normally be imposed, the punishment could be exempted altogether. Such legal leniency, particularly in an era marked by low levels of productivity and limited public understanding, should be regarded as a rare and progressive development in early Chinese jurisprudence.

3.3.2 The Evidence System of Feudal Society

From the Spring and Autumn Period to the Warring States Period, the power of the landlord class in China gradually expanded, and the feudal social structure was fully established during the Qin Dynasty. In this period, the Chinese evidence system was characterized by the institutionalization of practices such as "obtaining confessions to determine guilt," "conviction based on public testimony," and the widespread use of torture. Judicial officials retained broad discretionary authority in evaluating the probative value of evidence, and a formal legal evidence system—such as that found in feudal Europe—did not fully materialize. In the late Qing Dynasty, influenced by Western legal traditions, China began incorporating elements of modern evidentiary practice, including the presumption of innocence, the principle of free evaluation of evidence, and adversarial verbal argumentation. However, these reforms coexisted with residual features of the traditional feudal evidence system, resulting in a hybrid model in which judicial discretion remained dominant. The evidence system of China's feudal era exhibited several distinct characteristics, which are discussed below.

3.3.2.1 The Supreme Status of Oral Testimony

Throughout China's feudal dynasties, oral testimony played a central role in the evidence system and was often regarded as the most authoritative form of proof—earning the title "king of evidence." Among various forms of testimony, the defendant's confession was considered the most compelling, giving rise to the evidentiary principle of "confession first."

Historically referred to as the "first truth," a confession specifically denoted the defendant's admission of the alleged offense. In practice, a conviction was often contingent upon such a confession, giving rise to institutional rules such as "no record without testimony" or "no conviction without confession." For instance, in the Records of the Grand Historian, the *Biography of Li Si* describes how Zhao Gao extracted a confession through torture and deception. Despite Li Si′s initial resistance, repeated interrogations ultimately led to his coerced confession. Legal codes across dynasties reinforced the centrality of confession. The Tang Code stipulated that in cases involving vulnerable defendants—such as the elderly, the young, or the infirm—where a confession could not be obtained, conviction must rely on objective evidence. Similarly, the Ming Code mandated that "criminal charges must be verified through the prisoner's confession." The *Draft History of the Qing Dynasty: Annals of Criminal Law* explicitly stated that "a confession must be obtained to establish guilt."

In summary, ancient Chinese legal practice placed disproportionate weight on confessions, often treating them as decisive or exclusive evidence. This long-standing reliance underscores the pivotal role of confession in the traditional Chinese evidentiary framework.

3.3.2.2 The Legalized Status of Judicial Torture

From the Zhou Dynasty to the Qin Dynasty, the use of torture in judicial proceedings gradually became legalized and institutionalized. The *Sealing and Diagnosis Style* found in the Qin bamboo slips records: "In managing prisons, following written procedures and behavior is essential. Prioritizing non-responsive questioning, concealment, and appealing to emotional manipulation is ideal; resorting to direct coercion and force is considered the last resort. Instilling fear is viewed as a form of failure." From the Qin through the Ming and Qing dynasties, Chinese law consistently authorized the use of torture during interrogations. Over time, it developed standardized regulations governing the conditions, procedures, instruments, and limits of torture, effectively establishing a systematic approach to its application. For example, the *Tang Code* stipulates: "A suspect must not be subjected to more than three levels of torture, and the total number of blows shall not exceed two hundred. In cases where full torture has not been administered, the suspect may be released on bail." Similarly, the Northern Wei Dynasty limited beatings to fifty strokes, and the Sui Dynasty capped them at two hundred. Historical texts also reflect how torture could be misused. During the Eastern Han Dynasty, there was a case involving a woman from Yangling who, along with an accomplice, murdered her husband. Her uncle, upon discovering the crime, attempted to pursue the perpetrator. In order to frame him, the woman smeared her uncle with blood and cried out, "Why do you conspire with me to secretly kill your brother?" She then reported the incident to the authorities. The officials, during their interrogation, subjected the uncle to excessive torture, which ultimately led him to falsely confess to the crime.

Although the application of torture to extract confessions was legally sanctioned throughout Chinese history, legislation imposed formal restrictions on its use. These limitations pertained to the types of cases eligible for coercion, the subjects of interrogation, procedural safeguards, specific techniques, designated locations, and permissible frequency. Despite its brutality, torture had a veneer of legitimacy in feudal society due to its codification in law. However, these practices did not amount to a coherent or principled legal evidence system in the modern sense.

The use of torture as a method of evidence collection was not unique to China. It was also prevalent in other civilizations, including ancient Greece and Rome. In the Middle Ages, torture was a widespread judicial tool across cultures. The detailed legal provisions regulating torture became a distinctive feature of the evidence system in China's feudal era.

3.3.2.3 Presumption of Guilt vs. Presumption of Innocence

One of the fundamental reasons for the legal acceptance of torture in feudal Chinese society was the presumption of guilt. Once a defendant was accused of a crime, the burden of proof shifted to them—they were required to provide sufficient evidence of their innocence; otherwise, they would be deemed guilty. In this context, all defendants were obligated to provide a confession. Failure to do so—especially refusal to admit criminal conduct—often resulted in the use of torture. During the Qin Dynasty, the purpose of interrogating defendants extended beyond establishing innocence to compelling confessions of guilt. If one is exceptionally clean yet deceitful and refuses to comply, then one who ought to be plundered shall indeed be plundered. In cases where guilt or innocence could not be clearly determined, principles such as "leniency in cases of doubt" and "redemption in cases of doubt" were applied. Additionally, civil evidentiary rules followed maxims such as: "In disputes over property, it is better to yield to local officials to avoid injustice; in disputes over personal appearance or character, it is better to accommodate local officials to preserve credibility."

3.3.2.4 The Influence of Patriarchal Clan Culture on the Evidence System

The rule of patrilineal clans was a defining feature of the ancient Chinese legal system and remains a significant characteristic of traditional Chinese jurisprudence. During the Western Han Dynasty, legal provisions began to incorporate the principle of "mutual concealment among relatives." In the fourth year of the Benshi reign of Emperor Xuan of Han (70 BC), an imperial decree stated: "The relationship between father and son, and between husband and wife, persists beyond life and death. Even in the presence of criminal conduct, sincere affection binds their hearts. The utmost expression of familial kindness and loyalty must not be violated. Henceforth, children may conceal crimes committed by their parents, wives by their husbands, and grandchildren by their grandparents; conversely, parents may conceal crimes committed by their children, husbands by their wives, and grandparents by their grandchildren. Even in capital cases, all shall be reported to the court but judged with leniency."This provision reflects the profound influence of patriarchal family structures and Confucian moral philosophy on the development of evidence law. Beginning in the Han Dynasty, this concept of familial concealment was gradually formalized and institutionalized, giving rise to a distinctive evidentiary system imbued with patriarchal values.

3.3.2.5 Trial Emphasis on the "Five Hearings" Method and Witness Scrutiny

Throughout Chinese legal history, the "Five Listening" (wuting) method has been regarded as an essential tool for examining and assessing the veracity of parties involved in litigation. During the Western Han Dynasty, records indicate that "every line of a prisoner's statement was to be documented while observing their expressions, revealing numerous instances of false emotions." The *Tang Code of Punishments* further institutionalized this practice by stating: "When interrogating prisoners, one must first assess the consistency and rationale of their arguments, conducting multiple examinations. If a determination cannot be reached and further questioning is required, the case shall be documented, and a consistent verdict rendered before proceeding with interrogation." Similarly, during the Ming Dynasty, interrogators were instructed to "observe the suspect's expression and listen to their emotional tone." It was believed that "those whose speech is forceful and whose expressions remain unchanged are likely telling the truth, whereas evasive language and inconsistent demeanor indicate a weaker position in reasoning."

3.3.2.6 The Low Status of Witnesses and Rules Against False Accusation

In the Han Dynasty, China established the system of "mutual concealment among relatives," which imposed an obligation on family members not to testify against one another. However, in feudal society, witnesses were often treated in the same manner as plaintiffs and defendants: they were detained, required to kneel during proceedings, and subject to arrest and interrogation. The practice of interrogating witnesses was widespread in Chinese judicial proceedings and is documented in Tang Dynasty legal texts. For example, the Tang Code: Douzheng stipulates: "In cases where an individual falsely accuses another of abortion, if torture was not previously applied to the accused but the allegation is proven false, the accuser's punishment shall be reduced by one grade. However, if torture had already been used, the punishment shall not be reduced. This also applies when torture was used on witnesses." In addition, ancient Chinese litigation required "corroborated testimony" to secure a conviction—when no confession was available, at least three witnesses were needed to establish the defendant's guilt. In civil cases, consistent testimony from multiple witnesses increased the likelihood that the evidence would be accepted. The generally low social status of witnesses in ancient China was closely tied to prevailing hierarchical views, including the concept of "untouchability." Perjury was criminalized relatively early in Chinese legal history, with severe penalties imposed. During the Han Dynasty, it was stipulated that witnesses who gave false testimony would be punished as if they had committed the crime themselves. The Tang Code similarly addressed witness responsibility, stating: "If the testimony is false and leads to an erroneous conviction, the witness's punishment shall be reduced by two degrees."

3.3.2.7 The Relatively Developed System of Investigation and Inquest

Ancient Chinese society exhibited relatively advanced levels of productivity and civilization, which laid a material foundation for the early development and application of physical evidence and forensic techniques. Compared to other civilizations, China adopted the use of physical evidence in judicial proceedings at an earlier stage and developed more sophisticated inspection methods, thereby establishing a tradition of emphasizing on-site investigations.

Evidence played a central role in the adjudication of cases and was regarded as the principal basis for determining facts. From local judicial officials to ordinary citizens, the use of evidence in resolving disputes was widespread in legal practice, forming a distinct evidence system. Civil disputes—including those over property, rights and wrongs, land, and boundaries—were commonly resolved through the testimony of witnesses and the submission of historical maps. Such practices contributed to social order and public trust in the legal process. During the reign of Emperor Xiaozong of the Song Dynasty, the issuance of the *Inspection of Frontline and Back People's Travel Maps* further standardized and institutionalized injury and property inspections.

The evidence system in criminal law differed significantly from that in civil law. Criminal proceedings rarely relied on documentary evidence, whereas civil cases frequently employed it. Torture was used extensively in civil litigation—not only against the parties but also against witnesses. In legal codes of ancient China, provisions related to evidence law were predominantly focused on criminal matters. Civil evidentiary rules, by contrast, were seldom codified and instead were primarily reflected in judicial precedents. This discrepancy illustrates the traditional Chinese legal philosophy of "emphasizing punishment over civil rights."

3.4 Evidence System in Modern China

Evidence legislation in modern China, particularly during the late Qing Dynasty, adopted the legislative model of civil law countries. It primarily drew upon the legal frameworks of nations such as Germany and Japan. The legal system of evidence was codified separately within procedural laws, thereby establishing a distinctive evidentiary system in modern Chinese legal practice.

3.4.1 The Evidence System under the Beiyang Government

After the Opium War in 1840, Chinese society underwent profound transformations, leading to significant changes in the legal system. The evidence system of this period continued to reflect many practices rooted in the feudal autocratic tradition while also absorbing elements of Western legal theory, particularly the principle of "free evaluation of evidence." The 1911 Xinhai Revolution, led by Sun Yat-sen, marked a turning point by overthrowing the Qing Dynasty and ending over two thousand years of imperial rule, thereby establishing the Republic of China. Concurrently, the use of torture and corporal punishment was abolished, representing progress in the development of the evidence system. In 1912, the Beiyang Government came to power, and in 1922, it promulgated the Criminal Procedure Regulations and Civil Procedure Regulations, which replaced the earlier Trial Regulations for Trial Courts at All Levels. These reforms contributed to the formation of a relatively comprehensive and modern evidence system. The characteristics of the evidence system during this period can be summarized as follows.

3.4.1.1 A Relatively Complete Statutory Framework

The laws promulgated by the Beiyang government established a relatively comprehensive evidence system. The *Criminal Procedure Regulations* expanded the scope of evidentiary provisions by introducing rules on search, seizure, and investigation, in addition to the original sections on witness testimony and expert appraisal. Notably, the regulations introduced protections against coercive practices, stipulating that interrogation of defendants must not involve violence, coercion, inducement, deception, or other improper methods. The *Civil Procedure Regulations* featured a dedicated section on evidence, which was systematically organized into six categories: general provisions, personal evidence, expert appraisal, documentary evidence, investigation, and preservation of evidence.

3.4.1.2 The Preliminary Establishment of Free Evaluation of Evidence

The legislation of foreign governments was influenced by Western legal thought and initially adopted the system of free evaluation of evidence. According to the Criminal Procedure Regulations, "Criminal facts shall be determined based on evidence," and "Evidence shall be freely evaluated by the court." However, as noted in precedents from the Dali Court, although courts possess the discretion to assess evidence, such evidence must be both legally obtained and factually reliable to serve as a valid basis for determining criminal liability.

Furthermore, the system governing witness testimony was relatively well-developed. The *Civil Procedure Regulations* stipulated that individuals have a legal obligation to serve as witnesses in the litigation of others, regardless of their social status or personal involvement. The Dali Court emphasized that it is the civic duty of all individuals to appear in court as witnesses when summoned, irrespective of their rank or background.

3.4.2 The Evidence System under the Nationalist Nanjing Government

In 1928, the Legislative Yuan of the Nanjing government enacted the Criminal Procedure Law and the Civil Procedure Law. These two procedural laws were subsequently amended in 1935 and 1946. In 1929, Professor Yang Zhaolong introduced the course "Introduction to Evidence Law" at Shanghai Law and Politics University and published *Evidence Law* in 1930—the first textbook on evidence law in China. The evidence system during this period was marked by the following key characteristics.

3.4.2.1 Case Law as an Important Source of Evidence System

In addition to procedural regulations, the *Trial Regulations for Trial Courts at All Levels* included several provisions related to evidence. To address the limitations of these legal provisions, the Dali Court issued numerous judicial precedents. Even after 1921, despite the successive enactment of procedural laws in both northern and southern China, the Dali Court continued to issue precedents to guide judicial practice. These precedents became a significant source of the evidentiary legal system and contributed to the development of an evidence framework that, to some extent, diverged from the traditional civil law model.

3.4.2.2 Established a Large Number of Evidence Principles

The Nationalist Nanjing government established a comprehensive framework of evidentiary principles, which primarily included the principles of evidence-based adjudication, free evaluation of evidence, direct trial, and oral argument. Articles 282 and 283 of the Criminal Procedure Law stipulate that "the facts of a crime shall be determined based on evidence" and that "evidence shall be freely judged by the court." Similarly, Article 297 of the Civil Procedure Law requires that the results of evidence investigations be communicated to the parties for adversarial debate. Notably, the Nanjing Provisional Government issued the *Presidential Decree on the Prohibition of Torture* on March 2, 1912, which provided that "interrogation should be based on sufficient evidence and should not rely solely on confessions." This provision is widely regarded as the starting point of the evidentiary principle emphasizing evidence over confessions in judicial practice.

3.4.2.3 Established some Rules of Evidence

During the Nanjing government period under the Kuomintang, several evidentiary rules were established. These included provisions restricting the unlawful use of torture to obtain confessions from defendants, rules governing presumptions and admissions in civil litigation, stipulations assigning greater probative value to original documentary evidence than to its copies or summaries, and rules on the preservation of evidence. For example, Article 282 of the Civil Procedure Law stated that if a fact claimed by a party was previously included in a written statement, an oral argument, or admitted before appointment or authorization as a judge, it did not require further proof. Similarly, no evidence was needed for facts presumed by law in the absence of contradiction. Courts were also permitted to infer the truth or falsity of a disputed fact based on established facts.

Although the evidentiary principles and rules developed during the Beiyang government period were largely retained during the Nanjing period—including some flawed provisions—the Nanjing government nonetheless made substantive progress in the development of the evidence system. Certain rules introduced during this period even had a lasting influence on the modern Chinese law of evidence.

3.5 Evidence System in Contemporary China

By critically examining the evidence systems of both pre-modern China and Western countries, New China developed its own approach through continuous reflection on judicial practice. This led to the formation of two distinct evidence systems: one during the New Democratic Revolution period and another following the establishment of the People's Republic of China. Each system reflects different institutional frameworks and exhibits unique characteristics in terms of evidentiary standards, procedural norms, and judicial principles.

3.5.1 The Evidence System during the New Democratic Revolution

The Communist Party of China established the people's judicial system as early as the revolutionary base period, during which an accompanying evidence system also emerged. On December 13, 1931, the Central Executive Committee of the Chinese Soviet Republic issued Order No. 6, stipulating that "in terms of trial procedures… corporal punishment must be resolutely abolished, and reliable evidence and various effective methods must be adopted." Article 17 of the Current Governance Program of the Jin-Cha-Ji Border Region, issued on August 13, 1940, emphasized that "the trial of Chinese traitors must be based on reliable evidence." Similarly, the 1941 Governance Outline of the Shaanxi-Gansu-Ningxia Border Region declared the need to "improve the judicial system, resolutely abolish corporal punishment, and prioritize evidence over confessions." Further, Articles 8 and 10 of the Regulations on the Protection of Human Rights and Property Rights in the Shanxi-Gansu-Ningxia Border Region (February 1942) mandated that "judicial and public security organs must have sufficient evidence to arrest suspects," and prohibited "insulting, beating, or torturing suspects, forcing confessions, or relying solely on confessions in trials." The Interim Measures for Handling Litigation Cases in the Suzhong Area also reinforced these principles by stating: "If the plaintiff or defendant asserts facts in their favor, they bear the burden of proof." In civil dispute investigations, the plaintiff, defendant, and relevant parties were required to submit supporting documentary evidence. Collectively, these measures laid a foundational framework for abolishing the feudal-era evidence system and promoted the establishment of a more modern, evidence-based judicial process.

During the War of Resistance Against Japan, judicial work in the liberated areas adapted to local conditions and gave rise to the "Ma Xiwu Trial Method." This approach emphasized bringing cases to rural communities, conducting on-site investigations, and relying on the masses for fact-finding and case resolution. By integrating legal proceedings with grassroots participation and localized inquiry, this method established a trial practice rooted in investigation and research. It played a significant role in promoting the gradual development of a fact-based evidence system.

During the Chinese War of Liberation, the People's Government of North China promulgated the Regulations on the Rights and Responsibilities of County and City Public Security Organs and Judicial Organs in Handling Criminal Cases on November 20, 1948. The regulations stipulated that investigative responsibilities were to be assigned to public security organs, whose primary task was to gather facts and evidence regarding the defendant's alleged criminal activities and to prepare cases for prosecution. Judicial organs were granted the authority to review cases and evaluate the facts and evidence collected. Importantly, the regulations emphasized that if the defendant was merely under suspicion and no substantive evidence existed to establish guilt, a conviction and sentencing were impermissible. Further guidance was provided on January 13, 1949, when the People's Government of North China issued the Instructions for Clearing Up Unresolved Criminal Cases. This directive stated that: if new evidence definitively disproved the original judgment, the individual should be exonerated and released; if the evidence supporting the original conviction remained unverified, the verdict should be changed to not guilty; if some charges could be substantiated while others could not, the unsubstantiated charges should be dismissed; and if a new crime was discovered or if substantial errors were identified in the original trial, the prior judgment could be annulled and replaced with an appropriate new sentence.

Although the evidence system during the New Democratic Revolution was fragmented, incomplete, and contained numerous deficiencies, it nonetheless represented the embryonic form of the evidence framework under the people's democratic regime. It laid a good practical foundation for the creation of the evidence system of new China and provided a solid institutional basis.

3.5.2 The Evidence System after the Founding of the People's Republic of China

On the eve of the founding of the People's Republic of China, the Central Committee of the Communist Party of China issued the *Directive on Abolishing the Six Codes of the Kuomintang and Establishing Judicial Principles for the Liberated Areas.* Following the establishment of the new regime, a nationwide judicial reform movement was initiated, which explicitly criticized traditional trial practices such as formalistic court hearings and interrogation-based adjudication, as well as the subjective evidence system rooted in feudal and Nationalist traditions. On the basis of abolishing the Kuomintang's "Six Codes" and drawing on the Soviet Union's evidentiary framework, New China reconstructed its legal system, gradually forming an evidence law and evidentiary structure characterized by socialist principles and distinct Chinese characteristics.

3.5.2.1 The Legal System of Evidence after the Founding of the People's Republic of China

The evidence system in New China gradually took shape under the influence of Soviet evidentiary theory, through the continuous summarization of practical experience, and developed into a legal framework with distinct Chinese characteristics. The Criminal Procedure Law promulgated in 1979 established a dedicated Chap. 5 titled "Evidence," comprising eight articles. Similarly, the *Civil Procedure Law* (Trial) of 1982, and the *Civil Procedure Law* of 1991 (including subsequent amendments in 2007, 2012, 2021, and 2023), included a specific chapter on evidence (Chap. 6), containing twelve articles. The Administrative Litigation Law, enacted in 1989, also features a dedicated Chap. 5 on "Evidence," with a total of eight articles. Additionally, certain substantive laws, such as the original *General Principles of Civil Law*, include provisions addressing evidentiary issues—such as the reversal of the burden of proof. Collectively, these legislative enactments laid the foundation for the development of China's evidence law system.

To further standardize evidentiary practices, public security, procuratorial, and judicial authorities have issued interpretive rules and guidelines in accordance with the Criminal Procedure Law. For example, the *Several Provisions of the Supreme People's Court on Evidence in Civil Litigation* provide detailed norms governing civil evidentiary procedures. In addition, the Supreme People's Court has issued official responses and interpretive rulings on specific evidentiary matters, including the 1957 *Reply on Whether Persons with a Direct Interest in a Case May Serve as Witnesses* (Fayanzi No. 12573), the 1987 *Reply on the Use of Human Leukocyte Antigen Testing in Parentage Identification* (Fayanfu [1987] No. 20), and the 1999 *Reply on the Admissibility of CPS Multi-Channel Psychological Testing as Evidence in Litigation.* Various judicial organs have also issued internal regulations to address evidentiary issues specific to their operational needs. Furthermore, international conventions to which China is a party contain provisions relevant to evidence. For instance, the *Convention on the Taking of Evidence Abroad in Civil or Commercial Matters*, which China acceded to on July 3, 1997, provides procedural mechanisms for cross-border evidence collection. Together, these laws, judicial interpretations, and international commitments have coalesced to form the modern evidentiary system in New China.

Theoretically, legal scholars have categorized China's evidence system using various descriptors, such as the "evidence system that emphasizes evidence, investigation, and seeking truth from facts," the "comprehensive evidence system,"and the "practical evidence system." Other terms include the "evidence system based on law," the "evidence system in accordance with the law," and systems characterized by "legal certainty," "truth through evidence," and "truth in law."

3.5.2.2 The Characteristics of the Evidence System after the Founding of the People's Republic of China

The evidence system established after the founding of the People's Republic of China encompasses not only statutory provisions on evidence, but also judicial interpretations, guidelines, and authoritative responses that hold practical significance in judicial proceedings. This system exhibits the following key characteristics.

(i) **The types of evidence are exhaustively enumerated**

The evidence system of New China was significantly influenced by the Soviet Union's provisions on criminal evidence and its foundational requirements for proof. In particular, China adopted the Soviet legislative framework concerning six major categories of evidence: witness testimony and victim statements, statements of criminal defendants and suspects, expert opinions, material evidence, records of investigative and trial activities, and documentary evidence.The 1979 *Criminal Procedure Law* of China explicitly classified the following types of evidence: physical and documentary evidence; witness testimony; victim statements; confessions and explanations of suspects and defendants; expert conclusions; and investigation and examination records. Similarly, civil litigation legislation in China, especially the *Civil Procedure Law* (Trial), was shaped by Soviet evidentiary theory—particularly that of Soviet scholar Kleiman. The law recognized six categories of evidence: documentary evidence, physical evidence, witness testimony, statements of the parties, expert conclusions, and investigation records. These categories largely mirrored those of the Soviet model. Subsequent legal developments in China refined these categories. The term "expert conclusion" was revised to "expert opinion," and new categories such as "audio-visual materials," "electronic data," and transcripts were added. China's evidentiary framework is now considered closed, with all forms of legally recognized evidence falling within these enumerated categories.

Notably, while the Soviet model combined witness and victim statements into one category, China initially grouped physical and documentary evidence together but later distinguished them. Furthermore, the Soviet classification included records and documents from investigative and trial proceedings, which in China are manifested as records and documentary evidence of investigation and examination.

(ii) **Adhere to seeking truth from facts in the evidence system**

In China, the foundational principles of the evidence system are derived directly from the Constitution. Article 6 of the Criminal Procedure Law stipulates that people's courts, procuratorates, and public security organs must conduct criminal proceedings based on facts and in accordance with the law. Certain procedural regulations also incorporate practical experience in case handling. For instance, in judicial trials, emphasis is placed on objective evidence and thorough investigation, while confessions alone are not regarded as conclusive. If a conviction is supported solely by the defendant's confession without corroborating evidence, guilt cannot be established. Conversely, where the defendant denies the charges but the available evidence is deemed reliable and sufficient, a conviction may still be warranted. These provisions reflect the core principles of China's evidence system, particularly the mandate to "remain faithful to the truth of facts," which is a direct embodiment of the overarching ideology of "seeking truth from facts" that underpins the evidentiary framework.

(iii) **Emphasize the objective investigation responsibilities of the investigating authorities**

Any evidence system is intrinsically linked to the broader litigation system and exhibits distinct institutional characteristics. It emphasizes both authoritative adjudication and reliance on public participation. In particular, the evidentiary process underscores the role of case-handling authorities, who are expected to collect and utilize evidence through grassroots engagement and thorough investigation—an approach rooted in the tradition of people's justice. For instance, the *Criminal Procedure Law* explicitly states: "Judges, prosecutors, and investigators must, in accordance with legal procedures, collect various forms of evidence that can establish the guilt or innocence of the criminal suspect or defendant, as well as the severity of the offense." Similarly, the *Civil Procedure Law* provides: "If a party or their litigation representative is unable to collect evidence for objective reasons, or if the people's court deems it necessary for the trial, the court shall investigate and collect such evidence." The *Administrative Procedure Law* likewise affirms that "the people's court has the authority to obtain evidence from relevant administrative organs, organizations, and individuals."

(iv) **Emphasize the discovery of objective truth**

China's evidence system is often characterized as a system grounded in the principle of "seeking truth from facts," which is rooted in dialectical materialist epistemology. This theoretical foundation emphasizes the discovery of objective truth as a central goal of evidentiary processes. The system places particular emphasis on establishing the factual truth of a case based on solid and sufficient evidence, thereby upholding fidelity to reality. However, the development of evidentiary rules has lagged behind that of substantive law. As a result, many procedural aspects of evidence law remain underdeveloped, and rules governing evidentiary admissibility and evaluation are incomplete. This has granted case-handling authorities significant discretionary power in the use and assessment of evidence, often without clear procedural constraints. Notably, much of China's evidentiary framework is derived from judicial interpretations rather than codified legislation, reflecting a strong reliance on practical experience over theoretical formalization.

China's current evidence system is grounded in the theoretical framework of dialectical materialist epistemology. It is fundamentally oriented toward the pursuit of objective truth in the determination of facts. The collection and use of evidence emphasize the objective duties and responsibilities of case-handling authorities, reflecting a commitment to fact-based adjudication that differs significantly from the evidentiary traditions of Western legal systems. In recent years, China's evidence regime has increasingly emphasized several key principles: the principle of evidentiary reliance, the principle of procedural legality, and the standard of eliminating reasonable doubt. Notably, the introduction of the exclusionary rule for illegally obtained evidence—within the broader framework of human rights protection—demonstrates a growing alignment with the values of democracy and the rule of law as hallmarks of a modern, civilized legal system.

3.6 Questions and Reflections

Many scholars of evidence law share a fundamental assumption: accurate fact-finding should be the central goal of evidentiary rules. It is important to note that evidentiary rules are largely the product of accumulated judicial experience, designed with the primary purpose of safeguarding the objective truth of the case and preventing wrongful convictions. In the case cited above, a government official, under the direction of the Chancellor, disguised himself as a passing merchant to conduct a covert investigation in a village. Through casual conversation with an elderly shopkeeper, he discovered that the murder had been committed by a local youth. Acting on this information, the authorities searched the suspect's home, where they recovered the murder weapon and stolen property, thereby exonerating the wrongly accused monk. Chinese legal scholars, reflecting on such historical practices, have drawn a theoretical distinction between statutory evidence systems, which they characterize as relying on "artificial algorithms", and free evaluation systems, which are likened to "biological algorithms" due to their flexibility and reliance on human intuition and contextual judgment. This suggests that the essence of evidentiary systems lies in the nature of their epistemological algorithms rather than their underlying purpose. Based on this case and the broader themes discussed in this chapter, the following questions merit further exploration: (1) What investigative methods did ancient Chinese judges primarily rely upon to ascertain the facts of a case? (2) What does the fact-finding process in this case reveal about the characteristics and limitations of the ancient Chinese evidence system? (3) Can the future development of evidence law in China incorporate artificial intelligence to model algorithmic approaches as transparent and visual tools for determining case facts?

Extended Reading

Zhao, C. Y. (2003). Zhongguo gudai xingxun zhidu yanbian guilü zhi yanjiu. Criminal Science (4):110–116. (in Chinese)

Jiang, T. C. (2004). Zhongguo jindai zhengju zhidu yanjiu. Beijing: China Financial & Economic Publishing House. (in Chinese)

Shen, D. M. (2006). Zhongguo gudai de zhengju zhidu ji qi tedian. Journal of Social Sciences, (7):139–145. (in Chinese)
Jiang, T. C. (2010). Zhongguo gudai de zuiyi weiqing. Chinese Journal of Law, 32(2):196–208. (in Chinese)

Chapter 4
Theoretical Basis of Evidence Law

4.1 Introductory Case

Peking University Founder Company and the Red Chamber Research Institute discovered that Beijing Gaoshu Tianli Technology Co., Ltd. and Beijing Gaoshu Technology Co., Ltd. had copied and sold their copyrighted software, including Founder RIP, the Founder font library, and Fang Zhengwen software. In response, they commissioned employees of their subsidiaries to engage in transactions with the infringing companies under the guise of ordinary consumers. Evidence was collected through notarized purchases in coordination with notaries, after which the plaintiffs filed a lawsuit for copyright infringement. In the first instance, the Beijing First Intermediate People's Court affirmed the legitimacy of this so-called "trap evidence collection" method, holding that it was not prohibited by law and should be admissible. Accordingly, the court ruled in favor of Peking University Founder. On appeal, however, the Beijing High People's Court reversed this position. The appellate court held that the evidence collection method violated the principle of fairness and, if widely adopted, could disrupt normal market order. Therefore, the court declined to recognize the method and dismissed the plaintiff's claims. Peking University Founder subsequently petitioned for retrial. In its ruling, the Supreme People's Court found that the appellate court erred in denying the legality of the evidence collection method. It held that the notarized evidence obtained should have been admitted for factual determination. The Court emphasized that Peking University Founder had no improper motive, did not infringe upon the rights of others or the public interest, and that the method was necessary given the covert nature and evidentiary difficulties associated with software copyright infringement. The Court concluded that such methods aid in addressing the evidentiary challenges of intellectual property disputes and align with the legal principle of strengthening intellectual property protection.

H. Guo, *Evidence Jurisprudence in China*, Understanding China,
https://doi.org/10.1007/978-981-95-3981-9_4

4.2 Chapter Overview

This chapter addresses the theoretical foundations of evidence law, focusing primarily on epistemology, value theory, and ethics. Epistemology constitutes the core foundation of evidence law, providing the conceptual basis for understanding how legal actors ascertain truth in judicial proceedings. In contrast, value theory and ethics serve as the normative boundaries of evidence law. Together, these frameworks provide the legitimacy and rational foundation upon which the rules and institutions of evidence law are built, sustained, and developed.

4.3 Epistemological Foundations

The facts of a case do not establish themselves; rather, they must be substantiated through evidence. However, evidence alone does not inherently assert factual truth—it requires a structured process of proof. Accordingly, the act of establishing facts becomes a process of human cognition, whereby evidence is examined to uncover the truth. In this sense, epistemology—concerned with the nature, scope, and justification of knowledge—naturally serves as the foundational theoretical framework of evidence law. "Evidence law is a system of rules that regulates the provision of information to factual adjudicators in legal proceedings. Its better definition is 'courtroom epistemology'."[1] The core question that evidence law seeks to address is how investigators and parties can lawfully and accurately discover the truth. In legal proceedings, regardless of what materials are recognized as evidence, the criteria used to classify types of evidence, the epistemic frameworks applied to novel evidentiary forms, or the processes of discovery, collection, preservation, examination, and evaluation of evidence—each stage of evidentiary handling fundamentally involves human cognition. These activities are intrinsically linked to cognitive capacity, cognitive development, methods of reasoning, and modes of understanding. In this sense, such inquiries fall squarely within the domain of epistemology and should be guided by its principles. Accordingly, epistemology serves as a foundational theoretical pillar of evidence law. This theoretical foundation mainly includes "reflection theory", "epistemology", and "dialectics".

4.3.1 The Reflection Theory of Dialectical Materialism

The primary focus of dialectical materialist epistemology is human cognitive activity. It not only offers scientific and coherent explanations for how individuals come to understand unknown phenomena and pursue objective truth, but also provides

[1] David P.Bergland, Value Analysis in the Law of Evidence, Western State Law Review, 1973, p.162.

essential theoretical guidance. This foundational role explains why evidence law adopts dialectical materialist epistemology as its theoretical basis. According to the reflection theory of dialectical materialism, matter is primary and consciousness is secondary; matter determines consciousness, and consciousness is a reflection of material reality. Cognition enables individuals to identify and distinguish between entities, based on the mind's ability to objectively reflect the external world and arrive at accurate understanding. In the context of evidence law, the principle that negative facts cannot be proven illustrates this theory. Since "negative facts" refer to events that have not occurred, they cannot be objects of human reflection. This idea is also embodied in the legal maxim that "the burden of proof lies with the party who asserts, not with the party who denies." The process of legal proof shares fundamental characteristics with human cognition more broadly. Just as people can achieve correct understanding of the world, legal actors can ascertain the truth of a case through proper evidentiary procedures. Moreover, advancements in cognitive understanding can, in turn, stimulate the evolution of the evidentiary system. Technological developments have introduced new forms of evidence—such as audiovisual materials and electronic data—as well as novel algorithms with strong probative value.

Litigation is fundamentally a process of understanding evidence and establishing the facts of a case. It involves transforming "things in themselves" into "things for themselves," meaning that investigators or parties render unknown case facts into knowable ones through evidentiary analysis. Whether this involves the discovery and extraction of physical evidence as material traces of the case or the interpretation of verbal statements as narratives of fact, the process is inherently linked to the cognitive capacity of those conducting the investigation and the extent to which the case facts are externally manifest. Whether the process involves proof by others or self-proof, it is predicated on the existence of evidence—without evidence, there can be no facts. Even the evolution of the evidentiary system and the development of evidentiary rules are contingent on the extent and sophistication of human understanding of evidentiary issues. A correct understanding of both evidence and the underlying facts—achieved by perceiving the essence through appearances—is essential to achieving accurate fact-finding. Misjudged cases often arise not from the nonexistence of facts or the inadequacy of evidence per se, but from flawed or biased cognitive reflections that fail to accurately connect evidence to the facts. As a discipline dedicated to guiding the use of evidence, evidence law must provide a scientifically grounded epistemological framework that facilitates accurate comprehension of both evidence and factual truth. Anchoring this framework in the dialectical materialist theory of reflection ensures the scientific rigor of the cognitive process it seeks to support.

As the theoretical foundation of evidence law, the theory of reflection should not be equated with the theory of correspondence. It should not be mechanically understood as a form of direct reflection, nor should it be considered a theory of complete conformity or full equivalence. Rather, it is an active reflection theory rooted in dialectical materialism.

4.3.2 Dialectical Materialism and the Theory of Knowability

The epistemology of dialectical materialism holds that human consciousness can accurately reflect objective reality. Evidence law should fully acknowledge that investigating authorities, parties, and other participants in litigation possess a certain level of cognitive ability and the potential to correctly understand evidence and ascertain the facts of a case. This recognition is fundamentally grounded in the knowability of both evidence and case facts. Although the irreversibility of time precludes any factual scenario from being completely restored to its original state, this does not imply that its original state cannot be known or understood. Only by recognizing and addressing this issue, and by adhering to the principle of evidence-based judgment, can the legal system maintain reasonable acceptability and offer a sound explanatory basis for the accurate determination of case facts.

Evidence is knowable, and the truth of a case is also knowable; it can be discovered through evidence, scientific and technological methods, empirical rules, and logical reasoning. This premise underlies the meaningfulness of pursuing the truth of a case through litigation and proof. Whether in the transition from a "divine revelation" evidence system to a "statutory" evidence system, or from a "free evaluation of evidence" system to a "seeking truth from facts" system, the evolution of these models reflects the continuous pursuit of accurate understanding grounded in epistemology. When an existing evidence system is found inadequate to ensure consistency between fact-finding and objective reality—thus increasing the risk of error—society tends to develop a new system, built upon accumulated experience, that is believed to more effectively support the accurate determination of case facts. The progression of these systems embodies the core principles of dialectical materialist epistemology and illustrates humanity's ongoing effort to better understand the world.

Lawsuit proof is a continuous and iterative process that moves from intuitive understanding to rational comprehension, and then returns to judicial practice. The more tools available to ascertain the truth of a case, the more abundant the evidence becomes, thereby increasing the likelihood of uncovering the truth. In ancient times, limited scientific and technological development severely restricted the means by which people could access the truth, thus constraining the accuracy of judicial fact-finding. For example, the traditional method of using blood drops to determine kinship illustrates the rudimentary level of cognitive and scientific understanding of the time. With the advancement of science and technology, both cognitive capacity and evidentiary precision have improved significantly, thereby enhancing the potential for uncovering objective truth in legal proceedings. Today, modern forensic techniques—such as Y-STR typing—enable the identification of biological relationships even in the absence of one parent, providing a reliable means of establishing parentage.

The epistemology of dialectical materialism is not without conditions. While the truth of a case can, in principle, be discovered through evidence, this does not imply that it is knowable in all circumstances. Even with the advancement of science and technology, it remains impossible to achieve complete knowledge of every case. Litigation, as a specialized form of cognition, is inherently constrained by procedural rules and time limitations. To uphold the fundamental principles of fairness and efficiency, there are instances where, despite the theoretical possibility of uncovering the truth, practical limitations—such as procedural boundaries, value judgments, and cost considerations—render full discovery infeasible. However, such constraints do not negate the knowability of case facts. Rather, they underscore the necessity of grounding evidence law in the epistemology of dialectical materialism. Only through adopting a scientific theory of knowledge can we justify the legitimacy of making judgments based on available evidence and proven facts within specific procedural contexts. This framework enables a principled approach to adjudicating complex or difficult cases, avoiding the tendency to indefinitely suspend judgment. Recognizing the inherent limitations of human cognition and the partial visibility of case facts is essential for developing an effective and rational evidence system. Judicial decision-making is not an absolute reconstruction of historical truth, but rather the establishment of a plausible and acceptable representation of past events.[2]This pursuit of acceptable truth—anchored in epistemological realism—constitutes a foundational principle of evidence theory.

Lawsuit proof is a reflective activity by which the subject apprehends the objective existence of the facts of a case, rather than an absolute or self-referential awareness of those facts. Epistemology is not equivalent to omniscience, nor does it imply complete knowledge; rather, it is a theory of knowledge under specific conditions. At the same time, it is necessary to distinguish between the epistemology of idealism and that of materialism, and to oppose agnosticism and skepticism, both of which deny that knowledge can reflect objective reality.

4.3.3 The Dialectics of Dialectical Materialism

Human cognitive activity embodies the unity of absoluteness and relativity; the results of cognition are both absolute and relative. The absolute contains the relative, and the relative also contains the absolute. "On the one hand, the nature of human thought is inherently absolute; on the other hand, it is realized through individuals whose thinking is necessarily limited. In this sense, human thought is both supreme and not supreme."[3] In the field of epistemology, evidence law must acknowledge both the possibility and capacity of human beings to understand evidence and ascertain the truth of facts. At the same time, it must also recognize that human understanding is an endless process of development, because "knowledge is the eternal and unending contact of thought with the object."[4] That is to say, both materialism and dialectics

---

[2] Peter Murphy, Murphyon Evidence, seventh ed., 2000,p.2.

[3] Selected Works of Marx and Engels, Volume 3, Page 126, Beijing: People's Publishing House, 1972.

[4] Complete Works of Lenin, Volume 38, Page 208, Beijing: People's Publishing House, 1972.

must be upheld. Therefore, in determining whether there is a correlation between evidence and the facts of the case, it is essential to "follow the normal course of things, whereby one fact, in itself related to another, can generally demonstrate the existence or non-existence of that other fact—whether in the past, present, or future. The comprehension of such issues cannot be divorced from dialectics."[5] In the process of proof, the facts of the case that have already occurred are the object of cognition, while investigators and parties are the cognitive subjects. Evidence initially serves as the object of cognition and, as the legal process unfolds, becomes a means for understanding case facts. Clarifying the facts themselves is thus part of the cognitive process. Litigation is fundamentally the activity through which investigators and parties seek to understand events that have already transpired. This process of understanding must bear the general features of cognition, namely, that it is "realized among a series of individuals who think inconsistently," and is "a particular and individual realization" of understanding. Although the trial process is designed to uncover and determine the truth, it is ultimately impossible to devise rules that will always ensure correct outcomes.[6]

Although human understanding of phenomena is inherently relative, relativity contains elements of the absolute. Grounded in the theory of absolute truth, it is possible to arrive at a correct understanding of case facts and to ensure the accuracy of judicial decisions through scientific and rational methods. Litigation is an activity aimed at uncovering factual truth, and its evidentiary process is, by nature, a cognitive one. However, unlike scientific inquiry, litigation involves a retrospective understanding of the object of cognition—the facts of a case that have already occurred—rendering it a distinct form of cognitive activity. This distinction is further shaped by temporal constraints, procedural requirements, and the limited availability of investigative tools. The historical and complex nature of case facts, the particularity of the proving subject, the necessity of lawful procedures, and the constraints of evidentiary timeframes collectively introduce obstacles to the discovery of truth through litigation. These limitations may render the full reconstruction of case facts unattainable under certain conditions. Even in instances where facts are deemed established, the truth they represent remains relative. This relativity stems not only from the inherent limitations of human cognition but also from the historicity and evolving interpretation of the case facts themselves.

The above discussion illustrates the guiding role of dialectical materialism in evidence law, rather than the contrary. Without such a foundation, one risks falling into skepticism and relying on subjective personality traits to resolve the irrationalities inherent in fact-finding, ultimately descending into the quagmire of agnosticism. In practice, neither the rationality nor the personal integrity of judges can be assumed to be absolutely reliable or consistent. Therefore, entrusting uniform judicial determinations to inherently variable personal dispositions is akin to constructing a high-rise

---

[5] [English] Stephen: "Concepts of Evidence Law", published in "Foreign Law Translation Series", 1984 (2).

[6] [America] John Rawls: A Theory of Justice, translated by He Huaihong et al., 81 pages, Beijing: China Social Sciences Press, 1988.

building on unstable sand—inevitably courting collapse at any moment.[1] A scientifically sound system of evidence and procedural rules is essential to ensuring that truth, as determined through evidentiary reasoning, aligns with objective reality. In this regard, dialectical materialism offers a crucial theoretical foundation and guiding framework.

Both the formulation of evidence rules and the improvement of evidence systems are inseparable from the fundamental premise of human cognitive activity. Any evidence system, evidentiary rules, or procedures for the application of evidence are constructed on the material foundations and cognitive capacities available at the time, with the principal aim of uncovering the truth of case facts. Epistemology plays a decisive role in this process and occupies a foundational position in the theoretical structure of evidence law. Knowledge, by its nature and across generations, is relative and inevitably tends toward refinement. To assess it against an unchanging and ultimate standard of truth is, as Marx and Engels noted, merely to reveal one's own ignorance and absurdity.[7] Epistemology serves not only to guide our understanding of evidence and the use of evidence to comprehend facts, but—more importantly—it provides a normative legal framework that helps avoid cognitive errors. It functions to suppress irrational factors that may distort the evidentiary process, thereby ensuring the legitimacy of cognition, improving the accuracy of factual conclusions, enhancing the reliability of truth-finding, and ultimately increasing the acceptability of factual determinations.

4.4 Axiological Foundations

The proof of case facts differs from general factual proof in that it not only requires uncovering the truth but also mandates that the truth be discovered through legal, rational, and legitimate procedures. The methods and processes used to ascertain truth must align with the overarching purposes of the law. However, the rationality and legitimacy of these activities, tools, and methods in achieving legal objectives necessitate the coordination and balance of multiple values. As such, value theory has become an indispensable theoretical foundation for evidence law. As a normative framework for dispute resolution, evidence law must take fairness as its core value, while also considering other objectives—such as procedural efficiency—on the basis of truth discovery. When individuals use their intrinsic value judgments to interpret and reconcile the relationship between human actors and the legal world, particularly in assessing the subjects and objects involved in adjudication, questions of value inevitably arise. Knowledge, as a process, unavoidably entails value judgments and selections. Therefore, while evidence law is supported by epistemology, it must also extend into the domain of value theory. In litigation, the discovery of factual truth is neither absolute nor the sole objective. Depending on the circumstances, competing

[7] Selected Works of Marx and Engels, Volume 3, Page 432, Beijing: People's Publishing House, 1995.

considerations—such as the legitimacy of legal procedures or the protection of individual rights—may take precedence. This shift underscores the importance of value theory in guiding the legitimate application and interpretation of evidentiary rules.

4.4.1 The Value Theory of Procedural Justice

Dialectical materialist epistemology is one of the theoretical foundations of evidence law, and its emphasis on the pursuit of objective truth constitutes one of the primary goals of litigation. To achieve this goal, it is essential to uphold the principle of procedural justice. As a legal discipline that bridges both procedural and substantive aspects, evidence law must be guided and constrained by value theory, with procedural justice at its core. Accordingly, it is both reasonable and necessary for procedural justice to serve as the value-theoretical foundation of evidence law. Whether in the collection and preservation of evidence, the provision of mechanisms for evidence preservation, or the examination, evaluation, and use of evidence in establishing case facts, all activities must conform to the requirements of due process. The value-theoretical dimension of evidence law is most prominently reflected in proof activities, exemplified by the principle of handling doubtful cases.

The theory of procedural justice not only requires the legitimacy of the outcome—that is, the discovery of truth—but also demands that the means and methods by which truth is pursued through evidence law be legitimate. This includes rules governing the discovery and collection of evidence, standards for evidential admissibility, and methods for evaluating probative value. From the perspective of procedural justice, these systems and rules must ensure that evidence is not only objective and relevant but also obtained and applied within the framework of legal norms. Furthermore, procedural justice calls for the establishment of remedial mechanisms when due legal procedures are violated, such as the exclusionary rule for illegally obtained evidence. In this sense, procedural justice is an indispensable theoretical foundation of modern evidence law.

4.4.2 The Value Theory of Interest-Balancing

Any evidence system is fundamentally based on the material conditions and the cognitive capacities of individuals at the time, as these are essential to discovering the truth of a case. In judicial practice, the limited availability of judicial resources often results in a strained supply–demand relationship. Procedural justice must therefore be balanced with litigation efficiency, which constitutes a key dimension of judicial fairness. The admissibility provision under Rule 403 of the United States Federal Rules of Evidence exemplifies this economic rationale.[1] It helps restrain parties from excessively investing in irrelevant or low-value evidence collection, while simultaneously safeguarding judicial fairness. This balance enables a more efficient allocation of judicial resources. Accordingly, evidence law, while grounded in fairness as its core value, must also accommodate considerations of litigation efficiency and recognize additional non-litigation values—such as privileges protecting communications among close relatives and immunities granted to certain categories of witnesses. These features illustrate the pluralistic theoretical foundation of evidence law's value system. However, the existence of multiple competing values inevitably gives rise to potential conflicts. When such conflicts occur, the formulation of evidentiary rules must rely on established standards and principles of interest-balancing to determine which values warrant priority and special protection. In doing so, the legal system can justify the limitation or exclusion of competing values. Therefore, the value foundation of evidence law must be pluralistic, and within this plurality, the principle of balancing interests should serve as a guiding norm.

The balance of interests endows human cognition with genuine purposefulness and agency. It governs the cognitive activities of the subject and constrains arbitrariness and recklessness, thereby preventing excessive deviation from the path of procedural justice. People's exploration of the facts of a case is neither arbitrary nor limitless; rather, it must be regulated by procedural justice. The pursuit of factual truth should be guided by the normative goodness of law. When factual truth and legal goodness are in conflict, individuals must choose between them according to certain value-based principles. Evidence law does not merely concern itself with the existence of evidence, but also with what should be considered evidence. For instance, the establishment of the "privilege of exemption from proof" between certain relatives is grounded in the legal value of trust and reflects a normative commitment to legal goodness. Similarly, in the allocation of the burden of proof in civil litigation, while the general rule assigns the burden to the party making the claim, certain exceptional circumstances call for a rebalancing. In such cases, the so-called "three P factors"—comprehensive policy, possibility of proof, and probability—serve as value-based justifications for deviating from standard proof burdens in pursuit of factual truth. These mechanisms reflect the underlying logic of interest balancing. When one party is deemed to have superior access to information, requiring the less-informed party to bear the burden of proof would be both inefficient and unjust.[8] Only by preserving this balance of interests—between substantive justice and procedural fairness—can evidence law guide the collection and assessment of evidence within a virtuous and equitable legal process.

As a legal activity, the discovery of the truth in a case must reflect the requirements of procedural justice. Its core lies in uncovering the truth through due process in order to protect the legitimate rights and interests of the litigants. Evidence law, therefore, should adopt procedural justice as a foundational principle. This not only limits the abuse of public power or party rights but also better safeguards the litigation rights of the parties and other participants. It further facilitates a proper balance between fact-finding and the principles of trust and procedural fairness among the parties. Only by placing the discovery of facts under the supervision of legal procedures

[8] [America] Michael D. Bayless, Principles of Law, translated by Zhang Wenxian et al., 67 pages, Beijing: Encyclopedia of China Press, 1996.

can litigation provide a rational, democratic, and civilized method of proof, thereby enabling the cognitive subject to more effectively fulfill the goal of discovering truth through evidence.

Value theory enhances the role of parties as active participants in litigation, upholds the dignity of litigation participants, and serves as the most rational and prudent guiding ideology for uncovering factual truth. Procedural justice constitutes the fundamental source of the value theory in evidence law. However, the values pursued by evidence law are both diverse and hierarchical, necessitating the reconciliation of value conflicts across different levels. The balance of interests thus becomes the essential foundation for sustaining procedural justice.

4.5 Moral Foundations

The framework of evidence law, within the scope of value selection in fact-finding, may seek to maximize value but must not do so at the expense of human dignity or moral boundaries such as personal integrity. The pursuit of truth cannot justify using any means or accepting any consequences. Therefore, evidence law must be subject to moral constraints, and moral theory has increasingly become a theoretical foundation of evidence law. Morality forms the basis of evidence legislation, and the basic requirements of morality should be respected not only in the formulation of evidence rules but also in their application. Morality thus occupies a fundamental position in the structure of evidence law. It significantly influences the theoretical development, legislative framework, and practical implementation of evidence law, serving as a source of normative ethics within the field.

4.5.1 The Moral Foundations of Evidentiary Principles

In general, individuals morally evaluate objective activities—particularly cognitive activities—based on traditional value scales, including both self-assessment and external evaluation. Only those activities that align with established moral standards are typically accepted; those that do not are rejected. If cognitive activities were devoid of purposeful guidance or reference to value-based frameworks, and exempt from moral evaluation, distinctions between right and wrong, or good and bad, would cease to exist. Human behavior would then risk becoming arbitrary. In the context of evidence law, this would eliminate the rationale for designing investigative procedures or establishing evidentiary rules. As such, "Evidence law should be understood and designed as follows: it is a field that combines moral and epistemological reasons. In this field, after epistemology stops, morality takes over".[9] Thus,

[9] [America] Alex Stein: The Foundation of Evidence Law, translated by Fan Chuanming, etc., 78 pages, Beijing: China Renmin University Press, 2018. Friedrich Baosheng.

moral theory is not only indispensable but also a fundamental pillar of evidence law theory.

The principles, systems, and rules of evidence law are gradually formed and established through the practical activities of countless individuals under specific political, economic, and social conditions, and are invariably shaped by the prevailing moral values of the time. Morality performs a dual function: first, it defines one's goals or ultimate good, falling within the realm of ethics; second, it concerns the means and methods for achieving those goals, which are the focus of moral theory.[10] The balancing of competing values in evidence legislation reflects the ethical value choices made by the state, society, and legislators.[11] The differences in evidence systems among countries are not only the result of divergences in legal traditions, social structures, and economic development levels, but also of variations in moral values. "In most societies, specific legal protections are afforded to the elderly, children, and individuals with disabilities—not because they are more morally valuable to society, but because they possess weaker capacities for self-protection. Similarly, individuals are granted stronger rights protections because they are more vulnerable to state power. Rights theory emphasizes the protection of individuals precisely because they, not society, require special safeguards."[12] "a person who has been granted power always faces the temptation to abuse it and to transgress the boundaries of justice and morality."[13] Consequently, a basic normative requirement of evidence law is to constrain the abuse of public authority and to design procedures that prevent such abuse. From an ethical standpoint, this entails establishing minimum standards for evidence-related activities. It is impermissible to use inhumane or degrading means to discover the truth, and any system of evidence must be rooted in the maintenance of human dignity and fairness in adjudication. These ethical commitments are enshrined in various legal provisions. For instance, Article 52 of China's *Criminal Procedure Law* strictly prohibits the extraction of confessions through torture or the collection of evidence by threats, inducements, deception, or other illegal means, affirming that no one may be forced to self-incriminate. Article 106 of the *Interpretation of the Civil Procedure Law of the Supreme People's Court* stipulates that "evidence formed or obtained through methods that seriously infringe upon the legitimate rights and interests of others, violate prohibitive legal provisions, or seriously

[10] [German]Friedrich Baosheng: "The Ethical System", translated by He Huaihong and Liao Shenbai, 10 pages, Beijing: China Social Sciences Press, 1988.

[11] As stipulated in the approval of the Supreme People's Court's Fa Fu Zi [1995] No. 2, "The acquisition of evidence must first be legal, and only evidence obtained through legal means can be used as the basis for deciding a case. Recording the conversation of the other party without their consent is illegal, and the recorded materials obtained through this means cannot be used as evidence." This judicial interpretation has been continuously revised by the "Several Provisions of the Supreme People's Court on Civil Evidence" and judicial interpretations.

[12] [America]Ronald Dworkin: "Taking Rights Seriously", translated by Xin Chunying and Wu Yuzhang, pages 15–16, Beijing: China Encyclopedia Press, 1998.

[13] [America]E. Bodenheimer: "Jurisprudence - Philosophy of Law and Its Methods", translated by Deng Zhenglai, p. 347, Beijing: Huaxia Publishing House, 1987.

contravene public order and good customs shall not be used as a basis for determining case facts." The *Evidence Law* also mandates restrictions on the collection of evidentiary materials obtained through serious violations of legal procedures, or through methods that infringe upon the legitimate rights and interests of others, such as surreptitious photography, secret recording, or wiretapping. It further prohibits acquiring evidence by improper means, including inducement, fraud, coercion, or violence. Additionally, the unlawful collection of sensitive personal information—such as biometric data, religious beliefs, medical records, financial accounts, and location data—is also subject to legal restriction. For example, Articles 21 and 35 of the *Japanese Constitution* prohibit citizens from secretly recording others in ways that infringe on personal rights, and evidence obtained through such means lacks legal validity. German courts likewise emphasize that technological advancement should not come at the cost of interpersonal trust or the development of individual personality. They hold that the legal order must protect personality-based values and reject the misuse of surveillance technologies.

In addition, certain international conventions have addressed these concerns, such as the *Convention against Torture and Other Cruel, Inhuman or Degrading Treatment or Punishment*. Evidence legislation should fulfill corresponding international obligations. When navigating the tension between achieving substantive justice and protecting citizens' dignity and privacy rights, the law should aim to minimize harm to individual rights. Under no circumstances should it violate fundamental human rights. The protection of human dignity and respect for reasonable moral sentiments must serve as a foundational principle, and such issues should be guided by established moral norms.

4.5.2 The Moral Foundations of the Evidentiary System

Whether viewed historically or across cultures, from East to West, "authentic"evidence is universally regarded as a "good" that aligns with prevailing moral standards and facilitates the smooth functioning of litigation. "False" evidence, by contrast, constitutes an "evil" and poses the significant "disadvantage" of obstructing the fair and efficient conduct of legal proceedings. Importantly, the process of obtaining evidence must also adhere to morally acceptable means. Even in the context of evaluating the value or utility of evidence, moral considerations should serve as an internal boundary in the design of evidentiary rules, ensuring that the evidence system remains subject to ethical constraints.

Maintaining human dignity and safeguarding human rights throughout the processes of evidence collection, review, evaluation, and application is a fundamental responsibility of evidence law. Given the inherent self-interest of individuals, no one should be legally compelled to incriminate themselves or place themselves in a disadvantageous position. Accordingly, evidence law must prohibit the use of coercive measures to induce involuntary "self-incrimination" or "self-accusation", and must uphold humane treatment and fundamental moral sentiments. The evidence system should respect and protect essential moral values such as human dignity, familial relationships, and shared human sensibilities. For example, the evidence system incorporates protections such as the "privilege against testifying" or "witness immunity" between close relatives, as well as the "doctrine of estoppel".

With the advancement of science and technology and the corresponding contraction of private space, increasing attention has been directed toward the protection of personal privacy and related rights. However, the integration of high technology into evidence law has introduced new and invasive threats to these rights. The selection of evidentiary methods must therefore be guided by moral considerations. Evidence law should prioritize the protection of privacy rights and the preservation of human dignity in the refinement of its institutional framework. For example, the notice issued by the Ministry of Public Security on September 7, 1993, prohibiting the establishment of private detective agencies, explicitly forbids institutions such as "security affairs investigation offices," "civil affairs investigation offices," and "socio-economic affairs detective offices" from engaging in activities including the handling of civil and economic disputes, debt collection, locating relatives and friends, providing technical consulting on security measures, and conducting investigations involving personal privacy. In matters involving constitutionally protected privacy rights, moral boundaries must be respected, and the principle of proportionality should not be applied to justify value-based trade-offs. In contrast, where public interest exists in private domains, value balancing may be appropriate—but must remain constrained by the principle of proportionality. Corresponding evidentiary rules should be developed to regulate practices that may infringe upon the personal dignity, health, and privacy of parties and other litigation participants. In essence, the prohibition of illegally obtained evidence serves to protect citizens' privacy rights. Judging such violations requires considering both subjective expectations of privacy and whether such expectations are deemed reasonable by societal standards. Special evidence collection methods—such as surveillance, entrapment, electronic monitoring, covert photography, facial recognition, and compulsory sampling—must be strictly regulated by law. This includes clearly defining their scope, conditions of use, guiding principles, authorization procedures, and rights to legal recourse. Methods that compromise human health or dignity must be categorically prohibited. Additionally, women and minors should receive heightened protection, fully reflecting the fundamental demands of morality.

Evidence law is a highly practical discipline that governs real-life human interactions. In its legislation, it must remain grounded in reality and avoid excessively elevating moral standards or establishing evidence-related systems that surpass practical human nature. Otherwise, it risks rendering evidence legislation abstract and impractical. Therefore, evidence legislation should develop relevant systems within a moral framework, appropriately reflecting the influence of social ethics, family relationships, and the principle of integrity. In certain contexts, it may be necessary to make choices that align with moral expectations and genuine emotional bonds. For instance, in cases involving parent–child relationships, DNA evidence should not be considered the sole determinant. Whether to rely on such evidence must also take into account the emotional connection between parents. In some cases, the legal parent–child relationship may be regarded as more significant than biological ties.[14] As legal practice increasingly relies on big data and incorporates artificial intelligence into evidentiary processes, the ethical challenges in this area have become more complex and pressing.

The issue of moral theory falls within the broader category of value theory to some extent, but value theory does not fully encompass the content of moral theory. Moral theory serves as the normative baseline for maintaining evidentiary rules and adjudication, whereas value theory functions more as a measure of the internal boundaries of morality. Evidence law is grounded in moral theory, which not only ensures the scientific validity, rationality, and alignment with human nature in the legislative design of evidentiary rules, but more importantly, guarantees that such rules reflect China's traditional culture, current national context, and specific policy needs. This alignment enhances societal acceptance and allows evidence law to fulfill its intended roles and functions in practice. Within the theoretical foundation of evidence law, epistemology plays a critical role as it provides the methodological basis for pursuing objective truth in litigation. Meanwhile, value theory and moral theory serve as fundamental safeguards for the legitimate and accurate attainment of that truth. Together, these three dimensions—epistemological inquiry, rational value selection, and moral boundary-setting—collectively constitute the theoretical foundation of evidence law.

4.6 Questions and Reflections

British scholar Jeremy Bentham asserted that "evidence is the foundation of justice; to exclude evidence is to exclude justice." In the retrial by the Supreme People's Court, it was determined that the evidence collection method employed by Peking University Founder was lawful and effective. Consequently, the evidence obtained was admitted as the basis for the verdict. The Supreme Court overturned the second-instance judgment of the Beijing High People's Court and ordered Beijing Gaoshu Tianli Technology Co., Ltd. and Beijing Gaoshu Technology Co., Ltd. to jointly compensate Peking University Founder and the Honglou Research Institute for economic losses amounting to 600,000 yuan, as well as 13,000 yuan in investigation and evidence collection expenses. In 1995, the Supreme People's Court issued a reply to the Higher Peopl's Court of Hebei Province, stating that "recording a conversation without the other party's consent is illegal." Some argue that recording without consent may, in certain contexts, be more justified—particularly if it is not obtained through covert means such as secret recording, hidden filming, or installing spyware on mobile phones, or if it does not occur within private conversational spaces. If the recording involves purely private matters unrelated to the case, the right to privacy should take precedence. However, if the person making the recording is also a party to the

[14] Refer to the Reply of the Supreme People's Court on whether the People's Court can use human leukocyte antigen paternity testing in the trial work (June 15, 1987, Fa (Yan) Fu [1987] No. 20).

conversation and the content is relevant to the case, such evidence is more likely to be deemed admissible. Based on the facts of the case and the content of this chapter, and in reference to the viewpoints above, consider the following questions: (1) What legal theory did the court apply in determining that Beijing Gaoshu Tianli Technology Co., Ltd. and Beijing Gaoshu Technology Co., Ltd. illegally reproduced and distributed copyrighted software, including Founder RIP, the Founder font library, and Fangzhengwen software? (2) How did the court of third instance evaluate the probative value and legality of the "trap evidence collection" method adopted by Peking University Founder and its affiliates? (3) Does the "trap evidence collection" method raise ethical concerns within the framework of evidence law?

Extended Reading

Chen, R. H. (2001). Cong renshilun zouxiang jiazhilun——zhengju fa lilun jichu de fansi yu chonggou. Law Science, 22(1). (in Chinese)
Zhang, J. W. (2002). Zhengju faxue de lilun jichu. Modern Law Science, 24(2). (in Chinese)
Yi, Y. Y. (2004). Zhengju faxue de lilun jichu——yi caipan shishi de ke jieshouxing wei zhongxin. Chinese Journal of Law, 26(1). (in Chinese)
Wang, J. C. (2004). Xingshi zhengju lilun de zhexue jichu. Chinese Journal of Law, 26(6). (in Chinese)
Song, Y. H. et al. (2005). Zhengju faxue jiben wenti zhi fansi. Chinese Journal of Law, 27(6). (in Chinese)
Zhang, B. S. (2008). Zhengju guize de jiazhi jichu he lilun tixi. Chinese Journal of Law, 30(2). (in Chinese)

Part II
Evidence

Chapter 5
Summary of Evidence

5.1 Introductory Case

The plaintiff, Wang, filed a lawsuit against the defendant, Li, for failing to repay a loan. Wang alleged that Li borrowed 2,400 yuan in cash on March 24, 2003, and had since refused repayment for various reasons. Wang demanded immediate repayment and submitted a handwritten promissory note as evidence. The note, written in pencil by Li, stated: "I borrowed 2,400 yuan in cash from Wang. — Li, March 24, 2003." Li contested the validity of the note, asserting that he had borrowed only 400 yuan and that the "2" in "2,400" had been added by the plaintiff. Both parties requested a handwriting identification. However, the appraisal agency appointed by the court was unable to conduct the analysis due to the note being written in pencil. The court subsequently commissioned a public security bureau to conduct a psychological test on Li. The resulting report concluded that Li's statement— "I only borrowed 400 yuan from Wang, not 2,400 yuan"—was credible. Relying on this psychological test report, the court ruled that Li was obligated to repay only 400 yuan. The court also ordered the plaintiff, Wang, to bear the litigation and identification expenses.

5.2 Chapter Overview

This chapter is the content of the basic evidence knowledge, mainly including the definition of the concept of evidence, the basic characteristics of the authenticity, relevance and legality of evidence, the basic attributes of evidence ability and proof power, the basic attributes of evidence admissibility, and the significance of evidence in litigation. Evidence is the most important and basic category of evidence law.

H. Guo, *Evidence Jurisprudence in China*, Understanding China,
https://doi.org/10.1007/978-981-95-3981-9_5

5.3 The Concept of Evidence

Evidence constitutes the core of modern judicial activities and serves as a fundamental category within the field of evidence law, occupying a cornerstone position. It is not only essential to the scientific structure of the theoretical system of evidence law but is also closely connected to the theory of proof and the coordination of the broader litigation framework. Due to the existence of various definitions, the concept of evidence has been expressed in multiple ways.

5.3.1 Different Theories of the Definition of Evidence

The concept of evidence is inherently complex. Due to varying perspectives and research methodologies, both Chinese and international scholars have developed different views and expressions regarding its definition. To fully comprehend and accurately grasp the essence of evidence, it is essential to examine these differing definitions and deepen our understanding through a comparative analysis of the various conceptualizations.

5.3.1.1 The Debate and Basic View of the Concept of Evidence

Scholars, based on their respective research traditions, generally place significant emphasis on the concept of evidence. They focus particularly on legal interpretations, reflections, and foreign theoretical frameworks. As a result, various theories of evidence have emerged, including the "fact theory," the "evidentiary theory," the "material theory," the "reasoning theory," the "method theory," the "outcome theory," the "information theory," and the "unified theory," among others. Therefore, in the process of studying and understanding the concept of evidence, it is essential to grasp and interpret the major theoretical perspectives, such as the "fact theory", "evidentiary theory", "material theory", and "unified theory".

i. **"Fact Theory"**

"Fact Theory" is one of the traditional viewpoints in Chinese evidence law and holds a dominant position in Chinese legal academia. According to this view, evidence refers to all facts that can prove the true circumstances of a case.[1] Given that China's Civil Procedure Law and Administrative Procedure Law do not provide a formal legal definition of evidence, scholarly interpretations have primarily been derived from theoretical extrapolations based on the Criminal Procedure Law. The Criminal Procedure Law once stated: "All facts that prove the true situation of the case are evidence." On this basis, some scholars argue that the facts of a case are objective

[1] 1 Jiang Wei, Evidence Law, 206, Beijing: Law Press, 1999; Wang Guoshu, Criminal Procedure Law, 126, Beijing: Peking University Press, 1998.

realities that come into existence along with the occurrence of the case itself, and that evidence is produced correspondingly and exists objectively. If you know it, it is evidence; if you do not know it, it is not evidence in essence.[2] This perspective links the concept of evidence directly to the occurrence of case facts, equating it with the objective facts arising during the commission of the act in question. However, because such objective facts do not enter the subjective cognition of case handlers as a priori knowledge, they cannot function as evidence in practice. As a result, the"fact theory" fails to convincingly demonstrate that evidence itself constitutes factual reality.

ii. **"Evidentiary theory"**

The "evidentiary theory" defines evidence as the basis for proving the existence of case facts or facts related to legal matters. From a semantic perspective, this view holds that evidence serves a single purpose: to provide proof or a clear foundation for establishing facts. According to this theory, evidence can be true or false and may or may not be accepted by the court.[3] As commonly stated, "evidence must be verified before it can be used as the basis for determining the facts." Some scholars further argue that evidence functions as the basis upon which the court determines the facts of a case.[4] This theory includes two variations: the general "evidentiary theory" and the "adjudicative evidentiary theory". Both emphasize the role of evidence in the court's final decision-making process, linking its definition to whether it is ultimately adopted by the court. However, from the perspective of case facts, this approach does not clarify what evidence is in itself. It defines evidence based on its function in judicial outcomes, rather than on its intrinsic properties.

iii. **"Material Theory"**

The "material theory" holds that evidence consists of materials that can be used to prove the facts of a case. As stated: "All materials that can prove the facts of a case constitute evidence."[5] China's *Criminal Procedure Law* similarly provides: "Materials that can be used to prove the facts of a case are all considered evidence." Comparable provisions exist in other jurisdictions. For example, Article 74 of the *Criminal Procedure Code of the Russian Federation* states: "Evidence in a criminal case includes any materials obtained by courts, chief procurators, investigators, and inquiry officers in accordance with the procedures prescribed by this Code, which establish the presence or absence of circumstances to be proven in a case, as well as other facts relevant to the criminal matter." In theory, "material theory" differs from evidentiary data: while materials are considered evidence, evidentiary data do not necessarily constitute complete evidence. Semantically, referring to witness testimony or statements of parties as materials may appear inconsistent with traditional Chinese linguistic conventions.

---

[2] Wang Jing, On the Judgment of Evidence in Criminal Procedure, Legal Studies, 1980 (4).

[3] He Jiahong: New Evidence Law, 100 pages, Beijing: Law Press, 2000.

[4] Zhang Weiping, The Civil Procedure Law, p. 183, Beijing: Law Press, 2009.

[5] Chen Guangzhong, Editor: Criminal Evidence Law of the People's Republic of China (Provisions, Interpretation and Demonstration), 133 pages, Beijing: China Legal Publishing House, 2004.

iv. **The "Unified theory"**

The "Unified Theory" posits that evidence is the combination of factual content and factual form—that is, it refers to facts presented in a legal form that can demonstrate the true circumstances of a case.[6] While the theory retains the core idea that evidence is fundamentally fact-based, it can be viewed as a revised version of the "fact theory" or "evidentiary theory". Over time, this perspective has gradually gained wider acceptance and has become a more commonly held view.

5.3.1.2 Different Theories of Foreign Scholars on the Concept of Evidence

Foreign scholars have proposed various definitions of evidence, framing it as "reason", "method", "result" and so on.

The "reason theory" posits that evidence is the reason that convinces a judge of the facts of a case. It refers to the internal conviction formed by the judge regarding the truth of the parties' claims.[7] For example, British jurist Bentham argues that anything capable of producing a convincing belief—sufficient to affirm or deny the existence of a fact—qualifies as evidence.

The "method theory" views evidence as the means or method by which the facts of a case are determined. German scholar Bauer, for instance, asserts that aside from oral arguments, any legal method used in judicial investigations to confirm or deny factual claims constitutes evidence.[8]

The "result theory" holds that evidence refers to the outcome of the evidentiary process that explains or establishes the facts of a case. Japanese jurist Matsuoka Yoshiaki suggests that evidence is inseparable from proof and the results of evidentiary investigation.

Foreign theories of evidence typically focus on the trial stage and often define evidence from the perspective of the judge's subjective assessment or the centrality of trial proceedings. As a result, these views reflect a strong element of subjectivity. However, litigation activities such as the discovery and collection of evidence inevitably involve human subjectivity. While this introduces subjective elements, evidence must still retain objectivity—otherwise, the process of proof would lose its factual basis.

In Japan and Germany, the subjects and objects involved in providing data for adjudication are typically viewed as methods of evidence. This includes parties, witnesses, and expert witnesses, as well as their statements, testimonies, expert evaluations, inquest results, and documentary evidence, which are considered both reasons

---

[6] Bian Jianlin, editor: Law of Evidence, 58 pages, Beijing: China University of Political Science and Law Press, 2007.

[7] Chen Yinan: On the Civil Procedure Law (Part I), p. 428, Taipei: Sanmin Book Company, 1999.

[8] [Germany], Otma Yao Enxi, Civil Procedure Law, translated by Zhou Cui, 258 pages, Beijing: Law Press, 2003.

and methods of evidence. Some jurisdictions also categorize the persons involved—such as witnesses and expert witnesses—and procedural tools—such as certificates and investigative records—as evidentiary methods.

5.4 Definition and Characteristics of Evidence

Evidence, as the basis for case determination, must, from an epistemological perspective, exist objectively and maintain a certain degree of connection with the facts of the case to ensure its authenticity. Since evidence serves to prove case facts, it must be meaningfully related to those facts. This connection is referred to as "probative power" in civil law jurisdictions and "relevance" in common law systems. From the perspectives of value theory and moral theory, evidence must be lawfully permitted and collected, secured, preserved, and presented by authorized legal actors in accordance with prescribed procedures. It must also be objectively linked to the facts of the case. As a basis for judicial decisions, evidence must first satisfy the criteria of "evidentiary capacity" or "admissibility." Evidence carriers possess a clearly defined objective form, while their content may be transferred or associated across different carriers or between instances of the same carrier. For example, physical evidence may correspond to and be documented in an investigation report.

Evidence is the legal manifestation of materials used to prove the factual circumstances of a case. Analyzing its content, evidence must be relevant to the facts in question. In terms of form, it exists through a specific carrier, representing a legally recognized type of evidence. From the perspective of its function, evidence serves to establish or refute the facts of the case and therefore possesses probative value. In essence, it is a factual representation or narration that reveals the relationship between the evidence and the facts of the case. The content of evidence cannot be separated from its form. While the content remains relatively stable, the form may vary. Regardless of how the form changes, the content and form of evidence must maintain a unified relationship—two inseparable aspects of a single entity. This unity is the fundamental reason why evidence can be relied upon to determine the facts of a case.

The emphasis on the unity of form and content in evidence arises from the dual requirements in determining its admissibility and probative value. First, the form of evidence—such as physical evidence, documentary evidence, witness testimony, and electronic data—must meet legal standards of admissibility. Second, during the assessment and review process, the content of the evidence—such as the substance of witness statements, expert opinions, and party declarations—must be scrutinized for its relevance and credibility. Evidence consists of both an objective external form and a fixed internal content. Only when these two elements are unified can the evidence possess complete legal and practical significance. As noted: "From a scientific perspective, form and content in litigation evidence are dialectically unified. Content refers to the factual substance or situation, while form represents the method of proof. Litigation evidence must contain both elements. If the method of proof lacks relevant facts, it proves nothing. Conversely, if factual material is not obtained through legally prescribed procedures, it cannot be used as evidence in legal proceedings, nor can it serve as a basis for judicial decisions."[9]

In our country's judicial practice, whether in criminal, civil, or administrative cases, it is required to conduct evidence examination around the authenticity, legality, and relevance to the facts to be proven. "Evidence that can reflect the true situation of the case, is related to the facts to be proven, and whose source and form comply with legal provisions, should be used as the basis for determining the facts of the case." Based on the above analysis of evidence, from a practical perspective, evidence has the following basic characteristics.

5.4.1 Authenticity

The authenticity of evidence requires that its content reflects an objective reality, rather than subjective imagination, speculation, or assumption. It must manifest as an objective presentation or reflection. This authenticity encompasses three key aspects: first, the form of evidence—whether it involves persons, objects, or conditions—must exist objectively; second, the content of the evidence must be an objective reflection of the facts of the case; and third, the connection between the evidence and the facts in question must also be objective. It is important to note, however, that objectivity does not equate to truth. A distorted phenomenon may exist objectively, yet the content it reflects may not be truthful—though the distortion itself remains an objective fact.

In the field of evidence, authenticity is primarily reflected in objectivity. Objectivity forms the foundation for case-handling authorities or parties to discover, collect, identify, and interpret evidence. Evidence is inherently objective, as every action or event occurs within a specific time and space, leaving discernible traces—whether temporal imprints or spatial reflections. Even when evidence is destroyed, the act of destruction itself produces new evidence. From another perspective, case-handling authorities or parties must not rely on subjective assumptions or personal inclinations during the collection and evaluation of evidence, as this would compromise the reliability of the process. Evidence is material that exists independently of individual will, and its objectivity makes it possible to accurately ascertain the facts of a case. Since the facts of a case are objective, the evidence arising from those facts must also be objective. The form of evidence must manifest this objectivity; otherwise, it cannot be accessed or used as a basis for adjudication. Although the substantive facts of a case become part of the past once they occur, the information retained in the form of evidence continues to exist in a tangible and objective form. While various factors—during the stages of evidence generation, existence, collection, and preservation—may introduce elements of subjectivity, and human judgment can influence

[9] [Soviet Union] A. A. Dooborysky, Soviet Civil Litigation, translated by Li Yan, 198, Beijing: Law Press, 1985.

the evidentiary process under certain conditions, such influences do not negate the objective nature or actual existence of the evidence.

However, the objectivity of evidence is distinct from its authenticity. Even when the form, content, and connection of the evidence to the facts of the case are objectively verifiable, this does not necessarily confirm its authenticity. The reverse, however, holds true—authentic evidence must possess objectivity.

Authenticity, or veracity, refers to the truthfulness and objective existence of the content conveyed by the evidence. Fabricated or falsified items do not constitute valid evidence. When a case occurs, it inevitably leaves traces in the objective external world, commonly referred to as "original items" or "original documents." These materials must undergo verification for authenticity, which is the essence of establishing truth. Thus, authenticity is the most fundamental characteristic of evidence. Whether in the process of collecting, reviewing, or evaluating evidence, one must assess factors that affect its authenticity. The evidence subjectively collected by individuals and the evidence that objectively exists are not on the same conceptual level. While human understanding can reflect objective reality, it cannot alter that reality. Although our cognition of case facts may be constrained by external conditions, making it difficult to fully align with objective truth, this does not negate the decisive role of objective facts in the process of understanding. Human cognition may be accurate or flawed, but the object itself remains unaffected by such judgments. In other words, evidence materials submitted by individuals may contain falsehoods, but the falsity lies not in the evidence per se. Some items presented as evidence may, in fact, not qualify as evidence in substance—they may function only as "evidence of evidence" and thus fail to meet the standard of authenticity.

5.4.2 Correlation

The relevance of evidence refers to the substantial connection between a piece of evidence and its probative value concerning the facts of the case. Relevance operates through the logical relationship between the evidence and the facts to be proven. It is reflected in the degree of influence the evidence has on the likelihood of the fact's existence, as indicated by the strength or closeness of their association. Relevance is what allows a piece of evidence to support or refute the existence of a fact that is at issue in the litigation. If a piece of evidence increases or decreases the probability of a fact's existence, it is considered relevant. British jurist James Fitzjames Stephen explains relevance as follows: "The application of the two facts is so interrelated, namely according to the usual course of things, that one of the facts, either by itself or in connection with other facts, can generally be used to prove the past, present, or future existence or non-existence of another fact."[10] Evidence emerges alongside the occurrence and development of a case. It must bear some kind of relationship

[10] Ouyang Tao, et al., Introduction to the Criminal Procedure Law of Criminal Law between America and Britain, page 269, Beijing: China Social Sciences Press, 1984.

to the case facts. This relationship forms the basis for case-handling authorities or litigants to infer and understand the facts through the presented evidence. In this sense, relevance serves as a bridge between the evidence and the determination of case facts.

In general, the relevance of evidence can be categorized into natural relevance and legal relevance. Natural relevance refers to the substantive relationship between evidence and the facts of the case, which is often characterized by various types of connections—direct or indirect, necessary or incidental, causal or non-causal, consistent or inconsistent. These multilayered and multifaceted relationships result in varying degrees of probative value. The complexity of these relationships can pose significant challenges in fact-finding, increase the difficulty of case resolution, and place greater demands on evidence collection and investigation, thereby contributing to the ongoing trend toward the technical and professional refinement of evidentiary practices. Legal relevance, by contrast, imposes a negative limitation on the admissibility of evidence that possesses natural relevance. It refers to statutory or judicial restrictions on certain types of evidence that may lead to undue prejudice, confusion, or distraction from the factual issues at hand, thereby limiting their admissibility in court.

Generally speaking, evidence—as supporting material—precedes the "facts of the case" in the process of proof, even though this sequence is the reverse of how evidence arises naturally. In the natural course of events, the facts of the case occur first, followed by the generation of evidence, though both may sometimes arise simultaneously. Therefore, the logical order of proof in litigation should not be dismissed merely because of the causal relationship between evidence and case facts. Evidence serves as the sole basis for determining the facts of the case precisely because it originates from those facts. It is the only "residue" left by the events in the continuum of time and space. As the carrier of factual content, evidence is intrinsically linked to the case and possesses the probative power to demonstrate that the events in question once occurred.

5.4.3 Legality

Legality, also referred to as the legal nature of evidence, requires that evidence comply with established legal standards. It ensures the authenticity and relevance of evidence through statutory provisions and upholds the order and stability of the legal system via procedural safeguards. The legality of evidence is reflected in three key aspects: First, from an external perspective, legality pertains to compliance with legal requirements regarding the source, form, and content of the evidence. Second, it serves as a normative guide for regulating the lawful exercise of authority by individuals involved in collecting and reviewing evidence, emphasizing procedural legality. Only evidence that is collected, preserved, examined, and used by authorized personnel in accordance with legally prescribed procedures may serve as a valid basis for adjudication and perform its function of establishing case facts. Third, legality functions as a restriction against the use of illegally obtained evidence. The exclusionary rule serves to prevent such evidence from entering judicial proceedings, thereby fulfilling a "purification" role by filtering out defective or tainted materials and establishing thresholds for admissibility. In Germany, evidentiary collection is subject to the principles of "prohibition of acquisition" and "prohibition of use." Exclusion of unlawfully obtained evidence helps deter illegal or unethical investigative practices and reinforces the objectivity of evidentiary sources and forms. In China, the *Rules of Criminal Procedure for the People's Procuratorate*, issued by the Supreme People's Procuratorate, provide: "If the People's Procuratorate determines upon review that evidence was collected illegally, such evidence shall be excluded." Similarly, the *Interpretation of the Civil Procedure Law* states: "Evidence that is formed or obtained in a manner that seriously infringes upon the lawful rights and interests of others, violates prohibitive legal provisions, or gravely contravenes public order and good customs shall not be used as the basis for determining the facts of a case."

The legitimacy of evidence is not a characteristic pertaining to the ontological nature of evidence itself, nor does it refer to the legality of the evidentiary method or the inherent legality of the evidence carrier—whether it be testimonial or physical evidence. On this basis, a longstanding debate exists in the legal field between the "two-element" theory and the "three-element" theory of evidence. Although legitimacy differs from authenticity and relevance—in that it involves a normative judgment rather than a descriptive property—it should not be viewed negatively. Rather, the requirement of legitimacy reflects a normative condition that all evidence in litigation must satisfy. It is precisely this value-laden characteristic that enables legitimacy to function as a foundational element of admissible evidence, distinguishing legal evidence from other types of factual materials or information.

Authenticity constitutes the fundamental substance of evidence, relevance represents its essential attribute, and legality serves as the critical condition for its admissibility. Authenticity provides the ontological basis for the existence of evidence; relevance forms the logical foundation for establishing the facts of the case; and legality ensures the normative justification for using evidence in legal proceedings. These three elements are interdependent and indispensable, collectively forming the core characteristics of evidence.

5.5 The Fundamental Property of the Evidence

Evidence, as the basis for establishing the facts of a case and rendering a judgment, must be evaluated not only in terms of its authenticity, relevance, and legality, but also in terms of its evidentiary capacity, probative value, and—particularly in common law jurisdictions—its admissibility. For any material to serve as evidence in judicial proceedings or as the basis for a ruling, it must possess both evidentiary capacity and probative value. These attributes, shaped by the influence of foreign evidentiary theories and the principle of adjudicative centralism, aim to clarify—through procedural mechanisms—the distinction between materials that qualify as evidence and those that serve as the foundation for judicial decisions.

5.5.1 Evidentiary Capability

Evidentiary capacity, also known as evidentiary qualification or permissibility of evidence, refers to the legal qualification of certain facts to become evidence, i.e., "the qualification that a tangible object can be used as a method of evidence".[11]

The concept of evidentiary capacity originates from civil law systems, whereas in common law jurisdictions, it is typically referred to as admissibility. Evidentiary capacity represents a legal constraint on the introduction of certain evidence in court, based on statutory provisions or policy considerations, and is fundamentally a legal question. The determination of whether specific facts possess evidentiary capacity not only pertains to their probative value in establishing the facts of the case but also bears on their potential impact on safeguarding public interests and upholding a just social order.

The civil law system primarily relies on judges to assess evidence, generally imposing fewer restrictions on the admissibility of materials presented in court. Under this system, "all materials that can serve as evidence possess logical evidentiary capacity." [12]Given that civil law countries employ professional judges—who typically receive formal legal training and possess greater legal expertise than lay jurors—there is often no need for a pre-trial evidentiary review. In principle, even materials lacking evidentiary capacity may be presented in court, although they cannot serve as a basis for judicial decisions. Differences in how evidentiary capacity is defined across jurisdictions have led to variations in interpretation, particularly between Germany and Japan. German law holds that evidence acquires evidentiary capacity only after it has been obtained through legally prescribed investigative procedures, with strict evidentiary rules serving as a prerequisite. In contrast, Japanese law emphasizes whether evidence meets the threshold for being introduced in open court, treating evidentiary capacity as a precondition for conducting formal proof.

In civil law countries, the primary focus of evidence law is on the procedure of evidence investigation, which shapes how evidence is collected and examined through legally prescribed processes. "The concept of evidentiary capacity thus evolves from referring to the legal qualification of evidence as a basis for fact-finding to denoting the legal qualification of evidence to be presented and reviewed by the judge during the public hearing stage."[13]

The property of evidentiary capacity as evidence may be understood as follows.

---

[11] [Japan] Takahashi Hiroshi: "Key Lectures on Civil Procedure Law", translated by Zhang Weiping and Xu Ke, 27 pages, Beijing: Legal Publishing House, 2007.

[12] Chen Pusheng, Criminal Evidence Law, p. 205, Taipei: Sanmin Book Company, 1979.

[13] Chen Pusheng, Criminal Evidence Law, p. 67, Taipei: Sanmin Book Company, 1979.

5.5.1.1 The Ability of Evidence is the Qualification of Some Facts as Evidence

From the perspective of its nature, the admissibility of evidence is not an inherent attribute of the evidence itself but rather a legal quality externally imposed to satisfy certain value considerations. As such, issues of admissibility are generally addressed explicitly through legal provisions.

In civil law countries, legislation typically does not affirmatively define admissibility; instead, it adopts a negative approach by specifying which types of evidence lack admissibility or are subject to limitations. In general, positive legal provisions cannot comprehensively enumerate all admissible evidence, whereas negative provisions more effectively regulate admissibility. Restrictions on admissibility are primarily based on considerations such as the unreliability of the evidence, the potential to cause erroneous judgments, procedural delays, or the need to deter and sanction unlawful methods of evidence collection.

Admissibility is closely linked to relevance. While admissible evidence must be relevant, not all relevant evidence is necessarily admissible. If the probative value of relevant evidence is substantially outweighed by the risk of unfair prejudice, confusion of issues, misleading the fact-finder, undue delay, or needless presentation of cumulative evidence, it shall not be admitted as evidence and shall not have admissibility.[14] Therefore, the admissibility of evidence is a matter strictly regulated by legal norms.

5.5.1.2 Evidence Ability is Closely Linked to Strict Proof

In terms of the degree of proof, all evidence should be subject to a uniform standard. However, the requirements for strict adherence to legally prescribed methods of investigation vary, resulting in different evidentiary standards for different types of evidence-gathering methods. Strict proof is contrasted with free proof; it demands higher evidentiary standards. Evidence used in strict proof must not only possess probative value but also evidentiary capacity. Accordingly, some scholars refer to evidentiary capacity as the "qualification" necessary for strict proof, or as the "qualification required for evidence to be used in investigation and fact-finding." Given the significance of evidentiary capacity in establishing the admissibility of evidence and the increasing emphasis on pretrial evidence exchange procedures, it is more appropriate to regard evidentiary capacity as the foundation for strict proof. For certain facts, evidentiary capacity should be assessed before trial. Only through such pretrial review can evidence that lacks admissibility be excluded from trial proceedings, thereby ensuring that evidentiary capacity functions as a filter to prevent unqualified evidence from entering the adjudicative process.

[14] See Rule 403 of the Federal Rules of Evidence.

5.5.1.3 The Competent Evidence Shall be Based on the Proof of the Substantive Legal Facts of the Case

In criminal proceedings, the facts to be proved primarily concern criminal acts and their circumstances; in civil proceedings, they relate to the rights and obligations of the parties; in administrative proceedings, the focus is on the legality of the administrative act. The evidentiary requirements for procedural facts are generally lower than those for substantive facts. If certain facts cannot serve as a basis for establishing substantive legal claims, they may still be admissible for proving procedural matters.

Although evidentiary capacity is a legal issue, it should not be equated solely with the legality of evidence. Evidentiary capacity pertains to the method by which evidence is obtained and relates to the legal standards of collection, as well as the authenticity and relevance of the evidence. At the same time, the "three characteristics" of evidence is not only limited to the ability of evidence, but also includes the proving power of evidence.

In legislation, evidentiary capacity is generally defined in negative terms. Evidence lacking evidentiary capacity falls into two main categories: evidence that lacks relevance and therefore does not possess evidentiary capacity; and evidence that, although potentially relevant, is excluded due to legal prohibitions. The determination of evidentiary capacity depends on evidentiary rules, is a strictly legal concept, and involves normative value judgments.

5.5.2 Probative Value

The probative value of evidence, also known as the effectiveness or value of evidence, refers to the extent to which evidence has an effect on proving the facts of a case and the degree of that effect. It is the natural effectiveness of the evidence itself and its inherent attributes, specifically referring to "the degree to which the evidential material plays a role in determining the facts in question."[15]

Probative value is an inherent attribute of evidence. All evidence possesses some degree of probative value in relation to the facts of the case; however, the strength of that value varies depending on the type of evidence. Moreover, the objective manifestations of probative value are not uniform but exist in diverse forms. These various forms, nonetheless, are capable of being identified and understood through human cognition.

Generally speaking, whether a piece of evidence has probative value and the extent of that value depend on whether it is connected to the facts of the case and the closeness of that connection. Probative value is closely related to the concept of relevance. While relevance emphasizes the existence of a connection between the evidence and the facts of the case, probative value focuses on the evidentiary

[15] [Japan] Takahashi Hiroshi: "Key Lectures on Civil Procedure Law", translated by Zhang Weiping and Xu Ke, 27 pages, Beijing: Legal Publishing House, 2007.

effect of that evidence on the case facts. The two are not entirely interchangeable. Probative value pertains exclusively to the factual dimension of evidence and reflects the degree to which evidence possessing evidentiary capacity reflects or proves the facts in question. Such reflection or proof may be either affirmative or negative; that is, evidence may serve not only to establish relevant facts but also to refute unrelated or inaccurate assertions. Thus, confirmatory and rebuttal evidence differ in nature. Relevance indicates a potential for the evidence to be probative of the facts at issue. However, whether the evidence ultimately exerts a probative effect, and to what extent, generally cannot be determined with certainty until the facts of the case have been established.

In most legal systems, the probative value of evidence—particularly the assessment and weighing of such value—is generally subject to the judge's free evaluation of evidence, granting the judge a certain degree of discretionary authority to make determinations based on the circumstances of the case. As the saying goes: "Evidence appears in myriad forms, with varying degrees of value, and it is inherently difficult for the law to prescribe uniform standards for its evaluation."[16]The probative value of evidence is closely related to its natural relevance. It depends on the objective and intrinsic connection between the evidence and the facts of the case, as well as the closeness of that connection. Generally speaking, evidence that bears a direct and intrinsic relationship to the facts of the case carries greater probative value; conversely, evidence with a more remote or indirect connection possesses lesser probative force. Although the determination of the existence and weight of probative value is typically subject to the judge's discretion under the doctrine of free evaluation of evidence, the degree of correlation between different types of evidence and the facts of the case often varies. As such, the degree of reliability and corresponding probative value may differ accordingly. Therefore, legal rules may provide guiding principles regarding the relative probative value of different categories of evidence. However, such guidance must not be applied in a mechanical or absolute manner in practice.

Although the law stipulates that the probative value of evidence is subject to the judge's free evaluation, this does not mean that the judge's assessment and weighing of evidence is entirely unconstrained or arbitrary. In determining the weight of evidence and its effectiveness in establishing the facts of the case, judges must not violate rules of experience or logical reasoning, nor may they act contrary to science or common sense. Furthermore, such evaluations are also subject to procedural limitations.

Evidentiary admissibility and probative value are fundamental attributes of evidence and constitute two key concepts in the study of evidence law. While there is a close relationship between admissibility and probative value, they are conceptually distinct and serve different legal functions.

[16] Chen Pusheng, Criminal Evidence Law, p. 574, Taipei: Sanmin Book Company, 1979.

5.5.2.1 The Connection Between Evidence Ability and Proof Power

Evidentiary admissibility and probative value are two sides of the same coin in the legal characterization of evidence. The former concerns the legal qualification of evidence, while the latter pertains to its natural or factual capacity to prove. These two attributes are mutually presupposed and dialectically unified within the concept of evidence, jointly constituting its essential nature.

Evidentiary admissibility is a category of possibility—it refers to the legal qualification that determines whether certain facts or materials may be submitted as evidence in court. Only factual materials that satisfy the legal requirements for admissibility may potentially be presented at trial. Probative value, by contrast, is a category of actuality—it concerns the transformation of potential proof into actual probative force. It refers to the actual evidentiary weight that admissible evidence carries in proving the facts of a case. From the standpoint of origin, probative value precedes admissibility, in the sense that a piece of evidence must possess probative value to be deemed admissible. Evidence that lacks probative value necessarily lacks evidentiary admissibility. However, from the logical order of proof, admissibility must precede probative value: evidence must first be admissible—i.e., deemed legally competent or acceptable—before its probative value may be evaluated. As some scholars have noted, "admissibility reflects the formal qualification of evidence, whereas probative value reflects its substantive worth."[17]

Evidentiary admissibility imposes both positive and negative limitations on probative value. Positive limitations typically involve restrictions on the source or method of obtaining certain facts. Negative limitations refer to procedural prohibitions against using certain materials as evidence. For example, even if certain facts possess probative value, legal rules governing admissibility may bar them from being used in court due to specific legal or procedural concerns. From the perspective of evidentiary application, evidence without admissibility cannot possess probative value.

5.5.2.2 The Difference Between Evidentiary Capacity and Probative Value

Evidentiary capacity is a legal issue—it refers to the legal determination of what types of facts may qualify as evidence under law. The statutory conditions and limitations imposed by law constitute the prerequisites for certain evidentiary materials to possess admissibility. Only evidence that satisfies the requirements of admissibility may be recognized as legally admissible evidence. Generally, admissibility is primarily reflected in the authenticity, relevance, and legality of the evidence, with legality bearing the closest relationship to admissibility. In contrast, probative value is a question of fact. It becomes relevant only after the legal question of admissibility has been resolved and concerns the evaluation and assessment of evidence that is

---

[17] Diao Ronghua, chief editor: On the Comparative Criminal Evidence Law, 5 pages, Taipei: Hanlin Publishing House, 1996.

already deemed admissible. The focus is on determining the extent to which such evidence contributes to establishing the facts of the case.

Evidentiary capacity primarily concerns whether the identification and use of evidence comply with relevant provisions of substantive and procedural law, emphasizing legal norms based on value assessments. Generally, it includes the following considerations: (1) Whether the evidence was collected by a legally authorized person; (2) Whether the collection of evidence complied with statutory procedures; (3) Whether the evidence was obtained through illegal means; (4) Whether the content of the evidence infringes upon the lawful rights and interests of others; (5) Whether the form of the evidence conforms to legal requirements. Probative value, by contrast, mainly concerns the intrinsic evidentiary effect of the evidence itself. From a legal perspective, evidence obtained through torture or other illegal or prohibited methods lacks evidentiary admissibility. However, this does not necessarily preclude such evidence from having factual relevance or the capacity to prove certain facts of the case.

Evidentiary capacity and probative value are fundamental attributes of evidence. Only through a comprehensive examination and analysis of these two attributes can a sound foundation be established for the formulation of evidentiary rules under evidence law. Such analysis is essential for developing scientifically grounded evidentiary standards, thereby ensuring the lawful and effective determination of facts in legal proceedings.

5.6 Admissibility of Evidence

Anglo-American law countries focus on the attributes of evidence in terms of admissibility or acceptability. In Anglo-American law countries, because trials are conducted with a jury system, the facts of the case are mainly determined by the jury. To prevent jurors from being prejudiced by inadmissible evidence or influenced by emotional factors, the law imposes certain restrictions on some types of evidence. The intention is to filter evidence through a pre-trial admissibility review, setting certain conditions for evidence to be presented in court. Based on this understanding, the concept of "admissibility" or "admissible evidence" better reflects this meaning.

The difference between Anglo-American and continental law countries regarding the regulation of evidentiary capacity is related to their litigation models, jury systems, and levels of judicial involvement. The focus of evidence law in Anglo-American jurisdictions is on the admissibility of evidence (evidentiary capacity), and it limits the arguments presented to the jury and parties through admissibility rules. Evidence may be admitted or excluded, and irrelevant evidence should be excluded. Article 402 of the Federal Rules of Evidence states that "relevant evidence is admissible" and that "irrelevant evidence is not admissible." The "relevance" of evidence differs from its admissibility. In Anglo-American evidence law, the relevance and admissibility of evidence are not treated as interchangeable or parallel in application. Relevance generally serves as the basis for determining the evidentiary capacity and relates to whether the evidence originates from the facts of the case. Admissibility is the rule for assessing relevant evidence and addresses the question of whether "relevant evidence" is acceptable, incorporating strong elements of value judgment and discretion. Although admissibility includes relevance, there are limitations and numerous exclusionary rules, such as the hearsay rule, character evidence rule, and opinion evidence rule.

5.7 The Significance of the Evidence

Evidence is the foundation and core of all litigation activities. The development and advancement of every litigation procedure revolve around evidence. Without evidence, litigation cannot proceed. Evidence plays a crucial role in litigation and holds particular significance in the adjudication process.

5.7.1 Evidence is the Prerequisite for Litigation

Evidence is the prerequisite for the commencement of litigation, and litigation cannot be carried out without evidence. For the parties, the first step in a lawsuit is to provide evidence. For example, the Civil Procedure Law stipulates that "the parties shall timely provide evidence for their claims," and the main contents of the complaint also include evidence and its sources. If the parties wish to protect their legitimate rights and interests according to law, they must rely on evidence to prove the existence of the disputed facts and the validity of their claims. Only when sufficient evidence is provided can the court confirm their legitimate rights and interests. For the court, evidence is the foundation for determining the facts of the case and the basis for ascertaining those facts. The court must judge the case "based on the facts," and "based on the facts" means based on facts established by evidence. In a certain sense, it can also be interpreted as "based on the evidence." The facts of a disputed case generally occur before the lawsuit, and the judge does not know these facts in advance. These facts will not be automatically presented to the court during litigation, and the evidence will not automatically assert the facts.

In litigation, due to the adversarial nature of the proceedings, the parties' statements about the facts of the case often differ, and the evidence they provide is not the same. In such circumstances, for the court to uncover the truth, it must rely on the evidence. Otherwise, the facts determined by the ruling will become like water without a source, and the application of the law will be like a tree without roots. At each stage of litigation, evidence serves as the substantive condition for progressing from one phase to the next, and its role in advancing litigation is particularly significant.

5.8 Evidence is the Basis for Realizing Judicial Justice

Evidence is the basis for proving the existence of the facts of a case and serves as the foundation for uncovering the truth and delivering a fair judgment. For a court to ascertain the facts of a case, it must rely on evidence, because evidence represents the "footprint of the true story" and is the only means by which it can be discovered. It also serves as a critical link between past facts and judicial decisions. Evidence plays a fundamental role in ensuring the realization of the principle of evidentiary justice and in safeguarding judicial fairness—both procedural and substantive.

The basic function of evidence is not only to prove factual matters, but also to act as a prerequisite for initiating legal proceedings. The initiation, development, and conclusion of any litigation process require evidentiary support. Only with sufficient evidence can the smooth progression of the legal process be ensured. At the same time, evidence is essential for discovering the facts of a case and assessing its merits. These substantive issues must also be addressed through fair procedures. In other words, only through legitimate, rational, humane, and impartial methods of collecting, preserving, and evaluating evidence can the facts of a case be accurately discovered and scientifically confirmed. "Only within the framework of the rule of law can evidence be grounded in justice, aimed at discovering the truth while also accounting for broader legal policies. The determination of facts is the foundation for the application of law. Accordingly, various systems of evidence law have developed to facilitate its use." Evidence is not only the basis for ensuring procedural fairness, but also the cornerstone of achieving judicial justice.

In addition, the reasonable and systematic definition of the concept of evidence—especially the preservation of its essential procedural characteristics—is of great significance for establishing sound evidentiary rules, improving the evidentiary system, safeguarding legal rights, and fulfilling the ultimate purpose of litigation: the pursuit of justice.

5.9 Thoughts and Reflections

According to Hu Shi, "Without evidence, a case can only be suspended; with insufficient evidence, it can only be assumed, but not concluded."In the example cited above, the court referred to the results of the "psychological test" and other evidence to conclude that the money in the credit card belonged to the defendant, Wang. However, the Supreme People's Procuratorate's Reply on Whether the Conclusion of CPS Multi-Channel Psychological Testing Can Be Used as Litigation Evidence pointed out: "In handling cases, the People's Procuratorate may use the conclusions of CPS multi-channel psychological tests to assist in reviewing and assessing evidence, but such conclusions cannot be used as litigation evidence." The Supreme People's Court, in its Provisions on the Work of Entrusted Appraisal Examination in Civil Procedure, stipulates that the results of polygraph tests do not constitute a legal form of evidence as defined by the Civil Procedure Law and may only serve as a reference. Based on the circumstances of the case, and in conjunction with the content of this chapter and the relevant provisions of judicial authorities, consider the following questions: (1) What types of evidence did the court rely on to determine the facts of the case? (2) Can the results of the "psychological test" in this case serve as the basis for a judicial decision? (3) What attributes must evidence possess to serve as the final basis for judgment? (4) What can polygraph results prove, and what are their limitations in evidentiary function?

Extended reading

Chen, R. H. (2001). Cong renshilun zouxiang jiazhilun——zhengju fa lilun jichu de fansi yu chonggou. Law Science, 22(1). (in Chinese)
Zhang, J. W. (2002). Zhengju faxue de lilun jichu. Modern Law Science, 24(2). (in Chinese)
Yi, Y. Y. (2004). Zhengju faxue de lilun jichu——yi caipan shishi de ke jieshouxing wei zhongxin. Chinese Journal of Law, 26(1). (in Chinese)
Wang, J. C. (2004). Xingshi zhengju lilun de zhexue jichu. Chinese Journal of Law, 26(6). (in Chinese)
Song, Y. H. et al. (2005). Zhengju faxue jiben wenti zhi fansi. Chinese Journal of Law, 27(6). (in Chinese)
Zhang, B. S. (2008). Zhengju guize de jiazhi jichu he lilun tixi. Chinese Journal of Law, 30(2). (in Chinese)

Chapter 6
Types of Evidence

6.1 Introductory Case

A crane from the Shanghai Construction Company accidentally knocked a gable into a nearby house, causing damage to furniture and electrical appliances inside. In addition, an elderly man in the house fell while attempting to leave the scene, resulting in a fractured thigh. Following the accident, the two parties disputed the amount of compensation, prompting the homeowner, Mr. Li, to file a lawsuit, seeking economic damages from the defendant, Shanghai Construction Company. In support of the lawsuit, the plaintiff, Mr. Li, submitted the following materials and physical evidence to the court: 1. Video footage recorded by a reporter from the local TV station's "Daily Observation" program. 2. Photographs taken by Mr. Li of the damaged items. 3. A decoration contract and payment receipts signed three months before the accident for work on the house. 4. The damaged Panasonic microwave oven and Toshiba laptop. 5. A copy of Mr. Li's mother's medical diagnosis report confirming a leg fracture, along with a list of medical expenses. 6. Testimony from the neighborhood committee. 7. Testimonies from several eyewitnesses at the scene. 8. A list of claimed compensation costs along with the calculation method. 9. Crane site location map and license plate number. The defendant, Shanghai Construction Company, provided the following materials: 1. Several photographs taken at the scene by the defendant. 2. Close-up and enlarged images of the damaged area. 3. Photographs showing the locations of the Panasonic microwave and Toshiba laptop, as well as photos of the surrounding cables. 4. Photographs taken on the day of the incident showing the defendant repairing the gable.

H. Guo, *Evidence Jurisprudence in China*, Understanding China,
https://doi.org/10.1007/978-981-95-3981-9_6

6.2 Chapter Overview

This chapter focuses on the legal classification of evidence, which mainly includes the legislative models and types of legal evidence across various countries. Evidence classifications can be summarized into three categories: open evidence systems, semi-closed evidence systems, and fully closed evidence systems. The types of legal evidence in China mainly include physical evidence, documentary evidence, witness testimony, statements by parties (including statements by the parties themselves, statements by victims, and confessions and defenses by criminal suspects and defendants), expert opinions, written records (such as inspection, examination, identification, investigative experiments, and field notes), audio-visual materials, and electronic data.

6.3 An Overview of the Types of Evidence

The type of evidence, also known as the legal form of evidence, refers to the classification of evidence prescribed by law based on specific criteria. Evidence types are defined by legislators according to practical experience, litigation needs, and the external forms of evidence. The aim is to establish corresponding rules for various legal forms of evidence, thereby facilitating judicial practice by enabling legal actors to determine the most appropriate methods for evidence collection, fixation, preservation, and review, based on the unique characteristics of each type of evidence.

6.3.1 Legislative Status of the Types of Evidence

Evidence is the unity of external form and intrinsic content. Although evidence may appear similar when proving the facts of a case, it serves different functions in the evidentiary process due to variations in content and modes of existence. To clarify the characteristics of various types of evidence and to facilitate their collection, preservation, examination, and evaluation, the law classifies evidence based on its form and content, thereby establishing the legal types of evidence.

The classification of evidence is developed by legislators through legal provisions, based on the external characteristics of evidence and accumulated legislative experience. The modes of evidence classification across countries can generally be summarized into three categories: open evidence systems, semi-enclosed evidence systems, and fully enclosed evidence systems.

6.3.1.1 Open Forms of Evidence

The open form of evidence means that the classification of evidence is not confined to the existing forms of evidence in judicial practice. It maintains an open stance toward all kinds of evidence that may currently exist or may emerge in the future, and the law does not stipulate the certainty of specific evidence types. This form of evidence is mostly adopted by common law countries, which can accept new types of evidence as admissible at any time. For example, the *Federal Rules of Evidence* in the United States and the *British Civil Evidence Act* do not provide a rigid legal classification of the forms of evidence.

6.3.1.2 The Semi-closed Form of Evidence

The semi-closed form of evidence refers to evidence law that does not strictly adhere to a single classification model. This method of classification exists in the procedural laws of France, Germany, Japan, and other civil law countries.

6.3.1.3 The Fully Enclosed Form of Evidence

The fully enclosed form of evidence refers to a model in which the types of evidence are enumerated or limited through legislation, thereby determining the legally recognized forms of evidence by statute. For example, the evidence systems in Russia and China belong to this model.

Regardless of the type or form of evidence and the model adopted by legislation for it, the legislation of each country has stipulated the type of evidence. The British evidence law stipulates three types of evidence: oral evidence, documentary evidence, and real evidence; the American evidence law specifies witness testimony, real evidence, documentary evidence, and visual evidence; Russian law includes statements by suspects and criminal defendants, statements by victims, testimony by witnesses, expert conclusions and statements, real evidence, transcripts of investigative acts and trial proceedings, and other documents. The three major procedural laws in China stipulate legal types of evidence according to their respective characteristics. The Criminal Procedure Law includes real evidence, documentary evidence, witness testimony, victim statements, confessions and defenses of criminal suspects and defendants, expert opinions, inquest, inspection, identification and investigative experiments, audio-visual materials, and electronic data. The Civil Procedure Law stipulates party statements, documentary evidence, real evidence, witness testimony, audio-visual materials, expert opinions, inspection records, and electronic data. The Administrative Procedure Law includes documentary evidence, real evidence, audio-visual materials, electronic data, witness testimony, party statements, expert opinions, inspection records, and on-site records. It is reasonable for Chinese law to categorize evidence into eight types, as this facilitates the formulation of distinct evidentiary rules based on their differing characteristics and promotes the standardization of evidence review and adjudication. However, the disadvantages of adopting a fully closed legislative model are also apparent. The legislation could adopt a semi-closed form, allowing for the accommodation of emerging forms of evidence that may not easily fit within traditional "legal categories" as society evolves.

Some scholars believe that evidence may be classified into three categories: testimonial evidence, real evidence, and documentary evidence, based on whether the facts of objective existence are perceived, recorded, or capable of being perceived by others. Other scholars maintain that regardless of how society evolves or how advanced science and technology become, and irrespective of the form in which evidence is presented, its carrier can only be either language or physical matter. Additionally, some scholars argue that statements of the parties, expert opinions, and records of inspections, identifications, and investigative experiments should not be treated as independent categories of evidence.

6.3.2 The Significance of the Types of Evidence

The classification of evidence is prescribed by law and is highly standardized. Generally speaking, only those forms of evidence recognized by legal norms qualify as admissible evidence. Since each rule of evidence corresponds to a specific type or form of evidence, the absence of a defined evidentiary form renders the applicable evidentiary rule inoperative. Therefore, it is essential for the law to systematically categorize evidence. A scientifically grounded classification of evidence serves the following purposes.

6.3.2.1 It is Conducive to the Correct Understanding of the Characteristics of Various Kinds of Evidence

The scientific classification of evidence is an important method of logical reasoning used to understand and analyze evidence. It plays a vital role in guiding the accurate comprehension of various types of evidence. Only by applying consistent evidentiary standards and distinguishing among different forms of evidence can one further uncover their commonalities and distinctions, identify general rules as well as unique features, and enable the parties or adjudicating authorities to better grasp the essential characteristics of each category of evidence. This, in turn, helps to avoid blind understanding of evidence.

6.3.2.2 Conducive to the Formulation of Rules of Evidence

Legal norms specify the types of evidence in order to further clarify and regulate the ways in which different forms of evidence may be introduced into judicial proceedings. By standardizing the forms in which evidence exists, the law provides a typological framework that enables parties and judicial authorities to utilize evidence in a systematic and predictable manner. Each category of evidence possesses its own characteristics, as well as distinct methods of discovery, collection, and preservation. Moreover, different types of evidence are subject to varying standards of examination, evaluation, and admissibility. Only through the scientific classification of evidence can these unique features be accurately identified, thereby allowing for the development of specific evidentiary rules tailored to each form. For example, the opinion rule applies to witness testimony; the hearsay rule pertains to verbal evidence conveyed through written or oral statements; the voluntariness rule corresponds to confessions made by defendants; and the exclusionary rule governs the admissibility of illegally obtained testimonial and real evidence. Furthermore, by analyzing evidence within the same category, it is possible to discern recurring patterns that can serve as the basis for establishing general evidentiary principles.

6.3.2.3 It is Conducive to the Timely and Rapid Collection, Provision and Review of Judgment Evidence

The legal classification of evidence in a scientific manner enables litigants and investigative authorities to adopt appropriate methods for discovering and collecting evidence according to its type. It also provides clear standards for the examination and assessment of different categories of evidence. By taking advantage of the specific characteristics inherent to each type of evidence, parties can employ tailored approaches to the discovery, preservation, fixation, and evaluation of evidence, thereby enhancing its timely and effective use. This, in turn, offers a consistent basis for judicial bodies to assess evidence in adjudication.

The purpose of legally classifying evidence is to group together types of evidence that share essential attributes, thereby providing targeted guidance to parties and investigative authorities in accurately identifying, understanding, and utilizing such evidence. It also lays an important foundation for theoretical research into the nature and application of different forms of evidence. Accordingly, the scientific classification of evidence holds substantial significance in both legal theory and judicial practice.

6.4 Real Evidence

Real evidence, as a form of physical proof characterized by a high degree of objectivity, has a long and well-established history. Its legislative definition first appeared in the 1808 French Code of Criminal Procedure, where it was defined in relatively broad terms. Some scholars contend that material evidence encompasses tangible items presented for judicial examination—such as movable property, documents, photographs, films, and audio recordings—as well as information that may be perceived by the court.[1] Other scholars conceptualize it through typological classification, holding that "real evidence consists of documents and objects subject to inspection."[2] In ancient China, real evidence had already been recognized as an independent category of proof. Under the current Chinese legal system, all three major procedural laws explicitly designate real evidence as one of the statutory forms of admissible evidence.

6.4.1 The Concept and Characteristics of Real Evidence

Real evidence refers to physical evidence that proves the facts of a case through its inherent material properties, external characteristics, and its specific location, placement, or condition. The material properties of such evidence pertain to its intrinsic qualities, including physical, chemical, and biological attributes such as mass, composition, structure, function, and color. Its external characteristics refer to objectively observable features, such as shape, size, quantity, degree of wear or damage, and overall condition. The location, placement, or condition of real evidence relates to the environment, time, spatial context, and its relation to other pieces of evidence. For instance, a footprint found at a crime scene may indicate that a particular person was present at that location.

Real evidence generally exists in the form of objects and traces. These may include tools used in the commission of a crime, physical items directly produced by the act, and objects or traces that manifest its consequences; illegal items or traces resulting from the act; objects or traces that reflect the perpetrator's characteristics; materials and traces generated during the process of the act; and items or traces originating from or left behind by other acts. In addition, animals, plants, human bodies, as well as trace substances such as odors, heat, electricity, and energy—despite their intangible nature—may also constitute real evidence.

Earlier conceptions of real evidence were limited to physical items. As one definition puts it: "Real evidence refers to objects within the physical world that possess legally defined characteristics and are used as sources of proof."[3] Real evidence may be further classified into traces and non-traces. Over time, the prevailing practice

[1] May (2007).

[2] Kaneko and Takeshita (1995).

[3] Tillichev et al. (1984).

has been to treat physical objects as distinct from traces, leading to the latter being recognized as a separate subcategory of material evidence.

It is important to distinguish between real evidence and exhibits. These two concepts are not synonymous, and their relationship is one of part to whole. Real evidence is not confined to tangible objects—it also encompasses traces and intangible matter—but it cannot exist independently of physical carriers. By contrast, exhibits refer exclusively to physical items submitted to prove case facts, excluding traces.

Real evidence is noted for its objectivity, perishability, and specificity. It is often referred to as "silent evidence," as it cannot directly attest to case facts. Rather, it serves as indirect evidence and must be considered in conjunction with other forms of evidence to establish the truth of a case. The defining features of Real evidence are as follows.

6.4.1.1 The High Degree of Objectivity of Real Evidence

A criminal act inevitably occurs within a specific time and space, during which it interacts with certain objects in the surrounding environment. This interaction often leads to changes in the external form, physical characteristics, internal properties, or structural integrity of those objects, to varying degrees. These altered features can reflect the occurrence, progression, and transformation of case-related events, and may serve as carriers that record such factual developments. The evidentiary value of these physical changes does not depend on human intent but is governed by the objective laws of nature. Accordingly, real evidence bears the hallmark of objective existence or unique external associations, making it difficult to manipulate or alter arbitrarily. Compared to other forms of evidence, it demonstrates a higher degree of objectivity in both its form and substance.

In common law jurisdictions, real evidence is also known as "physical evidence," "demonstrative evidence," or "object evidence." Some forms of real evidence may be unintelligible to the average observer and require the use of scientific techniques or instruments to extract evidentiary value from their objective properties or their relationships to the surrounding environment. Nevertheless, such scientific methods themselves possess an inherent objectivity and are capable of preserving the original objectivity of the evidence. As a result, real evidence is often regarded as the most reliable type of proof and is referred to as "evidence that speaks for itself."

In judicial practice, concerns have been raised about potential errors in real evidence, thereby questioning its objectivity. However, such errors generally do not arise from the evidence itself, but rather from flaws in the methods or procedures used to collect it, or from misinterpretations based on human error. These are essentially cognitive limitations on the part of investigators—for example, faulty reasoning or technological constraints that prevent an accurate understanding of the evidence. These shortcomings do not undermine the inherent reliability of the evidence itself, but rather reflect subjective distortions in its interpretation. Thus, it is incorrect to conclude that real evidence lacks objectivity; what is fallible is the human perception and assessment of it.

Replicas or photographs of real evidence are not equivalent to the original items. Although such substitutes may be submitted in court, they must be corroborated against the original objects or traces. Even when verified as accurate, they are considered substitutes, not the evidence itself.

Only when the model, photograph, or reproduction is demonstrably identical to the original object or trace can it be regarded as a valid substitute. This defining characteristic of real evidence requires parties and investigative authorities to adhere to the principle of submitting and presenting the original item. Only when it is impossible to do so, or where statutory impediments exist, may a reproduction or copy be introduced in accordance with prescribed legal procedures. For instance, Article 70 of the *Civil Procedure Law* of our country provides: "The original physical evidence shall be submitted. Where it is truly difficult to produce the original, a reproduction or photograph may be submitted instead…".

6.4.1.2 The Stable Specificity of Real Evidence

Real evidence emerges alongside the occurrence of case-related facts. It serves as a direct reflection of the original physical reality of the case, proving the facts through the objective existence of an item or trace, or its specific connection to the external environment. In other words, the characteristics of real evidence relevant to the case already exist objectively at the time of the incident or are already established in a specific and objective relation to their surroundings. These features and connections exist independently and generally remain unchanged unless actively interfered with or passively damaged. Even if the object or trace constituting the evidence is altered by natural or human factors, its specific nature can often still be identified through recognizable patterns of change. Unlike language or writing, real evidence is less easily influenced by human subjectivity.

The evidentiary content of real evidence is typically preserved in a specific physical medium and displays strong stability. Its essential content is generally difficult to reproduce through other means of transmission. Substitutes, equivalents, or models cannot replace the evidence itself. Replicas or photographs merely reflect or shadow the original and, in principle, cannot serve as real evidence. This is because such substitutes are inherently variable and lack the stable specificity possessed by the original evidence.

6.4.1.3 The Indirect Evidentiary Function of Real Evidence

Real evidence typically plays an indirect role in establishing case facts, as it cannot independently demonstrate its relevance to the case. It usually must be combined with other forms of proof to be evidentially effective. Accordingly, the law imposes strict procedural requirements on its collection—for example, examinations and inspections must follow rigorously defined protocols. In practice, real evidence often performs its probative function through expert evaluation or forensic inspection, in which professionals with specialized knowledge use instruments or scientific methods to extract evidentiary value. The evidentiary effect of real evidence depends not only on scientific appraisal but also on the methods used for its discovery and collection. Therefore, judicial practice requires both an analysis of the inherent characteristics of the evidence and a critical evaluation of the scientific soundness of the collection methods employed. If the procedures used to obtain the evidence are improper or unscientific, the evidence may be damaged, contaminated, or even falsified.

This characteristic of real evidence closely connects it with records of crime scene examinations, inspections, identifications, and expert opinions. Although Chinese law classifies these as distinct categories of evidence, they often reflect the processes by which real evidence is collected, preserved, or interpreted. In some instances, they serve as methods for fixing or explaining real evidence. Their evidentiary function frequently relies on the existence of real evidence itself, which may be regarded as their foundational source.

Real evidence differs from documentary evidence. Treating them as separate forms of evidence does not preclude a single item from serving as different types of evidence under varying circumstances within the same case. For example, a written will may be regarded as real evidence when assessed for its authenticity; however, when the content of the will is used to determine the distribution of the estate, it functions as documentary evidence.

6.4.2 Classification of Real Evidence

Real evidence may be classified into various types based on different criteria. Such classification facilitates a deeper understanding of its evidentiary nature, enhances the ability to accurately identify its essential characteristics, and helps ensure its proper and lawful application. Depending on the classification standard applied, real evidence can be categorized as follows.

6.4.2.1 Based on the Type of Carrier: Bodily Evidence, Physical Object Evidence, and Documentary Real Evidence

i. **Bodily evidence**

Bodily evidence refers to physical traces either left by the human body or found on the human body. This includes impressions such as fingerprints and footprints, as well as biological materials secreted or shed by the body, including bodily fluids, excretions, secretions, and hair. It also encompasses traces left on the body, most notably wounds or injury marks that reflect trauma sustained by the individual.

ii. **Physical object evidence**

Physical object evidence refers to traces resulting from the interaction of physical objects during the commission of an act. This category includes tool marks, vehicle tracks, ballistic markings, erasures or scratches, separation traces between objects, and traces of gaseous or liquid substances.

iii. **Documentary real evidence**

Documentary real evidence consists of both the physical traces left on a document and the material components that constitute the document itself. The former includes handwriting and other markings produced during the drafting or creation of the document. The latter refers to the materials used in its production, such as ink, printing ink, stamp oil, toner, and the underlying medium of the document itself.

6.4.2.2 Based on the Form of Manifestation: Physical Object Evidence, Impression Evidence, and Trace Evidence

i. **Physical object evidence**

Physical object evidence refers to items composed of tangible substances or particulate materials. This type of evidence proves case-related facts through its origin, possession, function, or other distinguishing features that set it apart from similar objects, including changes in its characteristics or manner of use.

ii. **Impression evidence**

Impression evidence refers to marks left on solid materials as a result of external forces. Such impressions may serve as proof by reflecting the shape, spatial distribution, or structural characteristics of the source object, or by revealing the process through which the impression was formed.

iii. **Trace evidence**

Trace evidence refers to microscopic or intangible substances—such as odors, thermal energy, and other imperceptible materials—that are used to establish case facts. The evidentiary value of such materials is typically derived through scientific and technological analysis of their structural properties, chemical composition, concentration levels, or component ratios.

6.4.2.3 Based on Whether Real Evidence Can Be Presented in Court: In-Court Presentable and Non-Presentable Real Evidence

In-court presentable real evidence refers to physical items that can be retrieved, transported, and preserved, and are capable of being physically displayed before the court. Once introduced, such evidence may be examined and identified by the parties and is typically incorporated into the case file for future reference.

Non-presentable real evidence refers to objects or traces that cannot be extracted, transported, or preserved for direct presentation in court. These forms of evidence must be submitted through alternative means such as photographs, video recordings, or replicas, and should be accompanied by written descriptions or explanatory notes for the record.

In both legislative and practical contexts, certain forms of real evidence cannot be brought into the courtroom—such as oversized items that are not movable, or perishable goods like fruit. When direct presentation is not feasible, courts may still need to inspect and document such evidence, making the use of reproductions a necessary evidentiary substitute. Accordingly, the law should not categorically exclude derivative or secondary evidence, nor should evidentiary practice overly or mechanically insist on the principle of originality with respect to real evidence.

6.4.3 The Significance of Real Evidence

In the field of evidence law, some scholars have proposed abolishing real evidence as an independent evidentiary category or method. Their argument rests on the observation that real evidence is often converted into other forms—such as expert opinions, records of inspection or identification, or notarial documents—which, in their view, are sufficient substitutes, rendering a separate classification unnecessary. However, we contend that while the evidentiary content of real evidence may sometimes be transformed, its fundamental evidentiary nature remains intact. For example, an expert opinion may interpret the evidentiary value of real evidence through professional analysis, but the original material remains unchanged, and the facts it embodies continue to exist objectively within its physical carrier. Accordingly, the retention of real evidence as an independent category is both justified and necessary. As a distinct form of evidence, real evidence carries the following significance:

First, in litigation, both parties and investigative authorities may rely on real evidence to discover and substantiate factual elements of a case, as well as to determine the legal nature of the dispute. For instance, in tort cases, damaged property or adulterated products may serve as crucial physical evidence.

Second, real evidence plays a vital role in verifying the authenticity of testimonial evidence, such as witness statements or party admissions. Although it is often referred to as "silent evidence," given its inability to directly express factual assertions, its high degree of objectivity and strong probative force make it an indispensable tool for corroborating or challenging verbal testimony. Generally speaking, testimonial evidence requires confirmation through physical forms of proof—particularly real evidence.

Third, real evidence, when combined with other forms of proof, contributes significantly to fact-finding. Records of inspection, examination, search, and on-site documentation can reveal the characteristics, spatial positioning, and external relationships of real evidence. When considered alongside the physical evidence itself, such records assist in establishing factual conclusions. The location and environment of an object or trace, as well as its relationship to other evidence, may be critical in determining whether specific facts occurred. Real evidence thus holds substantial value in establishing the truth in judicial proceedings.

Moreover, real evidence represents a traditional and widely accepted evidentiary category with intrinsic independence. Advancing theoretical inquiry into the nature and function of real evidence is not only essential for enhancing its application in judicial practice—particularly in uncovering factual truth—but also for informing the continued refinement of evidentiary legislation.

6.5 Documentary Evidence

Documentary evidence is among the oldest recognized forms of legal proof. In ancient China, legal references to such evidence appear in texts such as *Zhouli · Officials of the Earth* and *Zhouli · Autumn Offices*, where it was stated that "disputes over land shall be resolved with maps." This indicates that the use of documentary evidence in legal proceedings dates back to the Western Zhou period. Similarly, the *Yunmeng Qin Bamboo Slips· Model of Seals and Inquiries* mandated the use of written registers as proof in cases involving fugitives. Internationally, documentary evidence was affirmed in the *Code of Hammurabi* from 18th-century BCE Babylon, and in classical Roman law.

6.5.1 Definition and Characteristics of Documentary Evidence

Documentary evidence refers to materials that serve a probative function through their recorded or expressed content—whether in the form of words, symbols, diagrams, or similar notations. Common examples include contracts, bills of lading, bank transfer records, financial transaction documents, and official certificates.

Documentary evidence proves facts through the meaning conveyed by its recorded content or expressed ideas, and typically exists in written form or as objects bearing written or graphical inscriptions on a tangible medium. In common law jurisdictions, "documentary evidence" refers to documents presented to the court from which relevant facts can be discerned. In Japanese legal doctrine, documentary evidence encompasses not only textual and graphical materials, but also includes "the examination of documents wherein the meaning and content expressed in writing serve as evidentiary material."[4] As one of the most prevalent and important forms of evidence, documentary evidence—when classified as an independent evidentiary type—exhibits several defining characteristics.

[4] Kaneko and Takeshita (1995).

6.5.1.1 Direct Evidentiary Value

Documentary evidence derives its probative force from the ideas or content expressed through written language, symbols, or diagrams. While such materials necessarily rely on a physical medium, their evidentiary value lies not in the medium itself, nor in the physical appearance of the text or symbols, but in the intelligible content they convey. As documentary evidence must communicate discernible meaning, it must be capable of human comprehension. Any written or symbolic material that expresses coherent thought, regardless of its physical form, size, or the number of individuals able to interpret it, may be deemed documentary evidence.

The use of documentary evidence presupposes an understanding of the content encoded in words, symbols, or graphical representations. Owing to its specificity, clarity, and intelligibility, documentary evidence typically allows for the direct assessment of its relevance to the facts in dispute—without requiring intermediate reasoning or inferential steps. This characteristic underscores the direct nature of its probative function in legal proceedings.

6.5.1.2 Stability of Documentary Evidence

Human beings constantly engage in communication and interaction for survival, cooperation, and development. Beyond verbal and nonverbal communication, written materials constitute a foundational medium. Once created, such materials not only have fixed content but also maintain a relatively stable form. They are typically unaffected by temporal or spatial changes and are capable of long-term preservation. Provided their physical integrity is maintained, documents may remain legible and comprehensible even after several decades or centuries. Historical contracts passed down through generations can still be interpreted today, with their meanings and intentions confirmed through the words, symbols, or illustrations they contain. Moreover, once generated, the form of a document is generally resistant to alteration. Even when tampered with or forged, such changes are usually detectable and may be reversed through scientific techniques. These qualities render documentary evidence highly stable and reliable.

6.5.1.3 Ideational Nature of Documentary Evidence

Documentary evidence proves facts through the ideas and meanings conveyed by written language, symbols, or diagrams. While the materials and tools used to create such evidence are objective, and the characters and symbols themselves are physically manifest, the expressed content originates in human thought and intention. As such, the meaning of documentary evidence reflects subjective human agency. Although the author exercises control over the content at the time of creation, once the document is separated from its creator, divergent interpretations may arise. This potential disjunction between the author's original intent and subsequent understanding can distance the document's expressed meaning from the factual truth. Even the author may later reinterpret the content under changing circumstances. Thus, while documentary evidence possesses a degree of subjectivity, it remains comparatively more objective than testimonial evidence, although less so than real evidence.

6.5.1.4 Physical Form of Documentary Evidence

Both the tools used to create documentary evidence and the materials that carry its content exhibit physical properties. Instruments such as pens, blades, blood, or sticks have tangible form; creation methods—writing, printing, engraving, stamping, cutting, painting, scanning, copying—are physical processes; and media like paper, cloth, walls, stone tablets, metal, flooring, and film are all material carriers. These attributes confer documentary evidence with distinctive physical characteristics that differentiate it from other forms.

Although documentary evidence is often presented in written form, not all written materials qualify as such. For example, written witness statements are categorized as testimonial, not documentary, evidence. When other evidence types are recorded in writing, this reflects a preservation method rather than a change in evidentiary nature. Thus, written testimony remains testimonial in character; victim statements remain testimonial, even if transcribed.

Documentary evidence and real evidence are closely related, as both exist objectively in material form and relate to case facts. However, they differ fundamentally in their modes of proof. Real evidence proves facts through its physical attributes, properties, or condition; documentary evidence proves facts through the content it records or expresses. If a material object is relevant because of the content it expresses—and its physical features are irrelevant—it is classified as documentary evidence. Conversely, if its physical characteristics are probative and its content is not, it constitutes real evidence. If both its content and physical features are relevant to the case, it may function simultaneously as both. Such dual-function evidence is frequently encountered. For instance, a written will serves as real evidence when handwriting analysis is conducted to verify the authenticity of the signature, as the focus lies on the physical trace rather than the semantic content. However, when determining how the estate is to be distributed according to the testator's expressed wishes, the same will functions as documentary evidence. While the medium may be identical, the evidentiary mechanisms differ. Accurately distinguishing between the two enhances the effective use of each in legal proceedings and supports the application of appropriate evidentiary rules based on their respective functions.

Additionally, some scholars have classified recordings, video footage, photographs, and computer-generated documents as falling within the scope of documentary evidence, referring to them as audiovisual documentary evidence. This classification is based on the premise that such materials prove facts through recorded audio, visual images, or computer-generated text and charts—features that, in their view, "it has all the characteristics of documentary evidence".[5] However, because these forms of evidence function differently from traditional written documents in how they convey information and demonstrate facts, they are generally categorized under audiovisual materials or electronic data. In Chinese practice, court transcripts, particularly those produced during first-instance trials, often function as documentary evidence. These transcripts, which comprehensively record procedural events and substantive evidence presented in court, frequently serve as a factual basis for second-instance adjudication. Legislatively, most jurisdictions do not designate court transcripts as a separate category of evidence. China similarly does not treat them as an independent evidentiary type; rather, they are considered a statutory format for preserving evidentiary content.

The evidentiary status of institutional certifications—documents issued by organizations—has been the subject of scholarly debate. Some scholars contend that institutional certifications fall under witness testimony, characterizing them as written statements issued by entities acting as witnesses. Others argue that such documents meet the definitional requirements of documentary evidence and should be treated accordingly. A third view holds that the classification should depend on the legal status of the institution in the litigation: institutions may appear as criminal suspects, defendants, victims, or witnesses, and the evidentiary categorization of their statements should correspond to these roles. In practice, some courts treat such certifications as witness testimony. However, because institutions are not natural persons, it is often impractical to subject their statements to courtroom cross-examination. For this reason, it may be more appropriate to treat institutional certifications as documentary evidence—for example, a personal credit report issued by a bank.

There is also ongoing debate in Chinese legal scholarship as to whether computer-generated documents should be treated as originals or as duplicates. Foreign jurisdictions differ in their legislative approaches to this issue. Given the general principle that documentary evidence must be submitted in its original form, treating computer printouts as copies is considered more appropriate under prevailing evidentiary standards.

6.5.2 Categories of Documentary Evidence

Documentary evidence, as a form of proof based on the recorded content and expressed meaning of a document, is produced across a wide range of fields and thus manifests in diverse forms. It can be classified in various ways depending on the analytical perspective adopted.

[5] Pei (2002).

6.5.2.1 Classification by Mode of Content Expression: Textual, Graphical, and Symbolic Documentary Evidence

i. **Textual documentary evidence**

Textual documentary evidence refers to documents in which facts are established through content recorded in written language. Examples include contracts, promissory notes, correspondence, and similar written materials. The term "written language" encompasses not only Chinese characters but also scripts of other ethnic groups and foreign languages. It further includes numerical records such as invoices containing altered figures, ledgers, and financial statements.

ii. **Graphical documentary evidence**

Graphical documentary evidence involves documents in which facts are conveyed through drawings, images, or similar visual representations. Examples include product trademarks, technical blueprints, forged seals, obscene illustrations, and defamatory caricatures.

iii. **Symbolic documentary evidence**

Symbolic documentary evidence refers to materials that utilize simple and often concealed symbols—excluding text and graphics—to convey information relevant to a case. Examples include secret markings placed along border routes to facilitate illegal crossings, or prearranged symbols used for covert communication. Such evidence typically requires decoding or expert interpretation to ascertain its actual meaning.

This classification is meaningful in guiding how the content of documentary evidence should be interpreted. Depending on the form of expression, courts may rely on common understanding or expert analysis to ensure accurate comprehension and correct legal evaluation of the document's probative content.

6.5.2.2 Classification Based on Whether the Document is Created in the Exercise of Official Authority: Public Versus Private Documentary Evidence

i. **Public document**

Public document refers to documents prepared by state authorities or other institutions pursuant to their official functions. According to the *German Code of Civil Procedure*, "Documents drawn up by a public authority within the scope of its official powers, or by a person vested with public certification authority acting within such scope, in accordance with proper formalities, constitute public documents." Examples include marriage and divorce certificates issued by civil affairs departments, notarial deeds issued by notary offices, court judgments, administrative penalty decisions, business licenses issued by market regulatory authorities, graduation diplomas granted by educational institutions, and official certificates of appointment, dismissal, commendation, or disciplinary action issued by government agencies or authorized organizations. To qualify as a public document, the record must be created by a competent state organ or authorized institution, in accordance with statutory procedures and within the bounds of its legal authority. Documents produced by unauthorized entities or beyond the scope of official duties do not constitute public documents. Public documents generally possess pre-existing legal validity prior to their submission as evidence, and are presumed authentic without requiring proof from the presenting party. The burden of proof lies with the party alleging falsity. Unless rebutted by sufficient contrary evidence, the factual content recorded in such documents—created within the official competence of the issuing body—is presumed to be true. Public documents originating outside China must be authenticated by a competent notarial authority in the country of origin. If they concern matters of personal status, such documents must also be certified by the issuing country's notarial authority and legalized by the Chinese embassy or consulate in that jurisdiction.

ii. **Private Document**

Private document refers to documents created by governmental bodies, organizations, enterprises, or individuals not in the course of performing official duties, as well as those prepared by private parties. Examples include letters of introduction issued by institutions, routine business correspondence, civil contracts concluded between institutions or between institutions and individuals, and private agreements drawn up by citizens. A private document need not be authored by the signatory personally, but it must bear their handwritten signature or official seal to be considered valid.

This classification matters because the methods of verifying authenticity differ. Public documents, if lawfully issued, are generally presumed authentic. In cases of dispute, the issuing authority may be requested to verify the document. If a public document has been lost or destroyed, the relevant authority should be consulted for verification. By contrast, the authenticity of private documents must be proven by the party submitting them. As stipulated in the *German Code of Civil Procedure*, "The authenticity of a private document not acknowledged by the opposing party must be proven." If a private document has been lost or destroyed, and no corroborating evidence exists while the opposing party denies its authenticity, the document cannot be admitted as valid evidence.

6.5.2.3 Classification Based on Method of Creation: Original, Official Copy, Duplicate, and Excerpted Documentary Evidence

i. **Original document**

Original document refers to the primary document as initially produced by its creator. It is the first version of the document, or the original textual record in which the relevant content was documented by the author. It represents the document in its original and unaltered form and typically carries the highest probative value among all categories of documentary evidence. As a general rule, parties should submit the original document whenever possible.

ii. **Official copy**

An official copy is a document that fully transcribes or reproduces the original and is accorded the same legal effect as the original. Although it is derived from the original, it is not itself the original but is treated as equivalent in evidentiary proceedings due to its formal certification or legal recognition.

iii. **Duplicate**

A duplicate is a reproduction of the original document that replicates its entire content but lacks the legal status of an official copy. Duplicates and official copies may differ in formal designation, and their evidentiary weight is typically subject to specific legal provisions or contractual agreements. For example, Sect. 6.3 of the *Bankers' Books Evidence Act 1879* (UK) provides that, in all legal proceedings, copies of entries from bankers' books may serve as prima facie evidence of the recorded entries, transactions, and accounts.

iv. **Excerpted documentary evidence**

An excerpted document refers to a partial reproduction of content taken from the original or official copy. Such documents reflect only a portion of the full content and lack the completeness necessary to fully convey the intent or meaning of the original. Their evidentiary value is therefore limited and context-dependent.

This classification is significant because different evidentiary rules govern the admissibility and weight of these forms in legal proceedings. While original documents are generally required, duplicates or excerpts may be accepted when submission of the original is genuinely impracticable.

However, where a submitted document is a copy and the party offering it fails to produce the original or indicate its whereabouts, and where no corroborating evidence exists and the opposing party disputes its authenticity, such a copy shall not be admitted as a basis for determining the facts of the case.

6.5.2.4 Classification Based on Purpose of Creation: Incidental Versus Purpose-Oriented Documentary Evidence

i. **Incidental documentary evidence**

Incidental documentary evidence refers to documents that were not originally created for evidentiary purposes, or whose primary function was not intended to serve as evidence in legal proceedings. Examples include accounting records, site maps, and personal diaries. In criminal litigation, most documentary evidence falls into this category.

ii. **Purpose-oriented documentary evidence**

Purpose-oriented documentary evidence refers to documents that are created with the express intent of serving as legal evidence. Typical examples include contracts, notarial deeds, and written wills.

This classification is relevant in evaluating the degree of objectivity embedded in a given document. As a general principle, incidental documents tend to exhibit a higher level of objectivity—especially when their content is adverse to the interest of the document's creator—thus enhancing their probative value.

6.5.2.5 Classification Based on Evidentiary Function: Self-Contained Versus Explanatory Documentary Evidence

i. **Self-Contained Documentary Evidence**

Self-contained documentary evidence refers to documents whose recorded or expressed content directly and unambiguously reflects the facts of the case, requiring no additional explanation or external reference to establish their evidentiary value. Examples include obscene illustrations or videos, fabricated accusations, or defamatory cartoons.

ii. **Explanatory Documentary Evidence**

Explanatory documentary evidence refers to documents whose content is relevant to the facts of the case but does not establish that relevance directly or intuitively. Instead, such documents require interpretation or the support of supplementary evidence to clarify their connection to the case. Examples include documents containing coded messages or symbolic references.

This classification is meaningful in terms of how the content of documentary evidence is to be interpreted. Generally, self-contained documents permit immediate factual inferences, whereas explanatory documents necessitate further analysis or corroboration before their evidentiary relevance can be fully established.

6.5.2.6 Classification Based on Legal Nature: Dispositive Versus Reportive Documentary Evidence

i. **Dispositive documentary evidence**

Dispositive documentary evidence refers to documents that serve to establish, modify, or extinguish specific legal relationships, or that independently give rise to legal consequences. Examples include property ownership certificates, court judgments, written wills, and donation agreements.

ii. **Reportive documentary evidence**

Reportive documentary evidence refers to documents that merely record, report, or reflect legally relevant facts that have already occurred or been observed. Examples include accounting vouchers, medical records, hotel guest logs, market analysis reports, credit evaluation reports, and news articles.

This classification is significant because these two types of documents perform distinct evidentiary functions. Dispositive documents are inherently linked to legal outcomes and may serve as proof of the creation, alteration, or termination of legal relationships. In contrast, reportive documents merely describe factual circumstances and, by themselves, do not directly produce legal effects. However, they may serve as a precursor to dispositive documents or corroborate their authenticity and factual accuracy.

6.5.3 The Significance of the Documentary Evidence

Throughout the history of litigation, documentary evidence has consistently played a vital role in establishing case facts. Due to its evidentiary importance, British legal history once experienced a period characterized as a "trial by documents," which eventually evolved into the best evidence rule, requiring the submission of original documents. In the development of civil litigation in China, evidence was long centered on documents, giving rise to a tendency known as "documentary evidence supremacy." Contemporary practice, however, has shifted greater emphasis toward party statements and the expression of intent. Nevertheless, with ongoing societal development, technological innovation, and cultural advancement, documentary evidence—combining legal foresight with the communicative function of written language—is expected to assume an increasingly important role in future proceedings.

6.5.3.1 Documentary Evidence Can Help Determine the Legal Nature of a Case

In many instances, documentary evidence can directly identify the legal nature of a case by clearly stating its connection to the facts in dispute. For this reason, it is often metaphorically described as "speaking for itself." In criminal cases such as corruption or defamation, documents may directly reveal the core legal issue. In certain proceedings, documentary evidence is indispensable. This is particularly true for contract disputes, insurance litigation, and cases involving counterfeit trademarks, forged currency, or securities violations. Such cases typically require submission of the counterfeit trademarks, forged currencies, fabricated official documents, or obscene publications, videos, or digital recordings associated with the offense. In fraud cases, transactional records mapping the flow of funds across multiple accounts serve as crucial evidence. Thus, documentary evidence frequently provides straightforward and compelling proof regarding the legal characterization of a case.

6.5.3.2 Documentary Evidence Serves as Direct Proof of Disputed Facts

In criminal proceedings, some documents may directly address whether the defendant is identical to the perpetrator of the criminal act. In civil and administrative litigation, the role of documentary evidence is even more direct. A signed promissory note may suffice to establish a creditor-debtor relationship. Similarly, a land use certificate or property title may directly prove legal ownership.

6.5.3.3 Documentary Evidence is Highly Credible in Establishing Facts

As documentary evidence is typically created before litigation arises, it possesses historical continuity and is generally free from the influence of litigation-driven motives. Compared to other types of evidence, it is often viewed as more reliable. This explains the long-standing judicial reliance on documentary evidence—particularly in civil and administrative cases—where it frequently serves as the principal or decisive basis for fact-finding. In practice, such reliance has occasionally led to an overproduction and overreliance on formal documentation. Nonetheless, this phenomenon reflects the comparatively high probative value of documentary evidence.

Documentary evidence, as a tangible object, exists independently of the will of the parties or the adjudicating body and exhibits a strong degree of objectivity. Unlike real evidence, which proves facts through physical characteristics, documentary evidence derives its value from the content it records or expresses. That content—whether directly, or with the aid of interpretive or supplementary materials—can be readily understood and applied to fact-finding. This is a distinctive and significant feature of documentary evidence. A clear understanding of this characteristic allows parties and judicial authorities to make effective use of documentary materials in establishing the facts of a case.

6.6 Witness Testimony

Witness testimony is a form of testimonial evidence expressed through spoken or written language. It occupies a pivotal role in the law of evidence and is recognized as a formal category of evidence under Chinese law. In both common law and civil law jurisdictions, witness testimony is among the most prevalent and universally applicable forms of evidence in litigation.

6.6.1 Definition and Characteristics of Witness Testimony

The concept of witness testimony can be understood in both a broad and a narrow sense. Broadly defined—often referred to as personal testimonial evidence—it encompasses all spoken or written expressions used to prove facts in a case. This definition is commonly adopted in common law jurisdictions. It emphasizes the verbal form of the evidence, focusing on its external linguistic expression, while placing less emphasis on the source of the statement or the procedural status of the speaker. Under this approach, "witnesses" include not only ordinary lay witnesses but also parties to the litigation (e.g., victim statements, confessions by defendants), expert witnesses, and law enforcement officers—all of whom may provide specialized forms of testimony.

Narrowly defined, as in the Chinese legal context, witness testimony refers specifically to statements made by third parties—i.e., individuals other than the litigants themselves—regarding facts they have personally perceived or experienced that are relevant to the case. Such testimony may be delivered orally or submitted in written form. Regardless of the format, witness testimony consists of two essential components: the subject of the testimony (i.e., the witness) and the content of the testimony (i.e., the statement made). It represents the inseparable unity between the testifying person and the factual account provided. As a distinct evidentiary category, witness testimony possesses several defining characteristics that distinguish it from other types of evidence:

6.6.1.1 Witness Testimony Must Be Given by a Legally Qualified Individual

Witness testimony must be provided by a person who possesses the legal capacity to testify. That is, the testimony must originate from a natural person who meets the statutory requirements to serve as a witness. Since witness testimony is human-derived, it is inherently linked to both the individual's potential interest in the outcome of the case and their cognitive and expressive abilities—namely, their capacity to observe, remember, and communicate facts. These factors critically affect both the admissibility and probative value of the testimony.

A witness is defined as a natural person who is capable of distinguishing right from wrong, who can accurately articulate facts, and who has personal knowledge of circumstances related to the case. Testimony arises when a witness conveys facts they have directly observed or experienced through their senses. The witness's ability to discern truth and to express it accurately forms the legal and practical foundation for their qualification to testify. As a general rule, a natural person is considered competent to testify if the following conditions are met.

i. **A Witness must have personal knowledge of the facts of the case**

A witness is an individual who, at a specific time and place and under certain circumstances, perceived or experienced facts relevant to the case through their own senses. As a general rule, a witness must testify based on facts that they have personally and directly perceived. Testimony based on hearsay or secondhand information is generally inadmissible, as its source lacks reliability. For instance, Rule 602 of the *U.S. Federal Rules of Evidence* stipulates: "A witness may not testify to a matter unless evidence is introduced sufficient to support a finding that the witness has personal knowledge of the matter." Witness testimony must be provided directly by the individual who perceived the facts—it may not be substituted or delegated to others. This reflects the principle of non-substitutability, which underpins the broader evidentiary rule that legal fact-finding should rely on the most reliable source of information available. While the Chinese legal system does not adhere strictly to the common law's hearsay doctrine, it does allow, under certain circumstances, testimony from individuals who did not personally perceive the facts in question.

ii. **A witness is generally a natural person, though an entity may serve in limited circumstances**

The qualifications for serving as a witness are inherently tied to the human faculties of perception, cognition, and expression. Witnessing is a fact-sensitive and person-dependent activity. Although legal persons (such as corporations or other organizations) are treated as juridical entities under the law, they do not possess the natural faculties required to observe facts, and thus cannot serve as witnesses in the literal sense. Even when a legal entity becomes aware of factual circumstances in the course of business operations, it is, in fact, the organization's members who possess that knowledge. In such instances, the testimony must be given by individuals—often referred to as "institutional witnesses"—who directly observed the relevant events in their personal capacity. "A legal person or other juridical entity, lacking perceptual faculties, is incapable of observing factual events and therefore cannot testify to them."[6] Article 72 of *China's Civil Procedure Law* affirms: "All entities and individuals with knowledge of the case are obligated to appear in court and testify." In practice, documents submitted by organizations must be signed or sealed by an authorized representative and bear the official seal of the institution. These documents, however, should not be treated as witness testimony, as they lack the essential characteristics of testimonial evidence, particularly the capacity for cross-examination in open court.

Documents issued by a legal entity, bearing both an official seal and the signature of its legal representative, may be admitted as documentary evidence. Such documents are assessed based on the content recorded and evaluated through judicial review. Similarly, evidence collected by investigative bodies from institutional sources should not be classified as witness testimony. Where necessary, the individual responsible for preparing such documentation must appear in court to offer live testimony.

iii. **Individuals who lack the capacity to distinguish right from wrong or to express themselves clearly cannot serve as witnesses**

[6] Chen (1979).

.Article 62 of the *Criminal Procedure Law* of our country provides: "Any person who has knowledge of the facts of a case is obligated to testify. Those who, due to physical or mental disability or immaturity, are unable to distinguish right from wrong or to express themselves properly shall not serve as witnesses." Likewise, the Civil Procedure Law stipulates: "Persons who are unable to express their intent accurately shall not serve as witnesses." Accordingly, individuals with physical or mental impairments, or of young age, may be permitted to testify so long as they possess both the ability to distinguish right from wrong and the ability to express themselves clearly. If either capacity is absent—whether the person cannot distinguish right from wrong, or cannot communicate effectively—they are disqualified from testifying.

Chinese law does not impose a strict age threshold for child witnesses. In contrast, Sect. 6.3 of the Evidence Ordinance of the Hong Kong Special Administrative Region specifies that children under the age of seven, and mentally disordered persons who appear unable to comprehend relevant facts or to communicate them reliably, are not qualified to testify. In general, courts are required to examine a child's competence, assessing whether the child has sufficient intelligence to observe, recall, and recount facts, and whether they understand the duty to speak truthfully.[7] If these conditions are met, the child may be allowed to testify. Persons who are unable to express themselves coherently are not eligible to testify. However, individuals with no or limited civil capacity due to their age, intellectual development, or mental condition may still be permitted to testify, provided their understanding of the facts corresponds with their mental capacity and the complexity of the factual issues involved. Witnesses must possess sensory perception, cognitive discernment, and expressive ability. The requirement to distinguish right from wrong does not demand a philosophical understanding of legal truth, but merely that the witness can accurately and objectively recount what they have personally seen or heard.

In principle, any person with knowledge of the case is obliged to testify. The individual's relationship with the parties, their motivation or purpose in testifying, or the manner in which they obtained the relevant information, does not in itself disqualify them from serving as a witness. As long as the person is not a party to the case, they may testify. Under Chinese law, only close relatives of a party are subject to restricted testimonial obligations; there is no system of testimonial privilege for special categories of witnesses, nor is there a witness immunity regime. Absent specific statutory exemptions, any citizen—regardless of whether they have a direct interest in the case—may be summoned to testify. However, where a witness has a direct interest in the outcome of the case, courts should evaluate their testimony with appropriate caution. Nevertheless, if such testimony is found to be truthful and reliable, it should be admitted.[8] Furthermore, witnesses testifying to facts they did not personally perceive—i.e., facts not directly observed or heard—must disclose the source of that information. Otherwise, the statement does not qualify as admissible

---

[7] Morgan (1982).

[8] See the Reply of the Supreme People's Court on whether a person with a direct interest in the case can be a witness, etc. (No.12573, June 22,1957).

testimony. Hearsay evidence generally lacks probative value because it deprives the opposing party (whether prosecution or defense) of the opportunity to cross-examine the original source. Absent statutory exceptions, such testimony is inadmissible due to its lack of verifiability in court and the consequent denial of the opposing party's right to confrontation.

6.6.1.2 Witness Testimony is Inherently Subjective

Witness testimony consists of statements made by individuals recounting facts they claim to have perceived. Such testimony is typically given after the events in question and results from a complex cognitive process involving observation, recognition, comprehension, memory, and verbal expression. Each of these stages is susceptible to subjective influence. Moreover, a witness's age, psychological condition, educational background, physical health, occupation, and personal preferences may all impact the reliability and quality of their testimony. In practice, what a witness recounts often diverges—sometimes significantly—from the objective reality of the events as they actually occurred. Even if a witness possesses adequate perceptual, cognitive, and expressive abilities, the accuracy of their testimony may still be affected by the passage of time or the strength of their original impression, leading to inconsistencies between the testimony and the actual facts.

Furthermore, as ordinary individuals embedded in social contexts, witnesses may be influenced by external pressures or personal interests. They may act out of fear of retaliation, be subject to threats, coercion, or even bribery, or may be guided by ulterior motives. These circumstances increase the risk that a witness will deliberately distort or misrepresent the truth. In this regard, witness testimony is often shaped by the witness's own volition and filtered through layers of social and psychological influence. Compared to physical or documentary forms of evidence—such as real evidence or documentary evidence—witness testimony is markedly more subjective in nature, and its evidentiary value must be assessed accordingly.

6.6.1.3 Witness Testimony is Primarily Delivered Orally

Witness testimony is typically provided in oral form, allowing the court to assess the witness's credibility based on their voice, tone, demeanor, and facial expressions. Oral testimony not only facilitates the confrontation and cross-examination of witnesses—enabling direct clarification of disputed facts and resolution of ambiguities—but also allows for a more immediate evaluation of consistency between statements and nonverbal cues. Oral delivery thus promotes the principles of immediacy and orality, which are foundational to adversarial proceedings and essential for effective fact-finding. "A witness shall not prepare a written report, in whole or in part, to substitute for testimony, nor may a witness feign recollection while in fact reciting from a written script."[9]

Nevertheless, the requirement for oral testimony is not absolute. Statutory exceptions permit written testimony under specific circumstances. Article 195 of China's Criminal Procedure Law provides that written statements of absent witnesses may be read aloud in court. In such cases, the court must solicit the opinions of the prosecutor, the parties, defense counsel, and legal representatives. Similarly, under the Civil Procedure Law, witnesses may, with court approval, testify through written statements, audiovisual transmission, or recorded media in any of the following situations: (1) The witness is unable to appear in court due to medical reasons;(2) Travel to court is infeasible due to distance or transportation constraints;(3) Attendance is prevented by force majeure, such as natural disasters;(4) Other legitimate reasons preclude in-person testimony. However, where a witness refuses to appear without just cause and submits a written or other indirect form of testimony, such evidence may not serve as a basis for judicial fact-finding.

Written witness testimony—commonly referred to as a written statement—may, in some instances, reflect the witness's sincere account of the facts. However, it is also possible that the statement has been deliberately constructed after thoughtful consideration and strategic judgment. Because such testimony is not subject to live cross-examination, and may be presented by someone other than the witness, there is a heightened risk that the intended meaning of the statement may be misinterpreted or distorted. This introduces challenges in verifying its authenticity and assessing its probative value.

It is also crucial to distinguish between written witness statements and documentary evidence. While they may appear similar in format, they differ fundamentally in legal nature. Documentary evidence is typically created during the occurrence, alteration, or conclusion of factual events, and functions as a contemporaneous historical record. Once generated, its content is fixed, and judicial scrutiny usually focuses on objective features, such as the date of creation, presence of alterations, or internal consistency. By contrast, a written statement represents a post hoc account of a witness's direct or indirect perception of facts. It is not itself part of the original event. As such, it lacks the historical immutability of documentary evidence and must be evaluated with greater caution.

6.6.1.4 Witness Testimony is Generally Provided in Court

Witness testimony is ordinarily presented during pretrial evidence exchange or during formal court proceedings. According to Article 61 of the *Criminal Procedure Law* of our country, "A witness's testimony must be cross-examined in court by the public prosecutor, the victim, and the defendant and defense counsel, and verified by the court before it may serve as a basis for a verdict."

[9] Diao (1984).

This means that witness testimony must, in principle, be delivered in court, in the presence of both the judge and the parties. It is not admissible if submitted unilaterally to the court or a party outside of formal proceedings. Only through courtroom presentation can the testimony be cross-examined by both sides and subject to judicial verification. Exceptions are permitted where both parties consent and the court grants approval.

Given the vivid, intuitive, complex, and subjective nature of witness testimony, witnesses are required to testify in person and provide oral statements based on what they personally observed or experienced. The reliability of their testimony must be affirmed through a signed declaration or formal oath. When adjudicating a case, courts should evaluate such testimony in light of these characteristics and through formal adversarial procedures, including cross-examination and judicial assessment. In criminal proceedings, which are often divided into multiple stages—each with the potential to conclude the case—witness testimony may be necessary to support interim or final decisions. Thus, statements made by witnesses at earlier stages may also constitute legally valid testimony. Where inconsistencies arise between in-court and pretrial statements, the pretrial testimony may still be admitted if the witness provides a reasonable explanation and the testimony is corroborated by other evidence.

6.6.1.5 Witness Testimony is a Factual Account, not an Analytical Opinion

Witness testimony must be limited to objective descriptions of facts that the witness has personally perceived through their senses. It should reflect what the witness directly observed or experienced, not their opinions, conjectures, or analytical conclusions regarding the case. As stipulated in the *Provisions of the Supreme People's Court on Evidence in Civil Litigation*: "Witnesses shall objectively describe facts personally perceived and shall not use speculative, inferential, or evaluative language when testifying." Judicial guidance further warns that: "Opinions and speculations offered by witnesses are not admissible as evidence and may compromise the impartial determination of facts."[10]

In practice, however, the line between experiential statements and opinion-based testimony is not always clear-cut. The distinction is often one of degree rather than kind. Most witness statements are inevitably shaped by some level of reasoning or mental processing. In many instances, a witness's opinion is inseparable from their direct experience and cannot be wholly excluded from their testimony. Generally, statements describing experiential facts—such as what the witness saw, heard, or felt—may be treated as valid testimony. As a core evidentiary principle holds: "A witness must testify to facts personally experienced; such testimony may not be substituted by someone who did not directly perceive the facts."[11]

---

[10] Chen (1979).

[11] Soppellee, p. 88.

This highlights the non-substitutable nature of genuine experiential testimony.

In practice, witness statements can be categorized into two types: Descriptive (experiential) testimony, which is generally admissible; and Judgmental (opinion-based) testimony, which must be subject to heightened scrutiny and is ordinarily inadmissible.

6.6.2 Classification of Witness Testimony

Classifying witness testimony according to different criteria enables a multidimensional understanding of its nature and evidentiary value. Such classification also provides an analytical foundation for comprehensively evaluating testimony within the adjudicative process. Witness testimony may be categorized as follows:

6.6.2.1 By the Natural Characteristics of the Witness

Witness testimony may be classified based on the biological and personal attributes of the witness, such as gender, age, or cognitive capacity:

Gender-based testimony includes male and female testimony. Due to physiological and cognitive differences between men and women, their perception, memory, and narration of the same event may vary.

Age-based testimony includes that of elderly, middle-aged, young adults, adolescents, and children. Age impacts both physiological and psychological faculties, which in turn affects comprehension, recall, and expressive capacity. Hence, testimony from different age groups may differ in accuracy and detail.

Capacity-based testimony distinguishes between witnesses with full testimonial capacity and those with limited or relative testimonial capacity. The former refers to witnesses capable of distinguishing right from wrong and expressing themselves accurately. The latter includes individuals—such as minors or persons with mental impairments—whose ability to perceive or articulate facts may be partial or impaired.

This classification underscores that variability among witness accounts is expected and natural. If different witnesses provide accounts that are identical in every detail, such uniformity may raise concerns of fabrication or collusion. Conversely, slight inconsistencies in detail often indicate independent and truthful recollection.

6.6.2.2 By the Evidentiary Value of the Testimony

Witness testimony may also be categorized based on the nature of its evidentiary function in relation to the facts of the case: Affirmative testimony supports the existence of a specific fact. Negative testimony denies the occurrence or existence of a fact. Mixed testimony affirms some aspects while denying others.

This distinction is important in evidentiary evaluation. Negative testimony, once verified, can directly negate a factual assertion. Affirmative testimony, on the other hand, usually requires corroboration from additional sources to establish the veracity of the facts asserted.

6.6.2.3 By the Professional Background of the Witness

Witness testimony may further be divided into professional testimony and non-professional testimony, depending on whether the subject matter relates to the witness's occupational expertise: Professional testimony is provided by individuals whose statements are based on their professional duties or roles—for example, a physician testifying about a patient's symptoms observed during consultation. Non-professional testimony is given by individuals speaking as laypersons, such as a pedestrian describing the speed of a moving vehicle at the scene of an accident.

This classification bears on the method of evidence assessment. Testimony involving specialized or technical content requires evaluators to possess or consult relevant subject-matter expertise—potentially through the assistance of expert witnesses. In contrast, lay testimony based on ordinary perception can be evaluated using general reasoning and common experience.

6.6.2.4 Classification Based on Whether the Witness Has an Interest in the Case

Witness testimony may be classified according to whether the witness holds a personal or legal interest in the case: Interested witness testimony refers to statements provided by individuals who have a direct or indirect stake in the outcome of the case or who maintain a personal, familial, or professional relationship with one of the parties. Disinterested witness testimony refers to statements given by individuals who have no such connection and who occupy a position of complete neutrality.

As a general rule, interested witnesses may exhibit partisan tendencies, potentially giving statements that seek to absolve themselves of liability or favor a particular party. Consequently, such testimony may lack objectivity. By contrast, testimony from disinterested witnesses is typically regarded as more credible and impartial.

This classification is significant when assessing the probative value of a witness's testimony. It is standard practice to first examine the relationship between the witness and the parties or the case. When a witness has a discernible interest in the outcome, and their testimony aligns with that interest, its evidentiary weight is often considered weaker than testimony from a neutral party.

6.6.2.5 Classification Based on the Form in Which Testimony is Provided

Witness testimony may also be distinguished based on its mode of delivery: Oral testimony refers to statements delivered verbally in court or during official proceedings. Written testimony refers to statements recorded in written form and submitted as documentary evidence. Written witness statements must comply with procedural and evidentiary requirements. When a party submits such a statement to the court, it must generally meet the following conditions: (1) It must clearly identify the witness, including full name, age, gender, occupation, and residential address; (2) It must bear the signature of the witness; if the witness is unable to sign, an alternative form of authentication (such as a seal or thumbprint) must be used; (3) It must include the date the statement was made or submitted; (4) It must be accompanied by a copy of the witness's identification document, such as a national identity card, to verify their identity.

6.6.3 The Evidentiary Significance of Witness Testimony

Witness testimony remains one of the most extensively utilized and frequently relied-upon forms of evidence in modern legal proceedings across jurisdictions. It plays a crucial role in the discovery and proof of facts and serves as an effective mechanism for verifying and assessing other types of evidence. Soviet legal scholars have lauded it as "the most important source for forming the judge's inner conviction and the foundation of the entire modern trial process."[12] In contrast, some German scholars have characterized it as the most frequently used yet least reliable form of evidence.[13]

6.6.3.1 Witness Testimony Has a Direct Function in Proving Facts

Witness testimony is based on a witness's truthful account of facts that they have personally perceived, either in whole or in part. As such, it can directly establish case facts and significantly contribute to fact-finding. As a form of testimonial evidence, it is derived from the witness's sensory experience of the event in question. Compared with physical evidence, documentary evidence, or audiovisual materials, witness testimony possesses the advantage of immediacy and expressiveness, often allowing the adjudicator to ascertain facts without requiring inferential reasoning.

[12] Vyshinsky (1957).

[13] Rosenberg et al. (2007).

6.6.3.2 Witness Testimony Functions as a Tool for Corroborating Other Evidence

Witness statements can aid both parties and judicial authorities in identifying, understanding, and evaluating other forms of evidence—such as physical exhibits or documents—by verifying their authenticity and clarifying their evidentiary weight. In addition, witness testimony can expose false narratives, identify contradictions among various forms of evidence, and thereby serve as a critical tool for testing the reliability and consistency of the evidentiary system as a whole. When a witness statement withstands cross-examination and is confirmed as credible during trial, it carries enhanced probative value in establishing the factual basis of the case.

6.7 Statements of the Parties

Statements made by the parties are recognized as a formal type of evidence in law. In the legal systems of the former Soviet Union and several Eastern European countries, such statements were treated as a distinct evidentiary category alongside other forms of evidence. Some jurisdictions have developed procedures for directly questioning parties based on the principle of the right to be heard, thereby formally incorporating party statements as admissible evidence. In China, party statements generally include the following: victim statements in criminal proceedings; confessions and defenses made by criminal suspects and defendants; and statements made by parties involved in civil and administrative litigation.

6.7.1 Victim Statements

In Chinese criminal procedure, victims are classified as parties to the case. Although victim statements are categorized under party statements, they are treated as a distinct evidentiary type exclusively in public prosecution cases.

6.7.1.1 Definition and Characteristics of Victim Statements

A victim statement refers to a declaration made by an individual who has suffered direct harm from a criminal act, describing both the facts of the offense and the identity of the alleged offender, submitted to the investigative authorities. The core contents of a victim statement generally include: (1) A detailed account of the events constituting the criminal offense; (2) Information pertaining to the offender's physical appearance and personal characteristics; (3) Requests regarding the protection of the victim's lawful rights and interests. For evidentiary purposes, only the first two elements—narration of the criminal act and identification of the offender—are considered relevant, while the third, being a legal demand, is excluded from the scope of admissible factual evidence.

From a procedural standpoint, victim statements include those made by victims in public prosecution cases, by private prosecutors in private prosecution cases, and by civil claimants in criminal cases involving attached civil suits. In the United States, a related concept exists known as the victim impact statement, which refers to the expression by the victim of the social, economic, physical, and psychological harm suffered as a result of the crime. These statements are typically submitted during sentencing to inform judicial discretion regarding punishment. They differ from victim statements in Chinese law, which are intended to establish the facts of the case. Victim statements exhibit several distinct features when compared with other types of evidence.

i. **A victim statement is a statement made by the individual directly Harmed by the criminal act**

The victim is the person directly harmed by a criminal act. As a party to the proceedings, the victim enjoys rights and bears obligations different from other participants such as witnesses or expert evaluators. In cases involving crimes against personal or property rights, the victim often comes into direct contact with the perpetrator and is present during the commission of the crime. As such, the victim is able to provide a relatively complete account of the criminal act and the specific circumstances surrounding it. While the content of a victim's statement may be similar to that of an eyewitness, the procedural status of the victim differs from that of a witness. Victims differ from witnesses in the following respects: (1) The relationship between the victim and the case differs from that of the witness. The victim is the direct sufferer of the crime and has a personal stake in the outcome of the case; the witness merely has knowledge of certain facts and holds no direct interest in the matter. (2) Victims participate in litigation because their lawful rights have been infringed; witnesses participate due to their knowledge of the case and a civic obligation to testify. (3) The victim's goal in litigation is to protect their lawful interests; the witness's role is to assist judicial authorities in establishing the facts. (4) Victim statements often carry an accusatory tone and cover a broad range of content; witnesses, by contrast, provide factual observations based on their knowledge of the case.

ii. **Victim statements are generally direct**

During the commission of a crime, the victim is typically familiar not only with the sequence of events but also with the physical characteristics of the offender. Moreover, having directly suffered harm, the victim holds unique experiential knowledge that is not shared or replaceable by others. In cases such as robbery, rape, kidnapping, or fraud, the victim's personal impressions may be particularly vivid and long-lasting, rendering their statement of significant evidentiary value in uncovering and verifying criminal conduct.

Even where the victim is not physically present during the crime, they may still possess a clear understanding of certain case facts. For instance, in theft cases, victims often have precise knowledge of the quantity and value of stolen items. In some online fraud cases, even if the criminal behavior is virtual or remote and online avatars are falsified, the victim may still be able to recognize patterns in conduct, speech, or behavioral cues that point to the identity of the perpetrator. Thus, the victim's statement constitutes a source of independently derived evidence.

iii. **Victim statements may contain both truthful and false elements**

Given the victim's personal stake in the case, their statements may at times be exaggerated, motivated by emotions such as anger, retaliation, or resentment. In urgent or stressful circumstances, the victim may misperceive events, leading to inaccurate recollections. Consequently, victim statements may contain a blend of truthful and false elements, and in some cases, may even be fabricated with the intent to falsely accuse others.

iv. **Victim statements are irreplaceable**

Victim statements must be provided directly by the victim and cannot be substituted by others. In this sense, they share similarities with witness testimony. In cases involving minor victims, statements are typically made in the presence of a legal guardian. However, any additional content provided by the guardian cannot be regarded as part of the victim's statement and should not be treated as such in evidentiary proceedings.

iv. **Complexity of victim statements**

When victims make statements to investigative authorities, their accounts often go beyond describing the factual aspects of the case. These statements frequently include accusations against the alleged offender, personal demands, or claims for compensation in ancillary civil proceedings. The intermingling of factual narration and subjective appeals gives victim statements a certain degree of complexity. It is important to distinguish a victim's statement from a complaint or accusation. A victim statement does not include allegations made in reports, complaints, requests for prosecutorial review, or private prosecutions submitted to authorities concerning past or ongoing criminal conduct or specific suspects or defendants. However, any factual assertions based on the victim's own perceptions, even if embedded in those accusations, may still be treated as victim statements.

In judicial practice, victims may also participate in identification procedures, resulting in the production of identification records. These records typically include the time and location of the identification, the basic information and assigned numbers of the participants, characteristics of the person being identified, the outcome of the identification, and the reasons for recognition or non-recognition. The record is usually signed by the identifying victim, present personnel, and the organizers. While such records are not themselves classified as victim statements, they may serve as auxiliary material for examining and assessing the reliability of victim statements and other evidence.

6.7.1.2 Classification of Victim Statement

To better understand, analyze, and apply victim statements, scholars have generally categorized them as follows:

i. **By the identity of the declarant: victim statements may be classified as statements made by natural persons and statements made by victim organizations.**

A statement by a natural person refers to an individual's account given to investigative authorities about the facts of harm they personally suffered. These statements may be further categorized into those made by adult victims and minor victims, or by male victims and female victims, depending on the individual's characteristics. A statement by a victim organization refers to a declaration made by a representative of an entity harmed by a criminal act regarding the harm suffered by the organization.

This classification is meaningful in that different declarants, due to their distinct attributes, tend to present unique features in their statements.

ii. **By whether the victim had direct contact with the perpetrator: victim statements may be divided into statements involving direct contact and statements without direct contact.**

Statements involving direct contact often provide detailed information about the crime, such as the perpetrator's physical appearance, behavioral patterns, and even subtle personal traits. These are typically considered direct evidence and, once verified, can serve as a direct basis for adjudication. Conversely, statements without direct contact generally provide information about the consequences of the crime and constitute circumstantial evidence.

When gathering statements involving direct contact, investigators should probe deeply into the specifics of the crime, especially its finer details. In reviewing such statements, meticulous scrutiny is necessary to ensure no inconsistencies are overlooked.

iii. **By the presence or absence of fault on the part of the victim: victim statements can be divided into statements made by victims with contributory fault and statements made by victims without fault.**

This classification is particularly relevant when assessing statements by victims with contributory fault. Such statements may reflect attempts to obscure responsibility or exaggerate certain facts. However, unintentional errors arising from non-negligent behavior should be objectively assessed. Similarly, statements by faultless victims should not be accepted uncritically, as they may still reflect exaggeration or inaccuracies due to psychological distress or emotional agitation during the offense.

6.7.1.3 The Evidentiary Significance of Victim Statements

As a party to criminal proceedings, a victim's statement carries significant evidentiary value.

First, in certain cases, the victim's statement serves as the starting point for criminal prosecution and constitutes a critical basis for the initiation of a case. In crimes such as rape, assault, fraud, or theft, the offense may not even come to light without the victim's report. The victim is often able to recount the fundamental circumstances of the offense, including its key elements and specific details, as well as provide information about the perpetrator's physical features, mannerisms, and verbal expressions. These accounts offer crucial evidence and investigative leads that contribute to the timely resolution of criminal cases.

Second, the victim's statement generally constitutes direct evidence and plays an important role in establishing the existence and nature of the criminal act. Once corroborated, it may serve as a vital basis for the final adjudication. Moreover, the victim's statement serves as an effective tool for assessing the credibility and reliability of other forms of testimonial evidence, such as witness statements or the defendant's confession.

As the concept of the rule of law has evolved and human rights awareness has deepened, defendants—once relegated to a passive role in criminal proceedings—have gradually assumed the status of subjects of the proceedings. With the growing emphasis on procedural justice, legal protections afforded to defendants have become increasingly comprehensive. However, in jurisdictions that adopt the principle of prosecutorial monopoly or exclusive public prosecution, victims are often limited to the role of complainants. In such systems, victims are typically summoned as witnesses and are required to undergo cross-examination by the defendant and defense counsel, thereby exposing them to the risk of what is commonly referred to as "secondary victimization." Against this backdrop, there has been a discernible trend in legislation toward the enhanced protection of victims' rights.

6.7.2 Statements and Defenses by Criminal Suspects and Defendants

Statements and defenses made by criminal suspects and defendants—commonly referred to as confessions or oral statements—constitute one of the most prevalent, complex, and significant forms of evidence in criminal proceedings. Across various jurisdictions, such statements are explicitly recognized in criminal procedure or evidence law as a distinct category of evidence.

6.7.2.1 Definition and Characteristics of Statements and Defenses

Statements and defenses by criminal suspects and defendants, also known as "confessions" or "admissions," refer to the accounts and explanations offered by suspects or defendants to the authorities during criminal proceedings concerning facts relevant to the alleged offense.

These statements and defenses generally comprise three components: (1) Admissions of guilt, in which the suspect or defendant acknowledges having committed a criminal act and describes the underlying motive, the manner of commission, the specific circumstances, and the resulting consequences of the offense; (2) Defenses involving denial of guilt or claims of mitigation or exemption from punishment, wherein the suspect or defendant either denies involvement in the alleged criminal conduct or, while acknowledging the conduct, argues that no criminal liability should be imposed or that the punishment should be mitigated, reduced, or waived pursuant to applicable law; (3) Disclosures or accusations against other co-suspects or co-defendants, often referred to as "incriminating others," in which the individual reveals or reports the alleged criminal acts of others involved in the same case.

The evidentiary value of such disclosures must be assessed on a case-by-case basis. Where the content of the disclosure is connected to the suspect's or defendant's own criminal activity, it is deemed part of their statement or defense. However, if the disclosure concerns individuals not implicated in the same offense—for instance, in an attempt to obtain leniency or establish meritorious conduct—and relates to offenses unrelated to the joint criminal enterprise, it does not form part of the suspect's or defendant's statement or defense. Instead, such information may serve as an investigative lead or be treated as witness testimony in a separate case.

Given that suspects and defendants are the objects of prosecution and central figures in criminal proceedings—with the entire process oriented around the determination of their criminal responsibility—their statements and defenses possess distinctive attributes that differentiate them from all other forms of evidence.

i. **The direct nature of statements and defenses by criminal suspects and defendants**

Criminal suspects and defendants, as parties directly involved in the case, possess the most intimate knowledge of whether they committed the alleged offense, as well as the relevant circumstances and mental states before, during, and after the incident. A truthful and objective confession by a suspect or defendant may provide a comprehensive account of the motive, intent, methods, sequence of events, specific circumstances, consequences of the offense, and the disposition of stolen property or illicit proceeds. Such information is of critical value for fact-finding in criminal proceedings. Even in cases where suspects or defendants deny guilt or seek a lighter sentence, their defenses are typically accompanied by specific justifications or factual assertions, which may also assist in uncovering the truth.

In cases involving co-offenders, the suspect's or defendant's statements may further elucidate otherwise inaccessible aspects of joint criminal activity—such as the allocation of roles, hierarchical positions, the full commission process, and the organizational structure and criminal operations of criminal syndicates, mafia-type organizations, or illegal pyramid schemes. Consequently, once verified, statements and defenses by suspects and defendants can serve as a comprehensive and direct evidentiary basis for establishing the facts of a case. This evidentiary strength, unparalleled by other forms of evidence, is a primary reason why such confessions are often regarded as the "king of evidence" within evidentiary frameworks.

ii. **The instability of statements and defenses by criminal suspects and defendants**

Statements and defenses by criminal suspects and defendants often exhibit inconsistency and internal contradiction, rendering them inherently unstable.

As a form of testimonial evidence, such statements are particularly vulnerable to the emotional state and shifting mindset of the declarant. Given the suspect's or defendant's direct and substantial interest in the outcome of the proceedings, their statements are frequently influenced by strategic considerations or external factors. For example, a suspect may initially deny guilt or minimize the offense out of a sense of opportunism, only to later confess truthfully after receiving legal education or when confronted with compelling evidence. Conversely, a suspect may recant a prior confession due to peer influence or coercion from fellow detainees in an attempt to evade liability. There are also cases where family members or associates attempt to interfere with the proceedings by inducing victims or witnesses to alter their testimony, subsequently communicating this to the suspect or defendant, leading to coordinated false statements or "collusion." In some instances, suspects or defendants who did not commit the offense may be pressured into making false confessions due to investigative misconduct or mistaken identification. In practice, such statements are often marked by instability, manifesting as "post-confession retraction," "confessions that shift over time," "contradictory accounts within a single session," or "frequent reversals," all of which underscore the evidentiary unreliability of this form of testimony.

iii. **The complexity of statements and defenses by criminal suspects and defendants**

Statements by criminal suspects and defendants often comprise both truthful and false elements, thereby exhibiting considerable complexity. With respect to confessions of guilt, except for those who voluntarily surrender and exhibit genuine remorse, many suspects and defendants tend to employ evasive tactics—such as denial, equivocation, or selective disclosure—to minimize their culpability or avoid punishment. Some may only describe mitigating circumstances while omitting aggravating facts; others confess solely to offenses already known to the authorities while denying or concealing those not yet uncovered. There are also instances where suspects falsely admit to non-existent offenses to divert investigators' attention or to test the extent of the authorities' knowledge. In certain cases, suspects may even falsely confess in order to protect accomplices or relatives by accepting responsibility for crimes they did not commit.

In terms of defenses denying guilt or the severity of the offense, suspects and defendants may present truthful explanations grounded in fact. Some, however, may offer denials without providing supporting evidence or coherent reasoning—yet such deficiencies, in themselves, do not automatically invalidate the defense. Conversely, there are cases in which guilty individuals present unfounded denials or seek to portray serious offenses as minor infractions.

When it comes to disclosing the crimes of others, some suspects or defendants fabricate accusations to shift blame or create the appearance of cooperation. Others deliberately invent criminal scenarios to frame innocent parties. Some exaggerate the conduct of others in hopes of securing leniency through purported meritorious reporting.

In light of these possibilities, statements and defenses made by criminal suspects and defendants must be assessed with caution. They should neither be blindly accepted nor entirely disregarded. Instead, the principle of prioritizing objective evidence and thorough investigation over uncorroborated verbal statements must be upheld, in order to avoid wrongful convictions or the unjust exoneration of offenders.

As for whether the statements and defenses of co-suspects or co-defendants may be used as mutual evidence, there is ongoing scholarly debate. One view holds that such statements may serve as corroborative evidence and may even constitute mutual testimonial support. An opposing view contends that they remain, by nature, self-incriminating statements and do not transform into admissible witness testimony simply by virtue of mutual assertion. The prevailing position in both legal theory and judicial practice is that the matter should be assessed contextually and distinctions should be drawn based on the specific factual and procedural circumstances of each case.

Statements made by co-suspects or co-defendants in the same case cannot, on their own, serve as the sole basis for a conviction. If a case relies exclusively on the confessions of co-defendants without the support of other evidence, it is insufficient to establish guilt or impose criminal liability. This is due to the following considerations: (1) Statements by co-defendants do not constitute witness testimony for the purpose of proving facts. In evidentiary law, confessions by suspects or defendants are categorically distinct from witness statements. Mutual accusations among co-defendants, even when interrelated, remain confessions in nature and should not be treated as equivalent to ordinary testimonial evidence. Therefore, such statements cannot serve as the sole basis for determining guilt. (2) Confessions that are later retracted by co-defendants lose probative value. When a co-defendant recants a previous statement, the original confession is left without corroborative support. Given the frequency of such retractions in practice, it becomes difficult to ascertain the truthfulness of the statements, thus undermining their reliability. (3) Statements by co-defendants concerning offenses unrelated to the present case may, in certain circumstances, be treated as witness testimony in separate proceedings. Where such disclosures pertain to independent criminal acts, they may function as testimonial evidence in another case but not as direct evidence in the present one. (4) Statements made by accomplices or subordinate offenders may be used to establish the conduct of principal offenders. In joint criminal activities, participants often occupy different roles. Those in secondary or supportive positions—such as handlers of stolen goods, harborers, or accessories—may provide statements that implicate primary offenders. In judicial practice, such statements may be treated as having the probative function of witness testimony. However, the declarants do not appear in court as formal witnesses, and their statements must be corroborated by other independent evidence. (5) Statements by co-defendants whose cases have already been concluded should not be used as the sole basis for convicting defendants whose cases remain pending.

In practice, co-defendants may be apprehended at different times. Some may have already been convicted or not prosecuted and thus are no longer part of the proceedings. Even in such cases, they should not be summoned as witnesses, nor should the sequence or timing of their statements affect their evidentiary character. Confessions from resolved cases should not be used as the sole incriminating evidence against defendants who are still under prosecution. Particular caution must be exercised in handling statements made by co-defendants whose cases are processed separately.

6.7.2.2 Classification of Statements and Defenses by Criminal Suspects and Defendants

The forms in which statements and defenses by criminal suspects and defendants manifest in criminal proceedings are varied. Classifying these statements from different analytical perspectives contributes to their proper differentiation and prudent evidentiary application.

i. **By form: oral versus written statements**

Oral statements refer to those obtained through lawful interrogation procedures. These include transcribed interrogation records, audio recordings of interrogations, and both written and recorded statements made during voluntary surrenders. Written statements are those composed directly by the suspect or defendant. Throughout the criminal process, a suspect or defendant may provide both oral and written statements. There is no inherent hierarchy of evidentiary weight between the two.

Notably, oral statements that are documented in writing do not change their nature as oral testimonial evidence simply by virtue of the medium used to record them.

ii. **By veracity: truthful versus false statements**

Truthful statements are those that align with the objective facts of the case, while false statements contradict such facts. A suspect's or defendant's statement or defense may fall into either category. It is erroneous to presume that a confession must be truthful or that a denial of guilt must necessarily be false.

iii. **By content: factual versus opinion-based statements**

Factual statements are objective accounts provided by the suspect or defendant regarding case-related matters. These include both admissions of guilt and factual defenses. For instance, a suspect's claim that they were not present at the crime scene qualifies as a factual statement. Such statements, if corroborated, may directly support the establishment of case facts and serve as a basis for judicial determination.

Opinion-based statements involve the suspect's or defendant's subjective interpretations, analyses, speculations, or commentary regarding the legal characterization of the case or their own liability. Because these statements do not directly relate to the factual circumstances of the case, they generally fall outside the scope of admissible evidence. From an evidentiary standpoint, their lack of factual relevance renders them inadmissible. Moreover, such statements often constitute part of the defense strategy. In view of the defendant's unique procedural status, individuals who are innocent but lack exculpatory evidence may rely on subjective reasoning or argumentation to defend themselves. In such contexts, opinion-based statements may still carry significant weight.

iv. **By legality: legally versus illegally obtained statements**

Legally obtained statements are those collected by authorized personnel in accordance with prescribed legal procedures and methods. Illegally obtained statements are those procured in violation of procedural safeguards or through prohibited means such as torture, threats, inducement, deception, or other unlawful practices. Illegally obtained statements are subject to immediate exclusion under the exclusionary rule and may not be admitted as evidence, regardless of their apparent reliability or factual accuracy. Legally obtained statements, by contrast, must be verified before they can be relied upon, and even when substantiated, may not serve as the sole basis for conviction.

v. **Classification based on whether the statement is made in court: in-court versus out-of-court statements**

In-court statements refer to statements made by the defendant during a formal court hearing. Out-of-court statements refer to those made by the criminal suspect or defendant prior to trial—typically during the investigation or prosecution stages—when questioned by investigators or prosecutors.

Statements made in court and verified through judicial examination may serve as a basis for conviction. Out-of-court statements also generally carry evidentiary value. However, if a defendant recants such statements during trial, questions arise regarding their admissibility. In cases where the defendant refuses to testify or retracts earlier statements in court, such out-of-court statements may still be relied upon, provided they are substantiated, the authorities can demonstrate that the statements were lawfully obtained, and they are corroborated by other evidence examined during the trial. Neither in-court nor out-of-court statements possess predetermined evidentiary weight; their probative value must be assessed in light of the surrounding circumstances.

vi. **Classification based on consistency: consistent versus contradictory statements**

Where suspects or defendants possess unimpaired memory, reasoning, and communication abilities, and express genuine remorse, their statements—regardless of the sequence—tend to be internally consistent. Consistent statements are generally more reliable and closer to the objective truth of the case than contradictory ones, as they tend to contain fewer fabricated elements. However, consistency alone does not guarantee authenticity. Some statements may be deliberately fabricated or manipulated under external influence. If the consistency across statements is unusually precise in its detail, this may raise suspicion of fabrication. Thus, consistent statements must still be independently verified and should not be accepted at face value. Contradictory statements refer to statements that contain partial or complete inconsistencies over time. Such contradictions should not be judged using a simplistic binary framework—i.e., assuming one version is true and the other false. It is entirely possible that both statements are false, while it is unlikely that both are wholly accurate.

There is also debate regarding whether a *Statement of Plea and Sentencing Agreement* may be admitted as evidence. One view maintains that the agreement constitutes either a confession or documentary evidence under the Criminal Procedure Law. Another view holds that once either the prosecution or defense withdraws from the agreement, it loses all evidentiary function and should not be admitted. A third position asserts that, given its formal and procedural nature, the document may serve as procedural evidence, though not necessarily as substantive proof of fact.

6.7.2.3 The Evidentiary Significance of Statements and Defenses by Criminal Suspects and Defendants

Both civil law jurisdictions, which follow an inquisitorial model, and common law jurisdictions, characterized by adversarial proceedings, regard statements and confessions as critical forms of evidence. In China, statements and defenses by criminal suspects and defendants are also formally recognized as a statutory category of evidence. Although such statements may contain falsehoods, exhibit complexity, and require caution, their evidentiary value must not be dismissed. When obtained through lawful procedures, statements and defenses can significantly contribute to a comprehensive understanding of the case and to the accurate determination of facts—especially in cases involving crimes committed in private or concealed environments.

i. **Statements and defenses serve as direct evidence of the facts**

Statements and defenses made by suspects and defendants constitute direct evidence. They assist investigators, prosecutors, and judges in discovering, examining, verifying, and evaluating other pieces of evidence. They also help delineate the scope of investigation, enable the identification of evidentiary inconsistencies, and support the timely resolution of doubts. In particular, they are crucial for proving subjective aspects of the offense—such as the suspect's motive or mental state—matters that often cannot be established through other types of evidence. Furthermore, such statements play an indispensable role in sentencing, where the defendant's admission of guilt, attitude of remorse, or performance of meritorious acts may significantly influence sentencing outcomes. In many cases, these factors cannot be directly proven without the suspect's or defendant's own statements.

At the same time, it is essential to treat defenses asserting innocence, mitigation, or exemption from punishment with fairness and objectivity. Such statements should not be summarily dismissed as evasive or untruthful. They form part of the evidentiary record and must be evaluated on their merits, like any other evidence.

ii. **Statements and defenses have corroborative value with other evidence**

Criminal cases concern past events, and statements and defenses often play a vital role in reconstructing the details and context of those events. Most cases are supported by fragmented and largely indirect evidence, making it difficult to construct a complete evidentiary chain or to directly establish core facts. Even with the aid of forensic technologies, indirect evidence often lacks the capacity to conclusively prove the principal facts of a case.

Frequently, there is a shortage of physical or documentary evidence, and some cases lack victim or eyewitness testimony altogether. Certain forms of evidence may also conflict with one another. Moreover, many criminal acts—especially bribery, drug trafficking, and cybercrime—are committed in highly covert or virtual spaces, where unrelated third parties are seldom present. In such instances, guilt is exceedingly difficult to prove without a confession or without catching the perpetrator in possession of illicit goods. Absent such circumstances, direct evidence is often lacking. A truthful confession by a suspect or defendant can serve to link static and isolated pieces of evidence, shedding light on otherwise obscure facts. Nevertheless, careful attention must be paid to the content and context of such statements—particularly when they involve the implication of co-defendants (commonly referred to as "incriminating others"). In the absence of corroborating evidence, mutual accusations between co-defendants must not serve as the sole basis for conviction, to avoid the risk of wrongful judgments.

Finally, statements and defenses provided by individuals under investigation by supervisory commissions are to be treated in the same evidentiary category as statements and defenses by criminal suspects and defendants.

6.7.3 Party Statements in Civil and Administrative Litigation

Party statements are recognized as a statutory form of evidence under both the Civil Procedure Law and the Administrative Procedure Law of the People's Republic of China. In civil proceedings, due to the constraints imposed by the principles of party disposition and adversarial procedure, party statements are generally not classified as an independent category of evidence in many foreign jurisdictions. Nevertheless, the open-ended nature of evidentiary rules in some legal systems allows party statements to exert substantial influence on case outcomes. For example, Sect. 623 of the California Evidence Code provides: "Where a party, by statement or conduct, intentionally leads another to believe a certain fact to be true and to rely on it, that party shall not be permitted to contradict that belief in any action arising from such statement or conduct." In contrast, both Chinese civil and administrative procedural laws explicitly recognize party statements as a distinct type of evidence. However, some scholars contend that party statements should be regarded as a method of proof rather than as an independent evidentiary category.

6.7.3.1 Definition and Characteristics of Party Statements

A party statement refers to a party's narrative, provided during litigation, concerning facts within their personal knowledge that are relevant to the case. This includes statements made by plaintiffs, defendants, co-litigants, legal representatives, and third parties in both civil and administrative proceedings.

Given that parties have a vested interest in the outcome and typically occupy the role of either plaintiff or defendant, their statements often go beyond factual accounts and may include personal claims, legal positions, subjective opinions, or requests. Not all statements made by parties in court are admissible as evidence. Party statements can encompass factual descriptions of the case, expressions of legal claims or proposed outcomes, evaluations of evidence, and arguments concerning the legal interpretation of disputed facts. Only those statements that pertain to the occurrence and development of the facts in dispute, or that are materially relevant to the resolution of the substantive legal relationship, qualify as evidentiary party statements. In both civil and administrative litigation, party statements generally fall into the following categories: (1) Statements concerning the factual circumstances of the case; (2) Assertions and explanations of legal claims, as well as opinions on how the case should be resolved; (3) Evaluative comments on the admissibility, probative value, and relevance of other evidence; (4) Interpretative views regarding the application of legal norms to the facts in dispute. Party statements are typically made with the intent to influence the proceedings in a manner favorable to the speaker. Nevertheless, for a party statement to serve a probative function, it must pertain specifically to facts relevant to the case. These include: (1) Facts establishing substantive or procedural legal relationships; (2) The origin, development, and progression of the civil or administrative dispute; (3) Other factual details that materially affect the adjudication of the case.

Whether the party is affirming, denying, acknowledging, or explaining facts, as long as the statement pertains to facts that are significant to the determination of the case, it constitutes a party statement. As a form of evidence aimed at establishing the truth of facts, party statements possess several distinguishing characteristics…

i. **Comprehensiveness of party statements**

Parties to litigation have a direct and substantial interest in the facts of the case. They are often well acquainted with how the dispute arose, developed, and transformed over time, and may possess a clear understanding of its origins, underlying causes, and causal relationships. When truthfully presented, a party's statement can provide the court with a comprehensive account of the facts. Compared with other forms of evidence—such as witness testimony or expert opinions—party statements may offer a broader and more detailed depiction of the circumstances, particularly with respect to events the party personally experienced.

ii. **Dual nature of party statements**

Given that the parties' interests are directly implicated and typically opposed to one another, their desire to prevail in litigation often leads them to present statements selectively. They may emphasize facts favorable to themselves while omitting, minimizing, or concealing facts that are unfavorable. As a result, party statements are frequently partial in nature. Motivated by self-interest and the instinct to avoid adverse consequences, parties may interweave truth with falsehood, distort the facts, fabricate events, or provide misleading narratives. Thus, party statements characteristically exhibit a dual nature: they may simultaneously contain elements of truth and falsity, objectivity and subjectivity, comprehensiveness and selectiveness. In some cases, opposing parties may offer entirely contradictory versions of the same events.

iii. **Limitations of party statements**

As a rule, party statements are limited to in-court declarations. Statements made outside the courtroom generally do not qualify as admissible party statements. Additionally, compared to other types of evidence, party statements are typically retrospective in nature—that is, they are made after the events in question have occurred.

Different jurisdictions adopt varying approaches regarding the obligation of parties to provide truthful statements. In countries such as Germany and Austria, parties are legally required to make full and truthful disclosures. However, scholarly opinion is divided. Some theorists argue that, under the principle of good faith, parties should be obligated to tell the truth, but this duty is more moral in character than strictly legal. Even the definition and scope of the so-called "truth-telling obligation" remain subjects of debate. Under Chinese law, parties are explicitly required to make truthful and complete statements concerning the facts of the case.

6.7.3.2 Classification of Party Statements

Although China's Civil Procedure Law and Administrative Procedure Law do not explicitly classify party statements, legal scholarship has developed several classification frameworks based on differing criteria.

i. **Classification by relevance to the facts of the case: party statements may be categorized as either factually relevant or factually irrelevant.**

This classification serves to clarify the evidentiary boundaries of party statements. Only those statements that relate directly to the facts in dispute may be admitted as evidence. Statements that are unrelated to the facts of the case lack probative value and should not be treated as evidence.

ii. **Classification by Form: Party statements may take the form of either written or oral declarations**

A written party statement refers to a document in which the party records relevant factual information in writing and submits it to the court as evidence. An oral party statement refers to a verbal account given by the party regarding facts relevant to the case. Modern procedural systems generally emphasize in-person appearances and oral declarations, enabling direct confrontation and cross-examination. This approach upholds the principle of orality and facilitates the discovery of truth through live testimonial interaction.

iii. **Classification by evidentiary orientation:**

Party statements may also be classified based on their substantive orientation into affirmative, negative, or admissive statements: An affirmative statement involves the party presenting specific facts to substantiate the existence of a disputed substantive legal relationship. A negative statement involves the party presenting facts to deny the existence of that legal relationship. An admissive statement is one in which a party explicitly acknowledges factual assertions made by the opposing party. This classification aids in the proper evaluation of the nature of party statements and helps define the scope of their evidentiary function.

6.7.3.3 Judicial Admissions by Parties

Party statements are a recognized form of evidence in many legal systems. Although they do not hold the privileged status of being the "king of evidence" under statutory evidentiary hierarchies, they remain an important evidentiary category and often play a decisive role in the establishment of facts. In particular, judicial admissions made by parties carry binding legal consequences for the admitting party and are accorded significant weight by the court. A judicial admission refers to a party's express acknowledgment—whether oral or written—of the truth of a fact asserted by the opposing party that is adverse to its own interests, or of the validity of the opposing party's claim, thereby producing certain legal effects. The former, which pertains to factual acknowledgment, is commonly referred to as a narrow admission, while the latter, which concerns the legal claim itself, is often called an acknowledgment of claim.

As a form of self-incriminating statement, a judicial admission is typically accepted as evidence against the party making it. In both civil and administrative proceedings, parties enter litigation with the goal of prevailing and protecting their lawful rights and interests. Accordingly, they generally present facts in a manner favorable to their position and seek to challenge the factual and legal grounds advanced by the opposing party. If, however, one party chooses not to dispute but instead affirmatively acknowledges adverse facts or claims asserted by the other party, such conduct constitutes a judicial admission. Judicial admissions may be made during the course of trial or presented in written submissions such as complaints, answers, or attorney briefs. Once a party unequivocally acknowledges a fact that is detrimental to its legal position, the opposing party is relieved of the burden of proving that fact. This applies whether the adverse fact is stated by the party itself or formally acknowledged in court filings. Where a party places limitations or conditions on its acknowledgment of an adverse fact, the court must determine, in light of the overall context of the case, whether such a statement qualifies as a judicial admission.

A judicial admission constitutes a special form of party statement, playing a critical role in the evidentiary process and the adjudication of disputes. In certain cases, it may substantially influence the final outcome of the litigation.

i. **Classification of judicial admissions**

According to different criteria, party admissions can be classified in various ways. Based on the circumstances of party admissions and the needs of judicial practice, party admissions can be classified as follows.

a. Classification by context: judicial admissions versus extrajudicial admissions

A judicial admission refers to an acknowledgment made by a party during the course of litigation. It typically occurs when a party, in response to factual assertions or legal claims adverse to its interests, explicitly affirms the truth of those assertions or the reasonableness of the opposing party's claims in the context of judicial proceedings.

An extrajudicial admission refers to an acknowledgment made outside formal litigation, such as in correspondence or informal conversations, involving facts unfavorable to the party or in response to claims made by the opposing party. While such admissions may be introduced as evidence and examined by the court, they generally do not carry the same binding legal effect as judicial admissions.

In civil law jurisdictions, the term "admission" typically refers to judicial admissions made within the framework of court proceedings. In contrast, common law jurisdictions primarily recognize extrajudicial admissions. Judicial admissions function as rules of proof rather than conventional items of evidence, whereas extrajudicial admissions are treated as evidentiary material, not procedural presumptions.

b. By subject and legal effect: admissions of facts versus admissions of legal claims

Admissions of fact relieve the opposing party of the burden of proof. When a party expressly acknowledges a fact adverse to its interest—whether during evidence disclosure, interrogations, or within pleadings such as complaints, answers, or legal briefs—the opposing party is exempted from producing evidence on that point. For example, Article 279 of the *Civil Procedure Code* of Taiwan provides: "Facts alleged by a party shall not require proof if expressly admitted by the other party in written submissions or oral arguments before the presiding judge or assigned judge." Admissions of legal claims pertain to the acknowledgment of the legal validity of the opposing party's requested relief. These admissions are grounded in the principle of party disposition and may serve as a sufficient basis for rendering judgment against the admitting party.

c. By scope: complete versus partial admissions

A complete admission refers to an unqualified acknowledgment by a party of all facts and claims asserted by the opposing party. A partial admission occurs where the party admits only part of the factual or legal assertions, or conditions the admission with qualifications or limitations. In such cases, the legal effect of the admission is limited to the portion that has been clearly affirmed. Generally, if a party admits to certain facts while denying others—without attaching conditions—the admitted facts constitute a valid judicial admission, while the denied portions do not. In cases involving qualified admissions, where the party introduces additional conditions or explanatory defenses, the court must determine whether the admitted facts and the qualifications are inseparably linked. If the party acknowledges an adverse fact but simultaneously introduces an independent defense or counterclaim that negates the legal significance of the opposing party's position, the court should assess the admission and the defense together as a unified assertion. Isolating only the adverse portion may misrepresent the party's overall intent and lead to an unjust outcome. However, where the adverse fact and the accompanying statement are legally distinct and severable, the acknowledgment alone may suffice as a valid judicial admission. In such cases, the defense or explanation does not negate the evidentiary force of the admission.

d. By legal effect: binding versus non-binding judicial admissions

Judicial admissions can be categorized according to their legal consequences. Binding judicial admissions exempt the opposing party from the burden of proof and may, under certain conditions, directly lead to a favorable judgment for that party. However, such legal effect is only recognized where the admission satisfies statutory requirements. Conversely, non-binding admissions—those failing to meet the legal criteria—do not produce such evidentiary or dispositive outcomes.

e. By manner of expression: express versus implied judicial admissions

Judicial admissions may also be divided into express admissions and implied admissions. An express admission is an explicit acknowledgment made by a party in writing or orally, either in the pleadings or during court proceedings. An implied admission occurs when a party fails to dispute or respond to a factual allegation made by the opposing party, and such silence may be interpreted as tacit acceptance.

Under Chinese law, only express admissions carry binding legal effect. Implied admissions do not automatically relieve the opposing party of the burden of proof. Courts generally seek clarification by asking the party to take a clear position. If the party, after being advised by the court, still refuses to affirm or deny the allegation, the court may infer an admission of fact. However, this presumption applies only to factual issues, not to the admission of legal claims. Where a party neither admits nor denies a fact adverse to its interest, and—after judicial inquiry—still fails to clarify, the fact may be deemed admitted. This judicial presumption of admission does not apply to substantive legal claims or relief sought.

f. By declarant: admissions by the party versus admissions by legal representatives

Judicial admissions may also be classified according to the person making the admission: Admissions by the party themselves include those made by the litigant or their legal guardian. Admissions by a legal representative refer to those made by an authorized attorney or agent acting on the party's behalf during the proceedings.

Many jurisdictions expressly provide that an admission made by a litigation representative is legally attributed to the party, unless the party has explicitly excluded such authority. Under Chinese civil procedure law, special authorization is required for a representative to dispose of legal claims. However, an admission of fact is conceptually distinct from the disposition of claims and does not necessarily require special authorization. Where a representative makes a comprehensive acknowledgment encompassing both facts and claims, such conduct may be construed as acceptance of the claim, and distinguishing between factual and legal admissions becomes unnecessary. Accordingly, unless the power of attorney expressly excludes the authority to make admissions, a representative's admission is deemed binding on the party. Article 3 of the *Several Provisions of the Supreme People's Court on Evidence in Civil Proceedings* provides: "Where a party authorizes a litigation representative to participate in the proceedings, unless otherwise specified in the power of attorney, the representative's admission shall be deemed the party's own admission. If the party is present and expressly rejects the representative's admission, it shall not be treated as a judicial admission."

In personal status litigation, such as cases involving the establishment of marital or parent–child relationships, judicial admissions are generally inapplicable. Even if a party admits the facts or claims involved, the court is obliged to conduct an independent investigation ex officio, considering factors such as public interest, public order, and social morality.

ii. **Legal effect of judicial admissions**

The legal effect of judicial admissions refers to the impact such admissions have on the evidentiary process and the outcome of a case. Judicial admissions typically carry the following legal consequences:

a. Exemption of the opposing party from the burden of proof

When one party expressly admits to the factual assertions or legal claims advanced by the opposing party, the latter is relieved from the obligation to present further proof regarding the admitted facts. Such an express judicial admission, made during the course of litigation, has the effect of exempting the opposing party from its evidentiary burden.

b. Judicial admissions may result in a judgment in favor of the opposing party

Civil legal relations are rooted in the autonomy of private rights and are governed by the principle of party disposition. Under the dual principles of party disposition and adversarial procedure that characterize civil litigation, an admission by one party to facts adverse to its interest effectively shifts the burden of proof and may suffice to support a judgment in favor of the opposing party. For instance, if a defendant admits to the plaintiff's legal claim, the court may render a judgment directly in favor of the plaintiff. Judicial interpretations of the Supreme People's Court affirm that once a judicial admission absolves the opposing party of the burden of proof, it may, under appropriate conditions, lead to a favorable adjudication for that party.

In general, the evidentiary value of a judicial admission lies in relieving the burden of proof. While judicial admissions are primarily understood as acknowledgments of facts asserted by the opposing party, when they also involve recognition of the claim itself, they may functionally result in acceptance of the legal claim. However, an admission of fact does not inherently amount to a full concession of the opposing party's claim.

c. Evidentiary value of out-of-court and implied admissions

Out-of-court admissions, whether oral or written, may be submitted by the opposing party as evidence during litigation. Upon verification, such statements may serve as auxiliary or corroborative evidence in establishing the facts of the case. However, such admissions do not automatically produce the legal effect of shifting the burden of proof.

Parties are permitted to introduce out-of-court admissions as evidence, and they may also retract or dispute them. In such instances, the party seeking to rely on the admission must provide justification for its evidentiary use. Implied admissions made during litigation indicate a party's failure to respond to or dispute the opposing party's factual or legal claims. As these do not amount to express admissions, they do not, by default, relieve the opposing party of its burden of proof. In such cases, the court's determination regarding the facts or the final judgment depends on whether the party bearing the burden has fulfilled its evidentiary obligations. However, where a party remains silent even after the judge has provided clarification or sought a direct response, such silence may be construed as an implied admission of fact.

iii. **Conditions for party admissions to exempt the burden of proof**

An admission is not a form of evidence but constitutes an exception to the general rule on the burden of proof. It arises from the exercise of a party's right of disposition and serves as a method by which the court may establish the facts of the case. Party admissions are of significant importance in safeguarding the procedural rights of the parties and in reducing litigation costs. For an admission to have the effect of exempting the opposing party from the burden of proof, the following conditions must be met: (1)The admission must be made in the course of litigation, rather than outside the proceedings; (2)The admission must relate to facts or claims raised by the opposing party, rather than to other matters; (3)The admission must be expressly made to the court, either orally or in writing; mere silence or implied conduct does not suffice; (4)The admission must be made voluntarily and represent the genuine intention of the party; (5)There must be no collusion between the parties that would prejudice the interests of the state or a third party, and the admission must not contravene any mandatory provisions of law. Party admissions shall be recorded by the adjudicating judge. The judge must inform the party concerned of the legal consequences of such admissions, in order to prevent any misunderstanding.

iv. **Withdrawal of a party's admission**

Chinese law does not prohibit a party from withdrawing a previous admission—that is, it does not adopt the doctrine of estoppel. The principle of estoppel originates from the obligation of parties to make truthful statements, and is commonly found in common law jurisdictions. It seeks to restrict inconsistencies in statements by means such as sworn testimony, but does not impose an absolute prohibition. Where a party withdraws an admission that previously exempted the opposing party from the burden of proof, the withdrawing party bears the burden of proof for the reasons of withdrawal. If the evidence provided is insufficient or fails to overturn the original admission, the admission shall remain effective. Where any of the following circumstances are present, and the withdrawal occurs prior to the conclusion of court debate, the court shall permit the withdrawal:

(1) the opposing party consents; (2) the admission was made under coercion or due to a fundamental misunderstanding. Where the court permits a party to withdraw an admission, it shall issue an oral or written ruling. If, before the conclusion of court debate, a party withdraws an admission with the consent of the opposing party or provides sufficient evidence to prove that the admission was made under coercion or due to a fundamental misunderstanding and is inconsistent with the facts, the opposing party shall not be exempted from the burden of proof.

The judicial interpretations do not specify what kinds of reasons may justify such withdrawal. However, the relevant provisions in the Taiwan region of China may serve as reference. A party seeking to withdraw an admission must provide evidence to establish one of the following grounds: (1) the admission was made in error and does not reflect the truth; (2) the opposing party agrees to the withdrawal; (3) the admission was made under fraud, coercion, or as a result of criminal conduct by another person; (4) the admission was made by a litigation agent or assistant without authorization. These circumstances must be reviewed by the court to determine whether the admission and its legal consequences remain binding on the parties. As to out-of-court admissions and implied admissions made during litigation, a party shall be allowed to withdraw such admissions at any time before the conclusion of court debate, but must state the reason for doing so.

There are differing views on whether a partial admission by a party should be deemed to cover the entire set of facts. For instance, where the plaintiff alleges that the defendant borrowed RMB 5,000, and the defendant admits to borrowing only RMB 2,000, some argue that a partial admission should be deemed to extend to the entire factual assertion, as partial and full facts are difficult to separate. Others contend that a partial admission should not extend to the whole, and that only the portion acknowledged by both parties constitutes the admission.

6.7.3.4 The Significance of Party Statements

Parties are not only the subjects of the substantive legal relationships in dispute, but also the principal participants in litigation. In order to obtain a judgment favorable to themselves, parties will, under normal circumstances, actively and voluntarily provide the court with factual information about the case and seek to prove those facts. Party statements are a widely used form of evidence in civil and administrative proceedings. They play a critical role in uncovering the truth, swiftly identifying the disputed facts, and properly resolving civil or administrative disputes.

i. **Party statements contribute to the prompt establishment of case facts and the timely resolution of disputes**

When parties present statements of fact to the court, they typically provide evidence in their possession or offer clues relevant to the case. Through such statements, the court can obtain pertinent evidence, identify and collect additional supporting materials, and thereby establish a solid basis for fact-finding and adjudication. If the party's statement includes explicit admissions, this further facilitates the prompt conclusion of the litigation.

Because parties to civil or administrative proceedings are the very subjects of the disputed substantive legal relationship, they generally have direct experience of the case facts and thus understand them more thoroughly than others. In order to protect their lawful rights and interests, parties actively provide the court with relevant information after the initiation of proceedings, explaining the reasons and grounds for their claims. Through such statements, the court can rapidly determine whether the substantive legal relationship in dispute exists, learn about the causes, progression, and points of contention in the dispute, and assess the consequences. These statements thus offer a crucial basis for ascertaining the facts and lay the foundation for timely resolution and cessation of litigation.

ii **Party statements help the court adjust the relationship between parties and enhance the social impact of adjudication**

Where the facts asserted by one party are admitted by the opposing party during litigation, such admissions carry the effect of exempting the asserting party from the burden of proof. The court may, based on the admission or on consistent statements by both parties, draw conclusions as to the facts of the case. This promotes the prompt resolution of disputes and helps prevent prolonged litigation. By examining and analyzing party statements, the court can further understand the causes and development of the dispute, as well as the parties' respective positions. This, in turn, enables the court to dispel hostility between the parties where appropriate, improve their relationship, and transform a confrontation over rights into a negotiation over rights. Such adjustments foster early dispute resolution and encourage reconciliation.

6.8 Expert Opinions

Forensic evaluation, as a legal institution, has persisted throughout litigation history for centuries. Archival documents reveal that cause-of-death examinations were performed by physicians in ancient Greece, with regulatory provisions on forensic practices identifiable in the *Codex Justinianus*. The 1532 *Constitutio Criminalis Carolina* marked the first statutory use of the term "expert evaluation." Within comparative legal terminology: common law jurisdictions classify this evidence as "expert testimony," civil law systems term it "expert conclusions," and China's procedural law formally designates it as "expert opinions."

6.8.1 Concept and Characteristics of Expert Opinions

An expert opinion is defined as a written document in which appraisers, utilizing scientific methods or specialized knowledge, analyze and determine specialized issues involved in litigation proceedings.

This evidentiary category is expressly stipulated in China's Civil Procedure Law, Criminal Procedure Law, and Administrative Procedure Law. Structurally, an expert opinion comprises these essential components: the appraiser, the appraisal activities, and the written opinions. Among these, the appraiser serves as the formal embodiment of the opinion as evidence, while the evaluative conclusion constitutes its substantive content. As a type of testimonial evidence,[14] expert opinions exhibit the following distinguishing features when compared with other evidence:

6.8.1.1 Expert Opinions Constitute the Appraiser's Individual Professional Judgments

Within common law systems, appraisers are formally recognized as "expert witnesses"—persons authorized by courts to present evidentiary opinions or factual testimony. Civil law jurisdictions refer to them as Sachverständigen (expert appraisers), functioning as judicial auxiliaries governed by statutory qualification regimes. China administers a credentialing system for judicial appraisers (sifa jiandingren).

Appraisers operate as technical extensions of judicial authority, enhancing judges' fact-finding capabilities through specialized knowledge. Distinct from ordinary people, appraisers must demonstrate certified expertise in particular professional domains.

i. **Appraisers as Bearers of Specialized Expertise**

Appraisers constitute certified professionals possessing both domain-specific knowledge and technical proficiency, fundamentally distinguishing them from ordinary evidentiary witnesses.

[14] Guo (2007).

Critical distinctions exist among appraisers, expert assistants (zhuanjia fuzhuren), and expert witnesses. Expert assistants—litigation participants aiding parties in challenging expert opinions—retain examination rights over appraisers, yet their technical commentaries lack statutory evidentiary validity. Serving essentially as technical advisors, litigants may apply for court approval to engage one or two qualified specialists as expert assistants. Unlike conventional witnesses, appraisers are governed by judicial recusal protocols and maintain functional substitutability.

ii. **Appraisers as Officially Accredited Practitioners**

Beyond mandatory certification, appraisers require formal enrollment in state-maintained registries with public accessibility. China implements bifurcated registration protocols: investigative agencies' forensic units undergo administrative registration, while non-governmental appraisal institutions necessitate regulatory vetting and public gazettal. Appraisers are categorized as "professional witnesses", subject to elevated qualification benchmarks.

Common law jurisdictions classify appraisers as expert witnesses without pre-litigation qualification barriers, though courts retain authority to evaluate expertise in situ. The French system mandates selection from judicially curated expert rosters. Contrasted with lay witnesses providing sensory fact accounts, expert witnesses deliver inferential assessments. While paralleling witnesses' experiential deductions, appraisers' conclusions derive from technical diagnostic methodologies rather than common knowledge. Appraisers shall strictly limit practice to registered specializations within authorized institutional parameters.

iii. **Appraisers shall be natural persons**

Appraisers are legally required to be natural persons rather than juridical entities. This mandate arises from two inherent necessities: (1) the specialized knowledge required for forensic evaluations can only be cognitively internalized by individual practitioners; (2) the appraisal process—involving evidentiary observation, technical investigation, analytical reasoning, and professional judgment—is fundamentally anthropocentric and non-delegable. In multi-appraiser assessments, collective decision-making mechanisms such as "democratic centralism" or "majoritarian adjudication" through collegiate panels are expressly prohibited; each appraiser maintains sole accountability for their evaluative determinations. Notwithstanding this statutory requirement, institutional appraisals persist operationally under specific regulatory circumstances.

A critical distinction exists between appraisers and "expert-evidentiary witnesses". The latter refers to individuals who, drawing upon specialized knowledge, testify about historical facts or circumstances they directly perceived. Their evidentiary value lies in the non-substitutable nature of their sensory experiences. While such witnesses may employ technical reasoning similar to appraisers when contextualizing their observations, they occupy a hybrid evidentiary position—simultaneously fulfilling witness and analytical roles. Jurisprudentially, however, their testimony retains the essential character of witness evidence rather than appraisal conclusions.

6.8.1.2 Expert Opinions Originate from Appraisers Formally Appointed by Case-Handling Authorities or Litigants

Appraisers generally maintain neutrality and hold the legal status of litigation participants. To conduct appraisal activities, they must be members of an appraisal institution, and appraisal services are uniformly accepted by their affiliated institution. The appraisal institution can only carry out appraisal activities after being appointed, hired, or commissioned by case-handling authorities or parties. Once appointed or hired as appraisers, they become subjects of litigation legal relationships, entitled to certain litigation rights and bearing specific litigation obligations. Appraisers have the right to participate in litigation, understand case details, review case files related to the appraisal; during the appraisal process, they have the right to participate in crime scene investigations related to the case, request supplementary appraisal materials, and conduct appraisals independently. Simultaneously, they must legally recuse themselves, fulfill the statutory obligation to testify in court, and take responsibility for their expert opinions.

Appraisers may conduct appraisal services nationwide and can legally accept commissions from case-handling authorities or parties anywhere within China. Only expert opinions provided by appraisers formally appointed or hired according to law possess evidentiary validity. The unified acceptance of commissions by appraisal institutions does not mean the institution itself serves as the appraiser.

Medical diagnosis certificates issued by doctors as medical experts are products of routine medical work and do not constitute expert opinions as evidence. When medical institutions or doctors are appointed or hired by case-handling authorities or parties through proper legal procedures to make factual judgments on specialized issues in a case, their conclusions qualify as expert opinions.

6.8.1.3 Expert Opinion as a Judgment Rendered by the Appraisers Following an Examination

An expert opinion is a judgment rendered by the appraisers after conducting the examination. The expert shall personally perform the examination in accordance with the law, following statutory procedures and technical specifications. The appraisers must comply with laws, regulations, and rules, adhere to professional ethics and discipline, respect science, observe technical protocols, and conduct the examination independently, objectively, and impartially. The appraisers shall be responsible for the opinion they provide. An expert opinion is different from physical evidence—it does not constitute the facts of the case themselves. It also differs from other forms of testimonial evidence: it reflects the appraiser's understanding and judgment on specialized issues, and is distinct from the perceptual understanding of case facts found in witness testimony or statements of the parties. Expert opinions involve the application of specialized knowledge to transform other forms of evidence. This transformation is not a simple material conversion, but a process of professional judgment. The result is a cognitive or inferential opinion on a specialized matter.

Even in cases involving DNA technology, the conclusions drawn are not automatically generated by the technology itself, as the data produced do not directly yield conclusions. A DNA expert opinion still involves the appraiser's interpretation and understanding of the test results or data, and thus constitutes a form of judgment. The appraisers must personally carry out the examination; otherwise, they shall not sign the expert report.

Expert opinions also differ from witness testimony, statements by parties, victims, suspects, or defendants. Although testimonial evidence may also involve transmission between subjects—as in hearsay—hearsay involves merely the transfer of statements without altering their content. In contrast, expert opinions involve a substantive transformation of the content of evidence. For instance, the examination of physical evidence converts it into verbal expression; such expression is analytical or cognitive in nature and bears the essential characteristics of an opinion. An expert opinion is a judgment made by the appraisers, based on their professional knowledge, regarding a specialized issue. In practice, it is not uncommon for different appraisers to reach differing conclusions on the same issue. This is normal, and such differences are reasonable. According to legal requirements, "Where multiple persons participate in an examination and hold differing opinions, such differences shall be indicated." Divergent expert opinions shall not be resolved through a "majority rule" approach.

6.8.1.4 Expert Opinion as a Conclusion on Specialized Issues

An expert opinion is a judgment made by the appraiser on a specialized issue. Its role is to reveal the causal relationship or evidentiary value between other evidence and the facts of the case. This judgment pertains solely to factual issues and must not involve legal issues. The factual issues in question are those that cannot be affirmatively or negatively determined by ordinary persons through intuition, direct observation, general experience, or logical reasoning alone. Instead, such determinations require identification and evaluation through scientific or technical means, specialized skills, or particular expertise—for example, determinations involving paternity, mental illness, or the authenticity of handwriting and seals. If no specialized issue exists in a case, expert evaluation is unnecessary.

Legal issues must be determined by judges, as the authority to decide legal matters rests with the judiciary. Professional judges are capable of resolving legal issues, whereas expert opinions, as a form of evidence, are confined to matters of fact. Should an expert opinion address legal issues, it would encroach upon the judge's authority and thereby lack evidentiary admissibility. For instance, opinions on the classification of injuries—such as whether an injury constitutes a minor or serious one—and determinations in mental illness cases regarding the presence or absence of criminal responsibility, or whether such responsibility is partial or full, all involve legal determinations. These are matters of legal fact. Therefore, investigative authorities shall not, under any circumstances, require appraisers to render opinions on legal issues.

6.8.1.5 Expert Opinion as a Conclusive Written Conclusion of Certainty

As a type of evidence, the expert opinion is primarily presented in the form of a written report. After completing the appraisal, the appraiser shall prepare a written expert opinion. This document, issued by the appraisal institution and the appraiser after examining and assessing the materials provided by the client, records the appraiser's professional judgment. It generally includes the following components: (1) Title: Specifies the name of the judicial appraisal institution and the subject matter entrusted for appraisal. (2) Serial Number: Includes the abbreviation of the appraisal institution, the year, the professional abbreviation, the document type abbreviation, and a sequence number. (3) Basic Information: States the client, the entrusted appraisal matter, date of acceptance, appraisal materials, date and location of the appraisal, persons present, and the individual being appraised. The appraisal materials section should objectively describe the samples and relevant documentation provided by the client, as well as the sources of such materials. (4) Case Summary: Briefly outlines the facts of the case related to the entrusted appraisal matter. (5) Appraisal Process: Describes how the appraisal was conducted and the scientific basis relied upon, including sample handling, appraisal procedures, technical methods used, and the applicable technical standards and norms. (6) Examination Results: Presents the objective findings derived from the examination of the materials provided by the client. (7) Analysis and Explanation: This is the key component of the expert opinion and a major criterion for assessing its quality. Based on the case summary and examination results, this section elaborates on causal relationships and addresses the relevant issues raised in the appraisal (examination, consultation, or document review). Where necessary, sources of cited information should be indicated. (8) Expert Opinion: The opinion must be clear, specific, standardized, and targeted, with practical applicability. (9) Signature and Seal: The appraiser shall sign or affix their seal to the document, indicate their judicial appraisal license number, and affix the official seal of the judicial appraisal institution. The date of issuance should also be indicated. (10) Appendix: Any content in the expert opinion requiring clarification may be addressed in this section. The main body of the expert opinion may be adjusted appropriately according to the type of appraisal and the characteristics of the relevant professional field.

The conclusion in an expert opinion report should generally be definitive, clearly establishing the relationship between the case facts, the truth or falsity of those facts, as well as the existence and extent of the facts, and the causal relationships between them. As a form of conclusive judgment, an expert opinion includes both affirmative and negative judgments and generally should not contain ambiguous statements.

In practice, there are also expert examination reports, such as alcohol testing reports for individuals. An expert examination report is a document issued by the expert institution or expert after inspecting the materials provided by the client, objectively reflecting the expert's examination process and results. Although the conclusions of such documents are heavily reliant on the examination, the examination itself does not automatically generate conclusions. The conclusions in these documents remain interpretative judgments made by the expert and are still considered expert opinions. In practice, there are also accident investigation reports (such as fire accident investigation reports) and valuations by appraisal institutions. While these can be used as supporting evidence, they are not considered expert opinions.

Most expert opinions in practice provide affirmative conclusions on specialized issues. However, due to insufficient materials or unmet examination conditions, experts may sometimes present tentative opinions rather than definitive conclusions. Such tentative opinions are not considered expert opinions in the evidentiary sense and cannot be used as a basis for determining the case.

6.8.2 Classification of Expert Opinions

From the perspective of the existence and form of evidence, expert opinions fall under the category of testimonial evidence and are closely related to physical evidence. Since most expert activities focus on physical objects that exist objectively, expert opinions are more objective compared to general testimonial evidence. Due to the differences in specialized issues and expert knowledge, expert opinions exist in various categories, which continue to expand as the scope of expert tasks increases. For example, in Japan, expert opinions are divided into three categories: first, expert opinions concerning general principles; second, expert opinions regarding the determination of specific facts; and third, expert opinions that derive conclusions by applying general principles to specific facts. Based on the current status of expert opinions in China, they can generally be classified as follows.

6.8.2.1 Based on the Determination Procedure of the Expert Opinion, It Can Be Divid

Conclusive expert opinions refer to expert opinions that make definite conclusions regarding the examined issue. This primarily includes affirmative expert opinions and negative expert opinions. These opinions involve clear answers to the examination requirements, such as affirming or denying the issue, stating "yes" or "no," indicating the presence or absence of something, or determining ranks and abilities.

Tentative expert opinions, also known as probabilistic expert opinions, refer to opinions provided by the expert after being commissioned to examine, identify, and assess certain specialized issues in a case. Due to various subjective or objective reasons, the expert is unable to offer a definitive affirmative or negative conclusion and instead presents their "tendencies" or views on the matter. Tentative expert opinions are considered "atypical" expert opinions. Because of their uncertain and inconclusive nature, they do not meet the standards required for evidence and cannot be used to prove case facts.

Due to numerous subjective and objective factors, expert opinions may sometimes yield definite affirmative or negative conclusions, while other times, they may only lead to tentative or possible conclusions, or even fail to provide any conclusion. Only affirmative and negative conclusions can prove the existence or non-existence of certain facts. Tentative or possible conclusions, while not proving the existence of certain facts, still serve a positive role in defense by raising doubts or suggesting the non-existence of those facts.

6.8.2.2 Based on the Reproducibility or Verifiability of the Expert Opinion, It Can Be Divided into Experimental Expert Opinions and Empirical Expert Opinions

i. **Experimental expert opinions**

Experimental expert opinions refer to expert opinions made based on scientific and technological tests and experiments. These types of expert opinions primarily rely on scientific and technological methods to provide examination and testing results. The expert activities depend on factors such as the level of laboratory infrastructure, quality control systems, institutional management standards, technical methods, and technical specifications, and generally allow for quantitative analysis. The results of such expert opinions are reproducible and possess strong objectivity, such as in DNA testing and physical evidence examinations.

Experimental expert opinions emphasize the stability, reliability, and safety of the testing techniques, and these techniques must be widely recognized by peers in the field. It is not the case that more advanced technology inherently provides greater reliability, and techniques that are unreliable cannot be used for expert opinions. For example, lie detection, narcotic and mental analysis testing, and bone age assessments, due to their unreliable technical foundations and the difficulty in obtaining consistent results under the same conditions, cannot be used as expert opinions with evidentiary value.

a. Lie Detection Expert Opinions. Lie detection technology originated in the United States, and its full name is "multivariable psychological testing technology." The basic principle is that when a person lies, or when certain events from their memory are recalled, the psychological activity triggered by these events will inevitably cause changes in various physiological parameters (such as blood pressure, respiration, brain waves, voice, pupil response, skin conductivity, etc.). These physiological changes are typically only influenced by the autonomic nervous system and are not controlled by the conscious brain. By testing the changes in these physiological parameters using instruments, the psychological changes of the subject can be analyzed to assess their knowledge of the issue, and thus determine the truthfulness of their statements. This activity measures physiological parameters, not the speech itself. The polygraph is designed by integrating psychology, physiology, modern electronics, and other applied sciences, and has continuously evolved and been updated with technological advancements. In addition to testing various physiological parameters, technologies such as pupil analysis, voice analysis, and computer wave-based lie detection have been developed. The software systems for measurement have also evolved, resulting in various models of testing methods and computer recognition systems. There are differing views within China's academic community regarding whether lie detection results can be used as evidence.

It is generally believed that the results of a polygraph test are not independent evidence. This is because evidence reflects the facts of the case, and case facts are objective and relevant, while lie detection tests the various physiological parameters of the person involved in the case, not the facts themselves. The results of a polygraph test differ from expert opinions in the following ways: (1) Different objects of examination: The object of an expert opinion is the fact itself, such as injury assessments, blood type tests, or psychiatric evaluations. These are objectively existing facts that require the expert to make a clear judgment and reach a conclusion. The object of a polygraph test is the person involved in the case, and it tests their physiological parameters. While physiological parameters may have some connection to whether a person is lying, the person involved is not the fact itself. (2) Different methods used: An expert opinion is based on the expert's specialized knowledge, such as forensic science or trace evidence analysis, to examine the facts and draw conclusions. In contrast, polygraph testing uses purely mechanical means to obtain test results. The former is the recognition of facts based on specialized knowledge, while the latter is a mechanical method to test the mindset of the person involved in the case. (3) Different uses in litigation: Expert opinions are an independent form of evidence and can be used in litigation. However, polygraph results cannot yet be used as evidence in litigation.

Polygraph results cannot be used as evidence, nor are they considered expert opinions. This is not because polygraph technology itself lacks scientific validity, but because there are still some unresolved issues with the technology: first, it has not been scientifically proven whether there is a direct and strong link between lying and clear emotional responses; second, It has not been conclusively proven whether there is a stable correlation between emotional and physiological responses; third, physiological responses cannot rule out the possibility of interference from other factors, meaning the results may not always correspond directly to the outcomes. Because polygraph technology has not yet gained widespread acceptance in psychology and physiology, the results of polygraph tests are not sufficient to be considered expert conclusions. This is also the reason why the Supreme People's Procuratorate has denied their status as evidence.[15]

b. Bone Age Expert Opinions. A person has many types of age, including chronological age, biological age, and psychological age. Chronological age refers to the time that has passed since birth, calculated according to the calendar and related to the time of birth. It accurately reflects the length of an individual's life.

[15] In October 1999, the Reply of the Supreme People's Procuratorate on whether the conclusion of CPS multi-channel psychological test identification conclusion can be used as litigation evidence held that the CPS multi-channel psychological test identification conclusion can be used to help review and judge the evidence, but can not be used as litigation evidence.

> The age specified in the relevant provisions of China's criminal law is based on chronological age. Biological age, on the other hand, is related to the timing of certain events in human growth and development. It is inferred based on the physiological and anatomical development status of a normal human body, reflecting the actual state of bodily tissues and physiological functions. Psychological age is used to express the absolute level of psychological development. By comparing psychological age with chronological age, one can determine the level of intellectual development. During the process of human growth and development, the skeletal system most accurately reflects the passage of growth time. Bone age, a shorthand for skeletal age, is an important component of biological age. It is an estimate of age based on the patterns of skeletal growth, development, and aging. Bone age refers to skeletal age, describing the age progression of skeletal development and representing the general state of normal human skeletal development. Since skeletal development is closely linked to the physiological maturity of the body, bone age can reflect the physiological maturity of the individual and is a key indicator of physiological development. Generally, through X-ray images of the shoulder, elbow, wrist, hip, knee, and ankle joints, which show skeletal development, and using scientific evaluation methods, an individual's age can be inferred with reasonable accuracy. This method can fairly accurately reflect the biological age of a person, but due to the influence of various objective factors on individual growth, biological age does not always match the actual chronological age. Bone age assessment is an expert or evaluator's opinion on an individual's age based on their skeletal development. This assessment is constrained by the individual's development level and influenced by the evaluator and evaluation standards, making it generally impossible to determine the exact date.

Bone age assessments generally cannot serve as independent evidence for determining age. In cases where the defendant's real name, address, or age is unclear, a bone age assessment may be commissioned. However, in judicial practice, due to technical limitations, bone age assessments cannot yet achieve precision; they only determine a time range with some margin of error. Judges should carefully examine the qualifications of the expert, whether the expert was influenced by external factors during the assessment, and combine the bone age assessment with other evidence for a comprehensive determination. Bone age assessments should only serve as a reference, not as the sole basis for determining the case.[16]

Additionally, attention should be given to the timing of document assessments. Currently, only a few expert institutions can determine documents that are less than three months old using multiple testing methods; a very few can assess documents within six months. Due to the influence of various objective factors, the detection rate for submitted samples is not high. The differences in paper, ink, toner, and storage

[16] See the provisions on bone age appraisal on July 22,1991, the Supreme People's Court research on how to identify the defendant's crime age to the Guangdong higher people's court telephone reply, in February 2000, the Supreme People's Procuratorate on "bone age appraisal" can use as evidence of criminal responsibility age approval and the Supreme People's Court on the foreign entrusted documents made time appraisal related matters notice (department [2008] no. 12).

conditions may have a decisive impact on the results, so it is generally not advisable to rely on them as expert opinions.

ii. **Empirical expert opinions**

Empirical expert opinions refer to those expert opinions made primarily based on the expert's professional knowledge, practical experience, and occupational skills. These assessments rely on the expert's personal experience, including professional education, technical qualifications, academic standing, practical experience, and work achievements. Compared to experimental expert opinions, empirical expert opinions are more subjective and lack reproducibility. Due to the close relationship with the expert's personal experience, these opinions generally only allow for qualitative analysis. For the same subject of evaluation, different experts may arrive at differing or even opposing conclusions. Examples include psychiatric evaluations, particularly those concerning functional mental disorders.

While empirical expert opinions lack verifiability and reproducibility, and are somewhat inferior in objectivity compared to experimental expert opinions, their reliability remains higher than that of a layperson's understanding of the specialized issue. This does not invalidate their scientific basis, reliability, or evidentiary value.

6.8.2.3 Based on the Object of Evaluation, Expert Opinions Can Be Divided into Opinions on Individuals and Opinions on Objects

i. **Expert Opinions on Individuals**

Expert opinions on individuals refer to those where the subject of the evaluation is a specific person. These opinions are based on certain characteristics, skills, habits, or physical traits of the human body to make judgments regarding the individual that need to be identified in the case. Expert opinions on individuals primarily include: skin papillary patterns, handwriting habits, speech patterns, physical appearance, teeth, blood, hair, bone structure, body tissues, body fluids, body secretions, body odors, and other skin patterns. Therefore, there are evaluations in expert assessments such as skin papillary pattern analysis, handwriting habit analysis, physical appearance assessments, dental evaluations, speech pattern analysis, blood analysis (primarily DNA testing), bone analysis, and other skin pattern evaluations.

Expert opinions on individuals can be classified into direct and indirect identification. Direct identification is performed based on certain characteristics of the individual being evaluated, such as in forensic medicine where identification of a complete body is made based on dismembered limbs. This form of evaluation is relatively rare. Indirect identification, on the other hand, is based on traces left by the individual, such as voiceprints, handwriting, odors, and residues, to establish a connection with the individual. Indirect identification is the primary form of expert opinion on individuals.

ii. **Expert opinions on objects**

Expert opinions on objects refer to the evaluation determining whether the material being examined is the object being searched for. Expert opinions on objects mainly include: tools used in crimes, means of transportation, shoe soles, sock soles, bullets, seals, lead types, printing plates, woven fabrics, textiles, and various other materials.

Expert opinions on objects can further be divided into those concerning "individual objects" and those concerning "composite objects." An "individual object" is a material with a single, fixed shape and simple external structure, and its characteristics are reflected through a specific part of its surface structure. Examples include shoe print evaluations, stamp impressions, bullet markings, and tool mark evaluations. The primary method of evaluation is comparing the reflected characteristics of the object. A "composite object," on the other hand, is an object with overall properties rather than a single structure or form. Each small part of it is independent and can reflect the overall characteristics of the object. Examples include fibers, explosives, poisons, plant fruits, animal hair, etc. The evaluation method often involves direct comparative analysis to determine the specific characteristics of the object.

6.8.2.4 Based on the Characteristics of the Object Being Evaluated, Expert Opinions Can be Divided into Opinions on External Appearance and Shape, Behavioral Habits, Material Composition, and Odor

i. **Expert opinions on external appearance and shape**

Expert opinions on external appearance and shape refer to evaluations based on the external appearance characteristics of an object. This is a traditional method of evaluation, which, despite the high development of science and technology, remains a key approach in expert assessments. This type of evaluation is generally carried out by comparing the reflected characteristics of the object, such as fingerprint analysis, dental impression analysis, barefoot print analysis, shoe print analysis, tool mark evaluations, injury tool evaluations, impression analysis, and portrait photo evaluations.

ii. **Expert opinions on behavioral habits**

Human habits are multifaceted, including physiological activity habits, psychological activity habits, skill movements, and certain special behavior patterns. Currently, only handwriting habits and speech habits are considered valid subjects for evaluation. Handwriting reflects writing habits, and voiceprints reflect speech habits. The stability of this type of evaluation is relatively weak.

iii. **Expert opinions on material composition**

Expert opinions on material composition are based on the characteristics of the material's composition. This evaluation mainly involves assessing the material's morphology, structure, arrangement, and content proportions. Any specific substance in nature is, in fact, a mixture, and not only do different types of substances have different components, but even substances of the same type and species can vary in terms of components, content, structure, and morphology. These differences reveal the physical, chemical, and biological properties of the substance, which can be used to distinguish between substances of different types or varieties. Examples of this type of evaluation include explosives testing, poison testing, grease and paint analysis, and fiber analysis.

iv. **Expert Opinions on Odor**

Expert opinions on odor refer to evaluations based on the odor characteristics of an object. In fact, this is another approach to material composition evaluation. Odor evaluations mainly involve identifying and determining to whom a particular odor belongs (establishing the relationship between the odor and a person). Identifying the odor of a substance typically addresses the issue of distinguishing between different species or types.

Additionally, expert opinions can be categorized into forensic medical opinions, psychiatric opinions, toxicological opinions, and others, as well as same-species and species classification expert opinions.

6.8.3 The Significance of Expert Opinions

Expert opinions are an independent form of evidence and an important method and tool for uncovering the facts of a case. They play an increasingly vital role in modern litigation. Unlike typical witness testimony, victim statements, or party statements, expert opinions are human judgments. Not only can they reveal the relationship between evidence and case facts, but they can also reveal the content of other evidence, playing a crucial role in litigation practice.

6.8.3.1 Expert Opinions Often Play a Critical Role in Determining Case Facts

Expert opinions can have a unique role in determining certain facts of a case. For example, fingerprint analysis can confirm whether a person was present at the scene; forensic psychiatric evaluations can determine whether the perpetrator has criminal responsibility; minor injury assessments and light injury evaluations can serve as evidence for determining criminal liability or lack thereof. Expert opinions have the effect of being the "king of evidence" in litigation practice, playing a particularly important role in verifying the authenticity of other evidence and emphasizing the probative value of material evidence, documentary evidence, and other forms of evidence.

6.8.3.2 Expert Opinions Have a Direct Function in Determining Case Facts

Expert opinions are an important means of reviewing and assessing other evidence. They serve as the basis for determining whether other evidence is authentic and reliable, and they play a role in corroborating and strengthening other evidence. After undergoing the process of scrutiny and authentication, expert opinions that are verified as true can be used as the basis for a ruling. Expert opinions often help determine personal relationships and can directly confirm the main facts of a case, such as in DNA paternity testing.

The evidentiary role and significance of expert opinions should be fully acknowledged, but they should not be exaggerated. After all, they are human judgments, not "scientific decisions." Due to various factors, they may also be inaccurate or unreliable. Scientific validity does not equate to accuracy, certainty, or definitiveness, and expert opinions should not be used as the basis for a ruling without proper examination and cross-examination.

6.9 Records

The records include examination records, inspection records, identification records, investigative experiment records, and on-site records. Examination, inspection, identification, investigative experiments, and on-site records have a long history as evidence. Ancient documents such as the "Code of Hammurabi" and China's "Bamboo Slips from the Tomb of the Sleeping Tiger" both include references to these records. China's *Criminal Procedure Law*, *Civil Procedure Law*, and *Administrative Procedure Law* also provide regulations regarding this type of evidence. In the Criminal Procedure Law, these are referred to as examination, inspection, identification, and investigative experiment records; in the *Civil Procedure Law*, they are called examination records; and in the *Administrative Procedure Law*, they are referred to as examination records and on-site records.

6.9.1 Concept and Characteristics of Records

A record is an objective record of activities related to the case, carried out by legal entities in accordance with the law. These activities include observation, inspection, identification, investigative experiments, and other actions conducted at places, on objects, on corpses, or on people, as well as at scenes of violations of administrative laws. Records include examination records, inspection records, identification records, investigative experiment records, and on-site records. This type of evidence mainly provides an objective description and record of how evidence was collected and obtained, reflecting the process of obtaining evidence, and is also referred to as "process evidence."

6.9.1.1 Concept of Examination, Inspection, Identification, Investigative Experiment Records, and On-Site Records

i. **Concept of examination, inspection, identification, and investigative experiment records**

Examination, inspection, identification, and investigative experiment records refer to the objective records made by the case-handling authorities to collect evidence through activities such as observing, inspecting, identifying, and conducting investigative experiments on locations, items, corpses, and individuals related to the case. These records have the following meanings:

a. The subject making the examination, inspection, identification, and investigative experiment records is of special significance. These activities are considered authoritative actions in litigation, with the subject being the case-handling authorities or administrative law enforcement personnel. Therefore, examination, inspection, identification, and investigative experiment records only have legal effect if they are made by these authorities in accordance with the law. In criminal litigation, the authorities making these records are public security and judicial organs; in civil and administrative litigation, the subject making the examination records is the court. In administrative litigation, examination records may also be made by administrative authorities during the performance of administrative duties.
b. Examination, inspection, identification, and investigative experiment activities are considered authoritative activities. Examination mainly refers to the on-site inspection and evaluation of locations, items, and corpses related to the case. In criminal litigation, this includes investigation of crime scenes and examination of crime residues by law enforcement personnel; in civil litigation, this refers to the court's on-site examination of disputed property. Inspection, also known as personal inspection, refers to the examination of individuals to determine their physical characteristics, injury conditions, or physiological state. This is carried out on criminal suspects, defendants, or victims. Identification is the process in investigations where, to clarify the facts of the case, the victim, witnesses, or suspects are asked to identify objects, documents, corpses, locations, or suspects related to the crime. Investigative experiments involve the investigative authorities using simulation and reenactment methods during their investigation to verify whether and how a crime could have occurred under certain conditions and what results might have followed.
c. The objects of examination, inspection, identification, and investigative experiments are locations, items, corpses, suspects, photographs, etc., that are related to the case. These objects themselves are not subjects of specific rights and obligations, and generally only serve as the objects of rights and obligations.

d. Examination, inspection, identification, and investigative experiments must be carried out in accordance with the law. The subjects of examination, inspection, identification, and investigative experiments involve the legal rights of relevant individuals. When conducting these activities on locations, items, corpses, and individuals related to the case, they must be done legally. Particularly when conducting personal inspections that may infringe upon the legitimate rights of the individual being inspected, it is essential to strictly follow the statutory procedures and use methods that cause minimal harm to personal rights, ensuring the protection of the inspected person's rights.

In criminal litigation, examination, inspection, identification, and investigative experiments are both investigative actions and activities for gathering evidence. Investigators must conduct examinations or inspections of locations, items, individuals, and corpses related to the crime. If necessary, experts with specialized knowledge may be appointed or hired to carry out the examination or inspection under the supervision of investigators. To avoid doubts and disputes regarding the objectivity and fairness of the examination and inspection, persons unrelated to the case should be invited to participate as witnesses in the on-site activities. For identification, the principle of mixing should be applied, and suggestions must be avoided; for investigative experiments, all actions that could cause danger or be indecent should be prohibited. In civil litigation, the court has the right to examine places of property damage related to the dispute, objects with disputed ownership, or items subject to contracts, sales, etc.

The legal status and nature of examination, inspection, identification, and investigative experiments are the same. In criminal litigation, they are all considered investigative actions or measures, differing only in their subjects of application. The object of examination is generally "inanimate" things related to the case, such as locations, items, and corpses; the object of inspection is the body of a "living person" related to the case; identification can involve either a person or an object, or a photograph; investigative experiments have stricter requirements, prohibiting any actions that could cause danger, insult personal dignity, or be indecent, and are limited to criminal litigation.

ii. **Concept of on-site records**

On-site records, also known as immediate records, refer to records made by administrative law enforcement authorities during the exercise of their administrative powers and implementation of administrative actions. These records document certain matters on-site that can prove the facts of the case. On-site records have the following meanings:

a. On-site records primarily originate from the objective written documentation of administrative law enforcement activities and serve as important evidence for administrative decisions. They are written records created by administrative authorities and their staff when handling individuals who violate administrative legal norms. On-site records are created on the spot during investigations and evidence collection at the law enforcement site, reflecting relevant case details. They serve as written documents for the administrative authority's preliminary determination of the case facts and can more accurately, objectively, and completely reflect the original state of the law enforcement scene. These records are an important basis for making administrative decisions.

b. On-site records are also a crucial part of judicial review of administrative actions by the courts and are primary, direct evidence proving the legality of the contested administrative action. In administrative litigation, the content of on-site records is primarily used to prove the contested administrative action, reflecting the process of investigation and evidence collection by administrative law enforcement personnel at the scene. In administrative lawsuits, they are also used to determine whether the contested administrative action complies with legal procedures.

On-site records refer to the records made by state administrative agencies at the scene before taking administrative actions, with the direct purpose of providing a basis for those actions. Only when a party is dissatisfied with the administrative action and files a lawsuit in court do these records have significance as evidence in administrative litigation.

On-site records and examination, inspection, identification, and investigative experiment records share similarities, yet there are notable differences between the two. Both are types of evidence created by legal entities in accordance with legal procedures. The differences between them are as follows: (1) Different Subjects of Creation: On-site records are created by the defendant in administrative litigation. Examination, inspection, identification, and investigative experiment records are created by public security and judicial authorities during litigation, to clarify certain case facts, while conducting examinations and inspections of locations, items, and corpses related to the case. (2) Different Timing of Creation: On-site records are made by administrative authorities before taking administrative actions, documenting matters on-site prior to the occurrence of litigation. In contrast, examination, inspection, identification, and investigative experiment records are created by public security and judicial authorities after accepting a case, during the litigation process. (3) Different Content: On-site records may include records of inquiries made by administrative authorities to individuals who violate administrative regulations. Examination and inspection records only consist of objective descriptions of the relevant locations and items, and do not include records of inquiries from the parties involved. (4) Factors Affecting the Effectiveness of Evidence: On-site records must be verified by the parties involved and signed or stamped on the record to be considered valid evidence. In criminal litigation, examination, inspection, identification, and investigative experiment records generally do not require the presence of the parties but do require witnesses. In civil or administrative litigation, the parties or their adult family members should be notified to attend, depending on the circumstances. If they refuse to attend, this does not affect the effectiveness of the evidence. These records are distinct from "case reports" or "situation explanations," which are explanatory materials. The former are considered legal evidence, but there is debate about whether they are testimonial or physical evidence. Some argue that they are written forms of testimonial evidence, while others believe they are non-testimonial objective evidence, requiring the creator to explain or clarify any issues.

6.9.1.2 Characteristics of Examination, Inspection, Identification, Investigative Experiment, and On-Site Records

Based on the inherent essential attributes of examination, inspection, identification, investigative experiment, and on-site records, these records have the following characteristics compared to other types of evidence:

i. **Examination, inspection, identification, investigative experiment, and on-site records are objective records**

Examination, inspection, identification, investigative experiment, and on-site records are truthful records made by case-handling authorities during their collection of evidence. These records are made when examining or inspecting locations, items, corpses, and individuals related to the facts of the case. They are objective descriptions of the relevant items, scene conditions, the state of individuals, and the inspection process and results, documenting the time, place, and specific events. Among them, on-site records are made on-site at certain events, such as when market supervision departments seize counterfeit goods or when financial regulatory departments investigate financial events. The content of these records is objective and does not include subjective analysis or opinions from the inspection personnel or those creating the on-site records.

ii. **Examination, inspection, identification, investigative experiment, and on-site records are standardized**

Examination, inspection, identification, investigative experiment, and on-site records are objective descriptions of activities conducted by case-handling authorities. These records are signed or stamped by those involved in the examination, inspection, identification, or investigative experiments, as well as witnesses, according to legal procedures. The creation of these records is governed by laws and regulations and must comply with their requirements, demonstrating a high degree of standardization. In particular, the creation of on-site records must follow corresponding laws, regulations, and rules.

iii. **Examination, inspection, identification, investigative experiment, and on-site records are highly objective forms of evidence**

Examination, inspection, identification, investigative experiment, and on-site records generally include both the process of examination and inspection, as well as the results. They can also reflect the state or environmental context in which various traces and items exist at the scene and their interrelationships, making them a type of evidence with comprehensive probative value. The content of these records is an objective account of the process and results of the examination, inspection, identification, and investigative experiments. They are considered real-time records with a high degree of objectivity. These records differ from physical evidence, documentary evidence, and expert opinions.

iv. **Examination, inspection, identification, investigative experiment, and on-site records have special characteristics**

The personnel involved in examination, inspection, identification, and investigative experiments, in addition to the case-handling personnel, can, when necessary, assign or hire experts with specialized knowledge to participate in order to help resolve issues that require specialized knowledge during these activities. Additionally, citizens who have no interest in the case should be invited to participate as witnesses. The *Criminal Procedure Law* requires: "The circumstances of examination and inspection should be recorded, and the record should be signed or stamped by the participants and the witnesses." The *Civil Procedure Law* also stipulates: "For the examination of physical evidence or a scene, the examiner must present the court's credentials and invite representatives from local grassroots organizations or the parties' workplaces to participate." However, examination, inspection, identification, investigative experiment, and on-site records must be created by the public security and judicial personnel involved in the examination, inspection, identification, or investigative experiments, as well as administrative law enforcement officers.

Examination, inspection, identification, investigative experiment, and on-site records differ from physical evidence and documentary evidence. Although these records are written forms that objectively document locations, items, corpses, and individuals related to the case, they serve the function of reflecting and preserving material evidence. For example, they record the shape, characteristics, spatial conditions of the physical evidence, and the relationships between different pieces of evidence. However, they themselves are not physical evidence. Examination, inspection, identification, investigative experiment, and on-site records are created by public security and judicial personnel and administrative law enforcement officers in accordance with legal procedures, distinguishing them from physical evidence and documentary evidence obtained through examination and inspection by case-handling personnel.

During litigation, examination, inspection, identification, investigative experiment, and on-site records, like expert opinions, are created by authorized personnel or agencies. Moreover, in some cases, the subjects of examination, inspection, and expert identification are the same. However, there are still differences between the two types of evidence. The examination and inspection are conducted by case-handling personnel themselves, while expert identification is performed by individuals with specialized knowledge. The former involves a direct, objective record created by the case-handling personnel or administrative law enforcement officers using their senses or instruments, without analysis or judgment. In contrast, expert opinions are conclusions made by experts based on their specialized knowledge through inspection and analysis.

6.9.2 Classification of Records

There are various classifications of records, mainly including interrogation records, inquiry records, on-site examination records, physical evidence inspection records, corpse inspection records, investigative experiment records, search records, seizure records, on-site records, and trial records. Based on the nature of the evidence and classification requirements, records that serve as statutory types of evidence are examination, inspection, and on-site records. Examination, inspection, and on-site records must be created according to legal procedures and rules. Therefore, record classification is limited to those that are considered statutory types of evidence.

6.9.2.1 Examination Records

Depending on the nature of the litigation, examination records can be divided into criminal examination records, civil examination records, and administrative examination records.

i. **Criminal examination records**

The main subject responsible for creating criminal examination records is the authority body, as the defense does not have the right to create examination records. Criminal examination records include written documentation of the scene, photographs of the scene, and drawings of the scene. The content of examination records primarily consists of an introduction, a description of the facts, and a conclusion. The specific content is as follows: (1) The introduction includes the case description and general information. It records the time the report was received, the time and location of the incident and discovery, the name, occupation, and address of the reporter and the victim, as well as their descriptions of the incident and discovery. It also includes details about the scene protection, the names, occupations, arrival times of personnel protecting the scene, and the situation found during scene protection. The names and positions of the examination personnel, the names, occupations, and addresses of witnesses, and the start and end times of the examination are also recorded, along with the order of the examination and the weather and lighting conditions at the time. (2) The description of facts section refers to what was observed during the examination. This includes the specific location, position, and surrounding environment of the scene, such as the city, district, street address, neighboring buildings, and road distribution. The internal conditions of the scene include the situation at the center of the scene and related locations, especially any changes or movements at the scene. Details about the scene's central area should be described specifically. For instance, in a murder case, the position and posture of the body, the presence of bloodstains, blood splatter shapes and areas, and the location and characteristics of the murder weapon should be noted. Information on relevant places, such as an indoor scene, should include whether doors or windows were opened, the arrangement and storage of items like furniture, boxes, bedding, and any other objects related to the case, and whether anything was disturbed or damaged. The location, quantity, characteristics, and distribution of various criminal traces and evidence should also be recorded, along with the victim's injuries and material losses, and any unusual phenomena at the scene. And (3) The conclusion section includes the names and quantities of traces and physical evidence collected, the details and number of photographs and drawings taken at the scene, the signatures or stamps of the participants in the examination and relevant personnel, and the signatures or stamps of the witnesses.

ii. **Civil examination records**

Examination records refer to the records made by the court to determine the facts of the case, in which the appointed examination personnel inspect, photograph, and measure locations, items, or objects related to the dispute. Based on the examination findings, these records are created. The main subject responsible for creating these records is the court's judicial personnel. The content of the records primarily includes the examination situation and results, and should document the time and location of the examination, the examiner, the participants present, the process and results of the examination, with signatures or stamps from the examiner and participants. For any site drawings, the time of creation, orientation, the name, and identity of the surveyor should be noted.

iii. **Administrative examination records**

Administrative examination records are factual records created by law enforcement personnel or courts during the examination of a case scene. These records primarily include the examination situation and results, and should document the time and location of the examination, the examiner, the participants present, the process and results of the examination, with signatures from the examiner, parties involved, and participants. For any site drawings, the time of creation, orientation, and the name and identity of the surveyor should be noted. These records are composed of text, photographs, videos, drawings, and models.

Additionally, examination records may include attachments such as on-site photographs and drawings. On-site photographs refer to using photographic methods to objectively and accurately record the state of the scene and to fix and extract various traces and items related to the case found at the scene. The photographs should reflect the original state of the scene and the various traces and material evidence discovered during the examination process. On-site drawings represent the situation of the scene and the interrelationship with the surrounding environment, as well as the distribution and proportional conditions of various traces and objects related to the case. With the advancement of technology, examination activities can now be conducted through video recording, which has become a part of the examination record.

6.9.2.2 Inspection Records

Inspection records are mainly used for personal inspections in criminal litigation, aiming to determine certain characteristics, injuries, or physiological conditions of the victim or criminal suspect. The main subject responsible for creating the inspection records is the investigative authority. The content of the inspection records includes: the time and location of the inspection, the names and positions of the inspection personnel; the name, occupation, and address of the person being inspected; the names, occupations, and addresses of witnesses; the content of the inspection and the results. According to the Criminal Procedure Law of China: "To determine certain characteristics, injuries, or physiological conditions of the victim or criminal suspect, a personal inspection may be conducted. If a criminal suspect refuses the inspection and the investigative personnel deem it necessary, a forced inspection may be carried out. If a woman's body is to be inspected, it must be done by a female staff member or a doctor." If a criminal suspect or defendant refuses the inspection and the investigative authority deems it necessary, the forced inspection should be documented in the records.

6.9.2.3 Identification Records

Identification records refer to the written records made by investigative personnel during the identification process, documenting the process and results of the identification. The content includes: the header, which contains the title, identification time, location, and the identification object (person, corpse, item, or environment) and purpose. The body of the record includes the specific situation of the identification process, the conditions under which the identification object is provided, the method of identification, the attitude of the person making the identification, and the identification result. The footer includes signatures from the participants and witnesses.

6.9.2.4 Investigative Experiment Records

Investigative experiment records are written accounts made based on the need to clarify the facts of the case, where certain events in the case are reenacted under conditions similar to the original circumstances, documenting the practical situation and experimental results. The content of the record includes: the header, which contains the title, time, location, participants (name of the unit, name and position of the individual), witnesses (as above), and the experimenter (name, gender, age, educational background; for criminal suspects or witnesses, their identities should be noted). The body of the record includes the reason for the experiment, its purpose, approval procedures, experimental conditions, and the specific problem to be solved; the experimental results. The footer includes signatures from the participants, witnesses, and the experimenter's fingerprint, with the date noted.

6.9.2.5 On-Site Records

On-site records are a unique type of evidence in administrative litigation law. They are records made by administrative agencies or administrative law enforcement personnel when performing their duties at the scene of an event. These records mainly consist of objective documentation by administrative authorities and their staff during the administrative enforcement process, addressing the event being processed or penalized, and the administrative enforcement procedures. The main subject responsible for creating these records is the administrative enforcement agency and its personnel. The primary content includes records made when examining, inspecting, measuring, photographing, or drawing the scene or objects. The record should specify the time, location, and details of the event and must be signed by the enforcement personnel and the parties involved. If the parties refuse to sign or are unable to sign, the reason should be noted. If other people are present at the scene, they may sign the record. If laws, regulations, or rules provide specific requirements for the form of on-sit.

The creation of on-site records should adhere to the following rules: The main body responsible for creation must be the administrative agency and its staff; on-site records must be made on-site and cannot be made after the fact; the record must include signatures from both the enforcement personnel and the parties involved.

On-site records share certain similarities with examination records in terms of their evidentiary properties, but there are distinct differences between the two: (1) Different Subjects of Creation: On-site records are created by the administrative authority, specifically by administrative enforcement personnel in the presence of the parties involved. Examination records, on the other hand, are created by the case-handling agency. In terms of nature, the former are considered administrative documents, while the latter are considered litigation documents. (2) Different Timing of Creation: On-site records can only be created by the administrative authority during the administrative process; examination records are created by the case-handling agency during the litigation process. On-site records must be created on-site and cannot be created retroactively; examination records are created after the incident, and if the parties disagree with the content of the examination records, they can request a re-examination. (3) Different Use in Determining Case Facts: On-site records are original, direct evidence used to prove the legality of the contested administrative action, and they can serve as the sole evidence to determine whether the contested administrative action is lawful. Examination records only reflect the examiner's identification of the external characteristics and features of the examined objects and cannot be used as the sole basis for determining case facts.

6.9.3 The Significance of Records

Records are a type of statutory evidence used in litigation to determine the facts of a case. They play an important role in distinguishing the authenticity of other evidence, clarifying the sources of material evidence, documentary evidence, and other forms of evidence, ensuring the legality of evidence collection, and maintaining the integrity of the chain of evidence. They are essential in uncovering the truth of the entire case.

6.9.3.1 Records Can Prove the Basic Facts of the Case

Examination, inspection, identification, investigative experiment, and on-site records are objective records of examinations and inspections conducted at locations, on items, or on corpses related to the case. These records can objectively reflect various conditions at the scene and provide crucial evidence for case-handling personnel or administrative enforcement officers to study and analyze the case. They are important for determining the cause and process of the incident, establishing the responsibility of the defendant (or the party), and correctly handling criminal, civil, administrative cases, or other non-litigation matters.

6.9.3.2 Records Can Be Used to Verify the Authenticity of Other Evidence

Examination, inspection, identification, investigative experiment, and on-site records are important pieces of evidence in litigation. They not only accurately reflect the objective conditions at the scene but also help verify the authenticity of other evidence. Since these records provide an objective and comprehensive account of the case's location, environment, and the characteristics of any evidence left at the scene, they can essentially reflect the general overview of the case. Other evidence generally only reflects partial aspects of the case. Therefore, examination, inspection, identification, investigative experiment, and on-site records play an important role in corroborating and verifying the authenticity of other evidence.

6.9.3.3 Records as an Important Means of Preserving and Securing Evidence

The scene of an incident cannot remain unchanged permanently. The material evidence and documentary evidence left at the scene are likely to change over time, and injuries from personal harm may disappear or change. Therefore, conducting a timely, detailed on-site examination and objectively, comprehensively, and accurately documenting the conditions of the scene allows relevant evidence to be fixed and preserved. This documentation can serve as a basis for later understanding and analyzing the situation, "restoring" certain facts of the case to their "original state," and also provide an objective basis for determining the facts of the case.

6.10 Audiovisual Materials

Audiovisual materials only emerged as a form of evidence after the development of science and technology to a certain stage. They are a product of modern technological advancements. In common law countries, these are treated as documentary evidence and subject to the best evidence rule. Some countries consider them to fall within the scope of physical evidence. With the rapid development of technology, particularly the widespread use of computers, audiovisual materials, due to the limitations of "sight" and "sound," cannot fully encompass new types of evidence, especially considering the uncertainties in their conceptual connotation and extension. Scholars hold differing views on both their name and their scope.

6.10.1 Concept and Characteristics of Audiovisual Materials

Audiovisual materials, also known as audio-visual data, refer to evidence that uses high-tech equipment such as recorders, video cameras, or computers to record and display content to prove the facts of a case. This includes videotapes, audiotapes, fax materials, film rolls, microfilms, telephone recordings, radar scanning data, computer-stored data, information, as well as videos from platforms like TikTok. Audiovisual materials have become an important form of evidence in modern litigation.[17]

Audiovisual materials have the following characteristics compared to other types of evidence.

6.10.1.1 Audiovisual Materials Have Special Material Properties

Audiovisual materials are intangible substances that rely on tangible materials to reflect certain thoughts, activities, material forms, or analyze unknown phenomena. They are a type of technological evidence that preserves sound, images, data, and information through sound, light, electricity, magnetism, and other forms. These intangible substances, such as sound, light, electricity, and magnetism, undergo energy conversion through technological means and are stored on tangible media such as audiotapes, videotapes, and floppy disks. Using audiovisual technology, these materials are restored into factual data that can be heard and seen. Without tangible media as a carrier, the audiovisual data would be fleeting; without physical

[17] The audio-visual materials of China's judicial practice refers to the evidence that proves the true situation of the case in the form of images and sounds. It includes the sound recording, video recording, photo, film, sound card, visual disc, electronic computer memory information and data related to the facts of the case, the criminal suspect and the criminal suspect's anti-investigation behavior.

media to support them, the stored audiovisual facts cannot be reproduced. The materiality of audiovisual materials distinguishes them from other types of evidence in a clear and noticeable way.

6.10.1.2 Audiovisual Materials Have Objective Realism

Audiovisual materials are original materials that use modern scientific and technological means to record the circumstances of a case and, through scientific equipment, "reproduce" the facts of the case. Generally, they are not influenced by subjective factors from the recorder, operator, or others, especially when it comes to surveillance footage. As long as the original materials are accurate, the extracted items or stored information typically will not contain errors. If the equipment used is functioning properly and the operation follows proper protocols, it can objectively reflect the facts as they were at the time, vividly displaying the various forms, spatial features, colors, sounds, and other characteristics of people and objects at the time. This provides a three-dimensional effect. In other words, these sounds, images, and stored data can vividly "restore" the original appearance of the case facts. The objective realism of audiovisual materials is unmatched by other forms of evidence.

6.10.1.3 Audiovisual Materials Have Vivid and Intuitive Characteristics

Audiovisual materials rely on advanced technology and are stored using high-tech equipment, making them evidence with a strong technological component. Although their intangible information is attached to tangible materials, their audio and visual content, through playback media, can repeatedly display the original conditions of the event, directly and vividly presenting the facts of the case. This is in clear contrast to physical evidence and documentary evidence, which only offer static and one-dimensional reflections of the case. However, this intuitiveness does not guarantee authenticity; for example, synthesized sounds or AI face-swapping could be fabricated.

The sound and images in audiovisual materials are sensorial symbols. They not only convey human language but can also reproduce all the light, shadow, movement, and sound changes of human society and the natural world. They possess a strong direct emotional impact, allowing them to intuitively display the auditory and visual characteristics of objects related to the case, and vividly recreate the process of events or activities connected to the case. This allows people to perceive the facts and object characteristics more realistically, comprehensively, and continuously.

6.10.1.4 Audiovisual Materials Have Variability

Audiovisual materials are vivid, continuous, and highly visual, and they can reflect the original facts of the case in a complete, systematic, and clear manner. However, because the collection, fixation, and display of audiovisual materials require high-tech methods, the use of such technologies also opens the possibility for manipulation. These materials can be altered or erased through technological means, leaving no trace and making it difficult to detect changes, which can be deceptive. At the same time, because audiovisual materials can be recorded and separated for playback, their distribution allows a larger audience to accurately understand the sound and visual information being conveyed. On the other hand, this also provides an opportunity for distortion, editing, or even stitching together fragments of facts. Especially since some audiovisual materials require advanced technology for restoration, the restoration process may introduce additional issues. The reliance on high-tech methods and the characteristics of recording and separation make both the advantages and disadvantages of audiovisual materials quite evident. Even if the materials themselves are flawless, the way the facts are captured or the way footage is edited and framed could affect the authenticity and accuracy of the information being conveyed.

Regarding the classification of audiovisual materials as evidence, there are differing opinions in the legal community, with the main views being the "computer evidence theory," the "audio-visual evidence theory," and the "audiovisual evidence theory." The computer evidence theory originates from Western countries, where the electronic technology revolution came earlier, developed faster, and was more widely applied, leading to the classification of devices used to create recordings and videos, such as audiotapes and videotapes, under the category of electronic computers. For example, Professor Paul Rostan from the Georgetown University Law Center refers to audiovisual materials as "electronic computer materials."

The audio-visual evidence theory argues that this type of evidence reflects the original conversation sounds and actions of the parties involved. It focuses on the content of audio and video materials, and thus should be referred to as "audio-visual materials." The audiovisual evidence theory, on the other hand, holds that these materials, which use audiotapes, videotapes, and other media to store sound and images, are a form of evidence that can be heard and seen by people, thereby proving the facts of the case. The tone, images, and stored data in audiovisual materials do not merely express thoughts through words and symbols but independently reflect part or all of the true situation of the case. They not only statically reflect the facts of the case but also dynamically illustrate the actual circumstances of the case. Audiovisual materials can include computer evidence, which is also treated as such in practice. For example, Article 25, Paragraph 4 of the "Regulations on Administrative Review of Radio, Film, and Television" states: "Materials used to prove the facts of a case, such as those recorded on audiotapes, videotapes, or electronic computer-stored data, including audiotapes, videotapes, fax materials, microfilms, and electronic computer disks, are referred to as audiovisual materials."

6.10.2 Types of Audiovisual Materials

As a form of statutory evidence, the scope of audiovisual materials is quite broad, and their forms are relatively complex. Therefore, conducting a classification study of these materials is of particular importance.

6.10.2.1 Based on the Source of Audiovisual Materials, They Can Be Divided into Originals and Copies

An original refers to audiovisual materials directly generated from the object's sound or image. Examples include on-site surveillance footage, synchronized recordings of interrogations, and the original data or documents entered into electronic files and records. A copy refers to audiovisual materials made from other sound and visual materials. Examples include copied audiotapes, videotapes, etc.

This classification distinguishing between original audiovisual materials and copies helps people correctly assess their probative value. Other evidence that corroborates the audiovisual material and has been lawfully obtained, or copies that have been verified to be accurate against the original audiovisual materials, can be accepted as evidence.

6.10.2.2 Based on the Form of Audiovisual Materials, They Can Be Divided into Audio Materials and Video Materials

Audio materials refer to sound recordings made using scientific principles from fields such as acoustics, electronics, chemistry, and mechanics. These recording devices capture ongoing speeches, statements, conversations, singing, calls, explosions, mechanical friction, natural sounds, telephone intercoms, and more. Afterward, the recorded sounds are played back to reproduce the original sound, thus proving the facts of the case. Audio materials can fix, preserve, and reproduce sound, restoring the original sound as evidence. This allows people to listen to the sounds, providing an effect that other evidence cannot prove, which is why they are known as "speaking evidence."

Video materials refer to footage recorded using cameras and video recorders based on the principles of photoelectric effects and electromagnetic conversion. They capture the objective, real-time occurrences, development, movement, and changes of events and reproduce the original images when played back, serving as evidence to prove the facts of a case. Through video recording, filming, and the conversion of magnetic signals into light signals, they combine sound and imagery, allowing for direct recording, transmission at any time, and synchronized viewing. This makes it possible for people to visually witness and clearly distinguish the facts of the case, earning them the name "moving evidence."

Other information and materials obtained through scientific technology refer to evidence collected using scientific devices to solve problems that conventional methods cannot address. For example, using computer technology, laser technology, and spectroscopy, one can detect seals or writing and make precise comparisons by confirming aspects like font shapes, stroke arrangement, and structural features. Laser beam technology can also be used to detect minute changes in molecular or atomic arrangements at the point of indentation, which allows for the discovery of impressions left on several layers of paper.

6.10.3 The Significance of Audiovisual Materials

As a product of modern technological development and a new type of evidence, audiovisual materials are widely used in practice, especially in social governance through surveillance and in criminal litigation with the establishment of systems for the full recording and video recording of interrogations of criminal suspects. The widespread use of surveillance footage in administrative law enforcement further emphasizes the importance of this new type of evidence in litigation. Audiovisual materials, as evidence with high technological content, not only require timely production but are also susceptible to tampering and forgery. The legality of their production and collection has a significant impact on their probative value, drawing considerable attention from scholars. Issues such as "secret recordings" or "covert filming" have become major points of concern.

Modern developed countries place great importance on this type of evidence, and it has been widely used in litigation, especially in civil lawsuits. Due to its inherent advantages, audiovisual materials have characteristics such as intuitiveness, continuity, stability, large information capacity, and high precision, allowing them to vividly and effectively reflect the facts of the case and reproduce the process of the case. As a unique means of proof, it possesses irreplaceable superiority over other forms of evidence and plays an increasingly important role in proving crimes, protecting public and private property, and safeguarding citizens' legal rights.

6.11 Electronic Data

With the development of computer technology, the widespread use of networks, and the emergence of the digital economy, especially with the advent of e-commerce, electronic data, which relies on computers and networks, plays an increasingly important role in proving the facts of a case. This is especially evident in the banking, securities, and other financial fields, such as digital currencies. This new form of evidence has been recognized in both legal practice and theoretical research on evidence law.[18] The *UN Model Law on Electronic Commerce* defines it as electronic data, and in China, it is also recognized as a new type of evidence and is referred to as "electronic data."

6.11.1 The Concept and Characteristics of Electronic Data

Electronic data, also known in practice as digital evidence or electronic evidence,[19] has different interpretations regarding whether it can be considered an independent category of evidence. The first viewpoint holds that electronic data is a subset of audiovisual materials. Audiovisual materials refer to materials such as videotapes and audiotapes that are visible and audible, but need certain tools or means to be perceived. Similarly, electronic data must be displayed in a "readable format" via computer systems, making it also "visible." Both share the same medium of transmission and, based on their physical properties, can be categorized as electromagnetic recordings. The second viewpoint argues that electronic data should be categorized as documentary evidence. Traditional documentary evidence records content on paper through written symbols, whereas electronic data records the same content on non-paper storage media (such as electromagnetic or light-based methods). The only difference between them lies in the recording method and the medium, but their function as a record is the same. For example, Article 469 of *China's Civil Code* stipulates: "Written forms include contracts, letters, telegrams, faxes, etc., that can physically display the content. Electronic data exchanges, emails, etc., that can display content and allow for retrieval of applicable data are considered written forms." The third viewpoint asserts that electronic data is not merely a part of audiovisual materials or documentary evidence, but that all seven forms of evidence may exist in an electronic format. The only difference is the medium; electronic data is not a brand new form of evidence but a new form that has evolved from traditional evidence. The fourth viewpoint believes that no other form of evidence can fully encompass electronic data, making it more appropriate to regard it as an independent form of evidence, which aligns with the future direction of evidence types.

China's laws, like those in foreign countries, have separate provisions regarding electronic data. For example, *China's Electronic Signature Law* states: "Data messages shall not be refused as evidence merely because they are generated, sent,

[18] For example, the Uniform Electronic Evidence Law of Canada and China's 2010 Provisions of the Supreme People's Court, the Supreme People's Procuratorate, the Ministry of Public Security, the Ministry of State Security and the Ministry of Justice on Several Issues concerning the Examination and Judgment of Evidence in Handling Death Penalty Cases (No.20, 2010) are identified as the new type of evidence.

[19] We believe that as the type of evidence, it is not appropriate to add "evidence" behind the electronic evidence, because all the types of evidence do not take evidence as their own name, called electronic data is more in line with the development trend of the digital economy.

received, or stored by electronic, optical, magnetic, or similar means." Similar provisions can be found in the *Canadian Uniform Electronic Evidence Act*, the *U.S. Uniform Electronic Transactions Act*, the *Singapore Electronic Commerce Act*, and the *UN Model Law on Electronic Commerce*, among others. In particular, the *UN Model Law on Electronic Commerce* stipulates: "In any legal proceedings, the application of rules of evidence shall not deny the admissibility of a data message as evidence on any of the following grounds." Electronic data as evidence has special characteristics compared to other evidence, whether it relates to its generation, storage, copying, transfer, or retrieval. There are also specific rules for the provision, authentication, cross-examination, and review of electronic data, making it necessary to treat electronic data as a new type of evidence. This is also an inevitable trend in the development of evidence law.

Electronic data refers to materials formed during the course of a case that are stored, processed, and transmitted in digital form and can prove the facts of the case. It mainly includes information formed or stored in electronic media through emails, electronic data exchanges, online chat records, blogs, social media posts, mobile text messages, electronic signatures, domain names, etc. The primary types of electronic data include, but are not limited to, the following information and electronic documents: (1) information posted on websites, blogs, social media platforms, friend circles, forums, and cloud storage platforms; (2) communication information from mobile messages, emails, instant messaging, and communication groups in network applications; (3) User registration information, identity authentication information, electronic transaction records, communication logs, and login logs; (4) Electronic documents such as documents, images, audio and video files, digital certificates, and computer programs. However, witness testimony and statements made by the parties that are recorded in digital form do not constitute electronic data. In practice, this primarily involves information formed or stored in electronic media, such as online chat records, blogs, social media posts, text messages, electronic signatures, and domain names. Compared to other types of evidence, electronic data has the following characteristics.

6.11.1.1 Concealability

Electronic data, as evidence, must be stored and processed using specific data, with all information transmitted through invisible codes. Compared to other types of evidence, electronic data exhibits the characteristic of intangibility. The external manifestation of electronic data as evidence is entirely different from other forms of evidence, such as computer hard drives, CDs, and mobile messaging apps like WeChat. Its creation and reproduction depend on these specific electronic media, which is a limitation compared to traditional evidence (such as documentary evidence) that can independently be reproduced without relying on other media. This dependence on specific media is one of the weaknesses of electronic data, directly weakening its probative value. For example, through hacking, an intruder can alter the original form of electronic data, adding, deleting, or modifying it without leaving a trace, making it difficult to assess the authenticity and reliability of the data.

Moreover, electronic data may not record the identity of its creator, and it can be difficult to determine who created the data. Although network transmission can identify the website (IP) and codes, the potential for impersonation complicates the identification of the creator. This, in contrast to other forms of evidence, also adds an element of concealability.

6.11.1.2 Fragility

The unique generation, storage, and transmission methods of electronic data lead to its inherent concealability, making it more susceptible to alteration compared to other types of evidence. The computer systems on which electronic data relies are vulnerable to attacks, tampering, and are difficult to detect. Data can be easily modified without leaving traces. Electronic data exists in the form of digital information, which is easily altered by humans. Once modified, it is difficult to detect or assess the changes if there are no copies or backup files for comparison. Written documents, using paper as their medium, not only record the signer's handwriting and various other features but can also be preserved for a long time. Any changes or additions will leave "traces," making them easy to detect through expert analysis or authentication methods. However, electronic data, which uses electromagnetic media, can be easily modified without leaving any trace, making it easier to steal, alter, or even completely destroy the data without leaving any evidence. This is especially true today, as advancements in computer and network technology have made data manipulation easier and more difficult to track or recover afterward.

6.11.1.3 Openness

Electronic data, stored on mobile phones, computers, and other mobile internet devices, is not bound by time or space constraints. Its content can be reused repeatedly, and it is easy to copy. With the widespread use of high-tech products like smartphones and tablets, which integrate handwriting, audio recording, photography, video recording, and internet functions, electronic data is easily replicated and, once uploaded to the internet, becomes highly open. It can be created, queried, uploaded, and downloaded at any time. In theory, as long as no obstacles or tampering occur during transmission, electronic data's copy is identical to the original, without any differences. Thus, electronic data has an indifference in replication, meaning that the original and its copy have the same authenticity. The data can be obtained through technical means without restriction, making it highly open.

6.11.1.4 Diversity and Complexity

The form of electronic data is diverse, especially with the advent of multimedia technology. This has made electronic data as evidence a combination of text, graphics, images, animations, audio, video, and other types of media information. This multimedia-based data almost encompasses all traditional types of evidence. It is not only in text form but also combines images, pictures, sounds, and drawings, exhibiting strong complexity and a variety of expressive forms. The internal form of electronic data within a network is a simple electromagnetic form, but its external manifestation is highly diverse. It can be displayed on a computer screen as images, animations, or video formats, printed on paper as traditional hard-copy documents, emitted through speakers as audio information, or displayed on microfilm as audio-visual materials. Its operational execution also takes the form of various command instructions, further demonstrating its external diversity.Due to its reliance on integrated, interactive, and real-time mobile phones, computers, and network systems, electronic data includes not only payment data, click data, and query data but also behavioral data, habit data, and preference data. This has significantly altered the way traditional evidence operates, and combined with a large amount of irrelevant information, the diversity and complexity of electronic data is more evident.

6.11.1.5 High-Tech Nature

Electronic data is an important product and advanced result of modern high-tech development. It reflects the development of modern science and technology in the realm of litigation evidence, with a primary characteristic of high technological content compared to other types of evidence. The generation, storage, and transmission of electronic data all rely on technologies such as computer technology, storage technology, network technology, and blockchain technology. It is inseparable from high-tech equipment, and its method of generation, storage medium, inquiry method, manifestation form, and source characteristics all differ from traditional data. The collection and review of electronic data must rely on certain technical methods, even cutting-edge technologies, and will continue to evolve with the advancement of science and technology. It is rarely influenced by subjective factors and can avoid some of the shortcomings of other evidence, such as the misrepresentation of testimony or the misrecording of documentary evidence, making it relatively more objective. Whether it is the replication, storage, or retrieval of electronic evidence, it requires relevant operators to use technological means. Its accuracy is reflected in its ability to intuitively, dynamically, and visually record case facts, effectively reducing the number of links in the evidence chain. Moreover, it is stable and resistant to interference, maintaining its original state over a long period without incorporating subjective factors. Because electronic data's digital signals are discontinuous, if someone intentionally or accidentally intercepts, monitors, eavesdrops, deletes, or edits the data, it is technically difficult to detect. Often, experts must use technological means for authentication, linking it closely to technology.

Additionally, electronic data also has the advantages of rapid collection, easy preservation, minimal storage space, convenient transmission and transportation, the ability to be reproduced multiple times, ease of use, examination, verification, and ease of operation.

6.11.2 Classification of Electronic Data

Electronic data primarily exists in the form of "data," a form of existence brought about by electronic technology. It cannot be directly read or heard by the human eye or ear and must be converted into a readable form for human understanding. Technically, electronic data is typically divided into the following four categories: content data, which refers to electronic data related to the case, such as documents, images, and graphics; derivative data, which refers to data automatically generated by the computer during the operation of content data; environmental data, which refers to the hardware and software environment that data generation, modification, deletion, transmission, and storage depend on; and communication data, which refers to data generated during the transmission of data over a network. As a new type of evidence, electronic data mainly includes the following types:

1.1. Based on the Different Forms of Electronic Data: Information published on websites, blogs, social media platforms, friend circles, forums, and cloud storage platforms; communication information from mobile messages, emails, instant messaging, and communication groups in network applications; user registration information, identity authentication information, electronic transaction records, communication logs, login logs, and other data; electronic files such as documents, images, audio and video files, digital certificates, and computer programs; and other information that is stored, processed, and transmitted in digital form to prove the facts of the case.
1.2. Based on the Mechanism of Proof in Electronic Data: electronic data that proves the facts of the case through electronic representations of intent; electronic trace evidence that proves the facts of the case through the existence or condition of electronic information; digital video evidence in the form of visual images and audible sounds that prove the facts of the case; testimony evidence in the form of visual telephony; evidence in the form of photographs taken on-site with a digital camera, and so on.
1.3. Based on the Common Forms of Electronic Data, They Can Be Divided Into: chat records; online accounts such as those for games, QQ, alipay, etc.; e-mails; transfer records from online banking; electronic files, including electronic contracts, electronic bills of lading, electronic insurance policies, etc.; electronic attendance records; website information; personal blogs; photos, videos, and audio recordings captured by smartphones, digital cameras, and digital landline phones.

6.11.3 The Significance of Electronic Data

China's judicial practice and relevant legislation have not only recognized the importance of electronic data as evidence but have also made some initial provisions regarding electronic data, the significance of which cannot be underestimated. With the development of modern information technology, especially the characteristics of the international internet that transcend time and geographic limitations, traditional written documents such as contracts, bills of lading, insurance policies, invoices, tax receipts, and electronic invoices in e-commerce are increasingly being replaced by corresponding electronic files stored on computer storage devices, requiring electronic data verification. At the same time, many legal facts related to electronic privacy, network and computer security, intellectual property on the internet, administrative management, and industry regulation on the internet, and other aspects, largely depend on electronic data for confirmation. Therefore, electronic data has particular significance in modern society, especially in the information age.

6.11.3.1 Electronic Data Can Prove the Truth of Information Technology Disputes

Since the 1990s, digital communication networks and computer devices have enabled paperless storage, transmission, statistics, and publication of information carriers, but this has also raised numerous legal issues. Electronic data has become the key evidence for resolving these legal problems. From network privacy rights and online intellectual property infringement cases to electronic contract disputes, consumer rights protection on platforms, administrative regulation of online advertisements, and the pursuit of crimes in e-commerce and the internet, many cases require the confirmation of electronic data. For example, when a contract is signed using modern information technologies like email or WeChat to send offers and promises, the different times of sending and receiving emails will certainly affect the time of contract formation and validity. Once a dispute arises over the contract's effective time, determining the time of email sending and receiving becomes crucial, and proving these critical facts requires scientific and reliable electronic data.

6.11.3.2 Electronic Data Contributes to the Development of Evidence Theory

In the field of evidence law, traditional concepts of evidence have been significantly impacted by electronic information. Not only does the form of electronic data differ drastically from traditional evidence, but its collection, examination, and evaluation also exhibit new characteristics. Essentially, electronic data is a set of digitized information, recorded in magnetic media through different digital encoding methods. At the same time, integrating electronic data into the scope of evidence law studies will prompt a reevaluation of the development direction of computer and network technologies. The development of information technologies such as encryption, digital signatures, identity verification, firewalls, disaster recovery, anti-virus measures, and protection against hacking will continue to be strengthened to ensure the smooth conduct of online and e-commerce activities and to protect the legitimate rights and interests of the parties involved.

6.12 Questions and Thoughts

With the development of modern information technologies such as artificial intelligence and the Internet of Things, and the continuous emergence of e-commerce, e-government, online education, and various online services in social production and human life, smart devices have permeated all aspects of daily life. Due to the continuous upgrading and expansion of smart terminals, the carriers of electronic data are constantly being updated and developed in the direction of intelligence. These smart devices typically have functions such as storage, computing, and networking. Social media platforms such as Weibo, WeChat, third-party payments, and fintech continuously leave behind information and videos that embody the idea of "no picture, no truth," forming new types of electronic data. Based on the specifics of the case, considering modern information technologies such as big data and blockchain, the following questions should be considered in relation to this chapter's content:

(1) What types of evidence exist in the case?(2) How should the classification of evidence types be determined? (3) Which materials do not belong to evidence types? (4) How should the standards for classifying evidence types be determined? (5) How should the issue of overlapping evidence types be addressed? (6) Does the electronicization of evidence in this case qualify as electronic data?

References

May, R. (2007). Xing shi zheng ju [Translation of Criminal Evidence] (Wang, L., et al., Trans.). Beijing: Law Press China.

Kaneko, H. and Takeshita, M. (1995). Riben minshi susong fa (Bai, L. X., Trans.). Beijing: Law Press China.

Tillichev, H. B., et al. (1984). Suweiai xingshi susong [Translation of Sovetskii ugolovnyi protsess] (Zhang, Z. L., et al., Trans.). Beijing: Law Press China.

Kaneko, H. and Takeshita, M. (1995). Minshi susong fa [Translation of 民事訴訟法] (Bai, L. X., Trans.). Beijing: Law Press China.

Pei, S. L. (2002). Xin zhengjuxue lungang. Beijing: China Legal Publishing House. (in Chinese)

Chen, P. S. (1979). Xingshi zhengjufa. Taipei: San Min Book Co., Ltd. (in Chinese)

Morgan, E. M. (1982). Zhengju fa zhi jiben wenti [Translation of Basic problems of evidence] (Li, X. D., Trans.). Taipei: The World Book Co., Ltd. (Original work published 1961).

Diao, R. H. (ed.) (1984). Bijiao xingshi zhengjufa gelun. Taipei: Han Lin Publishing Co., Ltd.

Vyshinsky, A. Y. (1957). Suweiai falü shang de susong zhengju lilun [Translation of Теория судебных доказательств в советском праве] (Wang, Z. X., Trans.). Beijing: Law Press of China. (Original work published 1950).

Rosenberg, L., Schwab, K.H. and Gottwald, P. (2007). Deguo minshi susong fa [Translation of Zivilprozessrecht] (Li, D.X., Trans.). Beijing: China Legal Publishing House.

Guo, H. (2007). Jianding jielun lun. Beijing: Chinese People's Public Security University Press. (in Chinese)

Extended Reading

Tan, Q. G., & Feng, L. (1999). Minshi susong zhong zhengju gainian ji qi fenlei de fansi. Law Review, 17(1): 118–122. (in Chinese).

Lei, J. C. (2004). Lun woguo xingshi zhengju fenlei moshi de quexian ji qi wanshan. Science of Law(Journal of Northwest University of Political Science and Law), (3): 82-89. (in Chinese).

Long, Z. Z. (2005). Zhengju fenlei zhidu ji qi gaige. Chinese Journal of Law, 27(5): 88–97. (in Chinese).

Shao, M. (2009). Woguo Minshi Susong Dangshiren Chenshu Zhidu zhi "Zhi" — Cong Minshi Susong Zhengming de Jiaodu Fenxi. Peking University Law Journal, 21(02): 236–245. (in Chinese).

Wang, J. X. (2002). Xingshi zhengren zhengyan lun. Beijing: China People's Public Security University Press. (in Chinese).

Fan, C. Y., Wen, X. J., & Zhao, Y. (2002). Shiting ziliao yanjiu zongshu yu pingjia. Beijing: China People's Public Security University Press. (in Chinese).

Guo, H. (2007). Jianding jielun lun. Beijing: China People's Public Security University Press. (in Chinese).

Yuan, Z. (2007). Kanyan jiancha bilu yanjiu. Chengdu: Southwestern University of Finance and Economics Press. (in Chinese).

Zhao, C. J. (2018). Xingshi dianzi shuju zhengju guize yanjiu. Beijing: Law Press China. (in Chinese).

Chapter 7
Classification of Evidence

7.1 Introductory Case

One early morning in a certain year, a traffic accident occurred on the Hangzhou-Xiaoshan Highway. At the scene, there was the victim's body and the motorcycle the victim was riding, with bloodstains next to the body. Not far from the body, there were skid marks left by a car's emergency braking. The victim's wristwatch had been damaged, and the hour hand pointed to 5:50. Investigators conducted an on-site examination and took a panoramic photo of the scene. The forensic conclusion was that the victim died from being struck by a car. A woman, Ms. Zhang, told investigators that her husband had informed her that at the time of the accident, he was walking 50 meters from the scene and witnessed a large "Jiefang" truck hitting the victim before fleeing the scene. Nearby, a milestone marked that the accident occurred 15 kilometers from Xiaoshan. The Xiaoshan Traffic Management Bureau reviewed video footage from the highway toll station and confirmed that around 5:50, two "Jiefang" trucks passed the accident site. One of these trucks was from a factory in Xiaoshan. Upon investigation, it was found that the truck had a newly exposed patch where the paint had peeled off. A dispatch record from the factory indicated that driver Liu had driven back to Xiaoshan from Hangzhou on the morning of the 13th, and after getting out of the car, his face appeared anxious. The vehicle log stated that driver Liu returned to the factory at 5:55 AM on the 13th. Investigators questioned Liu and Zhao, the passenger in the truck, but both denied being involved in the traffic accident that morning.

H. Guo, *Evidence Jurisprudence in China*, Understanding China,
https://doi.org/10.1007/978-981-95-3981-9_7

7.2 Chapter Overview

This chapter discusses the theoretical classification of evidence, mainly including categories such as primary evidence and hearsay evidence, verbal evidence and physical evidence, direct evidence and circumstantial evidence, and prima facie evidence and rebuttal evidence. This theoretical classification is particularly important for gaining a comprehensive understanding of the role of evidence in proving the facts of a case.

7.3 An Overview of the Evidence Classification

The classification of evidence is a theoretical typification of evidence, serving as a special means for deepening the understanding of evidence. It organizes and categorizes interconnected pieces of evidence logically, further summarizing the characteristics and regularities of different types of evidence. By distinguishing the commonalities and differences between various types of evidence, it helps facilitate a deeper understanding of evidence and enables each type of evidence to play its unique role in proving the facts of a case.

7.3.1 The Concept of Evidence Classification

Evidence classification, also known as the theoretical categories of evidence, refers to the different divisions of evidence in theory based on various standards or perspectives. It is a logical thinking method used to understand and study evidence, aimed at exploring the relationships between various legal types of evidence by analyzing their complexity and specificity. This classification provides a scientific approach and methods for evaluating and judging evidence.

The theoretical classification of evidence differs from the legal types of evidence, as it falls within the realm of academic research and represents a theoretical construct. One type of evidence in the legal categories of evidence may belong to multiple classifications in theory. For example, a party's statement can be classified as verbal evidence based on its form; based on its source, it may be categorized as primary evidence; and if it is a statement directly related to the facts of the case, it may also be considered direct evidence. However, in the legal categories of evidence, it is only classified as a statement by the party, and cannot be categorized as another type of evidence.

Evidence classification is related to the state of theoretical research. Because the perspectives of researchers differ, evidence may be classified in various ways in theory. This classification serves as a theoretical explanation and does not have legal enforceability. Although evidence classification differs from legal types of evidence, it is based on legal types of evidence as its research object and foundation.

7.3.2 Overview of Evidence Classification

The theoretical classification of evidence can be traced back to the British jurist Jeremy Bentham. In his book *The Principles of Judicial Evidence*, he categorized evidence into nine types: physical evidence and human evidence; voluntary evidence and compulsory evidence; sworn evidence, verbal evidence, and written evidence; direct evidence and circumstantial evidence; primary evidence and hearsay evidence, among others. Bentham's classification of evidence sparked significant interest among many evidence scholars and has been continuously explored in theoretical research on evidence, by figures such as Ulrich, Bailey, Glaser, and Vragi-Mirov. Due to differences in legal systems across countries and varying focuses in classification, different scholars at different times or even within the same period in the same country have adopted varying classification standards, leading to different theoretical classifications of evidence. For instance, another British jurist, Ronald Walker, classified evidence into direct evidence and circumstantial evidence; primary evidence and hearsay evidence; best evidence and secondary evidence; verbal evidence, written evidence, and physical evidence in his book *The English Legal System*. American legal scholar Griffiths, in *Legal Concepts*, categorized evidence into direct evidence and circumstantial evidence. Another American scholar, Wigmore, classified evidence into physical evidence, circumstantial evidence, and verbal evidence. German scholars typically divide evidence into direct evidence and indirect evidence; human evidence and physical evidence; eyewitness testimony and hearsay testimony, etc. Generally speaking, civil law countries primarily systematize evidence starting from the concept of evidence, focusing on functional differences and emphasizing logical methods of classification. Common law countries, on the other hand, emphasize the external form of evidence, focusing on its constitutive forms and primarily classify evidence based on its format.

Chinese scholars' classification of evidence is based on Soviet theories of evidence classification. Early classifications included: incriminating evidence and exculpatory evidence; prosecution evidence and defense evidence; primary evidence and hearsay evidence; direct evidence and circumstantial evidence. Article 52 of *China's Criminal Procedure Law* stipulates: "Judges, prosecutors, and investigators must collect all evidence in accordance with legal procedures to confirm the guilt or innocence of the suspect or defendant, and to determine the severity of the crime." According to the law, scholars have summarized the classification of evidence into incriminating and exculpatory evidence. Soviet scholars analyzed the classification of "incriminating evidence and exculpatory evidence" and concluded: "Only after the nature of such evidence has been tested under the scrutiny of the court investigation, and after its incriminating or exculpatory significance is determined in the outcome of the litigation, can it be considered incriminating or exculpatory evidence. However, the significance of evidence classification lies not in the evidence already adopted in practice, but in its pre-adoption, which allows for a better practical application of evidence based on an understanding of its characteristics. Otherwise, any theoretical analysis would have no practical significance."[1] With the deepening of evidence law research in China, new types of evidence have been added, such as evidence favorable to the accused and evidence unfavorable to the accused; strong evidence and weak evidence; substantive evidence and procedural evidence; primary evidence and corroborative evidence; general evidence and auxiliary evidence; key evidence and derivative evidence (regenerational evidence, process evidence), etc.

Given the state of theoretical research and scholars' reflections on evidence, this book will focus on the more commonly accepted classifications. These classifications include: primary evidence and hearsay evidence; verbal evidence and physical evidence; direct evidence and circumstantial evidence; and prima facie evidence and rebuttal evidence.

7.3.3 The Significance of Evidence Classification

The classification of evidence is a typification of evidence in theory. It not only provides a broad field for theoretical research on evidence, but also offers valuable reference material for evidence legislation. Furthermore, it serves as a standard for scientifically reviewing and judging evidence in practice. Both in theory and in practice, the theoretical classification of evidence holds significant importance.

First, the theoretical classification of evidence helps systematize the vast and complex forms of evidence, allowing for a better understanding of the characteristics, functions, and patterns of different types of evidence. This enhances the depth of understanding regarding various types of evidence, broadens the theoretical scope of evidence research, and provides theoretical resources for the scientific nature of evidence legislation.

Evidence classification is based on the characteristics inherent to the evidence itself. This classification emphasizes certain aspects that reflect the characteristics of the evidence, helping to deepen understanding and master the underlying patterns. Particularly, classifying evidence from different perspectives helps reveal its complexity from multiple angles, thus enriching the research outcomes in evidence theory.

Second, evidence classification reveals the characteristics and applicable patterns of different types of evidence, providing theoretical guidance for their practical application. It can guide judicial bodies and parties involved in a case to effectively collect, preserve, examine, and judge evidence based on the distinct characteristics of each type of evidence, thereby improving the efficiency of evidence use and enhancing the ability to prove the facts of a case.

[1] [Soviet Union] Ann Jan Visinski, The Theory of Litigation Evidence in Soviet Law, translated by Wang Zhi, 305 pages, Beijing: Law Press, 1957.

7.4 Original Evidence and Hearsay Evidence

7.4.1 Overview of Original Evidence and Hearsay Evidence

Original evidence and hearsay evidence represent one of the oldest forms of evidence classification. This classification is based on the different sources and formation processes of the evidence.

7.4.1.1 The Concept and Characteristics of the Original Evidence

Original evidence refers to evidence directly obtained from the original source that can maintain its original connection to the facts of the case. Original evidence directly originates from the initial cause or manifests in its original form. Any evidence that has not been copied, reproduced, altered, transcribed, paraphrased, or conveyed is considered original evidence.

Original evidence directly stems from the facts of the case, and there is a causal link between the formation of the evidence and the facts of the case. For example, a contract signed by the parties, even if followed by a supplementary agreement, still qualifies as original evidence; investigation and inspection records are also original evidence. The fact that the content of these records does not involve the inspection or examination object itself does not negate their original evidence nature. Original evidence has the following characteristics:

(i) **Original evidence has a direct relationship with the case facts**

Original evidence is generally evidence directly generated by criminal, civil, or administrative actions and has a direct connection to the facts of the case. It has not undergone any intermediary steps, with minimal interference, and can objectively reflect the true nature of the case facts. As the evidence closest to the facts of the case, it is considered highly reliable.

(ii) **There is a natural relationship between the original evidence and the facts of the case**

There exists a natural, unaltered relationship between original evidence and the facts of the case. This evidence is obtained without any human intervention or modification and without going through intermediary steps such as copying, reproducing, transcribing, or paraphrasing. As a result, it has a stronger authenticity and stronger probative value.

Original evidence does not change depending on the entity that obtains it. For example, if the party personally collects the evidence, it is still original evidence; if the court collects it, it remains original evidence; if the court commissions a local court to collect it, it is still original evidence. It has not been "contaminated" by any intermediary steps and maintains a natural relationship with the case facts.

(iii) **Original evidence is not immutable**

Due to factors such as natural environmental changes, inherent qualities, and differences in the conditions under which evidence is collected and preserved, original evidence can change or even become unrecognizable. For example, physical evidence as original evidence may become deformed or deteriorate due to age or exposure to the elements; a witness may make an incorrect statement due to memory loss; or the evidence may be altered due to outdated collection techniques or improper handling. Therefore, original evidence cannot be directly recognized or accepted without scrutiny.

7.4.1.2 The Concept and Characteristics of Hearsay Evidence

Hearsay evidence, also known as derivative evidence, refers to evidence generated through intermediate steps such as paraphrasing, transcribing, copying, or reproducing. Any evidence obtained from a source other than the original can be classified as hearsay evidence.

Hearsay evidence is obtained from sources outside the original, and it does not directly originate from the facts of the case. It is generally formed through indirect channels or intermediary steps such as paraphrasing, transcribing, copying, or reproducing. Since hearsay evidence is not directly linked to the facts of the case, it is also referred to as non-primary source evidence. Hearsay evidence is also known as "derivative evidence" or "secondary evidence."

"Derivative evidence" or "secondary evidence" is similar to regenerational evidence in the context of new types of evidence. Regenerational evidence refers to the series of actions taken by criminal suspects or defendants to cover up their crimes and evade legal consequences, generating evidence through activities aimed at obstructing investigation or prosecution. These actions are then discovered by investigators through necessary means, providing facts that either prove the existence of "original evidence" or demonstrate the existence of activities aimed at obstructing justice. Hearsay evidence has the following characteristics:

(i) **Hearsay evidence does not have a direct relationship with case facts**

Hearsay evidence does not directly originate from the facts of the case. It is generally formed through intermediate steps such as copying, reproducing, transcribing, paraphrasing, or other indirect channels, and does not have a direct connection with the case facts. Generally speaking, the more times evidence is copied, reproduced, transcribed, or paraphrased, the further it is from the facts of the case, increasing the likelihood of errors or distortion. As a result, its authenticity and reliability decrease, and its probative value tends to weaken gradually.

(ii) **Hearsay evidence is derivative relative to original evidence**

Hearsay evidence can stem from original evidence or from other hearsay evidence, but its ultimate origin remains original evidence. Hearsay evidence is generated on the basis of another piece of evidence. It can be derived from original evidence or from other hearsay evidence.

Hearsay evidence is distinct from hearsay in the common law system. In English-speaking legal systems, hearsay evidence has a defined meaning and set rules, often limited to non-directly perceived verbal evidence, and it has a different meaning compared to hearsay evidence in the broader sense. Hearsay evidence refers to statements made by a declarant about what they have perceived outside of court or statements made by others in written form, such as hearsay written evidence, or statements made by others in court. Hearsay evidence, as a classification based on the source of the evidence, is broader than hearsay in the traditional sense. It includes not only verbal evidence but also physical evidence. For example, a witness's out-of-court written statement is hearsay evidence in the common law system, but in China, it is considered original evidence, not hearsay.

Although original evidence is generally more reliable than hearsay evidence, hearsay evidence also plays an indispensable role in litigation.

7.4.2 Hearsay Evidence Can Serve as a Clue to Discover Original Evidence

Generally speaking, original evidence is not always readily available. At the beginning of litigation, it is often not immediately possible to access original evidence directly. In some cases, original evidence is collected or obtained based on the hearsay evidence discovered.

7.4.2.1 Hearsay Evidence Can Be Used to Examine the Reliability of Original Evidence

Under certain circumstances, the reliability of original evidence can be verified through the examination of hearsay evidence. For example, if original evidence has changed, hearsay evidence from before the change can confirm and strengthen the probative value of the original evidence.

7.4.2.2 Hearsay Evidence Can Serve as the Basis for Judgment when Original Evidence cannot Be Obtained

When original evidence cannot be obtained directly, or does not need to be directly extracted, hearsay evidence, once verified, can serve as the basis for judgment. For example, if the original document has been destroyed or lost, or if some original evidence cannot or will not be submitted, a copy or reproduction of it can be accepted as evidence. Of course, when using hearsay evidence, efforts should be made to collect or use hearsay evidence that is as close as possible to the original source.

7.4.2.3 The Rules for the Application of Original Evidence and Hearsay Evidence

The distinction between original evidence and hearsay evidence is reflected in the relationship between the evidence and the facts of the case, or whether the evidence has gone through intermediary steps. The subject who collects the evidence does not affect this distinction. For example, if Zhang says, "Liu told me that he saw Wang steal something from another student yesterday," the fact that Liu told Zhang this is original evidence, while Zhang's knowledge that "Wang stole something from another student yesterday" is hearsay evidence. The facts that Zhang learned, due to their differing content, are classified as different types of evidence.

7.4.2.4 The Rules for the Application of Original Evidence

Original evidence, as it originates from the facts of the case, is directly related to those facts and is more reliable than hearsay evidence. Therefore, when both original and hearsay evidence come from the same source, original evidence should be prioritized. For example, the Civil Procedure Law stipulates: "Documentary evidence should be submitted in its original form. Physical evidence should be submitted in its original form. If it is difficult to submit the original, copies, photographs, duplicates, or excerpts may be submitted instead." The general rule for applying original and hearsay evidence should not be understood or applied mechanically or rigidly.

Original verbal evidence should also be subject to court examination, and eyewitnesses should appear in court for cross-examination. For original written testimony when the witness is not present in court, other evidence must verify it.

7.4.2.5 The Rules for the Application of Hearsay Evidence

First, hearsay evidence that cannot be traced to its source, or where there are contradictions between sources, cannot be used as the basis for judgment. Identifying the source of hearsay evidence is the primary task.

Second, when two pieces of hearsay evidence are identical, the one that has been copied, reproduced, transcribed, or paraphrased fewer times, or that is closer to the facts of the case, should be preferred.

Third, when there are doubts about the hearsay evidence, if those doubts can be cleared, it may be used. If the doubts cannot be cleared, it should not be used as the basis for judgment.

Fourth, hearsay evidence may be submitted only when there are difficulties in submitting original evidence.

According to the *Supreme People's Court's Several Provisions on Civil Procedure Evidence*, "When submitting documentary evidence, physical evidence, or audiovisual materials for cross-examination, the parties have the right to request the presentation of the original evidence or original items. However, the following situations are exceptions: (1) When there are difficulties in presenting the original evidence or original items, and the court permits the presentation of copies or reproductions; (2) When the original evidence or original items no longer exist, but there is evidence proving that the copies or reproductions are consistent with the original evidence or items."

When both original evidence and hearsay evidence exist, original evidence should generally be used, and hearsay evidence should not be adopted. However, original evidence must also be verified and cannot be automatically considered superior to hearsay evidence based solely on this classification. When both original and hearsay evidence are available, it is not appropriate to adopt original evidence absolutely or to mechanically apply the notion that "the probative value of original evidence is always greater than that of hearsay evidence."

7.4.3 The Significance of the Lassification of Original Evidence and Hearsay Evidence

The distinction between original evidence and hearsay evidence reveals the reliability of different types of evidence and reflects the varying degrees of their probative strength in relation to the facts of the case. This classification serves as a standard for measuring the reliability and probative value of evidence. The closer the evidence is to the facts of the case, the stronger its reliability and greater its probative value. Conversely, the further the evidence is from the case facts, the more intermediary steps it has undergone, the lower its reliability, and the greater the potential for distortion through copying, reproduction, transcribing, paraphrasing, or other intermediate channels. The more times evidence has passed through these steps, the more likely errors, loss of information, added factors, or distortions in form may occur, making it harder to reflect the true situation of the case.

In the application of evidence, the investigating authorities or parties should make every effort to find and collect original evidence. For physical evidence, efforts should be made to locate the original item, and only when the original cannot be obtained should copies be provided. In the case of testimonies, the original witnesses should be located whenever possible, and their statements should be obtained directly from their personal experiences to avoid misinformation or hearsay. Only when the original witnesses cannot be found or cannot testify should written testimony be used. At the same time, hearsay evidence should not be disregarded. The importance of original evidence should not lead to neglecting the collection of hearsay evidence, as it may provide valuable clues for discovering original evidence.

Although hearsay evidence is not as closely related to the facts of the case as original evidence, it can serve as a clue for finding original evidence. By tracing back the source and using hearsay evidence, original evidence can be uncovered. "Striving to use original evidence as much as possible does not mean that real conclusions cannot be drawn from hearsay evidence, nor does it mean that hearsay evidence is 'second-rate' evidence." Additionally, using both hearsay and original evidence together can strengthen the probative value of the original evidence, and in certain circumstances, hearsay evidence can replace original evidence in proving the facts of the case. Therefore, the classification of original and hearsay evidence is particularly important for correctly selecting and applying evidence and for scientifically assessing the probative value of evidence.

7.5 Verbal Evidence and Physical Evidence

7.5.1 Overview of Verbal Evidence and Physical Evidence

Verbal evidence and physical evidence are classifications based on the external form, presentation, existence, provision methods, and the carriers used to express the facts of the case. Some scholars also categorize them as "human evidence" and "material evidence," but this classification differs slightly from the former.

7.5.1.1 Concept and Characteristics of Verbal Evidence

Verbal evidence refers to statements related to the facts of the case, either directly or indirectly perceived by the relevant individuals, obtained through inquiry or interrogation. These statements often need to be recorded as they are fleeting in nature, such as witness testimony, victim statements, statements and defenses from criminal suspects or defendants, and written expert opinions. Although these records are presented in written form, their essence remains verbal evidence. Verbal evidence has the following characteristics:

(i) **Verbal evidence is carried by people and proves facts through expression**

The content of verbal evidence is generally vivid and detailed, and it can describe the cause, process, and results of an event clearly, making it strongly related to the case facts. After verification, it can directly reveal the facts of the case and may even prove the facts of the case directly. Compared to physical evidence, which directly stems from the facts of the case, verbal evidence is somewhat indirect as it involves people transforming other facts into language.

(ii) **Verbal evidence reflects the case facts through human input, and it has proactivity and variability**

Due to personal factors (such as memory, comprehension, expression abilities, and honesty) or external influences, people's statements about the same fact may have certain variations. These issues should be filtered through cross-examination and verified by corroborating evidence or physical evidence before they can be used as the basis for judgment.

(iii) **Verbal evidence is provided through language and has complex content**

Language itself is ambiguous, and there are differences in how people understand language. Even if the expression is correct, different people may interpret the same issue differently, leading to ambiguities. Moreover, language often not only reflects external facts but also carries personal value judgments, selective inferences, etc., making the content expressed more complex. Therefore, understanding and interpreting verbal evidence should be limited to a specific context, avoiding over-interpretation or creative imagination.

7.5.1.2 Concept and Characteristics of Physical Evidence

Physical evidence refers to evidence presented in the form of tangible objects. It includes physical objects, written evidence, audiovisual materials, as well as field observations, inspections, investigations, and examination reports obtained through written materials, photographs, drawings, and other means. This type of evidence is sometimes generally referred to as "material evidence," but it differs in meaning from the legally defined category of physical evidence. Physical evidence has the following characteristics:

7.5.2 Physical Evidence Is Used to Prove the Facts of the Case through Tangible Objects, and Is Generally More Objective with Less Human Influence

Physical evidence is primarily objective and less affected by human factors, giving it a stronger degree of objectivity.

7.5.2.1 Physical Evidence Is Generally Indirect and Passive Evidence

This type of evidence typically reflects only a segment of the case facts. It usually cannot reveal the full picture of the case and cannot directly prove whether the case facts exist. It does not actively prove the facts of the case; rather, it requires the combination of various physical pieces of evidence and human reasoning to establish the facts of the case.

7.5.2.2 Physical Evidence Is Not Unchanging, it Can Change Due to Natural Causes, or Be Polluted or Destroyed by External Factors

At the same time, due to non-scientific methods of collecting physical evidence, as well as the limitations of scientific technology or human weaknesses, the physical evidence collected may differ from the original item. However, as long as these changes follow a pattern or regularity, even if variations occur, people can still uncover the truth by studying the patterns of change, and the evidence can still serve its purpose in proving the facts.

7.5.3 The Applicable Rules of Verbal Evidence and Physical Evidence

7.5.3.1 The Applicable Rules of Verbal Evidence

First, the verbal evidence is produced in the way of oral inquiry (interrogation), should prove the facts of the case in the court, adopt the direct oral rule, generally should not be used in written form as evidence.

Second, due to the characteristics of ambiguity, verbal evidence generally adopts cross-examination to examine its authenticity. The content of its censorship is human honesty and credit, but can not simply by people's honesty or character to confirm the correctness of his words.

Third, the verbal evidence is the carrier of evidence, and the relationship between the subject of testimony and the case and the parties should be taken as the object of review, so as to prevent the phenomenon of perjury, concealment, omission and other phenomena due to the existence of interests.

Fourth, the evidence should generally be verified by physical evidence, only the evidence can also identify the facts of the case.

7.5.3.2 Rules of Application of Physical Evidence

First, physical evidence, in general, can only prove one aspect or one side of the facts of the case, and can not prove the whole picture of the facts of the case, and it belongs to the "can not speak" evidence, which needs to find out the relationship between it and the facts of the case with the help of relevant verbal evidence.

Second, physical evidence is circumstantial. The proof force is based on technology, through the inquest, inspection, search, seizure, identification, with the help of scientific and technical equipment or personnel with professional knowledge, the physical evidence review, at the same time shall be on the means of reliability or professional ability to review.

Third, physical evidence generally belongs to indirect evidence, and the rule of indirect evidence should be applied when using physical evidence.

Physical evidence needs the direct perception of people's vision, touch and perception or the perception of its content with the help of certain instruments and equipment. Even if the physical evidence itself is objective, it may be distorted due to the error in the link of knowing its significance, so it cannot be directly taken as the final basis for decision without examination.

7.5.3.3 The Significance of the Classification of Verbal Evidence and Physical Evidence

Verbal evidence falls under the category of testimonial evidence, which includes witness testimony, victim statements, confessions and defenses of criminal suspects or defendants, and expert opinions. Since this type of evidence is presented in the form of language, it has vivid, concrete, and profound characteristics that provide clear and detailed insights into the facts of the case. It is particularly useful in explaining the purpose, motive, background, sequence of events, and subtle details of the case. It can guide the investigating authorities in analyzing and studying the case, understanding the overall situation of the case, and is often more valuable than physical evidence. However, because verbal evidence is subject to perception, memory, recollection, and expression, it is easily influenced and disturbed by various subjective and objective factors, making it more unstable. Additionally, due to the relationship between the person providing the statement and the case, as well as the individual's ability to express themselves, there may be false statements or distorted explanations, which makes verbal evidence less reliable than physical evidence. Therefore, when collecting and applying verbal evidence, it is essential to maintain a good environment for providing statements, ensure high-quality conditions for making statements, and avoid distortion. It is also important to examine the source of the statement to guarantee its reliability. Verbal evidence can help piece together physical evidence through the logical connections of time and space provided in the statement, and its role in proving the facts of the case can be discovered through the corroboration between different pieces of evidence.

Physical evidence is characterized by strong objectivity, good stability, and resistance to distortion. Unlike verbal evidence, physical evidence is less susceptible to the influence of subjective factors, and it is difficult to falsify. Even if physical evidence is forged, it is easier to detect. Once collected and secured, it can maintain its original form and characteristics over time, making it one of the most powerful pieces of evidence in proving the facts of a case.

Verbal evidence needs to be corroborated by physical evidence to verify its authenticity. Verbal evidence can explain the source, collection, preservation methods, and legal and scientific procedures involved in obtaining physical evidence, thereby strengthening the probative value of the physical evidence.

7.6 Direct Evidence and Indirect Evidence

7.6.1 Overview of Direct Evidence and Indirect Evidence

Direct evidence and indirect evidence refer to the theoretical classification of evidence based on the direct or indirect relationship between a single piece of evidence and the main facts of a case. This classification, which involves only the main facts of the case and not secondary facts, is considered logically problematic and lacks scientific rigor.

7.6.1.1 The Concept and Characteristics of Direct Evidence

Direct evidence refers to evidence that can independently and directly prove the main facts of a case. Because it is directly related to the main facts of the case, direct evidence can independently and directly establish the truth of those facts.

In criminal cases, direct evidence typically includes the confessions of the defendant or suspect, victim statements, witness testimony, certain documents, audiovisual materials, and electronic data. In civil litigation, direct evidence generally includes the statements of the parties, witness testimony, certain documents (such as contracts that prove the existence of a contract), and audiovisual materials. In administrative litigation, direct evidence may include the on-site records made by the administrative authority, statements from the parties, and audiovisual materials obtained from surveillance at the scene.

The main facts of the case differ depending on the type of case. Generally, the main facts of a case involve two key components: "who did what." In criminal cases, the facts typically include "who," "what," "when," "where," "how," "why," and "what was the outcome" — the "seven Ws." The facts that include both "who" and "what" are considered the main facts. In civil cases, the main facts concern whether a civil legal relationship between the parties has been established, changed, or terminated. Any evidence that proves whether such a relationship has occurred, changed, or ended is direct evidence. In administrative litigation, the main facts often relate to the legality of the administrative actions taken by the government agency. Any evidence that can independently and directly prove the legality of an administrative act is considered direct evidence.

Direct evidence has the following characteristics.

(i) **The direct evidence overlaps with the facts of the case**

The facts contained in the direct evidence coincide with the principal facts of the case. The content of the evidence is generally not contradictory, and it has a strong stability and a clear reality. Direct evidence has a large or small proof power, which is valuable in its only one place that can be questioned, that is, the authenticity and accuracy of the witness testimony (including the confession of the suspect and the defendant, the statement of the victim and the statement of the party).[2]

(ii) **Direct evidence proves that the facts of the case are direct**

When proving the main facts of the case, direct evidence does not need to go through any intermediate link, nor does it need to rely on other evidence to make logical reasoning and comprehensive judgment. After verification, it can independently and directly prove the existence of the main facts of the case or key facts, and make a positive determination of the facts of the case.

(iii) **Direct evidence is mostly manifested as verbal evidence**

Because the evidence of speech is greatly influenced by the subjective will of the speaker, the direct evidence expressed by the evidence of speech has the possibility of hypocrisy and misleakage, and its true reliability is particularly complicated. Therefore, when applying direct evidence as the final basis, its authenticity and accuracy must be verified in strict accordance with legal procedures.

Different direct evidence to prove the scope of the facts of the case is different, some large scope of proof, some small scope of proof. If the testimony of a witness may describe the whole course of the case in detail, but it cannot explain the subjective psychological condition of the perpetrator. The defendant's confession can not only describe the circumstances of the crime, but also accurately describe his psychological state. Under specific conditions, the victim can refer to recognize the criminal perpetrator, generally unable to state the whole process of the crime and its psychological state. In specific cases, on the one hand, direct evidence should be collected as much as possible, although direct evidence in reality, the number is small and difficult to obtain, or not even in every case; on the other hand, it should not be too superstitious about direct evidence and blindly expand its proof role. Only on the basis of extensive collection of all evidence and comprehensive use of various evidence can the panorama of the case be fully and fully displayed.

---

[2] [British], Richard May, Criminal Evidence, translated by Wang Li et al., 4 pages, Beijing: Law Press, 2007.

7.6.1.2 The Concept and Characteristics of Indirect Evidence

Indirect evidence, also known as circumstantial evidence, refers to evidence that cannot independently prove the primary facts of a case. It must be used in conjunction with other evidence to establish the main facts of the case.

In litigation, most evidence presented is indirect evidence, such as physical evidence, documentary evidence, inspection records, and expert opinions. Indirect evidence has the following characteristics:

(i) **Complexity and variety of indirect evidence**

Indirect evidence comes in various forms and types. It can be either testimonial or physical evidence. These pieces of evidence do not directly relate to the core facts of the case; they only demonstrate certain aspects or details of the case. To establish the primary facts of the case, indirect evidence requires reasoning or combination with direct evidence. The process of proving the facts is more complex. However, such evidence is generally abundant.

(ii) **Indirect nature of indirect evidence in proving direct facts**

Indirect evidence, when used to prove the facts of a case or disputed facts, relies on logical reasoning. It is only when several pieces of indirect evidence, each proving a related fact, are combined and analyzed that the direct facts of the case can be inferred. Indirect evidence cannot directly prove the primary facts of the case in a single step. This shows its indirect nature, as it does not immediately resolve the substantive disputes in the case.

7.6.2 Rules for the Application of Direct and Indirect Evidence

7.6.2.1 Rules for the Application of Direct Evidence

First, an independent piece of direct evidence cannot be used as the definitive basis for establishing the facts of the case. No evidence can prove its own authenticity, and direct evidence is no exception. Even though a single piece of direct evidence may prove the main facts of the case and provide a relatively comprehensive description of the situation, it cannot confirm the truth of its own content. Relying solely on it for a definitive determination of the case facts carries significant risks. Therefore, according to *China's Criminal Procedure Law*, if the defendant's confession is the only evidence, without corroborating evidence, the defendant cannot be deemed guilty or subjected to punishment. In civil litigation, even if a party admits to a fact, their statement must be supported by other evidence in the case to determine whether it can serve as the basis for establishing the facts.

Second, direct evidence must undergo a legal verification process and must be corroborated by other evidence before it can be used as the basis for a ruling. When the primary determination of facts depends on direct evidence, its authenticity must be verified. This verification requires support or reinforcement from other pieces of evidence.

When both direct and indirect evidence exist to prove the same fact, the probative value of direct evidence is generally stronger than that of indirect evidence.

7.6.2.2 Rules for the Application of Indirect Evidence

Indirect evidence cannot independently prove the main facts of a case. It must be combined with other evidence to fulfill its role in proving the main facts of the case. Since indirect evidence does not have a direct relationship with the main facts, its application is more complicated than direct evidence, which often causes practitioners to hesitate and continue their investigation before making a decision. If we compare the case facts to a wall, then indirect evidence is like each brick that forms the wall. Only when the quality and quantity of each brick meet the standards can the wall stand. If the bricks are flawed, it will affect the quality of the wall or even cause the whole wall to collapse.

First, indirect evidence refers to evidence that cannot independently prove the main facts of a case; it must be combined with other evidence to prove the main facts. In litigation, most evidence is indirect, such as physical evidence, documentary evidence, records, and expert opinions. These types of evidence are not directly related to the main facts of the case. They can only prove certain fragments or details of the facts, and cannot independently prove the main facts. To prove the main facts of the case, indirect evidence must be used in conjunction with other evidence through reasoning.

Second, each piece of indirect evidence used to determine the case must be lawfully obtained and verified as accurate. This is a requirement for each piece of indirect evidence itself. Evidence serves as the basis for establishing the facts of the case and must be examined to ensure that its source and form comply with legal regulations. Each piece of indirect evidence must undergo cross-examination in court and be verified for accuracy. If not verified, it should be excluded and cannot be included in the evidence system. When using indirect evidence to determine the case, each piece of indirect evidence forming the basis of the inference about the main facts must be reliable and supported by other evidence.

Third, the indirect evidence used to determine the case must corroborate each other, with no unresolved contradictions or inexplicable doubts. This refers to the examination and judgment of indirect evidence based on the relationship between the pieces of evidence. The corroborative and consistent relationships between indirect evidence show consistency. The corroborative relationship requires a high degree of consistency between the pieces of indirect evidence, i.e., they must align or match. The consistent relationship requires that the evidence points in the same direction, meaning if one piece of indirect evidence makes the results of other indirect evidence more likely, then the two pieces of evidence are consistent.

The absence of contradictions between indirect evidence means that the existence of each piece of evidence does not make the result of other evidence less likely. When forming an evidence system with indirect evidence to prove the main facts, the relationships between the various pieces of indirect evidence should generally be consistent in pointing to the target. In determining the case using indirect evidence, contradictions or conflicts between the evidence are not allowed. Even if contradictions exist, they must be reasonably resolved.

Indirect evidence, as a type of evidence, must be exclusive, ruling out all possibilities and reasonable doubts. If there are multiple possibilities or reasonable doubts between indirect evidence, such evidence cannot be used as the basis for determining the case. Even if indirect evidence proves a series of unrelated facts or facts that conflict internally, such evidence, regardless of how abundant, cannot serve as the basis for determining the factual truth of the case.

Fourth, indirect evidence used to decide a case must form a complete system of proof, meaning that it must be sufficient in quantity and form a coherent and rigorous structure. Single pieces of evidence cannot determine the case. Only when evidence has formed a complete chain of proof can it serve as the basis for decision-making. Indirect evidence must form a complete system, where each fact or circumstance in the case is supported by corresponding indirect evidence. In criminal cases, these elements primarily include the time, location, process, means, tools, consequences, purpose, motives, and the defendant's personal situation—these are the seven essential elements that must be fully proven. These facts should link together like links in a chain, with each ring connected to the next, creating an overall system of indirect evidence, which is referred to as the "chain of evidence". The specific number of pieces of indirect evidence required for this system to be complete must be analyzed on a case-by-case basis. All facts used for convicting and sentencing the defendant, including facts related to the elements of the crime and the facts that justify a heavier or lighter sentence or even exemption from punishment, must be proven by corresponding indirect evidence.

Fifth, the conclusion derived from indirect evidence must be the only one that excludes all reasonable doubts. The chain of indirect evidence should be consistent across the facts it proves. Only in this way can the facts determined in the case have a reliable basis and unassailable persuasive power. "Excluding all reasonable doubt" means eliminating the following types of doubts: (1) the existing indirect evidence does not fully cover the case facts; (2) there are indications that some condition, which could affect the truth of the case, may exist and cannot be ruled out; (3) situations that are likely to affect the truth of the case, based on common sense, exist. The proof system of indirect evidence must be strong enough to exclude all other possibilities and lead to the only conclusion about the existence of the case facts. This uniqueness refers to only one possibility with no multiple explanations.

Sixth, the reasoning based on indirect evidence must comply with logic and empirical judgment. When proving case facts using indirect evidence, logical reasoning is necessary. This is because each piece of indirect evidence only reflects a fragment or aspect of the case facts and cannot provide a full picture. Only through reasoning can one understand the connection between pieces of evidence and between evidence and the case facts, linking the different fragments of facts and inferring the unknown facts of the case from the known indirect evidence. At the same time, it is crucial to distinguish between logical reasoning and subjective speculation. While reasoning is logical, this does not mean the conclusions are true, objective, or inevitable; instead, it means that the relationship between the premise and conclusion is valid, and the truth of the conclusion depends on the truth of the premise. In a valid logical argument, if the premise is true, the conclusion is inevitable; if the premise is false, the conclusion does not have to be true. During logical reasoning, attention must be paid to three main factors: the truth of the premise, the logical consistency of the reasoning, and the reliability of the premise itself.

In addition to logic, the role of experience should also be considered. Experience reflects the typical nature or relationship between things in general circumstances or situations. When applying experience to judgments of specific facts, the special circumstances in the evidence of the case must also be considered. Based on the individual pieces of indirect evidence, reasoning the main facts of the case is, from the perspective of logical nature, simply a probabilistic conclusion with varying degrees of certainty—it is impossible to derive an inevitable conclusion. When this probability reaches a certain level and no reasonable doubt arises regarding the main facts of the case, the facts of the case can be determined, but this must not contradict common sense or ethical principles.

7.6.3 The Significance of the Classification of Direct Evidence and Indirect Evidence

The division of evidence into direct and indirect evidence is both natural and practical, as it aligns with the real-life situations and relationships in which they occur. This classification helps ensure the correct application of these two types of evidence. By categorizing evidence, we can more accurately grasp their characteristics, understand their respective advantages, and skillfully combine both forms to leverage their complementary roles.

Classifying direct and indirect evidence facilitates using indirect evidence to prove case facts, discover direct evidence, or assess and evaluate direct evidence, thereby making the basis for the case more comprehensive and certain. "While acknowledging the reasonableness of this classification, we must firmly oppose positioning one type of evidence against the other, or comparing more reliable evidence with less reliable evidence."[3] Indirect evidence can serve as a lead to discover or collect direct evidence, or it can act as a method to verify and corroborate the authenticity of direct evidence. The combination of indirect and direct evidence can provide a more comprehensive and sufficient demonstration of the truth of the key facts of a case. In the absence of direct evidence, indirect evidence can also be used through inference to confirm the direct facts of the case. This is especially important in cases such as "one-on-one" bribery cases, invasions of private spaces, and "insider trading" cases, where the collection of substantial indirect evidence can play a crucial role in affirmatively establishing the direct facts of the case.

7.7 Main Evidence and Counterevidence

Main evidence and counterevidence are theoretical classifications based on the relationship between evidence and the party responsible for bearing the burden of proof in civil and administrative litigation. This classification divides evidence according to whether it can prove the facts claimed by the party bearing the burden of proof, and it is a distinctive form of evidence classification in civil and administrative litigation.

7.7.1 Overview of Main Evidence and Counterevidence

In civil and administrative litigation, evidence is classified into main evidence and counterevidence based on whether it can prove the facts claimed by the party bearing the burden of proof. Although the terms "main evidence" and "counterevidence" are not directly used in Chinese legislation, a similar concept of "contrary evidence" is mentioned. For example, Article 64 of the Civil Procedure Law of China stipulates that documents that have been notarized should be regarded as the basis for determining facts, unless there is "contrary evidence" sufficient to overturn them.

7.7.1.1 Concept and Characteristics of Main Evidence

Main evidence refers to evidence that can prove the existence or establishment of the facts claimed by the party bearing the burden of proof. It is evidence that supports the establishment of the facts claimed in the lawsuit. Main evidence has the following characteristics:

---

[3] [Soviet Union] Ann Jan Visinski, The Theory of Litigation Evidence in Soviet Law, translated by Wang Zhi, p. 301, Beijing: Law Press, 1957.

(i) **Positivity in Proving Case Facts**

The party presenting proof bears the burden of proof for the establishment of the claimed facts. The purpose is to actively influence the formation of the judge's belief so that an affirmative determination can be made regarding the claimed facts.

(ii) **Attribute of Assertive Evidence in Nature**

Main evidence is provided by the party bearing the burden of proof to prove the establishment of their claim. To some extent, it has an offensive nature and aims to actively influence the judge's belief.

(iii) **Association with the Party's Burden of Proof and Litigation Interests**

Generally speaking, evidence that is beneficial to the party bearing the burden of proof and supports their claim is proof. The evidence presented by the plaintiff to prove the facts underlying their lawsuit claim is main evidence. Similarly, the evidence presented by the defendant to prove the existence of the facts in their defense is also proof. For example, if Party A sues Party B to repay a loan of 1000 yuan, based on the burden of proof, Party A presents evidence such as a promissory note to prove the existence of the loan. The promissory note presented by Party A is proof. If Party B, the defendant, argues that the 1000-yuan loan has been repaid and presents a receipt written by Party A to prove this fact, the receipt is also proof. In administrative litigation, if the plaintiff accuses a market supervision and administration department of making an illegal fine decision, the evidence presented by the plaintiff to prove that their business operations are legal is proof. Meanwhile, the evidence such as on - site records provided by the defendant market supervision and administration department when making the fine decision is also proof.

The determination of main evidence cannot simply assume that evidence provided by the plaintiff is proof and that provided by the defendant is counterevidence. Main evidence has nothing to do with the identities of the plaintiff and the defendant, but is only related to the burden of proof and whether it can prove the claimed facts.

7.7.1.2 Concept and Characteristics of Counterevidence

Counterevidence refers to evidence presented by one party to deny the facts claimed by the other party and to prove the existence of the facts they claim. Any evidence that can prove that the facts claimed by the party bearing the burden of proof do not hold is called counterevidence. Counterevidence has the following characteristics:

(i) **A defensive evidence**

Counterevidence is used to prevent the facts proved by proof from being established. That is, it is evidence presented by one party to prevent the judge from believing the facts claimed by the other party to be true. Take the previous example: In a lawsuit where Party A demands Party B to repay a 1000 - yuan debt, Party B claims that the 1000 yuan obtained from Party A is a gift, not a loan, and presents a letter of donation written by Party A. This letter is disproof because the facts it proves are contrary to those claimed by the other party. If it is true and reliable, it can rebut the facts claimed by the other party. If Party B provides a receipt of 1000 yuan from Party A, the receipt is proof. If Party B provides evidence that the 1000 - yuan promissory note from Party A is not written by Party A himself, the evidence provided is evidence defense rather than proof or disproof. Like proof, counterevidence can be presented by both the defendant and the plaintiff. Both main evidence and counterevidence are used to prove the same fact in a case, but they play opposite roles. Theoretically, it should be clear which evidence is main evidence, which is counterevidence, and which is evidence defense.

(ii) **A negative evidence**

Counterevidence has the function of undermining and eliminating the existence of the facts proved by proof. Its role is to weaken and shake the probative force of proof, with a defensive function, ultimately preventing the facts claimed by proof from being recognized by the court. It has nothing to do with the litigation status of the parties, and the plaintiff, defendant, or third - party can all be the subject of presenting counterevidence.

(iii) **Not associated with the burden of proof**

The party presenting counterevidence does not bear the burden of proof. Counterevidence has the meaning of denying or opposing proof, and its main purpose is to negatively hinder the formation of the judge's belief.

(iv) **Closely associated with presumptions, and some presumptions can be the object of counterevidence**

For example, according to the judicial interpretation in China regarding the "presumption of obstructing the presentation of evidence", if a party controls evidence and refuses to provide it without justifiable reasons, and the party bearing the burden of proof for the fact to be proved claims that the content of the evidence is unfavorable to the controller, the court may determine that the claim holds. For parties who destroy or hide evidence to obstruct the other party's proof activities, certain unfavorable consequences in the law of evidence will be imposed on them.[4]

Counterevidence is different from rebuttal evidence or evidence defense. Rebuttal evidence refers to the basis provided by one party to point out that the evidence presented by the other party is illegal or untrue. Since it does not prove the existence of new facts, it may not necessarily rebut the facts claimed by the other party. Counterevidence is that one party presents additional evidence to prove the existence of contrary facts, thereby denying and rebutting the claim of the other party.

[4] Huang Guochang, The New Development of Civil Litigation Theory, page 216, Beijing: Peking University Press, 2008.

For example, if Party A sues Party B to repay a due loan of 1000 yuan and presents a promissory note as evidence, and Party B argues that they never wrote the promissory note and that the promissory note presented by Party A is false, this is rebuttal evidence or evidence defense.

Rebuttal evidence or evidence defense is relative to the evidence provided by the other party. It only proves that the evidence lacks legality, authenticity, and relevance, and is the basis for rebutting the evidence provided by the other party. The purpose is to prevent the proof from being used as evidence, with the nature of impeaching evidence. Counterevidence, on the other hand, proves that the facts claimed by the other party do not exist, thus preventing the facts proved by the proof from being recognized.

7.7.2 *Rules for the Application of Main Evidence and Counterevidence*

In addition to following the general rules of evidence, the following rules should also be noted when applying main evidence and counterevidence.

Firstly, when parties are proving the existence or non - existence of the claimed facts, whether they are the plaintiff, the defendant, or a third party, they should present main evidence and counterevidence to support their claims. That is, the party bearing the burden of proof should prove the existence of the facts they claim, or the other party should rebut the facts claimed by the opposing party, except in cases where the opposing party makes an admission. In civil litigation, when both main evidence and counterevidence have been presented, the judge should first investigate the main evidence. If the probative force of the main evidence is obviously weak and fails to meet the requirements of proof, generally, there is no need to investigate the counterevidence. As the saying goes, "If the main evidence fails to achieve its purpose, there is no need to rebut it with counterevidence."[5]

Secondly, main evidence and counterevidence cannot be true at the same time, but they may both be false. When main evidence and counterevidence co-exist, the court cannot recognize both of them. The judge should, based on their own judgment, determine which one is more superior, certain, and credible. If the main evidence does not exist or is untrue, even without counterevidence, a judgment unfavorable to the defendant cannot be made.[6] That is to say, counterevidence depends on the existence of main evidence. First, there must be main evidence, and then there can be counterevidence. When the main evidence cannot be established, even if there is no counterevidence to rebut the claimed facts, a factual finding unfavorable to the party without the burden of proof cannot be made. When there is only main evidence but no counterevidence, the establishment of the proof cannot be directly recognized just

[5] Wang Jiayi, et al., New Theory of Civil Procedure Law, p. 344, Taipei: Sanmin Book Company, 2002.

[6] Chen Pusheng, Criminal Evidence Law, page 129, Taipei: Sanmin Book Company, 1979.

because there is no counterevidence, and the existence of the claimed facts cannot be directly determined either.

The counterevidence against main evidence and the main evidence against counterevidence belong to different categories. They are both independent types of evidence with unique evidential statuses. They should not be confused or conflated.

7.7.3 *Significance of the Classification of Main Evidence and Counterevidence*

In civil and administrative litigation, classifying evidence into main evidence and counterevidence aims to clarify the probative roles of these two different types of evidence, so that the court can comprehensively collect and correctly examine and judge evidence, and prevent subjectivity and one-sidedness. Although this classification is based on whether the evidence is presented by the party bearing the burden of proof and the facts it can prove, the evidence collected by the court ex officio can also be classified accordingly. That is, the evidence collected by the court that can prove the existence of the facts claimed by the parties is main evidence, and the evidence that proves the non - existence of the claimed facts is counterevidence.

This classification is also beneficial for clarifying the attribution of the burden of proof, implementing the burden of proof, specifying the order of presenting evidence, prompting the parties who put forward litigation claims to actively fulfill their burden of proof, facilitating the smooth progress of the litigation, helping to ascertain the objective truth of the case, and ensuring the quality of case adjudication.

7.8 Questions and Reflections

Regarding the issue of evidence classification, some scholars believe that an evidence method can have two different evidential attributes, such as the co-existence of main evidence and counterevidence. They call this type of evidence method "mixed evidence". Other scholars believe that judicial practice should focus on the classification of "problematic evidence" and divide it into illegal evidence, absent evidence, and defective evidence. Based on the case situation, combined with the content of this chapter, and considering the theoretical differences, think about the following questions: (1) Which pieces of evidence in this case are testimonial evidence and physical evidence? (2) Which pieces of evidence in this case are original evidence and derivative evidence? (3) Which pieces of evidence in this case are direct evidence and indirect evidence? (4) How do these different types of evidence exert their probative force on the facts of the case? (5) What are your views on evidence classification?

Extended reading

Vyshinsky, A. Y. (1957). Suweiai Falü Shang de Susong Zhengju Lilun [Translation of Теория судебных доказательств в советском праве] (Wang, Z. X., Trans.). Beijing: Law Press China. (Original work published 1950).

Tang, Y. C. (1994). Lun yunyong zhijie zhengju yu jianjie zhengju dingzui de guize. Studies in Law and Business, (4): 30–35. (in Chinese)

Chen, R. H. (1985). Shilun xingshi susong zhong de chuanlai zhengju. Law Review, 1985(4), 16–19. (in Chinese)

He, Y. (2008). Guanyu benzheng yu fanzheng zhi zaisi kao. Journal of National Prosecutors College. (2): 144–149. (in Chinese)

Chapter 8
Rule of Evidence

8.1 Introductory Case

Li worked for a certain internet company, which provided him with a work phone for business use. According to the company's employee handbook, if an employee engages in "private transactions" (commonly known as "flying orders"), they will be held liable for compensation amounting to 40% of the transaction value. After resigning, Li returned the work phone to the company. The company extracted call recordings from Li's phone and recovered the phone's call data, which provided evidence of Li's involvement in "private transactions." The company used this evidence to file a labor arbitration claim. The arbitration department, based on the call recordings, found that Li had engaged in "private transactions." Li, dissatisfied with the arbitration, filed a lawsuit in court. The court ruled that the company owned the work phone but failed to prove that Li was informed that the phone's calls would be recorded and its data recovered. As a result, the court did not recognize the legality of this evidence and ruled in favor of Li's lawsuit.

8.2 Chapter Overview

This chapter discusses the rules of evidence, focusing primarily on the hearsay rule, the exclusionary rule for illegal evidence, the corroborative evidence rule, the best evidence rule, and the opinion evidence rule. These rules are crucial for regulating the selection and application of evidence.

H. Guo, *Evidence Jurisprudence in China*, Understanding China,
https://doi.org/10.1007/978-981-95-3981-9_8

8.3 The Rule of Hearsay Evidence

The rule of hearsay evidence is one of the most developed evidence rules in the common law system, originating from trial by jury. This rule was established in England in 1680. The United States inherited this tradition and has further refined and developed it. For example, the *Federal Rules of Evidence* in the United States provide comprehensive provisions on the hearsay rule. Civil law countries have also gradually implemented this rule.

8.3.1 Concept and Characteristics of Hearsay Evidence

Hearsay evidence is an out-of-court statement proving the facts of the case. "Hearsay evidence, in a narrow sense, is only the statement of the person on behalf of the statement made outside the trial; in a broad sense, the written statement also includes the above statement."[1] Hearsay evidence mainly includes three situations: one is to report the oral statements of others; the other is to express the statements of others through documents; the third is to repeat and imitate the behavior of the insider. Hearsay evidence has the following characteristics.

8.3.1.1 Hearsay Evidence is a Kind of Meaning Behavior of the Speaker

Hearsay evidence whether in the court statement people report what others saw and heard, or the perception of case facts personally written materials or by others to direct perception of the statement record, and has some sense of non-language behavior, performance as a kind of meaning behavior, not a direct reflection of the case facts, belong to the court Chen, the substitute of evidence. This substitute is an expression of meaning for the speaker.

8.3.1.2 Hearsay Evidence is a Statement Used to Prove the Facts of the Case

Hearsay evidence is a statement that the matter asserted by the supporting party is true. Whether an out-of-trial statement is hearsay evidence should first determine its relationship to the facts of the case. If the truth of the statement is irrelevant to the facts of the case, the statement is not hearsay evidence. Under the United States Federal Rules of Evidence, the following statements are not made within, or are "not hearsay": (1) the testimony of a witness introduced and recorded in a previous proceeding. The introduction of the record of testimony in subsequent proceedings is not hearsay; (2) prior statement of a witness who has passed the cross-examination of

[1] Diao (1984), p. 218.

the court. If used to prove perjury, or to rebut the charge, Or a recognition made after detecting someone, The prior statement of the witness is not hearsay; (3) admission by a party. That admission or statement may be made by the intention of the party himself.

8.3.1.3 Hearsay Evidence is Generally not Admissible

Hearsay evidence does not have the ability to prove evidence, and generally shall not be submitted to the court for investigation. It is generally excluded before the trial, and cannot enter the court as the basis for determining the facts of the case. Evidence offered by any witness, whether oral, in writing or by any other means, such as a gesture, is inadmissible if the purpose of introducing such evidence is to prove the truth of a fact previously said by someone. Although hearsay evidence itself assumes comparative non-hearsay evidence, this is not the main reason for exclusion. When the statement is made for evidentiary purposes other than the truth of the case, then it is admissibility.

There are a large number of "exceptions" to the inadmissibility of hearsay evidence, and even more hearsay evidence than excluded in judicial practice in various countries. For example, the United States Federal Rules of Evidence stipulates dozens of exception rules, and there are also general exceptions.

Hearsay evidence is different from the incoming evidence. The form of hearsay evidence is mainly declarative evidence, record evidence and behavior representation. Its existence is for the purpose of denying its evidence ability, while the purpose of proving the force does not deny its evidence ability, but the evidence and hearsay evidence overlap. Our legislative and judicial practice does not preclude the application of hearsay evidence.

8.3.2 Application of the Hearsay Evidence Rule

The hearsay evidence rule is one of the important evidence rules of the British-American legal exclusion rule. Because the hearsay evidence belongs to a statement outside the trial, fails to undergo oath, cross-examination or cross-examination, and the judge fails to see in person, has doubts about authenticity and credit crisis, according to the principle of direct speech, especially the direct observation rule, this evidence should be excluded. However, there are exceptions where the principle exists, and the importance of the hearsay exception is gradually fixed by the making law. In civil proceedings, the hearsay rule is gradually abolished or no longer applicable.

8.3.2.1 The Exclusionary Rule of Hearsay Evidence

Hearsay evidence, as a statement outside the trial, violates the verification principle of the "direct cross-examination" of the mainland law countries and the "cross-examination", and generally is not admitted into the court as evidence, and the exclusion rule is applied. Article 68 and 81 of the *Provisions of the Supreme People's Court on Evidence in Civil Procedure* stipulate: "The testimony of a witness who fails to appear in court without justifiable reasons shall not be used as the basis for recognizing and determining the facts of the case.", "If the expert expert refuses to testify in court, the expert opinion shall not be used as the basis for ascertaining the facts of the case." Although these provisions still have a certain gap with the hearsay rule, the provisions have the significance of hearsay exclusion.

8.3.2.2 Exceptions to the Hearsay Evidence Exclusion Rule

Hearsay evidence, although uncredible, cannot be denied that some hearsay evidence is more credible than nonhearsay evidence in exceptional circumstances. Because some of the evidence before the court interference is less, for the witness case facts, the memory more clear, especially some witnesses have been unable to testify (witness has died), blindly emphasize its testimony has no realistic possibility, judicial practice and legislation should consider these exceptions.

Hearsay evidence has a great risk of mistransmission, so the exclusion is naturally applicable. If absolutely excluded, in practice, it may not be feasible, and may even appear the phenomenon that extreme things will reverse, resulting in the truth of the case. In order to improve the efficiency of litigation, reduce the cost of litigation, and realize the litigation purpose of finding the truth, the law generally stipulates the exception rule of hearsay evidence. If in British and American law countries, hearsay evidence has one of the following conditions, it can be adopted: (1) it is "reliability and situation assurance". By comprehensive and comprehensive consideration of the relevant circumstances of the hearsay evidence, it can be believed that it has a high credibility or does not have the danger that the hearsay evidence is not true under normal circumstances, even without the cross-examination of the parties will not pose harm to the interests of the parties. (2) The parties have been given the opportunity to counter-question or question in other procedures.

Exceptions to the hearsay rule generally fall into unconditional exceptions and conditional exceptions.

i. **Unconditional exception**

The unconditional exception refers to the evidentiary capacity of hearsay evidence to be admissible into evidence designed to legislatively admit such hearsay evidence, even where one directly perceiving the facts of the case can testify. Such anecdotal evidence mainly includes: (1) the statement of the event at the time or shortly after the incident; (2) the statement of the statement of the startling event in an extremely excited or stimulated state; (3) the statement of his own state of mind, feelings, perception or physical state; (4) a statement made for medical diagnosis or treatment; (5) when the witness has experienced but cannot adequately recall, The records they made when they are still fresh;(6)records and files of daily business activities such as commerce and associations; (7) records and reports of activities or observations made by public institutions or civil servants according to their statutory duties; (8) important statistical data such as birth, death, marriage, commercial and scientific publications, marriage certificates, academic papers, inscriptions, court decisions, names, branches and reputation of character, etc.

ii. **Conditional exceptions**

A conditional exception means that hearsay evidence is taken as evidence only when a person who directly senses the facts of the case is unable or unable to appear to testify. The evidentiary competence of such hearsay evidence depends on the condition of the person who directly feels the facts of the case to testify. Hearsay evidence is not admissible if they are available and if they are not admissible. The circumstances in which the person who directly feels the facts of the case is unable to testify generally include: (1) the speaker enjoys the privilege of being exempted from testimony and refuses to testify; (2) the speaker has not the privilege of being exempted from testimony, but would rather be punished than testify. (3) the speaker is unable to appear or to testify due to death or physical or mental illness or poor health; (4) the speaker claims that the contents of the statement are unclear; (5) the speaker is unable to give notice to testify by summons or other reasonable means.

China's legislation does not explicitly stipulate the rule of hearsay evidence, but its judicial interpretation implies this meaning, which is similar to the "conditional exception". For example, China has provided that the testimony of a witness who does not appear in court without justifiable reasons, provided in writing, etc., shall not be used as the basis for determining the facts of the case. Under the following circumstances: (1) unable to appear in court due to health problems; (2) truly unable to leave special posts; (3) unable to appear in court; (4) unable to appear in court due to force majeure such as natural disasters; (5) unable to appear in court for other justifiable reasons, they may submit written testimony or audio-visual materials or testify through audio-visual transmission technology.

In our country, although the judicial interpretation stipulates the exception to the hearsay evidence rule, the exception becomes the norm in practice and becomes an additional condition exception.

8.3.3 The Significance of the Hearsay Evidence Rule

The anecdotal evidence rule was first established in Britain, which has been closely related to the British jury system, and can also be said to be the direct product of the litigant trial model. Therefore, this rule is the most characteristic in the Anglo-American evidence law, and its contribution to the operation of the judicial process is second only to the jury system. This rule has also been recognized by the international community. As article 14, paragraph 3, of the *International Convention on Civil and Political Rights*, provides, "In the judgment of any criminal charge against him, everyone is fully equally eligible for thc following minimum guarantees.... (E) to question or have questioned witnesses against him, and to bring witnesses against him to appear and interview on the same terms as the witnesses against him...". Article 6-3 of the *European Convention on Human Rights* provides: "Any defendant has the right to question or ask the court to incriminate witnesses and to call the same conditions as the witnesses who incriminate him." The hearsay evidence rule has the following meaning.

8.3.3.1 It is Conducive to Maintaining the Authenticity of the Evidence Content

When anyone states the facts of the past, he is often influenced by his perception, memory, expression, and honesty. The human perception process is easy to produce defects. If the observed thing does not see the whole picture, they often fill in the missing points by speculation according to their past experience and state it as the observed content. The human memory is a copy of everything that happened in the past according to their own subjective, which is easy to produce "imaginary memory"; the human expression may distort the facts due to their own factors or external influence. Witness perception, memory, expression, and language factors such as fuzzy is the weakness of the testimony as a witness, the witness in court in the past, the flaws in the inevitable, if after another reference equivalent to add an unreliable factor, in a sense is equal to increasing the possibility of deviation and error, enlarge the possibility of the original flaws, make people unbelievable is true. The hearsay evidence rule has the function of excluding such evidence, so as to maintain the authenticity of the evidence content, and achieve the purpose of using the evidence to find the truth.

8.3.3.2 It is Conducive to Protecting the Procedural Rights of the Parties Concerned

The modernization and rationalization of litigation and the protection of procedural human rights have led to the revolution of legitimacy of procedure. The control procedure of the testimony of witnesses and the right of the parties to cross-examine the witnesses have become an important part of due process. Modern law regards the "right of cross-examination" as the basic procedural right of the parties concerned, and some countries elevate it as a constitutional right. The significance of the hearsay evidence rule is no longer only to guarantee the authenticity of the evidence, far beyond the significance of guaranteeing its truth, and has the function of guaranteeing the realization of the parties' rights of the constitutional nature.

8.3.3.3 The Judicial Principle that is Conducive to the Implementation of Direct Speech

The rule of hearsay evidence originated from the law of evidence that reminds the jury in the western jury system. Because the witness is not directly in the courtroom, it is difficult for the jury to be aware of the state of the subject of the statement made outside the court, whether the subject of the original statement has clear memory. If the jury uses hearsay evidence, it will nullify the principle of direct and oral trial and violate the requirement that judges should personally experience the evidence. The judge needs to observe the appearance of the witnesses through court investigation and other procedures, and experience their attitude, expression, posture and other factors. Only in this way can he judge the reliability of the witnesses' testimony and judge its authenticity by comparing it with other evidence. Only the adoption of anecdotal evidence rules can ensure that these goals are effectively achieved.

8.4 Exclusionary Rules of Illegal Evidence

The rule of the exclusion of illegally obtained evidence has a history of nearly 100 years, originating in the United States and evolving over time. After being refined through judicial precedents, rational reflection, and ongoing struggles for rights, this rule has gradually been acknowledged and accepted by various countries. In facing the value choices of objective truth, procedural justice, and human rights protection, countries have developed similar rules regarding the probative value of illegally obtained evidence and whether it can serve as a basis for a decision, holding similar attitudes in certain respects. China has established a relatively comprehensive rule for the exclusion of illegally obtained evidence.

8.4.1 Concept and Characteristics of Illegal Evidence

Illegal evidence has the broad sense and the narrow sense. Broadly speaking, the reason why illegal evidence is illegal is the illegal evidence formed by the subject of collecting or providing evidence, the content of evidence, the form of evidence, the procedures and methods of collecting evidence or providing evidence. In a narrow sense, the illegal evidence is due to the illegal evidence collected by the case handling organs and their personnel in violation of legal procedures or by using improper methods. Illegal evidence generally refers to the latter, that is, illegal evidence obtained in violation of legal procedures or by using illegal methods or means. For some flawed evidence or formally illegal evidence is not illegal evidence mentioned in the illegal evidence exclusion rule. Illegal evidence is illegal, but not illegal evidence is illegal evidence. Especially if the procedure is illegal or the verbal evidence does not meet the legal form requirements due to defects, it can be solved through the way of supplementary evidence, without exclusion. Because the exclusion of illegal evidence is a procedural prohibition, directed against illegally obtained evidence. If there is no violation of the procedural prohibition rules in the evidence collection, which belongs to the violation of the substantive law provisions or takes the improper way of the evidence obtained, such evidence can generally be used, and will not cause the exclusion of the evidence itself.

The exclusionary rule of illegal evidence refers to the evidence rule that violates legal procedures or the evidence obtained by illegal means is not evidence competent and is not admissible. The exclusion rule of illegal evidence in China is only the rule of excluding the confession of criminal suspects and defendants obtained by illegal means such as extorting confessions by torture and the testimony of witnesses and statements of victims obtained by illegal means such as violence and threat. In civil proceedings, methods or obtain evidence that seriously divide the legitimate rights and interests of others, violate the prohibitive provisions of the law or seriously violate public order and good customs are also excluded. In the case of evidence classification, it mostly involves illegal words, including material evidence and documentary evidence that may seriously affect judicial justice and cannot be corrected or given a reasonable explanation. The exclusion rule of illegal evidence confirms the illegal and no evidence ability has the following characteristics.

8.4.1.1 The Subject of the Rule of Exclusion of Illegally Obtained Evidence is Judicial Conduct

The rule of the exclusion of illegally obtained evidence generally applies only to judicial procedures abroad and is not typically applied in investigation or prosecution procedures. This is related to the trial-centered approach in foreign legal systems. For example, Article 191 of the *Italian Code of Criminal Procedure* stipulates: "Evidence obtained in violation of legal prohibitions shall not be used, and its inadmissibility may be pointed out at any stage or level of the proceedings." "Violations of the exclusion rule may serve as grounds for appeal at any stage or level of the procedure."

Due to the differences in the legal status of prosecutorial bodies in China and foreign countries, the Chinese procuratorate, in addition to being the public prosecutor, also serves as the national legal supervisory body, responsible for overseeing investigation and trial activities. Under certain conditions, the exclusion of illegally obtained evidence also applies in the investigation and prosecution stages in China. For example, the *Criminal Procedure Law of China* states: "Confessions obtained through illegal methods, such as torture, and witness testimony or victim statements obtained through violence or threats, must be excluded. If physical evidence or documentary evidence is collected in violation of legal procedures and could seriously affect judicial fairness, it must be corrected or reasonably explained; if correction or explanation is not possible, the evidence must be excluded."

8.4.1.2 The Exclusionary Rules of Illegal Evidence Shall Only Apply to the Evidence Illegally Collected by the Case Handling Organs and Their Staff

One of the purposes of the exclusionary rule of illegal evidence is to curb the abuse of power by the case handling organs and their staff, including civil servants abetting, instructing or helping private individuals to violate legal procedures. Such as the "silver disk theory" of the United States. Evidence illegally collected by private persons generally does not apply this rule. However, the evidence collected that seriously infringes on the legitimate rights and interests of others is also prohibited. Such as privately or secretly invading other people's residences or other people's private lives to steal the relevant material evidence or documentary evidence, privately intercepting other people's letters, etc.

8.4.1.3 The Exclusionary Rules of Illegal Evidence Are Limited to Evidence Collected in Violation of Legal Procedures or by Using Illegal Methods

The exclusionary rule of illegal evidence is a restriction on illegal evidence collection. The restrictions vary in different countries and in the context of the rule of law. The United States has thoroughly implemented the exclusionary rule of illegal evidence, and also established "the fruit of poisonous tree" theory, which extends the exclusion of illegal evidence to the consequences of evidence obtained from illegal evidence. "The fruit of poisonous tree" is the evidence collected by illegal methods as the poisonous tree, the other evidence collected by these illegal methods as clues as the fruit of poisonous tree, and exclude the application of the fruit of poisonous tree. The selection of such evidence by some States is generally authorized by the judge, at his discretion. In Germany, the "illegal evidence exclusion rule" usually refers to the "prohibition of the use of non-autonomous evidence" (unselbstversta ndige Beweisverwertungsverbote), which is the prohibition of the right of investigation or investigation in the collection of evidence or illegal acts in criminal proceedings. Germany's "evidence ban" includes an "evidence acquisition ban" and an "evidence use ban".

Generally speaking, the illegal evidence exclusion rule mainly suppresses the infringement of public power on private rights, and its value basis lies in restricting the power of the state and preventing the power of the state from infringing on the constitutional rights of citizens. The collection of evidence in civil litigation generally does not involve the issue of public power, and this rule does not apply. However, the collection of a serious violation of public ethics or public order and good customs evidence, such as without the consent of others or without breaking into the private domain of others to take photos, evidence involving the acquisition of citizens' constitutional rights shall also be excluded and applicable.

This rule is generally applicable to the case handling organs and their staff who infringe upon the basic rights of citizens in the legal procedures. Germany's "prohibition of the use of autonomy" refers to the fact that the process of obtaining evidence by the case handling authorities is not illegal, but the court forbids the use of this evidence based on the higher value and purpose of the Constitution. Such as the private secret recording case in 1960, the federal German Supreme Court decided in the case of another secret recording, due to serious infringement of personality rights and human dignity belongs to major illegal, although the state organs' evidence is not illegal, but the use of the evidence itself is enough to constitute another new, independent behavior, so refused to use this evidence.

The exclusion rule of evidence is different from the exclusion rule of illegal evidence, which is divided into external exclusion rule and internal exclusion rule. Among them, the external exclusion rule is shared by the British and American law countries and the mainland law countries, while the internal exclusion rule is unique to the British and American law countries. The former is "an exclusion rule established to improve the accuracy of fact determination" and "the latter rule excluding proving information for many values unrelated to the pursuit of truth".

8.4.2 Application of the Exclusionary Rule of Illegal Evidence

Whether the illegally obtained evidence can be put forward as evidence in court and whether it can be used as the basis for determining the facts of the case is the most likely value conflict in the litigation. Value conflict leads to the choice of value, and the choice of value needs to be judged based on the interest balance. If we focus on due process of law and the legitimate rights and interests of the parties and other participants in the proceedings, the evidence ability of the illegally obtained evidence should be denied; if based on the discovery of the truth and the realization of the entity, the evidence ability should be affirmed. On the problem of illegal evidence, no matter what choice is made, it will inevitably pay some price or sacrifice some interests. The exclusion of illegal evidence is a matter of value choice. The general rule is: in principle, exclude applicable, do not exclude under specific conditions.

8.4.2.1 Application of the Exclusionary Rule of Illegal Evidence

The application of the exclusionary rule of illegal evidence is different because of the different categories of evidence. These differences are mainly reflected in the exclusion and application of verbal evidence and physical evidence.

i. **The exclusion of evidence of illegal words applies**

The collection of evidence of illegal words will generally cause a great violation of personal rights or personal dignity, and is prohibited by the constitutions of various countries. Such evidence will generally be excluded and applied, forming the so-called absolute rule of exclusion.

The main reasons for the exclusion of illegal speech evidence are as follows: a. such illegal evidence infringes on the basic rights stipulated in the constitution and is unconstitutional behavior, and is excluded by all countries around the world. b. the speech evidence obtained by illegal means is extremely false, easy to cause the misidentification of facts, and often does not have the characteristic of "defective in form but substantially true". c. there are certain requirements in the international community. As article 15 of the *United Nations Convention on Torture and Other Cruel, Inhuman or Degrading Treatment or Punishment* provides, "Each state party shall ensure that any confession determined to be based on torture."

In addition to the evidence collected by illegal methods such as extorting confessions by torture, China also excluded the confessions made against their will by the threat of violence or serious damage to the legitimate rights and interests of themselves and their close relatives. Any confession of a criminal suspect or defendant collected by illegal restriction of personal freedom, such as illegal detention shall be excluded. Using the method of extorting the confession by torture to make the confession, and then the repeated confession made by the suspect or defendant and the same as the confession shall be excluded together, except in the following circumstances:

a. During the period of investigation, according to the accusation, report or discovery, the investigation organ confirms or cannot exclude the change of investigators, and the other investigators inform the litigation rights and the legal consequences of his confession, and the criminal suspect voluntarily confesses;
b. during the period of the examination, examination and trial, the criminal suspect or defendant voluntarily confesses.

In addition, the evidence of illegal words is strictly prohibited because the evidence may also be recollected, which has the characteristics of repeated collection.

ii. **The exclusion of illegal physical evidence applies**

The exclusionary rule of illegal physical evidence refers to the rule that the physical evidence obtained by the case handling organ and its staff violates legal procedures or takes illegal methods when using search and seizure, and reaches a certain degree of harm and does not meet the exceptional conditions does not have the ability of evidence. In general, the illegal physical evidence adopts the exclusionary rule in principle.

In addition to considering the exclusion of illegal physical evidence, the social security situation and the severity of the case, the law gives the judge the discretion to decide the exclusion according to the specific circumstances. The law, to avoid the arbitrariness of the judge, establishes some exceptions to this rule. The exclusion of illegal evidence can infringe upon "serious benefits of law" as a measure of measure. In criminal cases, and referring to the illegal behavior against the legal degree of subjective intention, objective plot, the weight of the rights and interests of the infringer, the defendant the litigation defense interests, the harm of crime, prohibit the use of the evidence to curb illegal collection effect and investigation organs such as in accordance with legal procedures found the measure of the inevitability of the evidence, judging from the human rights protection and the maintenance of social security. If the acquisition of material evidence or documentary evidence obviously violates the provisions of the law and may affect the fair procedure, it shall be corrected or given a reasonable explanation; otherwise, the material evidence or documentary evidence cannot be used as the basis for deciding the case.

There is also the exclusion of illegal physical evidence in civil litigation. For example, the *Italian Civil Procedure Law* stipulates that one party has obtained from the other party by illegal means and belongs to the other party. China restricts the evidence formed or obtained by seriously infringing upon the legitimate rights and interests of others, violating the prohibitive provisions of the law or seriously violating public order and good customs. The violations of public order and good customs mainly include: violations of human relations; violation of justice; distress of others without experience; extreme restriction of personal freedom; disposal of basic property for survival; and significant acts of prosperity.

8.4.2.2 Exceptions to the Exclusionary Rule of Illegal Evidence

The exception to the exclusionary rule of illegal evidence means that, the exclusionary rule applies as evidence special rules. These exceptions are mainly included abroad (mainly in the United States), including: a. with the exception of grand jury trials. The illegal evidence exclusionary rule does not apply to a grand jury trial because it is an act prior to the bench trial and does not involve a final conviction of the defendant. b. The good-faith exception. A good faith exception is evidence that the subject of the evidence collection was illegally obtained in good faith and reasonably based on or is not intentionally obtained. c. Exceptions to impeachment evidence. Evidence to rebut a witness is a contradiction against the statements of the defendant or the witness, or the contradiction between the physical evidence and the statements of the defendant or the witness weakens the credibility of the defendant or the witness and makes the court distrust the evidence. Some illegally obtained evidence can be used in court to refute the defendant or the witness, and such impeachment evidence used to refute the witness (the defendant) can be used as an exception. d. the exception to private and illegal collection. The exclusionary rule of illegal evidence does not apply to "private searches."

In judicial practice and in theory, it is generally believed that the following circumstances can be taken as exceptions: a. the exclusion of illegal evidence that may endanger the major interests of the state, if the state security and sovereignty are unified; b. the evidence collection is illegal without involving the personal rights of citizens, or a significantly minor infringement of citizens' personal rights, Its exclusion is not conducive to the maintenance of normal social order; c. the evidence is obtained in a way of infringing upon the legitimate rights and interests of the parties concerned. However, the parties agree; d. the illegal evidence. e. other circumstances that should be adopted based on integrating various factors.

For the case handling personnel out of negligence or emergency, the lack of or failure to perform some specific legal procedures in the form of illegal evidence, only formally flawed evidence (such as no signature, seal, etc.), is not illegal evidence in the true sense.

In addition, there are exceptions to "the fruit of poisonous trees" abroad. These exceptions mainly include the "independent source", "inevitable discovery", and "pollution interruption" exceptions.

8.4.3 The Significance of the Exclusion Rule of Illegal Evidence

The core of the illegal evidence exclusion rule is to solve the evidence ability of evidence, aiming to maintain the authenticity of evidence while fully protecting human rights, and promote the litigation activities to be carried out strictly in accordance with the law. Although the establishment of illegal evidence exclusion may cause some damage to the interests of the society and the interests of the parties, it is conducive to preventing the social interests and the rights of every citizen of the society from the abuse of power, and is more in line with the general interests of the protection of rights. The establishment and application of this rule is of particular importance.

8.4.3.1 For the Case Handling Organs and Their Staff to Conduct Their Activities in Strict Accordance with the Provisions of the Law

Illegal evidence exclusion rules can effectively stop the handling authority's illegal forensics behavior, also conducive to citizens, legal persons or other organizations supervision and law enforcement agencies, the law enforcement authorities to investigate or collect evidence, citizens, legal persons or other groups, have the right to refuse, and in the later proceedings, can supervise the consequences of authorities and its staff in accordance with the legal procedures.

8.4.3.2 It is Conducive to Completely Correcting Illegal Acts and Preventing or Reducing Unjust, False and Erroneous Cases

In practice, one of the reasons for unjust, false and wrong cases is related to the illegal evidence collection of case handling personnel, and the exclusion rules of illegal evidence. There is the possibility of indulging in some illegal crimes, but it can guarantee the voluntariness of the verbal evidence to the greatest extent and safeguard the procedural interests of the parties. The rule of illegal evidence is an inevitable requirement to protect citizens 'rights, and also an important measure to effectively protect citizens' rights and effectively curb illegal acts.

8.4.3.3 It is Conducive to Effectively Protecting the Rights of the Participants in the Litigation

The illegal evidence exclusion rules can promote the case handling organs and their staff to change the concept of the rule of law. Whether the exclusion rule of illegal evidence is established in litigation activities is a question of value balance. If the illegally obtained evidence is allowed as final evidence, although it is beneficial to identify the true situation of a specific case, it is at the expense of destroying the order established by the state law and violating the basic rights of citizens. The establishment of the illegal evidence exclusion rule is a sign of a country's civilization level, and also the guarantee rule for the concept of human rights litigation.

8.5 Rules of Corroboration Evidence

The rule of corroboration evidence originated in the late eighteenth century in the United Kingdom. It later became a simple and practical rule in Anglo-American legal systems and Japan. This rule limits the probative value of specific evidence, stipulating that certain evidence can only be used as the basis for a verdict once it has been corroborated by other evidence.

8.5.1 Concept and Characteristics of the Corroboration Evidence Rule

Corroboration evidence, in contrast to substantive evidence, is a theoretical classification based on whether the evidence can play a central role in proving the facts of the case and whether one party has a guarantee or reliance on the other party. The corroboration evidence rule limits the probative value of specific evidence, aiming to restrict the discretion in accepting evidence in order to guarantee the authenticity of substantive evidence, which can then be used as the basis for a verdict.

8.5.1.1 Concept and Characteristics of Substantive Evidence

Substantive evidence, also known as "ordinary evidence," refers to evidence that, in order to prove the main facts of the case, needs to be enhanced or guaranteed to increase its probative value. Substantive evidence has the following characteristics when proving the facts of the case:

First, substantive evidence plays a key role in proving the main facts of the case. It is considered evidence with incomplete probative value, possessing the ability to prove the main facts of the case. It does not have defects, and there are no doubts about its probative value, unlike defective evidence that needs to be supplemented.

Second, based on its nature, substantive evidence, without the enhancement or guarantee of corroboration evidence, cannot prove the main facts of the case.

8.5.1.2 Concept and Characteristics of Corroboration Evidence

Corroboration evidence refers to the evidence that has the power of strengthening or guaranteeing the facts of the main evidence, and can prove the facts of the case together with the main evidence. According to the British law, corroboration evidence refers to the evidence that supports and confirms the accuracy of other evidence in important matters. "Supporting evidence means that the evidence to enhance or guarantee the supporting power of the principal evidence is not necessary for the independent evidence; that is, the principal evidence is proved without necessity, without direct evidence, including circumstantial evidence."[2]

Corroboration evidence plays the role of supporting, confirming or enhancing and guaranteeing the main evidence, which directly affects the proving power of the main evidence. Corroboration evidence has the following characteristics.

i. **Corroboration evidence is evidence with independent sources**

Corroboration Evidence is evidence that has an independent source, differing from the substantive evidence, and is not subordinate to the substantive evidence. In the case of Baskerville, Judge Reading held that, in the strictest sense, corroboration evidence must meet five elements: relevance, admissibility, credibility, independence, and implication with the defendant. Therefore, corroboration evidence cannot be the product or replica of the substantive evidence that requires reinforcement. For example, a witness's two testimonies cannot be used to corroborate each other.

ii. **Corroboration evidence has the function of proving the facts of the case**

Corroboration evidence, in comparison to substantive evidence, has its own characteristics in terms of position, role, focus of proof, and function. On one hand, it can not only prove the case facts, but may also overlap or intersect with the focus, direction, and object of proof of the substantive evidence in certain aspects or to some extent. Furthermore, it both proves the case facts and strengthens the probative value of the substantive evidence. Generally speaking, corroboration evidence does not directly prove the main facts of the case, unlike substantive evidence, whose direction of proof directly points to the main facts of the case. It is generally considered indirect evidence.

---

[2] Chen (1979).

8.5.2 *Application of the Rule of Reinforcing Evidence*

The corroboration evidence rule refers to a regulation that specific types of evidence, which may have a significant degree of relevance, cannot be used alone as the basis for determining case facts. They can only serve as the basis for a decision when supported or corroborated by other evidence. The corroboration evidence rule is related to a certain quantity of evidence, but unlike the "quantity rule," it is more about the "quality rule" of proof. A rule similar to the corroboration evidence rule is the "residual rule," but it is not in itself a residual rule.

8.5.2.1 Application of the Corroboration Evidence Rule Abroad

The corroboration evidence rule abroad is generally applied to the reinforcement of testimonial evidence and can be divided into two types: the rule for corroborating confessions and the rule for corroborating witness testimony.

i. **The rule for corroborating confessions**

The evidentiary strength of confessions obtained by legal means is used to establish the corroboration evidence rule and enhance its probative value. Countries like Japan and Russia have mandatory corroboration provisions for confession evidence. For example, the Japanese Criminal Procedure Law states: "If the defendant's confession is the only evidence against him, regardless of whether the confession was made during the trial, it cannot be used to establish guilt." China, following the tradition of civil law countries, has adopted a legally mandated corroboration rule for confessions.

American scholars of evidence law argue that corroborating evidence for confessions should independently prove the "main criminal facts" or "substantive crime" and form an independent corroborative (supporting) confession rule. The facts of a criminal prosecution include: (1) the existence of a crime committed by the defendant; (2) the fact that the crime was caused by someone's criminal act; (3) the defendant is the person who committed the crime. The main criminal facts only include the first two parts of the criminal prosecution facts. The fact that the defendant is the perpetrator of the crime, i.e., "the defendant and the perpetrator are the same," does not require corroboration. In practical terms, independent corroborating evidence of the main criminal facts helps confirm the reliability of the confession evidence and achieves "substantial independent corroborative evidence that aids in establishing the reliability of the evidence."[3] The rules for corroborating confessions designed by U.S. and Japanese scholars of evidence law are essentially the same, with the view that corroborative evidence for confessions should relate to the main facts of the crime, not only ensuring the truthfulness of the confession but also enhancing its probative power. Such corroborative evidence must have evidentiary value and contribute to proving the facts of the case. The consensus in Japanese legal scholarship is that a confession, regarding the "corpus delicti" (the objective elements of

---

[3] Waltz (1993).

the crime), should be corroborated. The corroborative evidence and the confession evidence should be identical, jointly forming the basis for determining the facts. Confessions require corroboration in the following cases:·(1) The determination of criminal facts must be corroborated. (2) The objective elements of the crime must be corroborated. (3) The identity of the defendant with the perpetrator in the crime does not require corroboration. (4) The subjective elements in the crime, such as intent, do not require corroboration. (5) Facts unrelated to criminal matters do not require corroboration. (6) Facts relating to non-criminal elements, such as the absence of justifications for the crime, do not require corroboration.

ii. **The rule for corroborating witness testimony**

The concept of corroborating witness testimony can be traced back to the ninth century in England, with the "Anglo-Saxon law" and the "Oath-helper" oath. The oath-helper's testimony was used to strengthen the credibility of the witness, but it did not directly address the disputed facts of the case.[4] These "Oath-helpers" might have been completely unaware of the facts in dispute, testifying only to the character of the party involved. This type of testimony was meant to enhance the party's credibility, influencing the judge's acceptance of their statements, rather than proving the facts of the case, and thus served as "supporting evidence."

In the Anglo-American legal system, there are different rules for corroborating witness testimony, and different rules are applied depending on the type of testimony.

a. Mandatory Corroboration Rules for Specific Witness Testimonies: Certain testimonies are considered to be "easily fabricated but difficult to refute," and therefore require mandatory corroboration. This is the case for testimonies in crimes like perjury or treason.
b. The supplementary rule of perceptual opinion testimony of witnesses. Perceptional witness testimony refers to speculative opinions made by the witness based on perceptual experiences such as facts or special knowledge. As in the testimony of witnesses about speed. This testimony is capable of evidence, "if it is used as a way to express the relevant facts that he has personally perceived, it can be used as evidence of the facts perceived by him."[5] These opinion evidence with the ability of evidence belongs to the synthesis of witnesses' perception and experience, and is easy to produce errors and errors. Its proving force should be limited. Only through reinforcement can its proving force be restored.
c. The procedural reinforcing warning rules of witness testimony. This procedural reinforcement is not directed to a particular case, but rather to a particular range of witnesses. It generally includes the depositions of children. For this kind of reinforcement only has the function of reminder on the program. If the judge does not make such a reminder, the jury judges against the defendant and becomes

[4] "Help the oath person" of the oath is: "I swear before God, he (the plaintiff or the defendant) of the oath is clean and true." On this oath, we find that it only enhances the credibility of the defendant's statement, does not prove the facts of the case, and does not have the meaning of reinforcing the evidence in a real sense.

[5] See also provisions, article 3, paragraph 2, of the British Code of Civil Procedure of 1972.

one of the reasons for appeal, and the appellate court may reverse its judgment for violation of proceedings.

d. Discretionary corroboration rules for witness testimony. The law does not specifically mandate either substantive or procedural corroboration. Whether corroboration is required is left to the discretion of the judge. The judge decides which type of corroboration (substantive or procedural) to apply based on the specifics of the case, the disputed facts, as well as the content, quality, and credibility of the witness testimony.

8.5.2.2 The Application of China's Reinforcing Evidence Rules

According to the provisions of China's procedural law and judicial interpretation on the rules of strengthening evidence, the rules apply as follows.

i. **Rules of reinforcing evidence in criminal proceedings**

Reinforcement rule for defendant's confession. China's Criminal Procedure Law stipulates: "Only the defendant's confession, if there is no other evidence, can the defendant not be found guilty and punished." According to the provisions of this article, the case only exists on the defendant's confession such evidence, there must be other evidence to strengthen it, otherwise the defendant's confession does not have the proof power of evidence.

ii. **Rules of reinforcing evidence in civil litigation and administrative litigation**

China's civil procedure law and judicial interpretation stipulate the rules of strengthening evidence. *China's Civil Procedure Law* stipulates: "The people's court shall distinguish the authenticity of audio-visual materials, and examine and determine whether the facts can be used as the basis of the case." The people's court shall, in the statement of the parties, examine and determine whether it can be determined as the basis of other evidence in the case. In judicial practice, the following evidence shall not be used as the basis for determining the facts of the case: a. testimony taken by a minor that is not commensurate with his age and intellectual status; b. testimony favorable to the party taken by a witness who is related or otherwise close to a party, or testimony taken by a witness adverse to a party; c. testimony of witnesses who should testify in court without justifiable reasons; d. audio-visual materials that are difficult to identify; e. copies or copies that cannot be checked with the original and the original substance. These above evidence can not prove the facts of the case alone, and there is no complete proof force, and other evidence is needed for mandatory reinforcement. However, the second item is to strengthen the ability of evidence, which is different from the original intention of the reinforcing evidence rules.

(i) The reinforcing rule of minor testimony. Due to the reasons of intelligence and development, the understanding of some things may be overgeneralization or sudden fantasy. Due to the uneven development degree, intelligence level and understanding ability of minors of the same age, they cannot make unified requirements or evaluation only by their age. The testimony of minors should also be limited in its application, and other evidence should be strengthened before it can be used as the basis for deciding the case.

(ii) Rules for reinforcing the testimony of witnesses who have kinship or other close relations with the parties. The testimony of a witness who has a kinship or other close relationship with the party mainly includes the testimony favorable to the party made by a witness who has a kinship or other close relationship and the testimony unfavorable to a witness who has an adverse relationship with the party. Other closely related witnesses such as employee and employer testify to collect debt. Because these witnesses have a specific relationship with the parties, according to the rule of "interests are involved", their proving power should be appropriately restricted, and the testimony of the witnesses provided by the parties themselves who have kinship, close relationship or other interests with the parties should be strengthened.

(iii) The reinforcing rules for the testimony of witnesses who fail to testify in court without justifiable reasons. When a witness testifies, he shall fully fulfill his duty of testifying in court and accept the questioning of the parties, so that the judge can judge from them the truth of his testimony. Because the testimony of a witness who has not testified in court has not been fully questioned by the parties, its authenticity is difficult to guarantee, which cannot be used as the basis for determining the facts of the case alone. Only when the facts of the case can be proved through reinforcement.

In addition, it also involves the reinforcement of audio-visual materials, reproduction and its reproduction problems. In essence, this evidence needs to be combined with other evidence to determine whether it can be used as the basis for determining the facts of the case, but it is not mainly a matter of strengthening, reflecting the significance of true authentication, nor strengthening in the essential sense.

8.5.3 Significance of the Corroboration Evidence Rule

The corroboration evidence rule helps parties clarify which evidence needs to be corroborated. Once evidence is provided that cannot be used on its own as the basis for determining the facts of a case, it is still necessary to actively provide additional evidence to strengthen the probative value of the previously submitted evidence. By promptly fulfilling the corroboration obligation, the party ensures that their claimed facts are confirmed and their legitimate rights and interests are protected.

The corroboration evidence rule also helps judges reasonably confirm the parties' proof rules, while limiting the discretion judges have in evaluating the probative value of evidence to some extent. By legally clarifying the incompleteness of the probative value of certain evidence, the rule requires parties to supplement with corroborative evidence, ensuring that the truth of the case facts is fully revealed. At the same time, it can also limit the judge's certification rules, ensuring the fairness of the litigation.

8.6 The Rules of Best Evidence

.The Best Evidence Rule originates from the ancient English "trial by charter" and is one of the oldest evidence rules in English common law. It is a rule used in judicial practice to determine the probative value of different types of evidence when they are applied.

8.6.1 The Concept and Characteristics of the Best Evidence Rule

The rules of best evidence, also known as the original writing rule, refers to the rule that the facts of a particular case can only be proved by the most convincing and convincing relevant evidence that can be found. "It is now the law of evidence tolerance of the contents of the instrument, which requires the original proposal of the document, and if the original cannot be made until a satisfactory explanation, then other evidence shall be rejected."[6]

The best evidence rules mainly apply to the evidence rules of written materials or documentary evidence. This rule includes three aspects: the first is the provision of the original document; the second is the production process of the document by the supporting witness; and the oral testimony cannot be changed or amended. These contents have gradually developed into the best evidence rules for documentary evidence. In Herzig v. Sweet Co., the 1945 Circuit said: "The best evidence rule in its modern application refers only to the rule that the content of a written material must be proved by the introduction of the instrument itself, unless a compelling reason is made for the absence of the original instrument." The jurist Thayer defines the best evidence rule as, to prove the content of the document, the original of the document is the first evidence, unless the reason for not providing the original is reasonably explained, otherwise the second evidence is not admissible.

The application of the best evidence rules should generally meet the following conditions: a. the evidence of the best evidence rules should belong to the written materials. This written material is generally recorded in letters, messages, contracts, maps, photographs, magnetic pulses, mechanical or electronic recordings, or other forms of data compilation. b. The written materials of the best evidence rules shall take the recorded content as the method of proof. If the written material is not the content recorded as the method of proof, or the content recorded in the written material has nothing to do with the facts of the case, or is not to prove the facts of the case, the best evidence rule shall not apply.

With the development of society, the best evidence rules in the British-American law system are developing continuously, and its scope of application is not only limited to written materials, but also includes sound recording, photography, ordinary

[6] Morgan (1982).

photography, ray film, video tape and film. For example, Article 1001 (3) of the *Federal Rules of Evidence* stipulates that "original" means "the 'original' of the text or recording, that is, the text or the recording material itself, or by the producer or issuer has the same effect as the original. The 'original' of the photograph includes the negative or any film printed by the negative. If data in a computer is stored in a computer or a similar device books that accurately reflect the data are 'original'".

8.6.2 Application Rules for the Best Evidence

The applicable rule of the best evidence refers to the rule of confirming the size of the proof force between several evidence when it has the proving force against the same fact and different evidence proves the opposite fact claim. Among them, several evidence includes both several evidence of the same type and several evidence of different types of evidence.

8.6.2.1 Application Rules of the Best Evidence Rules

The Best Evidence Rule—actually a set of rules—imposes an additional burden on the providers of "written documents," "recordings," and "images." This rule helps prevent the submission of tampered copies and the withholding of original documents.[7] According to judicial interpretation, the application of the best evidence rule is as follows.

i. **The best evidence rule for public documents**

Public documents made by state organs and specific public officials within the scope of their functions and duties and in accordance with certain procedures and rules are generally presumed to be true. For the private document certificate, its authenticity shall be proved by the provider. In China, state organs refer to various organs that exercise state functions, generally party organs and power organs, administrative organs, supervisory organs, supervisory organs, judicial organs, procuratorial organs, and the internal organs and dispatched offices of the military and state organs. According to the provisions of Chin's "Official Document Processing Measures of State Administrative Organs", official documents include relevant orders, instructions, resolutions, decisions, announcements, announcements, notices, notices, notices, reports, instructions, replies, letters, meeting minutes and other documents. But the state organ is not because the official act is not a public document.

Official documents produced and issued by state organs shall generally meet the legal conditions and be made in accordance with strict legal procedures within the scope of authority or within the scope of affairs clearly granted by law. They shall have strong standardization and have superior certification power than other documentary

[7] Allen et al. (2006).

evidence. There are also corresponding regulations abroad. For example, according to the *German Code of Civil Procedure*, official documents can be deemed to be certificates made by officials or people with public trust authority in both form and content, which are presumed to be true in themselves. The reasons for applying the best evidence rule to document evidence are as follows: a. document documents are objective. The production and completion of official documents are generally outside of litigation, not for litigation, with objectivity. b. Official documents have legal authority. The production organ of official documents is the state organ and other functional departments, which is the embodiment of the will of the unit or the state, and has strong credibility. c. Official documents have strong standardization.

ii. **The best evidence rule for the original object of documentary evidence and the original object of material evidence**

Material evidence has a strong stability, timely extraction and proper fixation and preservation, generally will not change. The documentary evidence is formed before the commencement of the lawsuit, and generally has a strong authenticity. Due to the development of modern science and technology, the copy of forgery, alteration and imitation evidence by copying, computer synthesis and production is quite acceptable.

The original of documentary evidence and the original material of material evidence can exclude the problem of forgery, alteration or imitation of evidence. The original of documentary evidence and the original of material evidence are better than copies and copies.[8] If the collection, the transfer of the documentary evidence should be the original. A copy or copy may only be used if it is difficult to obtain the original. The material evidence collected and retrieved shall be the original object. Only when it is not easy to carry or keep the original object, or when it should be returned to the victim according to law, photos and videos sufficient to reflect the appearance or content of the original object may be taken.

iii. **The best evidence rules for notarized or registered documentary evidence**

Legal acts, legal facts and documents proved by notarization refer to the certificates made by the notary organ of the authenticity and legality of certain acts and facts and documents with legal significance according to the application of the parties concerned. The laws of all countries give strong evidence to the legal acts, legal facts and documents. The notarial certificate in China belongs to the act of state certification, and the notarial documents made by the notarial organs in accordance with the relevant legal acts, legal facts and documents in accordance with strict legal procedures generally have authenticity. Article 69 of the *Civil Procedure Law*

---

[8] For the issue of original documents, can refer to the standing committee of the National People's Congress on August 28, 2004 by the electronic signature law article 5 provisions: "the data that meet the following conditions, as to meet the requirements of laws and regulations: (a) can effectively show the content and available for access; (2) can reliably ensure that since the beginning of the final form, the content is intact, unchanged. However, the addition of endorsement to the data message and changes in the form of data exchange, storage and display do not affect the integrity of the data message."

stipulates: "The people's court shall take the notarization of the proof for legal acts, legal matters and documents as the basis for the confirmation of facts, except where evidence to the contrary is sufficient to overturn the notarial proof." If the other party provides evidence to the contrary, the court shall examine it. If there is no evidence sufficient to overturn the notarial certificate, the court shall confirm the proving power of the notarial certificate document.

The registered documentary evidence refers to the documentary evidence that the legal organ has gone through the registration formalities. If prove the marriage certificate that marriage relation is established, the building property right card of ownership person, land uses authority card to wait. The registered documentary evidence has a high social credibility, so it is presumed to have a strong proof power in the lawsuit.[9]

iv. **The best evidence rule for original evidence and transmitted evidence**

The original evidence is directly related to the facts of the case, and it has not been changed hands or copied, and its authenticity is relatively great. The transmitted evidence is derived from the original evidence or other transmitted evidence, which can be regarded as the original evidence through changing hands, copying, copying, etc. Because the connection with the facts of the case is not as close as the original evidence, there are many intermediate links, the possibility of error is greater, not as reliable as the original evidence. Therefore, the proof power of the original evidence is better than the incoming evidence.

v. **The best evidence rule for direct evidence and circumstantial evidence**

Direct evidence has a direct relationship with the main facts of the case and can directly prove the main facts without the need for other evidence. The application of direct evidence to prove the main facts of the case is relatively simple; as long as the evidence itself is verified as truthful, the main facts can be established. In contrast, indirect evidence is more complex in proving the main facts of the case, as it requires many intermediate steps and inferential processes. Therefore, direct evidence holds an advantage over indirect evidence.

vi. **The best evidence rule for witness testimony**

As a kind of verbal evidence, the witness testimony is easily influenced by the witness himself. In particular, if the witness has kinship or other close relationship with the party, he generally consciously or unconsciously, more or less makes statements in favor of and inclined to the party, and avoids problems unfavorable to the party, and cannot truly, comprehensively and objectively reflect the facts of the case. The testimony of the witness in court or the testimony of the friendship relationship

---

[9] Such as the Supreme People's Court in the Zhou Weihong and Zhou Weihua housing dispute case how to deal with the problem of reply "pointed out: the case of the parties 179 house bought in 1947, buy the deed is Zhou Weihui (Zhou Weihong) name, Kunming municipal people's government in 1953, still in the name of Zhou Weihong registration, and has been used by Zhou Weihong management. In the process of litigation, Zhou Weihua could not cite strong evidence to prove his property right claim. Accordingly, the 179 house should be owned by Zhou Weihong."

with the party is relatively objective and will not intentionally avoid the problem unfavorable or favorable to the parties. Therefore, the testimony provided by the witness that is favorable to the parties who have relatives or other close relations is generally less powerful than the testimony of other witnesses. In addition, the testimony of the witness questioned by the court can find the untrue situation, which has greater reliability compared with the written testimony outside the court.

8.6.2.2 Exceptions to the Best-Evidence Rule

The best-evidence rule prioritizes the adoption of the original. When the original or original evidence cannot be obtained, but the reasons and the authenticity can be explained, the copy or the second hand data, copy and copy can be applied as evidence. The application of such evidence falls within the exception to the best-evidence rule. According to the development of American jurisprudence and the legislative provisions, the best evidence rule has the following exceptions: i. the second hand may be adopted if the third party occupies the second hand; ii. copy admissible if third party in possession and lawful refusal to provide original instrument; iii. if the document is lost or if the document has been damaged or lost or produced, the second hand may be adopted; iv. a copy of the public record proved or sealed may be used as evidence. Photographs, video recordings or copies of material evidence, after verification with the original material, identified or otherwise confirmed by other ways, may be used as the basis for deciding the case. If a copy or copy of the documentary evidence is checked with the original, identified or otherwise confirmed as the truth, it may be used as the basis for deciding the case.

In addition, if the authenticity of the copy of the document has been confirmed by a previous court judgment or the notarial certificate of the notary office, and the other party has no doubt about the contents recorded in the copy, it can be used as evidence.

8.6.3 The Significance of the Best Evidence Rule

The best rule of evidence is not an exclusive rule of evidence, it is the rule of evidence for the judge to apply. Because there are different levels of relationship between the facts of the case to be proved, some are parallel, some are progressive, and some are cross-sectional, the best evidence rule is beneficial to determine the proving power of several evidence. At the same time, this rule can encourage the parties to provide evidence in accordance with the best evidence rules, which has the function of ensuring the authenticity of the evidence.

On the premise of guiding the use of the original evidence, especially the original evidence, the best evidence rule allows the use of derived evidence such as copies of specific circumstances or specific conditions, so as to solve the problem that the original cannot be provided and the substitute is used to determine the facts of the case. The review and judgment method of substitutes is conducive to the discovery of truth.

The best evidence rule is only to give the judge the direction of several evidence, and does not have absolute effect. If the parties can present evidence sufficient to overturn the strong proof force, then the evidence with the strong proof force cannot be taken as the final basis.

8.7 Opinion Evidence Rule

In Anglo-American evidentiary law, the opinion evidence rule is also an important evidentiary rule. In common law countries, it is generally required that witnesses testify orally in court and present facts based on their personal experience and perception. Statements of opinions or inferences cannot be admitted as evidence, except for the opinions of expert witnesses.

8.7.1 Concept and Characteristics of the Opinion Evidence Rule

The opinion evidence rule (the rule of the opinion evidence) refers to the rule that prevents a witness from offering opinions, inferences, or conclusions about facts they have directly perceived through their senses as evidence. "When a witness infers whether a disputed fact exists based on facts directly presented to their senses, it is legally termed an opinion. Statements made by the witness based on this inference are called opinion evidence."[10] The opinion evidence rule has the following characteristics.

8.7.1.1 Opinion Evidence Rule is Generally Expressed as the Opinions of Verbal Evidence

Evidence is an inference or judgmental opinion of the witness regarding the observed or perceived facts, not a description of the observed or perceived facts. This statement, due to the addition of some experience or imagination of the witness, accompanied by the analysis of the facts observed, is not a fact in itself and cannot be used as evidence to prove the facts of the case, and should apply the opinion evidence rule.

---

[10] Diao (1984), p. 259.

8.7.1.2 Opinion Evidence Rule Applies to Inferences of Facts

Opinion evidence is the judgment of the facts. Because the judge has the ability of ordinary people, the judge can also do the judgment of the facts, and it case evidence, and the accuracy of his judgment will be higher than the judgment of ordinary people on a single fact. If the witness found the defendant outside of the hotel, and stated that "he was drunk." In the witness statement, the statement "the defendant staggering" of the witness is an objective description of the fact and belongs to the witness testimony, while the statement that "he was drunk" is the opinion of the witness. The rule of opinion evidence applies to the judgment of witnesses.

8.7.1.3 Opinion Evidence Rule is an Exclusionary Rule

The opinion evidence rule is an exclusionary rule. In principle, opinion evidence cannot be accepted as evidence and does not possess evidentiary value. A witness may only testify to the facts they have directly observed or provide evidence regarding those facts. Statements provided by a witness that involve opinions, inferences, or judgments about the case cannot serve as the basis for a decision. For example, the *Australian Federal Evidence Act* of 1995 states: "Opinion evidence is not admissible to prove the existence of the fact expressed in the opinion."

Opinion evidence is different from the facts, and it is intertwined with the facts. From the process of the formation of the phenomenon and psychological impression, it seems that all the testimony of the witnesses has gone through the thinking and judgment of the witnesses, and has the tendency to opinion evidence. A statement of the same matter in the court is a fact, and the prosecution may insist it is an opinion. In practice, the courts always adopt the method of common sense and empirical judgment, excluding some evidence that is obviously an opinion. The reasons for excluding the opinion evidence are: the fact that the opinion evidence of the witness is not related to the facts of the case; the adoption of the opinion evidence violates the function of the judge, because it is his duty to judge the evidence or facts, and the judge is fully competent for this work.

Although the hearsay evidence rule and the opinion evidence rule stem from the same source, both originating from a witness's firsthand experience of facts, there are significant differences between the two. The hearsay evidence rule excludes out-of-court statements, excluding them as a method of proof; while the opinion evidence rule excludes non-factual statements, excluding them as the content of evidence.

8.7.2 Application of the Opinion Evidence Rule

The key to applying the opinion evidence rule is distinguishing between opinions and facts. The boundary between opinions and facts is largely a matter of degree and should depend solely on factual reasons. This is because, like most people, witnesses may not be aware of the extent to which their reasoning enters into their perception.[11]

8.7.2.1 Application of the Exclusionary Rule for Opinion Evidence

In Anglo-American evidentiary law, witnesses are divided into lay witnesses and expert witnesses. The opinion evidence rule mainly applies to lay witnesses, with expert witnesses being an exception to this rule. The role of an expert witness is to provide necessary information to the court to fill the knowledge gap of the judge and jury. Without the help of an expert witness, the court cannot make certain inferences, so the opinions of experts are admissible. The opinion evidence rule only applies to lay witnesses, as their opinion evidence is not directly related to the facts of the case and is generally inadmissible. Testimony that is speculative, comment-based, or inferential from lay witnesses cannot be used as evidence, except when it aligns with ordinary life experience and the judgment of the facts. This is because judges are fully capable of making guesses, comments, or inferences based on the content of the witness's testimony, their expressions, and demeanor. When combined with other evidence, these speculative, comment-based, or inferential opinions can become more reliable than those of the witness alone.

8.7.2.2 Exceptions to the Exclusionary Rule for Opinion Evidence

Although a witness's inference is not the fact itself, it is still based on the facts perceived by the witness, and the opinion is not without foundation or entirely speculative. In certain circumstances, opinion evidence can have probative value for the case, particularly when the witness provides experiential opinions based on their own observations of facts. Therefore, the opinion evidence of lay witnesses is not always excluded, and there are exceptions. For example, Richard May, a scholar of evidence law in the UK, argues that opinion evidence may not be excluded in the following cases: i. Personal impressions and the narrative of facts; ii. The witness's own condition; iii. Handwriting; iv. Evidence in terrorism-related cases.[12] As stipulated in *Federal Rules of Evidence* Rule 701 in the United States: "If the witness is not testifying as an expert, the witness's testimony in the form of opinions or inferences is limited to those situations where: (a) it is based on the witness's perception; and (b) it is helpful to clearly understanding the witness's testimony or to determining a fact in issue." Exceptions to the rule prohibiting lay witnesses from providing opinion testimony include issues such as identity, handwriting, quantity, value, weight, size, time, distance, speed, appearance, size, age, strength, temperature (hot or cold), disease, and health, as well as issues related to various mental and moral aspects of human behavior, such as character, temperament, anger, excitement, intoxication, honesty,

[11] Shen (1996).

[12] May (2007).

and general personality traits. Based on relevant provisions, judicial practice, and case law, the following are recognized exceptions to the opinion evidence rule.

i. **Evidence of opinion about someone's emotional and physical condition**

An ordinary witness may testify to a person. If someone appears angry or funny; stating the physical condition of strength, energy, weakness, illness, etc. But the relevant motive, intent, inference, or belief, is not competent in evidence.

ii. **Evidence of opinion on sound identification**

If a witness had previously spoken to a person or heard him on the telephone, he could testify that he was able to discern the person's voice. In practice, even if the witness is not familiar with or even does not know the speaker, it does not prevent him from comparing, distinguishing, and making some judgments about the sounds that he has heard and the sounds that he has heard afterwards.

iii. **Opinion evidence on the speed of a motor vehicle in motion**

An ordinary witness may testify as to the speed of a moving motor vehicle, but he must show some experience in observing the speed of moving objects or provide other reasonable reasons. If the witness's statement of the impression of the observation of the speed of the car is generally admissible.

iv. **Evidence of opinion on the witnesses' own condition**

Statements made by witnesses as to their own physical or mental condition are admissible. In addition, the speculative, critical and inferred testimony of witnesses shall not be used as evidence, except for the facts judged based on general life experience.

8.7.3 Significance of the Opinion Evidence Rule

The establishment of the opinion evidence rule provides a basis for the correct distinction between the function of witness testimony and the function of the judge's adjudication, which is conducive to the scientific and reasonable regulation of the behaviour of witnesses and judges in the law of evidence, restricts the arbitrariness of the judge's judgement on the competence of the evidence and the power of proof, and ensures the objectivity and impartiality of the judge's examination and application of the evidence. The establishment of the opinion evidence rule can safeguard the right of the parties to counter-examination through procedures, and at the same time help the judge to fully understand the statements of witnesses.

8.8 Questions and Reflections

In China, different regulations have been applied to evidence obtained through methods such as secret recording or surveillance. In practice, when the loan amount is relatively small, it is often paid in cash, and due to social considerations, the lender may not require the borrower to sign a loan contract or provide written evidence such as a promissory note, receipt, or acknowledgment of debt. Once a borrower fails to repay the loan principal and interest according to the oral agreement, the lender may face difficulties proving the existence of the loan relationship due to the lack of written evidence. In such cases, the lender often resorts to recording the borrower's admission of the loan, the loan amount, repayment terms, and agreed interest through secret recordings or video recordings without the borrower's consent. Whether evidence obtained through secret recording or surveillance should be considered illegal and excluded requires consideration of whether it constitutes a severe infringement of another person's legal rights, violates prohibitive legal provisions, or seriously contravenes public order and morals. Based on the specifics of the case and the contents of this chapter, consider the meaning of the judicial interpretations and reflect on the following questions: (1) Does the recorded evidence in this case fall under the hearsay evidence rule? (2) Should the recorded evidence be subject to the rule of excluding illegal evidence? (3) If the recorded evidence is supplemented with additional evidence, does it still apply to the exclusionary rule for such evidence? (4) If photos or videos obtained through secret recording or surveillance are posted online, and the online comments are used as supporting evidence for the factual claim, how should the photo or video and its comments be classified?

References

Diao, R. H. (ed.) (1984). Bijiao xingshi zhengjufa gelun. Taipei: Han Lin Publishing Co., Ltd.

Chen, P. S. (1979). Xingshi zhengjufa. Taipei: San Min Book Co., Ltd. (in Chinese)

Waltz, J.R. (1993). Xingshi zhengju daquan [Translation of Introduction to Criminal Evidence (3rd edn)] (He, J.H., Trans.). Beijing: Zhongguo renmin gongan daxue chubanshe (official English name not verified). (Original work published 1991).

Morgan, E. M. (1982). Zhengju fa zhi jiben wenti [Translation of Basic problems of evidence] (Li, X. D., Trans.). Taipei: The World Book Co., Ltd. (Original work published 1961).

Allen, R.J., Kuhns, R.B. and Swift, E. (2006). Zhengju fa: wenben, wenti he anli (di 3 ban) [Translation of Evidence: Text, Problems, and Cases (3rd edn)] (Zhang, B.S., Wang, J.X. and Zhao, Y., Trans.). Beijing: Higher Education Press. (Original work published 2002).

Diao Ronghua, Comparative Criminal Evidence Law, p. 259, Taipei: Xuelin Publishing House, 1984.

Shen, D.M. (1996). Yingmei zhengju fa. Beijing: CITIC Press. (in Chinese).

May, R. (2007). Xing shi zheng ju [Translation of Criminal Evidence] (Wang, L., et al., Trans.). Beijing: Law Press China.

Extended Reading

Zhang, M.W. (2016). Chuanwen liwai. Taipei: Yuanzhao Publishing. (in Chinese)
Song, Y.H. and Li, Z. (2003). Zhijie, yanci yuanze yu chuanwen zhengju guize zhi bijiao. Journal of Comparative Law, (5): 52–60. (in Chinese)
Yang, Y. G. (2002). Feifa zhengju paichu guize yanjiu. Beijing: Chinese People's Public Security University Press. (in Chinese)
Tang, W. J. (2004). Minshi susong feifa zhengju paichu guize chuyi. Law Science Magazine, (5): 95–96.
Guo, H. (2004). Kougong buqiang zhengju guize yanjiu. Journal of Gansu University of Political Science and Law, (3). (in Chinese)
Yi, Y. Y. (2011). Lun zuijia zhengju guize [The Best Evidence Rule]. Journal of Comparative Law, (6): 96–111. (in Chinese)
Wu, G. S. (2014). Lun putongren yijian zhengju de shencha yu yunyong guize. Research on Rule of Law, (10): 125–131. (in Chinese)

Part III
Proof

Chapter 9
Overview of Proof

9.1 Introductory Case

Yang worked as a designer at a construction materials company. Due to the fact that the design department was very idle when there were no projects and worked on weekends without rest when there were projects, after a dispute with the company, she calculated the total number of overtime hours she had worked that year. Including both regular overtime and weekend overtime, the total amounted to 310.5 h. She then requested the company to pay for the 310.5 h of overtime. However, the company did not agree, so she took the matter to court. The defendant company argued that Yang had only worked 285.5 h of overtime, of which 61 h were weekend overtime and 224.5 h were regular overtime. The plaintiff, Yang, had already applied for 277.5 h of compensatory time off and presented the company with her overtime and time-off application forms. The company agreed to pay for the 8 h of overtime that Yang had not taken as compensatory time off. However, Yang believed that weekend overtime should be offset by compensatory time off, but regular overtime could not be offset, and the company should pay her the full overtime wages. Additionally, she argued that the company only provided part of her overtime application forms and that there were many more that the company did not present.

9.2 Chapter Overview

This chapter covers the topic of evidence, primarily discussing the concept and characteristics of proof, as well as the distinctions between types of proof, such as explanatory proof, strict proof, and free proof, and their respective meanings in the context of evidence law. Proof is a key element of litigation activities, playing a crucial role in discovering the truth.

H. Guo, *Evidence Jurisprudence in China*, Understanding China,
https://doi.org/10.1007/978-981-95-3981-9_9

9.3 An Overview of the Proof

Proof is one of the most common cognitive activities in the social life of mankind, and it is an important category of evidence jurisprudence, as well as an important content of evidence law. Proof is the intermediate link in the identification and judgement of the truth, the soul and foundation of the whole litigation activity, and the key activity for the evidence to become the basis of the case. Evidence can prove the facts of the case, but can not automatically prove the facts of the case, it must be some subjects with the help of certain activities to the real situation of the case, these activities or processes for the proof.

9.3.1 The Concept of Proof

Proof refers to the activity of using evidence to demonstrate or establish the truth of a person, event, or thing. It can be categorized into proof in social life, proof in natural sciences, and proof in procedural law. As a concept in evidence law, proof has multiple meanings. Some scholars define it as: "When a party presents evidence that enables the court to form a firm conviction about the facts they assert, believing them to be true, this is called proof."[1] Others argue that proof refers to the internal conviction that results from evidence, or the ultimate result of the persuasive power generated by the presentation of evidence.[2] Still others define proof as the process of inferring and determining the facts of a case based on evidence. All of these concepts involve persuading others or oneself to believe in the truth of specific facts through evidence.

Proof is the activity of providing and using evidence to argue for the truth of the case facts in accordance with the law. Proof includes basic elements such as the proving party, the object of proof, the burden of proof, and the standard of proof. Proof is the process in which these elements interact.

9.3.2 Characteristics of Proof

The activity of proof differs from the logical activities people engage in when dealing with everyday matters, which can be categorized as social life proof. It is also different from the activities in natural sciences that rely purely on technical methods. Compared to these activities, proof in legal contexts has the following characteristics.

---

[1] Chen (1996).

[2] Strong (1992).

9.3.2.1 The Subject of Proof: Specific Authorities and Litigation Participants

In criminal litigation, the specific authority responsible for proof is the prosecutor's office; the litigation participants include the parties (the complainant in a private prosecution or the plaintiff in an ancillary civil suit). In civil and administrative litigation, the subjects of proof are the parties (including administrative authorities) and third parties. The law varies in terms of the scope, extent, and requirements for proof depending on the specific authority and litigation participant. In special circumstances, the subject of proof may also include the investigation authorities, criminal defendants, or the defendant in civil or administrative lawsuits. In litigation, the court, as the entity responsible for determining the facts of the case, is not the subject of proof. Witnesses and experts, who assist the judge in determining the facts of the case, are also not the subject of proof.

9.3.2.2 Proof Takes Place During Litigation

Proof is a litigation activity governed by procedural law. Whether it involves collecting or using evidence, it must be completed within the framework of legal procedures, subject to restrictions such as litigation deadlines, methods for collecting evidence, and applicable procedural rules. It differs from natural science proof, which can take place at any time and in any space. Both the means and methods of proof are restricted and must comply with legal norms in litigation. The methods of proof are limited, and the tools for proof are also bound by legal constraints.

9.3.2.3 The Purpose of the Proof is to Discover the Fact of the Case

The facts of the case have already occurred, and they are irreversible, cannot be restored, and cannot be validated through experimental methods. The existence of the facts must be confirmed by specific authorities and litigation participants through evidence. Therefore, the understanding of the true facts of the case requires proof. The degree of certainty required in evidence law differs from the unquestionable proof in natural sciences. It only requires a level of certainty that people in daily life would not doubt, and that serves as the basis for their actions.[3] However, it should not be concluded that the purpose of litigation proof is not to discover the truth. Although different cases or facts may have different proof requirements, the goal is always to discover the truth of the case.

Proof differs from clarification. Clarification typically means making oneself understand and be certain about the facts of the case, and in a certain sense, it can be called "self-proof." Proof not only requires making oneself understand the facts of the case but also requires making the adjudicator understand and be convinced of

[3] Kaneko and Takeshita (1995).

the facts. It involves both self-proof and third-party proof. In practice, it serves to connect the evidence with the facts of the accusation or claim.

9.4 Basic Category of Proof

Proof is a retrospective cognitive activity that uses evidence to infer facts that have already occurred, and evidence serves as the cornerstone of this cognitive activity. However, due to the different objects of proof, the law requires different levels of proof, and proof activities should be weighted accordingly. This approach not only helps improve the efficiency of litigation but also does not impede the fairness of the litigation process. It is necessary to clarify some fundamental categories related to proof. These categories primarily include proof and explanation, strict proof and free proof, proof in terms of actions and proof in terms of results.

9.4.1 Proof and Explanation

According to the different requirements for proof objects, specifically whether it is necessary for the judge to obtain complete certainty, proof can be divided into proof and explanation. Theoretically, scholars have different views on the understanding of proof and explanation. Some believe that "presenting evidence that leads the judge to complete certainty is called proof; however, if presenting evidence only leads the judge to a generally credible but weaker conviction, it is not proof but explanation."[4] Others argue that "the facts claimed by the parties in litigation generally require proof, but in certain cases where a swift and decisive decision is needed, and where the law does not specify, explanation will suffice."[5] Proof is seen as complete evidence, while explanation is regarded as incomplete evidence.[6]

9.4.1.1 Proof

Proof refers to the activity of using evidence to establish the existence of substantive legal relationships and the constituent elements of certain legal facts as outlined in substantive law. It is also the state of certainty regarding the facts of the case that arises after the legal procedures of court investigation, oral arguments, and mutual cross-examination. This "certainty refers to the belief held by ordinary people in

[4] Lin (2000).

[5] Chen (1996).

[6] Matsuoka (2004).

society without any doubts."[7] In this context, proof refers to proof in the narrow sense.

9.4.1.2 Explanation

Explanation, also known as "clarification," "elucidation," or "collateral evidence," refers to the burden placed on the party to make corresponding claims regarding procedural matters related to the case in order to help the judge make a ruling that is favorable to them. Explanation functions similarly to "prima facie proof," aiming to achieve a sufficient level of certainty. It is typically used to prove elements of unlawful behavior, causal relationships, and other exceptional facts, as well as certain procedural facts, such as grounds for recusal or the facts concerning evidence preservation.

Proof and explanation originate from the distinction between complete and incomplete evidence in German common law. Proof generally applies to the establishment of substantive legal facts, requiring not only the method of proof but also the provision of corresponding evidence. In contrast, explanation is mainly used for procedural legal facts and causal facts, where it is sufficient to merely outline the method of proof.

9.4.2 Strict Proof and Free Proof

Depending on the field to which the object of proof belongs, proof can be divided into strict proof and free proof. The concepts of strict proof and free proof originate from German procedural law. This concept was introduced by German scholar Deinz in 1926 and gradually evolved into the prevailing view within the German evidence law community. It was later adopted in Japan and Taiwan. After 1930, it was widely accepted by civil procedural law scholars.

9.4.2.1 Strict Proof

Strict certification means a certificate made by the method of certification prescribed by law and in accordance with legal procedures. In the process of strict proof, the form of evidence, the way of evidence collection and the procedure of evidence investigation adopted are all restricted and restricted by strict legal norms.

In criminal proceedings, the facts constituting the elements of an offence, whether direct or indirect, require strict proof. Generally speaking, "the determination of the facts necessary for the legal relationship that is the subject of the proceedings or for the assertion of rights must be based on strict proof". The use of strict proof

[7] Nakamura (2001).

in litigation must be in accordance with the legal procedures and methods of proof prescribed by law and the principle of verbal argument as a prerequisite for the determination of the facts of the case, and the method of strict proof is not only strictly binding on the court of first instance, but also on the court of final appeal. Strict proof is an objective safeguard for the discovery of the truth in a case.

Strict proof and strict burden of proof are two concepts in different areas. Strict proof is the certification activity and applies to the court and the parties to the litigation; strict burden of proof is the burden of proof and only applies to the party bearing the burden of proof.

9.4.2.2 Free Proof

Freedom proof, also known as "arbitrary proof", means the proof other than the proof method prescribed by law and is not bound by legal procedures. The facts involved in free proof are mostly facts related to procedural matters which arise with the litigation. For example, the facts about the arrest are withdrawn; the facts about the proceedings concerned; the facts about whether the proceedings are beyond the legal time limit; the facts related to the legality of the proceedings; and the facts of the legality of the proceedings concerned. These facts do not involve substantive issues and cannot be a basis for determining the victory or loss of the parties. In civil litigation, the object of free proof generally includes the procedural matters unrelated to the substantive dispute, such as the suspension of the court, the termination of litigation, and the withdrawal, etc.

Generally speaking, the evidence for strict proof must be the form of evidence clearly prescribed by law; the appropriate form may be chosen "by the practice of general practice". The evidence investigation procedure is a defining feature of strict proof; the law does not specify the freedom to justify the application. Generally speaking, the simple procedural facts only need to be proved by freedom, but all the whole procedural facts cannot be simply classified into the scope of free proof. If the procedural law facts involve the "compound of facts" of the result of substantive law, strict proof shall be applied.

Strict proof and free proof are the depth rules of proof, which makes the proof activity more explicit and procedural. It not only refines the proof rules, making the proof more clear, stable and predictable, but also the free proof also makes up for the gap between strict proof and interpretation, alleviates the stiffness of strict proof, and makes the judge form inner confidence with more clear depth requirements. At the same time, it also provides directional guidance for the certification activities of the parties (prosecution) in the lawsuit, and has a clear understanding of which evidence and which certification rules should be applied to the facts of the case, so as to make the certification rules have strong operability.

9.4.3 Proof in Terms of Actions and Proof in Terms of Results

Based on the different forms of proof, proof can be divided into proof in terms of actions and proof in terms of results.

9.4.3.1 Proof in Terms of Actions

Proof in terms of actions refers to the activity of the proving party using known evidence to argue the facts of the case, which specifically pertains to the act of proof itself. It mainly includes actions such as collecting evidence, presenting evidence, cross-examining, certifying, and collecting evidence, and represents a continuous process of proof.

9.4.3.2 Proof in Terms of Results

Proof in terms of results refers to the outcome of the proving party's use of known evidence to establish the facts of the case. It particularly refers to the result formed when the proving party uses evidence to prove the facts of the case, meaning the state of certainty that the judge or the litigant reaches regarding the facts of the case or the disputed facts between the parties.

9.5 The Significance of Proof

In litigation, disputed facts refer to all the facts that the prosecution in criminal proceedings or the plaintiff in civil or administrative proceedings must prove in order to win the case. These facts are determined based on substantive law and the claims made in the litigation. Whether it is the activities of the parties (prosecution and defense) such as presenting evidence, cross-examining, or the facts that the court needs to clarify, all revolve around the activity of proof. Proof plays a particularly important role throughout the entire litigation process.

9.5.1 Proof as the Fundamental Method for Discovering the True Facts of a Case

One of the meanings of proof is to use evidence to demonstrate or determine the truth of a person or thing. For judges who are initially unaware of or unfamiliar with the facts of the case, proof becomes the fundamental method for discovering the truth of the facts. The determination of the facts of the case by the judge is primarily based on the proof activities of the parties (prosecution and defense). Without the proof activities of the parties, relying solely on the judge to directly collect evidence would not only affect the fairness of the proceedings, but could also lead the judge away from the true facts of the case, potentially resulting in a misjudgment of the facts. Therefore, proof is the fundamental channel through which evidence plays a role in the facts of the case, and it is also the most reliable method for the court to discover the truth of the facts.

9.5.2 *Proof as the Primary Means of Determining the Facts of the Case Using Evidence*

Proof is the central component of the entire litigation process and is the prerequisite for determining the facts of the case. The reason the litigation system uses proof as a means of clarifying the facts of the case is because it has the function of discovering the truth of the case through legal procedures. The primary way to clarify the facts of the case is through proof. At the same time, evidence is static and requires dynamic proof to activate it. Dynamic proof relies on the active participation of the parties (prosecution and defense) to provide evidence. Proof thus has the effect of bringing static evidence to life. Therefore, the court's use of evidence to determine the facts of the case inevitably relies on proof to complete the process, and proof becomes the primary means of evidence-based adjudication.

9.6 Questions and Reflections

Professor Hirano Ryūichi, a Japanese scholar, proposed the concept of "appropriate proof" between strict proof and free proof, based on the aspects of simplified procedures and sentencing procedures. Appropriate proof is a method of proof that lies between strict proof and free proof, emphasizing the need to consider the opinions of the parties involved. There is theoretical debate about whether evidence that should be excluded under strict proof procedures can be applied in free proof procedures, and whether the principle of "no revival after defeat" should be allowed. In the example provided above, the court found that Yang lacked sufficient evidence to prove her overtime hours and only ruled that the company should pay Yang 8 h of overtime wages and economic compensation for the termination of her employment contract. Yang disagreed and filed an appeal, but the appellate court upheld the original judgment. According to the case, combined with the contents of this chapter, consider the theory about the proof of the assertion, think about the following questions: (1) What kind of activity is proof? (2) What are the contents of the proof activity? (3) What is the significance of the classification of proof? (4) What type of proof should the overtime application form be considered when proving overtime?

References

Chen, R. Z. (1996). Minshi susong fa (Lin, Q. M., Trans.). Taipei: San Min Book Co., Ltd.
Strong, J. W. (ed.) (1992). McCormick on Evidence. 4th edn. St Paul, MN: West Publishing Company.
Kaneko, H. and Takeshita, M. (1995). Minshi susong fa [Translation of 民事訴訟法] (Bai, L. X., Trans.). Beijing: Law Press China.
Lin, S. T. (2004). Xingshi chengxu fa. Taipei: Wu-Nan Book Inc.
Matsuoka, Y. (2004). Minshi zhengju lun [Translation of 『民事證據論』] (Zhang, Z. B., Trans.). Beijing: China University of Political Science and Law Press.
Nakamura, E. (2001). Xin minshi susong fa jiangyi [Translation of 『新民事訴訟法講義』] (Chen, G., Lin, J. F. and Guo, M. S., Trans.). Beijing: Law Press of China.

Extended Reading

Matsuoka, M. (1981). Yange zhengming yu ziyou zhengming (Guo, B. and Luo, R. Q., Trans.). Global Law Review, 3(5): 58–60. (in Chinese)
Wu, H. Y. and Wei, X. N. (2002). Susong zhengming yuanli. Beijing: Law Press China. (in Chinese)
Bian, J. L. (2004). Xingshi zhengming lilun [Chinese]. Beijing: People's Public Security University of China Press. (in Chinese)
Xiong, Y. M. (2004). Minshi susong zhong fayuan de shiming: fali, guize yu panli — yi Riben minshi susong wei zhongxin de kaocha. Journal of Comparative Law, 18(6): 66–76. (in Chinese)
Zhan, S. G. (2007). Lun minshi susong zhong zhi ziyou zhengming. Law Review, 25(4): 79–83. (in Chinese)
Min, C. L. (2010). Yange zhengming yu ziyou zhengming xintan. Peking University Law Journal, 22(5): 684–697. (in Chinese)

Chapter 10
Object of Proof

10.1 Introductory Case

The plaintiff claimed that the defendant owed 30,000 yuan and provided a torn and reassembled promissory note as evidence. The defendant argued that the debt had already been repaid, stating: when the plaintiff came to his house to collect the debt, he paid the 30,000 yuan to the plaintiff, then tore up the promissory note and threw it in the trash. The plaintiff's statement contradicted this, asserting: when the plaintiff came to collect the debt at the defendant's house, the defendant refused to pay, falsely claimed to be looking at the promissory note, and after taking it, said, "I won't pay you, let's see what you'll do," and then tore up the note and threw it on the ground. The plaintiff quickly picked up the torn promissory note. There is no other evidence to determine whether the defendant repaid the debt.

10.2 Chapter Overview

This chapter covers the topic of the objects of proof, primarily discussing the concept and significance of proof objects, including substantive law facts, procedural law facts, evidentiary facts, and the distinction between proof objects and facts exempt from proof. The proof object is one of the key issues that must be addressed in litigation, and it represents the goal and direction of litigation proof activities.

H. Guo, *Evidence Jurisprudence in China*, Understanding China,
https://doi.org/10.1007/978-981-95-3981-9_10

10.3 Overview of the Object of Proof

The object of proof is one of the important categories of evidence law. It is closely related to the litigation subject, litigation behavior and litigation purpose. It is the basic element of proof and occupies an important position in the proof activity. Only when the object of proof is resolved can other proof activities be carried out in detail and the litigation activities can be carried out in an orderly manner. Therefore, accurately determining the object of proof is the key to the correct development of proof activities, which is not only conducive to the scientific proof system, but also able to show the way for the proof activities.

10.3.1 Concept of Proof Object

The object of proof, also known as the object of proof, the fact to be proved, the fact to be proved or the disputed fact, refers to the facts of the legal requirements that the subject of proof must prove or confirm by using evidence.

The object of proof is a fluid or abstract concept. Different types of litigation have different objects of proof; different cases of the same type of litigation have different objects of proof; the same litigation case has certain differences in its objects of proof at different stages of litigation. The object of proof is closely related to the litigation claims, the issues in dispute, and the interests that need to be protected in the litigation. From the perspective of the litigation process, it includes both substantive law facts that have occurred or existed before the litigation was initiated, and procedural law facts that occurred during the litigation process.

In litigation, facts related to the handling of the case are often the object of proof. In litigation, the object of proof is the starting point of the proof activity, and it is also the direct direction and destination of the proof activity. Only when the object of proof is established, will the burden of proof, the subject of proof and other issues arise. At the same time, the object of proof is also related to the standard of proof. The essential facts of the disputed object of proof are the premise and basis for establishing the standard of proof, and based on this, other relevant contents of proof, such as the direction of proof, the content of proof, and the requirements of proof, can be deduced. Generally speaking, the object of proof mainly includes the following contents.

10.3.1.1 The Object of Proof is Facts Related to the Case

Whether the facts proved in the lawsuit are related to the case is related to the fundamental issue of whether the case can be properly handled. If these facts are related to the case and have a greater impact on the handling of the case, they need to be proved by evidence, and they will become the object of proof. The object of proof is not only the basis for the parties to make claims or debates, but also the basis for ascertaining the facts of the case and making correct handling, and the basis for resolving disputes and making judgments. This determines that the object of proof must be related to the facts of the case and belongs to the content of the facts of the case.

10.3.1.2 The Object of Proof is the Facts Regulated by Laws and Regulations

Facts are divided into legal facts and ordinary facts that are not involved in the identification of the case. The existence or occurrence of legal facts will cause the occurrence, change or elimination of legal relations. Only when facts become legal facts will they be of great significance to the handling of cases. Legal facts are different from ordinary facts of life. They are facts regulated by laws and regulations. The object of proof is the facts to be proved among legal facts, and they must be regulated by laws and regulations.

10.3.1.3 The Object of Proof is the Fact Confirmed by Evidence

In litigation, not all facts need to be proven before they can be confirmed. Some facts do not need to be proven by evidence, and the court can directly use them as the basis for a verdict. These case facts that do not require the parties to provide evidence are exempt from proof as clearly stipulated by the law, and they are not the objects of proof. Most facts must be proven by evidence, and their objective truth can only be determined after being proven. These facts that need to be proven by evidence are the objects of proof, while well-known facts or presumed facts that do not need to be proven by evidence are not the objects of proof.

The object of proof is different from the object of adjudication. The object of proof is to answer the question of which facts need to be proved by evidence and which facts do not need to be proved by evidence from the perspective of evidence; the object of adjudication is to answer the question of which facts fall within the scope of the judge's power of investigation from the perspective of adjudication. The facts involved in the object of proof generally belong to the facts investigated by the object of adjudication. The object of proof is also different from the object of litigation. They are mutually dependent, and the latter is derived from the former.

In common law countries, the objects of proof generally include three parts: disputed facts, facts related to the disputed facts, and collateral facts. Disputed facts, also known as ultimate facts, mainly include the constituent facts of the cause of action and the constituent facts of the defense. Facts related to disputed facts are also called evidentiary facts or facts that play a logical role in proof. Based on such facts, it can be inferred through reasoning whether the disputed facts exist or are true. Collateral facts, also known as subordinate facts, refer to facts related to the admissibility or credibility of evidence. In continental law countries, the objects of proof generally include essential facts and legal norms.

10.3.2 The Significance of Establishing the Object of Proof

The object of proof is the basic factor of proof activities and the primary link of litigation proof. Whether in theory or in judicial practice, the object of proof is of great significance to litigation activities. The object of proof is an important category of proof theory.

Establishing the object of proof is conducive to the establishment of a scientific system of proof. The object of proof is the intermediate link between the proof standard and the burden of proof, and it is also the starting point and end point of the proof activities. Whether the object of proof is established scientifically determines the scientificity and integrity of the entire proof system. Research on the object of proof is conducive to promoting the reasonable and scientific establishment of the proof system.

The scientific establishment of the object of proof can enable the investigating authorities and the parties to clearly define the scope of evidence collection and provision, ensure the specific direction of cross-examination, authentication and evidence collection, help determine the scope of prosecution and trial, and avoid being entangled in details due to unclear direction of proof or omitting certain case facts that should be proved by evidence due to unclear determination of the scope of proof, thereby ensuring that the purpose of proof is fully achieved.

Studying the object of proof is conducive to clarifying the difference between substantive law and procedural law, and then establishing different proof standards and proof procedures accordingly. In a sense, establishing the object of proof is equivalent to establishing the corresponding proof standard. Therefore, clarifying the object of proof in litigation proof can save judicial resources, ensure that the case can be handled quickly, and improve litigation efficiency.

10.4 Substantive Law Facts

Case facts are those facts that have legal significance for resolving a case and involve the substantive rights and obligations of the proving party. Due to the different nature, purpose, and tasks of criminal, civil, and administrative litigation, the objects of proof also vary. Even within the same area of litigation, the objects of proof can differ depending on the specifics of the case. Since substantive interests play a crucial role in determining the objects of proof, the vast majority of proof objects belong to substantive law facts, making substantive law facts the primary objects of proof.

10.4.1 Substantive Law Facts of Criminal Proceedings

The substantive law facts of criminal proceedings include the criminal facts of the case and the sentencing facts. The criminal facts of the case are the most important and the most difficult to determine issue in the object of proof. In order to clarify the scope of facts that judges need to ascertain during trial, criminal proceedings "should use evidence to prove the following facts: 1.1 the identity of the defendant and the victim; 1.2 whether the alleged crime exists; 1.3 whether the alleged crime was committed by the defendant; 1.4 whether the defendant has criminal responsibility, guilt, motives and purposes for committing the crime; 1.5 the time, place, means, consequences of the crime and the cause of the case; 1.6 whether it is a joint crime or whether the criminal facts are related, and the defendant's position and role in the crime; 1.7 whether the defendant has circumstances that aggravate, mitigate, reduce or exempt punishment; 1.8 facts about the handling of property involved in the case; 1.9 facts about incidental civil litigation; 1.10 procedural facts about jurisdiction, recusation, postponement of trial, etc.; 1.11 other facts related to conviction and sentencing." According to the requirements of the object of proof and the needs of judicial practice, the object of proof in criminal proceedings mainly includes substantive law facts related to conviction and sentencing. These substantive law facts mainly include the following aspects.

10.4.1.1 Facts of Conviction in a Case

The facts of conviction mainly include: i. whether the crime has actually occurred; ii. who committed the crime; iii. the process of committing the crime and the harmful consequences caused by the crime, that is, the time, place, means, method and conditions of the crime and the causal relationship between the criminal behavior and the criminal result; iv. whether the defendant has reached the age of criminal responsibility, whether he has criminal responsibility, the defendant's subjective guilt (intentional and negligent) and the motive and purpose of the crime; v. facts that exclude the illegality of the act, the punishability of the act, and the criminal responsibility; vi. other facts related to whether criminal responsibility should be pursued. These facts are related to the elements of the crime, mainly including the "seven whys": "who," "what," "where," "why," "for what purpose," "by what means," and "what result." In short, it can be expressed as: "Who" committed "what act" at "what time" and "where," using "what mean" to produce "what result." The aim is to resolve issues related to crime versus non-crime, this crime versus that crime, and serious crime versus minor crime.

10.4.1.2 Facts of Sentencing in a Case

Sentencing facts refer to the facts about what kind of punishment the defendant should be given. These facts mainly refer to the facts of statutory circumstances and the facts of discretionary circumstances. These facts mainly include: i. the defendant's personal information, namely name, gender, age, ethnicity, address, occupation, consistent performance, whether he has been punished with criminal penalties or other sanctions, etc.; ii. whether he has taken the initiative to actively recover the losses caused by the crime after committing the crime, whether he has shown remorse such as surrendering himself, admitting guilt and punishment, actively returning the stolen goods, and making meritorious contributions, or whether he has shown resistance such as escaping, destroying evidence, forging evidence, colluding with others, refusing to confess guilt, etc.; iii. whether there are statutory facts that may aggravate, mitigate, reduce or exempt the punishment, etc.

In addition, the facts of conviction and the facts of sentencing sometimes have a cross-cutting and encompassing relationship, with some substantive law facts being both facts of conviction and facts of sentencing, and the facts of conviction sometimes encompassing the facts of sentencing. Such facts, especially those that are aggravated by the sentence, should generally be classified as facts of conviction that require strict proof.

10.4.2 Substantive Law Facts in Civil Litigation

The substantive law that is the object of proof in civil litigation can be divided into essential facts, indirect facts and auxiliary facts according to their nature and function. The facts that constitute the elements of the occurrence of legal effects stipulated by the law are called essential facts. The specific facts that the judge infers whether the essential facts exist based on the rule of thumb are indirect facts. The facts that illustrate the admissibility, probative force and value of evidence are called auxiliary facts.

The facts asserted by the parties should be the objects of proof in civil litigation. Generally speaking, the substantive law facts asserted by the parties mainly include facts related to the substantive civil rights and obligations of the parties. These facts mainly include: 2.1 facts on which the rights and obligations between the parties arise, change or disappear; 2.2 facts on which civil rights are infringed or disputes arise; 2.3 facts that hinder the occurrence, change or disappearance of rights; 2.4 the basic situation of the parties; 2.5 foreign laws or the laws of Hong Kong, Macao and Taiwan, as well as customs or practices.

10.4.3 Substantive Law Facts in Administrative Litigation

The substantive law facts of administrative litigation mainly involve the facts of administrative acts of administrative agencies. The substantive law facts of administrative litigation can be divided into substantive law facts that the defendant should prove and substantive law facts that the plaintiff should provide proof of, among which the substantive law facts that the defendant should prove are the main ones.

10.4.3.1 Substantive Legal Facts that the Defendant Should Prove

The substantive law facts that the defendant should prove mainly include: i. facts related to the legality and rationality of the administrative act in question, such as the fact that the administrative agency has statutory powers, the fact that the punished act is implemented, the fact that the purpose of the administrative act in question is legitimate, and the fact that the handling of the administrative act in question is consistent with the nature, facts and circumstances of the case. ii. facts related to the legality of abstract acts. In particular, whether the legal basis and normative documents of administrative acts and certain administrative regulations, rules and normative documents are valid; whether the administrative acts of administrative agencies meet the factual requirements stipulated by laws, regulations and rules. iii. facts of the legality of the existence and application of normative documents.

10.4.3.2 Substantive Legal Facts that the Plaintiff Should Prove

In administrative litigation, the plaintiff generally does not bear the burden of proof, but this does not prevent him from providing evidence to prove certain facts. Generally speaking, the plaintiff needs to provide evidence for the following matters: i. prove that the lawsuit meets the statutory conditions, except when the defendant believes that the plaintiff's lawsuit exceeds the deadline for prosecution; ii. in the case of suing the defendant for inaction, prove the fact that he filed an application; iii. in the administrative compensation lawsuit filed together, prove the fact that the loss was caused by the infringement of the accused behavior; iv. other matters that the plaintiff should bear the burden of proof. In administrative litigation, the facts about the infringement damage caused by administrative behavior and the fact that the administrative agency did not act or abused its power or exceeded its authority should be the plaintiff's proof.

10.5 Procedural Law Facts and Facts Exempt from Proof

10.5.1 Procedural Law Facts

Procedural law facts mainly refer to the facts about the situation that promote the development of procedures stipulated in the litigation law. There is controversy in the legal community of my country on whether procedural law facts should be the object of proof. There are generally affirmative, negative and compromise views. The main reason for the controversy is that my country's litigation law has not clearly established the principle of procedural legality. The underlying reason is that substantive justice is the goal of litigation, and the function of procedural issues to restrict and influence the entity is not seen. Procedural law facts should be the object of proof, which helps to maintain the balance between substantive justice and procedural justice and reflects the value of procedural law itself.

10.5.1.1 Procedural Law Facts in Criminal Litigation

Procedural law facts in criminal proceedings include: i. the fact of whether or not a certain coercive measure should be taken against a suspect or defendant; ii. the fact of the need for disqualification; iii. the fact of the delay in the time limit for the proceedings; iv. facts that infringe the litigation rights of the criminal suspect or defendant, deprive or restrict the legal litigation rights of the parties, and may affect the fair trial; v. other facts that violate the legal procedures.

10.5.1.2 Procedural Law Facts in Civil Litigation

The facts of procedural law in civil litigation mainly include: i. facts relating to the eligibility of the parties; ii. facts relating to the competence of the court and its jurisdiction; iii. facts relating to the lawfulness of the composition of the panel and the disqualification of the trial judge; iv. facts relating to the adoption of coercive measures to exclude the obstruction of civil litigation; v. facts relating to the period of proof; vi. facts relating to other procedural matters.

10.5.1.3 Procedural Law Facts in Administrative Litigation

The procedural law facts in administrative litigation mainly include: i. the facts about the eligibility of the parties; ii. the facts about the jurisdiction of the case; iii. the facts about the trial recusal; iv. the facts about the adoption of coercive measures to exclude obstruction of the administrative litigation; v. the defendant and its agents during the litigation to collect evidence from the plaintiff or witnesses; vi. the facts about the duration of the litigation; vii. the other facts concerning procedural matters.

10.5.2 Evidentiary Facts

There are different views in theory and practice on whether evidentiary facts should be the object of proof.

10.5.2.1 Evidentiary Facts Are the Object of Proof

According to this view: i. the evidence must be verified in order to be used as a basis for a judgement. The evidence is verified, itself is a process of proof. ii. the case-handling organs, as well as the parties, defenders, litigation agents to collect a variety of evidence, there are true and false, without verification can not be used to prove the case of substantive law and procedural law facts. Therefore, the need to verify the evidence, should also be the object of proof in the proceedings. iii. evidence of some of the facts are the facts of the case, with the help of part of the facts of the case to prove another part of the facts of the case, and the part of the facts of the case, if you need to prove, it is the object of proof. Only after it is proved, to prove another part of the case facts, then it for evidence. Continental law countries in the doctrine generally believe that the evidence of the fact is the object of proof, the evidence of the fact as proof of the reliability of the evidence of the fact, such as the reliability of the fact of witness testimony.

10.5.2.2 Part of the Evidentiary Fact is the Object of Proof

This view holds that: i. the facts of human evidence are first of all the objects of proof. Because the facts presented by people are facts that have happened in the past, such facts no longer exist and belong to unproven and unclear facts to be proved. Physical evidence is not the object of proof because physical evidence is an objective object and trace. It has a shape, can be seen and touched, and is a real fact, although it needs to be inspected, examined or identified. However, these activities are not activities to prove physical evidence, but activities to understand physical evidence. ii. in litigation, when the evidential facts become the objects of proof to prove the true situation of the case, the evidential facts become the objects of proof. Evidence law scholars in Anglo-American legal systems divide auxiliary facts that are the objects of proof into three aspects: First, facts that affect the ability of witnesses. For example, the fact that a potential mental disability makes him unable to testify. Second, facts that affect the credibility of witness testimony. For example, a witness makes a statement about an event that happened 50 m away, but in fact her eyes are diseased and cannot see anything beyond 20 m, and the fact that the witness is biased or partial to one party. Third, prerequisite facts. Facts that must be proved as a prerequisite for the admissibility of evidence proving the main facts. If the original documentary evidence has been lost or cannot be found after legal procedures, a copy of the documentary evidence can be admitted as evidence by the court after proof.

10.5.2.3 Evidentiary Facts Are not Objects of Proof

This view holds that: i. direct evidence facts overlap with the main facts of the case, and indirect evidence facts actually overlap with the facts of the case. It is meaningless to list them independently as objects of proof. ii. Evidence facts are ultimately just methods of proving substantive law facts or procedural law facts, that is, means of proving the object. iii. Depending on the circumstances of the case, some evidence facts must be verified, while others may not be verified. This is not the case with the case facts that are the objects of proof. Generally speaking, there should be evidence to prove each of them. iv. Evidence needs to be verified before it can be used as the basis for determining the case. This is a question of review and judgment of evidence and should not be classified as the object of proof. It should be included in the scope of proof requirements. Evidence facts are the means to solve the case facts. The relationship between them and the case facts is the relationship between the means of proof and the object of proof. Evidence facts are not case facts. The proof of case facts cannot be confused with the examination and judgment of specific evidence. Evidence cannot become the object of proof just because it needs to be verified. Otherwise, there will be a logical cycle, that is, the facts that prove the evidence facts still need to be found out and should also be the object of proof. And so on, it will continue to cycle and cause the problem of circular reasoning.

Evidence facts are the means to solve the case facts. The relationship between them and the case facts is the relationship between the means of proof and the object of proof. Evidence facts are not case facts. The proof of case facts cannot be confused with the examination and judgment of specific evidence. Evidence cannot become the object of proof just because it needs to be verified. Otherwise, there will be a logical cycle, that is, the facts that prove the evidence facts still need to be found out and should also be the object of proof. And so on, it will continue to cycle and cause the problem of circular reasoning.

10.5.3 Facts Exempt from Proof

Facts exempt from proof, also known as facts that do not require evidence to be proven, refer to facts for which parties are relieved from providing evidence. These facts generally include: judicial notice of notorious or readily demonstrable facts by the court; Presumptions in favor of one party's claims; facts confirmed by legally effective documents, such as facts recognized in final court judgments, facts recognized in effective arbitration awards, or facts confirmed in notarized documents; formal admissions made by the parties for litigation purposes.

In litigation, some facts are so obvious and self-evident that they can be verified without the need for the parties to provide evidence. Although exempt facts form the factual basis for the court's judgment, their truth is affirmed due to their exceptional nature, or because there is no dispute between the parties, and thus there is no need for the parties to provide further evidence unless they present reasonable and sufficient rebuttal evidence or new facts. Generally speaking, facts exempt from proof are exceptions to the burden of proof or the objects of proof, and because they do not require evidence, they are not considered proof objects.

As exceptions to the burden of proof or the objects of proof, facts exempt from proof, which serve as the basis for a court's judgment, generally affect the substantive rights of the parties and should be explicitly defined by law, not left to the discretion of the judge. Since China's procedural and substantive laws do not provide clear provisions on this, judicial interpretations have filled the gap. Generally, the following facts do not require the parties to present evidence: i. natural laws, theorems, and laws; ii. well-known facts; iii. facts inferred according to legal provisions; iv. another fact inferred based on known facts and rules of daily life experience; v. facts confirmed by an effective ruling of an arbitration institution; vi. basic facts confirmed by a judgment of a people's court that has legal effect; vii. facts proved by valid notarized documents. The exceptions to the above items are as follows: for items 2 through 5, if the parties present rebuttal evidence that is sufficient to counter them; for items 6 and 7, if the parties present rebuttal evidence sufficient to overturn them. Facts exempt from proof mainly include the following:

10.5.3.1 The Facts that Well-Known

Well-known facts refer to common sense facts that are known to ordinary people with certain knowledge and experience. Well-known facts are facts that are known to everyone and whose authenticity is undisputed. These facts mainly include natural laws and theorems, historical events, current news, statutory holidays, national and provincial boundaries, daily life knowledge and experience, etc. Whether a fact is well-known often varies depending on time, region, and field. Some may be well-known for a long time, while others are well-known for a short time; some are well-known in a province, a country, or even the world, while some are only known to people in a relatively small area (such as local events, local customs, etc.); some are generally known to the whole society, while others are known to people in certain areas or fields (such as industry events, industry customs or practices, etc.).

Since well-known facts may be contrary to the truth, the parties are allowed to provide counter-evidence in the procedure. The content can be understood in conjunction with the content on "well-known" facts in Chapter 19 "Judicial Knowledge".

10.5.3.2 Notorious Facts Known to the Court in the Course of Its Duties

Notorious facts known to the court in the course of its duties are generally considered exempt from proof in many countries and regions. These are facts that the court, in performing its legal duties or official functions, becomes aware of. Such facts may include the content of judgments made by the court or judge, as well as other judgments or notices that the court or judge is required to know in their official capacity, such as bankruptcy declarations, declarations of missing persons, etc. These facts include those that the judge becomes aware of while handling the current case, as well as those learned in other civil, administrative, or criminal litigations. However, such facts do not include personal experiences outside the judge's official capacity. If a judge, acting as a tribunal, states or provides such facts in court, it would be considered as witness testimony.

Matters related to the court's duties primarily refer to facts published in official government bulletins. The facts in government bulletins often pertain to significant or typical matters and are typically subject to internal scrutiny, making them highly reliable and trustworthy. The court or judge is expected to be aware of these facts. These government bodies primarily include central state authorities and local authorities with legislative power. As the state's judicial body, the court should be aware of the facts published in government bulletins.

For notorious facts known to the court in the course of its duties, if a collegial panel is used as the trial body, a majority of the judges must have a clear recollection of these facts. For such notorious facts, the court does not require the parties to present evidence but allows the parties to dispute and rebut the facts. In China's civil and administrative litigation, facts known to the court in the course of its duties only include those facts confirmed by effective court judgments or arbitration awards.

Additionally, facts that are undisputed by the parties are not necessarily considered exempt from proof. In administrative litigation, if the facts are undisputed by the parties but involve national interests, public interests, or the legitimate interests of others, the court may order the parties to provide or supplement relevant evidence, or it may conduct an investigation on its own. The topics of presumed facts and judicial notice will be discussed in detail in Chapters 18 and 19. Facts acknowledged by the parties are addressed in Section 6, "Party Statements," and can be referred to for further context.

10.6 Questions and Reflections

The object of proof is the first issue that needs to be clarified in the process of proof. Only by clarifying the object of proof can we further determine who bears the burden of proof, to what extent proof is required, and how proof should be conducted. Additionally, only by clarifying the object of proof can activities such as evidence collection, presentation, cross-examination, and authentication be carried out effectively and purposefully. However, from a theoretical perspective, it is necessary to distinguish between "substantive law facts, procedural law facts, and evidentiary law facts," clarify the distinction between "facts to be proven and facts exempt from proof," and differentiate between "the singularity and identity of case facts."

In the example provided, the judge, based on the evidence presented in court, reasoned that if the defendant had repaid the plaintiff the 30,000 yuan, retrieved the promissory note, and then torn it up, it would defy common sense for the plaintiff to simply recover the torn-up note without any objection. The torn promissory note could still serve as evidence proving the existence of the unpaid loan. Based on the specifics of the case, and reflecting on the views expressed above in the context of this chapter, consider the following questions: (a) What are the objects of proof in this case? (b) Is the torn-up promissory note or the content of the promissory note the object of proof? (c) Are there any facts exempt from proof in this case?

Extended Reading

Li, J. M (1990). Lun xingzheng susong zhong de zhengming duixiang de fanwei. Chinese Journal of Law, (02): 49–54. (in Chinese)

Hu, X. Q. (2002). Susong zhengmingxue. Beijing: China Legal Publishing House. (in Chinese)

Luo, X. Q. (2004). Minshi panjue duixiang de bijiao fenxi. In Jiang, W. (Ed.), Bijiao minshi susong fa guoji yantaohui lunwenji. Beijing: China University of Political Science and Law Press. (in Chinese).

Xie, J. J. (2007). Shenpan duixiang yunxing guilü. Chinese Journal of Law, 29(4): 96–115. (in Chinese).

Lu, J. and Cao, F. L. (2009). Lun zhengming duixiang de fanwei shi subian shuangfang de susong zhuzhang. Political Science and Law, (1): 128–132. (in Chinese).

Chapter 11
Burden of Proof

11.1 Introductory Case

The case of privacy rights dispute between plaintiff Pang Moupeng and defendants Beijing Quna Information Technology Co., Ltd. and China Eastern Airlines Co., Ltd. Pang Moupeng entrusted Lu Mou to order an Eastern Airlines ticket from Luzhou to Beijing on MU5492 through the Qunar.com platform. The order details page of Qunar.com shows that the passenger information registered for the order includes the plaintiff's name and ID number, and the contact information and reimbursement information are all Lu Mou and his mobile phone number with the last digit 1858, and a text message is sent: "MU5492 flight from Luzhou Blue Sky Airport to Beijing Capital Airport T2... Star Travel Airlines Preferred, the only customer service phone number: 010-89930736." Then a text message was received from a mobile phone number with the last digit 9949 from an unknown source... Your booked MU5492 flight has been cancelled due to mechanical failure... Please contact customer service in time after receiving the text message to handle the rebooking service hotline 4008-129-218 [Note: Passengers who change their tickets need to pay a 20 yuan rebooking fee first, and each passenger will receive an additional compensation of 200 yuan after the rebooking is successful]. Pang Moupeng believes that Qu Na Company and China Eastern Airlines are suspected of leaking private information. Pang Moupeng submitted relevant web page printouts to prove that Qu Na Company and China Eastern Airlines are suspected of leaking the privacy of many passengers. Qu Na Company provided evidence to prove that the funds have taken multiple encryption measures to protect user information, and the security of Qunar.com has been certified by domestic and international authoritative security assessment agencies. The first instance court held that when Pang Moupeng entrusted Lu Mou to purchase air tickets through Qunar.com, he did not keep his mobile phone number, and the agent Xinglv Company did not obtain his mobile phone number. Xinglv Company did not keep his number when purchasing air tickets from China Eastern Airlines. Therefore, the court could not confirm that the defendant had access to Pang Moupeng's mobile

H. Guo, *Evidence Jurisprudence in China*, Understanding China,
https://doi.org/10.1007/978-981-95-3981-9_11

phone number during the purchase of air tickets in this case, and they were not the only medium to hold his personal information. Therefore, Pang Moupeng's lawsuit request lacked factual basis and the court did not support it. The plaintiff believed that he was a frequent flyer of the defendant and had reason to infer that Pang Moupeng's private information was stored in the defendant's system. It could not be ruled out that the private information was leaked by the defendant. He was dissatisfied with the first instance judgment and appealed. The second-instance court made a judgment on whether China Eastern Airlines and QuNa Company should bear responsibility as there was a high possibility that Pang Moupeng's private information was leaked.

11.2 Chapter Overview

This chapter is about the allocation of the burden of proof, including the concept and characteristics of the burden of proof, the theory of the distribution of the burden of proof, the burden of proof in criminal proceedings, the burden of proof in civil proceedings, the burden of proof in administrative proceedings and the inversion of the burden of proof. The burden of proof is the backbone of litigation and has a profound impact on the substantive rights of the parties.

11.3 Overview of the Burden of Proof

The burden of proof originated in the ancient Roman law era. The burden of proof can be summarized as "the person who claims has the burden of proof, while the person who denies has no burden of proof"; "the plaintiff's rights to his lawsuit and his claims must be proved by evidence"; "if a defense is raised, it is necessary to prove the defense." This view has evolved into the popular terminology of "he who claims, proves" in theory today.

11.3.1 Historical Evolution of the Burden of Proof

The burden of proof, also known as the burden of proof, is the core content of litigation proof theory, known as the backbone of litigation, and is the most complex issue in proof theory. The formation of the concept of burden of proof and the development of the theory have gone through a long historical period both in foreign countries and in China. Ancient Roman law established the principle of "he who asserts, he who proves", which has become an ancient "golden" rule for the burden of proof.

In continental law countries, the burden of proof (beweis notwendigkeit) is called "burden of proof", "burden of proof", and "burden of proof". In modern times, the theory of burden of proof has been developed and prospered in continental law

Germany. In Germany, the burden of proof mainly refers to the burden of providing evidence in the early days. This kind of responsibility belongs to the subjective burden of proof. In 1883, German scholar Julius Glasser first decomposed the concept of burden of proof and proposed subjective burden of proof (burden of proof in a formal sense) and objective burden of proof (burden of proof in a substantive sense), that is, the behavioral responsibility and result responsibility of the burden of proof. Later, it was developed and improved by Leonhard, Rosenberg and Hanns Pritting. In Anglo-American legal countries, the burden of proof is generally called the burden of proof, which mainly includes the burden of evidence, the burden of proof and the burden of persuasion. There was no statutory concept of burden of proof in ancient my country. The burden of proof as a legal concept in China can be traced back to the 1910 Qing Civil Procedure Law (Draft), Article 230 of which stipulates: "The parties shall establish evidence to prove their factual claims in their own favor." This provision is a direct transplant of the concept of burden of proof in the Japanese Civil Procedure Law.

In ancient times, there was no statutory concept of burden of proof in China. The burden of proof as a legal concept in China can be traced back to the Qing Civil Procedure Law (Draft) of 1910, which stipulates in article 230 that "the parties shall establish the factual claims in their favour." This provision is a direct transplantation of the concept of burden of proof from Japanese civil procedure law.[1] In the laws of New China, the first statutory concept was the Administrative Procedure Law of 1989. Article 32 of the law provides: "the defendant to make the specific administrative act has the burden of proof......" China's litigation law on the burden of proof and the burden of proof of the interrelationship between, respectively, put forward the same theory, juxtaposition, inclusion, size and so on a variety of doctrines. "The same" belongs to the general theory, that the burden of proof and the burden of proof is originally the same concept, there is no difference between the two. In criminal proceedings, the burden of proof is borne by the prosecution; criminal suspects and defendants do not bear the burden of proving their innocence, nor do they bear the burden of proving their guilt; they may put forward materials and opinions on innocence or misdemeanour, with the aim of requesting that the parties concerned be mitigated or exonerated from criminal punishment; this is a procedural right of the criminal suspects and defendants and their defenders. Since the procuratorial organs that undertake the function of public prosecution in public cases are in a completely unequal position to the defendant, the burden of proof in public cases is quite simple, i.e., "the people's procuratorate bears the burden of proof of the guilt of the defendant in a public case, and the burden of proof of the guilt of the defendant in a private case bears the burden of proof of the private prosecutor." Civil or administrative litigation in the "burden of proof" refers to the parties to their own claims to provide evidence to prove the obligation. In civil litigation, if a party fails to provide sufficient evidence,

[1] At the end of the Qing Dynasty, to assist the Qing government to draft the civil procedure law of foreign scholars for the Japanese Matsuoka Yoshimasa, his academic ideas directly affect the theory of civil procedure law in China and the concept of legislation, for the Taiwan region of China's civil procedure law has great influence.

his or her claim will not be proved and may be subject to unfavourable judgement. The duty of the court is to make a judgement, that is to say, to make a decision on the facts of the case proved by the two parties to the litigation. The court is not the main body of proof and should not bear the burden of proof. China's Criminal Procedure Law provides that "judges, procurators and investigators must, in accordance with legal procedures, collect evidence that confirms the guilt or innocence of suspects and defendants, and the gravity of the offence." The court is only required to assume a certain degree of responsibility for ascertainment, although there is a clear difference between this responsibility for ascertainment and the burden of proof borne by both the prosecution and the defence in providing evidence to prove their claims. Some scholars have also argued that the burden of proof includes the burden of proof, and that the burden of proof is part of the burden of proof.

11.3.2 Concept of Burden of Proof

The burden of proof refers to the obligation of the investigating agency or the parties to provide evidence to prove the existence of the facts they claim. The burden of proof generally includes the following:

11.3.2.1 The Parties Have the Responsibility to Provide Evidence in Support of Their Claims

The parties have the obligation to provide appropriate evidence to prove certain disputed facts so that the judge can make a favorable determination based on the proven facts. For example, my country's Civil Procedure Law stipulates: "The parties have the responsibility to provide evidence for their claims." The parties have the responsibility to provide evidence to prove the facts of the case that are favorable to their claims. At this time, the burden of proof is manifested as behavioral responsibility.

11.3.2.2 The Persuasive Burden of the Parties to Use Evidence to Prove Their Own Claims

When a party is proving the facts of a case, they should argue the authenticity, relevance and the evidential relationship with the facts of the case of the evidence they provide, fully utilize the evidence to argue for the existence of the claimed facts to convince the judge and make them believe and accept it. If a party fails to properly fulfill this burden of proof, once the judge has doubts about the facts claimed by the party, it is possible to make a judgment unfavorable to the party with the burden of proof, making them bear the adverse consequences of their claims. At this time, the burden of proof is manifested as the burden of persuasion.

11.3.2.3 The Risk of Losing the Case Borne by the Party When the Party Presents Unfavorable Evidence or Fails to Make the Argument

When a party cannot provide evidence for a self-interested claim, or the evidence provided cannot prove the existence of the self-interested claim, resulting in the factual truth of the claim being unclear, the party shall bear the judgment consequences that are unfavorable to the party. At this time, the burden of proof is manifested as the result responsibility.

In China, the burden of proof is positioned as a risk responsibility rather than a liability for losing the case because the litigation system in China adopts an inquisitorial model, where judges still have a certain degree of power to investigate evidence and bear the responsibility of pursuing the objective truth. For instance, the Civil Procedure Law of China stipulates: "If a party or its litigation representative is unable to collect evidence due to objective reasons, or if the court deems it necessary for the trial of the case, the court shall investigate and collect the evidence." The evidence collected by the court may clarify the facts of the case that were previously ambiguous, and thus, it is not ruled out that the court will make a fair judgment based on the facts ascertained, which may be favorable to the party claiming the facts.

In the academic circle, there are mainly four viewpoints on the nature of the burden of proof: the "right theory", the "obligation theory", the "right and obligation theory", and the "risk theory". The judicial interpretations in China also vary in their expressions on this issue. Judging from the provisions on the loss of the right to present evidence, the burden of proof is regarded as a right; while from the perspective of the outcome of the proof, it is a kind of risk. In China, treating the burden of proof as the allocation of the risk of the uncertainty of the facts better reflects the essence of the burden of proof.

11.3.3 The Significance of the Burden of Proof

The burden of proof is of great value in litigation. It determines the final outcome of the litigation and is the basis for the court to determine the facts of the case, correctly apply the law, and accurately handle the case. Therefore, it is of particular importance to reasonably clarify the sharing of the burden of proof and correctly allocate the burden of proof in order to give full play to the role of the subject of proof, promptly ascertain the case situation, and fairly handle the case.

Reasonable establishment of the burden of proof is conducive to clarifying the subject of proof and giving full play to the subject's initiative and enthusiasm in proving. By clarifying the burden of proof and reasonably sharing the burden of proof, the parties can provide evidence according to the clear distribution of the burden of proof, actively and proactively perform the obligation of proof, and use the adverse legal consequences of not fulfilling the burden of proof to encourage the subject of proof to fully perform the burden of proof, so that the facts of the case can be fully proved and it is also convenient for the facts of the case to be determined.

Scientifically establishing the burden of proof is conducive to improving the efficiency of case handling. The burden of proof is an inherent requirement for litigation economy and improving litigation efficiency. It requires the subject of proof to fulfill its obligation to prove in a timely manner according to its own burden of proof, and to find and provide evidence to prove its claims within a reasonable period of time, which can save unnecessary time and waste of manpower and material resources, avoid litigation delays, and help improve litigation efficiency.

Correctly establishing the burden of proof is conducive to the court's timely resolution of cases where the truth is unclear. The burden of proof clarifies that those who fail to fulfill their burden of proof should bear the corresponding adverse legal consequences. The court can make substantive handling of the case in accordance with the parties' burden of proof and handle cases where the truth is unclear in a timely manner, thereby avoiding the delayed justice issue of "pending" due to the fact that the case has not been proven.

11.4 Allocation of the Burden of Proof

11.4.1 Allocation of the Burden of Proof Abroad

The allocation of the burden of proof is an important theoretical issue in continental and common law countries. This theory has a certain reference value for how to scientifically and reasonably allocate the burden of proof in legislation or judicial interpretation in my country, and it is also of particular significance for solving difficult fact determinations in judicial practice. Due to the different litigation models and traditional legal cultures of the two major legal systems, there are also certain differences in the theory and practice of the allocation of the burden of proof.

11.4.1.1 Allocation of the Burden of Proof in Civil Law Countries

i. **The meaning of the burden of proof in continental law**

Since the German jurist Julius Glarza distinguished the burden of proof into subjective burden of proof and objective burden of proof, the simple burden of proof allocation such as "he who asserts must prove" in the Roman law tradition has been replaced by a more complex burden of proof theory system in the civil law system.

Subjective burden of proof, also known as behavioral responsibility or formal burden of proof, refers to the responsibility of a party to prove the disputed facts through their own proof activities in order to avoid losing the lawsuit. This responsibility can only function in litigation based on the principle of debate. Objective burden of proof, also known as result responsibility or substantive burden of proof, refers to the legal consequences when the facts to be proved remain undetermined or unproven until the end of the trial, that is, when the truth of the disputed facts is unclear, one party will bear the adverse consequences in the lawsuit. The objective burden of proof is generally borne by the party asserting the existence of the facts and cannot be transferred. Its function is not to solve the problem of which party provides the evidence, but to solve the problem of judgment when the facts are unclear. Therefore, the objective burden of proof only manifests as a special risk allocation mechanism.

After the 20th century, the burden of proof theory in Germany successively emerged as confirmation responsibility and proof responsibility,[2] formal proof responsibility and substantive proof responsibility.

The concept of burden of proof in the civil law system is associated with the inquisitorial system, and the allocation is based on the adverse consequences of the uncertainty of the facts. The uncertainty of the facts does not mean the uncertainty of the legal issues. The burden of proof is an abstract sense of proof responsibility, and the allocation of responsibilities between the two parties is basically the sharing of subjective burden of proof. This form of responsibility allocation does not have a decisive significance for the outcome of the lawsuit.

ii. **Allocation of the burden of proof in continental law countries**

After the "Legal Element Theory" was established in the civil law countries, other theories such as the "Danger Zone Theory", "Probability Theory", and "Damage Attribution Theory" emerged. However, the "Legal Element Theory" remains the prevailing view in the allocation of the burden of proof. The "Legal Element Theory" mainly refers to "the party should assert and prove the elements of the norm that are favorable to them". Generally speaking, the party should bear the burden of proof for the facts that belong to a certain legal constituent element. The party who asserts the existence of a right or other legal effect should bear the burden of proof for the legal facts that give rise to the right; the party who asserts that the right no longer exists or its legal effect has changed should bear the burden of proof for the legal facts of the right's extinction, change or limitation.

In recent years, civil law countries have established some exceptional provisions through legislation and judicial precedents, in addition to the general rule that the party asserting the existence of a fact bears the burden of proof, based on the actual situation of social development. France is a typical country among civil law countries in terms of exceptional provisions. These exceptions mainly include the following aspects.

a. When the defendant proposes a fact with certain probative force as evidence, such as in defamation cases, if the prosecution has proved the existence of the defendant's defamatory act, and the defendant defends, they should provide evidence to prove that the fact does not exist.

[2] Rosenberg (2018).

b. Regarding justifiable defense, the law requires the defendant to provide evidence that their behavior was a justifiable defense, except for the situation where it is presumed to be a justifiable defense.
c. When the defendant invokes the privilege of not testifying against a family member, the defendant should provide evidence to prove it.
d. In cases related to road traffic, when the police impose a penalty on a driver for violating the paid parking regulations, if the driver claims they are not at fault, they must prove that there were no clear paid parking signs on the premises. For crimes involving fines for violating parking regulations, it is presumed that the holder of the vehicle registration certificate is responsible; in cases where the vehicle has been rented to a third party, it is presumed that the renter is responsible. If the vehicle registrant and the renter claim that someone else is responsible, they should bear the burden of proof for their claim.
e. When the defendant claims that they committed the crime due to coercion or mental disorder, the defendant bears the burden of proof.
f. In cases of minor offenses and tax cases, the existence of a crime can be presumed based on on-site records. If the accused claims they did not commit the crime, they must provide evidence in writing or through witnesses.
g. When the defendant invokes a fact that makes the crime actually impossible, such as not being at the scene, the defendant should provide evidence to prove it.
h. In cases where goods without valid customs clearance evidence are seized within the jurisdiction of the customs, it is presumed that they are smuggled goods. If the accused claims that the goods are not smuggled, they should bear the burden of proof.
i. According to criminal law, a person living with someone who habitually engages in prostitution is regarded as a "prostitution facilitator for profit". If the defendant claims innocence, they must prove a legitimate source of income commensurate with their living standard.
j. In certain economic crimes, minor offenses of polluting waterways, or crimes of making fraudulent announcements, if the defendant uses "force majeure" as a defense, they should bear the burden of proof.

11.4.1.2 Allocation of the Burden of Proof in Common Law Countries

Based on historical traditions and long-term case practice, Anglo-American legal systems have formed a relatively systematic and complete system of evidence. Liability theory system. There are some differences between the UK and the US on the issue of burden of proof.

i. **The Burden of Persuasion and Burden of Proof in the United Kingdom**

The burden of proof in the United Kingdom's evidence law actually consists of two parts, namely the burden of persuasion and the burden of proof.

The burden of persuasion, also known as the statutory burden, refers to the burden of proof that a party to a lawsuit should bear in order to convince the trier of fact (judge or jury) of all the facts presented by the court. The party should provide sufficient evidence to convince the judge or jury and make them form a conviction, so it is called the burden of persuasion. Since this responsibility is stipulated by law and cannot be shirked, it is called the statutory burden. If the party cannot remove the statutory responsibility it bears according to the standard of proof, it will eventually lead to its defeat. Therefore, this responsibility is also called the ultimate responsibility or comprehensive responsibility. In criminal proceedings, this responsibility is always borne by the prosecution, that is, the prosecution should convince the trier of fact (judge or jury) according to the standard of proof that the facts of the crime it accuses are true based on all the evidence it presents, otherwise, this responsibility cannot be removed. This statutory burden of persuasion is not transferable at any time in the lawsuit.

The burden of proof, also known as the burden of producing evidence or the burden of advancing, refers to the party's submission of sufficient evidence to make the facts claimed by the party become a controversial issue for the jury to deliberate in the court, and then obtain a decision in its favor. It is also known as the "burden of evidence", the responsibility to provide evidence or the burden of advancing.

Taylor, a British scholar of evidence law, believes that in adversarial litigation, a party—whether in criminal or civil litigation—must do two things to defeat the other party: he must provide sufficient evidence to satisfy the legal judge, and the evidence he provides must ultimately convince the fact judge to the required extent. In other words, if a party wants to win the lawsuit, he has the responsibility to prove the facts he claims, and his proof should meet the necessary standards.[3]

ii. **The dual burden of proof in the United States**

In the United States, the more popular theory of burden of proof is the dual burden of proof proposed by Thayer. The burden of proof is divided into the burden of presentation and the burden of persuasion.

The burden of presentation refers to the party's responsibility to present evidence and convince the judge to submit the case to the jury, or to present a piece of evidence to make his or her claim a controversial point. The burden of presenting evidence is first borne by the party who claims the existence of the fact. At the beginning of the lawsuit, the party should present prima facie evidence to make the judge accept his or her accusation. The judge has the right to decide on it without the need for the jury to debate.[4] If the plaintiff or the prosecutor's evidence is insufficient, the defendant can make a "no response" motion, and the judge can also rule to dismiss the lawsuit.

The burden of persuasion refers to the responsibility of the party making a claim to present evidence to convince the jury that their claim is true in a lawsuit. In criminal proceedings, the prosecution bears the responsibility of convincing the jury of the defendant's guilt beyond a reasonable doubt. The burden of persuasion is actually only directed at the facts judged by the jury, that is, whether the defendant is guilty. Although sometimes the defendant's defense also needs to be judged by the jury,

---

[3] Taylor (2000).

[4] Strong (2004).

the defendant only needs to raise a reasonable doubt in the mind of the jury, without having to reach the level of beyond a reasonable doubt, and thus it is not the burden of persuasion in the ultimate sense.

iii. **Allocation of the burden of proof in common-law countries**

The allocation of the burden of proof in common law countries originates from case law. Regardless of the charges, the prosecution bears the responsibility of proving the facts of the defendant's guilt in criminal proceedings. This principle has become an integral part of British common law. British Chief Justice Sankey believes that "Looking through the web of British criminal law, we can often see a golden thread, that is, it is the prosecution's responsibility to prove the defendant's guilt... When the entire case is finally considered, whether it is the evidence submitted by the prosecution or the defendant, if it can arouse reasonable doubt on whether the defendant intended to kill the victim, then the prosecution has not proved its accusation, and the defendant is therefore entitled to a not guilty verdict."[5] In general, the prosecution bears the statutory responsibility of accusing the crime, that is, the burden of persuasion, and the defendant does not bear the obligation to prove his innocence. However, in most cases, the defendant may raise certain controversial issues, and if the controversial issues are to be transferred to the jury for trial, the defendant must provide sufficient evidence. However, the prosecution is not required to deny every defense before it is raised. Lord Goddard, a British judge, said in a case: "Adhering to the rule that the (legal) burden is always borne by the prosecution does not mean that the prosecution must present evidence to refute the defense before the (defendant) raises the defense of self-defense." If the defendant raises defenses such as coercion, provocation, emergency, accident, and mental disorder, sufficient evidence must be submitted to make the judge believe that the defense constitutes a disputed fact and should be submitted to the jury for trial. If there is no evidence to support his defense, the judge has the right to withdraw the dispute from the jury. Once the defendant has properly fulfilled the burden of proof, the statutory burden of the prosecution begins to take effect. To complete the task of proving the defendant guilty, the prosecution must not only prove the elements of the crime, but also prove that the crime was not committed on the basis of provocation or self-defense. Because the defendant successfully raised a protest dispute, the scope of the prosecution's statutory burden of proof has been expanded to a certain extent.

In some cases, because it is quite difficult for the prosecution to prove the facts of the case and there are reasons for not being able to do so, British case law changes its perspective and emphasizes that the defendant should fulfill a certain burden of proof in order to maintain the balance between "security and freedom" and clarifies it through legislation. The UK stipulates that the defendant's burden of proof is roughly divided into the following categories.

a. In serious fraud investigations, a suspect who is questioned and who refuses to answer questions or lies without reasonable justification commits an offence in itself and may be sentenced to a short term of imprisonment. This means that a

[5] Reay and Templeman (1999).

defendant accused of serious fraud who wishes to plead not guilty must bear the burden of proof.

b. Failure of a suspect or accused to give evidence allows the judge and jury to draw inferences against him or her. The judge and jury may draw an inference against the accused from the fact that the suspect did not tell the police during questioning what they were expecting to be mentioned, a fact which the defence may use as a basis for its defence at trial. The judge and jury may draw "seemingly appropriate inferences", i.e., inferences against the accused, because of the accused's failure to present evidence or his unjustified refusal to answer questions during the court proceedings.

The judge and jury may draw inferences against the accused when the suspect refuses to answer police questions about suspicious objects, substances, or traces that are found on the accused's body or at the place of arrest. When a police officer finds a person whom he has arrested in a certain place around the time of a pre-crime offence and is convinced that he has committed the alleged offence, the police officer asks him to give an explanation about it, and the suspect does not give an explanation to the police officer. In such cases, the court or jury may draw "such inferences as appear proper".

c. Strict burden of proof. Strict burden of proof refers to the provisions of the criminal law, the perpetrator has committed a specific harmful act or is in an illegal state, and there is no evidence to the contrary to show that he lacks subjective guilt, the judge can be presumed to have the guilt and make him bear criminal responsibility. The English common law strict liability includes the following four offences: public nuisance; libel; blasphemous libel; and contempt of court. The strict liability of the British enactment is mainly embodied in the Traffic Act, the Food Act, the Liquor and Drugs Act, the Fisheries Act and the Hunting Act, which are related to the infringement of the public welfare or serious public nuisance of industrial and commercial offences. Examples include obstruction of highways, making a lot of noise, illegal possession of firearms and ammunition, and possession or sale of counterfeit or substandard drugs and narcotics. In cases of strict burden of proof, if the defendant puts forward his own defence of innocence, he must bear the burden of proving the cause of the defence.
d. In British jurisprudence, the defendant should also bear the burden of proof in the following cases: (i) If the defence submits that the defendant is mentally ill or unfit to stand trial, it should provide evidence of the facts claimed by the defendant. (ii) If the statutory law provides that it is unlawful to carry prohibited goods without lawful authority, justification, special circumstances or exceptional circumstances, the defendant shall bear the burden of proof if he argues that there is lawful authority, justification, special circumstances or exceptional circumstances. (iii) If the defendant claims that he/she has obtained consent for the act or that the act was committed by accident, incident, coercion, out of anger or in self-defence, the burden of proof shall be on the defendant. The defendant has the burden of proof. (iv) If the defendant intends to override the presumption

of certain facts in the written law, or invoke the proviso, exception or exemption in the provision, the defendant shall bear the burden of proof.

Common law countries and civil law countries in the burden of proof there are some differences. The former is generally based on factual issues, the parties with the help of proof of the facts to obtain the rights; the latter is generally based on legal norms, the parties through the fulfilment of the relevant requirements of the legal norms, and ultimately to make their own rights to be safeguarded. In criminal proceedings, not only in the theory of the defendant in the refutation of the charges should bear the burden of proof, but also in the summary of the judicial practice on the basis of experience, through the statute law gradually clarify the defendant in which specific circumstances need to bear the burden of proof. The common denominator is the requirement that the defendant should bear the burden of proof in rebutting the charges. The common point is to require the defendant, in the case of refuting the charges, should bear a certain burden of proof for the facts claimed by the defendant. Theoretically, the basic structure of the burden of proof system has been formed, including the burden of claim, the burden of proof and the burden of persuasion.

11.4.2 Allocation of the Burden of Proof in China

According to the provisions of the three major procedural laws of China and the contents of the relevant judicial interpretations, the burden of proof can be divided into the burden of proof in criminal proceedings, the burden of proof in civil proceedings and the burden of proof in administrative proceedings.

11.4.2.1 Allocation of the Burden of Proof in Criminal Proceedings

The principle of 'whoever claims, whoever proves' is implemented in criminal private prosecution cases. A private prosecution must provide evidence to prove that the defendant has committed a crime, and bears the burden of proof of the fact that the defendant is guilty. In the case of a private prosecution that lacks evidence of guilt (including no evidence and insufficient evidence), if the private prosecutor is unable to provide additional evidence, the court shall persuade the private prosecutor to withdraw the private prosecution or rule that it is inadmissible. If the defendant files a counter-claim against the private prosecutor, he or she shall also bear the burden of proof of the facts claimed in the counter-claim. Criminal The burden of proof in a private criminal case is similar to that in a civil case.

i. **Burden of proof in prosecution cases**

The burden of proof in public prosecution cases is borne by the procuratorial authorities as the prosecution. The act of providing evidence to prove the facts of the case by the procuratorial authorities is an act of proof on their own authority, and the burden of proof is a duty that they should fulfil. The allocation of the burden of proof in criminal prosecution cases is as follows.

a. In principle, the prosecution bears the burden of proof in public prosecution cases. In an indictment case, the prosecuting authority, on behalf of the State, brings an indictment against the defendant, accusing the defendant of a crime, and the status of the prosecution in the litigation is that of the prosecution. As the prosecution, the procuratorate must provide the court with "solid and sufficient" evidence sufficient to prove that the defendant is guilty of the offence and that he or she has been given a heavier penalty, and it should actively send its officers to the court to support the prosecution. The significance of a prosecutor's presence in court to support the prosecution lies in the presentation to the court of sufficient evidence to prove the facts of the crime, so as to persuade the court that the evidence for the prosecution is true and sufficient and is sufficient to establish that the accused has committed a crime. This responsibility is a full one, which the prosecution cannot shirk to the accused. If the evidence presented by the prosecuting authority is insufficient, the court shall, in accordance with the law, 'render a judgement of acquittal on the grounds of insufficient evidence to establish the alleged offence'.
b. Victims in prosecuted cases do not bear the burden of proof. Although victims in public prosecution cases are also parties to the case, they have the right to accuse the crime, but do not bear the burden of proof. Because the offence is not only an infringement of the rights and interests of the victim, but also an infringement of the legitimate interests protected by the State, it is regarded by the State as a kind of public nuisance and undermines the normal social order of the State. For this reason, the investigation and prosecution of criminal offences should be carried out by special organs established by the State. Victims in criminal proceedings can provide some evidence and certain clues of their own knowledge to help the investigating authorities to solve the case and to assist the procuratorial authorities to carry out the public prosecution; they do not bear the responsibility of providing solid and sufficient evidence to substantiate the facts of the offence.
c. The defendant does not bear the burden of proof, but in the refutation of the charges of the defence also need to bear part of the burden of proof. Modern criminal proceedings based on the presumption of innocence, the defendant generally does not bear the burden of proof. The court can neither require him to prove his innocence nor compel him to incriminate himself, unless otherwise provided by law.

China's judicial practice that the defendant should bear part of the burden of proof in the following cases: (i) to the "large amount of property of unknown origin" harge, the defence needs to explain the source of the property; (ii) "self-defence" defence, the defence needs to provide evidence of their own have been unlawfully assaulted; (iii) to raise the defence of "mergency evacuation", the defence needs to provide evidence of an emergency or force majeure; (iv) to raise the defence of "mental illness" as a ground for not being criminally liable, or for mitigating or reducing the punishment, the defence needs to provide evidence of mental illness; e. to raise the defence of "alibi", the defence needs to provide evidence of where the accused was at the time; (v) to raise a defence of "absence from the scene", the defence needs to provide evidence of where he or she was at the time. (vi) The defence is required to provide evidence of "lawful possession" in order to raise the defence of "lawful possession" of seized prohibited items; (vii) To raise the defence that the Prosecution has taken evidence illegally, the Defence is required to provide relevant clues or materials such as the person, time, place, manner and content of the allegedly illegal evidence; (viii) The possible origin of suspicious objects or traces found in a person's immediate vicinity or place of residence, if the defence claims that they are not relevant, except in cases of complete ignorance; (ix) Other matters in rebuttal of the allegations, to be supported by relevant evidence, as the case may be;

The partial burden of proof on the accused and his or her defence in rebutting the alleged offence is only relative. It is distinctly different from the burden of proof borne by the public prosecutor in proving the existence of the offence or the establishment of the facts of the offence. These differences are mainly manifested in the following three aspects: (i) different nature. Defendants and their defenders in the case of rebuttal charges to bear a certain burden of proof, the law does not compel the defence must provide evidence to prove the establishment of the facts claimed; the prosecution put forward by the defendant is guilty of the allegations, the burden of proof is absolute. (ii) proof of different requirements. The defence in the case of rebuttal of the allegations of a certain burden of proof does not require the evidence must reach the level of certainty, adequacy; prosecution of criminal charges, not only to reach the level of certainty, adequacy of evidence, but also to reach a certain standard of proof. (iii) different legal consequences. The defence in the case of rebuttal charges should bear a certain burden of proof, but the court shall not be based only on the defence can not put forward a strong defence evidence and the defendant is found guilty or aggravate his penalty; if the prosecution can not put forward solid and sufficient evidence to prove its allegations, the court can only be made in favour of the defendant's verdict or acquittal of the defendant.

In essence, part of the burden of proof borne by the accused and his or her defence is only the responsibility to provide evidence, provide evidence that can cause the court to doubt the facts of the crime proved by the prosecution is the same as fulfilling the burden of proof, does not bear the burden of persuasion. The court does not bear the burden of proof, but in order to pursue the truth of the facts, it has the ex officio duty to "clarify the facts of the case". The court shall exercise its functions to the best of its ability in order to discover the truth of the evidence collected ex officio, and the collection of evidence is the duty of the court in the trial.

ii. Allocation of the burden of proof in civil proceedings

In civil litigation, the allocation of the burden of proof should follow the general principle of "whoever claims, whoever gives evidence", i.e., it is the responsibility of the parties to provide evidence to prove their claims. If the party with the burden of proof fails or refuses to prove it, the claim may be unsubstantiated. The main duty of the court is to examine and verify the evidence comprehensively and objectively in accordance with the legal procedures, but in the following two cases, the court has the duty to check the evidence and should take the initiative to investigate and collect the evidence: a. the parties and their legal representatives for objective reasons can not collect evidence; b. the court that the trial of the case requires evidence.

Civil litigation follows the principle of 'who claims, who proves' the allocation of the burden of proof, because civil litigation needs to solve the substantive issues of civil disputes, is a citizen, legal person or other organisations in order to safeguard their own private rights, and request for legal remedies for the activities. This activity is affected by the principle of disposition of the parties, and the State generally does not actively intervene in it. Therefore, only when the party concerned puts forward evidence to prove its own claim can the court ascertain the truth, and if the party bearing the burden of proof fails to provide evidence or provides evidence that is insufficient to establish the existence of the facts claimed by the party concerned, it will bear the risk that its claim cannot be established. For the allocation of the burden of proof in addition to the above principles should be followed, our judicial interpretation of the special cases of the burden of proof and the allocation of a clear, and requires the encounter of the special burden of proof configuration needs to the supreme people's court, by the supreme people's court, the supreme people's court approval of the way to solve the case, and can not be arbitrarily changed in individual cases of the distribution of the burden of proof of the rules determined by the law, aimed at solving the trial practice of the arbitrary application of the burden of proof. Risks of arbitrary application of the burden of proof in trial practice.

Allocation of the burden of proof has legal, substantive legal norms itself contains the content of the allocation of the burden of proof, in principle, the burden of proof by the law rather than by the judge, only in very special circumstances, in accordance with the law of the allocation of the burden of proof will lead to obviously unfair results, only then allow the judge in accordance with the principle of good faith, the principle of fairness, and other factors to allocate the burden of proof. The judge shall determine the burden of proof in accordance with the following principles, unless otherwise provided by law: a. the party claiming the existence of a legal relationship shall bear the burden of proving the basic facts of the legal relationship; b. the party claiming that the legal relationship has been changed or destroyed or its rights have been obstructed shall bear the burden of proving the basic facts of the change or destruction of the legal relationship or the obstruction of its rights; c. the party claiming the existence of a legal relationship shall bear the burden of proving the basic facts of the change or destruction of the legal relationship or the obstruction of its rights. The burden of proof shall be borne by the parties. For laws, regulations, judicial interpretations do not provide for the burden of proof, the court may, in accordance with the principle of fair responsibility and honesty and credit, the ability of the parties to prove a combination of factors to determine. Generally, the court shall consider the nature of the case, the degree of difficulty of proof, the proximity of the parties to the evidence, the degree of probability of the facts occurring, the ability to collect evidence and other factors.

iii. **Burden of proof in administrative proceedings**

The administrative organ, as the defendant in an administrative proceeding, shall bear the burden of proof in respect of the administrative act. When the defendant fails to prove that the administrative act he or she has performed is lawful and the court is unable to ascertain the facts of the case, the defendant bears the consequences of losing the case. On the contrary, because the plaintiff can not adduce evidence to prove the illegality of the administrative act and judge the plaintiff to lose the case.

The administrative litigation law stipulates that the administrative organ bears the burden of proof, mainly based on the nature of the administrative litigation law, the party's ability to prove, the fairness of the procedure, and the law on the administration of the law. The main reasons are as follows:

Firstly, the constituent elements of an administrative act require that the administrative act to be proved should be lawful. Legitimacy requires that the administrative body in the administrative act, should be in accordance with the legal procedures for the 'first evidence and then ruled', the full collection of evidence, according to the evidence of the factual situation, in accordance with the law to make a ruling. An administrative act must not be made against a citizen, legal person or other organisation without evidence or sufficient evidence. Therefore, when an administrative organ issues an administrative act that is appealed to the court, the defendant should already have sufficient evidence to prove the legality of the administrative act. The plaintiff can provide evidence to prove that the administrative act is unlawful, not because the evidence provided by the plaintiff is not established, and exempt the defendant on the lawfulness of the administrative act of the burden of proof.

Secondly, in the administrative legal relationship, the administrative organ in the active position, its implementation of the act without the consent of citizens, legal persons or other organisations, citizens, legal persons or other organisations in a passive position. As a result of the unequal status of the two parties in an administrative legal relationship, it is generally difficult or even impossible for the plaintiff to collect evidence, and even if some evidence is collected, it is difficult to preserve it. In order to reflect the equality of the two parties in the litigation, the law requires the defendant to prove the lawfulness of its behaviour, but does not require the plaintiff in a passive position to bear the burden of proof.

Thirdly, the administrative organ's ability to prove than the plaintiff, in some specific circumstances, the plaintiff almost no ability to prove. Some cases of evidence need certain professional knowledge, technical means and even equipment to obtain, these are often the plaintiff does not have. Such as cases involving environmental pollution, drug management in the case of shoddy drugs, poisonous and harmful food cases, etc., these are the plaintiff can not be collected and preserved, and thus require the plaintiff to provide evidence will be beyond its ability to bear, the law has the suspicion of the difficult, there is also the possibility of obvious unfairness.

Generally speaking, in a lawsuit against an administrative organ for an administrative act, the administrative organ bears the burden of proving the legality of the administrative act. However, in a lawsuit brought by a plaintiff against an administrative organ for failure to act, the plaintiff shall provide evidence that it has made an application in the course of the administrative procedure, except in the following cases: a. where the defendant should have taken the initiative to perform its statutory duties ex officio; b. where the plaintiff is not able to provide the relevant evidence for justifiable reasons, such as the defendant's imperfect system of registering applications, and is able to make a reasonable explanation. In administrative compensation proceedings, the plaintiff shall provide evidence of the fact that the administrative act in question has caused damage. Special attention shall be paid to special cases, for example, in the case of securities administrative penalties, the regulatory body shall, in addition to providing the court with the evidence and grounds on which the decision on the administrative penalty being sued is based in accordance with the law, also submit the evidence and materials provided by the plaintiff and the third party in the administrative proceedings. Taking into account the special nature of some types of securities offences, the regulatory body bears the burden of proof for the main facts of the offence, and appropriately transfers the burden of proof for some specific facts to the plaintiff and the third party by way of presumption.

11.5 Reversal of the Burden of Proof

11.5.1 Overview of the Reversal of the Burden of Proof

Reversal of the burden of proof is a form of allocation in which the burden of proof for a claim made by one party is borne by the other party who denies the validity of the claim or denies part of its factual composition. It is based on the legal elements of the allocation of the burden of proof of the amendment, originated in the 1960s German theory. It is the modern law of fairness, justice and protection of the weak concept of "who claims, who proves" rule of supplementation, adaptation or correction, belongs to the "who claims, who proves" of the regular burden of proof allocation of the exception.

The law may place the burden of proof on the party making the claim, which would normally be the burden of proof, and stipulate that it is not the burden of proof, but rather that the other party bears the burden of proof as to the existence or non-existence of the fact, and that if the other party fails to provide evidence in this regard, the factual assertion of the other party may be determined to have been established. Since the reversal of the burden of proof involves the substantive rights of the parties, especially the allocation of the risk of uncertainty about the truth of the facts, generally only the substantive law can make provisions. The "reversal" of the burden of proof is premised on the "positive" principle of "he who asserts, he who proves", which is an exception to the "positive" rule. It is an exception to the "positive" rule. In essence, this "exception" in the substantive law has been allocated, with the normative predecessor, from the distribution of the results of the state is inverted.

The reversal of the burden of proof has the following implications:

Firstly, reversal of the burden of proof means that the party making the claim does not bear the burden of proof in respect of a certain matter, while the other party who opposes it has the obligation to prove it. The reversal of the burden of proof means that the party making the claim does not bear the burden of proof on a certain cause (fault or causation, etc.), and the substantive law clearly stipulates that, unlike the conversion of the burden of proof in the procedure, it is only a "reverse exercise" of the burden of proof.

The burden of proof conversion refers to the specific litigation in the parties to provide evidence in the procedure for some reason occurred in the transfer of the burden of proof, he does not involve the allocation of the burden of proof. In the litigation, one party puts forward a request, the other party puts forward a defence, both parties need to bear the burden of proof of their own claims. In the course of proof, the burden of proof shifts sequentially between the parties as a result of such requests or defences. The conversion of the burden of proof does not exempt any party to prove the responsibility, it is still "who claims, who proves" principle of embodiment, it is only the conversion of the party to put forward the responsibility of evidence, belong to the conversion of subjective burden of proof. Reversal of the burden of proof is "escaping" the "who claims, who proves" rule of limitations, it exempts the party making the claim on the existence or non-existence of a certain cause of the burden of proof should be borne by the other party to place such a burden on the other side of the objection, which belongs to the legal It is a statutory burden of proof and is mandatory in character. The "reversal of the burden of proof" is merely a theoretical generalisation.

Secondly, in the reversal of the burden of proof, the other party to the denial or objection should bear the burden of proving the existence or non-existence of a certain cause. The reversal of the burden of proof to prove what the opposing party should prove, to prove the scope of the size, generally by the substantive law clearly stipulated. The law provides for the cause of proof mainly includes two categories: one is to prove that they are not at fault; the second is to prove that there is no causal relationship. Under certain circumstances, these two facts can also be proved at the same time.

Third, in the case of reversal of the burden of proof, the other party to bear the burden of proving the existence or non-existence of a fact, if the other party does not provide evidence to prove or prove that does not meet the standard, a party claimed that the fact is established. Reversal of the burden of proof is ostensibly a reversal of the burden of proof, in fact, the burden of proof in the distribution of the problem between the parties. Reversal of the burden of proof is not only the allocation of the burden of proof, more importantly, the allocation of the burden of proof will have a direct impact on the outcome of the litigation. Such as in the case of high risk of liability, the defendant must prove that the danger is caused by the plaintiff intentionally, otherwise the defendant will face the risk of losing the case.

Fourthly, in a case where the burden of proof is reversed, the party making the claim should also bear the burden of proving the existence of some of the facts. The reversal of the burden of proof does not mean that one party does not bear the burden of proving the facts of the case, but that the burden of proof is borne by the other party. The party making the claim to a particular fact should also bear a certain burden of proof, this responsibility is called to advance the responsibility.

Fifthly, in cases where the burden of proof is reversed, the other party is generally capable of shouldering the reversed burden of proof. The burden of proof should have claimed a party to bear, because it can not bear or bear up quite difficult, the substantive law is not forced, in order to maintain the fairness of the burden of proof will be reversed provisions, is equivalent to exempt from this party's burden of proof. On the contrary, the substantive law should not impose the burden of proof on the other party and make it unfair. Therefore, the law or judicial interpretation of the reversal of the burden of proof can not be unlimited.

11.5.2 *Application of the Reversal of the Burden of Proof*

The reversal of the burden of proof increases the responsibility of the other party and affects its substantive rights, which should be strictly limited in substantive law. Because of the complexity of individual cases, it is not appropriate to be absolute in applying the rules provided for in the law. For the law does not specify, the court can be based on the principle of fairness and the principle of good faith, the party's ability to prove the burden of proof and other factors to determine the burden of proof.

Reversal of the burden of proof is based on the direct provisions of the law and judicial interpretations, but does not exclude the judge in accordance with the principle of fairness and the principle of good faith, the needs of the specific case and the parties to prove the ability to determine the burden of proof and other factors in individual cases. The judge's discretion should be subject to strict procedural limitations.

11.5.2.1 Reversal of the Burden of Proof in Criminal Proceedings

In criminal proceedings, based on the requirement of the principle of presumption of innocence, the prosecution shall bear the burden of proof of the facts of the offence it accuses, and the accused shall not bear the burden of proof. But under special circumstances, the prosecution in some cases will also appear on the difficulty of proof, and the defendant is easy to provide the relevant evidence, some of the defendant is uniquely aware of the facts, the law will be the burden of proof appropriately assigned to the defendant, the burden of proof by the defendant has a certain degree of reasonableness. For example, article 395, paragraph 1, of the Criminal Law of China provides: "If the property or expenditure of a State official clearly exceeds his lawful income by a huge amount, he may be ordered to account for the source.

If he or she is unable to account for his or her lawful source, the difference shall be deemed to be illegal income." In this regard, the requirement that a State official account for the source of his property or expenditures in excess of his lawful income has the significance of reversing the burden of proof. This provision of the Criminal Law is conducive to the realisation of the value of efficiency in litigation, and in a certain sense it is a reversal of the burden of proof.

11.5.2.2 Reversal of the Burden of Proof in Civil Proceedings

The Civil Code, the Code of Civil Procedure, the Rules of the Supreme People's Court on Certain Issues Concerning Evidence in Civil Litigation and the Summary of the Symposium on Certain Issues Concerning Evidence in Cases of Administrative Penalties on Securities provide for the reversal of the burden of proof in special cases as follows.

Article 1253 of the Civil Code stipulates that: "If a building, structure or other facility, or its shelves or hangings, falls off or causes damage to another person, and the owner, manager or user is unable to prove that he or she is not at fault, he or she shall be liable for the tort. The owner, manager or user shall have the right to recover compensation from other responsible persons if there are other responsible persons." The victim as the plaintiff does not need to provide evidence to prove who caused the fault, the ownership or management of the burden of proof of no fault. These cases mainly include cases of infringement of the rights of animals, patent infringement, environmental pollution, common dangerous acts, defective products, highly dangerous work, some labour disputes, and disputes over defective goods. The laws involved in these cases include, in addition to the Civil Code, the Law on the Protection of Consumer Rights and Interests, the Company Law, the Law on Mediation and Arbitration of Labour Disputes, and the Regulations on Work Injury Insurance.

11.5.2.3 Reversal of the Burden of Proof in Administrative Proceedings

In accordance with the provisions of the Administrative Procedure Law, the reversal of the burden of proof in administrative litigation applies: the defendant has the burden of proof with respect to the legality of the administrative act under appeal. Upon receipt of a copy of the indictment, the defendant shall provide all the evidence on which the administrative act in question was based and the normative documents on which it was based. If the defendant fails to provide evidence or provides evidence late without a valid reason, the administrative act under appeal shall be deemed to have no corresponding evidence. However, in special cases such as securities penalties, based on the listed company directors, supervisors, senior management and information disclosure violations of the degree of connection between the performance of their duties, that they are directly responsible for the competent personnel or other directly responsible personnel and given a penalty, the punished person is not convinced to file a lawsuit, it should be to provide the disclosure of information on the act of the duty of loyalty, such as the obligation of diligence and other evidence. In individual cases, such as insider trading cases, the evidence provided by the regulatory body can prove one of the following circumstances, and the punished person can not make a reasonable explanation or provide evidence to exclude the existence of the use of insider information to engage in related securities trading activities, the court may confirm that the insider trading behaviour identified by the decision on the penalty is established: i. a person who has knowledge of insider information on securities trading as stipulated in the Securities Law, and who has carried out securities trading activities related to such insider information; ii. spouses, parents, children and other closely related persons of a person with knowledge of insider information under the Securities Law whose securities trading activities are substantially consistent with the insider information; iii. knowing the above insider information and trading in securities related to the information due to the performance of his job duties; iv. illegally obtaining inside information and trading in securities related to the inside information; v. contacting the person who has knowledge of the inside information or the person who knows the inside information before the disclosure of the inside information, and his/her securities trading activities are highly consistent with the inside information.

In administrative litigation, the defendant administrative organ bears the burden of proof belongs to a kind of proof of the legality of their own administrative acts. For example, the regulatory body of the listed company directors, supervisors, senior management personnel other than identified as directly responsible for the listed company information disclosure violations or other directly responsible personnel and give punishment, should prove that the punished person has one of the following circumstances: the actual performance of the duties of directors, supervisors and senior management personnel, and information disclosure violations have a direct connection; organisation, participation, Implementation of information disclosure violations or directly lead to information disclosure violations. In a certain sense, it is a legal duty that the administrative organ must perform, which is a special form of "who claims, who gives evidence".

11.6 Questions and Reflections

According to the American scholar Posner, "the legal system often has no clue as to the merits of the legal disputes it must resolve, but it avoids this stigma by using the burden of proof as a surrogate for the lack of such knowledge." For "uncertainty as to the truth of a question of fact does not mean uncertainty as to the truth of a question of law." In the above cited example, the court of second instance held that, from the point of view of the whole process of ticket sales, Pang Moupeng himself, Lu Mou, interesting to take the company, China Eastern Airline, China Airlines letter are in possession of Pang Moupeng's name, mobile phone number and the case of the main body of the itinerary information. After excluding the possibility of Pang Moupeng and Lu Mou's leakage, there is the possibility of the leakage of information by the company, China Eastern Airlines and China Airlines. From the point of view of the cost of collecting evidence, Pang Moupeng, as an ordinary person, does not have the ability to prove whether there are loopholes in the internal management of data and information of China Eastern Airlines and Chunna Company. According to the case, combined with the contents of this chapter, think about the following questions: (a) the facts of the case should have which party bears the burden of proof? (b) what is the nature of the burden of proof borne by the subject of the burden of proof? (c) whether the burden of proof means inevitable loss? (d) the case based on the occurrence of the incident before and after the Eastern Airlines was leaked by a number of media to make a determination, the burden of proof is how to allocate?

References

Rosenberg, L. (2018). Zhengming zeren lun [Translation of Die Beweislast] (Zhuang, J. H., Trans.). Beijing: China Legal Publishing House. (Original work published 1900).

Taylor, A. (2000). Principles of evidence (2nd ed.). London: Cavendish Publishing (Routledge-Cavendish).

Strong, J. W. (Ed.) (2004). Maikaomike lun zhengju [Translation of McCormick on evidence] (Tang, W. J., Trans.). Beijing: China University of Political Science and Law Press

Reay, R. and Templeman, Lord (1999). Evidence: textbook. London: HLT Publications/Old Bailey Press.

Extended reading

Chen, G. (2000). Zhengming zeren fa yanjiu. Beijing: China Renmin University Press. (in Chinese)

Prütting, H. (2000). Xiandai zhengming zeren wenti [Translation of Gegenwartsprobleme der Beweislast: eine Untersuchung moderner Beweislasttheorien und ihrer Anwendung insbesondere im Arbeitsrecht] (Wu, Y., Trans.). Beijing: Law Press of China. (Original work published 1983).

Rosenberg, L. (2002). Zhengming zeren lun: yi Deguo minfa dian he minshi susong fadian weijichu xiezhu, trans. Zhuang, J. Beijing: China Legal Publishing House. (in Chinese)

Liu, S. (2003). Xingzheng susong zhengming zeren fenpei guize gangyao. China Legal Science, (3): 69–75. (in Chinese)

Li, H. (2003). Zhengming zeren yu guifan bushiyong lun – Rosenbeck guifan shuo ji qi yiyi. Modern Law Science, (4): 81–86. (in Chinese)

Long, Y. and Duan, W. (2008). Luelun zhengming zeren yu zhuzhang zeren de xianghu guanxi. Law Review, 26(3): 31–36. (in Chinese)

Huo, H. (2018). Zhengming zeren de fali yu jishu. Beijing: Peking University Press. (in Chinese).

Chapter 12
Standard of Proof

12.1 Introductory Case

Black American football star Simpson has been indicted for allegedly killing his ex-wife Nicole and her boyfriend Goldman. Simpson's blood and hair were taken from the crime scene, the victim's blood from Simpson's home, and the same pair of bloody gloves found at the crime scene and Simpson's home, as well as a sock stained with the victim's blood found in Simpson's bedroom. Blood and DNA tests point to Simpson. The "dream team" of lawyers hired by Simpson argued that the police proved that the bloody gloves found in the defendant's home were still wet, seven hours after the murder, and that the bloodstains should have dried out, not remained wet. Thus, the possibility of a frame-up could not be ruled out. As the defence took full advantage of the flaws in the prosecution's evidence, the jury came to the understanding that Simpson was not necessarily the perpetrator of the crime, and that the perpetrator was most likely someone else, and cast doubt on Simpson's "wife-killing behaviour", and ultimately ruled that Simpson was not guilty. Subsequently, relatives of the two victims, Goldman and Nicole, filed separate lawsuits for civil damages for wrongful death. In addition to the original evidence of the criminal proceedings, only several Los Angeles police officers who had arrived at the scene of the crime before Detective Foreman were called to testify. The court held that the plaintiff's evidence of Simpson's civil liability outweighed the evidence of his non-liability.

12.2 Chapter Overview

This chapter is about the standard of proof, including the standard of proof in criminal proceedings, the standard of proof in civil proceedings and the standard of proof in administrative proceedings. In litigation of a different nature or the same nature of

H. Guo, *Evidence Jurisprudence in China*, Understanding China,
https://doi.org/10.1007/978-981-95-3981-9_12

litigation of a different nature of the case, the standard of proof there is a certain degree of difference.

12.2.1 Overview of the Standard of Proof

The standard of proof is a measure of proof whether to meet the legal requirements of the yardstick, but also bear the burden of proof of the main body to remove the responsibility of the watershed, in the history of the litigation has been through the God shows the real, the legal real, the inner conviction of the real as well as to exclude reasonable doubt and other different requirements. In modern litigation, due to criminal, civil and administrative litigation, the pursuit of different goals, the facts of the case of the proof of the requirements of the degree of difference, in the establishment of the standard of proof is not consistent. China's litigation legislation requires that "the facts of the case are clear and the evidence is sufficient". However, there are differences in the understanding of scholars, and in the theory of "objective truth", "legal truth" and "relative truth" and other different points of view.

12.2.2 Meaning of Standard of Proof

The standard of proof is an important category of litigation proof, is the party as well as the case organ to perform the burden of proof lighthouse, is to guide and regulate the proof of the activities of the code of conduct, but also for the court to determine the facts of the case is an important yardstick, is one of the important areas of evidence jurisprudence research.

Proof standard, also known as proof requirements, proof task, proof degree or degree of understanding. Chinese and foreign scholars in the theory of its different expressions, these different expressions also implies different content and degree of difference.

Since the end of the eighteenth century to the beginning of the nineteenth century, the European bourgeois revolution impacted the feudal system, the bourgeois enlightenment ideas, such as freedom, the concept of equality, respect for individual reason and promote humanitarianism, so that the inquisitorial mode of litigation by the debate mode of litigation, the emergence of the evidence system of free will, and the formation of free will of the evidence of the standard of proof. In different countries and at different periods of historical development, the standard of proof of free conscience has been expressed and required in different ways in legislation, theoretical research and jurisprudence. To sort it out, there is a preponderance of the theory of the preponderance of the cover, beyond a reasonable doubt, a high degree of cover and the evidence is true, sufficient and so on the generalisation.

Common law countries generally from the perspective of the parties to understand the standard of proof, the standard of proof as a party with the burden of proof to provide evidence to prove its claim that the facts should reach the level, degree, quantum. Such as the United States evidence law scholars Murphy that: 'the standard of proof refers to the fulfilment of the burden of proof must reach the scope or degree, is the evidence must be in the mind of the fact adjudicator caused by the degree of certainty or cover, is to bear the burden of proof of the party in the right to win the lawsuit before the fact adjudicator to form a certainty of the standard. It is the yardstick for the quality of the evidence and the degree of certainty required by the evidence from the point of view of the fulfilment of the burden of proof.[1]

Continental law countries mainly from the perspective of the judge to define the standard of proof, the standard of proof is understood as the judge to determine the facts of the case scale. Such as the German jurist Hans Povetin that: "if the evaluation of proof is only limited to detect whether the success of the proof, that is, the judge can deny the case of a fact has been proved, then the proof of the yardstick (sometimes also referred to as the standard of proof, proof of the amount of proof or proof of the intensity of the proof) is a yardstick to measure when the proof of the success of the proof of the yardstick to decide on a specific content of the Judge of the heart of the evidence, it determines the judge on what basis is considered to have received the heart of the evidence."

China's early definition of the standard of proof by the influence of the Soviet Union law, in recent years the civil law system and the common law system of the relevant theories of the country's research and judicial practice has had a greater impact on the academic community on the concept of the standard of proof of the concept of the controversy has arisen in different ways. Proof of the standard of proof there are different views, because the standard of proof and the parties to the burden of proof is closely linked, but also with the judge to determine the facts of the case is difficult to separate activities. Because of the close relationship between the parties "proof of the facts of the case and the judge's determination of the facts of the case, it is difficult to define the standard of proof purely from the parties" or the judge's point of view in order to cover the entire content of the problem.

The close relationship between the parties to prove the facts of the case and the judge's determination of the facts of the case, so that purely from the perspective of the parties or the judge to define the standard of proof, there are difficult to cover all of the content of the problem.

The standard of proof refers to the burden of proof of the main body of evidence to prove the facts of the case should reach the degree of evidence and the judge to determine the existence of the facts of the case of the yardstick. The standard of proof can be understood from the following aspects.

First, from the perspective of the judge to determine the facts of the case to understand the standard of proof, can be regarded as a judge to judge a party's burden of proof relative to the other party's burden of proof more than how much of a measure, but also to the facts of the case to make a positive determination of the boundaries. The boundaries of the positive determination of the facts of the case. Whether it is the standard of proof beyond reasonable doubt or the standard of proof

[1] Murphy (1992).

beyond reasonable doubt, this kind of psychological standard can be said to be related to the degree of confidence in the adjudicator of the facts of the case.

Secondly, the standard of proof is understood from the point of view of the burden of proof borne by the parties, which refers to the degree to which the party bearing the burden of proof should provide evidence to prove the facts claimed in order to succeed in winning the litigation. Whether it is "the evidence cited to the degree of persuasive", or "evidence to prove the degree of probability should be achieved", are the party to prove the requirements of the law or the task given to the party to prove the standard of proof naturally becomes the party to prove the burden of proof can be Unloading of the burden of proof can naturally become the boundaries, so it is also known as the "degree of clarity". In a certain sense, focusing on the party's burden of proof level to understand the standard of proof can be said to be more meaningful. However, the party's proof from the judge's factual determination is meaningless, no matter what degree of persuasive evidence provided by the parties, or when the burden of proof of the parties to be discharged, with the judge to determine the facts of the case. The standard of proof from the perspective of the parties or the judge to define also has a certain degree of reasonableness.

The establishment of the standard of proof affects the rights and interests of the parties and the judge's determination of the facts of the case can achieve the real problem. If the standard of proof is too high, relatively increase the difficulty of the parties to prove the facts of the case, resulting in the parties to bear a heavier burden of proof, prompting the parties to pay a heavy price to fulfil this obligation, but also to the court to determine the facts of the case will bring certain difficulties to meet the high standard of the requirements will cause delays in the proceedings, affecting the efficiency of the proceedings. On the other hand, if the standard of proof is set too low, the risk of misidentification of the facts of the case will be increased. Therefore, a scientific, reasonable and appropriate determination of the standard of proof is of particular significance to judicial efficiency and fairness.

The standard of proof stipulated in our laws is "the facts of the case are clear and the evidence is solid and sufficient". This expression can be understood in two ways. From the perspective of the parties to understand, especially the prosecution or the plaintiff, "the facts of the case is clear, the evidence is indeed sufficient" is to provide evidence to meet the legal requirements, if "the facts of the case is not clear, the evidence is insufficient", its litigation claims may be court If the facts of the case are not clear and the evidence is insufficient, the claim may be "rejected by the court in accordance with the law". In criminal proceedings, the court will 'acquit the defendant on the basis of insufficient evidence to establish the alleged offence'. In civil proceedings, the party bearing the burden of proof runs the risk of losing the case. From the judge's point of view, "the facts of the case are clear and the evidence is solid and sufficient" is the basis for a positive determination of the parties' claims; otherwise, "the facts of the case are unclear and the evidence is insufficient" can only lead to a negative determination. If the court of first instance judgement is found to be unclear or insufficient evidence, the court of second instance "may decide to set aside the original judgement and return it to the people's court of first instance for a new trial". It can also be said that the standard of proof is a legal requirement for judges to determine the facts of a case, and serves as a yardstick for judges to determine the facts of a case.

12.3 Standard of Proof in Criminal Proceedings

The standard of proof in criminal proceedings has different requirements in different countries. It is higher than the standard of proof in civil and administrative proceedings. As far as it is concerned, the standard of proof for affirmative fact-finding and negative fact-finding also have different requirements.

12.3.1 Standards of Proof in Foreign Criminal Proceedings

In the jurisprudence of evidence, the standard of proof initially applied in common-law countries was that there must be a "clear basis" for the conviction and sentence of the accused. Subsequently, different terms have been used interchangeably. Since the standard of proof was influenced by free evidence and was intended to indicate different degrees of "conviction", the degree of conviction in the treason case in Dublin was placed on the word "doubt", resulting in a standard of criminal proof that has remained in use to the present day, i.e. "beyond reasonable doubt". The standard of proof of "beyond reasonable doubt" is a method of expressing the standard of proof by trial and error and the method of disproof, and the establishment of this standard is related to the tradition of scepticism in the common law countries. The most widely quoted definition of reasonable doubt "beyond a reasonable doubt" is the expression in the United States "California Penal Code": "It is not only a possible doubt, but refers to the state of the case, after a general comparison and consideration of all the evidence, the juror mentality is in such a state that they can not be said to feel that they are not in a position to prove the case. State in which they cannot be said to feel that a permanent verdict as to the truth of the offence charged has reached the point of internal conviction."

In civil law countries, the standard of proof is generally expressed as "inner conviction", which is the basic element of "free conscience". Inner conviction is a criminal standard of proof that expresses "free conscience" in a positive way, while "beyond a reasonable doubt" is another way of expressing "free conscience". "Beyond reasonable doubt" and "inner conviction" have the same orientation. In terms of subjective conviction, "inner conviction" means beyond reasonable doubt, and they are two aspects of one standard, or two operational expressions of one standard. According to Japanese scholars, "the standard of 'high degree of probability' is a method of evaluation of double certainty, and the standard of proof of 'beyond reasonable doubt' is a method of evaluation of exclusion of the negative. The two are the epiphenomenon of the same judgement."[2]

Different procedures or cases of different nature have different standards of proof. The standard for prosecution in the UK is different from the standard for reaching a guilty verdict. Such as the United Kingdom "1994 Crown Prosecutors Code," Article V (I) provides: "Crown prosecutors should be satisfied that each charge against each defendant has sufficient evidence to be 'expected to lead to a conviction'." The United States has a hierarchical interpretation of the standard of proof, dividing the degree of proof into a total of nine levels: the first is absolute certainty, which is considered unattainable due to epistemological constraints; the second is beyond a reasonable doubt, which is required for a conviction in a criminal case and is the highest standard of proof in litigation; the third is clear and convincing evidence, which is considered to be sufficient to establish a conviction in certain jurisdictions when bail is denied in death penalty cases, as well as in certain civil cases. The fourth is a preponderance of the evidence, which is required for civil judgments and affirmative criminal defences; the fifth is probable cause, which applies to the issuance of warrants, warrantless arrests, searches and seizures, the filing of grand jury indictments and prosecutor's indictments, the revocation of probation and parole, and citizen's removals; the sixth is reasonable grounds for believing that a defendant is guilty; the seventh is reasonable suspicion, sufficient to acquit the defendant; the eighth is suspicion, sufficient to begin an investigation; the ninth is suspicion, insufficient to begin an investigation;

German scholars from civil law countries, Eckroff and Masson, used the dial as a tool to illustrate the standard of proof. The dial has two ends, 0 and 100%, and there are different levels from 0 to 100%. The first level is 1–24%, the second 26–49%, the third 51–74% and the fourth 75–99%. 0 is absolutely impossible and 100% is absolutely possible. Level 1 is very unlikely, level 2 is unlikely, level 3 is approximately likely, and level 4 is very likely, i.e., highly probable.[3] Generally speaking, after exhausting the means and ways of obtaining evidence, and still not reaching the 75% level of proof, the judge should find that the facts of the case do not exist; if it exceeds 75%, the existence of the facts of the case has been proved.

Probability is the ratio of the likelihood of an event occurring under certain conditions. In relation to the facts of the case, existence is existence and non-existence is non-existence, and there is no probability in itself. Judges judge a number of evidence constitutes the evidence of the combination of proof, can use statistical probability theory of the probability value of the synthetic formula, can also assist artificial intelligence algorithms. However, the judge's judgement activity can not simply be equated with probability projections, probability theory in the evidence is only a nearly pure theory of exploration, and shall not give way to modern workers intelligence (AI) algorithms, the use of which as a standard of proof is not feasible in practice, in evaluating the authenticity of the evidence is also not desirable.

---

[2] Taguchi (2000).

[3] Prütting (2000).

12.3.2 Our Standard of Proof in Criminal Proceedings

For criminal procedure cases, there are different proof requirements for different objects of proof, and different cases require the application of different levels of standards of proof, even for the same case at different stages of the proceedings, the requirements for proof are not the same. This creates a system of standards of proof with different levels of structure.

12.3.2.1 Standards of Proof in Substantive and Procedural Criminal Law

i. **Standard of proof in substantive criminal law**

Among the standards of proof in substantive criminal law, there are standards of proof for conviction and standards of proof for sentencing. Usually, we are talking about the main standard of proof for conviction.

a. The standard of proof for conviction. The standard of proof in criminal proceedings in China is “the facts of the case are clear and the evidence is sufficient”. Proceedings to prove or determine the facts of the case to meet this requirement, in particular, as a positive standard, the following aspects should be considered: first, the evidence on the basis of which the case has been established have been verified, which is the basis for the initiation of the standard of proof; secondly, the object of proof of the case should be proved by the corresponding evidence to prove the fact that there is no evidence to prove that can not be determined; thirdly, the evidence itself, the evidence between the various kinds of evidence, as well as the evidence and the facts of the case between the absence of contradictions; fourthly, based on the evidence of the case to prove that the conclusion is unique, no evidence to prove that the case is not a contradiction.

In judicial practice, attention should also be paid to the grasp and application of the “two basics”. A case should be decided on the basis of “clear basic facts” and “sufficient basic evidence”, that is, the main facts of the case or the key decisive and fundamental facts should be clear. “The basic facts are clear”, including the facts of crime and non-crime; the facts of this crime and the facts of the other crime; the facts of punishment and non-punishment; the facts of this punishment and the facts of the other punishment; and the facts of aggravating circumstances. “Sufficiency of basic evidence” mainly means that the evidence that has a decisive impact on the basic facts of the case should be sufficiently conclusive and adequate, leaving no room for error. It must not be confused with “the facts of the case are basically clear, the evidence is basically sufficient”, the latter is prohibited by law. Because the “basic facts are clear, the basic evidence is solid and sufficient” is the practice of handling criminal cases, the application of the “two basic” to determine the facts of the case, must reach a certain degree of certainty, and at the same time must exclude other possibilities, its conclusions and points to the uniqueness of the defendant, to ensure that the defendant's case will not be considered as a criminal case. Uniqueness, to ensure the correctness of the conviction and punishment of the accused.

The theoretical setting of the standard of proof in criminal proceedings in China should be in line with three basic requirements, namely, "accuracy of language, simplicity of expression, and operability of application". Theoretically, China's standard of proof can be improved from both positive and negative aspects, while absorbing the reasonable aspects of foreign standards of proof, so as to make it in line with the actual situation and practical needs of China's criminal justice, that is, the establishment of "beyond a reasonable doubt" standard of proof.

"Undoubtedly" is a positive way of expressing the standard of proof that is suitable for the criminal proceedings in China, which is summarised from the practice. From the subjective point of view, "beyond reasonable doubt" indicates that the judge is completely sure of the facts of the case of the state of mind that is "certain", at the same time expresses the confirmation of the facts of the case has a very high degree of credibility that is "beyond reasonable doubt"; from the objective aspect, 'no doubt' indicates that the facts of the case to the specific objectivity of the sufficient evidence, the facts of the case is determined in full compliance with the criteria for the determination of the case, with the objectivity of the judge's will is not shifted. It can be said that 'beyond a reasonable doubt' is an accurate interpretation of 'the facts of the case are clear and the evidence is solid and sufficient', which is more appropriate as a standard of proof in criminal proceedings.

"Undoubtedly" is concise and clear in language and rich in connotation. It combines the "beyond a reasonable doubt" standard of proof in criminal proceedings of Anglo-American countries with the "inner conviction" standard of proof in civil law countries. In terms of the established concept, it embodies the idea of combining "verificationism" and "pseudo-evidenceism", and it is verifiable and operable. "Certainty" means certainty, not reluctance, let alone uncertainty. This kind of certainty is established on the basis of corroborating evidence on the facts of the full, complete certainty, but also the judge on the case of the facts of the establishment of the "inner conviction" of the results. At the same time, the word "certainty" in the context of a strong reflection of the objectivity and not like the 'inner conviction' as subjective colours, but also help to prevent the subjective arbitrariness of the judge. "Undoubtedly" means that there is no doubt, that there is no other doubt, that there is no other possibility. It is both the interpretation and definition of "certainty", but also the use of exclusionary law to express the standard of proof, for further verification of the reliability of the factual determination to provide a solid foundation. "Undoubtedly" and "exclude other possibilities" and "beyond reasonable doubt" have the same effect of exclusion, in line with China's criminal justice tradition and the traditional habits of language and logic.

b. Standard of proof for sentencing. In determining the standard of proof of the sentencing facts, two basic factors should generally be taken into account. The first is the nature of the sentencing fact and the result of its application. If the nature of the sentencing fact and the result of its application may deprive the defendant of property, freedom or even life, a higher standard of proof shall apply. The second is the strength or weakness of the ability of the subject of the burden of proof. In determining the standard of proof of the facts in dispute, the standard of proof shall be based on the ability of the parties to prove them, and the law shall neither confer on the parties rights that they cannot realise nor impose obligations that they cannot fulfil. If the burden of proof is placed on the defendant, the law sets too high a standard of proof. The establishment of a scientific and reasonable standard of proof for sentencing is of particular importance to judicial justice.

Continental law countries generally will be unfavourable to the defendant sentencing facts and sentencing facts in favour of the defendant to distinguish, so as to determine different standards of proof. Common law countries, the proof of sentencing facts to dispute as a prerequisite, the disputed sentencing facts will be differentiated into minor and serious circumstances and establish different standards of proof.

China's sentencing facts of proof standards also need to be based on the sentencing circumstances and the degree of impact on sentencing, set the corresponding standard of proof. The sentencing facts in favour of the defendant, such as mitigating, reducing, exempting from criminal punishment, can adopt the "preponderance of evidence" standard. Because the prosecution and the defence are in different positions, most of the evidence in favour of the defendant is put forward by the defence on its own initiative, compared with the prosecution's ability to obtain evidence, the defence's ability to obtain evidence is weaker, and it is not appropriate to prove the sentencing circumstances in favour of the defendant to a higher standard. Sentencing facts that are unfavourable to the accused, such as aggravating facts, should generally be proved beyond a reasonable doubt.

ii. **Standard of proof in procedural law**

The standard of proof for substantive and procedural facts varies according to the requirements for proving them. Substantive law facts should be proved strictly, while procedural law facts can be proved freely. Substantive law facts using strict proof of the standard for the case for the facts are clear, the evidence is indeed sufficient; procedural law facts to implement the free proof or "interpretation" standard, lower than the standard of the advantage of the cover, to achieve the possibility of the existence of the possibility of greater than the possibility of non-existence can be achieved, do not have to meet the requirements of the exact. For example, a lower standard of proof is applied to procedural facts such as evasion, coercive measures and the duration of the proceedings, so as to avoid the prolongation of the duration of the proceedings as a result of a higher standard and the infringement of the lawful interests of suspects and defendants as a result of the prolongation of the proceedings.

The standards of proof for substantive and procedural facts should also be separated, and different provisions from those of substantive law should be applied to the standards of proof for procedural facts, such as jurisdiction, disqualification, delay in proceedings, violation of legal procedures and the taking of coercive measures. This requirement is reflected, for example, in our provisions on arrest. The standard of proof of arrest: "there is evidence of criminal facts ......" "there is evidence of criminal facts", refers to the following circumstances: there is evidence of criminal facts; there is evidence that the occurrence of Criminal facts; evidence that the criminal facts were committed by the suspect; evidence that the suspect committed the offence has been verified.

In practice, the proof of the facts of the case should not blindly pursue the amount of evidence, or even take the amount of evidence as the basis for judgement. At the same time, the procedural facts of the standard of proof is not fixed, it is also with the advancement of the litigation process, the standard of its upward trend, reflecting a dynamic process of development. However, the practice of evenly dividing the standard of proof between substantive and procedural facts should be avoided, as this will not be conducive to the unfolding of the proceedings.

12.3.2.2 Standard of Proof at Different Stages of the Proceedings

Criminal proceedings in China are different from the "trial-centredism" of foreign countries in that criminal proceedings are staged, with different requirements for proof in the filing, investigation, prosecution, trial and execution of cases, and the standard of proof is gradually raised as the process continues. At the stage of filing and investigation, the proof of evidence reaches a certain standard before the procedure can be initiated, even though it belongs to the initial stage of the initiation of the proceedings. At this stage, the general evidence is relatively small, and it is difficult to make a very accurate judgement on the reality of the case, and its main task is to collect evidence for the purpose of obtaining a perceptual understanding of the case through the investigation. Because of the limitations of this understanding, the standard of proof is generally low, and a case can be opened for investigation if it is believed that there is a need to pursue responsibility for the facts of the offence. In the trial stage belongs to the decisive stage of the factual determination of the case, both the evidence to prove the facts of the case has a certain amount of requirements, but also evidence to prove the facts of the case of the quality of the higher requirements to prove that the facts of the case should meet the "facts of the case is clear, the evidence is indeed sufficient," and beyond a reasonable doubt standard.

The different stages of criminal proceedings are bound to have different requirements and should have different standards. At the stage of completion of investigation and prosecution, it is stipulated that "the facts of the 'offence' are clear and the evidence is solid and sufficient", while at the stage of making a guilty verdict it is stipulated that "the facts of the 'case' are clear and the evidence is solid and sufficient". Whether the Criminal Procedure Law adopts different standards or the same standards for the three stages of investigation, prosecution and trial remains a matter of academic disagreement.

12.3.2.3 Standard of Proof in Death Penalty Cases

Death penalty cases involve life. Once the facts are wrongly determined, it will cause irreversible impact on innocent and priceless lives. People who die cannot be revived. The proof requirements for death penalty cases, whether in fact determination or evidence acceptance, must be stricter than other ordinary criminal cases. The proof of whether the alleged criminal facts occurred, whether the defendant committed the crime, the time, place, means, consequences and other circumstances of the crime, the identity of the defendant that affects the conviction, whether the defendant has criminal responsibility, the guilt of the defendant, whether it is a joint crime and the defendant's position and role in the joint crime, and the fact that the defendant was punished more severely must be proven to be reliable and sufficient, and the collegial panel should strive to reach a consensus on the extent to eliminate all doubts.

12.3.2.4 Principles of Handling Suspicious Criminal Cases

A criminal mystery, also known as an "unsolved case", refers to a case in which there is evidence but it is insufficient to prove the defendant's crime, nor is it possible to deny the defendant's crime. It is a so-called "true and false evidence, and a balanced right and wrong" case that can neither prove the defendant's guilt nor exclude the defendant's innocence.

Criminal doubts include substantive criminal doubts and procedural criminal doubts. Substantive criminal doubts refer to cases where the facts of the crime have been ascertained, but the investigators have different opinions and disagreements on how to determine the nature of the crime, which is reflected in the application of the law; procedural criminal doubts refer to cases where the facts of the case itself are unclear or the evidence is insufficient, and there is doubt as to whether the defendant has committed a crime, which cannot be determined and does not meet the standard of proof. The criminal doubts referred to here are the latter, that is, there is evidence of guilt, and the evidence of innocence cannot be excluded. The evidence of guilt and the evidence of innocence cannot be excluded, which makes the facts of the case have both the possibility of guilt and the possibility of innocence. There is hesitation in determining his guilt, and there is uncertainty in determining his innocence, resulting in a dilemma of criminal doubts. At the same time, the law requires judges not to refuse to judge and must make a decision.

i. **Get the benefit of the doubt**

When the case handling organ does not have solid and sufficient evidence to prove the defendant's guilt and does not exclude the defendant's innocence, the court shall make an acquittal judgment, and the following rules shall be established: a. Although the suspicion of guilt is a procedural matter, it still plays a role in the entity and cannot be ruled out; b. should not therefore suspend the judgment, pending, once the judgment has a res judicata; c. After the judgment is made, the "principle of double jeopardy prohibition" or the "principle of non bis in idem" shall be implemented;

d. There is only the qualitative difference between "there" and "nothing", and the choice between "there" and "nothing" should not be measured and evaluated from the quantity of "big" and "small". It is a reasonable restriction of the judge's power of judgment, which belongs to the rule of judgment, and is different from the rules of evidence that constrain both the prosecution and the defense.

ii. **Leniency for suspicion**

When there is no doubt about the conviction of a criminal case, and there is doubt about misdemeanors and felonies and it is difficult to solve, the principle of handling in favor of the defendant should be adopted. It is difficult to determine the facts constituting misdemeanors and felonies, and should be determined according to the facts of misdemeanors. The conditions for leniency of suspicion should be: (a) The facts of the crime in question are not part of a misdemeanor or part of a felony, but they intersect and cannot be distinguished. (b) In the facts of the crime in question, the felony cannot be separated from the misdemeanor, and the unclear facts of the misdemeanor or the unclear facts of the simple felony cannot be included in this scope. If there is any doubt about the facts of the punishment, it shall be punished in accordance with a lighter punishment.

12.4 Standard of Proof in Civil Litigation

The standard of proof in civil litigation generally depends on the task of proof in civil litigation. Because the task of proof in civil litigation is different from that in criminal litigation and administrative litigation, the degree of proof required is also different from them, and there are different standards of proof in the requirements for the determination of case facts.

12.4.1 Standard of Proof in Foreign Civil Proceedings

Common law countries basically apply the standard of proof of preponderance of probability to ordinary civil cases, but the language is different. In American law, "preponder of the evidence" is used, while in British law, "balance of probabilities" is used. For some important or special civil cases, different countries have different standards of proof. In some important cases, Britain generally applies two other methods derived from the basic standard of probability weighing: the flexible method and the priority possibility method. For the former, the standard of proof changes with the seriousness of the case. For the latter, the standard of proof remains fixed. In the case, Nicholls has pointed out that the standard of proof is the balance of probability, but when the probability is estimated, the judge must bear in mind that the more serious the claim, the less likely it is to occur. Thus, the degree of proof is stronger before the court concludes that the claim has been confirmed on the balance of probabilities. But this does not mean that the more serious the claim, the higher the standard of proof. It simply means that in considering the probability and determining whether an event occurred on the basis of a balance, the inherent probability and improbability of the event being an event must be taken into account.[4] However, in the following two types of cases, there are still large differences in which standard to apply: one is the marriage case, the British Court of Appeal and the House of Lords advocate the application of the standard beyond reasonable doubt in adultery cases; The other type of case is when the facts to be proved in civil proceedings are criminal, for which both the beyond reasonable doubt and the balance of probability test are applied, but the Court of Appeal and the House of Lords are currently inclined to apply the beyond reasonable doubt test.

The standard of proof of superior evidence is mainly applied in American civil litigation. This standard requires that the party with the burden of proof need to prove the facts of his claim to the extent that existence is more likely than non-existence. In some special cases, a third standard has developed between beyond a reasonable doubt and preponders of evidence, that is, a clear and convincing standard of proof, whose degree of proof is between preponders of probability and preponders of reasonable doubt. Its application cases mainly include loss of nationality, termination of parental rights and other cases, but the situation is slightly different in the United States. Some states apply to cases of fraudulent allegations, amendments to written contracts, etc. Some states apply this standard in cases of wrongful coercion, destruction of documents, contents of wills, oral deeds of gift, etc.

Civil law countries generally divide civil cases into general cases and special cases, and different cases adopt different standards. The high degree of probability applies to general cases; Special cases (such as oral trusts, oral wills, and alteration of documents by reason of error or fraud, etc.) apply a higher standard than a high probability, that is, a clear and convincing evidence; There are also individual special cases where a lower standard than high probability is applied. For example, Germany generally applies a lower degree of proof than the highly probable proof standard in traffic accidents, product liability, medical disputes, environmental pollution and other litigation cases. The standard of high probability is generally called the standard of apparent proof, which means that the court uses the general rule of life experience to infer the evidence of a certain fact to be proved from certain objective facts on typical matters that repeatedly appear. The standard of proof of civil proceedings in common law countries and civil law countries is based on free heart evidence, but there are some differences in their standards.[5]

In common law countries, the standard of proof of civil litigation pays attention to the external development process of things, and pays attention to procedural justice in litigation. The standard of proof of civil litigation in the civil law system countries emphasizes the intrinsic nature of things and is more inclined to the justice of entities in litigation. These problems are compatible with their litigation mode and cultural tradition, so it is not appropriate to simply comment on their merits and demerits.

---

[4] Qi (2002).

[5] Chen Rongzong (1984).

12.4.2 *The Standard of Proof in my country's Civil Litigation*

The standard of proof in civil litigation refers to the criteria used to measure whether the evidence provided by the subject of proof has met the requirements and to what extent in civil litigation. The standard of proof is the yardstick for the proof requirements of civil litigation cases. Once the degree of proof provided by the parties exceeds the yardstick, the facts of the case to be proved by the proof can be determined to be true.

The standard of proof in civil litigation includes the following meanings: 2.1 The parties are the parties who provide evidence, and the judge is the subject of judgment on the evidence; 2.2 The standard of proof is a statutory standard, which is set in advance by law and serves as a measure for determining facts; 2.3 When the degree of proof of evidence reaches the standard of proof prescribed by law, the facts of the case proved by the evidence can become the factual basis for the judge to make a judgment.

12.4.2.1 The Basis for Establishing the Standard of Proof in Civil Litigation in China

The purpose of civil litigation is to resolve disputes between parties. Such disputes often arise between parties due to property rights, identity relations and intellectual property rights. In order to avoid the risk of losing the case, the parties need to collect evidence, provide evidence, and use evidence to prove their litigation claims, and the cost of collecting and presenting evidence is also borne by the parties. The higher the degree of proof of the case, the more time and energy the party with the burden of proof needs to spend, and the greater the difficulty of proof. If a fact can be proved by the standard of proof that is predominantly probable, but the law requires the parties to prove it on the basis of certainty and sufficiency, it is equivalent to making the parties spend too much money and energy for no reason, violating the principle of litigation economy and affecting the fairness of litigation. In addition, due to the high standard of proof, the facts of the case are difficult to prove, which will also cause the legal relationship between the parties to be in an unstable and uncertain state for a long time to a certain extent, affecting the normal social, economic and living order, and not conducive to the resolution of disputes.

Civil litigation implements the principle of "who claims and who proves", that is, the party who claims the occurrence of rights bears the burden of proof for the legal facts of the occurrence of rights, and the person who denies the existence of rights bears the burden of proof for the legal elements of the obstruction of rights, the legal facts of the elimination of rights or the legal facts of the restriction of rights. Due to the egoism of both parties, the evidence in favor of their own is often presented in the lawsuit, and the evidence against their own is often hidden, or even destroyed. In this way, if one party controls the main evidence is not provided, the other party will be in a passive position, and the litigation structure is in an unbalanced state. This is not consistent with the purpose of protecting the legitimate rights and interests of the parties and pursuing the justice of the proceedings. This problem could be addressed by hindering the distribution of the burden of proof.

12.4.2.2 Factors in Establishing the Standard of Proof in Civil Proceedings

The establishment of the standard of proof in civil litigation should consider the following factors.

i. **The nature of the case**

There are objective differences in the nature of various cases. Cases of different natures have different social influences and different degrees of impact on the rights and interests of the parties, and the requirements for the degree of proof should also be different. For example, compared with general contract disputes and divorce cases, and compared with infringement of property rights and infringement of personal rights, the harm caused to society and families by the former is generally less than that of the latter, and its standard of proof is lower than that of the latter.

ii. **The importance of the case**

The importance of similar cases can be considered from the complexity of the case and the scope of influence, and the amount of the case can be used as an indicator to measure the importance of the case. Generally speaking, the more important the case is, the greater the interests of the country, society and individuals it involves, and the higher the degree of proof should be.

iii. **Probability of a case occurring**

Although the facts faced by the judge during the adjudication are one-time dispute facts, if the case is placed in the overall context of disputes, it will be found that the cases heard by the court have shown a stereotyped trend, and the probability of occurrence of different types of cases is different. For example, the probability of damages occurring is much greater than that of bill disputes; the probability of major cases occurring is lower than that of general cases.

iv. **Difficulty of proving a case**

Economic development has led to increasingly complex social life, and new types of disputes continue to emerge. In some new types of dispute cases, factors such as the lack of evidence resources and difficulty in obtaining evidence may affect the evidence to a certain extent, such as cases of infringement and disturbance of private space.

When establishing the standard of proof for civil litigation, the above factors can be considered individually according to the different circumstances of the case, and sometimes they also need to be considered comprehensively and weighed comprehensively.

12.5 The Standard of Proof in My Country's Civil Litigation

Proof in civil litigation should not be limited to a fixed standard of proof. Because no standard is sufficient to adapt to all complex social disputes, different standards can be adopted for different cases in combination with the specific circumstances of the case. However, the standard of proof in civil litigation should also establish a relative standard so that there is a minimum benchmark in judicial practice; for the substantive facts and procedural facts of civil litigation cases, the standard of proof with a preponderance of probability is generally adopted, and for civil litigation cases with serious, major and low probability of occurrence, the standard of proof with a high degree of probability is generally adopted.

i. **The standard of proof that "probability prevails"**

General civil cases can be established as the standard of proof that "probability" prevails. The standard of proof that "probability" prevails means that when the factual claim of the case is convinced by the judge that the probability of existence on the evidence is greater than the probability of non-existence, the factual claim can be found to be true. Specifically, in civil proceedings, when the party bearing the burden of proof finally proves the result can reach the general normal people in the case of common sense that there is a certain inevitable or reasonable probability or degree of certainty, it should make a determination that the claim is established. "'Probability' is a quality, or a state of possibility, that is possible rather than necessary."[6] In civil proceedings, if a higher standard of proof is applied, the parties in some cases may not be able to make the evidence provided meet the standard required by law even if they try their best. It is necessary to apply the standard of proof that "probability" prevails in civil proceedings. In the case of the court's determination of the facts of the case is not very strong, it is helpful for the judge to carefully analyze the evidence of the two sides and compare the probative power of the evidence provided by the two sides, rather than simply to determine that the burden of proof has not been fulfilled.

ii. **High probability proof standard**

The general standard of proof is the minimum standard to be achieved in the litigation process, not as long as this standard should be achieved to prove the facts or the existence of the facts of the claim to be determined, in specific circumstances and special cases also need a higher standard. However, if this standard is not met, the facts of the case can not be determined, but should be absolute. The court may adopt different standards of proof according to the relevance of the case and the interests of the parties and the degree of responsibility. Therefore, for cases of a serious and significant nature and with a low probability of occurrence in civil litigation, the standard of proof of a high degree of probability is generally applied.

---

[6] He (2003).

High degree of probability and the preponderance of probability as a standard of proof, there is a different degree of proof, the judgement scale is mainly the quality of evidence to prove and meet the requirements, should not be limited to the number of evidence. The former focuses on a comparison with the degree of proof of the other party, while the latter is mainly based on the weight and degree of its own proof. If, upon examination of the evidence provided by the party who bears the burden of proof, the court is satisfied that the existence of the fact to be proved has a high degree of probability, it shall find that the fact exists, taking into account the relevant facts. If the court is satisfied, after examining the evidence provided by a party to refute a fact asserted by the party having the burden of proof, that the truth of the fact to be proved is not clear, it shall find that the fact does not exist. If the law provides otherwise with regard to the standard of proof for the facts to be proved, it shall follow its provisions.

12.6 Standard of Proof in Administrative Litigation

Administrative litigation is the activity of the court using judicial power to deal with administrative disputes between administrative subjects and administrative counterparts. It protects the legitimate rights and interests of citizens, legal persons and other organizations through the trial and adjudication of cases, and maintains and supervises the administrative organs in exercising their powers in accordance with the law. Since the nature of the cases handled by administrative litigation, the purpose and tasks of the litigation are different from criminal and civil litigation, the requirements of its own rules are also reflected in the standard of proof.

12.6.1 Standard of Proof in Administrative Litigation

12.6.1.1 The Meaning of the Standard of Proof in Administrative Litigation

The standard of proof in administrative litigation refers to the evidence provided by the parties in administrative cases in accordance with the provisions of the Administrative Litigation Law. The degree to which the facts of the case should be met and the basic requirements for the court to determine the legality of the administrative act in question.

The standard of proof in administrative litigation includes the following meanings.

i. The standard of proof in administrative litigation is the standard to measure whether the parties have fulfilled the burden of proof in administrative litigation

The party bearing the burden of proof in the lawsuit provides evidence to prove the facts of the case, there must be a standard of measurement, reached this standard, the burden of proof is possible.

ii. The standard of proof of administrative litigation is the standard for the court to determine the facts of the case

The court must solve the administrative dispute according to the facts of the case, and the court must have a standard for determining the facts, which is equivalent to finding out the facts of the case disputed by the parties.

iii. The standard of proof of administrative litigation includes the requirements of quality and quantity of evidence

The obtaining of truth is formed on the basis of analyzing and judging the quality (whether it is legal) and quantity (whether it is sufficient) of the evidence provided by the parties, which reflects the requirements of both quality and quantity of evidence.

Understand the standard of proof from the point of view of the parties. The standard of proof of administrative litigation is the degree to which the parties, especially the defendant, fulfill the burden of proof and prove the establishment of the administrative act accused. If its proof fails to meet this requirement, the facts it proves will not be supported by the court, and the legality of its administrative act is difficult to be maintained. From the judge's point of view, the standard of proof of administrative litigation is the measure that the judge supports the parties' case facts claim, otherwise it can not make a positive determination of the case facts. If the facts of the case are not determined according to this standard in the first instance, in the second or retrial, the facts determined by the judgment may be overturned, and the judgment made on this basis may also be revised or revoked.

12.6.1.2 The Establishment of Proof Standards for Administrative Litigation

China's legislation requires that the standard of proof of administrative litigation should be "clear case facts and sufficient evidence". Although this standard is the same as the provisions of criminal procedure law, it is different from criminal procedure and civil procedure in establishing proof standard because of the particularity of administrative procedure. There are different views on the standard of proof of administrative litigation in Chinese academic circles. The main points of view are: i. criminal, civil and administrative litigation to implement the same standard of proof, that is, the evidence is true, sufficient standard. It requires that the facts of the case be proved by the necessary evidence that has been verified, and that the contradictions between the evidence and the facts of the case be reasonably excluded. ii. Similar to civil litigation, the authentication standard of evidence in administrative litigation is not to achieve the degree of "evidence is true and sufficient" and beyond reasonable doubt as in criminal litigation, but only requires the prevailing probability. iii. The standard of proof for administrative litigation should be the same as that for criminal litigation, and higher than that for civil litigation. iv. The standard of proof of administrative litigation is intermediate, lower than that of criminal litigation but higher than that of civil litigation, and depends on the type of specific judgment. The existence of these different views fully reflects the complexity of the standard of proof in administrative litigation. Therefore, the diversity of the nature of administrative acts should be considered in setting the standard of proof of administrative litigation, reflecting the requirements of diversification.

The main purpose of administrative litigation is to review the legality of administrative acts. Due to the variety of administrative acts, the nature of various administrative acts is different, the procedures are different, administrative laws and regulations for different acts of different procedures and different requirements for obtaining evidence. For example, in the administrative punishment, the punishment made by the administrative law enforcement personnel on the spot according to the summary procedure is different from the administrative punishment made according to the ordinary procedure, the standard of proof required by the two different administrative procedures to determine the fact should also be different. At the same time, due to the great difference in the nature of various administrative acts, the degree of non-equality of rights and obligations between administrative organs and their counterparts in different administrative management is quite different. Such as administrative punishment and administrative registration act. The former adds new obligations due to the relative person's assumption of deprivation of property or liberty or impairment of rights and interests; In the latter, the obligation of the relative person is very light, and some even simply enjoy certain rights. Therefore, the requirements for proof of the two should be differentiated. Generally speaking, the standard of proof in administrative litigation should be slightly higher than that in civil litigation and lower than that in criminal litigation. In other words, the standard of proof of administrative litigation should be lower than the "certainty" of criminal litigation and higher than the "probability" of civil litigation.

Different levels of proof standards can be adopted according to different administrative actions. The reason why the standard of proof of administrative litigation is so established is that the nature, purpose, task and law of litigation activities of administrative litigation are different from other litigation, and the standards adopted should be different. The status of the parties in administrative litigation is unequal, which is different from that of the parties in equal status in civil litigation. Compared with the administrative subject status of the plaintiff and the defendant, their inferior status is higher than that of the defendant in criminal litigation. This complex relationship determines that the standard of proof in administrative litigation is in the middle zone between criminal litigation and civil litigation, and its standard of proof is moderate Intersexuality. Generally speaking, the standard of proof with high probability is the principle, and the standard of proof with preponsibility and the standard of certainty are supplemented. For administrative acts that restrict the personal freedom or life safety of the parties, as well as for cases involving property rights and other non-property rights, the standard of proof may be considered. In administrative rulings and administrative compensation cases, the standard of proof that probability prevails can be considered.

12.6.2 *Standard of Proof in Administrative Litigation*

Administrative litigation involves different issues, so the requirements for proof will also vary, forming different levels of proof standards, namely, the proof standard of high probability for general administrative cases, the proof standard of preponderance of probability for special cases, and the proof standard of beyond doubt.

12.6.2.1 The High Probability Standard of Proof in General Administrative Litigation Cases

In the relation of administrative law, because the administrative subject enjoys the power of state administration according to law, it conducts management independently on behalf of the state and participates in administrative litigation activities independently. In the administrative procedure, the administrative subject always occupies the leading, dominating and dominant position, enjoys certain functions and powers to manage specific matters, and can write external documents and make handling decisions in its own name. However, the administrative counterpart is always in the position of being led, dominated and managed in the administrative procedure, and can only dispose of his own rights within the scope permitted by laws and regulations. This inequality in status leads to administrative subjects enjoying certain privileges in handling affairs, and it is easier to investigate certain matters than administrative counterparts, and it is easier to comprehensively investigate, collect and obtain relevant evidence to ensure that the facts and evidence of their handling decisions are clear and sufficient. Therefore, the administrative procedure law of our country stipulates that the defendant should bear the burden of proof to prove that his administrative act is legal and effective. The administrative counterpart may also provide relevant evidence, but in most cases, it is not as comprehensive and systematic as the evidence provided by the administrative subject. In view of this, the high probability proof standard in administrative litigation conforms to the legislative intention of our country, and can also reflect the principles of justice, openness and fairness.

The application of highly probable proof standards should meet the following conditions: first, compared with the evidentiary effect of the evidence provided by the two parties, the evidentiary effect of the evidence provided by one party has a greater advantage; Second, the advantage is sufficient to convince the court that the facts of the case asserted by it exist, or have a greater likelihood of real existence.

12.6.2.2 The Standard of Proof that the Probability Prevails in Administrative Litigation

The standard of proof of preponderance of probability refers to the standard of proof that the court determines the facts of the case according to the evidence provided by the party with the preponderance of probative force. Its "preponderance" means that the evidence provided by one party is more persuasive and probative than the evidence provided by the other party. The probative force of the evidence provided by one party and the case facts proved by it are more likely than those of the other party, and the reasons for the establishment of the litigation claim are more sufficient, and the probative force of its evidence is more preponderant.

This standard of proof is generally applicable to administrative adjudication cases involving property rights, administrative penalties, administrative enforcement, and administrative contract cases, etc. It can also be applied to cases of inaction and administrative compensation litigation. Because administrative cases involving disputes over property rights and personal rights are, in nature, cases involving disputes over civil rights and obligations between equal subjects that have been handled by administrative agencies, the preponderance standard of proof can be adopted in reference to the standard of proof in civil litigation. The main reason for applying this standard in administrative litigation is that administrative actions as the object of administrative litigation are diverse, including unilateral administrative actions with a strong public power color, and bilateral or multilateral administrative actions with a weak public power color. The latter is more permeated with the will of the parties, and the standard of proof adopted in the litigation will be more similar to or close to civil litigation. However, administrative litigation is different from civil litigation after all, and its standard of proof is higher than that of civil litigation to a considerable extent. This is because the object of administrative adjudication is a civil dispute, and administrative litigation examines the legality of administrative actions such as administrative adjudication. Civil disputes have been subjected to the influence of public power, and its standard of proof is higher than that of civil litigation under the same circumstances, which is reasonable and legitimate.

12.6.2.3 The Standard of Certainty in Administrative Litigation

The main reason for adopting the standard of certainty in administrative litigation is that administrative behavior itself is a multi-level and multi-angle administrative means, including administrative handling behaviors with the characteristics of general administrative behavior, as well as bilateral consensual behaviors close to civil behavior, and even some administrative behaviors that are more severe than criminal sanctions. Such as compulsory isolation or compulsory drug rehabilitation, compulsory treatment, etc. These administrative behaviors can restrict the personal freedom of citizens for a long time, and to a certain extent, the impact on citizens' rights is no less than that of criminal litigation, and is more severe than fines, control, and detention in criminal penalties. Therefore, the standard of certainty should be applied to such cases in administrative litigation.

The application of the standard of beyond doubt must be in cases that have a significant impact on the personal rights of the administrative counterpart. If it is for rights other than personal rights, such as the right to education, the right to work, the right to social security and political rights, this is not limited. At the same time, the administrative act must have a significant impact on the personal or property rights of the administrative counterpart. Precisely because the administrative act has a "significant impact" on the personal and property rights of the administrative counterpart, this significant impact is close to the rights of citizens protected by the Criminal Procedure Law, and it is legitimate to adopt the proof standard of criminal proceedings.

12.7 Questions and Reflections

The US civil jury made a verdict on the case, unanimously finding that Simpson was responsible for the deaths of the two victims, and ordered Simpson to compensate the plaintiffs $8.5 million. In addition, Simpson was ordered to pay $12.5 million in punitive damages to each of the two victims' families, totaling $33.5 million. However, the standard of proof in civil litigation in my country adopts different standards of "beyond a reasonable doubt" and "more likely". "If the parties prove the facts of fraud, coercion, malicious collusion, or oral wills or gifts, and the people's court is convinced that the possibility of the existence of the facts to be proved can be excluded from reasonable doubt, the facts shall be deemed to exist." "As for the facts related to litigation preservation, recusation and other procedural matters, if the people's court believes that the possibility of the existence of the relevant facts is relatively high based on the explanations of the parties and relevant evidence, it may determine that the facts exist." Based on the case and the content of this chapter, think about the following questions: (a) What are the differences in the standards of proof between criminal and civil proceedings? (b) Is there a contradiction between the fact that the criminal proceedings could not find Simpson guilty based on the same evidence, while the civil proceedings found Simpson liable for compensation? (c) How should this case be handled according to the provisions of Chinese law?

References

Murphy, P. (1992). A practical approach to evidence (4th ed.). London: Blackstone Press.
Taguchi, M. (2000). Xingshi susongfa [Liu, D., Zhang, L. and Mu, J., Trans.; Bian, J. L., Rev.]. Beijing: Law Press China.
Prütting, H. (2000). Xiandai zhengming zeren wenti (Wu, Y., Trans.). Beijing: Law Press China.
Qi, S. J. (2002). Yingguo zhengju fa. Xiamen: Xiamen University Press.
He, J. H. (Ed.). (2003). Waiguo zhengju fa [English/official title unconfirmed]. Beijing: Law Press China.

Extended Reading

Fan, C. Y. (2000). Keguan zhenshi guanjian. China Legal Science, (1): 114–120. (in Chinese)
Zhang, W. P. (2003). Zhengming biaozhun jiangou de wutuobang. Chinese Journal of Law, (4): 60–69. (in Chinese)
Li, H. (2005). Shishi zhenwei buming chuzhi banfa zhi bijiao. Studies in Law and Business, (3): 104–111. (in Chinese)
Zhou, H. B. (2008). Xingshi zhengming biaozhun wenti zhi zheng zhong de sida wuqu. Tsinghua Law Journal, (5): 119–139. (in Chinese)
Wang, M. Y. (2013). Yi ge miuwu, liang ju feihua, san zhong xueshuo – dui anjian shishi ji zhengju de zhexue, lishixue fenxi. Beijing: China University of Political Science and Law Press. (in Chinese)
Guo, H. (2021). Woguo yizui congyou de lilun xingcha ji guize chongshu. Tribune of Political Science and Law, (1): 161–173. (in Chinese)

Part IV
Procedural theory

Chapter 13
Principles for the Application of Evidence

13.1 Introductory Case

One night, Ms Qian and three colleagues came to a hotel dinner, Ms Qian drank half a bottle of beer and went to the washroom, three colleagues heard a loud bang in the washroom, found Ms Qian has fallen to the ground, the shop staff immediately sent her to the hospital, a week after Ms Qian died. Qian's mother appealed to the court, arguing that the cause of her daughter's death was the absence of any anti-slip measures or warning signs in the hotel, and that the hotel should be held liable for compensation. The hotel argued that they had fulfilled their safety obligations by sending Ms Qian to the hospital in a timely manner after the incident, and that Ms Qian was not liable because she had a history of high blood pressure and other medical conditions. The court held that, in accordance with the principle of "who claims, who proves", the plaintiff has the burden of proof as to whether there is a causal relationship between the service behaviour of the defendant restaurant and the death of Ms. Qian. The evidence provided by the plaintiff does not prove that the money is due to the restaurant tiles slippery and fell to death, also did not apply to the court within the statutory period of proof to the defendant restaurant tiles anti-slip performance appraisal. According to the hospital history, Ms. Qian suffered from high blood pressure, before the accident, had drunk half a bottle of beer, so the cause of the fall, there are a variety of possibilities exist. Because of the plaintiff, Ms Qian's body was cremated, making it difficult to ascertain the true cause of her death through forensic examination.

H. Guo, *Evidence Jurisprudence in China*, Understanding China,
https://doi.org/10.1007/978-981-95-3981-9_13

13.2 Chapter Overview

This chapter deals with the basic principles of the application of evidence, including the principles of the adjudication of evidence, the principle of direct speech and the principle of truthful discovery. The principle of evidence judgement is the principle of safeguard for the determination of the facts of the case, the principle of direct speech is the principle of confirmation of evidence, and the principle of true discovery is the principle of the purpose of the application of evidence.

13.3 Principles of Evidentiary Adjudication

13.3.1 Basic Meaning of the Principle of Adjudication of Evidence

The principle of adjudication of evidence has attracted much attention since ancient times. In early societies, the principle of adjudication of evidence did not have a strict meaning because of the impact of religious, moral and other factors. The establishment and development of the referee of evidence as a principle for the application of evidence is a matter of modern times. "Criminal judgement, should be based on evidence, that is, the so-called evidence refereeism, has become a certain rule of modern criminal procedure."[1] Countries around the world have different evidence referee principle of legislation mode, some countries through the form of law to be clearly stipulated, such as Japan, France; Some countries through the collection, examination and judgement of the evidence of the rules to be embodied, such as the United Kingdom, the United States. Evidence referee principle is not a simple and abstract principle, its principle also condenses a series of closely linked specific rules. These rules to evidence referee principle as the core and connection point, and influence the evidence referee principle in the evidence law status.

Evidence referee principle, also known as "evidence referee doctrine", refers to the litigation for the determination of facts, should be based on evidence; no evidence, shall not determine the facts. This principle contains two basic laws: first, the facts in the litigation should be based on evidence, which is the positive law of the principle of evidence refereeing; secondly, if there is no evidence, can not be found on the relevant facts, which is the negative law of the principle of evidence refereeing. In litigation, the basis for determining the facts, in addition to the express provisions of the law, can only be evidence. Anything other than evidence, such as subjective conjecture, delusion, speculation, etc. shall not be used as the basis for determining the facts. "No evidence of the judge, or only rely on the magistrate's ideal speculative words, as the basis of its decision, are contrary to the evidence of the judge."[2] Most countries and

[1] Diao (1984a).

[2] Chen (1979).

regions on the evidence of the principle of adjudication have corresponding legislative provisions. Such as Japan's Criminal Procedure Code, Article 317 provides: "the determination of facts shall be based on evidence." Article 427 of the French Code of Criminal Procedure provides that in the trial of misdemeanours, "unless otherwise provided by law, the offence may be established on various grounds...... The judge may only base his judgement on the evidence submitted to the trial and debated by the parties." Article 154 of the Criminal Procedure Law of China-Taiwan provides that: "The facts of a crime shall be determined by evidence, and the facts of a crime shall not be presumed in the absence of evidence." Article 69 of the Judicial Interpretation of the Criminal Procedure Law of China provides: "The facts of a case must be established on the basis of evidence." Instead, the judgement is based on other criteria. Article 85 of the Provisions of the Supreme People's Court on Evidence in Civil Litigation provides: "The people's court shall base its judgement on the facts of the case that can be proved by the evidence." Article 97 stipulates: "the people's court shall set out the reasons for the adoption of the evidence in the decision", these provisions constitute the principle of evidence judgement of the Chinese expression. The principle of adjudication by evidence can be understood in the following ways.

13.3.1.1 Evidence for the Principle of the Adjudication of Evidence

The facts in the proceedings shall be determined on the basis of evidence, which is irreplaceable as the basis for determining the facts of the case. The first meaning of the principle of adjudication by evidence is that evidence is the basis for the determination of facts, and adjudication is based on this. Facts in the litigation should be based on evidence, which is positively affirming the understanding of the fact that the basis can only be evidence, which is the positive significance of the principle of evidence refereeing. French scholars believe that the judge's inner conviction can arise from the scene of the verification (on-site investigation) ...... interrogation of the accused, but also the judge to obtain the formation of this sense or that sense of inner conviction of the material......[3] Of course, the free evidence can be from the preliminary investigation or from the various materials collected during the pre-trial process...... In another respect, anything other than evidence, such as subjective conjecture, delusion, speculation, etc., is not a basis for the determination of the facts. Among them, the evidence in the evidence is not only has the ability to evidence, but also should be the evidence of the legal process of verification, and the evidence based on the proof of the requirements or standards.

The second meaning of the principle of evidence judgement is that if there is no evidence, the relevant facts can not be determined. This is from the opposite side of the evidence to make the referee qualification, belong to the negative meaning of the evidence referee principle. There is no evidence of course can not determine the facts of the case, when the evidence in quantity and quality can not meet the need for proof, the same can not determine the facts of the case. Therefore, the absence of

[3] Diao (1984b).

evidence includes not only the absence of any evidence, but also the insufficiency of evidence, including incomplete evidence, defective evidence. No evidence not only refers to the lack of corresponding entity, sufficient evidence, but also refers to the evidence in the procedural matters or form fails to meet the requirements of the law.

The third meaning of the principle of adjudication by evidence is that the evidence used as a basis for a judgement must be lawful and illegal evidence should be excluded; even if such illegal evidence is true, it cannot be used as a basis for determining the facts of the case.

13.3.1.2 Adjudication of Evidentiary Principles

Refereeing under the evidence refers to the authoritative determination made by a judge in an open courtroom to hear the parties (prosecution and defence) on both sides of the evidence, questioning and debating, on the basis of sufficient verification and investigation of the evidence, on both sides of the dispute in accordance with the law. The basis of the decision stems from the facts proved by the evidence, and the facts are obtained as a result of the evidence. The adjudication process needs to go through a series of processes such as accepting the evidence, investigating the evidence, judging the evidence and finally using the evidence to determine the facts and make a decision. Evidence referee principle of adjudication should be established on the basis of the evidence debate, without the evidence can not make a decision on the facts of the case.

Judges should adhere to the principle of refereeing evidence, based on the facts of the case proved by the evidence, which is the cornerstone of the reasonableness of the strength of evidence of free will judgement. However, the principle of evidence itself needs a certain system and rules to be coordinated, so as to ensure that the principle in the litigation process has been fully and effectively implemented. These relevant systems mainly include the public trial system, the public system of reasons for judgement and the factual nature of the relief system and so on. These systems, on the one hand, help the parties to the judge whether to follow the principle of evidence for external supervision; on the other hand, is also conducive to the higher courts in the appeal trial of the original trial whether to follow the principle of evidence for supervision, urge the judge to strictly adhere to the principle of evidence for adjudication. At the same time, the judge did not implement the reasoning system, can be regarded as a violation of the principle of evidence refereeing, resulting in the original trial behaviour is invalid. In Taiwan, if the reasons for judgement omits or fails to record the evidence on which the facts are based, or if the judgement states that the facts are not appropriate, it is considered that the judgement is not based on evidence. For there are problems in the evidence of the decision, the parties have the right to request the court to be re-trial, the court also has the responsibility to be re-trial, which is the basic requirements of the principle of evidence. China's Civil Procedure Law stipulates: "The people's court shall conduct a retrial if the party's application meets one of the following circumstances: (a) there is new evidence sufficient to overturn the original judgement or decision; (b) the basic facts found by the original judgement or decision are not proved by evidence; (c) the main evidence found by the original judgement or decision is fabricated; (d) the main evidence found by the original judgement or decision is not proved by evidence; (e) the main evidence found by the original judgement or decision is fabricated; (f) the main evidence needed to hear the case, the parties for objective reasons can not collect their own, written application to the people's court to investigate and collect, the people's court has not investigated and collected ......" These provisions reflect the basic requirements of the principle of evidence refereeing.

13.3.1.3 Exceptions to the Principle of Adjudication of Evidence

Many countries and regions provide for exceptions to the principle of adjudication of evidence in their procedural or evidentiary codes and substantive laws. For example, artical 201 of the United States Federal Rules of Evidence provides for "knowledge of adjudicative facts". These exceptions mainly include "well-known facts" or "no need to prove the fact" or "free from evidence of the fact", but also includes rules of thumb, local customs, trade habits, industry practices, international practices and so on. Practice, international practice, etc.

The exceptions to the principle of evidence generally involves well-known facts, notarised facts, predetermined facts, presumed facts, the parties to the litigation on the self-confessed facts and so on without the parties to prove the facts.

Adhere to the principle of adjudication of evidence must be determined that the facts of the case should be proved by the corresponding evidence, the facts of the case rely on the evidence to confirm the evidence, there is no evidence shall not be determined that the facts of the case; Adhere to the principle of adjudication of evidence must do to the doubtful evidence is not admissible, that the facts of the case should be true and sufficient evidence; Adhere to the principle of adjudication of evidence on the existence of flaws in evidence shall not be used as a basis for the decision of the case. Adhere to the principle of adjudication of evidence, must also be done to determine the facts of the case of the evidence is legal, for illegally obtained evidence should be excluded, can not be used as a basis for the conclusion of the case.

13.3.2 The Significance of the Principle of Adjudication by Evidence

The principle of adjudication by evidence is the basic requirement of procedural rationality and an important symbol of human beings moving from irrational fact-finding to rational fact-finding. It requires that the adjudication of factual findings must be based on evidence that has been confirmed to be true through lawful procedures, and that facts cannot be found without evidence. Although the provisions of different countries, but as the application of the principle of evidence has been universally recognised by all countries.

The principle of evidence judgement puts evidence in the centre of the litigation, and has a decisive role in the decision of the facts of the case. Because this principle confirms the basic position that only evidence is the basis for ascertaining and determining the facts of a case, it also makes evidence the core of the entire litigation. Any process of litigation can not leave the evidence, otherwise the procedure can not or can not move forward, evidence is the litigation to promote the booster. Evidence referee principle also on the judge's free refereeing behaviour to be restricted, thus preventing the judge's subjective judgement, for the discovery of the real, to achieve the accuracy of the referee to lay a solid foundation.

13.4 Direct Speech Principle

13.4.1 Basic Meaning of the Principle of Direct Speech

13.4.1.1 The Concept of the Direct Speech Principle

The principle of direct speech means that the judge personally hears the oral statements and arguments of the parties, witnesses and other participants in the proceedings in court, thus forming an internal confirmation of the truthfulness of the case and making a decision on the case accordingly. The principle of direct speech can be divided into direct principle and speech principle, the two are closely related, all to find the real purpose. In the modern litigation system, the trial form generally take direct speech principle, it is the evidence can be effective evidence of the principle of evidence.

Direct principle, also known as the principle of presence or the principle of direct trial, refers to the handling of the case of the judge, jurors can only be in person in the courtroom directly obtained evidence as the basis for the decision of the litigation principle. Judges participating in a trial are required to personally participate in the examination of evidence and to listen to courtroom debates with a view to discovering the truth of the facts. This principle emphasises the integration of the trial judge and the sentencing judge, focusing on the unity of "trial" and "judgement". In contrast, there is indirect trial, in which the judgement judge uses the results of the trial by other judges as the basis for his or her judgement, i.e., there is a separation between the trial judge and the judgement judge.

The verbal principle, also known as the oral principle or the principle of verbal trial, is the principle that requires the parties and others to use words in the courtroom to argue their case. This principle is a necessary condition for the application of the principles of openness, argumentation and directness. The opposite of trial by speech is trial by writing. Proceedings in writing are based on written materials and evidence to establish the facts.

The direct speech principle requires the judge to make findings of fact only after a verbal debate between the parties. In the court trial, the judge through the parties and witnesses "face to face" activities, from the parties and witnesses, the appearance of the lawsuit, the attitude and situation of the case of the language can not convey information, from the actual trial to obtain the "heart evidence". Since the appearance of the person making the statement, his or her attitude and situation at the time of the statement have a different impact on the listener, and this impact is objective and often reflects the true situation, the judge derives such experience and appreciation from it. The principle of direct speech puts into practice the experiential nature of justice, emphasising that it is the judicial experience that gives rise to the experience of forming the "evidence of the heart", as well as the psychological basis for it.

13.4.1.2 Exceptions to the Direct Speech Principle

The principle of direct speech does not, as a principle, completely exclude written proceedings and allows for the existence of reasonable exceptions to the rule. The main manifestations of these exceptions to the rule are as follows.

i. **In principle, non-contentious matters are heard indirectly and in writing**

Direct speech is the principle of trial in contentious cases, and in non-contentious cases, where there are no opposing parties but only the applicant, there is no possibility or need for verbal argument, and the judge examines the applicant's application and the factual evidence provided in writing. Since the principle of written proceedings is adopted, there is no need to require the integration of the trial judge and the adjudicating judge, nor is there any need to apply the principle of directness. Of course, in non-litigation proceedings, the principles of indirect trial and written trial do not exclude direct trial by speech, and if necessary, the trial judge should also question the applicant and witnesses before making a decision.

ii. **If there is a change of judge during the course of the trial, the proceedings need not be reopened**

If, in the course of the trial, some of the members of the panel are unable to continue to fulfil their duties, the members of the panel are replaced and the trial is reopened. If the trial judge needs to be changed for a valid reason, the parties may present the results of their previous oral arguments before the new judge without having to reopen the proceedings.

13.4.2 The Significance of the Principle of Direct Speech

The principle of direct speech contributes to the discovery of truth and efficiency. The principle of direct speech requires direct contact between the judge, the parties and the witnesses in the courtroom, where the judge personally listens to the parties "statements and witnesses" testimony, directly observes the parties "and witnesses" expressions and attitudes, and directly observes the actual state of the evidence, which makes it easy to accurately grasp the facts of the case. At the same time, the judge, the parties and the witnesses meet directly, coupled with the advantages of simple and quick communication of words, which helps the judge and the parties to find out the dispute as soon as possible and solve the problem in a timely manner, so as to promote the litigation to proceed quickly.

The principle of direct speech emphasises the personal nature of the judge. The reliability of testimony is judged only by the judge's "face-to-face" activities with the parties and the witnesses and by the information conveyed by the witnesses through their explanations of the matters involved, answers to questions and other activities. Studies have shown that more than 50 per cent of communication between people relies on body language, such as eyes, voice, small movements and body posture. The vivid description of the influence of body language on people's testimonies[4] is the empirical and psychological basis for the adoption of the principle of "direct speech" and the emphasis on judicial experience in determining the facts of a case.

The principle of direct speech embodies the integration of the process and the outcome of the proceedings, and the final judgement in a case is the result of the accumulation of both objective and subjective factors in the process of hearing by the judge. By listening to the verbal evidence in person, the ability to discover the evidence and the facts of the case is enhanced, as well as the ability to judge the authenticity of other evidence. Together with the principles of openness and argumentation, it is an important principle for achieving procedural and substantive justice.

13.5 Principle of True Discovery

Litigation activities are, in the final analysis, activities in which the subject of litigation, in accordance with certain legal procedures, makes use of a variety of legal means and methods to discover the truth of the case. In countries governed by the rule of law, the discovery of the truth is carried out under substantive and proper procedures, and the law emphasises the legality and legitimacy of obtaining evidence and opposes the discovery of the truth at any cost or without regard to the consequences. The discovery of the truth is the basic goal of litigation activities, regardless of the mode of litigation or in what country, the discovery of the truth is regarded as the basic principle of the application of evidence.

[4] Spencer (2003).

13.5.1 The Basic Meaning of the Principle of True Discovery

In the process of using evidence to prove the facts of a case, there are two different levels of problems: First, it is necessary to prove whether the criminal facts alleged by the prosecution or the "case facts" disputed by the parties have ever occurred or existed. When the court makes a judgment on "existence or not", its judgment needs to be supported by sufficient evidence to ensure that the trial activities can discover the "truth" of the facts; second, the judge obtains a correct understanding of the facts of the case through the trial procedure with the help of evidence presented in court, and then obtains a judgment of "certainty or uncertainty" of the facts, and the litigation subject obtains a certain "belief" in his heart.

Regarding the issue of "reality", in theory, it is often used interchangeably with "truth", "authenticity" and "wahrheit", and there are different definitions in different disciplines (ontology, epistemology and ethics). In particular, the different translations of "truth" and "wahrheit" in the works of Western scholars in China make this concept quite confusing. According to the current broad understanding, "truth" or "authenticity" mainly contains five levels of meaning: one is synonymous with "have" and "exist"; two refers to something with certain regulations; three refers to the correctness of subjective reflection; four refers to the correctness of thought; five is synonymous with "good".[5] After this multiple meaning and ambiguous understanding was introduced into the field of law, it also brought some differences in the understanding of the legal community. In the determination of case facts, different views have emerged, such as "substantial truth" and "legal truth", "substantial truth" and "formal truth", and "objective truth" and "subjective truth" and "relative truth". Then, are the facts proved by evidence "objective truth" or "legal truth" or "relative truth"? Are the facts of the case confirmed by evidence "formal truth" or "substantial truth"? Does the discovery of facts require "relative truth" or "absolute truth"? These issues are reflected in methodology, mainly in terms of whether to obtain truth by "reproducing (restoring) case facts" or to test truth by proving "subjective conformity to objective facts" through evidence.[6]

The truth in the jurisprudence of evidence should be the truth proved by evidence, not excluding the truth presumed under certain conditions and the truth of judicial cognition. However, this kind of evidential truth, to a certain extent, belongs to the judge's inner conviction or the heart of the evidence is not in doubt and fully believe that it is "true" truth. This kind of truth is based on the evidence against the decision to determine the degree of reliance on the facts. Therefore, the judge's determination of the facts of the case should be based on the evidence presented by the parties. Only in full respect for the parties to the procedural subject status and fully safeguard the procedural rights of the parties to the premise, and in the active participation of the parties in the process of fact-finding and the judge's public testimony to the formation of the determination can make the 'real' has legitimacy. Only the parties to the judge's determination of the facts of the case due to their full participation and

---

[5] Guo (2003).

[6] Guo (2009).

subsequently produced a sense of identity and trust, it is possible to believe or should believe that due process with the help of the facts of the case is true. "In short, the determination of the real ...... most important, it is dependent on the availability of procedural safeguards, the thicker the safeguards, the more likely it is to determine the real possibility of trust worthy of the parties is also greater. It is not a question of whether the truth ascertained by this process is in fact only the truth referred to by the doctrine of formal truth, or even the truth sought by the doctrine of objective truth."[7] "Truth" as found to be true has the following meaning.

Firstly, the evidence proves that the facts of the case are not a reproduction or restoration of the facts of the case, nor can they be tested by the facts of the case, but it must not be concluded that the factual findings of the vast majority of cases are necessarily contrary to the facts of the case. In practice, on the contrary, the judge through the evidence of the facts of the case, in general, with the facts of the case to achieve fit or to maintain consistency.

In judicial practice, the accuracy of the determination of the facts of the case is absolute, and the incidence of wrongful conviction in countries around the world is still at a relatively low level. In fact, the factual determination of the case is not because of the theoretical "relative truth" and in practice there is "half" of the relative "untruth". From a systemic point of view, the use of evidence admitted in court proceedings to determine the facts of the case can guarantee that the judge's determination of the facts of the case is basically consistent with the facts of the case. "If there is no factual findings that are generally consistent with the truth, over time, the nation will lose confidence in the fairness of the adjudicative process, the trustworthiness of the courts, the effectiveness of policy instruments, and the effectiveness of channels of dispute resolution, whether in civil or criminal proceedings."[8] In other words, the facts of the case, as determined by the evidence through the due, open and fair process of the court, can easily be made to be true in a manner consistent with the facts as they actually occurred.

Secondly, the original historical facts of the case belong to the "original". This connotation of "original", "beginning" and "first" has long been lost. The facts of the case appearing in the court are the "real" historical facts of the original case, which are the external manifestation of the "original", and its external manifestation may be distorted due to the influence or intervention of other factors and manifested as the "false phase". However, people with the help of evidence can identify the "false phase", but also through the evidence to break through the "false phase" to obtain the correct understanding of the "true picture", the case occurred in the original original historical facts to obtain its essence. Historical facts of the case to obtain its essential understanding, so as to discover the reality of the case.

The discovery of truth depends on people's ability and level of knowledge of the laws of nature and of human beings themselves, as well as on the degree of scientific and rationality in the design of litigation procedures and rules of evidence. Whatever the circumstances, there is no way to escape the consistent pursuit of the

[7] Chiu (1996).

[8] Chiu (1996).

purpose of fact-finding in a case, i.e., the discovery of truth. Since "the trial court had many problems in determining the facts, such as perjured witnesses, missing or dead witnesses, lost or destroyed physical evidence, lawyers who were evil and stupid, and jurors who were stupid or distracted, all of these circumstances made it difficult to determine the objective facts, and made the determination of the facts subjective and irrational activities".[9] Thus, the process of discovering the truth requires the judge to transform "knowledge" between people and objects into "belief" between people with the help of evidence. Do not deny that in some cases, even if there is evidence to support the possibility of deviation from the facts of the case. But can not therefore deny the discovery of the truth as the basic principle of the application of evidence. Such as the German Criminal Procedure Code

Code of Criminal Procedure, Section 244, paragraph 2, provides: "in order to find out the truth, the court shall, ex officio on its own initiative to take sufficient evidence to prove the truth of all facts, and all methods of proof that are meaningful to the decision." The reason is that "criminal procedure is in the service of finding the truth of the matter."[10] Even in the parties have equal status in civil litigation, the law also gives the court certain power of investigation and evidence, which is based on the need to meet the discovery of the real. Such as China's Civil Procedure Law provides: "...... people's court that the trial of the case requires evidence, the people's court shall investigate and collect."

The court through the evidence to discover the real, can make the main body of the litigation will focus on the trial of the case on the facts of the judgement, from its judgement whether there is sufficient evidence to determine the existence of the facts claimed. There is evidence to prove the real also need to go through the test of falsification, with the help of cross-examination from the opposite to enhance the possibility of its "true". Once the evidence is insufficient, the judge to make a negative determination of the facts of the case, does not mean that the parties to the claim or allegation of the facts are necessarily false. It is because the facts claimed or alleged by the parties have not been determined to be true, and there is no need for positive confirmation of the truth or falsity of the disputed claim. In such a case, it can no longer be proved to be "true or false" and can only be dealt with on the basis of the burden of proof, which is not contradictory to the discovery of the truth, but merely a method of dealing with the difficulty of discovering the truth.

13.5.2 Significance of the Principle of True Discovery

The principle of true discovery is the basic principle of the application of evidence, but also the main goal pursued by the litigation activities, which has a particularly important significance in the process of the application of evidence.

---

[9] Zhang (2000).

[10] Henkel (1968).

13.5.2.1 The Principle of True Discovery is a Guide for Parties to Use Evidence to Protect Their Legitimate Interests

In criminal proceedings, the prosecution seeks to discover the truth in order to achieve justice; criminal suspects and defendants seek to discover the truth of the case in order to avoid being wrongly investigated and being unfairly punished for minor crimes; victims and their legal representatives seek to discover the truth of the case in order to ensure that the defendant's criminal behavior is properly investigated and their legitimate rights and interests are protected; parties to incidental civil proceedings and their legal representatives seek to discover the truth of the case in order to protect their own or the agent's civil legitimate rights and interests. In civil proceedings, plaintiffs, defendants, third parties and their legal representatives and litigation agents seek to discover the truth of the case in order to protect their own or the agent's civil substantive rights and interests and to resolve disputes fairly. In administrative proceedings, plaintiffs and their legal representatives seek to discover the truth of the case in order to have illegal administrative actions revoked in accordance with the law and to protect their legitimate rights and interests; defendants seek to discover the truth of the case in order to prove the legality of their own administrative actions and to protect public rights and interests; third parties and their legal representatives seek to protect legal administrative actions or have illegal administrative actions revoked to avoid infringement of their legitimate rights and interests. In the litigation process, each litigation subject can only achieve this goal with the help of evidence and the correct application of evidence.

13.5.2.2 The Principle of True Discovery is an Important Driving Force for Promoting Scientific Means of Proof

The discovery of truth is an intrinsic and essential requirement of the litigation evidence system. The setting up of any evidentiary system and the establishment of rules of proof, although they vary according to the circumstances in which they are set up, are not intended to restrict the discovery of the truth, but rather to safeguard the discovery of the truth to the greatest extent possible. Even if the rules applicable to evidence are restrictive in nature, their purpose is to minimise error. Although in some cases, procedural justice and the discovery and determination of the truth of the case may be contradictory, within a certain limit at the expense of the substantive justice of the case, but does not mean that the evidence system does not maximise the protection of the realization of substantive justice as the value of the goal. Therefore, the discovery of the truth is the basic principle of the application of evidence.

13.6 Questions and Reflections

The principle of adjudication by evidence implies that the facts of a case are to be established through evidence, and that evidence is to be used as the basis for the adjudication of the facts. The evidence must be verified to be true, in order to be used as the basis for a judgement. As the evidence of the evidence of the basis of the case must meet the requirements of the case is clear, the evidence is indeed sufficient. The discovery of the real litigation has a primitive impetus, but never the ultimate dispute resolution of the only pursuit. The rules of evidence in some ways block many of the discovery of the real evidence of great value as the basis for the case, artificially depleting the basis for finding the truth. In the case cited above, the court rejected the plaintiff's claim. According to the case, with reference to the above views, combined with the contents of this chapter, think about the following questions: (a) the court for the cause of Ms. Qian's death has not been clarified and rejected the plaintiff's claim is contrary to the principle of discovery of the truth? (b) whether the factual findings of the case followed the principle of evidence? (c) Under the circumstance that there were several possibilities for the cause of Ms Qian's death, on what principle did the court reject the plaintiff's claim? (d) in general, there is no evidence, there is no case facts; conversely, there is evidence, because it is not true enough, also does not necessarily determine the existence of the case facts, then, what kind of relationship exists between the evidence and the truth? The legitimacy of its decision in what?

References

Diao, R. H. (ed.) (1984a). Bijiao xingshi zhengju fa gelun. Taipei: Han Lin Publishing Co., Ltd. (in Chinese)
Chen, P. S. (1979). Xingshi zhengju fa. Taipei: San Min Book Co., Ltd. (in Chinese)
Diao, R. H. (ed.) (1984b). Bijiao xingshi zhengju fa gelun. Taipei: Han Lin Publishing House. (in Chinese)
Spencer, G. (2003). Zuijia bianhu [Translation of The Best Defence] (Wei, F., Trans.). Beijing: World Affairs Press. (in Chinese)
Guo, J. H. (2003). Zhenli fuhelun de kunnan ji qi jiejue. Beijing: China Social Sciences Press. (in Chinese)
Guo, H. (2009). Anjian shishi rending fangfa. Beijing: China People's Public Security University Press, 2009.(in Chinese)
Chiu, L.-K. (1996). Chengxu zhidu gongneng lun. Taipei: San Min Book Co., Ltd. (in Chinese)
Zhang, B. S. (2000). Falü tuili de lilun yu fangfa. Beijing: China University of Political Science and Law Press. (in Chinese). ISBN 9787562019763.
Henkel, H. (1968). Strafverfahrensrecht (2., neubearb. Aufl.). Stuttgart: W. Kohlhammer.

Extended Reading

Cohen, J. (1997). Zhengming de ziyou [Translation of The Freedom of Proof] (He, J. H., Trans.). Waiguofa Yiping [journal title used historically; later renamed Global Law Review], (3): 12. (in Chinese)

Li, Z. J. (2000). Quexin zhenshi, yi zhong xin lilun de jiegouxing youshi – lun minshi susong shishi shenli de mudi. Law Review, (3): 43–49. (in Chinese)

Chen, J. H. (2003). Shishi de falü yiyi. Peking University Law Journal, (6): 661–679. (in Chinese)

Chen, Y. S. (2003). Falü shishi yu keguan shishi de qihe yu beili —— dui zhengju zhidushi ling yi shijiao de jiedu. Journal of National Prosecutors College, 11(4). (in Chinese)

Zhang, W. P. (2021). Minshi zhengju caipan yuanze bianshi. Journal of Comparative Law, (2): 107–121. (in Chinese)

Chapter 14
Collection and Preservation of Evidence

14.1 Introductory Case

Guangzhou Municipal Public Security Bureau has issued "on rewarding the public to shoot traffic violations of the notice" (hereinafter referred to as 'notice'), so that the public act as a "volunteer monitors", on the illegal vehicle shooting and in the form of photographs to the public security departments to report, the whistleblower can get a certain amount of reward. Lai received the Guangzhou Municipal Public Security Bureau Traffic Police detachment motor brigade issued by the 'public security traffic management administrative penalty decision', the decision to the public Kong Mou provided photographs as evidence, that Lai's vehicle violation of traffic signs, markings, decided to impose a fine of 100 yuan. Lai was not convinced that the Guangzhou Municipal Public Security Bureau's use of clues provided by the public as the basis for administrative punishment was inappropriate, and that evidence collection must be carried out by administrative organs authorised by law. Lai filed an application for administrative reconsideration to the Guangzhou Municipal Public Security Bureau, requesting a review and revocation of the Notice; at the same time, requesting the revocation of the Guangzhou Municipal Traffic Police detachment motor brigade to impose penalties. Municipal Public Security Bureau after reconsideration that: the Notice is legal, the traffic police department that Mr Lai violation of the laws and regulations based on incorrect, and therefore ruled that the Notice is lawful, and revoke the Guangzhou Traffic Police Detachment Mobile Brigade penalty decision. Lai believes that the public based on the Guangzhou Municipal Public Security Bureau issued the Notice to take evidence is not legal, there is a suspicion of overstepping the authority. He requested the court to order the cancellation of the administrative reconsideration decision of the Guangzhou Municipal Public Security Bureau. The People's Court of Yuexiu District of Guangzhou City tried the administrative case and rejected Lai's request. The court held that the Circular on Rewarding Citizens for Photographing Traffic Violations issued by the Guangzhou Municipal Public Security Bureau "is an administrative guidance act without coercive power" and "does not fall within the

H. Guo, *Evidence Jurisprudence in China*, Understanding China,
https://doi.org/10.1007/978-981-95-3981-9_14

scope of administrative litigation in the People's Courts", so it did not review the Circular. Mr Lai appealed. In the same year, the Guangzhou Intermediate People's Court issued a judgement of second instance, rejecting Mr Lai's claim and upholding the judgement of the court of first instance. The Guangzhou Intermediate People's Court held, however, that citizens' "photographs of violations" could not be used directly as evidence of penalties, because, according to the Administrative Penalties Law, investigation and evidence-gathering is an integral part of the exercise of the right to impose penalties by administrative law enforcement agencies, and cannot be delegated to citizens.

14.2 Chapter Overview

This chapter is related to the collection and preservation of evidence, including the concept of evidence collection, basic requirements, common and special methods, and the conditions and procedures for the preservation of evidence. Evidence collection and preservation is the basic channel for obtaining evidence for the authorities and parties involved in the case, and is also a prerequisite for correctly determining the facts of the case.

14.3 Collection of Evidence

The collection and preservation of evidence is a coherent activity carried out by the subject of evidence collection and the subject of evidence preservation. Although the law on their provisions are separate, but in judicial practice is not completely independent. The preservation of evidence along with the collection of evidence, only after the collection of evidence quickly preserved or in the collection of the same time for the preservation of evidence, it is possible to achieve the purpose of the collection of evidence. Evidence collection can occur throughout the litigation activities as well as pre-litigation, while the preservation of evidence often occurs before the trial, in the course of the court generally no longer involved in the preservation of evidence, with the exception of special circumstances.

14.3.1 *Overview of Evidence Collection*

14.3.1.1 Concepts and Characteristics of Evidence Collection

Evidence collection, also known as evidence retrieval, refers to the case-handling organs, lawyers, the parties and their legal representatives, litigation agents, in accordance with the legal procedures and lawful means and methods, discovery, fixing, and extraction of all kinds of evidence related to the case of activities.

Evidence collection is a prerequisite for ascertaining the facts of a case, a basic task for handling cases and resolving disputes, and an important measure for the advancement of procedures and the discovery of truth. Due to the different modes of litigation and litigation traditions, countries have different requirements for the procedures, methods and means of evidence collection, especially whether the court, as a neutral adjudicating organ, can investigate and collect evidence outside the courtroom. However, the laws of various countries have a consistent direction in regulating the procedure and controlling the means of evidence collection. Evidence collection as an important litigation activity has the following characteristics.

i. **Evidence collection is an activity carried out in strict accordance with the law**

Evidence collection is different from the general social life, work in the investigation activities, its activities itself is not only the way of litigation rights (competence) exercise, but also a serious litigation behaviour. The nature and purpose of the evidence collection activity itself determines that it is a very strong legal work, because it may affect the normal work and life of others, and may even limit, infringe on the legitimate rights and interests of others, the law requires that it be carried out in accordance with the law. For this reason, the law makes clear provisions on the subject of evidence collection, the procedure for collecting evidence, the means and methods of collection, and sets certain boundaries and some prohibitions, since the task of ascertaining the truth through the collection of evidence is limited by other important interests, in particular the interests of the fundamental rights of the individual, which are guaranteed by the Constitution.

For the case-handling authorities, evidence collection is a highly legal, policy-oriented and disciplined act of authority, and the law, while granting them the authority to do so, stipulates strict procedures and restrictive conditions, as well as certain legal consequences, with the aim of safeguarding the exercise of their authority within the scope of the law and preventing the abuse or misuse of their power. For example, Article 52 of the Criminal Procedure Law stipulates: "...... It is strictly forbidden to extort confessions by torture or to collect evidence by threat, enticement, deception or other illegal methods. ......" Evidence collection must not only be carried out by legal officers of legal organs, but also by legal personnel of legal organs. The whole process of collecting evidence must comply with the requirements of the law.

The collection of evidence is a right for the parties. The parties, as well as "lawyers and other litigation agents acting on behalf of the litigation shall have the right to investigate and collect evidence ......" The collection of evidence shall not be formed or obtained in a way that seriously infringes on the lawful rights and interests of others, violates the prohibition of the law, or seriously violates public order and morals. Although the law does not impose strict limitations on the procedure and scope of the exercise of this right, it is not permissible to collect evidence "in serious violation of the legal procedure" or "in a manner that infringes on the lawful rights and interests of others or contravenes the legal prohibitions", otherwise, the evidence collected does not have the status of evidence.

ii. **Evidence collection is a complex litigation activity**

Evidence collection is not only a highly legal and policy-oriented endeavour, but also a complex activity. Its complexity is not only the collection of evidence subject to complexity, including both the case-handling organs, including general citizens, legal persons or other organisations, and its evidence collection activities itself also has complexity, both ex officio active collection of evidence activities, but also the exercise of the right to evidence collection activities, including the collection of evidence activities can not be carried out or impediments to the parties to apply for the case-handling organs of the evidence collection activities. At the same time, evidence collection is also a complex process. The facts of the case occurred in the past, for the case officer, the facts of the case is from no knowledge of the understanding of the facts of the case to know little to gradually know the full and progressive process.

The collection of evidence itself is extremely complex and difficult. Whether or not evidence can be collected depends not only on the nature of the case itself and the environmental conditions in which it takes place, but is also limited by the competence, level and methodology of the person collecting the evidence. Whether it is the investigation of a major criminal case or an ordinary civil or administrative litigation case, the collection of evidence is an extremely complex activity relative to other litigation activities. Such as can prove the real situation involving illegal cases of website pages, Internet records, e-mail, electronic contracts, electronic transaction records, electronic books and other electronic data should also be extracted, copied, fixed. Not only to extract, copy and fix the process of electronic data to produce the relevant text description, but also to record the cause of the case, the object, the content, as well as the extraction, copy and fix the time, place, method, electronic data specifications, categories, file format, extraction, copy and fix the producer of electronic data, electronic data holders should be signed or stamped, with the extracted, copied and fixed electronic data.

The collection of evidence is a prerequisite for the examination and judgement of evidence to determine the facts of the case. Without the collection of evidence, there is no provision of evidence, not to mention the examination and judgement of evidence. Review judgement evidence for further collection of evidence to indicate the direction. Evidence collection and review and judgement of the evidence of the activities of each other as a condition, interaction, and may be reciprocal.

iii. **Evidence collection as a purposeful legal activity**

The collection of evidence is intended to facilitate the ascertainment of the facts of a case and the discovery of the truth, thereby guaranteeing that the case will be handled in a fair and lawful manner. For the case-handling organ, the purpose of evidence collection is to ascertain the facts of the case and to discover the truth; for the parties, the purpose of evidence collection is to prove their own litigation claims or disputed facts. Evidence collection regardless of what motive, shall not in order to achieve the purpose of unscrupulous or reckless methods, must be within the scope of the lawful use of the law does not prohibit the means to achieve their own purposes.

In civil litigation, common law countries, the collection of evidence by the parties to the independent decision, and has the relevant institutional safeguards; in civil law countries, the collection of evidence on the parties to the existence of certain restrictions, emphasising the case-handling organs of the parties to the collection of evidence to assist.

14.3.1.2 The Significance of Evidence Collection

Evidence collection is a prerequisite for the advancement of litigation, a prerequisite for reviewing and judging evidence, and a prerequisite for using evidence to prove the facts of the case.

It is of particular importance in litigation. Evidence collection is the most basic activity in litigation. Whether it is a criminal public prosecution case or a criminal private prosecution case, or a civil litigation case or an administrative litigation case, evidence needs to be collected throughout the litigation process. This is the basis for the advancement of litigation. Only through evidence collection can we obtain the basis for advancing litigation and ensure the smooth progress of litigation activities. Since evidence collection is a difficult and complicated task, only by taking it seriously can we avoid changes or loss of evidence in time and provide sufficient evidence support for litigation activities, otherwise litigation activities cannot be carried out. Therefore, evidence collection is fundamental in the entire litigation activities.

Evidence collection is the basis for the determination of case facts. The facts of the case can only be identified after the cross-examination, review and judgment of the evidence. The review and judgment of evidence is based on the collected evidence. The quality and quantity of the collected evidence directly affect the judgment of the facts of the case. Whether the evidence is collected quickly and timely, whether it is detailed and comprehensive, and whether it is true and objective is the key to whether the facts of the case can be accurately determined. The quality of evidence collection will not only affect the determination of the facts of the case, but also restrict the quality of case handling. It is also a key factor in whether the legitimate interests of the parties can be effectively protected. Therefore, evidence collection is not only of great significance, but also plays a very important role in litigation.

14.3.2 Basic Requirements for Evidence Collection

Litigation activities are basically carried out around the evidence, evidence collection as the basic activities of the litigation, the need for the law to strictly regulate this, in order to ensure that its activities can be carried out in strict accordance with the law, not because of its impact on the normal order of society.

14.3.2.1 Evidence Collection Must Be Conducted in Accordance with the Law

China's procedural law contains relatively clear provisions on the collection of evidence. The Criminal Procedure Law, in the chapter entitled "Investigation", sets out in some detail the methods of evidence collection, and the Civil Procedure Law and the Administrative Procedure Law, in the chapter entitled "Evidence", also contain relevant provisions on the methods of evidence collection, which must not violate these provisions. Must be carried out in accordance with the law. The "law" mainly includes the following.

i. The main body of evidence collection should be legal subjects. The Criminal Procedure Law gives the public prosecution and law enforcement organs and their investigators, prosecutors, judges to collect evidence, they have the right and duty to the relevant state organs, enterprises, institutions, people's organisations and individual citizens to collect and retrieve evidence. These powers are not unlimited and are subject to the limitations of the law. Supervisory bodies, lawyers and administrative law enforcement agencies also have the right to collect evidence. For example, the Supervision Law provides that: "In the exercise of their supervisory and investigative powers, the supervisory authorities shall have the right, in accordance with the law, to seek information from the relevant units and individuals, and to collect and retrieve evidence." The lawyers law provides: "lawyers investigate and obtain evidence, with the lawyer's practice certificate and the law firm, can be to the relevant units or individuals to investigate and undertake legal affairs related to the situation."
ii. Evidence collection shall not be prohibited by law. The authorities and their personnel to collect evidence not only shall not violate the prohibitions of the law, such as not to torture confessions and by threat, enticement, deception, and other illegal methods of evidence collection, and must be authorised by law means or measures to collect evidence. Other subjects shall not infringe upon the lawful rights and interests of others or use methods prohibited by law in the collection of evidence. Otherwise, the evidence collected will have no evidential

capacity, and if the circumstances are serious, they will also be subject to the corresponding legal sanctions. "The collection of evidence by means of serious violations of social morality, restriction of the mental and physical freedom of others, and other methods that violate the personality of others to collect, which itself is illegal, and therefore have to be denied its ability to prove."[1]

iii. Evidence collection shall follow legal procedures. Evidence collection activities should be in accordance with legal procedures, serious violations of legal procedures, shall bear the corresponding legal consequences. Such as the Criminal Procedure Law stipulates: "Judges, procurators and investigators must follow the legal procedures to collect evidence that can confirm the guilt or innocence of the suspect or defendant, and the seriousness of the crime." The statutory procedures include both internal approval procedures and corresponding notification procedures, as well as implementation procedures and related formalities.

14.3.2.2 Evidence Collection Should Be Objective and Comprehensive

When collecting evidence, the subject of evidence collection should adhere to the materialist reflection theory, proceed from reality, seek truth from facts, and be faithful to the truth. Objectivity here means starting from the objective and actual situation of the case and collecting evidence truthfully according to its true nature. It is not allowed to replace objective reality with subjective conjecture, nor to collect evidence according to subjective needs, or to find evidence or arbitrarily choose evidence according to one's own subjective will, and it is even more forbidden to falsify evidence. Comprehensiveness means collecting evidence proving the facts of the case from different angles, neither exaggerating nor minimizing. For the case-handling agency, collecting evidence is not a simple matter.

When collecting evidence, the main body of evidence collection should adhere to the materialist theory of reflection, from a practical point of view, seeking truth from facts, and faithful to the truth. Here the objective refers to the objective reality from the case, in accordance with the original face of the evidence to be truthfully collected, neither subjective conjecture to replace the objective reality, not according to the subjective need to collect evidence or their own subjective will to look for evidence or arbitrarily take the evidence, and not to be false to falsify the evidence. Comprehensive refers to the collection of evidence to prove the facts of the case from different perspectives, neither to exaggerate nor to narrow. For the organ handling the case, the collection of evidence should not be preconceived and biased, but should collect all kinds of evidence that can prove the respective interests of the parties.

[1] Kaneko and Takeshita (1995).

14.3.2.3 Evidence Collection Should Be Proactive and Timely

All things in the world are in the movement of change, static and unchanging is only temporary, litigation evidence as material also has the same "volatility" characteristics. In criminal proceedings, after the perpetrator of a crime, in order to avoid punishment often destroy the scene, conceal, destroy evidence of crime, transfer stolen goods, enter into an alliance of attack and defence, making false testimony and false confessions to cover up their crimes; some physical evidence will change with the passage of time, or even disappear; the facts that exist in the minds of the people with the passage of time gradually fade away, or even forgotten. Once the timing of the collection of evidence is delayed, will result in the original can be collected evidence can not be collected, the original can be confirmed facts can not be confirmed. In civil and administrative litigation, the parties should also be based on the different circumstances of the case, timely collection of evidence or take the initiative to apply for the case organ to retrieve evidence. At the same time, the case-handling organ for the parties to apply for access to evidence, should also be carried out promptly and without delay. Therefore, the collection of evidence should be carried out proactively and in a timely manner, and hesitation will result in the "evaporation of truth".

14.3.2.4 Evidence Collection Should Be Thorough and Meticulous

The quantity and quality of evidence are related to the quality of the case, which determines the need for in-depth and detailed evidence collection. In-depth refers to the actual case to go, in-depth to the masses, investigation and research, to collect all the evidence related to the case. Meticulous refers to the process of collecting evidence, both a serious attitude, but also have a meticulous style, detailed questioning, carefully found and understand the subtle signs and some of the possible evidence of the clues, do not miss any doubt and the existence of evidence of the traces, there must not be the slightest carelessness, otherwise it is difficult to collect the evidence should be collected, due to the collection of evidence incomplete will be to ascertain the facts of the case will result in irreparable losses.

14.3.2.5 Evidence Collection Should Be Proactive and Timely

The complexity of social relations and the development of science and technology, making the collection of evidence in litigation is increasingly difficult, especially in cases involving high-tech and intelligent cases, such as network infringement and telecommunications fraud cases. Evidence must be collected with the help of strong modern scientific and technological means as well as professionals, to ensure the effectiveness of the collection of evidence. Evidence collection should not only use scientific and technological means, at the same time should also guarantee the effectiveness of the evidence obtained. Evidence collection of scientific mainly includes the following meanings: first, the evidence collection methods and means should be scientific; Second, the process of collecting evidence should be reliable; Third, the collection of evidence should have the results of the effectiveness of the collection of evidence should be; Fourth, the collection of evidence should be related to the facts to be proved or the facts of the case. For example, for borrowing and lending need to collect debit notes, receipts, notes and other credentials and other evidence that can prove the existence of the legal relationship between borrowing and lending of the flow of funds.

Evidence collection can use high-tech means to find, extract all kinds of evidence, such as shape display and amplification technology, composition and structure analysis technology (such as chromatography, spectral analysis), forensic biology technology (such as DNA typing technology), laser technology and blockchain and other modern information technology. However, the use of high-tech means must not infringe upon the legitimate rights and interests of others (such as the right to privacy) or impede the normal living or working order of others.

The basic requirements for evidence collection vary according to the subject of evidence collection. The case-handling organs and administrative organs have special requirements, and their evidence collection is not only an authority, but also a duty that should be fulfilled; not only should they collect evidence that is favourable to them, they should also collect evidence that is unfavourable to them, and they should not be biased or slack, and their requirements for evidence collection are more stringent than those of the parties concerned, and their behaviour is more standardized than that of the parties concerned.

14.3.3 Basic Methods of Evidence Collection

Evidence collection should be based on the different characteristics of evidence and adopt corresponding collection methods in a targeted manner to ensure that the collected evidence has evidentiary capacity and that its objectivity and authenticity are not affected by inappropriate collection methods. Different evidence collection subjects have different evidence collection powers (benefits), and they can use different collection means and methods.

14.3.3.1 Basic Methods of Evidence Collection by Case-Handling Authorities

The organ handling the case shall use methods authorised by law to collect evidence, and the parties concerned shall not use methods prohibited by law to collect evidence. These methods include general and specific methods.

i. **General methods of evidence collection by case-handling authorities**

Methods of investigation, inspection, search and seizure and sealing. Investigation, inspection, search and seizure are compulsory methods of collecting evidence in litigation, and are important means of collecting evidence, mainly applicable to the collection of physical evidence, documentary evidence, audio-visual materials and electronic data.

a. Survey, inspection is the legal subject of the case-related places, objects, persons, corpses and other activities to collect evidence. As a method of evidence collection, investigation can be used in all kinds of litigation; inspection is used only in criminal proceedings. The person conducting the survey or inspection shall make a record of the circumstances and results of the survey or inspection, which shall be signed or sealed by the person conducting the survey or inspection, the parties concerned and the invited participants.[2]

A search is a search of a person's body, belongings, or premises where evidence of a crime is concealed. It is mainly used in criminal proceedings. The searcher should be in possession of a "search warrant", and the family members or neighbours of the person searched should be present as witnesses and make a statement of what happened during the search. The record of the search must be signed or stamped by the person searched, the witnesses and the searcher. The search of a woman's body shall be conducted by a staff member.

Seizure is a litigation activity in which the subject of the law temporarily detains objects, texts or audio-visual electronic data related to the case. The seizure shall be carried out in the presence of a witness, and a list of seizures shall be drawn up in duplicate. The list shall include the name, quantity, quality and characteristics of the items, and shall be signed and stamped by the persons concerned; one copy shall be handed over to the holder and one copy shall be attached to the file.

Sequestration is a method of registering and preserving documents, information and electronic equipment that may be transferred, concealed, tampered with or destroyed by the subject of the law. For example, the Anti-Money-Laundering Law stipulates that: "When an investigator seals documents and information, he or she shall, together with the staff of the financial institution present at the investigation, make a list in duplicate on the spot, with the signatures or seals of the investigator and the staff of the financial institution present at the investigation, one copy of the list shall be handed over to the financial institution and one copy of the list shall be attached to the file for further investigation."

b. Methods of questioning. Interrogation is used primarily for the collection of statements from parties (victims) and testimony from witnesses. Questioning personnel in the questioning of witnesses, parties (victims), should be different attitudes of witnesses, parties (victims) to take different methods. In judicial

[2] For on-site investigation, reference may be made to the Ministry of Public Security's Rules for On-Site Investigation and Inspection of Criminal Cases by Public Security Organs (Gongtong Zi [2005] No. 54).

practice, the general use of witnesses, victims of free statements and answers to a combination of methods. Witnesses first free statement, when the statement is not perfect, can be appropriate guidance, but shall not imply, induce, and shall not use violence, coercion and threatening methods.

The enquiry shall be conducted individually and transcripts of individual enquiries shall be made in accordance with the law. The general use of enquiry shall make a transcript of the enquiry. Interrogation notes shall be handed over to the person being questioned to check. If there is any omission or error in the record, the person being questioned may request additions or corrections. The person questioned shall sign or stamp the transcript after confirming that it is correct; the questioner shall also sign the transcript.

c. Methods of interrogation. Methods of interrogation may be used only in respect of suspects and accused persons. When the organ handling the case interrogates a criminal suspect or defendant who is in custody, it shall issue an arraignment warrant and conduct the interrogation in the detention centre. If the suspect or defendant is not in custody, the officer in charge of the case shall present a document certifying that he or she is from his or her organ, and may summon the suspect or defendant to a designated place in the city or county where the suspect or defendant is located, or to his or her residence, for the purpose of questioning. When questioning a suspect or defendant, the officer in charge of the case shall first inform him or her of his or her right to apply for disqualification and of his or her right to engage a lawyer.

The methods of questioning a criminal suspect or defendant are as follows: (i) Questioning the natural situation. When interrogating a suspect or defendant, the suspect or defendant shall be asked about his or her name, age, occupation, home address, personal history and other natural circumstances, and shall truthfully fill in the interrogation transcript of the relevant matters. For not speaking the real name, address, can fill in their self-reported name and note; (ii) ask whether the guilty, so that the statement and defence, and then ask questions; (iii) interrogation should be conducted individually; (iv) interrogators shall not be less than two; (v) arrest shall be interrogated within 24 h; (vi) shall not be tortured to extract confessions and to threaten, enticement, deception, as well as other illegal methods of interrogation of suspects, defendants; (vii) making audio and video recordings. The audio and video recordings shall be made without interruption, and two copies shall be made: one sealed for safekeeping in case of dispute, and one for use by the court. At the same time, the interrogation of criminal suspects and defendants should be guaranteed their legitimate procedural rights. These procedural rights include: (i) the right of criminal suspects and defendants to reply to interrogations in their own language and to write confessions in their own characters; (ii) The right of the suspect or defendant to plead innocence, mitigation or exemption from criminal responsibility; (iii) suspects and accused persons have the right to refuse to answer questions unrelated to the case; (iv) The right of the suspect or the accused to have the transcript of the interrogation read or to have it read to him or her for the purpose of checking and making additions or corrections. (v) the right of criminal suspects and defendants to file complaints against interrogators for unlawful questioning and degrading remarks and behaviour; (vi) underage criminal suspects and defendants shall have the right to request that their legal representatives be notified of their presence when they are being questioned in accordance with the law.

d. Methods of identification. When the facts of the case involve specialised issues, the method of identification may be used to collect evidence. In the absence of an appraisal body, or where provided for by law or judicial interpretation, a person with specialised knowledge may be engaged to issue a report on the specialised issues of the case.

ii. **Special methods of evidence collection by case-handling authorities**

Special methods of evidence collection are applied mainly by the investigating authorities in criminal proceedings, while the approval procedure is carried out. These special methods are mainly the following.

a. Methods of identification. Identification is an organised and planned method for the people concerned to analyse and identify the people and things related to the case. It is one of the important methods of collecting evidence. This method can be divided into the identification of people, the identification of objects and the identification of places.

Identification of people. This kind of identification is mainly applied in criminal cases such as rape, fraud, robbery and other cases. When identifying a suspect, the number of people to be identified shall not be less than seven, and when identifying a photograph of a suspect, the photograph shall not be less than ten.

Identification of objects. The identification of objects mainly includes the identification of objects left at the scene, the identification of other material evidence in the case, the identification of the tools of the crime, stolen goods, etc. When identifying objects, the same kind of objects shall be identified. When identifying objects, no fewer than five items of the same kind should be identified and no fewer than five photographs should be taken.

Since the result of identification affects the handling of the case, some wrongful convictions are caused by mistakes in identification. Therefore, the method of identification must be cautious attitude, identification can not give any hint to the identifier, should be used mixed identification, the results of identification should not be blind faith. The identification shall be recorded.

b. Methods of investigative experiments. The Criminal Procedure Law provides that 'in order to ascertain the facts of a case, when necessary, with the approval of the head of public security, investigative experiments may be conducted.' The results of investigative experiments generally cannot be used as evidence of the existence of facts in a case, but can be used as negative evidence.

c. Wanted, interception methods. Wanted, intercepted is a method of investigative activities to collect evidence. This method is used for criminal suspects to commit a crime, absconding, transfer of material evidence and other circumstances. Wanted and intercepted can be seized criminal suspects, as well as stolen money and goods and all kinds of physical evidence in the case. This method than other methods of collecting evidence, time is stronger, the requirements of timely, rapid and decisive.
d. Technical investigation methods. Evidence obtained by the investigator himself or by other persons assigned to him in accordance with the law by means of covert or technical investigation may be submitted directly to the court as evidence. If the evidence is obtained in the above manner, the person who obtains it shall make a transcript of the time, place and process of obtaining the evidence, and the name of the person who obtains it, and attach it to the file.

In addition, the organ handling the case has the right to collect and retrieve evidence from relevant units and individuals. In civil and administrative proceedings, the court has the right to obtain evidence from the relevant units and citizens. In the retrieval of evidence, should be issued in duplicate "notice of retrieval of evidence" and "retrieval of evidence list". A copy of the transferred units and individuals to save; a file for the record. Evidence involving state secrets and commercial secrets of the unit being transferred and personal privacy, should be strictly confidential. At the same time, the production of evidence retrieval of the transcript, the evidence retrieval personnel should sign the name and date on the transcript.

14.3.3.2 Methods of Evidence Collection By the Parties

The law does not prescribe the methods by which the parties may collect evidence, but there are some restrictions on the use of such methods, namely, "seriously infringing on the lawful rights and interests of others, or violating legal prohibitions, or seriously violating public order and morals". The main method used by the parties to collect evidence is to inspect and copy the materials relating to the case. If, for objective reasons, the parties or their defence lawyers or litigation agents are inappropriate or unable to collect evidence relating to the facts of the case, they may apply to the relevant case-handling organ for the collection and retrieval of evidence. The application shall meet the conditions of relevance to the facts of the case, significance to the proof of the facts to be proved, or other conditions necessary for the investigation and collection of evidence, as well as the fulfilment of the corresponding procedures, which are governed by different provisions in different proceedings.

i. **Methods of applying for investigations to collect evidence in criminal proceedings**

In accordance with the provisions of the law and judicial interpretations, a lawyer may apply to the procuratorate or the court for the collection and retrieval of evidence as required by the circumstances of the case. The procuratorate, on the basis of an application by a defence lawyer for the collection and retrieval of evidence, may collect and retrieve evidence if it deems it necessary to do so. The applicant may be present when the evidence is collected or retrieved. If the court considers that it is inappropriate or impossible for the defence counsel to collect or retrieve evidence from witnesses or other relevant units or individuals and that it is necessary to do so, the court shall give its consent. Where an application is made for access to evidence collected by the supervisory organs, public security organs or procuratorial organs during the period of investigation, detection and prosecution to prove the innocence or mitigating circumstances of the accused, the court shall collect and access the evidence on the basis of the application of the defence counsel.

ii. **Application for investigation and collection of evidence in civil proceedings**

If the parties and their legal representatives are unable to collect evidence on their own for objective reasons, they may apply to the court to investigate the evidence. The parties and their legal representatives to apply to the court to investigate the evidence shall meet the following conditions: a. the application for investigation and collection of evidence belongs to the relevant departments of the state and must be retained by the court ex officio access to archival materials; b. involving state secrets, commercial secrets, personal privacy of the material; c. the parties and their legal representatives can not be collected due to objective reasons of other materials.

In addition, the court may collect on its own any evidence that it deems necessary for the trial of the case. Such evidence mainly involves facts that may be detrimental to the national interest, public interest or the legitimate rights and interests of others, or procedural matters that have nothing to do with the substantive disputes, such as the addition of parties ex officio, the suspension of the proceedings, the termination of the proceedings, or the disqualification of the parties. Generally speaking, the court does not take the initiative to investigate the evidence, and the parties shall apply for access to it.

The application shall contain the name of the person being investigated or the name of the unit, the place of residence and other basic information, the content of the evidence to be investigated and collected, the need for the court to investigate the reasons for the collection of evidence and its proof of the facts. Generally should also provide the investigation and collection of evidence clues. These clues mainly include the content of the evidence, the facts that can be proved, the location of the evidence, and who is in control of the situation.

iii. **Procedures for requesting an investigation to collect evidence in administrative proceedings**

In administrative litigation, the plaintiff or a third party may collect or apply to the court for access to evidence. These evidence are: a. by the relevant departments of the state and must be retrieved by the court; b. involving state secrets, commercial secrets, personal privacy; c. for objective reasons can not be collected.

The application shall be submitted within the time limit for evidence of the application for access to evidence. For eligible, the court shall decide to retrieve in a timely manner. Failure to obtain the appropriate evidence after access, shall inform the applicant and explain the reasons.

If the conditions are not met, the court shall serve a notice on the applicant and his or her representative, stating the reasons for not granting access. The applicant may apply to the court accepting the application for reconsideration once. The court shall make its decision on reconsideration in a timely manner.

14.4 Preservation of Evidence

14.4.1 Overview of Evidence Preservation

14.4.1.1 Concept and Characteristics of Evidence Preservation

Evidence preservation refers to a protective measure taken to protect the objectivity of evidence in order to prevent it from being lost naturally, destroyed artificially, unusable or difficult to obtain in the future.

Evidence preservation, as an evidence system, originated from the temple law, and was later inherited by the German common law and has been passed down to the present day, and has been adopted by continental legal systems. It is a method of fixing evidence and a system of protecting evidence. my country's "Civil Procedure Law" and "Administrative Procedure Law" have made corresponding provisions for evidence preservation, and the "Special Law on Maritime Litigation" has a special chapter to provide for this. It mainly applies to the pre-trial procedures of civil and administrative litigation. Criminal, civil and administrative litigation all have the problem of evidence preservation, which is fixed and protected by the case-handling agency in cooperation with the parties. Since the vast majority of criminal cases are public prosecution cases, the case-handling agency collects evidence, and in administrative litigation, the administrative agency collects evidence before making administrative actions. In the process of collecting evidence, the administrative agency has fixed and protected some evidence. In most cases, the parties may be hindered from collecting evidence, and the case-handling agency needs to assist in preservation to prevent their legitimate rights and interests from being lost due to the loss of evidence. In civil litigation, the main body of evidence collection is the parties. Since the rights and abilities of the parties to collect evidence are often subject to certain conditions, they especially need the assistance of the court, and under certain conditions, they also need the implementation of the notary office. Civil litigation is the most typical example of the evidence preservation system.

Evidence preservation is an important part of evidence collection, an integral part of evidence collection, and a link in evidence collection. If the evidence found is not fixed and extracted in a timely manner or properly stored, it will be lost or destroyed due to natural or man-made reasons, thus losing its effectiveness in proving the facts of the case, and ultimately making it difficult to obtain real protection of the legitimate rights and interests that should be protected by the law due to the lack of evidence to support them. Evidence preservation, as an activity to fix and protect evidence, is often carried out along with evidence collection activities. It itself contains elements of evidence collection, but it is still different from evidence collection. Evidence preservation has the following characteristics.

i. **The subject of evidence preservation is a statutory subject**

In addition to the organ handling the case, the main body implementing the preservation of evidence also includes other organs with the authority expressly provided for in the law, such as notary publics and administrative organs. Evidence preservation procedures must not only be initiated in accordance with the law, but also must have legal subjects in accordance with the law. China's civil procedure law provides: "in the evidence may be lost or difficult to obtain later, the parties can apply to the people's court for the preservation of evidence in the process of litigation, the people's court may also take the initiative to take preservation measures." Evidence preservation procedures can be initiated by an applicant before the lawsuit or by a party in the lawsuit upon application. The notary public and administrative authorities must take the application of the applicant or the party concerned as a prerequisite for the preservation of evidence,[3] and may not do so on their own initiative, otherwise, they are ineffective. As a general rule, the court may not take the initiative to do so ex officio prior to the proceedings.

ii **.Evidence preservation is a legal act**

Evidence preservation should be initiated according to statutory conditions, which are that the evidence will be lost or difficult to obtain in the future, and it has a legal interest and is necessary to determine the status quo of things. For example, Article 51 of the Copyright Law stipulates: "In order to stop infringement, if the evidence may be lost or difficult to obtain in the future, the copyright owner or the copyright-related right holder may apply to the People's Court for evidence preservation before filing a lawsuit." Whether the facts of the case to be proved by the evidence are important is not a necessary condition for the implementation of evidence preservation, but evidence preservation needs to comply with statutory circumstances and forms. For the preservation applied by the applicant to force the other party or a third party to provide evidence in his favor, the preservation applied for illegal property, or the preservation applied for the privacy of others for improper purposes, the relevant organs or departments shall not carry out preservation because the purpose of preservation is improper and does not meet the requirements of the law.

iii. **Evidence preservation is an independent procedure**

Evidence preservation has an independent procedural status. It is a procedure for the parties and the case-handling agency to pre-investigate and collect evidence and fix

[3] Whether the notary public as the legal organ of evidence preservation in the theory there are still different views. See Shan Gang (2009).

and preserve evidence. It is usually carried out at the same time as evidence collection, but most of the time it occurs before the court hearing. In special circumstances, it can also be carried out during the trial as a "procedure incidental to the litigation procedure."[4] Evidence preservation has the attributes of evidence collection and is a special method or form of evidence collection.

14.4.1.2 Nature and Significance of Preservation of Evidence

There are three main views on the nature of evidence preservation: non-litigation event theory, litigation event theory and compromise theory. The non-litigation event theory believes that the purpose of evidence preservation is mainly to preserve evidence in a timely manner, which does not necessarily require the participation of the other party, does not emphasize the opposition between the parties, and does not have the form of litigation. The litigation event theory believes that the purpose of evidence preservation is not just to preserve evidence, but to conduct evidence investigation and fact determination in advance for future litigation. The compromise theory believes that evidence preservation has both the nature of litigation events and non-litigation events.

China's "maritime litigation special procedures law", "trademark law", "patent law", "copyright law", "the supreme people's court on the pre-litigation to stop infringement of the exclusive right to use registered trademarks and the preservation of evidence of the interpretation of the applicable law", as well as other judicial interpretations for the pre-litigation preservation of evidence to make a more comprehensive provisions. From these provisions, whether it is pre-litigation evidence preservation or litigation in the preservation of evidence, are subject to the adjustment and regulation of litigation law, is a kind of dispute in order to solve the case in advance of the investigation of evidence activities, as a system should not be carried out because of the nature of the change in the nature of its pre-litigation, the preservation of evidence has the nature of litigation. From the legislative study, in Germany, the preservation of evidence has always been distinguished into two meanings, and will be attributed to litigation and non-litigation two different procedural nature. The former is in order to ensure that the future can be based on reliable evidence of notarial proceedings in advance of evidence investigation and fact-finding activities; The latter refers to the preservation of evidence in order to permanently retain the memory of the act of preservation. Its nature in the doctrine there are different views. A view that the preservation of evidence has litigation. Evidence preservation although there are two types of pre-litigation and post-litigation, but in principle, the nature of the two are not different. Pre-litigation evidence preservation, although may not be connected with a particular litigation events, with non-litigation elements, but its position and post-litigation evidence preservation, are the same, are in order to achieve the litigation procedures, is attached to the case of the procedure. It uses the same methods of investigation of evidence as the proceedings. Another view is

[4] Shindo (2008).

that the preservation of evidence is both litigious and non-litigious. Preservation of evidence for the purpose of "preserving evidence" when evidence may be lost or difficult to obtain at a later date does not have the same purpose as the establishment of facts between opposing parties, and this form of preservation of evidence has a non-litigious character.

In the traditional sense, the preservation of evidence is in the evidence is likely to be lost or later will be difficult to obtain the measures taken to preserve the evidence, most of the situation belongs to the situation is relatively urgent, if not immediately take measures to preserve evidence, the evidence will be lost or difficult to obtain the risk. Modern evidence preservation is no longer to the urgency of the evidence as a requirement, especially the notary preservation of evidence, no longer to the evidence in a state of danger of loss or difficult to obtain as a prerequisite. The purpose of evidence preservation is to ensure the authenticity of the evidence and the power of proof, it plays an important role in the subsequent case. Because litigation is a process, the implementation of this activity requires a certain amount of time, the need to preserve evidence whether in content or in the form of the process will be in a relatively unstable state, may be due to the passage of time or the environment of the migration and change, if not in time for the preservation of evidence will bring certain difficulties in dealing with the case later, and even to the parties or interested parties to bring high costs. Therefore, for those who may be lost or difficult to obtain the evidence, the evidence preservation authorities should be based on the application of the parties or ex officio initiative to timely preservation, in order to give better play to its role in proving the case in the litigation.

14.4.2 Procedures for the Preservation of Evidence

14.4.2.1 Conditions for Evidence Preservation

According to the Civil Procedure Law and the Administrative Procedure Law, evidence preservation should be based on the possibility that the evidence may be lost or difficult to obtain in the future.

i. **Evidence may be lost**

Evidence may be lost means that the evidence may no longer exist or cannot be used. For example, a witness may die of illness, physical evidence may lose its original form or be lost due to decay and deterioration, and the other party's behavior may be destroyed, changed or damaged.

ii. **Evidence may be difficult to obtain in the future**

Difficulty in obtaining evidence in the future means that although the evidence is not lost or may exist in the future, it will be difficult to retrieve in the future for subjective or objective reasons, or it will be difficult or costly to obtain in the future. For example, if the witness is about to leave the country to settle down, etc.

Whether it is necessary to take evidence preservation, the main basis for its measurement is that the evidence may be due to their own reasons for natural changes, such as not to take a certain means of preservation to deal with can not maintain its normal state, or the holder of the evidence in the interests of the driving force of the possibility of intentional destruction, transfer, concealment, tamper with the evidence, so that there is a change in the normal state of the evidence of the possibility. The requirement here is a "possibility", not a "necessity". However, the possibility is not baseless subjective speculation or conjecture, although there is no need to have sufficient evidence to prove, but still need to reach the level of interpretation.

Generally speaking, if one of the above conditions is met, the parties or interested parties may apply to the court or notary public for the preservation of evidence, or the court may take the initiative to take preservation measures ex officio in the litigation.

14.4.2.2 Procedures for Preserving Evidence

Evidence preservation is divided into pre-litigation evidence preservation and litigation evidence preservation, and can also be divided into evidence preservation by notary offices and evidence preservation by the People's Court. Evidence preservation can be requested by the parties (including litigation participants) before litigation or during litigation; the court can also take the initiative to do so ex officio, but notary offices cannot take the initiative.

i. **Time limit for applying for evidence preservation**

In civil proceedings, the parties or interested parties shall apply to the court for the preservation of evidence within the time limit for the presentation of evidence; in administrative proceedings, before the expiry of the time limit for the presentation of evidence. There is no time limit for applying to a notary public for the preservation of evidence.

ii. **Submit an application for evidence preservation**

If a party or interested party believes that evidence preservation is necessary, they shall submit an application. The application generally includes the following: a. the name and location of the evidence to be preserved; b. the content and scope of the evidence preservation; c. the relationship between the preserved evidence and the facts of the case; d. the reasons why the evidence needs to be preserved. Article 3 of the Interpretation of the Supreme People's Court on the Application of Law for Preventing Infringement of Registered Trademarks and Preservation of Evidence (Fa Shi [2002] No. 2) provides: "When a trademark registrant or an interested party applies to the People's Court for a pre-litigation cessation of infringement of registered trademarks, he shall submit a written application. The application shall state: a. the parties and their basic information; b. the specific content and scope of the application; c. the reasons for the application, including a specific statement that if the relevant behavior is not stopped in time, it will cause irreparable damage to the legitimate rights and interests of the trademark registrant or interested party."

"When a trademark registrant or an interested party applies to the People's Court for the preservation of evidence before litigation, he shall submit a written application. The application shall state: a. the parties and their basic information; b. the specific content, scope and location of the evidence to be preserved; c. the object that the evidence to be preserved can prove; d. the reasons for the application, including a specific statement that the evidence may be lost or difficult to obtain in the future, and that the parties and their litigation agents cannot collect it on their own due to objective reasons."

iii. **Provision of evidence for preservation of evidence**

The party or interested party shall present certain evidence to justify the preservation of evidence. The reasons show that the application for preservation of evidence meets the statutory conditions and necessity. For example, the supreme people's court on the cessation of infringement of the exclusive right to use registered trademarks and the preservation of evidence of the interpretation of the law applicable to the issue of: "the applicant puts forward an application for the cessation of infringement of the exclusive right to use registered trademarks, the following evidence shall be submitted: a. the trademark registrant shall be submitted to the certificate of registration of the trademark, the interested party shall be submitted to the trademark licensing contract, the record of materials and the trademark registration certificate; exclusive use of the licence contract copy of the trademark; the use of the contract of the exclusive use of the licensee shall submit a copy. b. Evidence that the respondent is committing or is about to commit an act of infringement of the exclusive right to use the registered trademark, including the allegedly infringing goods."

iv. **Decision on reviewing the application for evidence preservation**

Evidence preservation is generally reviewed by the court where the evidence is to be preserved, so as to facilitate timely evidence preservation. As stipulated in the Special Law on Maritime Litigation, if a party applies for maritime evidence preservation before filing a lawsuit, it shall submit the application to the maritime court where the evidence to be preserved is located. The court shall review the application for evidence preservation and make a ruling within 48 h if the conditions for evidence preservation are met. If the ruling is to take evidence preservation measures, it shall be executed immediately. If the conditions for evidence preservation are not met, the applicant's application shall be rejected. The applicant's application for evidence preservation to a notary office is generally not subject to geographical restrictions.

v. **Provide security for evidence preservation**

If a party files an application before filing a lawsuit, and the court deems it necessary to take evidence preservation measures, it shall notify the applicant to provide security and file a lawsuit within a certain period of time. If an application is filed after filing a lawsuit, the court shall review and decide. Pre-trial preservation of evidence may be implemented by a notarial agency; in some special cases, if it is difficult for a notarial agency to preserve evidence, the party may apply to the court for evidence preservation. If laws and judicial interpretations have provisions on pre-trial preservation of evidence, the court shall implement them in accordance with such provisions. The Interpretation of the Supreme People's Court on the Applicable Law on Pre-trial Suspension of Infringement of the Exclusive Right to Use a Registered Trademark and Preservation of Evidence stipulates: "When an applicant files an application for pre-trial suspension of infringement of the exclusive right to use a registered trademark, he shall provide security. If the applicant's application for pre-trial preservation of evidence may involve the property loss of the respondent, the people's court may order the applicant to provide corresponding security."[5]

vi. **The effectiveness of evidence preservation**

The effectiveness of evidence preservation only applies to the evidence to be preserved and has nothing to do with the facts of the case to be proved. Both parties may use the preserved evidence and shall state it in the debate of the lawsuit. That is to say, after the evidence is preserved, the court can only adopt it as the basis for judgment if the parties cite it in the litigation.

vii. **Remedies for evidence preservation**

If a party or interested party is dissatisfied with the court's ruling on evidence preservation, they may apply for a reconsideration from the original court after receiving the ruling; the court shall make a reconsideration decision after receiving the reconsideration application. If the respondent is dissatisfied with the ruling on evidence preservation and applies for a reconsideration, and the grounds for reconsideration are established, the court shall return the preserved evidence to the respondent. If the application for evidence preservation is wrong, the applicant shall compensate the respondent for the losses suffered as a result.

Before the prosecution, interested parties who believe that evidence preservation is necessary can also file a request with the notary office, which will implement it. When the notary office takes preservation measures, it can only do so in accordance with the application of interested parties, and cannot take preservation measures on its own initiative. There is no time limit for preserving evidence.

14.4.3 Basic Methods of Evidence Preservation

The Special Maritime Procedure Law, the Arbitration Law, the Notarization Law and the Several Provisions of the Supreme People's Court on Evidence in Civil Litigation have made provisions for the methods of preserving evidence, the main methods of which are: sealing (sealing), seizure, photographing, recording, videotaping, copying, appraisal, inspection, and making records.

[5] There are different views on pre-litigation preservation. There is a view that the preservation of pre-litigation evidence by the court is essentially an abuse of judicial power to interfere with the litigation rights of the parties. See Zhang and Xu (2000).

14.4.3.1 Preservation of Oral Evidence

The preservation method for evidence such as witness testimony, victim statements, defendant confessions, and party statements should generally be through questioning (interrogation) and making questioning (interrogation) records; audio and video recordings can also be made at the same time. The production of the record must be completely consistent with the original words and original intentions of the narrator, and it cannot be taken out of context, and it cannot be arbitrarily selected or deleted. After the recording is completed, the statutory verification procedures must be carried out, and the record must be handed over to the narrator for reading; if he is unable to read, he can be read to him. If there are errors or changes need to be made, they should be changed; after the changes are confirmed by the narrator, he should sign and seal or fingerprint. The completed record shall not be re-copied or changed, and the audio and video recordings should be attached to the file for preservation.

14.4.3.2 Preservation of Physical Evidence

Physical evidence, documentary evidence, audio-visual materials, and electronic data can be preserved through on-site investigation, seizure, sealing, copying, identification, retrieval, and receipt, and by drawing, photographing, identifying, fixing, and recording, and a record can be made. For example, various traces related to the case can be fixed and extracted by photography, video recording, or static electricity or plaster. At the same time, necessary explanations should be given for the time of shooting, and a record should be made. A list must be made for the seized, copied, retrieved, and accepted physical evidence and documentary evidence, stating the name, quantity, nature, characteristics, and name of the owner of the item or document, the time and place of extraction, etc. The original owner, witness, and extractor shall jointly sign or stamp the list. Two copies of the list shall be made, one for the owner and the other attached to the file. If the original item is perishable and difficult to preserve, it can be photographed and recorded before processing, and a record can be made. For electronic data, a third party can use instant encryption to fix its content and formation time, and generate a unique digital identifier for the data.

Physical evidence, documentary evidence, electronic data, or books, magazines and audio-visual materials with pornographic or obscene content involving State secrets shall be kept in special custody, shall not be leaked, shall not be proliferated, and shall be dealt with in accordance with the relevant provisions after the conclusion of the case.

When the court takes measures for the preservation of evidence, it may require the presence of the parties or their legal representatives in order to supervise the preservation of evidence, but the absence of the parties or their legal representatives shall not affect the court's taking of measures for the preservation of evidence.

14.5 Questions and Reflections

The Supreme Court held in (2008) Civil Shen Zi No. 926 that when a notarial act is performed in a place other than a notary's office, and the computer and mobile hard drive used for the notarial act are not under the control of the notary prior to the notarial act, and there is no record in the notarial certificate as to whether or not the cleanliness of the computer and mobile hard drive was checked, such a notarial certificate, although it can prove that the act as recorded in the notarial certificate took place in the presence of the notary, is It is not enough to prove that the act took place in the Internet environment. In the above cited case, the citizen provided evidence as the basis for the administrative organ to impose punishment, and there was a difference in the fact that the administrative organ delegated the authority to collect evidence to the citizen. According to the case, reference to the supreme court on the notarial act, combined with the contents of this chapter, think about the following questions: (a) the parties due to objective reasons can not collect evidence, how to collect evidence? (b) the case of preservation of evidence should follow what legal procedures? (c) the notary preservation of evidence can be used directly as a basis for decision without examination? (d) administrative organs or public security organs "reward notice" evidence obtained in accordance with the authority of the case-handling organ to collect evidence? (e) in litigation, how to apply to the court for evidence preservation?

References

Kaneko, H. and Takeshita, M. (1995). Minshi susong fa [Translation of 民事訴訟法] (Bai, L. X., Trans.). Beijing: Law Press China.

Zhan, S. G. (2009). Minshi zhengju fa yanjiu. Wuhan: Wuhan University Press. (in Chinese)

Shindo, S. (2008). Xin minshi susongfa [Translation of 新民事訴訟法] (Lin, J. F., Trans.). Beijing: Law Press. (in Chinese)

Zhang, J. L., & Xu, J. X. (2000). Lun suqian susong zhengju baoquan de weifaxing. Law Review, (3): 138–141, 146. (in Chinese)

Extended reading

Zhang, J. L., & Xu, J. X. (2000). Lun suqian susong zhengju baoquan de weifaxing. Law Review, (3): 138–141, 146. (in Chinese)

Bi, Y. Q. (2001). Zhengju baoquan chengxu wenti yanjiu. Journal of University of Science and Technology Beijing (Social Sciences Edition), (2): 61–67. (in Chinese)

Cui, J. (2002). Zhengju shouji zhidu. Modern Law Science, (3): 118–123. (in Chinese)

Chen, X. P., & Rao, B. (2003). Lun jianli woguo minshi suqian zhengju baoquan zhidu. Contemporary Law Review, (6): 141–143, 159. (in Chinese)

Xiong, Y. M. (2006). Faguan zhiquan diaocha zhengju de bijiao yanjiu. Journal of Comparative Law, (6): 82–90. (in Chinese)

Chapter 15
Procedures for the Application of Evidence

15.1 Introductory Case

In December 1995, the Zhongshan Branch of the Bank of China (hereinafter referred to as "the Bank") and Zhongshan Industrial Raw Materials Company (Defendant One) signed two loan contracts, with Defendant One borrowing 2 million USD and 1.25 million USD, respectively. Zhongshan Urban and Rural Construction Development Corporation (Defendant Two) provided guarantees. Defendant One later obtained the 3.25 million USD loan. In May 1996, Defendant One submitted a loan application to the Bank for 1,611,031.25 USD and signed a loan contract, with Defendant Two providing a guarantee.

In 1999, the Bank initiated debt collection for these three loans. However, the amount involved in the debt collection was not the 1,611,031.25 USD as stated in the contract, but 1.611 million USD, and both defendants received the debt collection notice. In 2000, the Bank transferred the debt to the Guangzhou office of China Orient Asset Management Corporation (Plaintiff) and notarized the notice. In 2002 and 2003, the Plaintiff repeatedly urged the repayment of the debt and later filed a lawsuit in court. Defendant One did not dispute the 3.25 million USD loan but claimed that it did not receive the loan of 1.611 million USD, and the Plaintiff had not provided the corresponding remittance certificate.

The Guangdong Provincial High Court ruled that while the Plaintiff claimed the loan was 1,611,031.25 USD, the debt collection notice stated 1.611 million USD, and the loan term was from December 1996 to the next December, which did not match the Plaintiff's claim that the loan occurred in May 1996. The court therefore rejected the Plaintiff's claim for 1.611 million USD. As for Defendant Two's guarantee, the court ruled that since Defendant Two's guarantee period for the 3.25 million USD loan was two years starting from December 1996, and the Plaintiff had no evidence to prove any claims during that period, Defendant Two was exempt from the guarantee responsibility. The Plaintiff appealed, and the Supreme People's Court further investigated the case.

H. Guo, *Evidence Jurisprudence in China*, Understanding China,
https://doi.org/10.1007/978-981-95-3981-9_15

In 1996, Defendant One reported to the Bank that due to financial difficulties, the principal and interest of 1,611,031.25 USD from the 1995 loan had not been paid and requested assistance. During the second trial, the Plaintiff submitted a loan agreement between the Bank and a third party, Construction Bank, where the Bank borrowed 1,611,031.25 USD from Construction Bank. This document was a photocopy and had been submitted to the court in the first trial, but the court had not verified it. In the second trial, the Plaintiff submitted the debt collection notice to prove that the claim for the guarantee rights had not exceeded the statute of limitations. Both defendants acknowledged the stamp on the debt collection notice but argued that the Plaintiff had introduced this evidence in the second trial, which was beyond the evidence submission deadline, and refused to cross-examine it.

The Supreme People's Court found that for the 1,611,031.25 USD loan, the evidence provided by the Plaintiff had formed a chain of evidence, and therefore, the court ruled that Defendant One should bear the repayment responsibility. Regarding the evidence submitted by the Plaintiff in the second trial to prove that the Plaintiff had not exceeded the guarantee period, and thus Defendant Two should bear the guarantee responsibility, the court ruled that although the defendants argued that the evidence submission deadline had passed, the court could decide to proceed with cross-examination based on the specifics of the case. The court ultimately determined that Defendant Two should bear the guarantee responsibility.

15.2 Chapter Overview

This chapter pertains to the specific application procedures of evidence, mainly including the evidence submission procedure, the evidence examination procedure, and the evidence authentication procedure. Among them, the evidence submission procedure involves the subjects of evidence submission, the time limit, and the methods; the evidence examination procedure mainly consists of cross-examination; and the evidence authentication procedure mainly concerns the admission and acceptance of evidence.

15.3 Evidence Submission Procedure

Parties or the prosecution initiating a lawsuit need to have sufficient evidence to support their claims. Specifically, when filing a lawsuit or initiating a public prosecution, they must provide enough evidence. The presentation of evidence is the foundation and prerequisite for cross-examination and authentication during the trial.

15.3.1 Overview of the Evidentiary Process

The evidence presentation procedure, also known as the evidence submission procedure, refers to the process where the party bearing the burden of proof provides evidence to the court within the statutory period to prove the facts of the case and support the litigation claims. The evidence presentation procedure is the initiation process for the application of evidence and the initial stage of evidence entering the trial process. It plays a significant role in the smooth progression of litigation. The evidence presentation procedure has the following characteristics.

15.3.1.1 The Evidence Submission Procedure as a Necessary Phase for Parties or the Prosecution to Initiate Judicial Proceedings

The evidence presentation procedure generally occurs during the trial stage and primarily includes the subjects responsible for presenting evidence, the methods of presenting evidence, the time limits for presenting evidence, the exchange of evidence, and the corresponding legal consequences.

In criminal litigation, the prosecution must transfer case files and evidence to the court when initiating public prosecution; in private prosecution cases, the complainant must provide evidence to prove the defendant's criminal conduct.

In civil litigation, the parties must provide evidence to the court that meets the conditions for filing a lawsuit. This evidence primarily includes the identity documents of the plaintiff, whether the plaintiff has the legal capacity to file a lawsuit, and whether the plaintiff's agent has the authority to act; the defendant's identity documents, whether the defendant has the legal capacity to be sued, and whether the defendant's agent has the authority to act; evidence supporting the factual grounds for the plaintiff's claims; and evidence regarding the court's jurisdiction.

In administrative litigation, the plaintiff must provide relevant evidence that meets the conditions for filing a lawsuit. In cases where the defendant's failure to act is being challenged, the plaintiff must provide evidence of having submitted a request in the administrative process. In administrative compensation lawsuits, the plaintiff must provide evidence of the harm caused by the administrative action. The plaintiff must classify and number the evidence, provide a brief explanation of its source, subject matter, and content, and sign or stamp the evidence with the submission date.

The evidence provided in the evidence presentation procedure is considered pre-litigation evidence, also referred to as evidence materials. Only when the parties or the prosecution submit these materials to the court and meet the basic legal requirements can the trial process be initiated.

15.3.1.2 The Evidence Submission Procedure as an Important Condition for the Commencement of the Judicial Process

Only after the parties or the prosecution provide evidence to the court and the court, upon review, deems that the conditions for holding a court session are met can the judicial process commence. Otherwise, the court may require the parties or the prosecution to supplement the evidence or may reject the case.

In criminal litigation, if supplementary evidence is required for a public prosecution case, the court shall notify the procuratorial organ to submit the supplementary evidence. In private prosecution cases, if the court has already accepted the case but finds, upon review, that there is a lack of evidence of the crime and the private prosecutor fails to provide supplementary evidence, the court shall persuade the private prosecutor to withdraw the lawsuit or issue a ruling to dismiss the prosecution. In civil and administrative litigation, the court shall review the evidence provided by the parties. If the conditions for filing a lawsuit are met, the court shall accept the case. After the case is accepted, the parties are still required to provide relevant evidence within the time limit for evidence submission.

In the evidence submission procedure, a distinction should be made between evidence for filing a lawsuit and evidence in support of the claims. In civil and administrative proceedings, whether the plaintiff provides sufficient evidence to support its claims is a matter of evidence submission during the litigation process, which generally should be completed within the time limit for evidence submission.

15.3.2 The Time Limit for Evidence Submission

15.3.2.1 The Concept and Function of the Time Limit for Presenting Evidence

The time limit for presenting evidence refers to the period during which the parties or the prosecution must fulfill their responsibility to provide evidence to the court. Within this period, the parties or the prosecution must submit evidence to the court. If no evidence is submitted or if the evidence submitted does not meet the legal requirements, it is considered a waiver of the right to present evidence, and the legal consequence is that the court will not accept it.

The purpose of setting a time limit for presenting evidence, as stipulated by law or judicial interpretation, is to prevent the parties or prosecution from submitting evidence at any time or making surprise presentations during the trial, which could lead to unresolved disputes in the case, even causing the court to reopen hearings, thereby wasting judicial resources and affecting the efficiency of the litigation. At the same time, this system encourages the parties or the prosecution to actively present evidence, compelling them to fulfill their burden of proof and facilitating the timely adjudication of the case. Since the law prescribes a time limit for concluding a case, the court should make a scientific and reasonable arrangement for the entire litigation process based on the specifics of each case, limiting the time within which the parties must present their evidence. Allowing parties to submit evidence at any time would disrupt the normal order of the trial and undermine the court's ability to perform its functions.

15.3.2.2 The Application of the Time Limit for Presenting Evidence

The time limit for presenting evidence is closely related to the burden of proof. It is an important step in enforcing the burden of proof and forms the basis for determining the legal consequences that parties will bear. The Civil Procedure Law, the Administrative Procedure Law, and their judicial interpretations in China provide regulations regarding the time limit for presenting evidence, which mainly applies to civil and administrative litigation. In civil litigation, different requirements for presenting evidence exist based on the use of simplified or ordinary procedures.

In civil litigation, the court should serve the parties with a notice of evidence submission during the preparation stage before the trial. The notice should specify the principles and requirements for distributing the burden of proof, the circumstances under which the parties may request the court to investigate and collect evidence, the time limit for presenting evidence as set by the court based on the specifics of the case, and the legal consequences of submitting evidence after the deadline. The time limit for presenting evidence can be agreed upon by the parties, subject to the court's approval. Once the time limit expires, if a party provides rebuttal evidence or corrects defects in the evidence already submitted, such as issues with its source or form, the court may, at its discretion, set a new time limit for presenting evidence. The court should make a comprehensive judgment based on the party's ability to present evidence and the reasons why evidence could not be submitted within the time limit. If necessary, the court may consult the other party's opinion. If a party changes its litigation request based on the trial's progress, the court should allow the change and, depending on the specifics of the case, may set a new time limit for presenting evidence.

In administrative litigation, due to the reversal of the burden of proof, the defendant bears the burden of proof for the administrative action under litigation. The defendant must provide evidence, including all evidence and the normative documents on which the administrative action is based, on the day they receive a copy of the complaint. If the defendant fails to provide evidence or provides it late without a legitimate reason, it is considered that the administrative action lacks corresponding evidence. If the plaintiff or a third party presents rebuttal arguments or evidence that was not raised during the administrative process, and the court allows it, the defendant may supplement the evidence during the first-instance procedure. If the defendant has a legitimate reason to request an extension of the time limit for presenting evidence, they may apply to the court for an extension within the period following the receipt of the complaint. Normative documents submitted by the defendant to the court are not subject to the time limit for presenting evidence.

In civil litigation, if a party fails to present evidence within the prescribed time limit without statutory or valid reasons, the legal consequence is that they lose the right to present that evidence. This legal consequence has two implications: first, the party loses the right to present evidence if it is submitted late; second, the court will not consider late evidence, even if it is truthful, when determining the case.

This system is significant in encouraging parties to actively present evidence and improving the efficiency of litigation. However, in practice, it should not be applied mechanically, as doing so may result in undesirable effects and lead to substantive unfairness.

15.3.2.3 Exceptions to the Time Limit for Evidence Submission

i. **Exception for agreement to cross-examine evidence**

If a party fails to submit evidence within the prescribed time limit, the legal consequence is the loss of the right to present the evidence, and the court will not organize a cross-examination of that evidence during the trial. However, in order to fully reflect the spirit of the litigation contract, if the opposing party agrees, the court should organize a cross-examination of the evidence. For evidence submitted after the deadline, the court will not organize a cross-examination, except when the opposing party agrees to cross-examine.

ii. **Exception for "new evidence"**

"New evidence" refers to evidence that appears after the time limit for presenting evidence set by the first-instance court, or evidence that a party was unable to submit within the time limit due to objective reasons. This mainly includes the following situations: ① Evidence discovered by a party after the first-instance evidence submission deadline. "New discovery" here involves two aspects: first, the evidence did not exist objectively before the deadline; second, the evidence existed before the deadline, but the party could not have known about it in normal circumstances. ② Evidence that the party could not provide during the first-instance proceedings due to objective reasons, but was still unable to provide even within an extended time limit allowed by the court. ③ Evidence discovered after the first-instance trial concludes. ④ Evidence that the party requested the court to investigate before the first-instance evidence submission deadline but was not granted, and the appellate court, upon review, deems it necessary to allow the evidence and requests it. The following conditions must be met: the party requested the court to investigate the evidence before the first-instance submission deadline; the first-instance court did not approve the request; and the appellate court, after review, deems it necessary to approve the request. ⑤ Evidence provided by a party after the court has granted an extension to submit evidence but which was still not provided within the extended time limit due to objective reasons. If the failure to consider this evidence could result in an obviously unjust ruling, the evidence may be treated as new evidence.

Whether foreign-related civil cases are subject to the time limit for presenting evidence as stipulated by domestic civil procedure laws has not been clearly defined by law, and there are differing opinions on this. One view holds that a time limit should apply, reasoning that since other cases have set time limits, foreign-related cases should follow suit. This would ensure the prompt realization of the legitimate right to a speedy trial for both parties, although the time limit could be set longer depending on the situation. Another view argues against setting a time limit, citing the difficulties in defining such a limit for foreign-related cases due to differing conditions in various countries, particularly differences in communication conditions. Moreover, many foreign legal systems do not have set time limits for litigation, making it inappropriate to impose such limits.

The question of whether evidence submitted after the time limit, and not falling within any of the exceptions, should automatically result in the loss of the right to present that evidence, still requires further discussion. This procedural abandonment of litigation rights can result in the forfeiture of substantive rights, and the system design may be seen as prioritizing litigation efficiency over substantive justice, potentially failing to strike a balance between the two. In such cases, sanctions could be applied. For example, the party could be required to bear reasonable costs and other losses arising from travel, lost work time, witness appearances, and litigation expenses. The court may, at its discretion, set a new time limit for the party to correct any defects in the rebuttal evidence or evidence already submitted regarding its source or form.

15.3.3 Evidence Exchange Procedure

15.3.3.1 Concept and Significance of the Evidence Exchange Procedure

The evidence exchange procedure, also known as the evidence disclosure procedure, refers to the procedure in which, after the expiration of the litigation defense period and before the court trial, under the auspices of the court, both parties (the prosecution and the defense in criminal cases) explicitly show each other the evidence they hold and exchange it with the other party. Evidence exchange mainly includes elements such as making evidence public, communicating evidence, sharing evidence, opposing the confidentiality of evidence, and the effect of losing the right to evidence in case of non-exchange. This procedure is of particular significance for strengthening the court's management of the evidence investigation and collection procedure.

As a legal system, evidence exchange originated from the practice of English equity law in the second half of the sixteenth century, and was codified in the *Federal Rules of Civil Procedure of the United States* in 1938. There are different understandings of the evidence exchange procedure in the theoretical and practical circles in China. Some believe that in the evidence exchange procedure, when the court organizes the evidence exchange, it is just a simple exchange of evidence, and the parties do not need to submit any written opinions, nor are they required to express their opinions and views on the exchanged evidence. Some believe that the purpose of evidence exchange is to fix the issues in dispute, and when the court organizes the evidence exchange, the parties should be allowed to conduct a certain degree of evidence examination. The evidence exchange should be carried out under the auspices of a judge. During the evidence exchange process, the judge should record the facts and evidence to which the parties have no objections in the case file; for the evidence to which there are objections, record them in the case file classified according to the facts to be proved, and record the reasons for the objections. Through evidence exchange, the main issues in dispute between the two parties are determined. As a statutory procedure, the activities and results of evidence exchange should be fixed in a certain form. When the court organizes the evidence exchange and requires the parties to express their opinions on the exchanged evidence, expressing their attitudes of approval or objection, it is not only conducive to fixing the issues in dispute of the case, but also means that the approved evidence will not be re-examined in the court trial, which is more conducive to improving the efficiency of litigation and realizing the purpose of evidence exchange.

The evidence exchange procedure in China is different from the discovery procedure in the United States. It focuses on encouraging one party to actively and dynamically use the procedural rights stipulated by law to collect, discover and investigate evidence, with a strong sense of initiative. It is also not completely the same as the evidence disclosure procedure, which focuses on the parties showing each other the evidence and other information they will use in court in stages after the pleading procedure and before the court trial, with a relatively strong sense of passivity. As an important part of the pre-trial conference, the evidence exchange procedure in China requires the court to "organize" evidence exchange for cases with a large number of evidence and complex and difficult cases, aiming to clarify the focal points of disputes, avoid evidence surprises, achieve concentrated trials, save judicial resources, and be conducive to judicial fairness.

15.3.3.2 The Specific Procedure for Exchange of Evidence

The specific procedure for the exchange of evidence primarily applies to civil and administrative litigation, while in criminal cases, it is part of the pre-trial conference procedure.

i. **Initiation of the evidence exchange**

The evidence exchange procedure can be initiated either by the parties' application or by the court's decision. If the parties apply and the court approves, the court can organize the exchange of evidence between the parties before the trial. Additionally, in cases where the facts are complex or there is a large volume of evidence, the court can proactively organize or decide that the parties exchange or present evidence to each other before the trial and record the exchange of evidence in the case file.

ii. **Time for exchange of evidence**

The determination of the time for exchanging evidence is generally based on two approaches: first, the parties (prosecution and defense) agree on a time; second, the court designates the time. If the parties agree, the arrangement needs to be approved by the court. The parties may agree to exchange evidence during the designated exchange period.

For cases with a large amount of evidence or complex issues, the exchange period should be limited to the period between the end of the defense period and the start of the trial. If the exchange period begins before the filing of the complaint and the submission of the defense, it may be difficult to achieve the purpose of the evidence exchange, as the parties may not yet fully understand each other's claims. Conducting the evidence exchange after the trial begins would defeat the purpose of the exchange. If a party submits rebuttal evidence or new evidence after receiving the evidence exchanged by the other party, the court should notify the parties to exchange evidence within a specified time. The exchange of evidence should generally be controlled appropriately. However, in major, complex, or particularly complicated cases, the court may allow multiple rounds of evidence exchange if necessary.

iii. **Methods of evidence exchange**

The evidence exchange procedure is not applicable to all cases and is generally used in cases with a large amount of evidence or complex facts. The methods of evidence exchange are mainly written exchange and oral exchange. For written exchanges, this may be done in the form of an interrogatory, where one party requests the other party to respond in writing to specific questions. Interrogatories cannot be used as evidence. In the case of oral exchange, the parties review the evidence together. Depending on the circumstances, video conferencing or other methods may also be used. Evidence that is acknowledged by the parties or admitted can be accepted as evidence without cross-examination in court, provided it has been verified. Evidence with objections should be categorized and recorded in the case file, along with the reasons for the objections.

iv. **Legal responsibility for the exchange of evidence**

The evidence exchange should be managed by the judge, with the court clerk recording the exchange in the form of an official record. Evidence exchange is not a trial session. During the exchange, the parties may only make brief, summarizing statements about the exchanged evidence. Evidence that both parties do not object to should be recorded in the case file, and typically, such evidence will not be cross-examined during the trial.

15.4 Evidence Examination Procedure

15.4.1 The Concept and Characteristics of Cross-Examination

Cross-examination can be understood in both broad and narrow senses. In the broad sense, cross-examination refers to any situation in litigation, arbitration, or other dispute resolution activities where the parties (prosecution and defense) and their defenders or legal representatives dispute or have doubts about the evidence provided. Through procedural mechanisms, they question, identify, challenge, explain, or debate the authenticity, legality, relevance, and probative value of the evidence. In the narrow sense, cross-examination specifically refers to the activities mentioned above during the court investigation stage of the trial.

The essence of cross-examination lies in the "challenge," i.e., questioning and doubting the evidence, where "doubt" and "question" have an inherently adversarial nature. "Evidence must be presented in court, identified, and cross-examined during the court investigation process to verify its authenticity; otherwise, it cannot be used as the basis for a ruling." Based on this, the concept used in this section refers to the narrow sense of cross-examination, specifically the activities of disputing and verifying evidence during the court investigation phase of a trial. Cross-examination, as a key phase in litigation, particularly in the trial process, has the following characteristics.

15.4.1.1 Cross-Examination is the Activity of Disputing and Debating Evidence Provided to the Court by the Parties (Prosecution and Defense), Their Defenders, and Legal Representatives

The activity of cross-examination originates from the right of the defendant to confront the plaintiff and witnesses. Although this right existed in ancient Roman law, it became part of the modern litigation system only in more recent times. Even in common law countries such as the United States, this right has been the subject of much legal struggle. For instance, the 6th Amendment of the U.S. Constitution states: "In all criminal prosecutions, the accused shall enjoy… the right to be confronted with the witnesses against him…" This ensures that witnesses appear in court to face the defendant, allowing the defendant to challenge their testimony, or enabling the witness to provide evidence against the defendant, safeguarding the full realization of the parties' litigation rights.

The parties involved in cross-examination are the parties (prosecution and defense), their defenders, legal representatives, and, in special cases, third parties. The court is not a party to cross-examination. Witnesses, experts, and investigators are not subjects of cross-examination; rather, they are the ones being cross-examined. The court is responsible for presenting evidence that it has obtained and should provide it for cross-examination while explaining the circumstances under which the evidence was gathered and hearing the parties' opinions. If the judge deems it necessary, they may question witnesses, experts, or other individuals with special knowledge or investigators. However, such questioning is not considered part of the cross-examination. Therefore, the view that judges can also act as parties to cross-examination in special circumstances is not valid.

15.4.1.2 Cross-Examination is an Activity Conducted in Court

Cross-examination is an activity where the parties or other participants in the litigation engage in adversarial actions, such as questioning and verifying, regarding evidence that is disputed or has raised doubts during the court session. According to China's *Civil Procedure Law*, "Evidence shall be presented in court and cross-examined by the parties." Evidence that has not been cross-examined cannot be used as the basis for a judgment.

During cross-examination, the parties should focus on questioning the authenticity, relevance, and legality of the evidence, as well as its probative value and weight. Any evidence that has been discussed during the preparation phase or the court's investigation or questioning process will be considered as having been cross-examined.

15.4.1.3 Cross-Examination as a Litigation Activity that Forms Conviction in the Judge's Mind

Cross-examination is a litigation activity that helps form the judge's conviction about the evidence, and it also serves as an important rule to limit the judge's internal conviction process. Evidence that has not been cross-examined cannot be used as the basis for a judgment. Evidence that was not contested during the pre-trial exchange and is recorded in the case file can be used as the basis for a judgment after the judge explains it during the trial.

Cross-examination is not only a litigation right of the parties but also an important means for the parties to achieve their goal of winning the case. It is a specific requirement of the principle of orality. At the same time, it is a necessary part of examining, verifying, and determining the evidence's capacity and probative value. Cross-examination plays a critical role in the evidence application process. It is the procedure through which the parties challenge and rebut the evidentiary value and probative strength of the evidence. Cross-examination enables the judge to thoroughly examine the evidence and use this process to decide which evidence to accept or reject and to assess its probative strength. It also helps prevent the judge from developing biases that could influence the proper judgment.

15.4.2 *Specific Procedures for Cross-Examination*

China's cross-examination procedure incorporates reasonable elements from the adversarial system of common law countries, changing the trial method to an accusatorial or adversarial format. The procedure has adopted the basic content of the cross-examination system, with cross-examination being conducted by the parties (prosecution and defense). The typical sequence of cross-examination is as follows: ① The prosecution (plaintiff) presents evidence, and the defense, as well as any third parties, cross-examine the plaintiff. ② The defense (defendant) presents evidence, and the plaintiff and third parties cross-examine the defendant. ③ The third party presents evidence, and both the plaintiff and defendant cross-examine the third party.

However, the judge still retains the authority to control, direct, organize, and guide the trial process. When necessary, the judge also has the power to investigate and verify evidence.

During cross-examination, the parties (prosecution and defense) should first focus on the legality, relevance, and authenticity of the evidence. Then, they will challenge, explain, and rebut the evidence regarding its probative value and weight. Evidence involving state secrets, commercial secrets, personal privacy, or other matters that are required by law to remain confidential cannot be cross-examined openly during the trial.

15.4.2.1 Cross-Examination Procedures

i. **Cross-examination procedure for physical evidence**

Physical evidence has an external form, strong intuitiveness and visibility, and can be directly perceived by the judge. It can exist independently without relying on other carriers and should be presented in court. The presentation of physical evidence provides a way for the judge to perceive the existence and state of the physical evidence, enabling the judge to obtain a perceptual understanding. At the same time, with the help of verification means such as the parties' identification of the physical evidence, and through the debate between the two parties (the prosecution and the defense) on the authenticity of the physical evidence, its relevance to the facts of the case, and the legality of the evidence collection, a comprehensive understanding of the evidence is formed.

For physical evidence and documentary evidence, the original objects or documents should be presented. If it is truly difficult to present the original objects or documents, copies or reproductions may be presented with the permission of the court. Audio-visual materials should be played in court.

The specific procedure is as follows: First, the party presenting the evidence shall explain the source, characteristics of the evidence presented, and the issues that the evidence proves. Then, the other party shall express opinions on the authenticity, relevance, and legality of the evidence. The two parties (the prosecution and the defense) can question and debate each other.

ii. **Cross-examination procedure for testimonial evidence**

The cross-examination of testimonial evidence is generally carried out through cross-examination. The methods of direct examination, cross-examination, redirect examination, and re-cross-examination are used to question and debate issues regarding the admissibility and probative force of the evidence. Cross-examination is mainly conducted on witnesses, expert witnesses, personnel who conduct on-site inspections, search personnel, and those who conduct investigative experiments, etc.

a. Direct Examination: Direct examination refers to the questioning by the party that summons the witness (including expert witnesses, etc., the same below). Its purpose is to make the person being questioned state the facts of the case that he or she knows and display the evidence.
b. Cross-examination: The questioning conducted by the other party after the direct examination is called cross-examination, aiming to expose the defects and deficiencies of the witness's testimony for the other party and weaken the reliability and credibility of the testimony.

After cross-examination, if either or both of the two parties (the prosecution and the defense) still have some questions that need further cross-examination, redirect examination and re-cross-examination can be carried out.

Redirect examination mainly aims to address the contradictions exposed during cross-examination through further questioning to discover the truth and falsehood. The questioning should focus on the necessary matters of the testimonial evidence in dispute, mainly on issues related to the credibility of the testimony, such as the accuracy of a person's observation, memory, or expression, as well as matters related to a person's credibility, such as self-interest, prejudice, and pre-judgment. If the court deems it necessary, it can require witnesses to confront each other.

For expert testimony, if necessary, the parties may apply to the court for assistance from one or two experts with specialized knowledge. With the court's permission, the parties can question individuals with specialized knowledge, and the experts selected by each party can cross-examine each other on relevant issues of the case.

Both direct examination and cross-examination require the court's permission. The judge typically only reviews the "request to question" in a formal or procedural manner and does not make substantive rulings. During the trial, if the court deems it necessary, it may summon co-defendants in the same case or co-defendants in related cases to testify and cross-examine in court.

iii. **Cross-examination procedure for illegally obtained evidence**

The cross-examination procedure for illegally obtained evidence mainly includes the following aspects:

(a) Initiation of the Procedure: During the court investigation process, the defendant has the right to raise the opinion that his/her pre-trial confession was illegally obtained and provide relevant clues or evidence.

(b) Preliminary Court Review: After the procedure is initiated, the court shall conduct a review. If the collegial panel has no doubts about the legality of the defendant's pre-trial confession, it can directly investigate the criminal facts charged in the indictment; if there are doubts about the legality of the confession's acquisition, the public prosecutor shall bear the burden of proof regarding the legality of the evidence collection.
(c) Prosecution's Proof: The public prosecutor shall provide the court with interrogation transcripts, original audio and video recordings of the interrogation process, or other evidence, and request the court to notify other present persons or other witnesses during the interrogation to appear in court to testify. If the suspicion of extorting a confession by torture still cannot be excluded, the public prosecutor shall request the court to notify the interrogators to appear in court to testify and prove the legality of the acquisition of the confession.
(d) Cross-examination by Both Parties: After the public prosecutor presents the evidence, the prosecution and the defense can cross-examine and debate on the issue of whether the defendant's pre-trial confession was obtained legally.

iv. **Cross-examination procedure for sentencing evidence**

In China's criminal trial process, the conviction procedure and sentencing procedure are relatively separate, with the sentencing procedure being a relatively independent process. For sentencing evidence, both the prosecution and the defense must conduct cross-examination. According to the presumption of innocence principle, the responsibility to prove the defendant's guilt lies with the prosecution. The defendant does not bear the burden of proving their guilt or innocence but may present evidence favorable to themselves. The cross-examination typically focuses on the following types of evidence: ① The cause of the case; ② Whether the victim was at fault and to what degree, and whether the victim's actions contributed to the escalation of the conflict, as well as the extent of their responsibility; ③ Whether the defendant's close relatives assisted in apprehending the defendant; ④ The defendant's behavior and whether they have shown remorse, pleaded guilty, or expressed regret; ⑤ The victim's civil compensation situation, and whether the defendant has received forgiveness from the victim or the victim's close relatives.

15.4.2.2 Rules of Cross-Examination

The Rules of Cross-Examination are a set of procedural and evidentiary rules governing the questioning of an opposing party's witness during a trial or hearing in adversarial legal systems. These rules ensure that cross-examination is conducted fairly, efficiently, and focused on relevant facts, while preventing harassment, speculation, or misleading of the witness. The parties involved in cross-examination must adhere to certain rules and should not violate these rules.

i. **Relevance rule**

Relevance means that the content of the evidence must be related to the facts of the case; otherwise, no cross-examination is necessary. When questioning a witness, the questions should be relevant to the case, and the witness has the right to refuse to answer questions that are unrelated to the facts of the case. Additionally, the presiding judge must intervene if the prosecution, parties, defense counsel, or legal representatives ask questions that are unrelated to the case. If either party (prosecution or defense) believes that the other's questions are irrelevant to the case, they have the right to object. After determining the situation, the judge will decide whether to support or reject the objection.

ii. **Rule against leading questions**

The rule against leading questions stipulates that the parties must not ask witnesses leading questions. A leading question is one that suggests the answer the questioner wants to receive, influencing the witness's response. When questioning a witness, inappropriate language or methods that may lead or suggest answers to the witness should not be used.

To avoid influencing the witness and to ensure the accuracy and rationality of the testimony, parties (prosecution and defense) must avoid asking questions that may lead the witness or distort the objective truth of their testimony. Such testimony should not be accepted as evidence.

iii. **Rule against threatening or insulting questions**

When questioning a witness, the dignity of the witness must be respected. Threatening or insulting questions are prohibited, especially when questioning the witness's character. Such questions should only address the credibility of the testimony, not the witness's personal privacy or character.

iv. **Individual questioning rule**

Witnesses should be questioned individually to prevent them from discussing the case with one another before testifying. Witnesses are not allowed to attend the trial proceedings as observers. When questioning a witness, other witnesses should be removed from the courtroom and not present.

v. **Rule against repetitive questioning**

Except when necessary due to the case's specifics, questions on the same matter should not be asked repeatedly. The judge has the authority to stop any repetitive or irrelevant questioning. Repetitive cross-examinations that do not present new points should be prohibited to ensure the efficiency of the trial.

15.5 Evidence Authentication Procedure

15.5.1 Concept and Characteristics of Evidence Authentication

In China, the term "authentication" was first used as a normative term in the *Supreme People's Court's Provisions on Strictly Enforcing the Open Trial System* in 1999. Article 5 of these provisions states: "Evidence used to prove the facts of the case that has not been publicly presented or cross-examined in court cannot be authenticated, except for facts that do not require evidence. In absentia hearings, the court may authenticate based on other facts and evidence. If the court can authenticate immediately, it should do so." Authentication, as a litigation system, is of significant importance in the judicial process.

Authentication, also known as evidence verification, refers to the process in which a panel of judges or a presiding judge, during a court hearing, analyzes, reviews, and verifies evidence provided by the parties (prosecution and defense), their defense lawyers, or litigation agents, as well as evidence collected by the court itself that has been cross-examined in court. This process is carried out according to specific principles, standards, and methods to analyze and assess the authenticity, reliability, and evidential strength of the evidence. The court should follow the legal procedures, conduct a thorough and objective review of the evidence, and, in accordance with legal provisions, judicial ethics, logical reasoning, and common sense, independently assess the probative value of the evidence, publicly disclosing the reasoning and results of the judgment. Authentication, as a legal system, has the following characteristics.

15.5.1.1 The Subject of Authentication is the Presiding Judge or the Panel of Judges

The subject of authentication is the presiding judge or the panel of judges handling the specific case. These individuals primarily include the judges participating in the court hearing and the jurors. The parties (prosecution and defense) and other litigation participants are not the subjects of authentication, nor are other court personnel.

15.5.1.2 The Object of Authentication is Evidence that Has Been Cross-Examined

The object of authentication is evidence that has been presented in court, provided by the parties (prosecution and defense) or collected by the court outside of the trial, and that has been cross-examined in court. Evidence that has not been presented in court cannot be subject to authentication, nor can evidence that has not been cross-examined. However, evidence that has been acknowledged by the parties during the exchange of evidence and recorded in the case file may be subject to authentication.

15.5.1.3 The Content of Authentication Primarily Concerns the Attributes of the Evidence

The content of authentication includes the determination of the authenticity, legality, relevance, or evidentiary value of the evidence, as well as its sufficiency, the quality of the evidence in proving the case facts, and the existence, degree, and direction of its probative value.

15.5.1.4 Authentication is a Litigation System

Authentication is not merely an activity where the judge determines the evidence; it also includes related procedures such as objections to authentication and remedies for authentication issues. It involves not only the recognition of evidence but also the conclusions and reasons behind such recognition. It is a litigation procedure, phase, and system that determines the facts of the case.

15.5.2 Specific Procedure of Evidence Authentication

The evidence authentication procedure can be divided into the authentication of the admissibility of evidence and the authentication of the probative force of evidence. The authentication of the admissibility of evidence refers to the determination of whether the evidence materials have the qualification as evidence. This kind of determination is generally carried out before the court session, and it is carried out for a single piece of evidence material. In special circumstances, it can also be carried out during the court session. The authentication of the probative force of evidence refers to the determination of the existence and degree of the probative force of evidence. This kind of authentication should be carried out in the comprehensive judgment of various kinds of evidence.

15.5.2.1 The Authentication Procedure of the Admissibility of Evidence

The authentication of the admissibility of evidence can be carried out in court. In-court authentication refers to the system in which a judge or the collegial panel publicly determines the evidence in court. In-court authentication not only includes the immediate authentication in court but also the authentication when the court resumes after an adjournment for deliberation.

This kind of authentication is mainly applicable to the authentication of a single piece of evidence, and the methods of "authentication one by one" or "one piece of evidence, one cross-examination and one authentication" can be adopted. This method divides the authentication of evidence into several units. After each piece of evidence is presented and cross-examined by both parties, the court shall make a confirmation immediately and explain whether the evidence is accepted and the specific reasons.

The validity of in-court authentication generally extends to the judgment and ruling, that is, the judgment and ruling are restricted by the authentication, and the judgment can only be made within the scope of the authentication.

15.5.2.2 The Authentication Procedure of the Probative Force of Evidence

The authentication of probative value refers to determining whether evidence has probative value and, if so, the extent of that value. This authentication generally occurs after the trial and is considered post-trial authentication, requiring the court to comprehensively evaluate all evidence that has been cross-examined during the trial.

Post-trial authentication refers to the system where the court determines the evidence through the judgment after the trial debates have concluded. Comprehensive authentication of evidence includes both classification authentication and centralized authentication. Classification authentication refers to grouping evidence of the same type together and authenticating it based on the cross-examination, depending on the specifics of the case. Centralized authentication refers to making a judgment based on the comprehensive authentication of all the evidence in the case. After all the evidence has been cross-examined, the court conducts a thorough analysis of the cross-examination results, accepting the relevant evidence as the basis for the decision or rejecting it, with reasons provided for the decision.

In a trial, after both parties (prosecution and defense) have presented evidence, cross-examined, and debated, the court can immediately authenticate evidence that both parties do not dispute or that the panel of judges has no doubts about. If either party (prosecution or defense) raises objections and presents rebuttal evidence, and an immediate judgment cannot be made, or if both parties present evidence for the same fact and it is difficult to determine immediately, or if the panel of judges has differing views on the evidence and cannot clarify the issue immediately in court, post-trial authentication can be used.

Whether performing single authentication of evidence or comprehensive authentication, the authentication of the probative value of evidence should be carried out based on the specifics of the case, considering the relevance of the evidence to the facts to be proven, and the relationships between different pieces of evidence. Evidence that is internally consistent and points to the same facts to be proven, and that can reasonably eliminate contradictions or provide reasonable explanations, should serve as the basis for the decision. The authenticated evidence should be made public, especially in the judgment document, with the reasons for accepting the evidence clearly explained.

The authentication of evidence not only includes the acceptance of evidence as the basis for the decision but also includes the rejection or exclusion of evidence. The exclusion of doubtful evidence also falls within the scope of authentication.

15.6 Questions and Reflections

The saying goes, "A lie requires ten more lies to cover it up." If there is indeed a false statement, there will always be gaps in the chain of evidence that the plaintiff cannot explain. Legal scholar Wigmore has stated: "Cross-examination is the greatest invention by mankind for uncovering the truth of a case and is the most effective legal tool for discovering the truth." Based on the case and in connection with the content of this chapter, and referring to the aforementioned saying and the scholar's argument, consider the following questions:

(1) How are the processes of providing evidence, cross-examination, and authentication conducted in the court's decision that Defendant Two should bear the guarantee responsibility?
(2) Can a witness be considered a subject of cross-examination?
(3) How should a litigation agent conduct cross-examination in court?
(4) How should the court authenticate evidence that raises doubts?

References

Chen, R. H. (1998). A Comparison of the Criminal Evidence Disclosure Systems in Britain and the United States. Tribune of Political Science and Law, (6): 84-95+117. (in Chinese)

David J. Gerber. (2000). Extraterritorial Discovery and the Conflict of Procedural Systems: Germany and the United States. The American Journal of Comparative Law, 34(4): 745-788. (in Chinese)

Han, B. (2005). A Study on the Civil Evidence Disclosure System. Beijing: China Renmin University Press. (in Chinese)

Shang, H. (2013). On Cross-examination and Confrontation. Beijing: China University of Political Science and Law Press. (in Chinese)

Chapter 16
Review and Judgment of Evidence

16.1 Introductory Case

The defendant, Liu, in the bankruptcy case of the managing entity, agreed to have the bankrupt company's assets auctioned by a certain auction house after discussions with the auction house's manager, Jiang. After the auction house successfully auctioned the bankrupt assets, between December 2010 and March 2003, Liu received kickbacks from the auction house manager on four separate occasions, totaling 205,000 RMB. After Liu was apprehended, he claimed in his confession that the 205,000 RMB he had received had been fully returned to Jiang, and he provided a copy of a receipt for the payment, allegedly signed by Jiang, with the payment date listed as January 5, 2011. This copy was examined by an appraisal agency, which concluded that the signature "Jiang" on the receipt matched the handwriting of the person named Jiang. However, based on the trial proceedings, Jiang denied the authenticity of the receipt copy. Furthermore, Liu's claim that he returned the money before the final instance of receiving a bribe presents an objective inconsistency. Considering both the supporting and contradictory evidence, it is difficult to establish whether Liu actually returned the funds.

16.2 Chapter Overview

This chapter addresses the review and judgment of evidence, primarily covering the concept and characteristics of evidence review and judgment, methods for reviewing and judging individual pieces of evidence, methods for the comprehensive review and judgment of evidence, as well as the procedures and main methods for reviewing and judging statutory evidence.

H. Guo, *Evidence Jurisprudence in China*, Understanding China,
https://doi.org/10.1007/978-981-95-3981-9_16

16.3 Overview of Evidence Review and Judgment

16.3.1 Concept of Evidence Review and Judgment

The review and assessment of evidence is a crucial activity in litigation and a key step in determining whether evidence can be used as a basis for the verdict. It holds a central position in the entire evidence system. The process of evidence review and judgment involves analyzing and evaluating the collected and presented evidence based on its intrinsic properties, in conjunction with the specific circumstances of the case. This activity can be understood as a process of "distilling the essence from the mass, distinguishing the genuine from the false, and moving from the surface to the core," which requires a deep understanding and judgment of the evidence. The review and judgment of evidence is the key step in establishing its probative value. It involves a detailed examination of both the evidence subject to cross-examination during the trial and the evidence that does not require cross-examination. This process must adhere to the judge's professional ethics, employing logical reasoning and life experience to conduct a comprehensive, objective, and impartial analysis. The goal is to establish the evidentiary relationship between the evidence and the facts of the case while excluding any irrelevant or unlawful evidence.

Scholars in China have differing views on the concept of "evidence review and judgment." Some believe that evidence review and judgment refers to the activity where judicial officers analyze and study the collected evidence, identify its authenticity, establish its objective connection to the facts of the case, determine its probative value, and then make conclusions regarding the truth of the facts of the case. Others define evidence review and judgment as the activity where specialized state agencies, parties, and their defenders or legal representatives analyze, study, and assess the evidence to verify its authenticity, determine its evidentiary capacity and probative value, and evaluate the strength of its probative value. The former view holds that the purpose of evidence review and judgment is to determine the probative value of the evidence in order to ascertain the facts of the case. The latter view, however, believes that the purpose of evidence review and judgment should also include determining the evidentiary capacity of the evidence. Some scholars even suggest using the term "evidence review and determination" and argue that evidence determination or certification is a concept frequently used in current judicial practice.

Evidence review and judgment refers to the activity in which the court, with the participation of the parties, their defenders, legal representatives, and other participants in the litigation, analyzes and studies the evidence to determine its authenticity, relevance, legality, and the existence and strength of its probative value. The evidence review and judgment process has the following characteristics.

16.3.1.1 The Subject of Evidence Review and Judgment is Specific

The subject of evidence review and judgment is limited to the judicial officers or jurors of the court, making it specific. Although, in practice, investigators, prosecutors, parties and their defenders, as well as legal representatives, also review and judge evidence, their review and judgment is primarily preparatory for presenting evidence and cross-examination. In contrast, the court's review and judgment of evidence aims to establish the authenticity of the evidence, providing a basis for determining the facts of the case or for handling the case. The purposes of the review and judgment differ, the significance varies, and the level at which the issues are resolved is distinct; the court's review and judgment thus holds a more critical significance.

16.3.1.2 The Object of Evidence Review and Judgment is Specific

The object of evidence review and judgment refers to the evidence that has been lawfully collected and provided to the court. All evidence must be verified as authentic before it can be used as a basis for the verdict. Therefore, the court must review and assess whether the evidence collected by other case-handling agencies, the parties, their defenders, and legal representatives can be used as evidence. Only after this review and judgment can it be determined. Evidence review and judgment is a necessary procedure for evidence to serve as the basis for a verdict.

16.3.1.3 Evidence Review and Judgment is a Purpose-Driven Cognitive Activity

Evidence review and judgment primarily focuses on the authenticity of the evidence, its intrinsic connection to the facts of the case, and its ability and strength in proving the facts of the case. This activity is characterized by a clear purpose. The purposes of evidence review and judgment are: first, to examine and identify the evidentiary capacity of the evidence; second, to verify and determine whether the evidence has probative value and its strength, with the ultimate goal being to determine which evidence can serve as the basis for the verdict.

16.3.2 The Significance of Evidence Review and Judgment

Evidence review and judgment holds an important position in the litigation process. It is the core of the evidence system and the lifeblood of the litigation procedure. The evidence collected by case-handling agencies, parties, their defenders, and legal representatives may not always be truthful due to various complex influences and constraints. Some evidence may be a mix of truth and falsehood, while others may even be entirely false. If not properly reviewed and judged, false evidence could be used as the basis for a verdict, leading to misidentification of the facts of the case, and potentially resulting in wrongful cases, unjust convictions, or fraudulent lawsuits. This, in turn, harms the legitimate rights and interests of the parties and undermines substantive justice in the judiciary. Therefore, evidence review and judgment plays a crucial role in the litigation process.

16.3.2.1 Evidence Review and Judgment Can Exclude False Evidence

Evidence review and judgment is a critical step in verifying evidence and plays an essential role in excluding false or fabricated evidence. For example, a witness may provide false testimony due to receiving bribes from one of the parties; a defendant may fabricate evidence, claiming they were not at the scene or did not have the time to commit the crime, in an attempt to avoid responsibility. Only through a rigorous review and judgment of the evidence can such false evidence be identified and excluded, ensuring that the litigation process is not derailed or misled.

In litigation, both physical evidence and testimonial evidence can be false, with testimonial evidence being particularly susceptible. Testimonial evidence relies on the witness's personal perception of the events, and their memory is expressed through language. Each step in this process carries the potential for distortion, whether due to subjective or objective factors, which can lead to inaccuracies or errors in the testimony. Only through evidence review and judgment can the truth of the evidence be accurately distinguished.

16.3.2.2 Evidence Review and Judgment Can Clarify the Truth of the Facts

The legal provisions regarding the procedures and methods of evidence collection are scientific and strict. Case-handling agencies or parties should obtain evidence in accordance with the rules of evidence, while fully safeguarding human rights. If evidence is collected in violation of the legally prescribed procedures, it cannot guarantee the objectivity and authenticity that evidence should have. When judges face conflicting evidence, some of which may be true and others false, they must conduct a rigorous examination and judgment according to court procedures to ensure the objective authenticity of the evidence. Only through this process can the connection between the evidence and the facts of the case be uncovered, the probative value of the evidence be determined, and the reliability and accuracy of the case facts be ensured.

16.4 Basic Methods of Evidence Review and Judgment

The review and judgment of evidence generally include two basic methods: the review and judgment of individual pieces of evidence and the comprehensive review and judgment of all the evidence in the case. These two basic methods are commonly used in judicial practice. In evidence review and judgment, judges should combine these two stages, alternating between them as needed based on the circumstances of the case.

16.4.1 Method of Reviewing and Judging Individual Evidence

The review and judgment of individual evidence refers to the process of examining and determining the authenticity, relevance, and legality of each piece of evidence. The "*Several Provisions of the Supreme People's Court on Civil Procedure Evidence*" stipulate that "judicial officers can review and determine individual evidence based on the following aspects: (1) Whether the evidence is the original document or item, and whether copies or reproductions match the original; (2) Whether the evidence is related to the facts of the case; (3) Whether the form and source of the evidence comply with legal regulations; (4) Whether the content of the evidence is true; (5) Whether the witness or the person providing the evidence has any interest in the case." The specific methods for reviewing and judging individual evidence are as follows.

16.4.1.1 Review and Judgment of the Source of Each Piece of Evidence

Every piece of evidence has a source, and reviewing the source of the evidence is a fundamental step and method for determining its authenticity. Identical evidence may differ in authenticity and reliability depending on its source. The source of the evidence should be reviewed and judged from the following aspects: (1) The source of the evidence should be determined. This includes how the evidence was discovered, how it was formed, who provided or collected it, where the evidence was collected, the circumstances at the time, and the environment of the location. (2) The process of obtaining the evidence should be clear. This includes the method used to extract the evidence, the tools used, the extraction method employed, and how the evidence was preserved after collection. (3) The source of the evidence should be legitimate. This includes whether the evidence was obtained in compliance with legal regulations and whether there are any other illegal circumstances affecting the objectivity of the evidence.

Every piece of evidence must have a source, and no piece of evidence should have multiple sources. Evidence without a source is unreliable, while multiple sources make it untrustworthy.

16.4.1.2 Review and Judgment of the External Form of Evidence

The review and judgment of the external form of evidence should be carried out from the following aspects: (1) Examine whether the form of the evidence is objective and whether it has been distorted or contaminated; (2) Examine whether the evidence complies with the legally prescribed form, such as whether evidence in administrative litigation conforms to the special requirements for evidence forms stipulated by laws, regulations, rules, and judicial interpretations; (3) Examine whether the evidence is the original item or original document. If it is a copy or reproduction, determine whether its form and characteristics are consistent with the original item or document. If there is any inconsistency, the evidence should be reviewed in conjunction with other evidence before a judgment is made.

16.4.1.3 Review and Judgment of the Subjective and Objective Conditions Underlying the Formation of Evidence

The environment and conditions in which evidence exists, as well as the environment and conditions under which it is extracted and preserved, have a significant impact on the objectivity and authenticity of the evidence. The subjective and objective conditions underlying the formation of evidence should be reviewed and judged from the following aspects: (1) The environment and conditions under which the evidence was formed-examining what the evidence should look like in such an environment and whether the current evidence matches the environment and conditions at that time; (2) The environment and conditions under which the evidence was collected and preserved-examining what state the evidence should present according to the environment and conditions at the time; (3) The environment and conditions for preserving the evidence-examining whether the evidence could change in such an environment and what changes may occur, and whether such changes are reflected in the existing evidence; (4) The environment and conditions of the evidence carrier. For example, if the auditory or visual environment of the witness differs, the witness's perception of the situation is likely to vary; the relationship between the witness and the parties may also affect the truthfulness of the testimony. When reviewing and judging evidence, all possible falsehoods caused by subjective and objective factors must be excluded, and the authenticity of the evidence should be determined. For instance, in administrative litigation, the review and judgment of evidence obtained by an administrative agency, such as the weather conditions, temperature, and the environment in which the food inspection was conducted, must be considered.

16.4.1.4 Review and Judgment of the Legality, Appropriateness, and Scientific Nature of Evidence Collection and Preservation

The legality of evidence primarily involves the legal form of the evidence and the legality of the methods and procedures used for its collection. This includes: (1) Examining whether the evidence conforms to the statutory form, whether it was obtained in accordance with the requirements of laws, regulations, judicial interpretations, and rules, and whether there are any other illegal circumstances that could affect the validity of the evidence; (2) Examining whether the procedures and methods used to collect the evidence are lawful. Any evidence obtained in violation of statutory procedures or using methods prohibited by law may affect its objectivity and authenticity, especially confessions obtained through torture, or evidence gathered using threats, inducements, deception, or other illegal means, or methods that severely infringe upon others' legal rights, as these are more likely to contain false elements.

Reviewing and judging whether the preservation of evidence is appropriate and scientific: (1) Determining whether the evidence was damaged, deformed, or replaced during the preservation period; (2) Examining whether the evidence was contaminated during transfer, or whether there were errors or losses; (3) Checking whether the collection, fixation, preservation, and provision of the evidence were recorded and whether the recorded content matches the actual evidence.

16.4.2 Method of Comparative Review and Judgment of Evidence

The method of comparative review and judgment of evidence involves comparing and contrasting two or more pieces of evidence that prove the same factual matter in a case, examining whether their content and the situations they reflect are consistent, and determining whether they reasonably and consistently collectively prove the facts of the case.

In general, evidence that is consistent after comparison and analysis is often more reliable, while contradictory evidence may indicate that one or both pieces of evidence are problematic. Of course, evidence that is consistent should not be blindly trusted, as factors such as collusion, false testimony, or torture-induced confessions could lead to false consistency. Similarly, contradictory or differing evidence should not be automatically rejected, but its contradictions or differences should be carefully analyzed to determine the cause and nature. Differences between different pieces of evidence are often inevitable. The key to comparative review is not just identifying the similarities and differences between the evidence, but analyzing these similarities and differences to see if they are reasonable and in line with objective principles. There are two basic forms of comparative review: Firstly, vertical comparative review of evidence. This primarily involves comparing multiple statements made by an individual regarding the same case facts over time, examining whether the content of the statements is consistent and identifying any contradictions. Secondly, horizontal comparative review of evidence. This mainly involves comparing different pieces of evidence or evidence provided by different individuals to prove the same case facts, checking whether their content is coordinated and consistent, and identifying any contradictions.

16.4.3 Comprehensive Review and Judgment of Evidence

The purpose of reviewing and judging individual evidence is to determine the authenticity of the evidence and its relevance to the facts of the case. However, it is insufficient to stop at this stage. This is because the review and judgment of individual evidence alone cannot fully establish its authenticity. It should be analyzed in conjunction with other evidence in the case, with comparisons made, distinctions drawn, and mutual corroboration sought. The previous step only provides a subjective understanding of the facts of the case, and even when the evidence confirming the truth is accumulated, it does not automatically lead to a conclusion about the existence of the facts. Only by linking all the evidence in the case and conducting a comprehensive review of the relationships between the evidence and the facts can the judge's understanding of the facts move from a subjective to a rational understanding, ultimately allowing for a conclusion about whether the evidence can prove the true state of affairs in the case. The entire body of evidence in the case should be comprehensively reviewed and judged based on the degree of relevance each piece of evidence has to the facts of the case, as well as the relationships between the various pieces of evidence. The methods of comprehensive review and judgment of evidence include the following.

First, in comprehensive review and judgment of evidence, all the evidence in the case should be considered. All evidence that has undergone cross-examination should be linked and compared, rather than selectively reviewing only part of the evidence. The entire body of evidence should be examined to uncover the relationship between the evidence and the facts of the case by analyzing the factual phenomena presented by individual pieces of evidence. The relationships between various pieces of evidence should be analyzed to further assess whether the evidence is authentic and reliable, whether there are any doubts, what those doubts are, the reasons for those doubts, and whether reasonable explanations can be drawn from other evidence. For example, when comprehensively reviewing and judging loan evidence, factors such as the loan amount, payment of funds, flow of money, the parties' financial capacity, local or party-specific transaction methods, trading habits, changes in the parties' assets, and witness testimony should be considered to make a comprehensive judgment on whether the loan transaction occurred.

Second, in comprehensive review and judgment of evidence, it should be objective and comprehensive, avoiding subjectivity and one-sidedness. While reviewing and judging evidence, attention should be paid to evidence that is favorable to one party, but the evidence favorable to the other party should also be considered. All evidence should be reviewed, not just a portion of it, and personal subjective assumptions should not replace the objective connection between the evidence and the facts of the case. Otherwise, it will be impossible to draw the correct conclusion regarding the facts of the case. In addition to conducting unit-based "small comprehensive" reviews and judgments, comprehensive review and judgment of evidence should treat evidence as a dynamic element, making a holistic judgment based on the changes in the evidence's generation, discovery, and development.

Third, in comprehensive review and judgment of evidence, attention should be given to identifying the hierarchical structure between primary and supporting evidence, as well as contradictions between the evidence and the facts of the case. The causes of these contradictions should be analyzed, and efforts should be made to reasonably exclude any contradictions.

First of all, it should be examined whether there are contradictions between similar pieces of evidence and whether different types of evidence proving the same case facts point in inconsistent directions. Specifically, attention should be paid to whether there is a primary-secondary relationship, auxiliary relationship, derivative relationship, or inclusion relationship between the pieces of evidence.

What's more, the evidence should be analyzed to determine where contradictions or inconsistencies exist, where there is agreement, and to further analyze whether the areas of agreement can be reasonably explained. The consistency should also be evaluated to determine whether it is justified-whether there are areas that should not be consistent but are, and whether there are areas that should be consistent but are not.

Furthermore, it is important to examine whether the agreement or contradiction in the evidence is due to a difference in understanding or a discrepancy within the evidence itself. Then, based on the chronological or dependency relationships between the pieces of evidence, a judgment should be made on which evidence can be accepted and which cannot.

In comprehensive review and judgment of evidence, it is crucial to give significant attention to contradictions within the evidence. However, it should also be recognized that some contradictions between evidence, between evidence and facts, or between the facts and the case itself are normal. Evidence that contains no contradictions is not necessarily more truthful or reliable-it could all be fabricated. Discovering contradictions within the evidence is a prerequisite for resolving them, which requires a full understanding of all the evidence in the case. After identifying contradictions, the reasons for them must be analyzed. These contradictions generally include the following situations:

a. Contradictions within individual pieces of evidence. For such contradictions, a comprehensive review and judgment of all the evidence in the case should be conducted before deciding how to use it.
b. Contradictions between different pieces of evidence. In this case, it is essential to analyze the contradictions between the statements of the parties and the testimonies of witnesses, between different testimonies, between testimonial evidence

and other types of evidence, between physical evidence and testimonial evidence, and between direct and indirect evidence. The causes of these contradictions should be identified, and false evidence should be excluded.

c. Contradictions between evidence and the facts of the case. Case facts are revealed and established through evidence. If there are contradictions between the evidence and the case facts, the contradictory points should be examined to determine whether the issue lies with the evidence or the case facts themselves. If necessary, an investigation should be conducted for verification.

16.5 Method of Review and Judgment of Statutory Evidence

16.5.1 Review and Judgment of Physical Evidence

Physical evidence possesses strong objectivity and stability. Although it cannot lie by itself, nor is it susceptible to intimidation, it has the characteristic of existing in various forms and is easily affected or interfered with by external factors. In reality, physical evidence may deteriorate, become contaminated, or even be altered, forged, or swapped. Therefore, physical evidence should also be reviewed and judged according to legal procedures and using reliable methods.

16.5.2 Review and Judgment of the Authenticity of Physical Evidence

The authenticity of physical evidence must be examined, and its identity must be effectively verified. It should be determined whether the physical evidence is the original item, and whether photographs, videos, or reproductions of the physical evidence match the original item or document. The physical evidence should also be examined to see if it has been identified or authenticated. Additionally, for photographs, videos, or reproductions of the physical evidence, it must be verified whether they were created by two or more individuals, and whether there is a written statement and signature from the creators regarding the process of creation and the storage location of the original item or physical evidence. Photographs or reproductions of the original item that fail to reflect the shape and characteristics of the original item cannot be accepted as evidence.

16.5.2.1 Review and Judgment of the Source of Physical Evidence

The source of physical evidence must be traced back to its origin, and its original source should be clarified. It should be determined whether the physical evidence was personally collected from the scene or handed over by another person, either voluntarily or under compulsion. The time, location, and process of the evidence's formation and discovery should be established. It should also be clarified whether the collected physical evidence is the original item, a copy, or a substitute, and whether the copy or substitute matches the original item. Since physical evidence originates from the case itself, its source is critical. Only by clarifying these issues can we prevent similar, fabricated, or swapped items from being used as the basis for a verdict. Evidence without relevant records and inventories, or evidence whose true source cannot be determined, should not be used.

16.5.2.2 Review and Judgment of the Collection Process of Physical Evidence

The collection procedures and methods of physical evidence have a significant impact on its authenticity. Therefore, the collection process and methods should be reviewed and judged. The review and judgment of the collection process of physical evidence primarily include the following aspects: (1) Examine whether the collection of physical evidence complies with the legal procedures. If legal procedures are violated, assess whether the extent of the violation affects the authenticity of the physical evidence; (2) Examine whether any changes to the physical evidence occurred during the collection process due to improper methods, such as extraction, fixation, or storage, leading to alterations such as distortion of footprints or contamination of bloodstains; (3) Examine whether the technology used in collecting the physical evidence is scientifically sound, and if the scientific methods used are effective for the specific evidence; (4) Verify whether physical evidence or documentary evidence obtained through inspection, examination, or search is accompanied by relevant records or inventories; (5) Verify whether the records or inventories are signed by the evidence collection personnel, item holders, and witnesses. If the item holder's signature is missing, check whether the reason is noted; (6) Check whether the characteristics, quantity, quality, name, etc., of the items are clearly indicated.

16.5.2.3 Review and Judgment of the External Characteristics and Properties of Physical Evidence

The review and judgment of physical evidence should examine whether it has undergone changes due to natural conditions such as time, weather, or temperature, such as fading, deformation, or deterioration. It should also examine whether the physical evidence has been forged or altered, and whether the internal properties and external characteristics of the evidence are consistent. If there are inconsistencies, the reasons for the discrepancies should be determined, and it should be assessed whether the physical evidence was damaged or altered during the collection, storage, or authentication processes.

16.5.2.4 Review and Judgment of the Objective Link Between Physical Evidence and the Case

Physical evidence is generated by the occurrence of case facts and must be objectively linked to the facts of the case. Therefore, the review and judgment of the authenticity of physical evidence is aimed at revealing the connection between the evidence and the case. This is particularly important for biological evidence such as bloodstains, fingerprints, hair, bodily fluids, and other trace evidence or items found at the crime scene, which are subject to examination and identification. These pieces of evidence should be verified through methods such as DNA testing or fingerprint identification to determine if they correspond to the biological materials, biological characteristics, or items of the defendant or victim. These issues should be examined by determining whether a probative relationship exists between the physical evidence and the facts of the case.

Additionally, the review and judgment should examine whether all physical evidence related to the facts of the case has been fully collected and whether any evidence has been overlooked. Photographs, videos, or reproductions of physical evidence, when verified to match the original item and confirmed as authentic through identification or other methods, can be used as the basis for the verdict. However, photographs, videos, or reproductions of physical evidence that do not accurately reflect the shape and characteristics of the original item cannot be used as the basis for the verdict.

16.5.3 Review and Judgment of Documentary Evidence

Documentary evidence relies heavily on the original document, and its content cannot inherently display its authenticity. Generally, an authentication procedure is required. The review and judgment of documentary evidence can be conducted from the following aspects.

16.5.3.1 Review and Judgment of the Production or Creation Process of Documentary Evidence

When creating copies or reproductions of documentary evidence, "there must be no fewer than two creators." Written evidence collected or retrieved by case-handling agencies from relevant units must be signed by the provider and stamped with the unit's seal. Written evidence collected or retrieved from individuals must be confirmed by the person involved and signed or sealed after confirming its accuracy. A receipt should be issued for evidence provided by relevant units and individuals, stating the name of the evidence, the time of receipt, the quantity, the number of pages, and whether it is an original. The receipt should also be signed by the case handler.

According to judicial interpretations, the review and judgment of the production or creation process of documentary evidence includes:

Firstly, determining whether the creator actually produced the documentary evidence. If the document was not created by the alleged producer, it indicates that the document was forged. If the document was created, the process of its creation should be examined to determine under what circumstances it was produced, the background of its production, and whether there were any factors such as violence, threats, or deceit. If such factors exist, the documentary evidence lacks authenticity.

Secondly, reviewing the process of obtaining the documentary evidence, including who provided it, when, where, and under what circumstances it was obtained. It should be examined whether others were involved in the process, whether there is a possibility of alteration, or whether the document may have been replaced.

Thirdly, reviewing whether the form of the documentary evidence is complete and complies with legal requirements, and whether there are any flaws. If there are flaws, it should be determined whether they can be corrected and whether such corrections comply with legal requirements.

16.5.3.2 Review and Judgment of Copies of Documentary Evidence

When a party provides a copy of documentary evidence, it must be proven that the original document once existed or currently exists and is authentic, as well as provide a valid reason for not presenting the original. The review and judgment of copies of documentary evidence mainly include the following aspects: (1) The original document no longer exists, and it is impossible to provide the original, such as when the original is lost or destroyed, unless it was deliberately lost or destroyed by the provider; (2) The original exists, but it is under the control of the opposing party or a third party, and the original cannot be obtained through legal procedures or means. For example, when the original is controlled by one of the parties or a third party, and that party or third party refuses to provide it; (3) The original exists, but providing the original may lead to its destruction or inconvenience, such as when a notice is posted on the wall, and providing the original may result in its damage; (4) Other legitimate reasons.

Additionally, further examination should be conducted to ensure that the copy matches the original, and that the method and procedure used to produce the copy comply with legal requirements. Considerations include the number of copies made, the condition of the photocopier, whether the content of the copy shows any obvious omissions, whether the content is consistent and coherent, and whether the format and layout of the copy comply with the requirements for documentary evidence. Generally, copies of documentary evidence are admissible to the same extent as the original, but this does not mean they carry the same evidentiary weight. Copies of documentary evidence, when verified against the original and confirmed as authentic through identification or other methods, can be used as the basis for the verdict. However, if changes to the documentary evidence or signs of alteration cannot be reasonably explained, or if the copy of the documentary evidence does not reflect the original and its content, it should not be used as the basis for the verdict.

16.5.3.3 Review and Judgment of the Collection Process and Preservation of Documentary Evidence

It is essential to determine whether the collection process and method of documentary evidence comply with legal and relevant regulations. This includes identifying who collected or provided the evidence and under what circumstances it was obtained. The review should also examine who has been responsible for the custody of the documentary evidence, whether any other individuals have had access to it during the custody period, and what measures were taken to secure and preserve it. If the documentary evidence was obtained through search and seizure, it must be reviewed to confirm whether the personnel involved had the legal authority to conduct the search and seizure, and whether the proper legal procedures and requirements were followed during the search and seizure of the evidence. If there are doubts about the source or collection process of the documentary evidence that cannot be reasonably explained, the evidence should not be used as the basis for the verdict.

16.5.3.4 Review and Judgment of the Content of Documentary Evidence

The content of documentary evidence should be analyzed to determine whether it is clear and specific, and whether it accurately reflects the true intentions of the creator. It should be checked for consistency in language and expression. The document should also be examined for any signs of alteration, forgery, deletion, modification, addition, or other defects. Additionally, the content of the documentary evidence should be examined to ensure it complies with legal requirements. For instance, contracts should contain the signatures of both parties, and notarized documents must meet legal standards. If necessary, the testimony of knowledgeable witnesses may be used to assist in the review and judgment.

16.5.4 Review and Judgment of Witness Testimony

Witness testimony, during its formation, undergoes a complex process of perception, memory, recollection, and expression. Its content is easily influenced by subjective and objective conditions, leading to distortion or misinterpretation. The review of witness testimony should examine the witness's intellectual condition, character, knowledge, experience, legal awareness, professional skills, as well as their relationship with the parties involved, the content of the testimony, and the source of the testimony. It should also consider other evidence in a comprehensive manner to prevent false or erroneous testimony. The review and judgment of witness testimony should include the following aspects.

16.5.4.1 Review and Judgment of the Witness's Qualifications

Examine whether the witness understands the true facts of the case. Determine if the witness has any physical or mental deficiencies, and if such conditions, or being too young or too old, affect their ability to distinguish right from wrong and express themselves accurately. Examine whether the witness is a party to the case or another participant in the litigation. At the same time, assess the witness's perceptive ability, such as whether their sensory organs are functioning normally, the objective environment during their perception of the case, their psychological state, and their level of knowledge. Review the witness's memory ability and related circumstances, such as whether the testimony aligns with the witness's age, work experience, and life history. Examine whether the mental state of the witness affects their perception of the outside world. Generally speaking, under stress or fear, sensory perception may be distorted, for example, when feeling in the dark. When mentally stable and focused, perception tends to be clearer and less likely to be forgotten. In contrast, if the witness was present at the time of the incident but was disinterested in the facts or distracted, their perception may be blurred or even nonexistent. Also, examine the time gap between the occurrence of the incident and the provision of the testimony. It is important to assess not only the witness's state during the testimony but also their condition when perceiving the case. For instance, when testifying under the influence of alcohol, intoxication, or anesthesia. Examine the witness's ability to express themselves verbally in order to assess the reliability of their testimony.

16.5.4.2 Review and Judgment of the Collection Process and Source of Witness Testimony

The review should examine whether the procedure and method of obtaining the witness testimony comply with legal and relevant regulations. This includes determining whether any violence, threats, inducements, deception, or other illegal means were used to obtain the testimony; whether the rule requiring individual questioning of witnesses was followed; whether the record was verified by the witness, confirmed by signature (or seal), and stamped with their fingerprint; whether, in the case of a minor witness, the legal representative was notified to be present and whether they were actually present.

The source of the witness testimony should be reviewed to determine whether it is based on firsthand knowledge or hearsay, whether it is an objective description or subjective assumption, whether the testimony was voluntarily given or made under duress, threat, inducement, or deceit, and whether the witness was influenced by bribery, coercion, or direction from the parties or others. The environment in which the witness perceived the facts of the case, such as distance, obstructions, lighting, weather conditions, and temperature, should also be considered. The reliability of the source of the testimony affects the authenticity of the content. If the collection process or method of obtaining testimony contains the following flaws, the testimony may be accepted if it is corrected or reasonably explained; otherwise, it should not be used as the basis for a verdict: (1) The questioning record does not include the names of the interrogator, recorder, or legal representative, or the start and end times, and location of the questioning; (2) The questioning location does not meet the required standards; (3) The questioning record does not include the informing of the witness regarding their rights, obligations, and legal responsibilities.

16.5.4.3 Review and Judgment of Contradictions in Testimony

The review should examine whether contradictions exist in the content of the testimony from the following aspects: whether the testimony from the same witness is reasonable, and whether there are contradictions in testimony given by the same witness at different times regarding the same facts; whether testimony from different witnesses regarding the same case facts is consistent; whether the testimony contradicts other evidence in the case. If multiple witnesses, who have a vested interest in one party, provide statements that are identical in content and expression, there is a possibility of collusion, and such testimony should not be treated as corroborative. If multiple witnesses provide testimony that is broadly consistent, the contradictions between their statements should be analyzed. If the contradictions can be reasonably explained and do not violate the rules of experience, the testimony can be treated as corroborative.

The testimony should also be compared with general experience or common sense. If the testimony contradicts common knowledge or experience, it may be judged to be false. If the witnes's testimony in court contradicts their pre-trial testimony, and the witness can provide a reasonable explanation and other evidence corroborates their in-court testimony, the court should accept the in-court testimony. If the witness cannot provide a reasonable explanation but their pre-trial testimony is corroborated by other evidence, the pre-trial testimony may be accepted.

16.5.4.4 Review and Judgment of Potential Bias or Personal Interests in the Witness

If a witness has a direct or indirect interest in the parties involved in the case or the outcome of the trial, or if they hold bias against one of the parties, their testimony may be unreliable. Questioning the witness's potential bias, personal interests, and motivations helps uncover the truth. The relationship between the witness and the parties or the case should be examined to assess the reliability of the testimony.

16.5.4.5 Review and Judgment of the Witness's Knowledge and Experience

The witness's age, cognitive level, memory, and expression abilities should be reviewed to determine whether their physiological and mental state affects their testimony. Relevant knowledge and experience can influence a witness's ability to observe things. A witness with expertise in a certain area typically has sharper observation skills and a deeper understanding. For example, a driver can judge vehicle speed more accurately than an average person. If a witness lacks specialized knowledge but their testimony pertains to specialized knowledge, the credibility of their testimony may be low.

16.5.4.6 Review and Judgment of the Witness's Reputation and Character

A witness's character is related to the reliability of their testimony. A person with good character is more likely to provide truthful testimony, whereas a witness lacking honesty may have their testimony questioned, leading to reduced credibility.

Generally, a witness providing testimony favorable to a party with whom they have a familial or close relationship tends to have less probative value than testimony from other witnesses. In other words, the testimony of other witnesses is generally considered more reliable than testimony from a witness who is related to or has a close relationship with one of the parties, especially if the testimony benefits that party.

16.5.5 Review and Judgment of the Victim's Statement

16.5.5.1 Review and Judgment of the Source of the Victim's Statement

The reliability of the source of the victim's statement should be reviewed. It should be determined whether the statement is based on firsthand perception, relayed by others, or inferred by the victim. The method of collecting the victim's statement should also be examined to ensure its legality. It should be reviewed whether the victim was influenced by external factors, such as being coerced, induced, or deceived, and whether the victim has the ability and means to prove the facts of the case.

16.5.5.2 Review and Judgment of the Motivation Behind the Victim's Statement

The circumstances under which the victim made the statement should be reviewed, along with whether the content of the statement is consistent with the facts. The relationship between the victim and the defendant prior to the incident should be examined, including whether they knew each other, the nature of their relationship, and whether there were any emotional entanglements, economic, or other disputes. It should be assessed whether the statement is objective, or if it includes any speculative content. Generally, if the victim had no prior relationship with the defendant or had a normal relationship without any negative history, the likelihood of false testimony is lower. In contrast, if there was a history of conflict or a complicated relationship, the victim may be more likely to make false statements, exaggerate the criminal facts, or even fabricate facts to increase the severity of the defendant's guilt.

16.5.5.3 Review and Judgment of the Content of the Statement for Reasonableness, Consistency, and Contradictions

The content of the victim's statement should be reviewed to determine whether it is reasonable, consistent, and free of contradictions. A comparative approach should be taken, examining whether the statement is stable and whether multiple accounts are consistent. It should be checked for any discrepancies or inconsistencies, and the content should be compared with other evidence in the case to see whether it aligns and can be corroborated.

16.5.6 Review and Judgment of the Defendant's Confession and Defense

All verdicts in cases must be based on solid evidence and thorough investigation, and confessions should not be trusted blindly. The review and judgment of the defendant's (including the criminal suspect's) confession and defense must be comprehensive, meticulous, and realistic, without being misled by superficial appearances. It must also be scientific and cautious, and judgments should not be made hastily or based on preconceived notions. According to the rules of litigation and judicial practice, the review and judgment of the defendant's confession and defense should proceed from the following aspects.

16.5.6.1 Review and Judgment of the Legality of the Process of Collecting the Defendant's Confession and Defense

Since illegally collected confessions and defenses can affect their authenticity, the legality of the collection process should be carefully reviewed. Special attention should be paid to whether the time, location, method, and the identity of the interrogators meet legal and relevant regulations. For instance, whether at least two investigators were involved in interrogating the criminal suspect, whether the interrogation of the defendant was conducted individually, and whether there were any instances of obtaining confessions through illegal means such as torture. If necessary, the health check records and transcripts of the defendant's entry and exit from the detention center can be retrieved. If torture is found to have been used, the reliability of the confession and defense is very low, and they cannot be used as the basis for the verdict. Additionally, the formal legal requirements for the collection of the confession and defense must be examined, including whether the prescribed number of people, time, and other legal formalities were followed, and whether the confession and defense are truthful.

16.5.6.2 Review and Judgment of Whether the Defendant's Confession and Defense Are Reasonable

The review and judgment of the defendant's confession and defense should be based on the laws of cause and effect and human behavior, as well as the general rules of life, to determine whether the confession and defense align with the facts, common sense, and reason. Those who sincerely repent and surrender voluntarily usually provide truthful confessions of their crimes. When presented with solid and sufficient evidence, even if there is some degree of coerced confession, it is often more accurate. Confessions made under the influence of criminal policy guidance and after receiving education typically tend to be more truthful. In practice, however, some defendants misunderstand leniency policies such as the reduction of sentence for confession and guilty plea, and confess to crimes they did not commit. Others, driven by loyalty or other reasons, may take responsibility for crimes they did not commit. Some defendants, due to misunderstanding, may confess to acts that are not crimes under the law. In such cases, while the confession may initially seem reasonable, further analysis may reveal it does not align with reason.

Defendants have the right to offer a defense to plead not guilty, claim a lesser offense, or seek a reduction or exemption from criminal punishment. In practice, some defendants offer a defense to protect their legitimate rights, while others fabricate facts or misinterpret the law to evade responsibility. The motive behind the defendant's defense can influence the truthfulness of the defense. A defendant's accusations against others can only serve as a clue for further evidence collection and review.

16.5.6.3 Review and Judgment of Whether the Defendant's Confession and Defense Contradict Other Evidence

The review should examine whether the confession and defense are consistent over time, whether there are any contradictions, and the reasons for those contradictions. It is important to check whether all of the defendant's confessions and defenses have been included in the case file. If any confessions or defenses that should have been included are missing, a relevant explanation should be provided. Specifically, the following points should be carefully examined:

i. **The review should be conducted in conjunction with the entire case evidence to assess whether there are contradictions between the confession and defense and other evidence**

a. Review whether the defendant's confession and defense contradict the confessions and defenses of other defendants in the same case. If contradictions exist, the specific manifestations and causes of these contradictions should be identified-whether the contradictions are due to the shifting of blame, differences in the degree of involvement in the crime, or discrepancies in knowledge of the situation. These contradictions should be analyzed in conjunction with the confessions, defenses, and other evidence in the case.
b. Review whether the defendant's confession and defense contradict other evidence. If contradictions are found, a careful analysis should be made of the specific forms of the contradiction and their causes, to determine whether the issue lies with the confession itself or with the other evidence. Even if the confession and defense are consistent with other evidence, they should not be taken at face value. Caution is needed to determine whether this consistency is superficial or substantial and whether there is a possibility of a false appearance of consistency.
c. Compare and analyze the defendant's confession and defense with other evidence in the case, such as physical evidence and victim statements, to check whether the direction of the confession and other evidence align. If they are consistent, this indicates that the confession and defense are truthful and reliable; if not, it suggests a higher likelihood that the confession and defense may be false.

ii. **Review of the defendant's confession and defense when they change their statements**

The review of confessions and defenses that have changed should be conducted from the following aspects:

a. Review the dual nature of confessions and defenses. The situation of a defendant changing their statement is complex: First, the reversal of the confession may be confrontational, made in an attempt to evade or reduce responsibility and disrupt the normal course of litigation; second, it may be defensive, as a form of exercising the right to defense, such as correcting false statements made earlier. Therefore, these issues should be analyzed specifically, and when there is a reversal from false to true, it should be corrected based on the principle of "correcting errors when found."

b. Analyze and review the true reasons for the change of confession. The reasons for a defendant changing their statement are varied and complex. The review should aim to determine whether the reversal is truthful. Some common reasons for changing a statement include: first, a previous confession made under illegal methods, such as torture, leading to a change of statement at the prosecution or trial stage; second, a misunderstanding, where the defendant confessed to facts that do not constitute a crime; third, taking responsibility for a crime not committed, often due to loyalty or other reasons; fourth, changing the confession to evade responsibility; fifth, changing the confession due to collusion or communication from others.
c. Review of confessions that change over time. For repeated or inconsistent confessions, it is important not to simply rely on the confession made during the investigation, nor should the reversal made during the trial be blindly accepted. The principle of seeking the truth should be upheld, with a careful analysis of multiple confessions to identify which parts can be verified as truthful. Regardless of the sequence of statements, "the verified truth is trusted, and unsubstantiated statements are rejected." In judicial practice and evidence law theory, some argue that only the statement made in court is considered truthful. In fact, this is not always the case. The review of the defendant's confession and defense must adhere to the principle of seeking the truth, verifying the facts, and considering the entire case. Whether it is a prior confession or a later reversal, the focus should be on whether the content of the statement aligns with the facts of the case and is consistent with other evidence. If the confession and defense align with the facts of the case and other evidence, particularly in terms of detailed consistency, the statement can be considered truthful. If, after a reversal, the defendant's confession leads to the discovery of strong physical evidence that corroborates other evidence proving the crime, the statement can be deemed truthful. If the defendant reverses their statement during the trial but cannot reasonably explain the reversal, or if their defense contradicts the case evidence, but their pre-trial statement is corroborated by other evidence, the pre-trial statement may be accepted. If the defendant reverses their statement during the trial, and there is no reasonable explanation for the reversal, and no other evidence corroborates their pre-trial statement, the pre-trial confession should not be accepted.

Additionally, when interrogating deaf-mute individuals, ethnic minorities, or foreigners, it is essential to ensure that an appropriate interpreter is provided. When questioning minor co-defendants, it must be confirmed that their legal representatives were notified to be present. If the legal representative was absent, it should be noted. The production and modification of the interrogation record should comply with legal and relevant regulations, and the record should indicate the time and place of the questioning. When the defendant is first questioned, they must be informed of their right to request disqualification of the investigator and to hire a lawyer. If the defendant did not verify, confirm, and sign (or stamp) the record, it cannot be used as the basis for the verdict.

16.5.7 Review and Judgment of the Parties' Statements

The review and judgment of the parties' statements in civil and administrative litigation should be conducted from the following aspects.

16.5.7.1 Review and Judgment of Whether the Parties' Statement is Objective and Voluntary

The review of the parties' statements primarily involves verifying the authenticity of the statement itself, which includes the following aspects: (1) Whether the statement was made voluntarily, without external pressure or undue influence, and whether the party admitted to something due to a misunderstanding or misguidance; (2) Whether there are contradictions in the statement, and whether the party has a good reputation; (3) Whether the statement is coherent and consistent from beginning to end, etc.

16.5.7.2 Review and Judgment of Whether the Parties' Statement Matches the Case Facts

The review should assess which parts of the statement are factual assertions and which parts are litigation demands. It should be examined whether the statement contradicts the facts of the case, including the occurrence, development, and changes in the case; whether such contradictions are reasonable; whether the statement contains any omissions, distortions, additions, or falsehoods; and whether the statement has been acknowledged by the opposing party. Evidence acknowledged by the party in the litigation should be confirmed by the court, unless otherwise stipulated by law or judicial interpretation.

16.5.7.3 Review and Judgment of Whether the Parties' Statement is Consistent with Other Evidence

The review should determine whether the statements made by both parties are supported by relevant evidence, whether there are conflicts between the parties' statements, and whether there are contradictions between the parties' statements and other evidence. If there is inconsistency between a party's current and prior statements, the review should be conducted in light of the party's litigation capacity, the evidence, and the specific circumstances of the case.

The parties' statements should be reviewed and judged in conjunction with other evidence.

16.5.8 Review and Judgment of Expert Opinions

As the opinion of the expert, the expert opinion does not possess inherent probative value in advance. The review and judgment of expert opinions should be conducted from the following aspects.

16.5.8.1 Review and Judgment of the Legality of the Expert Opinion

The review of the legality of the expert opinion mainly includes the following: (1) Whether the expert institution and the expert are legally registered, included in the roster, and publicly announced; (2) Whether the expert has the qualifications and practical ability to address the specialized issues involved in the assessment; (3) Whether the expert's qualifications are appropriate for the matter being assessed; (4) Whether the expert is among those who should be recused.

The review should also examine whether the expert report contains the statutory content. This includes the following: the name or title of the client, the content of the commissioned assessment; the materials provided for the assessment; the basis for the assessment and the scientific techniques used; an explanation of the assessment process; a clear conclusion; a statement of the expert's qualifications; and the signatures and seals of the expert and the expert institution. If the expert report lacks the required signatures and seals, it cannot be used as the basis for the verdict.

16.5.8.2 Review and Judgment of the Necessity of the Expert Opinion

The review of the necessity of the expert opinion includes: (1) Whether the scope of the commissioned matter is consistent with the scope of the expert opinion, and whether the expert opinion exceeds or narrows the scope of the commissioned matter; (2) Whether the facts addressed by the expert opinion involve specialized issues, and whether these specialized issues are necessary for determining the facts of the case, and whether expert knowledge is required to resolve them; (3) Whether the expert opinion addresses factual issues or legal issues. Expert opinions that are unrelated to the case facts cannot be used as the basis for the verdict.

16.5.8.3 Review of Whether the Materials Submitted for Testing Meet the Requirements for the Expert Opinion

The review of the authenticity and objectivity of the materials submitted for testing is the foundation for reviewing the expert opinion. The review of the materials submitted for testing includes examining the reliability and authenticity of the evidence, the source of the expert documents, and the situation of the individual providing the materials (e.g., doctors, witnesses, etc.). It should also assess the quantity, quality, retention time, storage conditions, and methods of handling and processing the materials, as well as the safety of the materials during transportation. Then, it should be determined whether the submitted materials are authentic and reliable, whether they have been contaminated, whether they are suitable for the assessment, and whether they meet the necessary quality and quantity requirements for the assessment. If the submitted materials do not meet any of the above conditions, it will affect the quality and accuracy of the expert opinion, and they cannot be used as the basis for the verdict.

16.5.8.4 Review and Judgment of the Reliability of the Expert Methodology

The review of the reliability of the expert methodology mainly involves assessing whether the scientific techniques, experimental methods, reasoning principles, and the formulas, theorems, and literature that serve as the basis for the expert assessment are scientific and reliable. The content of the review should include: (1) Whether the underlying principles of the assessment are reliable; (2) Whether the scientific techniques used in the assessment are reliable; (3) Whether the methods employed for the assessment of the matter are reliable; (4) Whether the order and steps of the assessment are scientifically sound.

When different techniques are used to assess the same matter, the reliability of the resulting expert opinion may vary. For example, while ABO blood type testing and DNA technology are both used for identification, DNA testing is generally considered more reliable. Additionally, when DNA profiling is used, the reliability and sensitivity of silver staining compared to PCR technology can differ. However, this is not absolute, and refers to the relative reliability of the technology, not the inherent reliability of the expert opinion.

16.5.8.5 Review and Judgment of the Validity of the Expert Technology and Standards

The review of the validity of the expert technology and standards mainly includes: (1) Whether the expert technology used is effective; (2) Whether the instruments and equipment used in the assessment are effective; (3) Whether the method employed in the assessment is effective. If national or industry standards exist, it should be confirmed whether they were applied correctly. In the absence of such standards, the adopted standards should be assessed for scientific and rational validity. Since different standards have different quality requirements, reviewing the expert standards can help determine the reliability of the expert opinion.

16.5.8.6 Review and Judgment of Whether the Expert Opinion Contradicts Other Evidence

The expert opinion should be compared and analyzed with other evidence to check for any contradictions, especially with respect to whether the expert opinion contradicts examination records and related photographs. It should be assessed whether any contradictions can be reasonably explained or clarified.

The review should also examine whether the facts upon which the expert opinion and its analysis are based are objective and comprehensive. The interpretation of the features of the test materials should be reasonable, the standards applied should be accurate, the analysis should be logically sound, and the conclusions drawn in the expert opinion should conform to scientific norms.

An expert opinion is a form of evidence, and it does not hold more weight than other types of evidence. The reliability of the expert opinion should not be determined based on the administrative ranking of the expert institution, nor should the title of the expert be used as the basis for judging the strength of the expert opinion. Even expert opinions from national-level institutions do not have predetermined probative force.

16.5.9 Review and Judgment of the Examination, Inspection, Identification, Investigation Experiments, and On-Site Records

In general, examination, inspection, identification, investigation experiments, and on-site records are objective records of the examination, inspection, and on-site activities. The review and judgment should be conducted from the following aspects.

16.5.9.1 Review and Judgment of Whether the Creation of Examination, Inspection, Identification, Investigation Experiments, and On-Site Records Complies with Legal Requirements

The review should examine whether the individuals conducting the examination, inspection, identification, and investigation experiments have the authority to do so; whether witnesses were invited to observe the examination, inspection, identification, and investigation experiments; whether the legal procedures for the examination, inspection, identification, investigation experiments, and on-site records are complete; whether the examination and inspection were conducted in accordance with the law, and whether the records were made in accordance with legal and relevant regulations; whether the individuals conducting the examination, inspection, identification, investigation experiments, and the witnesses signed or stamped the records. Particular attention should be paid to reviewing the process and method of the identification and investigation experiment records to ensure they comply with relevant regulations. If the examination, inspection, or identification records contain significant inconsistencies with legal or regulatory requirements that cannot be reasonably explained, they cannot be used as the basis for the verdict.

16.5.9.2 Review and Judgment of Whether the Content of the Examination, Inspection, Identification, Investigation Experiments, and On-Site Records is Comprehensive and Accurate

The review should determine whether the written content, photographs, drawings, etc., accurately reflect the original condition of the scene or other objects of the examination or inspection. The relevant content should be comprehensive. The content of the examination, inspection, identification, and investigation experiment records should be comprehensive, detailed, accurate, and standardized, accurately documenting the reasons for conducting the examination, inspection, identification, or investigation experiment; the time, place, personnel present, location of the scene, and surrounding environment; the location, characteristics, and detailed circumstances of the scene, items, persons, bodies, etc.; and the process of the examination, inspection, search, identification, or investigation experiment. The written records should match the physical objects, drawings, videos, or photographs. The methods of preserving evidence should be scientific and standardized. It should be confirmed whether the scene, objects, or traces have been damaged or falsified, and whether the scene is the original; whether personal characteristics, injuries, or physiological conditions have been concealed or altered, etc.

16.5.9.3 Review and Judgment of Whether the Content of the Examination, Inspection, Identification, Investigation Experiments, and On-Site Records is Authentic

When reviewing the examination, inspection, and on-site records, the recorded content should be compared and analyzed with the defendant's confession, the victim's statement, witness testimony, and other verbal evidence to check for contradictions. The recorded physical evidence, such as material and documentary evidence, should also be compared with the evidence collected to see if they match. The authenticity and objectivity of the examination, inspection, and on-site records should be determined based on the comparison with verbal evidence and physical evidence. Particularly when supplementary examinations or inspections are conducted, it should be reviewed whether there are contradictions between the previous and subsequent examinations and inspections, and whether the reasons for the re-examination or re-inspection are explained. If the conditions of the investigation experiment significantly differ from the conditions at the time of the event, or if there are other factors that affect the scientific validity of the experiment's conclusion, the investigation experiment record cannot be used as the basis for the verdict. The identification record should not be used as the basis for the verdict if it falls into any of the following categories: (1) The identification was not conducted under the supervision of investigators or law enforcement officers; (2) The person being identified was shown to the witness before the identification; (3) The identification was not conducted individually; (4) The person being identified was not mixed with other objects with similar characteristics, or the number of objects for identification does not meet the prescribed requirements; (5) The witness was given significant hints during the identification.

However, when it is difficult to find similar reference objects, such as bodies or places, or when the reference objects are identical, like banknotes, or when the witness can accurately describe the unique features of an item, such as a mobile phone, without using mixed identification, this does not affect the admissibility of the evidence.

16.5.9.4 Review and Judgment of the Time and Process of Creating Examination, Inspection, Identification, Investigation Experiments, and On-Site Records

The review should examine the time of the incident and the time when the examination, inspection, identification, and investigation experiments were conducted, analyzing the possibility of natural damage or human falsification of the scene, objects, and traces. It should also consider any changes in physical evidence, injuries, or physiological states and whether these have been falsified. The time of the creation of the records should be examined to determine whether they were made at the time of the examination, inspection, identification, and investigation experiments, or if they were created afterward. If created afterward, the circumstances under which the records were made should be clarified, and it should be assessed whether there were any errors, fabrications, or falsifications.

16.5.9.5 Review and Judgment of the Competence of Personnel Creating the Examination, Inspection, Identification, Investigation Experiment, and On-Site Records

The review should assess the professional competence and level of the personnel who created the examination, inspection, identification, investigation experiment, and on-site records, as well as their work attitude. Generally, if the personnel responsible for creating the records have poor professional skills or lack responsibility, there is a possibility of omissions or errors in the examination, inspection, and on-site records.

Furthermore, the records should be reviewed to check whether the content recorded aligns with the defendant's confession, the victim's statement, expert opinions, and other evidence. Contradictions should be identified, and the authenticity and relevance of the records should be assessed in light of other case evidence. If the examination, inspection, identification, or investigation experiment was conducted without a witness, or if the records lack the signatures or seals of the personnel and witnesses, or if the personnel violated recusal regulations, the authenticity and relevance of the records should be reviewed in conjunction with other evidence.

16.5.10 Review and Judgment of Audiovisual Materials

Audiovisual materials are high-tech evidence. Not only must they be produced in a timely manner, but they also have the potential to be altered or falsified. The legality of the production and acquisition of audiovisual materials has a profound impact on their admissibility as evidence. The review of audiovisual materials should generally focus on the following aspects.

16.5.10.1 Review and Judgment of the Source of Audiovisual Materials

The source of audiovisual materials generally falls into three categories: (1) Materials created by the parties or the case-handling agency; (2) Materials seized by the case-handling agency; (3) Materials provided by third parties. For audiovisual materials created by the case-handling agency during the investigation, it should be examined whether the production of these materials complied with legal procedures. For audiovisual materials obtained through search or seizure, it should be reviewed whether they were collected illegally. For audiovisual materials provided by third parties, it should be reviewed under what circumstances they were created, whether they were fabricated, edited, or compiled, and whether the parties involved were subjected to threats or inducements that violated the law or relevant regulations. Additionally, the review should consider whether the equipment used to produce the audiovisual materials is in good condition, whether the technology is scientific, and whether the methods used are effective. It should also be reviewed whether the technical equipment conditions required for producing the audiovisual materials were met, and whether any issues with the equipment affected the authenticity of the materials. Furthermore, it should be checked whether the operators have the required skills, whether the operating methods were scientific, and whether the proper procedures and regulations were followed. Materials without a clear explanation of the extraction process should not be used.

16.5.10.2 Review and Judgment of the Originality of Audiovisual Materials

The review should determine whether the audiovisual materials are original, whether copies exist, and the number of copies. If the audiovisual materials retrieved are copies, it should be checked whether there is an explanation for the inability to retrieve the original, including the production process and storage location of the original, and whether the producer and the original holder of the audiovisual materials have signed or stamped the materials. The original sound of audio tapes, the original images of video tapes, and the original data stored on computers should be reviewed. For example, when reviewing computer software, the directory, signature, license number, publisher, disk contents, and other relevant areas can be compared. These areas include: storylines, data arrangement, graphical and textual color, and sound clarity. The encryption and decryption process should also be compared, especially the orientation, content, and selectable items of common files and pull-down or pop-up menus. The source code and target program should be compared, as well as the on-screen display during installation. When reviewing audio tapes, the analysis should focus on fluctuations, mute sounds, hissing, echo, laughter, crying, sighing, coughing, and other noises to assess the speaker's emotions, environment, proximity to the recording device, and to determine the speaker's psychological state, physical condition, and the authenticity of their statement, checking for any signs of threats or coercion. If the audiovisual materials are copied or duplicated, the original materials should be located and compared before making a judgment.

16.5.10.3 Review and Judgment of the Reliability of the Audiovisual Material Carrier

Due to the unique nature of the storage medium and reliance on high-tech equipment and techniques, audiovisual materials are vulnerable to being forged or altered, and such tampering is often difficult to detect. In litigation, specialized technicians must use specialized equipment and methods to examine whether the audiovisual materials have been falsified, altered, or tampered with, such as through audio duplication, overlapping sounds, image shifting, or tampering with computer programs. The review should also verify whether the video recordings, computer data, and other carriers meet the required quality and performance standards, and whether they are complete, without any cuts, additions, deletions, or edits. If there are signs of copying, editing, or rearranging, the materials should be replayed in court for the parties to identify, and the opinions of the prosecutor, the parties, the defense, and legal representatives should be heard to make a comprehensive judgment. Audiovisual materials should not be used as the basis for the verdict if they fall into any of the following categories: (1) They have been tampered with, forged, or their authenticity cannot be determined; (2) There are doubts about the time, place, or method of their creation or acquisition, and no reasonable explanation can be provided.

16.5.10.4 Review and Judgment of the Background of Audiovisual Material Creation

Audiovisual materials can provide a comprehensive reflection of the case situation. For example, an audio tape can record accompanying background noises, and a video tape can capture relevant objects within the same field of view. Therefore, the background of the creation of audiovisual materials should be reviewed to verify their authenticity. For instance, when reviewing an audio tape, if there are voices from other individuals, the individuals should be brought to court to testify or provide written statements. If there are sounds from other objects or natural sounds, it should be checked whether such objects existed at the time and place, whether those sounds occurred, or if any of these sounds were produced. For video tapes, the same method can be applied to review the sounds, and in addition, the movement of people in the background, the direction of vehicles, the location of objects, and weather conditions should also be examined to assess the probative value of these materials.

16.5.10.5 Review and Judgment of the Relevant Technical Equipment Performance in the Creation of Audiovisual Materials

The collection, preservation, and reproduction of audiovisual materials rely heavily on technical equipment, and the scientific accuracy and reliability of these materials are closely related to the quality and performance of the equipment used. Therefore, the sensitivity and accuracy of the equipment should be reviewed to ensure they meet the required standards. Any records of equipment malfunctions or virus infections should be checked, along with whether the equipment has exceeded its useful life, its performance capabilities, and the scope of its application. The review of the technical equipment should not only focus on the collection and preservation stages of the audiovisual materials but also on the processes involved in playing and extracting the materials. Even if the equipment used for collecting and preserving the materials is top-quality, if the equipment used for playback and extraction is inadequate, it cannot accurately reflect the original situation of the case. Due to the specialized knowledge and advanced technology involved in audiovisual materials, for any difficult or questionable issues, experts should be hired to assist in the review and judgment.

16.5.10.6 Review and Judgment of the Legality of Collecting Audiovisual Materials

The review should assess whether the methods used to collect audiovisual materials, such as secret recordings or videos, seriously infringe upon others' legitimate rights or violate prohibitive legal regulations. Evidence obtained by intentionally violating public interest or social ethics, such as invading others' privacy or using eavesdropping techniques, cannot be used as evidence.

i. **Review and judgment of audiovisual materials made publicly**

Publicly made audiovisual materials refer to those produced with the knowledge or expectation that the person being recorded or filmed is aware. For example, audiovisual materials recording a party's actions or speech in public places; video recordings taken during a contract-signing ceremony; audiovisual materials made using surveillance equipment set up in public places like roads, airports, customs, and banks, where the general public is the target. Although these materials may involve private aspects or even personal privacy, they are generally considered legal because they were produced in public spaces.

ii. **Review and judgment of secretly made audiovisual materials**

Secretly made audiovisual materials refer to those produced without the knowledge of the person being recorded or filmed. For example, recordings made by one party without the knowledge of the other party, or audiovisual materials obtained through secret means such as eavesdropping or hidden cameras. The legality of these materials should be assessed based on different circumstances. Generally, recordings made for the purpose of stealing personal privacy, state secrets, or with ulterior motives, such as secretly installing eavesdropping devices or hidden cameras, violate privacy rights and national sovereignty or trade secrets, and cannot be used as evidence.

Audiovisual materials that violate *the National Security Law*, such as those obtained by illegally using hidden eavesdropping or surveillance equipment to "secretly record" state secrets, commercial secrets, or to severely violate others' privacy, are prohibited by law and cannot be used as evidence. For materials obtained by "secret recording" that violate others' private areas, a value judgment should be made to determine whether they can be used as evidence, and they should be treated with caution.[1]

Additionally, the review of audiovisual materials should be considered in conjunction with other evidence. If other evidence supports the facts proven by the audiovisual materials, their probative value can be confirmed. If other evidence contradicts the audiovisual materials, a thorough analysis should be conducted to identify the cause of the contradiction, determine which evidence is more accurate or closer to the truth, and if necessary, verify through expert evaluation, before making a realistic judgment on its probative value.

16.5.11 Review and Judgment of Electronic Data

Given the characteristics of electronic data and its relationship with the facts in question, as well as the presence of other corresponding materials to support it, the

[1] For this issue, reference can be made to the Supreme People's Court's response to the Hebei Provincial High Court's request on March 6, 1995, titled "Reply on the Use of Materials Obtained by Secretly Recording Conversations Without the Consent of the Other Party," and the changes in the "Supreme People's Court's Several Provisions on Civil Litigation Evidence."

review should assess its authenticity and relevance in conjunction with other case evidence. The following aspects should be reviewed for electronic data.

16.5.11.1 Review and Judgment of the Authenticity of Electronic Data

The authenticity of electronic data should be assessed based on the following factors: (1) Whether the hardware and software environment of the computer system that generated, stored, and transmitted the electronic data is complete and reliable; (2) Whether the hardware and software environment of the computer system that generated, stored, and transmitted the electronic data is in normal operating condition, and if it was not, whether this affected the generation, storage, or transmission of the electronic data; (3) Whether the computer system's hardware and software environment has effective error-prevention monitoring and verification methods; (4) Whether the electronic data was fully preserved, transmitted, and extracted, and whether the methods used for preservation, transmission, and extraction are reliable; (5) Whether the electronic data was generated and stored during normal business activities; (6) Whether the entity preserving, transmitting, and extracting the electronic data is appropriate; (7) Other factors affecting the integrity and reliability of the electronic data.

Electronic data may be considered authentic under the following circumstances, unless there is sufficient contrary evidence: (1) Electronic data submitted or maintained by a party that is unfavorable to them; (2) Electronic data provided or confirmed by a neutral third-party platform that records and preserves the data; (3) Electronic data generated during normal business activities; (4) Electronic data preserved through archival management methods; (5) Electronic data preserved, transmitted, or extracted according to an agreement between the parties; (6) Electronic data whose contents have been notarized by a notary agency.

However, if the electronic data is not transferred in a sealed state, if the record or list lacks the signatures or seals of the case handlers, data holders (providers), or witnesses, or if the name, category, format, etc., of the electronic data is unclear, it can be accepted if corrected or reasonably explained. If the issue cannot be corrected or explained, it should not be used as the basis for the verdict.

16.5.11.2 Review and Judgment of the Relevance of Electronic Data

In practice, the determination of the relevance of electronic data to the facts in question should be assessed from the following aspects: (1) The type of relationship between the electronic data and the facts to be proved, and the degree of closeness of that relationship. Whether the electronic data can prove a particular issue in the case; (2) Whether the facts proved by the electronic data are substantive issues in the case; (3) The substantive significance of the electronic data in resolving the disputed issues in the case. Due to the emergence of technologies such as hacking and remote computer control, reviewing the relevance of electronic data can be challenging. For example, an individual may steal someone else's internet account or leave a false IP address or email address. Given this, when reviewing the relevance of electronic data, it is crucial to adhere to the principle of comprehensive verification, combining factors such as the technical skills of the creator of the data to confirm its relevance to the case facts.

16.5.11.3 Review and Judgment of the Reliability of Electronic Data

Reliability refers to the authenticity of the content of electronic data, which is an inherent quality characteristic of the data. Article 8 of *China's Electronic Signature Law* stipulates that the authenticity of data messages should be reviewed based on the following factors: (1) The reliability of the method used to generate, store, or transmit the data message; (2) The reliability of the method used to maintain the integrity of the content; (3) The reliability of the method used to verify the sender; (4) Other relevant factors. For electronic data stored in various electronic media such as chips, floppy disks, hard drives, CDs, tapes, and mobile storage devices in digital or analog signals, corresponding equipment is required to display the data, and it should be submitted in the form of printed electronic evidence. The review should also assess whether the processes and steps involved in the creation, storage, transmission, acquisition, collection, and presentation of the data are lawful, and whether the collector, creator, holder, and witnesses have signed or stamped the documents. Specifically, the reliability of electronic data can be assessed from the following aspects.

i. **Assessing the reliability of electronic data generation**

The review should examine whether the electronic data was generated automatically or manually according to standard procedures, whether the system that generated or inputted the data is under normal control, whether the program used to generate the data is reliable, whether the network conditions were stable, whether the data was entered following operating procedures and reliable methods, and whether there is a possibility of the system being infected with a computer virus.

ii. **Assessing the reliability of electronic data storage**

The review should check whether the electronic data was stored using scientific methods, whether the storage medium is reliable, whether the personnel responsible for storing the data are impartial and independent, whether the data was encrypted, and whether unauthorized access to the stored data occurred.

iii **Assessing the reliability of electronic data transmission**

The review should examine whether the technological means or methods used to transmit and receive the electronic data are scientific and reliable, whether the network operators or intermediaries involved in transmitting the data are impartial and independent, whether the data was encrypted during transmission, whether it carries digital signatures, certificates, or other special identifiers, and whether it is possible that the data was intercepted illegally.

iv. **Assessing the reliability of electronic data collection**

The review of the reliability of the collected electronic data should consider whether the collector has any interests in the case, and whether the methods used to collect and extract the electronic data are scientific and reliable. Given the vast amount of electronic data on the internet, the collector's methods for selecting the data and the objectivity and legality of the process should also be assessed. For the collection and extraction of electronic data, the following aspects should be reviewed: Whether at least two investigators or law enforcement officers were involved in the collection or extraction of electronic data; Whether the methods of collection and extraction comply with relevant technical standards; Whether the collection and extraction of electronic data are accompanied by records or inventories, and whether they are signed or stamped by the investigators, law enforcement officers, data holders, providers, and witnesses; If no signatures or stamps are present, whether the reason is noted; Whether the category, file format, and other details of the electronic data are clearly indicated; Whether the designated witnesses meet the required qualifications and whether relevant activities were video recorded; Whether the collection and extraction of electronic data using technical investigative or law enforcement measures were properly approved. Different sources of electronic data often have varying degrees of reliability, and even electronic data from the same source may have different probative value due to various factors.

v. **Assessing whether the electronic data has been altered**

The review should assess whether the electronic data has been forged or altered. This includes determining whether there have been any modifications, splicing, cutting, or deletions. If there are doubts, experts with specialized technical knowledge should be appointed or hired to conduct an evaluation, and the judgment should be made based on the expert opinion. The determination of the reliability of electronic data can be transferred to the review of other factors, allowing the reliability of the electronic data to be inferred. This can be done in the following ways: First, by confirming the reliability of the computer system that the electronic data depends on, and inferring the reliability of the electronic data; Second, by confirming that the electronic data was maintained or provided by the opposing party, and inferring the reliability of the data; Third, by confirming that the electronic data was generated and stored during normal business activities, and inferring the reliability of the data.

16.5.11.4 Review and Judgment of the Integrity of Electronic Data

The integrity of electronic data is a special indicator of its authenticity and objectivity, and it mainly includes both the integrity of the data itself and the integrity of the electronic system upon which the data depends. Its integrity primarily involves the following aspects: (1) The system that records the electronic data must be in normal operating condition. If the system has been in an abnormal state, it may affect the integrity of the data; (2) Data records must be made at the time of or immediately after the business activity. Electronic records made specifically for a project, such as litigation, cannot ensure their integrity; (3) Under normal operating conditions, the system must have a complete record of the business activity. A complete record refers to the unified information of the data message, associated information, and system environment.

The review and judgment of the integrity of electronic data mainly involves assessing whether the content of the data is authentic, and whether there are any instances of cutting, splicing, tampering, or adding changes that may indicate forgery or alteration. To review and verify the integrity of electronic data, the following aspects should be focused on: (1) Reviewing the seizure and sealing status of the original storage medium; (2) Reviewing the process of collecting and extracting the electronic data, such as checking video footage; (3) Comparing the integrity checksum of the electronic data; (4) Comparing the electronic data with its backup; (5) Reviewing the access operation logs after freezing the data.

The integrity of the data itself involves both formal integrity and content integrity. Formal integrity refers to the requirement that the electronic data must remain in its original state at the time of generation, and any changes, including format adjustments, will be regarded as a breach of integrity. Content integrity refers to the condition that, from the moment the electronic data is created, its content remains intact without unnecessary additions or deletions. Unnecessary additions or deletions refer to significant changes made to the electronic data. However, format adjustments, such as adding headers, footers, source notes, formation process, and acquisition dates, are considered non-critical changes and do not affect the integrity of the electronic data.

16.6 Questions and Reflections

The review and judgment of evidence should focus on the authenticity, relevance, and legality of the evidence. To assess the authenticity of evidence, all the case evidence should be reviewed comprehensively. To assess the probative value of the evidence, specific factors such as the relationship between the evidence and the facts to be proved, and the connections between the evidence should be considered. Evidence that is interconnected and collectively points to the same fact to be proved, with no unresolved contradictions or unexplained doubts, can be used as the basis for the decision. In the case referenced, the first-instance court accepted the proof provided by the plaintiff on April 20, 2007, as evidence, upholding the defendant's decision on the recognition of the work injury. The plaintiff appealed. The second-instance court accepted the audio materials submitted by the plaintiff, the evidence from two other companies, and witness testimony as evidence, conducting a comprehensive analysis of the evidence. The court ruled to overturn the original judgment and revoke the work injury recognition decision. Based on the case situation and the above points, and in reference to the content of this chapter, think about the following questions: (1) How should audiovisual materials be reviewed and judged? (2) Can the probative value of audiovisual materials be superior to that of written evidence? (3) Should the court accept evidence submitted by the plaintiff in the litigation procedure but not in the administrative procedure? (4) What method should be used to review and judge the evidence existing in the case?

References

Liu, J. Y. (2004). Shilun woguo shencha panduan zhengju de yuanze ji qi lilun genju. Tribune of Political Science and Law, (2): 77–84.(in Chinese)

Yan, Y. K. (2000). Lun xingshi zhengju shencha de chengxu he guize. Criminal Science, (4): 90–94. (in Chinese)

He, J. H. (2008). Zhengju de shencha yu rending yuanli gangyao. The Jurist, (3): 95–103. (in Chinese)

Guo, H., & Wang, J. X. (Eds.). (2010). Interpretation and Application of the Evidence Provisions for Handling Death Penalty Cases and the Exclusion of Illegally Obtained Evidence Provisions. Beijing: Chinese People's Public Security University Press. (in Chinese)

Chapter 17
Methods of Determining Case Facts

17.1 Introductory Case

The case of former Nanchang University President Zhou, who was accused of bribery and embezzlement, set a groundbreaking precedent by using probability theory, mathematical statistics, combinatorics, and error theory to argue the "absurdity" of the prosecutor's evidence in his self-defense. Zhou faced 24 charges from the prosecution, including bribery of over 20 million yuan and embezzlement of over 58 million yuan. Not only did he deny the majority of the confessions he had previously made, but during the trial, he also stated that both the briber and the bribe recipient had confessed, and that the bribe occurred in May. However, later it was found that no bribe records existed for May, and both parties' records were changed to around October 10. According to error theory, the error between May and October was a 5-month absolute error, and a 50% relative error; the error between the 1st and 10th was a 10-day absolute error, and a 2.8% relative error. Both individuals were interrogated separately, and the error rate changed in the same significant manner. He argued that these errors "could only indicate collusion by the case handlers." Further, he calculated that both the briber and the recipient had initially stated that the bribery took place in May, but later both changed their testimony, and the probability of this happening was 1 in 140. After it was found that there were no withdrawal records for May, both parties simultaneously changed their testimony to October, and the probability of this was 1 in 20,700. His conclusion was that, without illegal evidence collection, for these errors to occur simultaneously, more than 20,000 records would need to be created. Additionally, he created a "Comprehensive Evidence Evaluation Table for the Case" and used his own invented calculation method to assess the testimony of a witness, ultimately concluding that the likelihood of the testimony being true was only 0.317 (with 1 being the maximum score).

H. Guo, *Evidence Jurisprudence in China*, Understanding China,
https://doi.org/10.1007/978-981-95-3981-9_17

17.2 Chapter Overview

This chapter discusses the use of evidence to determine case facts, focusing on empirical rules, logical rules, and modern algorithms. Empirical rules include their concepts, characteristics, types, and methods of application; logical rules involve logical principles. The determination of case facts must comply with these rules.

17.3 Empirical Rules

Empirical rules originate from practical experience and serve as a bridge or adhesive between evidence and case facts. They function to fill in the gaps when the probative value of evidence is insufficient and are a fundamental method for determining case facts, as well as a necessary safeguard for the determination of case facts. Any case fact determination that violates empirical rules is invalid.

17.3.1 The Concept and Characteristics of Empirical Rules

Empirical rules are common-sense, unwritten laws with inherent binding force, resembling the function of case law in common law countries. Article 85 of *the Supreme People's Cour's Several Provisions on Civil Litigation Evidence* states: "Judges…shall, in accordance with the law, follow judicial ethics, and apply logical reasoning and everyday life experience to independently assess the probative value of evidence and its strength…" In this context, "everyday life experience" is part of the empirical rules.

17.3.1.1 The Concept of Empirical Rules

Empirical rules are general knowledge derived from long-term practical experience in human daily life and production. They are obtained through experience-based induction and logical abstraction about the properties of things and the regular connections between things, including everyday life rules, natural laws, and rules in specialized disciplines.[1] The empirical rules in judicial adjudication refer to a necessary and specific component of everyday life experience. Their uniqueness lies in the fact that judges rely on their own knowledge, personal life experiences, or experiences widely recognized and accepted by the public, using them as a form of legal reasoning. The meaning of empirical rules can be summarized as follows:

[1] Ishii (2000).

i. **Empirical rules are general knowledge induced from individual experiences accumulated to a certain extent**

Empirical rules stem from other life and work experiences prior to the determination of case facts. They are formed through repeated occurrences of similar case facts, accumulated over time, and represent a kind of confidence or belief, not a physical object or fact. This belief, as common-sense knowledge, has a reliable predictive quality for recognizing unknown or future types of facts.

As general knowledge, although empirical rules carry special experiential significance derived from individual experiences, they are not unique to a particular individual. At least within a certain range, they are universally recognized or considered well-known knowledge, or accepted within a specific group, and are generally understood, known, or acknowledged by the public as social common sense. They largely reflect the nature, status, and regularity of things. Although some experiences are reliable, if they are not recognized by most people, they cannot become empirical knowledge or be used as empirical rules in the determination of case facts.

ii. **Empirical rules as law-like knowledge regarding the properties, states, and interrelations of things**

When people generalize or extract empirical laws regarding the properties, states, and interrelations of things, these experiences go beyond general experience and form empirical rules that possess a law-like quality. The law-like nature of empirical rules can be understood from two aspects: First, when people's understanding has not yet reached the theoretical level, the law only implies something close to an empirical generalization, that is, a summary of certain observations. This can be seen as a regularity that can be observed or a statement representing this regularity. Second, when the law rises to a theoretical level, it becomes an abstraction of experience, possessing general characteristics. It is objective in nature and carries universal features.

As a result of people's experience-based understanding, empirical rules, on the one hand, possess publicly observable aspects that are different from individual experiences. On the other hand, empirical rules are derived from practice and are a high-level abstraction of practical experience, differing from fragmented practical experiences. As a general understanding derived from the inductive summary of sensory knowledge, empirical rules are both the culmination of sensory knowledge and its necessary result. They also serve as the starting point for obtaining rational understanding and as the rational systematization of knowledge. This rational understanding, when applied to specific case fact determination, can only provide a definitive recognition of the case facts when exceptions to the case are excluded.

Empirical rules differ from general legal rules. General legal rules in case fact determination operate through deductive reasoning and are inherently true. Empirical rules, on the other hand, operate through inductive reasoning, and their results have a probabilistic nature. They have not yet encountered contradictory examples, or the contradictory examples can be ignored in normal circumstances, though exceptions may still exist.

iii. **Empirical rules as incomplete knowledge gained through inductive methods**

Empirical rules are knowledge derived from experience, generalized by individuals through social practice, regarding the properties, states, and interrelations of things. These rules, obtained through inductive synthesis, are generalizable and carry social universality, with inherent probabilistic and incomplete characteristics. The empirical rule itself is an induction of people's life experience, which inevitably cannot fully consider every aspect of the issues at hand, nor can it comprehensively or exhaustively encompass every problem. Consequently, it inherently contains a certain degree of probability.

Although empirical rules primarily reflect law-like qualities, experience remains their main component, and the law-like nature is influenced by the experiences. While humans acquire knowledge through the induction of past experiences, which serve as the source of human knowledge, past experiences are only a part of the infinitely evolving collective human experience. Therefore, the inductive process is incomplete, and the knowledge gained is inherently probabilistic at the present time.

17.3.1.2 Characteristics of Empirical Rules

Empirical rules have a certain relationship with the litigation model. In the inquisitorial litigation model, the trial is centered on the judge, with the system expecting the professional judge to have extraordinary observation, analytical, and judgmental abilities. The empirical rules in this system often extend beyond the everyday experiences of ordinary people. In the adversarial litigation model, case facts are determined by ordinary people from various social strata (jury members). The system requires the determination of case facts to rely on the everyday life experiences of ordinary people, which align with the composition of the jury. The jury members typically do not possess specialized experiences or extraordinary intelligence; thus, the empirical rules used in determining the case facts are more closely aligned with the general common sense of the parties involved. Empirical rules are not individual experiences but can be general knowledge or common-sense knowledge accumulated from individual experiences. They are a generalization of individual experiences that have been validated by practice and possess social sharedness. The following are the characteristics of empirical rules:

i. **Objectivity and subjectivity**

The objectivity of empirical rules refers to the fact that they are the result of long-term accumulation of human production and life experiences, reflecting objective existence. Common sense knowledge is based on specific social life experiences and, after repeated verification, gradually forms as a certain type of knowledge. Empirical rules serve as the basis for factual judgments, not allowing judges to exercise arbitrary or unrestricted discretion, but instead being based on the universality of human understanding. The objectivity of the content of empirical rules reflects the objective nature of the propositions in relation to the objective world.

The subjectivity of empirical rules refers to the fact that their form and application process are subjective. They exist in people's consciousness as an idea and reflect the active response of the human mind to the external world. The process by which judges apply empirical rules to deduce facts is a subjective thinking process. This thinking process inevitably is influenced by the judge's own qualities, knowledge, experience, and value orientation.

The subjectivity and objectivity of empirical rules are their most important characteristics. The objective content of empirical rules is reflected through subjective forms, and through the judge's subjective thinking process, it reflects the objective standard role of experience in the litigation process. This ensures that the judge's subjective thinking is constrained by objectivity, safeguarding judicial fairness.

ii. **Infinity and limitation**

The infinity of empirical rules refers to the fact that, in terms of the overall litigation, the number of empirical rules is infinite. Empirical rules are general knowledge accumulated by humans through long-term production and life practices, covering everything from specialized knowledge to general life experiences, from highly probable scientific theorems to relatively less probable common-sense rules, thereby encompassing all aspects of human life. In terms of quantity, they are inexhaustible. Since empirical rules come from the general body of human knowledge and the search for unknown facts in evidence evaluation has endless variations, the specific experience rule to be applied must be determined based on the case at hand. Therefore, the number of empirical rules that can be used as a premise when judging facts is infinite. The limitation of empirical rules refers to the fact that, in each individual case, the number of empirical rules applied is finite.

iii. **Abstractness and specificity**

Empirical rules are not the unique experiences of individuals, but rather are shared knowledge of the general public or a certain group of people. They are a summary and abstraction of recurring phenomena. Empirical rules go beyond individual thinking and are recognized within the understanding of ordinary people. They represent the elevation and crystallization of collective wisdom. Although empirical rules are abstract knowledge, their application is specific and conditional. Empirical rules are not fixed, abstract laws but are fluid laws derived from specific life experiences.

Empirical rules reflect the nature of things or the relationships between things in general or usual circumstances. When applying empirical rules to the judgment of specific facts, it is necessary to consider whether there are any special circumstances in the evidence and events of the case. The abstractness of empirical rules ensures that they can serve as major premises in syllogistic reasoning, possessing rule-like qualities, while their specificity requires judges to take a concrete, case-by-case analysis approach in determining case facts to ensure the validity of the empirical rules applied to the particular case.

17.3.2 Classification of Empirical Rules

Empirical rules are broad in scope and infinite in quantity. They can be classified according to different standards.

17.3.2.1 Based on the Extent of the Binding Force of Empirical Rules on Judges, They Can Be Divided into Generally Binding Empirical Rules and Non-generally Binding Empirical Rules

Generally binding empirical rules refer to those that have been proven by practice. These rules, especially those confirmed by natural sciences, generally have the effect of binding the judge. When empirical rules are based on scientifically proven knowledge, judges are generally not permitted to exercise "discretion." In the absence of exceptions, facts established according to widely accepted methods in a specific academic field should be used as the basis for determining case facts, even if the judge personally may not fully trust them. For example, in the case of a DNA test excluding biological paternity, the judge is generally not permitted to make a contradictory factual determination.

Non-generally binding empirical rules, by definition, do not have the force to bind judges. In such cases, judges must carefully examine the specific facts, circumstances, and various factors of the case and may refer to the "high probability" suggested by the empirical rule to judge the truth or falsity of the case facts.

In the determination of case facts, if it is a non-generally binding empirical rule, the judge cannot rely on it automatically. If the judge wants to accept a non-generally binding empirical rule, they should provide a reasoned explanation, stating why they believe this empirical rule "can" serve as the basis for determining the facts. In China, there is an emphasis on the transparency of judicial reasoning.

17.3.2.2 Based on Whether Empirical Rules Need To Be Proven in Litigation, They Can Be Divided into General Empirical Rules and Special Empirical Rules

General empirical rules, as common-sense rules, are formed through long-term accumulation of experience and gradual perception. Their content is familiar to the general public and is considered self-evident common knowledge, possessing a high degree of objectivity. The external forms of these rules are "common sense", "general reasoning," and "general practice," which can be summarized in the often-used expressions in practice such as "reasonable" or "logical."

Since general empirical rules have been repeatedly verified over time, they represent the usual trends or laws in the development of a type of thing, and have a high degree of probability during changes in the occurrence and development of things. These rules themselves do not require proof. This is because such empirical rules align with the basic life experience of the general public, and since judges, as members of society, also live in society and share this common life experience, they can directly rely on general empirical rules to determine case facts. For example, in China, the method of verifying case facts based on empirical rules ensures consistency among evidence and leads to a "single conclusion" regarding the facts of the case.

Special empirical rules, also known as non-common-sense empirical rules, refer to rules about certain things' regularities and peculiarities that go beyond the general knowledge and understanding of the public. These rules require specialized training, specific expertise, or the use of instruments, equipment, and other auxiliary methods to observe, experience, and master.

Special empirical rules belong to specialized knowledge. They are based on particular knowledge or experience and have a strong theoretical and professional nature. These rules are usually unfamiliar to the general public. Because special empirical rules are a type of specialized knowledge, judges generally cannot directly use them as the basis for determining case facts in litigation. A more rigorous proof procedure is required, with corroboration from other evidence or by using corresponding methods of proof, such as commissioning or hiring expert witnesses for identification. In practice, special empirical rules are mostly derived from natural sciences, where they play an important role in determining the composition or authenticity of things. Special empirical rules are also relative and carry an inherent "uncertainty." If they are "improperly used" (including errors in principles, methods, etc.) or if the person applying them lacks the necessary expertise, mistakes can occur. These mistakes are highly concealed and deceptive, making them difficult to correct in practice.

17.3.2.3 Based on the Degree of Probability in Empirical rules, They Can Be Divided into General Life Laws, Basic Experience Rules, Simple Experience Rules, and Pure Bias

General Life Laws refer to experiences that can be mathematically proven, logically consistent, or devoid of exceptions. Their expression is "If … always occurs." These laws align with human general cognitive patterns, and without these cognitive rules, judges would be unable to form their own judgment. These life laws primarily include natural laws and human thinking patterns. For example, the sun rises in the east-even on cloudy days when the sun is not visible, people do not doubt the existence of the sun. These general life laws can also manifest as scientific principles, such as the link between an individual's fingerprint, blood type, DNA, and their identity. Judges should confidently choose this type of empirical rule in the determination of case facts; failure to do so would be a violation of the empirical rule, although exceptions may exist.

Basic Experience Rules do not exclude exceptions, but they have a high degree of probability. Their expression is "If … occurs, then in most cases, this is the outcome." This rule must have a common foundation and verifiability and should, if necessary, withstand scientific scrutiny. These life experiences possess high probative value and typically do not require further scientific validation. For instance, if a person crosses a railroad track after the safety barrier has been lowered and is subsequently struck by a train, it may be considered the fault of the victim; if a doctor leaves surgical instruments, thread, or gauze inside a patient's wound, it can be considered medical malpractice, and so on.

Simple Experience Rules generally allow for other possible outcomes. Their expression is "If … occurs, then sometimes this is the case." These rules are marked by a lower degree of probability and cannot independently help judges form a definitive judgment. Instead, they play a supporting role when the judge has not fully formed their judgment. In such cases, the opposing party may provide a counterexample to challenge the simple experience rule, and if the challenge is successful, the original proof becomes questionable. Therefore, simple experience rules should not be adopted in this context. For example, if a car is parked on the emergency lane of a highway, it could be due to a mechanical failure, the driver's health issues, a traffic stop by the police, or other reasons. These possibilities cannot be oversimplified or overlook other potential causes.

Pure Bias is a one-sided understanding of things. Its expression is "If … occurs, then the relationship does not hold." This rule lacks probability and holds no value in the judge's reasoning process. Relying on it would have a negative effect. Judges should avoid such biases when determining case facts.

General life laws generally include natural laws, laws of thinking, and rules that are widely accepted by people, with the highest degree of probability. Basic experience rules have a high degree of probability but cannot entirely exclude exceptions, generally referring to life experiences. Simple experiences have a lower degree of probability and serve merely as tools to assist understanding.

17.3.3 Application of Empirical Rules

Judges, when applying empirical rules to determine case facts, must maintain an objective attitude, respect objective laws, start from reality, and be pragmatic, taking exceptions into full consideration. They must uphold objectivity and avoid subjectivity, preventing personal biases, preconceived notions, or assumptions. Since empirical rules are derived from daily life experiences and represent general rules that are objective and widely accepted, they are not subjective or narrow personal opinions. When a court makes a determination of facts, if it does not rely on empirical rules, it is likely to result in an inappropriate or inaccurate judgment that does not align with the facts. The application of empirical rules should pay attention to the following issues.

17.3.3.1 The Difference Between Empirical Rules and Evidence

Empirical rules differ from evidence in terms of stability, functionality, method selection, and procedural design. In terms of stability, the effect of empirical rules is far less stable compared to evidence-based proof. Regarding functionality, their application should take into account the degree of similarity of the case facts and the possibility of exceptions, functioning as a supplementary tool. In method selection, using evidence to determine case facts should be prioritized, as it holds precedence in the application sequence. Empirical rules, on the other hand, function as a limiting factor in this context. In procedural design, the procedure for evidence-based proof is external, public, and observable, whereas empirical rules are internal, constrained by the reasoning provided for their application. As people's understanding of the properties, states, and interrelationships of things, empirical rules are applied with the understanding that they must not violate established rules. Everyday life experience is intuitive and emotionally colored, classified as general knowledge. Individual intuitive experiences cannot be treated as empirical rules in litigation.

Judges should remain vigilant when applying empirical rules in case fact determination. Only when sufficient evidence has already proven the case facts should empirical rules be applied to fulfill their intended role. If there is insufficient evidence to prove the case facts, or if no evidence exists, the application of empirical rules should be avoided. Otherwise, it may lead to partial or erroneous determinations of case facts, affecting the factual accuracy of the court's judgment.

17.3.3.2 The Varying Maturity of Empirical Rules

As science and technology continue to develop and evolve, people can not only acquire experiential knowledge through daily life but also through scientific research and experimentation-knowledge that cannot be obtained through ordinary life experience alone. Incorporating this specialized knowledge into the realm of empirical rules for case fact determination helps enrich the content of these rules. However, due to the differing stability of empirical rules across various fields, the method for determining case facts should be adapted to different circumstances and supported by procedural rules to minimize the likelihood of erroneous determinations of case facts.

In practice, there may be inconsistencies between everyday experience and scientific knowledge. For example, people in daily life observe the sun rising in the east and setting in the west, leading them to conclude that the sun orbits the Earth, which led to the development of the geocentric theory. However, scientific research later established that planets orbit around stars, forming the heliocentric theory. Therefore, judges in case fact determination must differentiate between general life laws and specialized empirical rules, while also distinguishing between verifiable experimental empirical knowledge and unverifiable anecdotal empirical knowledge.

Equating everyday life experience with empirical rules is a misunderstanding of the concept of empirical rules, which could lead to conflating empirical rules with general life experiences. In a broader sense, empirical knowledge not only includes general knowledge gained from everyday experiences but also encompasses the inductive and abstract reasoning derived from these experiences. Additionally, it includes knowledge obtained from specialized practices such as scientific experiments. This knowledge is not the facts themselves but serves as the bridge connecting the judge's observations and conclusions.[2]

In the context of science, reliable quantitative analysis is generally referred to as true science, as it can achieve the "same result under the same conditions." When the method involves questionable observations, it can be considered a quasi-science, as it produces "similar results under similar conditions." For methods based on dubious correlations, it may be termed non-science, as it can yield "dissimilar results under similar conditions." Lastly, for deceptive similarity-based methods, they are labeled pseudoscience, as they can produce "different results under the same conditions."[3] When judges use special empirical rules to determine case facts, they must not only follow strict procedures of proof but also allow the opposing party to raise objections and provide necessary defenses. At the same time, judges must maintain a high level of vigilance. They should be able to distinguish between "science and non-science" and improve their ability to differentiate between "science and pseudoscience (junk science)" as well as "science and quasi-science."[4]

17.3.3.3 Empirical Rules and the Possibility of Exceptions

Empirical rules are the product of people's incomplete induction of past experiences. They are understood as general knowledge, and when applied to case fact determination, they may not always align perfectly with the actual facts of the case. Despite their inherent probability and uncertainty, empirical rules are still one of the more reliable methods for determining case facts compared to other ways of thinking. They can play an important role in case fact determination.

For example, during the period when Zhang was leasing and operating a frozen food factory, Cao frequently came to purchase ice from the factory. Cao had given Zhang an IOU, which stated: "Owes ice money 1.800 yuan." The two parties had a dispute over the content of the IOU. In the litigation, Zhang argued that "1.800 yuan" was a typographical error for "1,800 yuan" and that the actual amount Cao owed for the ice was 1,800 yuan. Cao, on the other hand, argued that "1.800 yuan" meant "1.8 yuan," not "1,800 yuan." After reviewing the case, the court found it illogical for the parties to have written a formal IOU for a debt of just 1.8 yuan. If Cao truly owed 1.8 yuan, the normal writing convention would be "1.80 yuan," not

---

[2] Lin (2005).

[3] Zhang (2008).

[4] Science and non-science belong to different research fields. Science is the primary method for generating knowledge in modern society; non-science is also a method, used when scientific methods cannot explain certain issues. Non-scientific methods are applied to study aspects that science cannot explain, such as religion, art, and philosophy. Pseudoscience, while in the same research field as science, distorts scientific principles and is a flawed research method with no inherent value.

"1.800 yuan." Furthermore, Cao had no other effective evidence to support his claim. The court ultimately ruled that Cao should return 1,800 yuan to Zhang. In this case, it is generally unreasonable for a formal IOU to be written for just 1.8 yuan, and the standard writing convention would make "1.80 yuan" the expected form, rather than "1.800 yuan." The court relied on these two empirical rules to rule that Cao owed Zhang 1,800 yuan.[5]

Empirical rules are the product of recurring normal phenomena in people's daily lives. While there are norms, exceptions may also occur, and these should be fully considered during application. Strict evidentiary procedures should be followed to avoid mistakes in applying these rules.

17.4 Logical Rules

Logical rules are formal modes of thinking, and the order of evidence arrangement can be determined by these logical rules. They are necessary conditions that must be followed in case fact determination and serve as essential safeguards. Any case fact determination that violates logical rules is invalid.

17.4.1 Basic Concept and Characteristics of Logical Rules

Logical rules (Gesetze der Logik), also known as logic laws, refer to the rules governing the process of drawing conclusions from one or more known premises through logical reasoning. "Logical rules focus on logic and reasoning, such as using scientific methods in physics, chemistry, biology, physiology, medicine, forensics, criminology, psychology, and other fields to reason or validate evidence in line with these rules." Logical rules are reasoning rules that derive necessary conclusions from premises based on their logical nature. Logical rules possess the following characteristics.

17.4.1.1 Logical Rules as the "Reasoning from General Knowledge Premises to Specific Knowledge Conclusions"

Logical rules are primarily expressed through deductive reasoning, and their basic structure consists of two parts: premises and conclusions. The major premise is provided through inductive reasoning and can be viewed as the result obtained from "empirical rules." Although empirical rules are considered "common knowledge," in comparison with the logical application of these rules, they still retain the nature of "specific knowledge." The conclusions of inductive reasoning are derived from

[5] See Jiangsu Province (2006) Binmin Yichu No. 0308 and (2006) Yanmin Yizhong No. 0507.

direct experiential knowledge, often constrained and limited by various conditions and factors, with their premises remaining probabilistic.

17.4.1.2 Logical Rules as the "Reasoning Rule Where Premises and Conclusion Maintain Unified Nature"

Logical rules, as a method of case fact determination, can yield conclusions that are truthful. However, under certain conditions, exceptions with probabilistic elements cannot be entirely ruled out. Logical rules emphasize the homogeneity between premises and conclusions, and the correctness of this homogeneity hinges on the truthfulness of the premises. Some of the premises used in case fact determination are derived from inductive reasoning, and knowledge obtained through induction may contain certain flaws. Therefore, the results obtained from logical reasoning may also have issues. However, the logical method itself, which maintains consistency between premises and conclusions, is scientifically sound and essential for determining case facts. The conclusions drawn from this method are acceptable, justified, and reasonable relative to the premises. Facts determined by the court must be accepted by an average, mentally healthy person, and they must possess universal and appropriate qualities. The thinking framework for maintaining such appropriateness aligns with logical rules.

17.4.1.3 Logical Rules are Different from General Logical Reasoning and Possess Legal Characteristics

Logical rules primarily involve deductive reasoning, but at times they may also include what is referred to as "ignorant logic." This type of logic is particularly evident in difficult fact determinations where the burden of proof is used to establish the existence of facts. Logical rules differ from "backward reasoning." As a thinking method, backward reasoning leads to conclusions with probabilistic outcomes, in contrast to deductive reasoning, which leads to conclusions with necessary certainty.

17.4.2 The Significance of Logical Rules in Case Fact Determination

As a method for determining case facts, logical rules are fundamental principles that humans must follow to think correctly. What differentiates humans from other animals is their ability to think, and through thinking, humans can apply inductive and deductive methods to derive certain logical rules about objective things and phenomena. When judges determine case facts, they must also utilize shared human thinking methods, providing a reliable path to accurately assess the probative value of evidence and determine the existence of case facts. This helps avoid making unreasonable subjective inferences influenced by emotions or other individual factors. The role of logical rules lies in offering judges a reasonable and appropriate logical approach to case fact determination, ensuring consistency between premises and conclusions through logical coherence.

Although humans may not have theoretical logical knowledge, they do possess the capacity for reasoning. Humans have an innate logical ability, but because this natural logic lacks precision, it is difficult to maintain consistency between premises and conclusions, which is why it is not adopted as a formal rule in law. Theoretical logical rules, as a thinking method, bypass the diversity of real-world society and are detached from the time- and space-bound emotional world. They are purely focused on the matter at hand, ensuring that reasoning remains free of contradictions and preventing distortion in the thinking process. When judges apply this as a logical method, it ensures that the determination of case facts aligns with the truth of the premise facts.

Logical rules rely on the truth of the premises. In other words, the evidence used for case determination or the facts proven by evidence must be true. If the premises are false, the conclusions drawn using logical rules will also be false, as they must remain consistent with the premises. In judicial practice, logical rules serve both as a guide for judges in determining case facts and as a constraint on their discretion. This method of determining case facts is essential for eliminating subjective speculation by judges and limiting the abuse of free evaluation of evidence, particularly in maintaining the objectivity and appropriateness of the factual transmission process, an aspect that no other method can replace.

17.4.3 Basic Logical Principles in Determining Case Facts

Determining case facts, although inherently subjective to some extent, is not a matter of arbitrary judgment by the judge. It must be based on evidence, follow legal procedures, and adhere to specific logical principles. The existence of the facts must be determined with sufficient reasoning.

Logical principles are the basic thinking methods judges use to establish connections between evidence and case facts, between different pieces of evidence, and between the evidence itself. In applying these logical principles to determine case facts, judges must not violate fundamental logical rules. On the contrary, applying these principles must follow basic logical laws.

The basic logical principles include the Law of Identity, the Law of Contradiction, the Law of the Excluded Middle, and the Principle of Sufficient Reason. These four principles are necessary conditions for correct reasoning. While adhering to them does not guarantee complete truth, violating them will inevitably lead to errors in judgment. Judges must follow these four logical principles when determining case facts.

17.4.3.1 The Law of Identity

The Law of Identity requires that the concepts and judgments used by judges in the process of determining case facts must remain consistent. The concepts and judgments must maintain their identity and cannot be substituted. This principle ensures the certainty of the thinking process in determining case facts and is a necessary condition for judges to make correct judgments. The Law of Identity demands consistency in thinking; otherwise, it will lead to incorrect identification of case facts.

17.4.3.2 The Law of Contradiction

The Law of Contradiction states that "two contradictory or opposing judgments cannot both be true; one must be false." This logical principle helps to ensure the certainty of reasoning by negating false premises. The Law of Contradiction is a rule of consistency in thinking. By adhering to this law, reasoning remains organized, and self-contradiction is avoided. In the same line of reasoning, no idea can both reflect a matter and not reflect that matter; a thing cannot simultaneously be true and false. Otherwise, self-contradiction occurs.

When applying this logical principle, judges should be adept at identifying contradictions in the logic of evidence and between the evidence and the facts. If there is a contradiction between pieces of evidence, especially when contradictory evidence is presented to support the same fact, the case facts cannot be definitively established. Judges should also pay attention to contradictions within the evidence itself. For example, if the defendant fabricates facts to avoid responsibility, initially claiming they were not at the scene and later stating that although they were at the scene, they did not see the victim, this would make their testimony self-contradictory. Using the Law of Contradiction, the truthfulness of these contradictory statements can be determined.

17.4.3.3 The Law of the Excluded Middle

The Law of the Excluded Middle states that "between two contradictory judgments, one must be true." This principle ensures clarity in reasoning. It assumes the objective truth of matters can be determined. A violation of the Law of the Excluded Middle would imply a refusal to acknowledge the truth of one of two contradictory judgments. Any thought either reflects or does not reflect a specific matter, and two contradictory thoughts cannot both be false; one must be true. This principle plays a significant role in determining the strength of evidence, resolving contradictions within the evidence, and ultimately establishing the facts of the case.

When judges apply the Law of the Excluded Middle to determine case facts, they should maintain a clear stance and avoid ambiguity. Especially when the strength of the evidence is difficult to judge and a "doubtful guilt" case arises, if the existing evidence cannot exclude the possibility of the defendant's innocence but cannot definitively establish guilt, the principle of "presumption of innocence" should be applied, and the case should not be downgraded.

17.4.3.4 The Principle of Sufficient Reason

The Principle of Sufficient Reason states that the reasons for determining case facts must be true and must have a necessary logical connection to the facts that need to be proven. These reasons should be substantial enough to convincingly demonstrate the existence of the case facts, making them "reasonably acceptable."

This principle pertains to the reasoning process, requiring the reasons to be true, justifiable, and sufficient to logically lead to the conclusion that the facts in question should be established. To assert that a fact is true, there must be sufficient reasoning. In adhering to the Principle of Sufficient Reason, the evidence must demonstrate a necessary connection to the case facts. Without such a connection, a definitive determination of the facts cannot be made.

17.4.4 Basic Methods of Fact Determination Using Logical Principles

As a method for determining case facts, logical principles are generally applied to the determination of individual case facts. However, they may also be used for the full determination of facts in certain exceptional cases. When logical principles are used in determining case facts, the emphasis is on ensuring that the reasoning process does not violate basic logical laws. The goal is to ensure consistency between the nature of the premises and the conclusions drawn, reflecting the "principle of logical consistency." Reasoning refers to the process of deriving a new judgment from one or more known premises. Only if the premise facts are true, and the reasoning method is correct, can the conclusion about the facts be valid. Logical reasoning is the dividing line between correct and incorrect thinking, providing a clear distinction between valid and invalid thinking.

Logical principles are operational, meaning that thinking according to logical rules ensures the correctness and validity of reasoning. Conversely, chaotic reasoning leads to uncertain logical outcomes.

Logical principles serve as norms for correct thinking. In judicial fact determination, these principles are no exception. Based on the basic requirements of logical principles and their application in judicial practice, the methods for judging whether logical principles are violated are as follows.

17.4.4.1 Determining the Appropriateness of Evidence for Fact Determination

To assess whether logical principles are violated in the determination of case facts, the first step is to determine whether the evidence available for use in the case is appropriate for determining the facts. Evidence that is not suitable for determining case facts cannot be used as the basis for factual determination, as this would violate logical principles.

17.4.4.2 Determining the Appropriateness of the Determined Case Facts

The judgment of appropriateness is based on the premise of "reasonableness." If something is unreasonable, it is inappropriate. For example, excluding testimony from a witness with a vested interest in the case without proper examination is inappropriate. Similarly, directly using evidence collected by the judge without cross-examination, or disregarding evidence submitted by the parties, also violates logical principles.

As a thinking method for determining case facts, logical principles provide a pathway for judges to use in deciding facts. However, they do not directly provide the answer to the existence of the facts themselves. Logical principles simplify the issues between evidence and facts, masking the complexity of the process. The facts derived from applying logical principles represent only one aspect of the case facts, and as they exclude substantive considerations, they cannot guarantee the truthfulness of the facts. However, judges must not discard logical principles just because their conclusions are probabilistic. While they cannot violate passive laws, logical principles are active and cautious in determining whether the outcome violates logic, making it feasible to assess the validity of the case facts.

Unlike experience principles, which can change-especially specialized experience principles that may evolve with advances in science and technology-logical principles are more certain, universal, and stable. As such, violations of logical principles in case fact determination should generally be avoided.

Furthermore, with the advancement of modern information technology, the role of artificial intelligence algorithms in assisting judicial decisions is increasingly apparent. Whether algorithms can become a third method for determining case facts is a subject of growing interest. Algorithms, through automated decision-making procedures and legitimacy standards, may be suitable for adjudicating simple cases. However, questions about public acceptance, adaptability of experience principles, and system biases still require further research.

17.5 Questions and Reflections

Sherlock Holmes once said, "When you have eliminated the impossible, whatever remains, however improbable, must be the truth." Ronald J. Allen argued that all disputed factual issues and proof reasoning problems are essentially mathematical in nature. In adjudicating truth and falsehood, applying quantitative reasoning could scientifically assess the proof standard and factual likelihood. "The law does not predefine the probative force of evidence; the adjudicator makes reasonable judgments based on experience principles and ethical norms, forming conviction and thus determining the case facts."In the above example, Zhou used probability theory, statistics, permutations, combinations, and error theory to demonstrate the "absurdity" of the public prosecutor' evidence. By calculating the absolute and relative errors in the testimonies of the "briber" and the "recipient," he concluded that the case evidence was false. According to *China's Criminal Procedure Law Interpretation*, if evidence extracted from hidden objects or documents corroborates the defendant's confession, and there is no evidence of fabricated confessions or coercion, the defendant can be found guilty. Based on this case and the points above, consider the following questions: (1) Was the application of the experience principle appropriate in this case? (2) Which logical principles were applied in this case? (3) What rules should be followed when applying experience principles? (4) Can algorithms become a future method for determining case facts?

References

Ishii, K. (2000). Riben shiyong xingshi zhengju fa [Translation of 刑事実務証拠法] (Chen, H. R., Trans.). Taipei: Wu-Nan Book Inc. (in Chinese)

Lin, Y. X. (2005). Xingshi susong fa: shangce, zonglun bian. Beijing: China Renmin University Press. (in Chinese)

Zhang, B. (2008). Kexue zhengju de san da jiben lilun wenti. Evidence Science, (2): 138-146. (in Chinese).

Extended Reading

Zhang, W. P. (2008). Renshi jingyan faze. Tsinghua Law Journal, 2(6): 6–24. (in Chinese)

Guo, H. (2009). Anjian shishi rending fangfa. Beijing: Chinese People's Public Security University Press. (in Chinese)

Zhang, B. S. (2009). Tuiding shi zhengming guocheng de zhongduan. Chinese Journal of Law, (5): 175–194. (in Chinese)

Zheng, W. G. (2019). Tuiding zhidu yanjiu. Beijing: China Renmin University Press. (in Chinese)

Yan, C. X. (2008). Sifa renzhi yanjiu. Beijing: China Procurational Press. (in Chinese)

Bi, Y. Q. (1999). Shilun minshi susong zhong de sifa renzhi. Peking University Law Journal, (1): 53–60. (in Chinese)

Zhao, Z. J. (2002). Sifa renzhi wenti yanjiu. Journal of National Prosecutors College, (6): 70–77. (in Chinese)

Chapter 18
Rules of Presumption

18.1 Introductory Case

On October 12, 2000, at 10:00 PM, the plaintiff Zhao Guorong's vessel, "Suhai Men Fishery 03016" (hereinafter referred to as the "03016" vessel), was operating in Section 2 of Fishing Area 150 at the Lushi Fishery in Jiangsu Province. At that time, an anchorless vessel was approaching the "03016" vessel. Soon, the anchor line of the anchorless vessel became entangled with the bow mast of the "03016" vessel, causing the right bow of the "03016" vessel to be pressed against the left bow of the anchorless vessel. The two vessels were repeatedly shaken by the strong wind and could not separate. The crew of the "03016" vessel cut the anchor line of the anchorless vessel, and the two vessels separated, with the anchorless vessel leaving the scene.

After the incident, the crew of the "03016" vessel discovered that the bow of their vessel had been damaged and water had begun flooding into the hold. While attempting to save the vessel, the crew called the "03004" vessel for assistance. Due to the large waves and strong winds, the "03004" vessel could not reach the scene until 5:00 AM the next day. The "03004" vessel rescued the nine crew members of the "03016" vessel and continued to operate in the sea with them. The "03016" vessel sank at 7:00 AM on the same day. Since it was the peak fishing season, the "03004" vessel continued to operate at sea with the rescued crew members.

On October 20, the "03004" vessel returned to port. On the same day, the plaintiff submitted an "Accident Report" to the Lushi Branch of the Jiangsu Fishery Supervisory Bureau. On October 23, the Jiangsu Fishery Supervisory Bureau conducted an investigation into the crew of the "03016" vessel and reported to the East China Sea Fishery Supervisory Bureau. Subsequently, the East China Sea Fishery Supervisory Bureau requested the Ningbo Maritime Safety Administration and the fishery supervisory departments in Zhejiang, Shanghai, Jiangsu, and Fujian provinces to assist in investigating the anchorless vessel at the time of the incident.

H. Guo, *Evidence Jurisprudence in China*, Understanding China,
https://doi.org/10.1007/978-981-95-3981-9_18

On February 18, 2001, the East China Sea Fishery Supervisory Bureau issued an "Investigation Opinion" to the Jiangsu Fishery Supervisory Bureau, identifying the defendant Lin Chengfang, Xu Liangang, Lu Zhaoyun, Ding Decai, and Yang Guding's shared vessel, "Zhejiang Xiang Fishery 055" (hereinafter referred to as the "055" vessel), as the vessel responsible for the accident. The plaintiff Zhao Guorong sued, demanding compensation for losses related to the vessel, fishing operations, fish cargo, and onboard personal items.

The Shanghai Maritime Court in the first instance held that the evidence provided by the plaintiff regarding the collision of the two vessels was exclusive and could be used to infer that the "055" vessel was the other vessel involved in the incident. The court found that the fact of the collision between the "03016" and "055" vessels was established. However, since the specific circumstances of their operations and the anchorless condition of the vessels before the collision were difficult to ascertain, the collision responsibility ratio could not be determined using the avoidance rule. Therefore, in accordance with the relevant provisions of China's Maritime Code, when the responsibility for a ship collision cannot be determined, the compensation responsibility is to be borne equally. Based on this, the court ordered the defendants, Lin Chengfang and others, to jointly compensate plaintiff Zhao Guorong for economic losses caused by the ship collision, amounting to RMB 152,507.27. The defendants, Lin Chengfang and others, were dissatisfied with the first-instance judgment and filed an appeal. During the second-instance trial, the appellants withdrew their appeal.

18.2 Chapter Overview

This chapter covers the concept of presumption, its characteristics, classifications, methods, and the rules of its applicability and effectiveness. Presumption is an auxiliary method of proof, which is an exception and complement to the principle of evidence-based adjudication. It is used to confirm the existence of a presumed fact based on the existence of foundational facts.

18.3 Overview of Presumption

As a method for recognizing case facts, presumption originates from the collective life experience and common sense of a community. It is the formulation of rules based on the relationship between phenomena and facts that co-exist or are naturally connected. By legal means, presumption grants foundational facts an expansive force, allowing facts that would otherwise be difficult or impossible to recognize to be accepted. It helps reduce unnecessary proof or alleviates the burden of proving difficult-to-establish facts, making it an auxiliary method in judicial fact-finding.

18.3.1 Concept and Characteristics of Presumption

Presumption refers to a case fact recognition rule, which confirms a presumed fact based on the affirmation of the relationship between a foundational fact and the presumed fact. It is a method of recognizing the existence of one fact (the presumed fact) based on the existence of another (the foundational fact).

Presumption, as a written rule, originates from Roman law, dating back to the sixth century BC in *the Digest of Roman Law*. It has since been incorporated into the legal theory, legislation, and judicial practices of many countries. "Among the family of legal terms, presumption is one of the most difficult to manage, aside from the burden of proof."[1] In Chinese legislation, the earliest law to provide for presumption is *the Maritime Code of the People's Republic of China.*[2]

Countries, considering the "rule of thumb," "probability," or "convenience of proof," have gradually transformed factual presumption (which is essentially inference) into legal presumption, establishing a large number of presumption rules. Presumption is a legal rule, where once one party has proven the foundational facts, and in the absence of contrary evidence, the presumed facts are established as proven.[3] The understanding of presumption as a method of fact-finding is largely the same across countries, though there are some differences in expression. According to the basic concept of presumption, it has the following characteristics.

18.3.1.1 The Foundational Fact Must Be Proven to Be True by Evidence

Presumption is based on the typical co-occurrence relationship or normal accompanying phenomenon between the foundational fact and the presumed fact. Once the foundational fact is proven by evidence, it implies that the presumed fact is confirmed, and the judge can directly establish the presumed fact based on the foundational fact. However, the existence of the foundational fact is proved through highly reliable evidence, and the premise for applying presumption is that the foundational fact has been proven to be true. Although the truth of the presumed fact depends on the truth of the foundational fact, proving the foundational fact true does not necessarily guarantee the truth of the presumed fact. Presumption serves as a temporary substitute for the truth, offering an interim alternative to directly asserting the actual truth.[4]

Presumption does not invert or transfer the burden of proof for the presumed fact based on the proof of the foundational fact, as proving the foundational fact is inherently part of the normal proof process. The presumed fact is usually difficult to prove with evidence under normal circumstances. If the law still requires the

---

[1] Strong (2004).

[2] Article 246 of the Maritime Code of the People's Republic of China stipulates: "After an insurance accident occurs to a ship, if it is considered that actual total loss is inevitable, or the expenses required to avoid actual total loss exceed the insured value, it shall be deemed as a constructive total loss."

[3] Murphy (2000).

[4] Rescher (2013).

parties to prove the existence of the presumed fact through evidence, as per the principle of evidence-based adjudication, the case would be unfairly handled due to the impossibility of proof.

18.3.1.2 Presumed Facts Are Only a Part of the Case Facts

As a method for recognizing case facts, the ultimate purpose of presumption is to address the issue of confirming the existence of the facts of the case. Presumed facts are neither the basis (evidence) for determining the facts nor the entirety of the facts of the case; they are only a part of the case facts. Some legislation and interpretations contain certain misunderstandings. For example, *China's Civil Procedure Law* stipulates: "If legal facts and documents are notarized through statutory procedures, they should be used as the basis for recognizing facts by the People's Court, except where contrary evidence is sufficient to overturn the notarization." The "legal acts, legal facts, and documents" referred to here are the basis for the court's recognition of facts, not the facts of the case itself. This is not presumption in the strict sense. The presumed fact is merely a part of the overall facts of the case or an element in the legal requirements, such as subjective elements or factual states, but not the entire case fact.

18.3.1.3 The Basis for Presumption Must Be the Normal Relationship Between the Foundational Fact and the Presumed Fact

Presumption is a result derived from human experience in social practice, summarized from either personal or others' experiences, carrying a certain "regularity" and is a product of practical reason. Once the foundational fact is proven by evidence, the judge can directly confirm the presumed fact based on the existence of the foundational fact, without needing additional evidence to prove or explain the presumed fact. This "regularity" manifests in the phenomenon as the normal relationship between the foundational fact and the presumed fact.

A normal relationship refers to a highly probable accompanying relationship between two things under typical circumstances. It is an experience of a similar cause-and-effect relationship obtained through long-term, repeated practice or application in daily life, not just a highly probable or contingent relationship. In other words, when one thing occurs, another thing will usually happen under normal circumstances, or whenever one phenomenon exists, another phenomenon will also occur, without exceptions in the same context. The "normal relationship" is not repetitive behavior. This normal relationship between the foundational fact and the presumed fact is the basis for the presumption and the reason why presumption can be applied. These reasons are the legal foundation for presumption, also the source of its legal rules, and differ from the general method of proof based on evidence in determining the facts of a case.

18.3.1.4 Presumed Facts Have a High Likelihood of Being True Compared to Objectively Existing Facts

Presumed facts are different from objectively existing facts in that they carry a high likelihood of being true, which is often referred to as "probability" in common law jurisdictions. However, presumed facts serve a key role in guiding the direction of case fact recognition. Their application typically affects the substantive rights of the party against whom the presumption is applied, and the law allows the opposing party to rebut the presumption. This rebuttal is generally based on the lack of legal foundation or necessity for the presumption, and it does not require the party to provide evidence proving the non-existence of the presumed fact. Proving the existence of a presumed fact is difficult, and confirming its existence is nearly impossible. Moreover, requiring the opposing party to disprove the presumed fact with evidence is also challenging.

18.3.1.5 Presumed Facts Are Considered to Exist

Once the foundational facts are confirmed, the judge is required to accept the presumed facts as true based on the law, without discretion. For example, *the German Civil Code Draft* once stipulated that if the law presumes a fact, it is considered proven..[5] However, exceptions arise when the presumed facts contradict one another.

Presumption differs from fictio. A fictio involves treating two distinct facts as identical or assigning different evaluations to two identical facts. It equates dissimilar things as if they were the same, replacing the real with the assumed. A fictio does not create an evidentiary burden and cannot be overturned; it simply represents a legal necessity to treat one fact the same as another. It is not subject to rebuttal by contrary evidence and is not part of the rules of evidence. Essentially, fictio is an entity law rule expressed in procedural legal terms, fundamentally distinct from presumption.

Presumption differs from assumption. An assumption is a form of speculation about a fact that did not exist in the past or does not exist currently. It is a hypothesis without any necessary preconditions, existing within the realm of thought, and has no legal effect. A presumption can only be overturned by rebuttal evidence, while an assumption can only be affirmed by validation. A presumption does not need to be proven true, whereas an assumption does not require proof of its falsity. Therefore, the law should avoid judges relying on assumptions to establish case facts or resolve cases.

Presumption differs from indirect evidence. Indirect evidence is a form of proof that is based on the truth of the evidence being established. Presumption, in contrast, interrupts the proof process and depends on the truth of the foundational facts. It does not meet the requirement for sufficient grounds or the exclusivity of indirect evidence.

Presumption differs from inference. Inference, while it follows the logical process of deriving new judgments from existing ones, requires additional supporting

[5] Rosenberg (2002).

evidence, and the conclusions reached are not unique, often leading to multiple interpretations. In contrast, the outcome of a presumption is unique and does not require supporting evidence for validation.

18.3.2 The Legal Significance of Presumptive Evidence

Abroad, presumptions are frequently applied in the process of determining case facts. With the deepening of research into presumption theory and the needs of judicial practice, presumptions have also gained increasing importance in Chinese legislation and judicial practice. There are provisions concerning presumptions in Chinese legislation and judicial interpretations, and they play an increasingly important role in judicial practice. Presumptions in evidence law have the following significance.

18.3.2.1 Presumption Helps Simplify Certain Aspects of the Proof Process

Legally defining presumptions and their corresponding provisions helps judicial practice make inferences from known facts to unknown facts, without needing to rely on evidence to prove them. Presumed facts can simplify the tedious steps of proof, save time in litigation, reduce litigation costs, and improve litigation efficiency. In a lawsuit, some disputes between parties may not involve contentious facts, or after one party makes a claim based on certain subordinate facts, the other party may not necessarily refute those facts. In such cases, the facts can be presumed to be true, reducing unnecessary proof and preventing difficult-to-prove facts from becoming obstacles in determining the overall case facts or disputed facts.

In some cases, although the facts could theoretically be clarified, practical investigation and verification can be extremely difficult and often require significant human, material, and financial resources, which may make the lawsuit violate the principle of litigation economy. In these situations, using presumptions to determine case facts can save considerable judicial resources and avoid delays in litigation.

18.3.2.2 Presumption Can Alleviate Certain Obstacles in Proof

Due to the close and regular connection between things, people can use their daily life experiences to judge that when one thing exists, it logically causes the occurrence of another, provided that there are no exceptions. Once this connection is elevated from ordinary experience to legislative provisions, judicial practice can make timely rulings on the same facts, avoid repetitive work, and prevent different or conflicting rulings on the same facts. It also ensures that parties involved in similar factual determination issues receive the same conclusions. At the same time, when facts need to be proven but certainty cannot be obtained, the presumption rule can stabilize the situation, resolving the uncertainty in legal relationships.

Case facts can be subjectively recognized, with human cognitive abilities serving as the basis. Due to the limitations of time, procedures, and methods in litigation activities, the understanding of case facts cannot go on indefinitely. Moreover, some evidence cannot be obtained due to time, space, and environmental factors, making it an ideal to fully clarify all the facts of a case in litigation. In such cases, presumptions can, to some extent, solve this problem, alleviate the difficulty of proving certain case facts, and help judges avoid the dilemma of being unable to determine certain case facts. This facilitates timely judgments by the court, ending the case, and saving litigation costs, thus achieving the values pursued by legislation.

18.3.2.3 Presumption as a Method for Confirming Uncertain Facts

When the facts of a case involve the subjective state of the parties, it is impossible to directly recognize their inner world, as the inner world is subjective and can only be known if the individual acknowledges it. Therefore, presuming the inner intention of the parties based on their external behavior is one of the best methods. As an evidentiary rule, presumption has the function of influencing the allocation of the burden of proof. It determines the transfer and change of the burden of proof in procedural terms and can serve as a supplement to the burden of proof, contributing to a more reasonable distribution of the burden of proof.

In the process of determining case facts, although presumption is based on the normal connections between things or rules of experience in daily life, the facts confirmed and the conclusions drawn still have a certain degree of distance from objective truth. As a result, it remains relative and uncertain. In terms of reflecting objective truth, presumption can only meet a high probability standard, not absolute certainty. Therefore, the application of presumptive rules in determining case facts must still be approached with caution.

18.4 Types of Presumption

On the issue of classifying presumptions, the Italian legal scholar, after accepting the concept of Roman law, classified presumptions based on their effects into legal presumptions and factual presumptions, thus opening the way for the classification of presumptions. In theory, the classification of presumptions generally includes three types: (1) strong presumptions; (2) weak presumptions; (3) moderate presumptions. The first case in the common law system to use the rule of presumption was the British case against Ireland. In the common law system, presumptions generally include: (1) conclusory presumptions; (2) persuasive presumptions; (3) evidential presumptions; (4) temporary presumptions. Among these, conclusory presumptions cannot be rebutted by evidence and are considered irrebuttable presumptions; the other three types of presumptions can be overturned by evidence provided. In theory, presumptions can generally be classified as follows.

18.4.1 Legal Presumptions and Factual Presumptions Based on Whether the Presumption Is Explicitly Provided by Law

Legal Presumption, also known as legislative presumption, refers to a presumption explicitly stipulated by law, which confirms the existence of one fact based on the existence of another. Factual Presumption, also known as judicial presumption or adjudicative presumption, refers to a presumption based on life experience and common sense, where the existence of one fact confirms the existence of another. For example, if objects A and B typically exist together, once object A is established, a judge can confirm the existence of object B in the litigation process based on life experience and common sense.

Both legal and factual presumptions essentially involve the presumption of facts. In form, both imply that if fact A exists, fact B can be presumed to exist. However, their nature and effects differ: from a normative perspective, legislation is more fixed, while the judiciary is more flexible. Legal presumptions are fixed presumptions with strict mandatory effect, while factual presumptions are flexible presumptions with discretionary power.

Legal presumptions can be applied when the associative relationship between basic facts and presumed facts is relatively stable or certain. Factual presumptions can be used when the relationship between basic facts and presumed facts is less stable or uncertain.

Factual presumptions can be seen as the "precursors" to legal presumptions, and legal presumptions are mature factual presumptions. When deciding whether to adopt legal presumptions and formalize a certain presumption, legislators or judicial interpretations must consider two factors: first, whether the relationship between the basic fact and the presumed fact generally follows the rule that the existence of A necessarily leads to the existence of B; second, whether the presumption has a high-value objective.

Although both factual presumptions and legal presumptions are based on the normal connection between facts, factual presumptions are a method for judges to establish facts through reasoning. The reasoning process and methods should be explained, which distinguishes it from legal presumptions. Otherwise, judges may arbitrarily confirm the facts of the case without providing reasons, turning the judges' proactive role in determining facts into arbitrariness. It would be more appropriate to express this distinction by using terms like "reasoning" or "inference" to highlight the difference from legal presumptions. In U.S. law, the basic distinction is between legal presumptions and factual presumptions. A legal presumption is a legal rule that results in a rebuttable presumption of fact upon the recognition of a basic fact. A factual presumption, on the other hand, is merely an argument-a conclusion drawn from the establishment of a basic fact.

18.4.2 Based on Whether the Conclusion of the Presumption Is Final, It Can Be Divided into Irrebuttable Presumptions and Rebuttable Presumptions

Irrebuttable Presumption, also known as a decisive presumption or "certain presumption," refers to a presumption where the law does not allow evidence to be presented to rebut or overturn the presumed fact. Legal presumptions often fall into the category of irrebuttable presumptions. These presumptions are legislated due to public policy considerations and are fixed through legislation. Because such presumptions have the nature of an indisputable legal conclusion, they are effectively equivalent to substantive law and express substantive rules using the term "presumption." In a certain sense, they are not considered presumptions under evidentiary law. In an irrebuttable presumption, the relationship between the basic fact and the presumed fact is often either inevitable or stable, or it is established by law due to some value-oriented consideration, making it "inevitable or stable." The conclusion of such a presumption has final legal effect, and the parties cannot rebut it. However, what the parties cannot rebut is the presumption itself, and the basic facts of the presumption can still be rebutted. For example, Article 301 of *the Federal Rules of Evidence of the United States* states: "In all civil actions, except as otherwise provided by statute or these rules, a presumption imposes upon the party against whom it is directed the burden of introducing evidence sufficient to rebut the presumption."

Rebuttable Presumption, also known as a "hypothetical presumption," refers to a presumption that can be rebutted or overturned by contrary evidence. This type of presumption can be further divided into persuasive presumptions and evidential presumptions. For instance, *Section 85C of the Indian Evidence Act of 1872* provides: "If a digital signature certificate is accepted by the signer, the court shall presume that the information listed on the digital signature certificate, except for the information that the signer indicates has not been verified, is accurate, unless the contrary is proven." Generally speaking, in a rebuttable presumption, the relationship between the basic fact and the presumed fact is in an uncertain state, and the parties can rebut or even overturn the presumed fact using evidence and inferences. Since the presumed fact is not proven by evidence, it inherently has a certain probability. Moreover, the normal relationship between the presumed fact and the basic fact is not an intrinsic, inherent connection. As such, it should be rebuttable and not irrebuttable. As for some legal provisions in China that use "irrebuttable presumption," they should be interpreted according to the context and content to determine their specific meaning and should not be broadly categorized as a form of presumption.

18.4.2.1 Based on Whether the Presumption Is Established by Legislation or Judicial Precedent, It Can Be Divided into Legislative Presumption and Judicial Presumption

Legislative presumption refers to presumption rules explicitly prescribed in relevant laws by legislative bodies; Judicial presumption refers to presumption rules established by judicial authorities through legal interpretation and the creation of precedents. Based on the different natures of presumed facts, presumptions can be divided into legal qualification presumption, intent presumption, responsibility presumption, and general matters presumption. Based on the content of the presumption, they can be divided into presumption of substantive facts and presumption of procedural facts, etc.

Furthermore, based on the content of the presumption, it can be divided into factual presumption in law and rights presumption in law. The former is expressed as "When fact A exists, presumption of fact B's existence"; the latter is expressed as "When fact A exists, presumption of right B's existence." For example, Article 250 of *the Japanese Civil Code* stipulates: "When the share of each co-owner is unclear, it is presumed to be equal."

18.5 Regulating the Application of Presumption

18.5.1 Basic Facts Rule for Applying Presumptions

As an important evidentiary rule, the presumption rule itself has certain limitations. Therefore, the application of presumptions must be strictly regulated and must follow legal procedures to fully reflect fairness and justice. Article 10 of the Supreme People's Court's Provisions on Civil Litigation Evidence stipulates: "For facts presumed according to law or for facts derived from daily life experience, the parties are not required to provide evidence."

18.5.1.1 Establishment of Basic Facts Rule

The application of a presumption must ensure the truth of the basic facts. A presumption in evidence has the same effect as proof, meaning the presumed fact does not require evidence to prove its truth. However, this truth originates from the truth of the basic facts. Only if the basic facts are true can the presumed facts derived from them be considered reliable. The basic facts used for presumption should meet the following conditions: (1) The basic facts must be proven by sufficient evidence. (2) Facts that are agreed upon in the plaintiff's and defendant's statements, i.e., facts that both parties agree on and do not dispute. (3) Judicial cognizance, i.e., facts that judges, by virtue of their duties, should know. (4) Facts that are widely known.

18.5.1.2 Rules of Connection Between Basic Facts and Presumed Facts

The connection between basic facts and presumed facts must be a normal or highly probable relationship. The relationship between basic facts and presumed facts is the underlying basis for the presumption. Logically, there are three forms of logical relationships between things: (1) When fact A exists, fact B must also exist, and there is an equivalence between them; (2) When fact A does not exist, fact B must not exist, and there is a contradictory relationship between them; (3) When fact A exists, fact B may exist, and there is a probabilistic relationship between them.

The relationship between basic facts and presumed facts must align with the first two types of relationships. From a logical perspective, this relationship forms the major premise for making a presumption, and the basic fact serves as the minor premise. If the major premise is unreliable, then the "inference" of this syllogism loses its foundation and becomes unbelievable. The normal relationship between the basic facts and presumed facts is a relationship of a causal nature, acquired through long-term, repeated practice and application in daily life. This causal relationship is outwardly manifested by the "inevitable" connection between the two facts. When one phenomenon exists, the other phenomenon will necessarily follow, exhibiting a companion-like relationship. Special or individual cases may occur, but generally, under normal conditions, they have not occurred. This connection is a general rule of human experience, but not all experience-based rules can be used as a basis for presumption in litigation. For an experience-based rule to serve as a premise for presumption, it should meet the following criteria: (1) Situations for applying the presumption explicitly defined by law; (2) Widely accepted rules of experience. For example, Article 19 of *China's Anti-Monopoly Law* states that the following conditions may lead to the presumption that an operator has a dominant market position: (1) If an operator's market share in the relevant market reaches one-half; (2) If two operators' combined market share in the relevant market reaches two-thirds; (3) If three operators' combined market share in the relevant market reaches three-quarters. In situations where the market share of some operators does not exceed one-tenth, they should not be presumed to have a dominant market position. If there is evidence to prove that the operator does not have a dominant market position, the presumption should not stand.

18.5.1.3 No Rebuttal or Insufficient Rebuttal of Presumed Facts

Generally, presumption facts, due to their accompanying relationship with the basic facts, carry a high degree of probability. However, from a theoretical perspective, there is also a possibility of relative inaccuracy. For the party to whom the presumption is unfavorable, the law should grant them the right to rebut the presumption's inaccuracy, through legal remedies. If the rebuttal or the evidence provided has the potential to shake the presumption fact, the presumption loses its effect. For example, *China's Copyright Law* stipulates: "The citizen who creates a work is the author. If a work is created under the direction of a legal person or other organization, and represents the will of the legal person or organization, the legal person or organization is considered the author. If there is no contrary evidence, the person or organization named as the author on the work is presumed to be the author."

Rebuttal by the unfavorable party does not necessarily need to reach the level of proving that the presumed fact does not exist. That is to say, it is not required to meet the standard of "contrary evidence sufficient to overturn" the presumption. Evidence may be presented for rebuttal, but it does not necessarily need to reach the level of overturning the presumption.

The party adversely affected by the presumption may rebut the presumption in three ways: (1) Directly rebutting the presumed fact with evidence. This rebuttal carries a dual burden of proof both in terms of behavior and results, and must convince the judge that the presumed fact is false, rather than leaving its truth or falsity unclear. (2) Rebutting the basic facts. If the basic facts are false, the party only has the burden of proving the behavior, and if they can make the truth of the basic facts uncertain, the presumption cannot be effectively applied. (3) Rebutting the experience rule on which the presumption is based. This constitutes a situation where the presumption should not be applied.

18.5.2 Presumption Rule of Obstruction of Proof

Obstruction of proof, also known as hindering proof or hindrance in presenting evidence, refers to the situation where one party, not bearing the burden of proof, obstructs the other party from proving the facts they assert. This can result in the party bearing the burden of proof being unable to prove their claim, which leads to the consequences of failing to meet the burden of proof.

The presumption rule of obstruction of proof refers to the rule that, when one party has conclusive evidence proving that the other party possesses or controls evidence favorable to them, and the second party refuses to provide such evidence without a justifiable reason, the court may presume the facts asserted by the first party to be true, and the second party will bear the unfavorable consequences. Chinese judicial interpretations have made corresponding provisions. For example, the Supreme People's Court's Provisions on Civil Litigation Evidence state: "If one party controls the evidence and refuses to submit it without a justifiable reason, and the party bearing the burden of proof claims that the evidence is unfavorable to the controlling party, the people's court may accept the claim as true." "If the party controlling documentary evidence refuses to submit it without justifiable reason, the people's court may accept the content of the documentary evidence as true." The presumption rule aims to alleviate difficulties in fact-finding and break procedural deadlocks but requires informing the parties about the legal consequences of refusing to provide evidence without justification. For instance, if a detainee dies during administrative detention, and their family requests an autopsy, but the public security agency refuses and forcibly cremates the body without other evidence proving death by disease, the court may apply the obstruction of proof rule and presume the defendant's unlawful conduct.

The presumption rule of obstruction of proof applies under the following conditions: (1) The party must have conclusive evidence proving that the other party holds evidence favorable to them; this cannot be based on speculation or conjecture. (2) The other party refuses to provide the evidence without justifiable reason, even after being informed of the consequences. "No justifiable reason" refers to the lack of a legal basis for withholding the evidence. (3) The disputed fact cannot be clarified, and the judge may make a presumption that it is true. For example, in administrative litigation, if the defendant administrative agency collects substantial evidence but refuses to provide evidence that is unfavorable to them, and the plaintiff, lacking the authority to collect such evidence, cannot obtain it, the plaintiff may request this evidence if it is recorded in the evidence held by the defendant. In this case, the presumption rule may apply.

There is a difference in academic and practical views on whether the presumption rule of obstruction of proof applies to personal relationship cases. Some scholars believe that in parental rights litigation, if one party refuses to undergo a paternity test for personal reasons, the court can presume the father to be the biological father, in accordance with the Supreme People's Court's interpretation. However, other scholars argue that in such cases, the presumption rule should not apply to parental rights litigation, as this could lead to undesirable outcomes, such as the court arbitrarily assigning a father to the child. For example, Plaintiff Zhang (male) and Defendant Lin (female) have a daughter after marriage. Zhang overhears a phone call between Lin and another defendant, Wu, learning that the child is Wu's. Zhang then takes his daughter for a paternity test, which confirms that he is not the biological father. Zhang files a lawsuit against Lin and Wu, requesting the court to confirm the father-daughter relationship between Wu and the child and seek compensation for damages. Wu denies this claim. The court, in order to clarify the facts, requests Wu to undergo a paternity test, but he refuses. Whether the refusal of Wu to undergo the paternity test should lead to a presumption that Wu is the father of Zhang's daughter remains an unresolved issue. While the law acknowledges the presumption of legitimacy for children born during the marriage, the presumption rule should generally be applied with a higher standard of proof in parental rights litigation, requiring precise evidence such as paternity tests, rather than relying on presumption.

There are different ways to solve the issue of obstruction of proof in factual determination. Some countries, such as Germany and Japan, which follow the civil law system, apply the burden-shifting rule. Others consider the obstruction of proof as a fairness issue between the parties, and the court, through the application of the principle of good faith, considers the manner of obstruction, the degree of responsibility, and the importance of the obstructed evidence, and ultimately makes a determination based on discretion. In particular, when evidence is destroyed due to negligence, it cannot be said that the destroyed evidence is unfavorable to the party holding the evidence. Therefore, the assumption that the fact obstructed by the person obstructing the proof should be considered as existing, based on the experience rule, does not hold. Some adopt the rule of lowering the standard of proof, making it easier for the party asserting the fact to achieve their evidentiary goal, thus forcing the opposing party into the disadvantage of not presenting evidence, which could result in the fact being determined.

18.6 Questions and Reflections

The presumption of obstruction of proof originates from a 1978 judgment by the Federal Supreme Court of Germany, where the court introduced the "burden of proof shift" rule in cases where the failure to fulfill the duty to provide information causes difficulties in proving a case. In the UK, the case Armony v. Delamirie established that the destruction or concealment of evidence to obstruct another party's ability to prove their case could lead to an adverse effect in terms of evidence law. In the example case above, the plaintiff identifies the defendant's vessel as the one involved in the collision, while the defendant denies that their vessel was present at the collision site. Both parties assert their positions and provide evidence to support their claims. Based on the case details, and referencing the viewpoints above, consider the following questions: (1) How did the court determine the facts of the case? (2) What method did the court use to confirm that the defendant's vessel was the one involved in the collision? (3) Is there any other possibility in this case?

References

Rosenberg, L. (2002). Zhengming zeren lun [Translation of Die Beweislast] (Zhuang, J. H., Trans.). Beijing: China Legal Publishing House. p. 226. (Original work published 1900).

Strong, J. W. (Ed.). (2004). Maikaomike lun zhengju [Translation of McCormick on Evidence] (Tang, W. J. et al., Trans.). Beijing: China University of Political Science and Law Press.

Murphy, P. (2000). Murphy on evidence. London: Blackstone Press.

Rescher, N. (2013). Tuiding he linshixing renzhi shijian [Translation of Presumption and the Practices of Tentative Cognition] (Wang, J. X., Trans.). Beijing: China Legal Publishing House. (Original work published 2006).

Extended Reading

Wang, X. M. (2004). Lun tuiding de luojixue jichu——jian lun tuiding yu nizhi de guanxi. Political Science and Law, (1): 165-172. (in Chinese)

Qin, C. (2004). Meiguo zhengjufa shang tuiding de xueshuo yu guize de fazhan. The Jurist, (4): 114–120. (in Chinese)

Pei, C. L. (2006). zailun tuiding. Chinese Journal of Law, (3): 119–127. (in Chinese)

Lao, D. Y. (2007). Tuiding yanjiu zhong de renshi wuqu. Science of Law (Journal of Northwest University of Political Science and Law), (5): 117–126. (in Chinese)

He, J. H. (2008). Cong ziran tuiding dao renzao tuiding—guanyu tuiding fanchou de fansi. Chinese Journal of Law, (4): 110–125. (in Chinese)

Zhang, B. S. (2009). Tuiding shi zhengming guocheng de zhongduan. Chinese Journal of Law, (5): 175–194. (in Chinese)
Zhang, H. Y. (2012). "Tuiding" he "shiwei" zhi yuci jiedu—yi woguo xianxing minshi falü guifan wei yangben. Law and Social Development, (3): 104–116. (in Chinese)
Zheng, W. G. (2019). Tuiding zhidu yanjiu. Beijing: China Renmin University Press.

Chapter 19
Judicial Cognition

19.1 Introductory Case

On an early summer evening, Mr. Wacoll took his 6-year-old son Jim for a walk in a neighborhood in San Francisco, located at the intersection of "Mission Street and 21st Street." As they were crossing the street on their way home, Jim was tragically struck and killed by an oncoming car. After the traffic accident, a police investigation determined that the car was traveling at a speed of 30 miles per hour at the time of the incident. Soon after, Mr. Wacoll filed a civil lawsuit against the owner of the vehicle, Mr. Lee, in the San Francisco District Court. During the first trial, both parties agreed on the fact that the defendant's car was traveling at a speed of 30 miles per hour at the time of the accident. The only point of dispute was whether the street in question, "Mission Street and 21st Street," was within the boundaries of San Francisco's commercial district. This was important because, within the commercial district, the legal speed limit for motor vehicles was 15 miles per hour. According to the law, if the street was indeed part of the commercial district, the defendant's actions would constitute illegal speeding, and the defendant would be liable for damages. Before the parties could present evidence or debate this point, the judge presiding over the case issued a judicial instruction directly to the jury, stating that "Mission Street and 21st Street" had always been a part of San Francisco's commercial district. Based on this judicial instruction, the jury ruled in favor of the plaintiff.

19.2 Chapter Overview

This chapter discusses the fundamental concepts related to judicial cognition, including the definition and characteristics of judicial cognition, the determination of its scope and standards, and the procedures for initiation, objections, and supervision.

H. Guo, *Evidence Jurisprudence in China*, Understanding China,
https://doi.org/10.1007/978-981-95-3981-9_19

Judicial cognition is a principle in evidence law and one of the auxiliary methods for establishing facts.

19.3 Overview of Judicial Cognition

Judicial cognition is a fundamental issue in evidence law. In general, the determination of case facts by judges is based on the evidence presented by the parties (prosecution and defense), which undergoes a strict proof process. In special cases, however, judges can directly recognize the existence or truth of certain facts that are objective, publicly known, or universally acknowledged without requiring evidence from the parties. This rule, where facts are recognized directly by the judge without the need for evidence, is known as judicial cognition. It is an exception and supplement to the doctrine of evidence adjudication. "Judicial cognition and formal acknowledgment do not require evidence to prove."[1]

19.3.1 Concept and Characteristics of Judicial Cognition

Judicial cognition, also known as "judicial notice" or "notice in court," refers to a rule for recognizing case facts in which the judge directly acknowledges the truth of applicable laws or facts without requiring evidence from the parties (prosecution and defense).

The concept of judicial cognition originates from the Roman legal maxim "What is known need not be proved." This system began in the periods of civil law and canon law and later evolved into an exception rule in the doctrine of evidence adjudication. The principle is based on the idea that "what the judge already knows does not need to be proved" (manifesta probatio non indigent). Judicial cognition, as a legal institution, has been recognized and adopted by the legislations and judicial practices of many countries and regions. "Judicial cognition is a principle in evidence law, granting the court (judge or magistrate) the authority to declare that a fact exists without requiring the parties to provide evidence to prove its existence."[2] It has the following characteristics.

19.3.1.1 Specialty of the Judicial Cognition Entity

Judicial cognition can only be exercised by a judge; no other parties in the lawsuit may exercise this power. This is because judicial cognition carries direct legal binding force and directly determines the outcome of the case's factual determination. The

---

[1] Cross and Tapper (1979).

[2] Dennis (1999).

parties have the right to request that the court take judicial notice of specific facts in the case, but they do not have the authority to initiate judicial cognition themselves. Statutory judicial cognition holds absolute effect; even if a judge does not take judicial notice, the parties have the right to provide information to assist the judge in this process. Therefore, it is considered a judicial function. The entity that applies judicial cognition has a particular role, as it can only be taken by the judge and serves to substitute for the parties' role in providing evidence or carrying out proof. According to *China's Interpretation of Civil Procedure Law*, "The following facts do not require parties to provide evidence to prove: (1) natural laws and theories, theorems, or laws; (2) facts that are well known; (3) facts that are presumed by law."At the same time, judges are not required to provide evidence to prove facts that fall under "facts recognized by the court through its official duties."[3]

19.3.1.2 Specificity of Judicial Notice Objects

Judges cannot take judicial notice of all facts; they can only do so for specific matters or facts. These specific facts mainly include case facts and evidentiary facts. Case facts are the factual elements defined by law, i.e., the objects of proof. Evidentiary facts are facts used to prove specific case facts (judicial notice generally should not include this content). The fact that these matters are subject to judicial notice does not mean that there is no dispute among the parties. For example, in the 1940 UK case Marquess v. Goddard for compensation, the plaintiff was kicked by a camel while playing in the defendant's park. To seek compensation, the plaintiff argued that the camel was a wild animal. According to *UK law*, the defendant would be liable for compensation if they could not prove they had taken adequate care regarding the camel's nature of being dangerous. During the litigation, the parties disputed the focal issue of whether the camel was a domesticated or wild animal, and the case was delayed. In this situation, Lord Scoff took judicial notice of the fact that the camel was a domesticated animal, ruling that the camel in this case was domesticated.

Based on the prominence of the judicial notice object and the extent of its recognition, these can be divided into prominent facts (facts that do not require evidence), such as the Earth's revolution and rotation; legal norms familiar to the judge; and indisputable facts (historical documents, scientific books, etc., that are clear and unambiguous), such as the formula for calculating the circumference of a circle.

19.3.1.3 Public Recognition of Judicial Notice Objects

The objects of judicial notice include laws, widely known facts, scientific laws, and experiential theories. Regardless of whether the parties acknowledge them, these facts exist objectively. This differs from self-admission. Judicial notice matters are not only objectively existing but also widely known at the time. However, it should

[3] Matsuoka (2004).

be noted that what is "widely known" at a given time may become "unknown" later, and not all widely accepted facts will necessarily become scientific laws. The reason for requiring public recognition is that when a judge directly affirms a fact, it serves to relieve the parties from the burden of proof, objectively increasing the burden of proof on the other party. In general, there should not be any disagreement. For facts that are not in accordance with the actual situation or facts that have reasonable objections, the law should not provide for judicial notice, nor should the court take judicial notice.

While judicial notice objects have public recognition, they are not the same as widely known facts. For example, if a judge obtains a fact (Fact A) during the course of their duties in one case, and in another case, Fact A is involved, it can become a judicially noticed fact in that case, but it is not necessarily a fact that everyone else would automatically know.[4]

The objects of judicial notice include laws, widely known facts, scientific laws, and experiential theories. Regardless of whether the parties acknowledge them, these facts exist objectively. This differs from self-admission. Judicial notice matters are not only objectively existing but also widely known at the time. However, it should be noted that what is "widely known" at a given time may become "unknown" later, and not all widely accepted facts will necessarily become scientific laws. The reason for requiring public recognition is that when a judge directly affirms a fact, it serves to relieve the parties from the burden of proof, objectively increasing the burden of proof on the other party. In general, there should not be any disagreement. For facts that are not in accordance with the actual situation or facts that have reasonable objections, the law should not provide for judicial notice, nor should the court take judicial notice.

While judicial notice objects have public recognition, they are not the same as widely known facts. For example, if a judge obtains a fact (Fact A) during the course of their duties in one case, and in another case, Fact A is involved, it can become a judicially noticed fact in that case, but it is not necessarily a fact that everyone else would automatically know.[5]

Judicial notice is distinct from facts that are exempt from proof. First, there is a difference in the subject of recognition. Judicial notice is explained from the perspective of the judge, focusing on the judge's actions and the recognition of a specific matter by the judge. Facts exempt from proof, on the other hand, are considered from the perspective of the parties involved, which removes the obligation of the parties to provide evidence to prove a specific fact. Second, the scope of application differs. The scope of facts exempt from proof includes judicial notice, but is not limited to judicial notice. Some facts may be exempt from proof, but the judge cannot directly recognize them and must still conduct an investigation.

Judicial notice is also distinct from self-admission. First, there is a difference in the applicable parties. The subject of judicial notice is the judge, while the subject of self-admission is the parties to the case. Second, there is a difference in the matters

[4] Luo (1972), p. 26.

[5] Posner (2004).

to which they apply. Judicial notice generally applies to matters that are objective and widely recognized. Some matters recognized through judicial notice cannot be subjects of self-admission, as the parties are not allowed to admit to facts that fall under judicial notice. Third, there is a difference in legal effect. The matters under judicial notice are conclusive, while self-admitted facts may be overturned if the self-admission is revoked.

Judicial notice functions as a remedy for private rights through public authority. It not only helps save litigation costs but also prevents the waste of litigation resources. This is because "evidence for facts that are apparent and obvious incurs costs without yielding benefits."

19.4 Rules for the Application of Judicial Notice

The public recognition of judicial notice makes it an active duty for judges to exercise this power. Judges are obligated to recognize facts that are commonly known or widely recognized in society, indisputable facts, or facts that have been established in the course of their duties. "For facts that are known to the average person, it is unreasonable for the court to remain silent or ignore them."[6] For example, the determination of whether a tomato is a fruit or a vegetable may lead to disagreement among the parties, but it is self-evident to ordinary people, and the judge can exercise judicial notice in this case. The subject of judicial notice is the judge, and the judge's ability to recognize facts (through knowledge and experience) plays a critical role in its application. The necessary knowledge and experience for judicial notice include: knowledge from daily life, experiential knowledge, and methods derived from experience. Knowledge from daily life (including common knowledge and habits) comes from accumulated experience, and judges can use this common sense to judge the truth of the facts in a case. This is because modern society has not yet reached a point where all facts can be confirmed through scientific rationality and absolute quantification. A judge's experience is closely related to their profession and is gradually formed through their practice of judging complex social disputes. These issues require judges to enhance their social experience and knowledge structure, particularly through years of judicial experience.

19.4.1 Scope of Judicial Notice Facts

The first issue to address is whether the scope of judicial notice should be regulated by law or be at the judge's discretion. Judicial notice is part of a judge's responsibilities, involving the direct recognition of widely known facts, facts already known in the trial process, scientific principles, and common facts. There may be discretionary

[6] H. Cunderhill, A Treatise on the Law of Criminal Evidence 5th ed., Ch. 7, §60.

decisions on whether to apply judicial notice in certain cases. The law mainly controls and limits a judge's discretion through authorization, particularly when it involves facts that influence the burden of proof. Judicial notice is meant to avoid undue encroachment on the substantive rights of the parties. Generally speaking, the scope of judicial notice is legally defined, and judges do not have the power of discretionary judgment.

Judicial notice originates from common law systems, and its content is largely determined through case law and legislation. For instance, *the Model Rules of Evidence*, *Uniform Rules of Evidence*, and *the Federal Rules of Evidence in the United States* all provide clear stipulations regarding judicial notice. Section 201(b) of *the Federal Rules of Evidence* states: "For judicial notice to be applied, the facts must not be subject to reasonable dispute, meaning (1) facts that are generally known within the jurisdiction of the trial court; or (2) facts that can be accurately and readily confirmed by reliable sources whose accuracy cannot reasonably be questioned." This law provides comprehensive provisions concerning the objects of judicial notice, the timing of its application, and the procedural safeguards in place. However, in judicial practice, "courts generally prefer to use judicial notice for ordinary facts, not for special facts. Courts are more inclined to apply judicial notice to secondary facts rather than decisive facts."[7] In civil law countries, the regulations on the scope of judicial notice are generally more principle-based and are often applied in civil and administrative litigation. For example, the German Code of Civil Procedure states that facts already well-known to the court do not require evidence. Similarly, the Japanese Civil Procedure Code stipulates: "Well-known facts need not be proven." However, in China, there has been some deviation in the understanding of the scope of judicial notice. It has been broadly interpreted, with all instances where "parties do not need to provide evidence" or "the court may directly recognize" certain facts being treated as within the scope of judicial notice, leading to an expansion of its application.

Generally, the scope of judicial notice pertains to facts that arise during the direct examination or in the exercise of duties within a legal procedure, ensuring that judicial notice is used appropriately within the established framework.[8] It is generally appropriate to limit the scope of judicial notice to a smaller range. This is because research on judicial notice in China is still underdeveloped, and there is no consensus on its scope. Although judicial notice can be a useful tool to improve judicial efficiency and apply it in case fact-finding, there is a risk of abuse that could harm judicial fairness. Therefore, it is necessary to establish appropriate controls over the potential sources of such damage.

The main facts subject to judicial notice include: (1) Well-known facts: These should generally be limited to the jurisdiction of the court, ensuring that while the universality of the judicial notice objects is respected, their specificity and practicality are also reflected. (2) Government facts: This includes facts about the state's territory, the division of administrative regions, the cities and towns within the jurisdiction,

---

[7] Shen (1996).

[8] Luo (1972), p. 32.

as well as the activities, duties, terms, and official behaviors of key government personnel. (3) Easily accessible common knowledge: This includes facts related to history, geography, economics, science, education, and other readily recognized facts. (4) Customs consistent with public policy and social norms: This includes local customs, traditions, and societal norms. (5) Industry practices and rules: These pertain to established conventions and regulations within specific industries. (6) Other facts that do not raise reasonable disputes: These are facts that, by their nature, do not lead to conflicting interpretations or disputes.

19.4.2 Standards for Determining Judicial Notice Matters

The question of what standards should be applied to determine matters for judicial notice is an issue that needs to be resolved by judicial notice itself. Based on the essence of judicial notice, and in conjunction with relevant regulations, the standards for determining judicial notice matters are as follows:

19.4.2.1 Well-Known Facts Standard

Currently, there are different understandings in academic circles in China regarding the concept of "well-known facts" (wegen Offenkundigkeit). There are generally three viewpoints: (1) Universality View: This view holds that the standard for judicial notice is based on facts that are known by the general public, including judges. (2) Relativity View: According to this perspective, the standard for judicial notice should be based on facts that are known by the general members of society, but it does not rule out other individual possibilities. (3) Regionality View: This view suggests that the standard for judicial notice should be limited to facts known by the general public within a certain region. There is also the opinion that "well-known" facts should be confined to those known within the jurisdiction of the trial court, where both the general public and judges are aware of them.[9]

Common law countries and civil law countries have different standards for recognizing "well-known facts." In common law countries, the standard is typically based on facts that are known to the general public (matters of common knowledge). This is because jurors (judges) are considered to be part of the general public, and facts that are known to the general public should also be known to jurors (judges). Thus, the standard of knowledge is that of the general public. In practice, for jurors in common law countries, the notion of "should know" has effectively evolved into the practical understanding of "could know."

In contrast, civil law countries believe that if a judge does not know a fact, it cannot be considered a well-known fact, with the judge's knowledge serving as the basis for determining whether a fact is well-known. This difference in standards

---

[9] Cai (2006).

leads to different outcomes in practice. Judges are trained legal professionals with a heightened sensitivity to and focus on case facts, which differs from the general public's approach. However, in civil law countries, the judge's knowledge of what is considered "well-known" is still the guiding standard.

Using the facts known to the judge for judicial notice may not be as beneficial for recognizing facts as using the knowledge of the general public. The general public's understanding as the benchmark for "well-known facts" is more appropriate. This is because ordinary people can better reflect what is "known" by the public (with the notion of "three people as a group"). As Enderle suggests, recognition refers to facts that are part of common knowledge or general experience, which the court can confirm without requiring evidence. Since these facts are already known by the general public, there is no need for proof. The court should not obscure what is common knowledge, and such facts within its jurisdiction should be recognized.[10] In China's judicial practice, the "universality theory" has been adopted. Although judges in China are a specialized group, they are still part of the larger social group and share the general characteristics of society. Judges should be aware of what is known to the general public. Thus, this standard encompasses the following meanings: (1) "Well-known" refers to matters that are common knowledge, which the majority of people already know and understand; (2) The majority of people do not question the current state of such matters, and their truth has been confirmed by many examples or widely accepted; (3) The public has an indisputable certainty about such matters, and there is no substantial controversy; (4) The geographical scope of "well-known" facts is limited to the jurisdiction of the trial court, while the temporal scope is based on the time of the trial.

The standard for "well-known facts" differs from that for "notorious facts." Notorious facts refer to facts whose truth is undisputed within the general knowledge of the public. "Notorious facts" are those that are commonly known, meaning facts that are universally recognized within a country, a region, or a society, or facts based on commonly accepted rules of experience that are widely known.[11] These facts have been universally recognized for their fairness, but the parties still have the right to raise objections and the duty to provide evidence to prove them. However, the level of proof required does not need to reach the level of the judge's internal conviction. Generally speaking, the standard for notorious facts differs from that for well-known facts in terms of degree. A fact becomes a well-known fact when it has become so widely known that everyone is aware of it. Well-known facts are those with the highest degree of notoriety among notorious facts.

19.4.2.2 Determining the Standard of Verifiability

Determining verifiability means the ability to accurately and easily verify a fact, providing a quick and unquestionable explanation that one party does not have the

[10] H. C. Underhil, A Treatise on the Law of Criminal Evidence 5th ed, ch. 7 p.60.

[11] Li (1992).

opportunity to deceive the court in front of a clever adversary, or that the fact can be accurately and quickly verified through a method that is not reasonably doubted in terms of its correctness.[12] It is an important development in judicial notice, involving new factual areas and the new development of traditional judicial notice standards.

19.4.2.3 Matters Subject to Judicial Notice

The matters subject to judicial notice should be specific issues, not only including the facts of the case but also the laws related to the case. Legal issues include domestic law, international treaties, and foreign laws. Factual issues include well-known facts, administrative matters, and other matters that are widely known.

19.4.3 The Effect of Judicial Notice

The effect of judicial notice is expressed as the legal consequence of being "self-evident" and directly serves as the basis for the judge's confirmation. To prevent judges from abusing their power to take judicial notice of relevant facts, the law generally grants the parties the right to challenge and rebut these facts. Specifically, the effect of judicial notice manifests in two aspects.

Firstly, effect on the Parties. For the parties, judicial notice relieves them of the burden of proof. They do not need to prove the facts recognized through judicial notice. This essentially redistributes the burden of proof. Whether it is a fact that needs to be proven or an evidentiary fact used to prove the main fact, both are exempt from needing proof due to judicial notice. In a certain sense, this may increase the burden of proof for one party. However, before the judgment becomes final, judicial notice only has a formal probative effect. To ensure fairness in the litigation process and protect the parties' right to be informed and to challenge, the court must give the parties an opportunity and right to make representations and rebuttals before and after taking judicial notice.

Secondly, effect on the Court. For the court, once judicial notice is taken of a fact that meets the conditions for judicial notice, the court directly confirms the truth of the fact without the need to verify it further. The neutral position of the court dictates that it cannot actively investigate and collect evidence. If the facts meet the legal criteria for judicial notice and the parties request it, the court must grant judicial notice of the matters that meet these conditions. Even if the parties do not raise the issue of judicial notice, the court should consider granting relief and has the duty to take judicial notice of matters that meet the required criteria.

---

[12] Strong (2004).

19.4.4 Procedural Rules for Judicial Notice

Judicial notice is a special method for judicial fact-finding that does not require evidence. It involves the judge directly affirming the truth of facts within the scope of judicial notice. As this process can have certain negative implications for the rights of the parties involved, appropriate procedures and a corresponding remedy mechanism must be established to ensure the legitimacy of judicial notice. The specific procedures for judicial notice are outlined below.

19.4.4.1 Procedure for Initiating Judicial Notice

The initiation procedure for judicial notice refers to who initiates judicial notice and how decisions and remedies are made after it is initiated. The term "well-known facts" does not imply that everyone is aware of the facts, as expressed in both case law and legislative language. Some facts are known by the vast majority of people, some by the general public, and some by individuals with significant knowledge. Even when something is considered "common knowledge," it does not necessarily mean that everyone is aware of it. There may be a discrepancy between the knowledge of the general public and that of the judge. Therefore, the procedure should be complementary, with both the judge taking the initiative in recognizing facts and the parties applying for judicial notice to fill in the gaps.

Judicial notice can be divided into mandatory and discretionary categories. For facts that must be recognized, the judge cannot refuse for any reason; for facts that may be recognized, the judge can use their discretion to determine whether to recognize them. There are two procedural types: judicial notice initiated by the judge and judicial notice requested by the parties.

i. **Judicial notice initiated by the judge**

Judicial notice initiated by the judge refers to the judge affirming well-known facts and facts that should be known in the trial process without the parties making an application. In such cases, the judge takes the initiative to recognize the facts that fall within the scope of judicial notice.

Facts that must be judicially noticed by the judge include: (1) well-known facts; (2) natural laws, scientific principles, and technical methods of analysis; (3) facts known by the judge in the course of their duties, including judicial matters, administrative matters, and matters subject to res judicata (final judgment).

When the judge initiates judicial notice, they must inform the parties, their defense attorneys, and legal representatives about the facts to be judicially noticed and the effects of doing so. This allows the parties to express their views and engage in debate or challenge the facts, thereby safeguarding their legitimate rights.

ii. **Judicial notice requested by the parties**

If a party believes certain facts fall within the scope of judicial notice, they may apply to the court to have those facts judicially noticed, thus relieving them of the burden of providing evidence for those facts.

Facts that parties may apply for judicial notice include: (1) facts that can be verified; (2) legislative facts; (3) rules of experience; (4) customs and industry practices. These are facts that the judge may judicially notice. When a party applies for judicial notice, it does not mean that the judge must initiate the process. The judge should first review whether the facts fall within the scope of judicial notice. If the judge determines the matter does not fall within the scope, they should decide not to recognize it. Regardless of whether the judge decides to initiate judicial notice, they should record the decision in writing.

19.4.4.2 Objection Procedures for Judicial Notice

Judicial notice plays a crucial role in relieving one party from the burden of providing evidence. Although it does not directly increase the litigation burden of the opposing party, it does affect the allocation of the burden of proof. From the perspectives of procedural fairness and justice, the opposing party should have the right to challenge or dispute the facts recognized by the judge through judicial notice.

Judicial notice, based on considerations of litigation efficiency, not only involves recognizing facts as true but also includes the potential recognition of facts that may be true. This means that some facts recognized through judicial notice may ultimately turn out to contradict the truth. To prevent unfair outcomes and ensure the legitimacy of the judicial notice process, it is essential to allow the parties involved to challenge the facts recognized by the judge. Prior to the judge conducting judicial notice, both parties, including their legal representatives or defense lawyers, should be allowed to object to the facts being recognized. This ensures that the party or interested parties who may suffer from the judicial notice can exercise their right to challenge the facts in a legitimate manner, guaranteeing fairness in the process and the immutability of the result.

For example, in *Taiwan's Civil Procedure Law*, Article 278 states that even if the facts are not raised by the parties, the court can still consider facts known to it by virtue of its judicial function. However, the parties must be given the opportunity to debate these facts before a judgment is made.

After the judicial notice decision is made, the parties and their defense attorneys or legal representatives have the right to provide relevant materials to assist in the realization of judicial notice. If they disagree with the judicial notice, they have the right to provide materials explaining why the matter should not be recognized and may request a review.

19.4.4.3 Supervision Procedures for Judicial Notice

Judicial notice matters should be handled by the court in a collegial manner, with differing opinions being recorded. If the parties disagree with the judicial notice decision made by the court of first instance, they have the right to appeal to the higher court. After review, the higher court should annul or correct decisions that do not meet the requirements for judicial notice, and it has the authority to recognize facts that should have been noticed but were not.

Additionally, when facts recognized by judicial notice conflict or do not align with facts proven by other evidence, the judge should not simply affirm the judicially noticed facts and dismiss the facts supported by other evidence.

19.5 Questions and Reflections

Judicial notice, as a system in which a judge exercises authority to intervene in the evidence by recognizing specific facts, should pertain to facts that are informed, determined, and authoritative, rather than partial or potentially controversial facts. In this case, the defendant disagreed and appealed to a higher court. Their argument was that: without the parties presenting evidence and engaging in a debate, the trial judge's unilateral judicial instruction to the jury was incorrect, and they requested that the appellate court invalidate the jury's verdict made based on this instruction. Judge O'Neill, who handled the appeal, stated that for facts that are well-known to the majority of people within the jurisdiction, the judge in a civil case is fully authorized to make judicial notice directly. Based on the circumstances of this case, and considering the content of this chapter, consider the following questions: (1) What are the facts involved in judicial notice? (2) At which stage of the trial can a judge conduct judicial notice? (3) How does judicial notice in this case differ from judicial notice in China in terms of scope?

References

Matsuoka, Y. (2004). Minshi zhengju lun [Translation of 民事証拠論] (Zhang, Z. B., Trans.). Beijing: China University of Political Science and Law Press, p. 21. (in Chinese). (Original work published 1925).

Posner, R. A. (2004). Zhengju fa de jingji fenxi [Translation of An economic approach to the law of evidence] (Xu, X. & Xu, Y., Trans.). Beijing: China Legal Publishing House, p. 110. (in Chinese)

Strong, J. W. (Ed.). (2004). Maikaomike lun zhengju [Translation of McCormick on Evidence] (Tang, W. J., Trans.). Beijing: China University of Political Science and Law Press, p. 633. (in Chinese)

Cross, R. & Tapper, C. (1979). Cross on evidence. 7th ed. London: Butterworths, p. 146.

Dennis, I. H. (1999). The law of evidence. London: Sweet & Maxwell, p. 392.

Luo, Y. J. (1972). Minshi jüzhen zeren lun. Taipei: The Commercial Press, p. 26. (in Chinese)
Shen, D. M. (1996). Yingmei zhengju fa. Beijing: CITIC Press, p. 63. (in Chinese)
Cai, X. (2006). Xingzheng Susong Zhengju Guize ji Shiyong [Evidence Rules and Application in Administrative Litigation]. Beijing: People's Court Press.
Li, X. D. (1992). Bijiao zhengju fa yanjiu. Taipei: Wu-Nan Book Inc., p. 22. (in Chinese)

Extended Reading

Ye, Z. Q. (1996). Sifa renzhi lun. Chinese Journal of Law, (4): 22–36.
Bi, Y. Q. (1999). Shilun minshi susong zhong de sifa renzhi. Peking University Law Journal, (1): 53–60. (in Chinese)
Zhao, Z. J. (2002). Sifa renzhi wenti yanjiu. Journal of National Prosecutors College,10(6): 70–77. (in Chinese)
Yan, C. X. (2008). Sifa renzhi yanjiu. Beijing: China Procuratorial Publishing House. (in Chinese)
Zhou, C. F. (2008). Sifa renzhi lun. Beijing: Chinese People's Public Security University Press. (in Chinese)

Postscript

To meet the needs of teaching in financial and economic law programs in China, and based on the teaching plans and talent development schemes of these programs, the specialized textbook Evidence Law (2nd edition) was written for the financial and economic law discipline. In the writing process, the specific characteristics of financial and economic law programs were considered, with an emphasis on the integration of theory and practice. The latest theoretical achievements in evidence law and the experiences of judicial practice have been incorporated. The textbook fully reflects the applied nature of evidence law, and while maintaining theoretical depth, it strives to systematically, accurately, and comprehensively present the basic knowledge, core content, and fundamental principles of evidence law. The goal was to achieve the completeness, systematization, scientific approach, and practicality of the textbook, with the hope of providing insight into the development direction of evidence law and offering a reference for solving practical evidence-related issues.

This textbook has been revised in light of the revisions to the three major procedural laws and their related interpretations, as well as recent developments in the study and application of evidence law. The content has been updated to reflect the latest research findings in evidence law while maintaining the original framework to preserve its practical value as a textbook.

In the writing process, the views and works of domestic and foreign experts and scholars in the field of evidence law have been referenced, and I express my heartfelt thanks to them. Due to limitations in my knowledge and other factors, there are certainly some shortcomings and flaws in the textbook, and I welcome feedback and corrections from experts and scholars.

Guo Hua

(Professor and Doctoral Supervisor of the Law School of Central University of Finance and Economics)

November 2nd, 2021

H. Guo, *Evidence Jurisprudence in China*, Understanding China,
https://doi.org/10.1007/978-981-95-3981-9

References

[Soviet Union] A. Ya. Vyshinsky: The Theory of Evidentiary Proof in Soviet Law, Beijing: Law Press, 1957.
[USA] Edmund.M.Mogrna: Basic Problems of the Law of Evidence, translated by Li Xuedeng, Taipei: Taiwan's "Ministry of Education", 1970.
[USA] John W. Strong (Editor-in-Chief): McCormick on Evidence, translated by Tang Weijian and others, Beijing: China University of Political Science and Law Press, 2004.
[USA] Ronald J. Allen, etc.: Evidence Law: Text, Problems, and Cases (3rd Edition), translated by Zhang Baosheng and others, Beijing: Higher Education Press, 2006.
[Germany] Hans Prütting: Modern Problems of the Burden of Proof, translated by Wu Yue, Beijing: Law Press, 2000.
[Germany] Leo Rosenberg: The Theory of the Burden of Proof (Fifth Edition), translated by Zhuang Jinghua, Beijing: China Legal Press, 2018.
[Germany] Otmar Jauernig: Civil Procedure Law, translated by Zhou Cui, Beijing: Law Press, 2003.
[Japan] Kenji Kaneko and Morio Takeshita: Civil Procedure Law, translated by Bai Lüxuan, Beijing: Law Press, 1995.
[Japan] Hideo Nakamura: Lectures on the New Civil Procedure Law, translated by Chen Gang and others, Beijing: Law Press, 2001.
[Japan] Matsuoka Yoshimasa: Civil Evidence Theory, translated by Zhang Zhiben, Beijing: China University of Political Science and Law Press, 2004.
[Japan] Sachio Takahashi: Key Lectures on Civil Procedure Law, translated by Zhang Weiping and Xu Ke, Beijing: Law Press, 2007.
[Japan] Shinjiro Shindō: New Civil Procedure Law, translated by Lin Jianfeng, Beijing: Law Press, 2008.
Chen Pusheng: Criminal Evidence Law, Taipei: Sanmin Bookstore, 1979.
Luo Yongjia: Theory of Civil Burden of Proof, Taipei: The Commercial Press, 1987.
Li Xuedeng: Comparative Study of Evidence Law, Taipei: Wunan Book Publishing Co., 1992.
Shen Daming: Anglo-American Evidence Law, Beijing: China Citic Press, 1996.
Chen Rongzong and Lin Qingmiao: Civil Procedure Law, Taipei: Sanmin Bookstore, 1996.
Cai Dunming: On Criminal Evidence Law, Taipei: Wunan Book Publishing Co., 1997.
The First Civil Adjudication Tribunal of the Supreme People's Court: Understanding and Application of the New Provisions of the Supreme People's Court on Civil Litigation Evidence (Volume I and II), Beijing: People's Court Press, 2020.

H. Guo, *Evidence Jurisprudence in China*, Understanding China,
https://doi.org/10.1007/978-981-95-3981-9

Xie Anping and Guo Hua: Evidence Law (Second Edition), Beijing: Law Press, 2014.
Cai Xiaoxue: Evidence Rules and Application in Administrative Litigation, Beijing: People's Court Press, 2006.
Bi Yuqian: A Study on the Hindrance of Proof in Civil Litigation, Beijing: Law Press, 2010.
Chen Ruihua: Criminal Evidence Law (Fourth Edition), Beijing: Peking University Press, 2021.
Zhang Baosheng: An Outline of Evidence Science, Beijing: Economic Science Press, 2019.

The manufacturer's authorised representative in the EU is Springer Nature Customer Service Centre GmbH, Europaplatz 3, 69115 Heidelberg, Germany. If you have any concerns regarding our products, please contact ProductSafety@springernature.com

Printed and bound by CPI Group (UK) Ltd, Croydon, CR0 4YY
21/09/2026
02219962-0018